Law in a World of Multiple Legal Orders

Law in a World of Multiple Legal Orders is an accessible introduction to law for students and general readers worldwide. It offers a foundational understanding of what law is and how it operates, while acknowledging that contemporary law is unavoidably cross-border.

Starting with the basic idea of law and its relationship with justice, the book introduces the main legal traditions, courts, and constitutions, before moving on to civil procedure and litigation, legal borrowing between systems, international and supranational law – including European law – and the growing role of alternative dispute resolution, such as arbitration and mediation. Conceived as an international introduction to law that also serves as a natural gateway to international law, the book is designed to help students from different legal traditions understand the nature and functions of law, while giving them the conceptual tools needed to engage more deeply with the major fields of law, such as contract law (and the law of obligations more generally), criminal law, administrative law, corporate law, family law, and a multitude of others. It performs the conventional function of an introduction to law, laying the foundations for understanding the role of law and legal institutions in the contemporary world.

By offering a modern and accessible introduction to law for the realities of a global and interconnected world, it helps students build a solid understanding of law across legal systems and brings together, in a single volume, what would normally take years to learn.

This will be essential reading for introduction to law courses, as well as for courses in international, transnational, and comparative law.

Jean-Yves Gontier is a French-Canadian lawyer at the Paris Bar and a legal scholar with extensive experience in transnational practice and legal education. He holds a PhD in law and has taught law at Sciences Po Paris, where he served as Academic Coordinator and Head of Law at the Undergraduate College and oversaw Dual BA programs with leading French and U.S. universities.

Law in a World of Multiple Legal Orders

A Global Introduction to Law

Jean-Yves Gontier

Preface by George A. Bermann, Walter Gellhorn Professor of Law, Columbia University

Routledge
Taylor & Francis Group
LONDON AND NEW YORK

Designed cover image: Shutterstock

First edition published 2027
by Routledge
4 Park Square, Milton Park, Abingdon, Oxon, OX14 4RN

and by Routledge
605 Third Avenue, New York, NY 10158

Routledge is an imprint of the Taylor & Francis Group, an informa business

British Library Cataloguing-in-Publication Data
A catalogue record for this book is available from the British Library

Library of Congress Cataloging-in-Publication Data
Names: Gontier, Jean-Yves author
Title: Law in a world of multiple legal orders : a global introduction to law / Jean-Yves Gontier.
Description: 1. | New York : Routledge, 2026. | Series: Routledge research in finance & banking law | Includes bibliographical references and index.
Identifiers: LCCN 2026007217 | ISBN 9781032492988 hardback | ISBN 9780367419059 paperback | ISBN 9781003393047 ebook
Subjects: LCSH: Law—Study and teaching | Comparative law | International law | Conflict of laws | Supranationalism | Arbitration (International law)
Classification: LCC K100.L39 G66 2026
LC record available at https://lccn.loc.gov/2026007217

ISBN: 978-1-032-49298-8 (hbk)
ISBN: 978-0-367-41905-9 (pbk)
ISBN: 978-1-003-39304-7 (ebk)

DOI: 10.4324/9781003393047

Typeset in Times New Roman
by Apex CoVantage, LLC

To my daughter, Rose, and in loving memory of my parents and my brother, Yann.

Contents

Preface

As Jean-Yves Gontier reports in his Introduction, this book originated in a course we jointly offered at the then-new Reims campus of Sciences Po Paris in fall 2010 designed to link American and European studies. Entitled "Law in a World of Multiple Legal Orders," the course was meant to be pioneering by placing law in a comprehensively international and comparative law setting. Though pioneering, the course was inspired by an offering I taught for several years at Columbia Law School in New York (significantly with a colleague from, and educated in, Germany) under a strikingly similar name: Lawyering Across Multiple Legal Orders. It was conceived of as one of a small series of "elective" courses specifically designed for first-year law students. This elective would stand out from the rest of the mandatory first-year curriculum, consisting entirely of courses that taught exclusively American law. But with Jean-Yves' collaboration, the course at Reims became even more markedly rich and cosmopolitan. It was also followed by students of even more strikingly diverse nationalities

The book, like the course, stems from the view that, in the current age, university students need as early as possible in their educational journey to become at least somewhat conversant not only with the foundations of law, but also with the reality that today's law is unavoidably cross-border in character. The book reflects a search for the building blocks of law in a multijurisdictional world. It strives, through its international and comparative law perspective, to help students become "literate" in law as it functions on a progressively more integrated landscape. As Jean-Yves aptly points out, his book is essentially dialogical, allowing legal systems (mostly national) to "speak" to one another.

"Law in a World of Multiple Legal Orders" begins with three chapters exploring the prerequisites of any attempt to capture law in a world of multiple legal orders. Because a definition of terms is an essential starting point for any such endeavor, the book begins by exploring the meaning of "law," its purposes, its philosophical and ethical foundations, and the challenging relationship between law and justice. There follows recognition of the reality that, for better or worse, comparative law has traditionally been organized around a dichotomy between the civil law and the common law and the notion more generally of "families" of law, each with its distinctive features and histories. Finally, because in all legal systems whatever their pedigree, i.e., whether based primarily on statute or case law, it is constitutions that provide the framework of law within any jurisdiction and courts that most authoritatively put the law to work, attention is drawn to constitutions and courts, and the latter's capacity to hold legislatures and administrative bodies to account through judicial review. So much for the essentials.

Refreshingly, the book does not then do what one might have expected, i.e., simply march through fields of law, such as contract law (and the law of obligations more generally), criminal law, administrative law, corporate law, family law, and a multitude of others, through a lens of comparative and international law – not that that would be without value. Instead, it probingly examines what I choose to call the main "ingredients" of a world of multiple legal orders, i.e., that which allows law to work in this profoundly cosmopolitan environment. The genius of this approach, in other words, is that it enables the reader to understand what it is that enables a multi-jurisdictional world of law to actually operate. Jean-Yves astutely assembles the most essential of these ingredients: the willingness and capacity of national courts to apply the law of other jurisdictions, the processes by which law can be effectively "transplanted" across borders, the challenge of building and developing international law and ensuring that it is properly "received" in national legal orders, the bold attempts to construct a "supranational" legal order, best exemplified by the European Union and, finally, the prospects of "privatizing" justice through mechanisms such as arbitration and mediation.

I know of no work that undertakes so ambitious a project of making the world of multiple legal orders intelligible. Nor can I imagine such a work being so well organized and expressed with the degree of clarity that produced with such clarity well-organized that "Law in a World of Multiple Legal Orders" exhibits. It is, in a word, one of a kind.

George A. Bermann, Walter Gellhorn
Professor of Law, Columbia University

Acknowledgments

I wish to extend my deepest gratitude to the colleagues who generously offered their time, expertise, and encouragement during the preparation of this textbook.

This work would not have been possible without the collaboration of:

George Bermann, with whom I co-designed and co-taught the original course at Sciences Po that became the foundation for this book.

Michèle Guillaume-Hoffnung, for her thoughtful advice and encouragement.

Thierry Rambaud, for his generous support and guidance.

Martina Smuclerova, for her contribution to Chapter 9 on International Law.

Bruno Sousa Rodrigues, for his input on Chapter 12 on International Arbitration.

Guillaume Tusseau, for his careful review and valuable insights on Chapter 5, centered on Constitutionalism.

Flora Vern, for her helpful feedback and general advice.

Salim Yaacoub, for his early contributions to Chapters 3 and 6 on Civil Law and Civil Procedure.

To each of them, I express my sincere gratitude.

I am also thankful to the editorial team at Routledge for their professionalism, attentiveness, and support throughout the publication process.

Finally, I wish to emphasize that all legal analysis, doctrinal discussions, and conclusions presented in this book – as well as any errors or inaccuracies – remain entirely my own. I bear full and sole responsibility for the content of this work.

Introduction

This textbook was born out of both a conviction and a gap.

A little over ten years ago, Sciences Po Paris began decentralizing its undergraduate programs to regional campuses across France – leading to the establishment of the Euro-American campus in Reims.

At the time, I was Academic Coordinator in the Office of Studies and Academic Affairs, working under Richard Descoings. His ambitious vision transformed Sciences Po into a selective, internationally recognized research university – with greater internationalization, new dual degree programs, regional campuses, and diverse student communities that reflected a globalized world.

As Head of Law at the Undergraduate College, my mission was to ensure the quality of law courses for undergraduate students, and to manage several dual degree programs – including the dual degree in literary humanities with La Sorbonne, and the international Dual Bachelor with Columbia University (the Dual BA).

From its very first intake, the Reims campus welcomed students from all over the world. One-third came from North America, one-third from France, and one-third from Europe and other regions of the world. These students were discovering Sciences Po, its educational program, its innovative teaching methods, and, above all, the unique experience of studying social sciences in English – in France.

It thus became necessary to provide an introduction to law – taught in English and accessible to all – a foundational course, reimagined for this new generation of global citizens.

At the same time, an increasing number of international students were joining Sciences Po's Undergraduate College for a semester or a year through exchange programs with our partner universities. In these exchange programs, students took the same courses as those admitted through national or international admissions – whether French or foreign – and were fully integrated into the academic life of the campuses.

This mix of students from across the world gave lecturers a unique educational opportunity: to engage with a multicultural, multilingual audience from diverse academic and cultural backgrounds, all united by a common working language – English. It was in this rich, open and globalized environment that the need emerged for an introduction to law course, specifically adapted to this type of audience. Not an introduction to international law, but rather an international introduction to law – designed for an audience from different countries, whether or not they had prior legal training, and whether or not they were planning a career in law.

This is how the course *Law in a World of Multiple Legal Orders* was born: not to teach French, American, or international law to law students, but to introduce law to French, American, or international students with diverse backgrounds. In other words, to develop an understanding of

DOI: 10.4324/9781003393047-1

law in a global context – a world where multiple legal orders coexist, intersect, interact, engage in dialogue, sometimes conflict, but continuously shape and influence one another.

To develop this course, I collaborated with a renowned professor of international law at Columbia University, George Bermann, a leading figure in comparative law, international arbitration, and European Union law. This collaboration was both an academic and human experience, a dialogue between legal traditions – Common Law and Civil Law – and a joint project to teach a global, living, and cross-border understanding of law grounded in real-world contexts.

I subsequently taught this course, either alone or alongside George Bermann, for several years between 2010 and 2015 at Sciences Po, in Paris rue Saint-Guillaume, on the Reims campus, in the former Jesuit College on Place Museux, as well as on other English-speaking campuses of Sciences Po. George Bermann was simultaneously teaching the course at Columbia University.

This manual is the direct heir of that original teaching experience. Over the years, through teaching, student questions, and shared reflection, I became convinced that this perspective – and this approach – deserved to be shared with a wider audience.

Although it emerged in the specific context of Sciences Po, it is not intended solely for its students. It is designed for a global audience – for students around the world, in all regions, who are part of increasingly international and multicultural learning environments.

Whether they are enrolled in a business school, a university of social sciences, an institute of political studies, international relations, or journalism – or more broadly, in any academic program offering law courses – this book can serve as an introduction to law.

Of course, this manual is also intended – and perhaps even primarily – for law students, both French and international, whether at the undergraduate or graduate level, and whether pursuing general or specialized studies.

At the time, I searched for a suitable bibliography for the course, but I couldn't find one.

Too often, introduction to law textbooks – in France and elsewhere – were confined to strictly national perspectives, whether focused on French, American, English, or Chinese law.

Even comparative approaches remained trapped in a logic of confrontation between systems, structured around opposing blocks: civil law versus common law, codified law versus case law, continental traditions versus Anglo-Saxon traditions.

The result was a fragmented reading of the law that failed to provide a truly transnational, transsystemic, fluid, and integrated vision of law as it unfolds today in a globalized world.

I realized that a number of fundamental topics were rarely, if ever, addressed in existing textbooks. Important developments in contemporary legal practice were often ignored. For example, the growing use of foreign precedents by supreme and constitutional courts, hybrid or transnational legal statuses like that of Basel-Mulhouse Airport, and original forms of shared governance in cross-border areas, such as the Central Commission for the Navigation of the Rhine.

These complex and cross-border legal realities often escaped traditional analytical frameworks. However, they powerfully illustrate the need to think about law beyond national systems alone.

It was this gap that gave me both the idea and the motivation to write this book – to address a need I had clearly identified, both within the discipline and in practice.

The recent publication in 2025 of a *Treatise on Transnational Administrative Law*, led by Professor Jean-Bernard Auby with Émilie Chevalier, Olivier Dubos, and Yseult Marique, reinforced this observation. It explores the growing importance of transnational legal dynamics in matters of administrative law.

However, the challenge was not only to transcend national boundaries. It was also essential to move beyond a strictly technical or formalist vision of law. Too often, legal education focused on manipulating rules as abstract tools, without questioning what law truly is, what it produces, and how it operates within its own normative framework.

There is an "internal" approach to law – one that understands it as a normative, structured, and rigorous science, with its own categories, reasoning methods, and foundational distinctions and dichotomies. This forms the core of traditional legal training, focusing on the content of norms, the hierarchy of sources, objective and subjective rights, general principles, textual interpretation, legal qualification of facts, solving case studies, writing case commentaries, legal essays, and analytical briefs.

That approach must be complemented by an "external" view on the law – one that considers law as a social, cultural, and political phenomenon. Law is not merely a set of technical rules; it is also a language, an ideology, an instrument of power, and a tool for regulating human relationships. It is rooted in history, expresses values, pursues goals – such as order, justice, freedom, and equality – and is embedded in social relations.

Efficient legal training requires openness to such a threefold, complementary perspective – internal, external, and transnational – which this manual seeks to embody. While this is not a "Law and Society" textbook, it may nonetheless serve as a valuable complement to courses in that field by providing students with conceptual tools to understand better how law operates.

Studying and practicing law also implies developing critical thinking, intuition and above all, creative imagination. A lawyer does not just apply rules: he must understand them, interpret them, sometimes question them, make them dialogue, and use them strategically when faced with often complex, sometimes unprecedented situations.

This is the key difference between legalism and a more flexible, responsive, and practical understanding of law. Legalism rests on the mechanical application of legal norms, promoting reasoning in isolation from context, without reflecting on the purpose or practical function of the rules. It is a limited and rigid view, unable to grasp the complexity of legal reality.

In practice, however, every rule and every situation requires some degree of interpretation. Applying the law depends heavily on context, involves understanding the facts, assessing the situation, and making choices.

This transnational and interdisciplinary approach does not call into question the fundamentally legal nature of this manual. It remains, above all, a law textbook – grounded in legal reasoning, concepts, rules, institutions, and systems. The interdisciplinary lens is not a change of discipline, but a mindset: a way of observing, understanding, presenting, and teaching law in all its richness, without diminishing its rigor or normative essence.

This textbook seeks to offer a broad, open, and lively vision of law. Law is not a fixed set of rules – it is constantly evolving, marked by tensions, and shaped by projects, conflicts, and change. It is altogether a science, a language, a tool, a means of constraint or liberation and a space for imagination. Ultimately, law is a way of thinking about the world.

This manual is therefore intended for those who seek to study law not only to know it, but to understand it, question it, and perhaps rethink it in light of the contemporary world.

Like many others, I was introduced to law through the foundational textbooks of eminent French and European professors. Their works shaped a whole tradition of legal teaching, and I hold them in the highest regard.

But today, the spirit, demands, and expectations of legal education have changed. The stakes are no longer the same. The students are no longer the same, nor is the world.

Approaching law inevitably means confronting a reality that crosses borders in one way or another. The spirit of contemporary law can no longer be limited to the rigor of legal classifications or the elegance of formal reasoning. It calls for more openness, more creativity, and stronger connections – especially in a world shaped by transnational exchanges, institutions, and challenges. It invites us to think about law in terms of its uses, its tensions, its role in society, and its changes, in a world increasingly shaped by legal and global interdependence.

This manual does not reject classical foundations. It seeks to build on them and enrich them. It offers another way into the study of law – one that is rooted in our time, open to the world, and guided by the idea that law is never stronger than when it engages in dialogue, moves across borders, adapts, and reinvents itself.

In short, this is a law textbook for a new generation of students, in a new world – a globalized world where disciplinary, linguistic, and geographic boundaries are increasingly blurred; a world where students are mobile, multilingual, and multicultural; where law is studied in Paris, New York, Nairobi, Montreal, Buenos Aires, and Brussels; where legal education is increasingly delivered in English, even within French universities; and where curricula are increasingly international and courses are taught in English.

This is an introduction to law for those who feel at home almost anywhere in the world, and who must learn to navigate a world of multiple legal orders.

This new academic textbook serves a double aim. It performs the conventional function of an introduction to law, laying the foundations for understanding the role of law and legal institutions in the contemporary world. At the same time, however, it acknowledges the necessity – especially for those students who may contemplate a career in law – to appreciate the increasingly multi-jurisdictional character of law. Each chapter deals with a theme designed to help students navigate across legal systems and understand the complex interfaces between and among them, to identify common patterns, but also to grasp the specific features of each tradition.

It was conceived as a pedagogical tool with no other ambition than to be useful.

Whether you are an exchange student, an international student, or simply a student on the move – wherever you come from, wherever you're headed, whatever your home or host university, whether or not you've studied law before, and whether or not you plan to pursue it later – as long as you understand English and are curious about the big questions law raises in our societies: this book is for you.

I hope it proves useful to you – wherever you are, whatever your legal system, academic path, or future direction. It is with humility and a genuine desire to share that I offer this introduction to law – in a world of multiple legal orders.

Statement on the Use of Generative AI Tools

The author acknowledges the use of generative AI tools exclusively for the purposes of linguistic refinement and stylistic consistency of the manuscript originally drafted by the author. No substantive legal analysis, interpretation, or research content was generated by the tool. All legal reasoning, doctrinal discussion, and conclusions are entirely the intellectual work of the author, who has reviewed and verified the accuracy and integrity of the text in full compliance with Routledge's editorial and ethical guidelines.

Part One

Law, Its Forms, and Its Families

1 What Is Law? What Forms Does Law Take?

Ubi societas, ibi jus.
(Wherever there is society, there is law.)
Latin legal maxim

Unjust law is not law.
St. Augustine, *Treatise on Grace and Free Will*
(A.D. 426–427)

While all agree that law is essential to the regulation and protection of social relationships within human societies, scholars diverge greatly on its true nature and on how to define, understand, and even teach it.

In 1989, an experiment conducted by the French journal *La Revue Droits* invited 50 legal scholars to define law in a few pages. The goal was to synthesize their conceptions into a coherent picture. Yet the project failed, as the definitions proved too numerous and divergent. Dean Georges Vedel expressed this difficulty with striking honesty:

> For weeks and even months I have been laboriously struggling with this apparently innocent question: "What is law?" I attended my first law lecture more than sixty years ago and delivered my first course more than fifty years ago. I have never ceased being a jurist – as lawyer, professor, author, counsellor, and judge – and yet here I am, as disconcerted as a first-year student handing in a blank paper.[1]

He concluded, however, with a key insight: "If I can hardly define what law is, I think I know what a society would be without law."[2]

The question "What is law?" has fascinated philosophers and jurists since antiquity. It appears simple, but conceals great depth. Socrates was among the first to raise it explicitly: in Plato's *Minos*, he asks, "I ask you, what is law?"

As Robert C. Hockett – Edward Cornell Professor of Law at Cornell Law School – rightly observed:

> Law is one of those institutions that is at once so pervasive and so close to us that, if asked what it is, we are apt not to know how to answer. In this respect, law might be likened to

1 French Law Review *Droits*, Revue Française de Théorie Juridique, No. 10 and 11, 1990, articles by leading lawyers and scholars on the question: Define Law.
2 French Law Review *Droits*.

DOI: 10.4324/9781003393047-3

mathematics. Most of us know how to count, multiply, and divide, and so forth. But if somebody asks us, "what is a number", we might well draw a blank. Or perhaps we'll say something like, "you know, like zero, one, two, and so on, that's what numbers are."[3]

Asking *What is law?* thus means questioning its foundations, purposes, and forms. It lies at the very core of legal philosophy. Any serious reflection on law must therefore address questions such as: Why do we have rules? Where does law come from? What are its purposes? Is there a difference between *law*, *a law*, and *the law*? Who has the legitimacy to create and enforce laws? What is the relationship between law and justice, or between law and politics? Can a law be unjust? What are the boundaries between legal norms and social norms?

Yet behind these apparently abstract questions lies one of humanity's oldest and most vital concerns: how can we live together without destroying each other? From the ancient codes of Hammurabi to modern constitutions, from divine commandments carved in stone to the social norms embedded in today's digital platforms, law has always been humanity's answer to disorder and violence – a fragile but enduring attempt to reconcile power and justice, freedom and order.

This chapter explores what is most distinctive and foundational about law, in light of the principal philosophical and cultural debates that have shaped it. It is designed for students who will operate in a world of multiple and interacting legal orders and who must understand both the theoretical and practical dimensions of law.

We begin by exploring the concept of law (section 1), focusing on the terminological problem, the different meanings of the word *law*, and its treatment across cultures and languages. This section also contrasts external and internal approaches to law – as a social science and as a pure, technical discipline.

Next, we turn to the foundations and intellectual roots of law (section 2), examining its political origins, its philosophical justifications, and the debates surrounding unjust laws. The discussion draws on major schools of thought – natural law, positivism, realism, and critical legal studies – as well as on the relationship between law and religion.

The third part considers the purposes and features of law (section 3), emphasizing that law serves practical goals such as justice, liberty, and social order. Here, law is approached as a binding and systemic phenomenon, distinct from other social norms, yet deeply connected to the political and moral life of societies.

Finally, the chapter examines the various forms that law takes (section 4), distinguishing between formal sources (constitutions, statutes, regulations, treaties) and informal ones (custom, general principles, equity, precedent, doctrine, contracts, religion, and soft law).

Taken together, these sections offer a comprehensive view of law as a multifaceted and evolving phenomenon – at once social, institutional, moral, and linguistic. They show why defining law is so difficult and why the question "What is law?" remains as relevant today as in Socrates' time.

1 Exploring the Concept of Law

The nature of law is a deep and complex subject that has interested and preoccupied thinkers and scholars for centuries. It all begins with a simple yet difficult question: *What is law?* To understand it, we must look at its basic ideas, the words we use to describe it, and the different ways it has been understood across time and cultures.

3 Hockett, Robert, 2009, *Law*, Chicago Review Press.

1.1 The Terminological Problem

Understanding the concept of law begins with addressing the challenges of its terminology. The word "law" carries different meanings and implications depending on the context, which makes its definition and interpretation complex.

1.1.1 The Word "Law" in the Ordinary Language

The word *law* in ordinary language refers to a wide range of ideas, each of which sheds light on a different aspect of what law may be. The following common expressions can help students beginning their study of law to grasp some of its everyday meanings:

(a) *To be a law unto oneself* – to act independently or unpredictably, outside the usual social rules.
(b) *The law of the jungle* – a situation governed by power or force rather than by rules, where only the strongest survive.
(c) *To lay down the law* – to speak or act in an authoritative or dogmatic way.
(d) *There's no law against it* – a phrase used to justify an action as permissible or not prohibited.

Such expressions, though familiar, do not provide a universal or precise definition of law. They offer clues about its purpose and scope but remain limited, since they usually refer to a "rule of conduct imposed by authority."

Brian Z. Tamanaha, an American legal theorist and professor at Washington University School of Law in St. Louis, explores the nature of law as a social phenomenon, showing how legal systems, norms, and practices take diverse forms across different societies. As Tamanaha notes, many different forms are conventionally considered to be law: International Law, Customary Law, Canon Law, the Sharia, Natural Law, state legal systems, and the *lex mercatoria*, among others. These various forms may overlap or differ greatly, yet they all involve rules or principles that claim some form of authority.[4]

This explains why theoretical and empirical debates on the nature of law can continue indefinitely if we accept that law is, in the end, "whatever groups of people conventionally attach the label law to."[5]

1.1.2 The Different Meanings of the Word "Law"

The search for the meaning of a word often begins with its dictionary definition. In this regard, *Black's Law Dictionary* offers several meanings for the term *law:*

(a) the system that regulates human activities and relationships through the organized force of a political society or through social pressure supported by that force;
(b) the body of legislation and recognized legal principles that guide judicial and administrative actions (as in "the law of the land");[6]

4 Tamanaha, Brian Z., 2008, "Law," *Legal Studies Research Paper Series*, paper no. 08-0095.

5 Williams, Glanville L., 1945, "International Law and the Controversy Concerning the Word 'Law'," *British Yearbook of International Law*, vol. 22, pp. 146–163. Tamanaha, Brian Z., 1995, "An Analytical Map of Social Scientific Approaches to the Concept of Law," *Oxford Journal of Legal Studies*, vol. 15, pp. 501–535.

6 "Phrase first used in the Magna Carta to refer to the then established law of the kingdom as distinguished from Roman or Civil Law. It refers today to fundamental principles of justice commensurate with due process of law, i.e., those rights that

(c) the set of rules governing a specific area within a legal system (for example, *copyright law*);
(d) the judicial and administrative process itself;
(e) legal actions and proceedings;
(f) a statute (as in "Congress passed a law");
(g) the legal profession (as in "she spent her entire career in law").

The expression *at law* refers to something recognized or enforceable under the legal system (for example, "an agreement enforceable at law" or "an attorney-at-law"), while *to go to law* or *to take someone to law* means to initiate legal proceedings against someone.

Although dictionaries provide concise and useful definitions, they remain limited. They describe how the word *law* is used but offer little insight into its deeper nature, its origins, or the criteria that distinguish what truly counts as law from what does not.

1.1.3 The Etymology of the Word Law

It is generally accepted that the English word *law* derives from the Old English *lagu*, itself borrowed from the Old Icelandic[7] *log* (plural *lag*), meaning "something laid down" or "fixed." The term is therefore of Nordic origin and related to the modern verb *to lay*. This etymology reveals an often-overlooked aspect of the legal phenomenon: law as a social construct – something deliberately established to organize human life.

For example, when a parliament *lays down* a statute to regulate the use of natural resources, or when a constitution *lays the foundation* for a new political order, both acts reflect this original sense of *law* as something set in place by society. Even customary law, though unwritten, is *laid down* through repeated social practice and shared acceptance.

The key idea here is one of social foundation: law is not a natural given, but a framework consciously created and maintained by communities to bring order, predictability, and legitimacy to their collective existence.

1.1.4 What Else Is There in le Droit *Than* la Loi*?*

It should be clear by now that the word *law* has countless meanings. Yet, the most significant of these are those referring to its normative dimension, usually expressed in the phrases *the Law* and *a law*. The difference between the two relates to the distinction between the legal norm and the legal order. Analytical jurisprudence typically defines a legal norm as a *command guiding human conduct*, while the legal order represents the *organized system* formed by these norms.

Thus, *a law* refers to an individual rule – for instance, *a law on environmental protection, a law regulating marriage*, or *a law establishing the right to education*. In contrast, *the Law* refers to the entire legal order that gives meaning and coherence to such rules – the overarching framework that governs society as a whole.

---

the Legislature cannot abolish or significantly limit, because they are so fundamental to our system of liberty and justice; also refers to the law as developed by the courts or in statutes in pursuance of those principles or rights. The United States Constitution (Art. VI, Sec. 2) establishes itself, and laws made under its authority, and treaties of the United States, as the supreme law of the land." Gifis, H. Steven, 2016, *Barron's Law Dictionary*, 7th ed., Barron's Educational Series.

7 In singular the word meant in Old Icelandic " 'something laid or fixed' . . . the plural had the collective sense 'law'. . . . As *law* is the usual English rendering of Latin *lex*, and to some extent of Latin *jus*, and of Greek *νόμος*, its development of senses has been in some degree affected by the uses of these words." Oxford English Dictionary, 2024, *Oxford English Dictionary*, Oxford University Press.

However, not all languages merge these two notions into a single term. In French, for example, *la loi* refers to a specific legal norm or statute, while *le Droit* designates the broader legal order. The same distinction exists in Spanish (*la ley / el Derecho*), German (*das Gesetz / das Recht*), Italian (*la legge / il Diritto*), and Arabic ([القانون] لحق" and "وكاناالقانون).

This linguistic diversity shows that law can be understood both as a rule – prescribing or prohibiting specific behavior – and as a system, embodying the collective structure of rights, duties, and institutions that regulate social life.

1.1.5 Different Cultures Have Different Conceptions of Law

The disagreements about law stem from the lack of agreement on its meaning.[8] This statement has both micro and macro dimensions. At the micro level, it means that a concept of law will always be "our concept of law."[9] This means that the definition of law carries an unavoidable subjectivity. At the macro level, this disagreement on the meaning of law points towards cultural relativism. In this respect, it seems difficult to ignore that the concept of law changes in time and space.

Indeed, Joseph Raz (1939–2022), an Israeli philosopher and one of the most prominent legal theorists of his time, whose work focused on law, morality, and politics, observed that "different cultures have different concepts of law . . . there is no one concept of law."[10]

Raz's work, *The Authority of Law: Essays on Law and Morality* (2009), critically examines the intersection of legal authority with moral principles, offering profound insights into the nature and legitimacy of legal systems.[11]

The social and cultural nature of law places its study at the crossroads of several disciplines. To understand the legal phenomenon, one must also understand society and culture as a whole. In this respect, the lesson of Max Gluckman (1911–1975), a South African and British social anthropologist, still holds relevance:

> Many volumes have been written on this subject, and it may seem a sweeping impertinence if I say, somewhat categorically, that much of this controversy has arisen from arguments about the word "law", apparently based on the assumption that it must have one meaning, and one meaning only. But the contrary is obviously true. Indeed, in any language most words which refer to important social phenomena – as "law" obviously does – are likely to have several referents and to cover a wide range of meanings. We should therefore expect that the English word "law", and other related words, will not have a single precise meaning. If jurisprudence is full of controversy centering on how "law" should be defined, the terminological disputes are increased when tribal societies, with their very different cultures, are investigated. Since our own words for "law" and related phenomena are already loaded with meaning – indeed many ambiguous meanings – students of tribal societies run into difficulties as soon as they try to apply these words to activities in other cultures.[12]

Accordingly, legal studies are to be understood as part of the broader realm of the social sciences. This may sound a bit confusing at this point, but what must be retained from this whole discussion is that there are as many definitions of law as there are different cultures and societies.

8 David, René, 1981, "Sources of Law," in *International Encyclopedia of Comparative Law*, Martinus Nijhoff.

9 Raz, Joseph, 2005, "Can There Be a Theory of Law?," in *Blackwell Guide to Philosophy of Law and Legal Theory*, eds. Martin P. Golding and William A. Edmundson, Blackwell Publishing.

10 Raz, "Can There Be a Theory of Law?"

11 Raz, Joseph, 2009, *The Authority of Law: Essays on Law and Morality*, Oxford University Press.

12 Gluckman, Max, 1965, *Politics, Law and Ritual in Tribal Society*, Blackwell, Oxford.

1.2 Law as a Social and Pure Science

Law belongs both to the social sciences and to the more formal, analytical, and natural sciences.

First, law is a social science. It should be studied, especially at university, alongside subjects such as history, economics, sociology, political science, literature, or philosophy. These fields help explain how law reflects society's values and how it changes with social, economic, and political developments. For example, studying labor law without understanding the history of workers' rights or social movements would give only a partial view of the subject.

Second, law is also a technical discipline, studied from the inside. This means looking closely at the content of legal rules – what each norm prescribes or prohibits – and how these norms interact with one another within the broader legal system. For instance, analyzing a rule on property ownership requires knowing how it connects to contract law, tax law, or inheritance rules. Practicing law, therefore, involves identifying the relevant norms, understanding how courts have interpreted them and applying them logically to specific cases.

Here, law can be compared to the pure sciences, which also study *laws* – the laws of physics, chemistry, or biology. Yet, while natural laws describe how the world *is* (for example, the law of gravity), legal laws prescribe how human beings *ought to act* (for example, criminal law prohibiting theft). In both cases, there is a search for order, coherence, and predictability. Scientists observe the regularities of nature; jurists establish the regularities of social life. Both rely on rigorous reasoning and systematic methods to explain or to organize reality.

These two perspectives – the external view, which studies law as a social phenomenon, and the internal view, which examines law as a coherent normative system – reflect the dual nature of legal study identified by Herbert L. A. Hart (1907–1992) – a British legal philosopher and one of the most influential legal thinkers of the 20th century. Understanding both is essential to fully grasp the complexity and richness of the legal discipline.

Hart profoundly shaped modern legal positivism by showing, in *The Concept of Law*, that every legal system relies on a shared but unwritten "rule of recognition" that enables officials to identify which norms count as valid law.

1.2.1 The External Look at Law: Law as a Social Science

Law can be studied from an external perspective, that is, by observing how it operates within society and how it interacts with other social forces. From this viewpoint, law is not an isolated system of rules but a social institution that reflects and shapes human relationships, values, and power structures. It seeks to achieve justice and maintain order, is closely linked to politics, and serves multiple functions in organizing social life – as highlighted by scholars such as Brian Tamanaha.

1.2.1.1 LAW AIMS AT JUSTICE AND ORDER

We take an external look at law when we see it not as a technical field but as one of the great forces that shape human society – a universal system of regulation created to organize life in common, to preserve order, and to pursue justice. Law is everywhere around us: it governs our families, protects our property, punishes crime, collects our taxes, and guarantees our freedoms. It decides who can marry, vote, work, inherit, or even speak in public. In a very real sense, law is the invisible architecture of society – the framework that allows millions of individuals to live together without chaos.

In this broader perspective, law is the language of social cohesion. Just as we share words to communicate and institutions to cooperate, we also share rules – *law in common* – to make peaceful life possible. Every society, from the ancient city-states of Athens or Babylon to today's global democracies, has relied on law to replace force with reason.

At its heart, law aims at justice and order, the twin pillars of civilized life. *Order* ensures stability and predictability, preventing society from falling into conflict or anarchy. *Justice* gives moral meaning to that order, ensuring that rules serve fairness rather than domination. One without the other leads to imbalance: order without justice becomes tyranny, and justice without order dissolves into disorder. When a criminal court punishes wrongdoing, when a constitution protects the weak from the powerful, or when an environmental law restrains human greed in the name of future generations, law performs its highest function: it reconciles freedom with responsibility.

Seen in this way, law and politics are inseparable. Politics decides the goals of society; law gives them form and force. A political ideal – equality, liberty, security – becomes real only when it is written into law and applied in practice. Whether it is the abolition of slavery, the recognition of women's rights, or the fight against climate change, every great political transformation has passed through the gate of law.

1.2.1.2 LAW AND POLITICS ARE CONSUBSTANTIAL

Law and politics are closely connected; in fact, they are consubstantial. This is evident when we look at how laws are made. Political institutions such as governments and parliaments create laws through political processes and debates. Laws are often the result of political compromise and reflect the balance of power within a society, especially in democratic systems.

However, legal rules cannot be reduced entirely to politics. Law and politics are two distinct spheres, each with its own methods, traditions, and language. Together, they have a transformative power: they can turn ideas and words into binding rules, enforceable by courts and public authorities, shaping the way people live and behave.

The relationship between law and politics is also two-way. While political processes produce laws, legal norms in turn define and limit political action. For example, the work of a parliament or Congress is governed by legal rules such as the majority principle, which requires more than half of the votes for a decision to be adopted. Law also intervenes directly in politics through mechanisms like judicial review, which allows courts to strike down rules that conflict with higher norms such as constitutions or treaties. Although this process is imperfect and often debated, it shows how law both enables and constrains political power.

In this sense, one may ask whether law is politics that has succeeded. Every law begins as a political decision about what society values or forbids. When a government enacts a law to protect the environment, recognize same-sex marriage, or ensure equal pay, it turns a political choice into a legal obligation. Yet once adopted, the law no longer belongs solely to politics. It must be applied fairly, interpreted by judges, and respected by all. Law, therefore, can be seen as politics that has accepted limits, guided by the principles of justice, order, and legitimacy.

1.2.1.3 LAW IS A MULTIFUNCTIONAL TOOL

It has been argued that law is, in fact, a multifunctional tool.[13] This view invites us to look at what law actually *does* in society in order to understand what it *is*. From this perspective, the meaning of law depends on the functions it performs and the purposes it serves.

Brian Tamanaha, among others, has argued that law is a means to achieve multiple ends. According to him, there is no single, correct concept of law; rather, law takes different forms and plays different roles depending on the social, cultural, and institutional context. Debates

13 Tamanaha, Brian Z., 2008, "Law," *St. John's Legal Studies Research Paper Series*, paper no. 08-0095.

about whether International Law, customary law, or religious law truly qualify as "law" therefore lose their significance, because law's identity lies in its function rather than in a fixed definition.[14]

Such an approach necessarily calls for an interdisciplinary study of law. Beyond cultural differences, even within a single society, law performs many roles: it regulates behavior, resolves disputes, distributes resources, expresses moral values, and shapes political power. To understand these diverse functions, students are encouraged to engage with related disciplines such as sociology, economics, philosophy, and history, as these fields deepen one's understanding of how law operates in practice and enrich legal reasoning.

1.2.2 The Internal Look at Law: Law as a Pure Science

Law can also be studied from an internal perspective, by examining its structure, logic, and operation from within the legal system itself. This approach treats law as a pure science, focusing on how legal rules are created, interpreted, and applied. It involves understanding legal reasoning, distinguishing between different branches and categories of law, and analyzing how rights and obligations function within the legal order. Through this lens, law appears as a coherent and rational system aimed at ensuring consistency, fairness, and predictability.

1.2.2.1 LEGAL REASONING, HOW THE LAW OPERATES, AND EXPLORING DICHOTOMIES

We can also have an internal look at law. This implies approaching the law not from the perspective of society and the role legality plays therein, but from the perspective of the legal community and how it operates legal instruments as a pure science characterized by accuracy, rationality, controlled variables, and predictability. The internal look at law focuses on the law alone (pure law) without the corpus of the social sciences, without history, politics, philosophy, sociology, morality, or ethics. As a doctoral candidate in Law at the University of Adelaide rightly observed:

> From their very first lectures, law students are told not to equate legal ethics with morality, to ignore emotional responses to cases and to ignore any idea of reforming the law.
>
> Instead, they are taught legal positivism or "pure law." Pure law is the teaching of law without the "baggage" of the social sciences: without history, politics, philosophy, morality or ethics.[15]

When studying law from the perspective of legal professionals, one quickly sees that law follows its own logic and way of reasoning. Legal thinking often relies on opposites, which are balanced through argument and interpretation – a kind of dialogue between two sides.

Jurists work with many such opposing ideas, such as *natural law and positive law*, *substantive and procedural law*, *public and private law*, or *law and rights*. In court, the claimant and the respondent, through their lawyers, present these opposing arguments – one as the thesis, the other as the antithesis – and the judge's decision becomes the synthesis, the final resolution of the legal dispute.

14 Tamanaha, *Law*.
15 Krook, Joshua, 2017, "Is Law a Social Science? Lessons from a Canadian Law School," *The Conversation*. Available at: https://theconversation.com/is-law-a-social-science-lessons-from-a-canadian-law-school-81753.

A good example of seeing a legal rule from both the inside and the outside is the rule of civil liability in French law, formerly Article 1382 of the Civil Code (now Article 1240), which states:

> Any act whatever of man, which causes damage to another, obliges him by whose fault it occurred to repair it.

From the inside, jurists analyze this rule in a technical and structured way. They break it down into its essential elements – *fault*, *damage*, and *causal link*. Each element has precise legal definitions developed through case law and doctrine. To establish liability, one must prove that a fault was committed, that actual damage occurred, and that there is a direct causal relationship between the two. This method reflects the logic, precision, and predictability that characterize the internal study of law.

From the outside, however, the same rule can be viewed as a social and political instrument. It expresses moral and cultural values, such as individual responsibility and the idea that no one should cause harm to others. It also serves broader social purposes – to maintain trust, ensure social order, and compensate victims fairly. The principle has economic and political implications as well, influencing behavior, insurance systems, and social solidarity.

Thus, when seen from the inside, the rule appears as a coherent part of the legal system; when seen from the outside, it reveals its role in shaping society and reflecting collective values.

1.2.2.2 SUBSTANTIVE AND PROCEDURAL LAW

The distinction between substantive law and procedural law is one of the most fundamental in legal study. It separates the *content* of the law – the rules that govern behavior – from the *methods* used to apply and enforce those rules.

Substantive law tells us what is allowed or forbidden, what rights people have, and what duties they owe to others. It defines the limits of acceptable conduct in society. For instance, family law rules allowing or forbidding divorce under certain conditions, or criminal law provisions punishing theft or fraud, all belong to substantive law.

Procedural law, on the other hand, tells us *how* the law operates in practice. It sets out the steps that must be followed to bring a case before a court, the deadlines to respect, the documents to submit, and the way judgments are executed. For example, it explains how a petition for divorce must be filed, what evidence is required, and how the judge will hear both parties before deciding.

In short, substantive law defines what the law says, while procedural law defines how the law speaks. The two are inseparable: a right without a procedure to enforce it remains powerless, and a procedure without a right to protect has no purpose.

1.2.2.3 PUBLIC AND PRIVATE LAW

Public Law is the branch of law that governs the organization and functioning of public authorities, their relations with individuals and private entities, and their interactions with one another. It ensures that governments and public bodies act lawfully, fairly, and within their powers, protecting citizens from abuses of authority and maintaining accountability in the exercise of public power.

Examples of Public Law include:

Constitutional Law, which defines the structure of the State and guarantees fundamental rights and liberties. For example, a citizen challenges a new law passed by parliament that restricts press freedom, arguing before the Constitutional Court that it violates the constitutional right to free expression.

Administrative Law, which regulates how public bodies such as ministries, local councils, or regulatory agencies make and apply decisions. For instance, a local business appeals a decision by the City Council denying it an operating license, claiming the decision was unfair and made without following proper procedure.

Criminal Law, which enables the State to punish offences and maintain public order. For example, the State prosecutes an individual accused of bribing a public official to preserve integrity in government.

Public International Law, which governs relations between states and international organizations. For instance, two neighboring countries submit a border dispute to the International Court of Justice after diplomatic negotiations fail.

Private Law, sometimes referred to in Europe as *Civil Law* because of its roots in Roman law (*Corpus Juris Civilis*), governs the relationships between private individuals and protects their property and personal interests. It regulates how people interact in their daily and professional lives, ensuring fairness and security in private dealings.

Its main branches include:

Contract Law, which sets out the rules under which private parties can create binding agreements and regulate their own affairs. For example, two companies sign a contract for the delivery of goods, but when one fails to deliver on time, the other seeks compensation for breach of contract.

Tort Law, which deals with non-contractual liability – the duty to compensate for harm caused to another person through fault or negligence. For instance, a driver who causes an accident by running a red light must pay damages to the injured pedestrian.

Property Law, which governs the acquisition, use, transfer, and loss of ownership rights over things, whether movable or immovable. For example, a homeowner sells a house, and the law ensures the transfer of ownership is valid and recorded, protecting both buyer and seller.

Family Law, which covers matters such as marriage, divorce, parental authority, and child custody. For instance, during a divorce, the court determines child custody arrangements and ensures both parents continue to meet their responsibilities toward the child.

For a long time, this division between public and private law stood at the center of legal education and practice, especially in Civil Law countries. Law faculties were organized around it, and lawyers or judges would specialize in one field or the other. The divide even produced different styles of legal reasoning: public law often emphasizing the general interest, while private law focused on individual rights.

Today, however, this traditional distinction is increasingly questioned. In practice, public and private law constantly overlap – for example, when private companies manage public services, or when human rights influence private contracts. Modern legal systems now tend to classify law according to the activity it regulates rather than by the type of actors involved. New hybrid fields such as banking law, transport law, electronic communications law, and space law illustrate this more realistic and dynamic approach, which continues to grow throughout Europe.

Beyond these traditional divisions, another key distinction in legal thinking concerns the relationship between law and rights.

1.2.2.4 LAW AND THE CONCEPT OF RIGHTS

Law and rights are two sides of the same reality. Law is the system of rules that governs how people live together; rights are the legal powers individuals hold within that system. Law sets the limits of what can or cannot be done, while rights allow people to act, demand, or defend something within those limits.

This relationship is often explained through the classic distinction between objective law and subjective rights. Objective law is an abstract notion describing the general framework of rules that governs relationships between human beings, while subjective rights are personal and concrete rights that individuals hold within that framework.

Although this distinction may seem abstract, it becomes very concrete in everyday life. Imagine I am in France buying a *baguette* or a *croissant* from a local *boulangerie*. The French Civil Code provides that "any contract lawfully entered into must be performed," a rule found in Article 1103 of the Civil Code.

> Contracts which are lawfully formed have the binding force of legislation for those who have made them.

This provision – part of the general rules of contract law defining what constitutes a valid sale and the obligations of each party – is objective law, and it governs our transaction.

Once I have paid, I acquire a subjective right: the legal power to demand the performance of an obligation, namely that the baker hand me my croissant. What seems like a simple, everyday act is, in fact, the concrete execution of a legal obligation – a perfect illustration of how abstract legal principles materialize into real, tangible rights in daily life.

A similar distinction appears in civil liability. The rule that "whoever causes harm to another must repair it" (former Article 1382 of the French Civil Code) is a principle of objective law. But if my neighbor accidentally breaks my window, I personally acquire the subjective right to claim compensation for the damage.

This distinction also operates in public law. The constitution's guarantee of *freedom of expression* belongs to objective law – it is a general rule defining the limits of public authority. Yet, when a journalist relies on that constitutional guarantee to challenge an act of censorship, they are exercising a subjective right.

In short, objective law provides the abstract structure of norms that regulates social relations, while subjective rights make these norms tangible and personal. Through them, the law comes to life in everyday situations – whether in demanding a croissant, seeking compensation, or defending one's freedom of speech.

1.2.2.5 EXPANDING THE CONCEPT OF RIGHTS

Modern legal thought has pushed this framework even further by asking new questions: Do the earth and the environment have rights? Do all living beings, including animals and plants, have rights? Those issues emerged under the influence of a contemporary school of thought known as "deep ecology,"[16] a term coined by 1973 Norwegian Philosophy Professor Arne Næss. This movement defends the idea that all living beings – including animals and plants – have an

16 Naess, Arne, 1973, "The Shallow and the Deep, Long-Range Ecology Movement: A Summary," *Inquiry*, vol. 16, no. 1, p. 95.

intrinsic value independent of their usefulness to humans. This approach challenges the anthropocentric foundations of traditional law, which historically viewed nature only as an object of protection or exploitation.

The State of Ecuador has been a pioneer in recognizing the rights of nature. Its 2008 Constitution enshrines *Pacha Mama* (Mother Earth) as a "subject of rights" – a radical innovation in legal thinking. The Constitution of the Republic of Ecuador grants nature two specific rights: the right to be respected, which includes maintaining and regenerating ecosystems, their structure, and their functions; the right to be restored, an autonomous right that exists independently of human claims for compensation.

This new vision moves beyond protecting nature as an object of law to acknowledging it as a subject deserving of respect and legal standing. Inspired by Indigenous worldviews, it invites a broader reflection on the boundaries of legal personality.

Europe has recently seen similar developments. In 2022, the Spanish Parliament granted legal personhood to the *Mar Menor* lagoon, following the example of Ecuador and New Zealand, where rivers and ecosystems have been recognized as legal entities. This growing movement to recognize the Rights of Nature brings together insights from law, philosophy, anthropology, environmental science, and Indigenous traditions – redefining the place of humanity within the legal order. Law is not a static set of rules, but a living system that evolves with culture, knowledge, and collective consciousness.

Exploring the concept of law reveals both its complexity and its dual nature. Law can be seen from the outside as a social institution that maintains order, ensures justice, and reflects political and cultural values, or from the inside as a rational and structured system of norms. Through its distinctions – between substantive and procedural law, public and private law, objective law and subjective rights – law appears both as an abstract framework that governs society and as a concrete reality that gives shape to rights, duties, and justice in everyday life.

2 Foundations and Intellectual Roots of Law

Where does law come from? How did it develop? Is it universal? What gives it authority? Does it have a divine or purely human origin?

At first glance, one might answer simply that law comes from political power. Yet this explanation is incomplete, for it immediately leads to another question: where does political power itself come from? For centuries, thinkers sought its origin in divine authority. As Saint Paul wrote in his *Epistle to the Romans*: *Nulla potestas nisi a Deo* (There is no power but from God). Political and legal authority were seen as reflections of a transcendent order. In this view, law was not merely a human creation but a divine command governing earthly life.

Over time, however, this religious conception gradually gave way to more human-centered or secular theories of authority, based on reason, nature, or the will of the people – a transition that marks one of the major turning points in the history of law.

This question inevitably reflects an ideological and cultural conception of authority. In the 21st century, some political systems – such as theocracies – continue to ground the legitimacy of law in divine will rather than in human sovereignty.

2.1 Law's Foundation in the Political Order

Law is founded in the political order and is created, shaped, and enforced by governmental authorities to organize collective life and regulate social relations. It provides the framework within which political power is exercised and held accountable, transforming collective choices into binding rules. In this sense, law expresses both the authority of the State and the values of the community it governs.

2.1.1 Law Is Specific to Human Societies

The origins of law are closely tied to those of politics and political power. Asking whether law presupposes politics is like asking whether the chicken or the egg came first – the two are inseparable. Both likely emerged when humans moved from nature to history, from instinct to organized community.

Wherever human beings have lived together, some form of law and politics has appeared. Every society, however simple or complex, has developed rules to regulate behavior and a system of authority to enforce them. For example, when the head of a Neolithic tribe punished a member for violating communal norms, that act already contained the basic elements of law and political power – a rule, an authority, and a sanction. Similarly, in ancient Mesopotamia, the Code of Hammurabi (around 1750 BC) provided detailed regulations for daily life, from trade and property to family relations – one of the earliest known legal systems.

This observation confirms the ancient Latin maxim introduced at the beginning of this chapter: *ubi societas, ibi jus* – where there is society, there is law. Law is a necessary consequence of social life; it arises wherever people live together and seek to organize their coexistence. Some may argue that such interpretations are ethnocentric, applying modern Western categories to non-Western or ancient societies. That concern is legitimate but not entirely convincing. The goal is not to claim universal truths but to identify recurring patterns: wherever humans coexist, they tend to create systems of norms and governance – forms of law and politics that evolve according to their cultures and needs.

2.1.2 Law Is Made by Governmental Authorities

In most societies, the power to make laws belongs to those who hold political power. In democracies, this authority is vested in elected representatives – parliaments, governments, or presidents – who enact laws on behalf of the people. For instance, in France, laws are passed by the National Assembly and the Senate before being promulgated by the President of the Republic. In the United States, Congress drafts and adopts federal laws that are signed or vetoed by the President.

In more authoritarian regimes, the law-making process is often concentrated in the hands of a single ruler or a small elite. For example, in Saudi Arabia, legislation is largely derived from Sharia law, and new rules are issued by royal decree. In China, the National People's Congress, dominated by the Communist Party, enacts laws reflecting the party's political and ideological direction.

Thus, while the mechanisms of law-making differ widely – from parliamentary debate to executive decree – the underlying principle remains constant: law is shaped by political authority. It reflects the ideology and priorities of those in power, whether these are democratic values like equality and liberty or authoritarian goals like order and control. This is why accountability and representation are vital in democracies – they ensure that the laws reflect the will and interests of the people rather than the ambitions of those who govern.

2.2 Controversy Over Unjust Laws: Exploring Ethical and Philosophical Perspectives

The question of whether individuals must obey laws that are deeply unjust lies at the heart of legal philosophy. It forces us to confront a fundamental tension between justice and authority – between what is *right* and what is *legal*. Throughout history, thinkers have debated whether the legitimacy of law depends on its moral content or simply on its formal validity. From Aristotle's reflections on natural justice to the positivist theories of Austin, Hart, and Raz, the dialogue has shaped how societies understand the very nature of law.

This section explores the main philosophical responses to this enduring problem, beginning with the schools of natural law, which claim that law must conform to universal principles of justice; moving through the German historical school, which grounds law in the customs and spirit of the people; and examining legal positivism, which separates law from morality while still acknowledging its authority. It then considers the modern critics and alternative schools – from realism to critical legal studies – and concludes with a reflection on the complex relationship between law and religion, where divine and secular norms continue to interact in shaping human conduct.

Ultimately, this exploration reveals that the question of unjust laws is not only theoretical but deeply practical: it determines when citizens, judges, and states must choose between obedience and conscience.

2.2.1 The Moral Dilemma of Unjust Laws

The philosophical question of whether one must obey laws that are extremely unjust is a timeless problem that has divided thinkers for centuries. It was first raised by St. Augustine of Hippo (A.D. 354–430) in his *Treatise on Grace and Free Will* (A.D. 426–427), and later echoed by other Christian thinkers in the Latin maxim *lex iniusta non est lex – an unjust law is not a law.*

The debate around this idea reveals the diversity of historical conceptions of law and justice. It raises a crucial issue: is legality defined by justice or by authority? In other words, is something "law" simply because it is enacted by those in power, or must it also be morally just to deserve obedience?

If we consider examples such as Nazi or Fascist legislation, decisions rendered by corrupt judges, or executive orders issued by dictators, the question "What is law?" becomes "When do coercively enforced rules deserve to be called laws that we are morally bound to obey?"

Over time, different schools of thought have provided different answers. Two major and opposing traditions stand out: Natural Law theory and Legal Positivism. Each reflects a distinctive way of understanding the relationship between law, morality, and authority. Between these two poles lie many intermediate positions – and even within each school, scholars have long disagreed about how exactly law relates to justice and moral truth.

A modern illustration of this dilemma can be found in the apartheid laws of South Africa (1948–1994). These laws were enacted by a legitimate parliament and enforced by courts, yet they institutionalized racial segregation and discrimination. Formally, they fulfilled all the conditions of valid legislation – they were written, promulgated, and enforced by recognized authorities – but morally, they were profoundly unjust.

This example exposes the core tension between Natural Law and Legal Positivism. For natural law theorists, such laws cannot be considered true law because they contradict fundamental principles of justice and human dignity. For legal positivists, however, these rules remain *law* in the formal sense – not because they are just, but because they have been created according to the proper legal procedures. This does not mean that positivists *approve* of their content; rather, they separate the question of what the law *is* from the question of whether it *ought to be obeyed.*

This leads to a deeper moral and legal question: where does the duty to obey the law end? The trial of Adolf Eichmann, held in Jerusalem in 1961, brought this issue to the forefront. It is one of the most important trials in modern history. Eichmann was a senior Nazi official responsible for organizing the "Final Solution," the mass deportation and extermination of Jews during World War II. After the war, he escaped to Argentina under a false name but was captured by Israeli agents in 1960 and brought to Israel to stand trial. The trial revealed the terrifying efficiency of the Nazi system and the role of ordinary people in carrying out extraordinary crimes.

Eichmann's defense shocked the world. He claimed he was "just following orders" and had no personal responsibility for the atrocities committed. He even invoked Kant's moral philosophy, arguing that he had simply obeyed the laws of his country and the commands of his superiors. The philosopher and political thinker Hannah Arendt, who attended the trial as a reporter, later wrote that Eichmann was not a monster but a terrifyingly ordinary man – a symbol of what she called "the banality of evil" (*Eichmann in Jerusalem: A Report on the Banality of Evil*, 1963). His case raised one of the most difficult moral questions of all: Should a person obey the law when the law itself commands injustice and inhumanity?

2.2.2 The Schools of Natural Law

Natural law theory has long provided one of the main answers to the problem of unjust laws. It holds that true law must be grounded in moral principles that are universal and independent of human authority. Over time, several schools of thought have emerged within this tradition, each reflecting different conceptions of the source and nature of justice. From Aristotle's distinction between what is just by nature and what is just by convention, to the Christian interpretation linking natural law to divine will, and finally to the modern secular school, which roots law in human reason, these perspectives collectively shaped the Western understanding of law as something that must always serve justice and human dignity.

2.2.2.1 ARISTOTLE'S DISTINCTION: JUST BY NATURE VS. JUST BY LAW

Observing the social structures of ancient Greece – where women were subordinated to men, slaves to citizens, and foreigners (barbarians) to Greeks (Hellenes) – Aristotle (384–322 BC) reflected deeply on the meaning of justice. In his *Nicomachean Ethics* and *Politics*, he drew a fundamental distinction between what is "just by nature" (physis) and what is "just by law" (nomos).

According to Aristotle, natural justice refers to what is inherently right and fair, independent of human opinion or legislation. It is universal, valid everywhere and at all times, because it stems from the very nature of human beings as rational and social creatures. In contrast, legal or conventional justice depends on human decisions – the laws and customs created by particular societies, which can vary across time and place.

For Aristotle, these two forms of justice are not always the same. A law enacted by a political authority can be "just by law" (that is, valid and enforceable) without being "just by nature" (that is, morally right). Therefore, positive law – the laws made by human institutions – must always strive to conform to natural law, since only natural justice expresses what is truly fair and good for all.

In Aristotle's Greece, slavery and the subordination of women were considered lawful and socially accepted – "just by law" in that context, but not just by nature, since they are not grounded in universal fairness or human dignity.

In this sense, Aristotle laid the philosophical foundation for the later idea that there exists a higher moral order above human legislation – a principle that would profoundly influence Christian thinkers like St. Thomas Aquinas and the entire natural law tradition of Western legal thought.

2.2.2.2 EARLY CHRISTIANISM INFLUENCE ON NATURAL LAW

Christian thought played a major role in shaping the idea of natural law, especially through the writings of St. Paul, St. Augustine, Gratian, and St. Thomas Aquinas.

St. Paul (10–67 AD), in his Letter to the Romans (2:14–15), spoke of a law "written in the hearts" of all people, meaning that even non-Jews ("Gentiles") could know what is right or wrong through their conscience.[17] This suggested that moral truth comes not only from written commandments but also from human reason and divine imprint.

St. Augustine of Hippo (354–430 AD) built on this idea. He taught that before humanity's fall into sin, humans lived freely under natural law, guided by reason and goodness. After the fall, sin corrupted human nature, making positive law (laws imposed by rulers) necessary to control disorder and wrongdoing. Thus, Augustine saw natural law as the original, perfect moral order, and human law as an imperfect tool to manage a fallen world.

In the 12th century, the Italian monk Gratian – often called the father of canon law – identified natural law with divine law, that is, the revealed law of the Bible (both Old and New Testaments). This marked a closer fusion of theology and legal theory within the Church.

St. Thomas Aquinas (1224–1274) later offered the most systematic and enduring version of Christian natural law in his Summa Theologica. He explained that although humans cannot fully grasp the eternal law (God's perfect rational plan), they can perceive part of it through reason. For Aquinas, human law must be a specific application of natural law, and it loses its legitimacy if it contradicts it. He proposed a hierarchy of laws – eternal, natural, and human – each deriving from the higher one. This logical structure, based on consistency between different levels of norms, resembles in some ways the later positivist model of Hans Kelsen in the 20th century.

Aquinas's philosophy created a grand synthesis of Aristotle's reason, Christian theology, and Roman legal thought, becoming one of the cornerstones of Western legal philosophy.

Later scholastic philosophers such as John Duns Scotus (1266–1308), William of Ockham (1285–1349), and Francisco Suárez (1548–1617) introduced a key variation: they emphasized divine will rather than human reason as the ultimate source of law. In their view, what is right and just depends primarily on God's will, not solely on rational moral order.

2.2.2.3 THE MODERN AND SECULAR SCHOOL OF NATURAL LAW

We often distinguish between two main periods of natural law thought: the classical school – represented by Aristotle and St. Thomas Aquinas – and the modern school – represented by Grotius, Althusius, Pufendorf, Locke, and Montesquieu. The essential difference between them lies in their source of legitimacy. While the classical school grounded natural law in God or divine reason, the modern school sought to free natural law from theology. For these thinkers, law no longer proceeds from divine order or from "nature in general," but from human nature and human reason.

The Dutch jurist and diplomat Hugo Grotius (1583–1645) is considered the founder of modern natural law. In his famous work *De Jure Belli ac Pacis* (1625, *On the Law of War and Peace*), he applied natural law principles to relations between nations, thus laying the foundation of International Law. Grotius held that natural law would remain valid "even if God did not

17 "For when the Gentiles who do not have the law by nature observe the prescriptions of the law, they are a law for themselves even though they do not have the law. They show that the demands of the law are written in their hearts, while their conscience also bears witness and their conflicting thoughts accuse or even defend them on the day when, according to my gospel, God will judge people's hidden works through Christ Jesus." The Bible, n.d., Romans 2:14.

exist or took no interest in human affairs." In other words, moral law is binding because it is rational, not simply because it is divine.

Grotius's reasoning was based on the belief that everything in nature has a purpose, and that natural law respects these purposes. For example, if the purpose of sexual relations is procreation, then any act that frustrates that purpose (such as contraception) would be "unnatural." Similarly, treason could be condemned as "unnatural" because it violates natural hierarchies of loyalty and trust.

Yet, more broadly, modern natural law emphasizes human equality: all people are naturally the same and therefore deserve equal treatment under the law. This principle of equality before the law appears in nearly all modern declarations of human rights.

Natural law's legacy can be seen in the founding documents of modern democracy. The U.S. Declaration of Independence (1776) declares that "all men are created equal" and possess "unalienable Rights" such as life, liberty, and the pursuit of happiness. Governments exist to protect these rights, and people have the right to alter or abolish a government that fails to do so. The French Declaration of the Rights of Man and of the Citizen (1789) begins with the statement that "All men are born and remain free and equal in rights." Law, as the expression of the general will, must be the same for everyone and accessible to all citizens according to their talents and virtues. The Charter of Fundamental Rights of the European Union (2000) reaffirms this principle in Article 20: "Everyone is equal before the law." Article 21 adds that any discrimination based on sex, race, religion, or other grounds "shall be prohibited." These texts clearly reflect the moral core of natural law: human dignity, equality, and justice are inherent and universal.

Natural law theorists argue that many areas of law are directly inspired by moral principles. Criminal law reflects the moral belief that wrongdoers deserve punishment. Contract law expresses the moral rule that promises must be kept. Tort law embodies the moral duty to compensate others for harm caused. This is perfectly illustrated by Articles 1382 and 1383 of the French Civil Code, which establish that anyone who causes harm to another must repair it, whether by intention, negligence, or imprudence.

After Grotius, Thomas Hobbes (1588–1679) redefined natural law in more pragmatic terms. For him, the *right of nature* (*jus naturale*) is the liberty each person has to preserve their own life, and the *law of nature* (*lex naturalis*) is a rational rule that forbids self-destruction. Hobbes described a "state of nature" where individuals live in constant conflict – "a war of every man against every man." To escape this chaos, people agree to a social contract, giving power to a sovereign to ensure peace and security. Hobbes thus emphasized order and authority over moral ideals, making him a transitional figure between natural law and early legal positivism.

Samuel von Pufendorf (1632–1694) continued the rationalist approach of Grotius and Hobbes. He viewed natural law as a universal system of moral and legal principles, applicable to all humanity, not just Christians. His *Elementa Jurisprudentiae Universalis* (1661) sought to establish a rational foundation for law that could unite nations and peoples.

Enlightenment philosophers such as Voltaire and Montesquieu further developed and criticized natural law ideas. Voltaire observed that no code of laws is perfect because laws depend on time, place, and circumstance: rules that once made sense may become absurd as societies change. Voltaire argued that there "is no good code in any country" and that "the reason for this is evident." The laws have been made according to the time, the place, and the need, etc. When the needs have changed, the laws, which have remained, have become ridiculous.[18]

18 Voltaire, 1924, "Laws," in *Voltaire's Philosophical Dictionary*, selected and trans. H. I. Woolf, Knopf, New York.

Montesquieu was also very interested in the nature of law and searched for what the essence of law could be as soon as he began studying law.[19] In *The Spirit of the Laws* (1748), Montesquieu defined laws in a broad and philosophical way: "Laws, in their most general sense, are the necessary relations arising from the nature of things." He thus expanded the idea of natural law beyond morality to include the entire order of nature, from divine to human and material realms.[20]

By the early 19th century, belief in natural law declined under the influence of Immanuel Kant (1724–1804) and Jeremy Bentham[21] (1748–1832). Kant emphasized individual autonomy and moral duty rather than "nature," while Bentham, a utilitarian and legal positivist, rejected natural rights as imaginary constructs and pure fiction.[22]

However, natural law thinking resurfaced after the atrocities of the Nazi, Fascist, and Communist regimes in the 20th century. The existence of formally valid but morally repugnant laws led jurists to call such norms "legal monsters." This realization revived the idea that law must be judged against universal moral standards – now expressed not as natural rights, but as human rights.

2.2.3 *The German Historical School vs. Natural Law Debate*

Legal theory has long struggled to explain where law comes from – whether it originates in universal moral principles, as natural lawyers claim, or in the concrete history and customs of a people, as the German historical school argued.

The German Historical School of Law emerged in the 19th century as a reaction against the earlier natural law movement (known in Germany as *Vernunftsrecht*, or "law of reason"). Influenced by the ideas of Romanticism, it rejected the abstract, universalist reasoning of natural lawyers and instead emphasized the historical and cultural roots of law.

The leading figure of this movement was Friedrich Carl von Savigny (1779–1861), whose major works include *History of German Law and Institutions* (1815) and *History of Roman Law in the Middle Ages* (1815–1831). Savigny argued that law does not arise from rational speculation or from the will of legislators, but from the customs, traditions, and shared consciousness of a people. This idea became known as the doctrine of historical continuity.

According to Savigny,

> Law comes into being through custom and popular acceptance, through internal, silently working forces, and not through the arbitrariness of a lawgiver.[23]

In this view, law is a living product of the people – the natural outgrowth of their culture, beliefs, and way of life. It develops organically, just as language does, expressing what Savigny called the *Volksgeist*, the "spirit of the people."

19 Montesquieu confessed in a letter to the Grand Prior Solar, Ambassador from Malta, in Rome, in 1749: "When I left school, law books were placed in my hands and I sought to find their spirit." Montesquieu, Charles de Secondat, 1749, Letter XXIX to the Grand Prior Solar, in Albert Sorel, *The Great French Writers*, Leopold Classics Library (1st ed. 1887; reprint 2017).

20 Montesquieu, Charles de Secondat, 1914, *The Spirit of Laws*, trans. Thomas Nugent, revised by J. V. Prichard, G. Bell & Sons, Ltd.

21 Bentham, Jeremy, 1907, *An Introduction to the Principles of Morals and Legislation*, Clarendon Press, Oxford. Bentham argues that it is the greatest good for the greatest number of people, which is the measure of right and wrong.

22 Utilitarianism is the doctrine which seeks *the greatest good for the greatest number*. "Good" is here understood as hedonic utility: the presence of physical pleasure and absence of pain.

23 Savigny, Friedrich Karl Von, 1831, *Of the Vocation of Our Age for Legislation and Jurisprudence*, trans. Abram Haryward. Littlewood & Co, London.

This conception has an important consequence: law is not universal. Because each nation has its own *Volksgeist*, every legal system reflects the unique character and history of its people. Law, therefore, can only bind those within the community that created it.

In short, the German Historical School replaced the universal rationalism of natural law with a particularist and cultural vision of law – one that values tradition, continuity, and social evolution over abstract moral principles.

2.2.4 The Modern School of Natural Law

In complete opposition to the historic school of law, natural law theory argues that law is transcendent and universal. It does not emerge from the customs or spirit of a particular people, but from principles of justice that apply to all human beings, everywhere and at all times. There are many variations of natural law theories, most of them rooted in theological ideas – which will be examined in more detail in Section 3 – but modern natural law theory places its foundation primarily in human reason. Philosophers such as Grotius, Pufendorf, and Locke believed that through rational reflection, it was possible to identify the true and immutable laws that should govern human society.

While the German Historical School located the origin of law in history, tradition, and culture, modern natural lawyers viewed law as a product of rational deduction, discoverable through the observation of human nature and the exercise of reason. Law, in their view, is not created but discovered – it exists independently of human will, like mathematical truth. Because of this, natural law theory tends to affirm that all legitimate systems of law must respect certain universal moral standards, such as justice, equality, and respect for human dignity. These standards serve as a yardstick to evaluate whether positive law – law enacted by public authorities – deserves obedience.

Notably, John Locke (1632–1704), one of the first so-called liberal authors, sought to design a political system that would protect individual rights by limiting the power of the State. In his *Two Treatises of Government* (1689),[24] Locke argued that people form societies and governments through consent, in order to preserve their natural rights to life, liberty, and property. For Locke, political authority must always remain grounded in natural law: when rulers violate these fundamental rights, citizens regain their right to resistance. His reasoning profoundly influenced later democratic constitutions, including those of the United States and France, and became a cornerstone of modern constitutional thought.

2.2.5 Positivism and Its Contemporary Critics

After centuries of philosophical reflection on the moral foundations of law, legal positivism emerged as a reaction against natural law theories. Whereas natural law links the validity of law to universal principles of justice, positivism insists that law is a social fact, created and recognized by human authority, regardless of its moral content. This school of thought seeks to describe *what law is*, rather than *what it ought to be.*

Developed in the 19th and 20th centuries by thinkers such as Jeremy Bentham, John Austin, Hans Kelsen, H. L. A. Hart, and Joseph Raz, positivism profoundly transformed modern legal philosophy. It introduced a more analytical and scientific approach to law, focusing on its structure, sources, and authority. Yet, this separation between law and morality has been strongly

24 Those treatises are an attack on absolutism and outline Locke's theory of having a civil society grounded on both natural rights and the social contract theory.

debated. Critics such as Ronald Dworkin later challenged positivism's limits, arguing that moral principles are essential to understanding and applying the law.

This part examines the main theses of positivism, its leading theorists, and the most influential critiques that continue to shape contemporary legal thought.

2.2.5.1 THE POSITIVIST THESIS

The other major tradition in legal philosophy is legal positivism. This school of thought arose in deliberate contrast to natural law theory, focusing on the sources of law rather than its moral content. Its most influential figures include Jeremy Bentham and John Austin in the 19th century, followed in the 20th century by Hans Kelsen, H. L. A. Hart, and Joseph Raz.

All legal positivists share two central beliefs. First, law in any given society is fundamentally a matter of social fact or convention, meaning that its validity depends on the way it is created, recognized, and applied within a specific legal system rather than on its moral worth. Second, there is no necessary connection between law and morality; a law can be valid even if it is unjust, so long as it has been produced according to the accepted rules of legal authority.[25]

These principles have profound methodological and practical implications. If law is understood as a human creation, it can be freely shaped or reformed to meet the needs, goals, and evolving values of a given society. Law is therefore primarily a matter of authority and institutional legitimacy rather than of moral truth. Positivism seeks to describe and analyze law as it exists in practice, avoiding the moral or theological assumptions that characterized earlier natural law theories.

Legal positivists also share with other philosophical positivists – in fields such as science or epistemology – a commitment to the idea that the phenomena under study must be accessible to human reason and observation. In this sense, positivism brings a scientific spirit to the study of law: it aims to understand how legal systems function as social structures, how rules are created and applied, and how authority operates within them. Rather than asking what law should be, positivism concentrates on explaining what law is, providing a descriptive and analytical framework that has profoundly influenced modern jurisprudence.

2.2.5.2 JOHN AUSTIN AND HERBERT HART

John Austin (1790–1859) focused strictly on law and its methods, seeking to study legal systems in a precise and scientific manner. Unlike many jurists of his time and even of later generations, he deliberately excluded cultural, sociological, political, economic, and moral considerations from his analysis. For Austin, law is essentially a command issued by a sovereign and backed by the threat of sanction. This definition emphasizes authority and obedience rather than morality or justice. The essence of his doctrine, often called "analytical jurisprudence,"[26] is captured in his well-known statement: "The existence of law is one thing; its merit or demerit is another." This distinction established a clear boundary between the questions of what the law *is* and what the law *ought to be*, forming one of the central pillars of legal positivism.

Herbert Lionel Adolphus Hart (1907–1992), a leading legal philosopher and Professor of Jurisprudence at Oxford University, profoundly transformed legal positivism in the 20th century.

25 Coleman, J. L. and Leiter, B., 1999, "Legal Positivism," in *Blackwell Companion to Philosophy*, ed. D. Patterson, Blackwell, Oxford.

26 Austin, J., 1832, *The Province of Jurisprudence Determined*, John Murray, London.

His most influential work, *The Concept of Law* (1961),[27] offers a more nuanced and sophisticated understanding of legal systems than Austin's command theory. Hart introduced a number of key ideas. First, he distinguished between the internal and external aspects of legal norms, an approach influenced by the sociologist Max Weber's distinction between the legal and sociological perspectives of law. Second, he proposed a fundamental distinction between primary rules, which govern conduct, and secondary rules, which determine how primary rules are created, modified, or annulled. The most important of these secondary rules is the rule of recognition, a social rule that allows members of a legal system to identify which norms possess legal authority and which do not. Through these concepts, Hart replaced Austin's view of law as mere coercion with a more complex and dynamic model of law as a system of rules grounded in both authority and social practice.

2.2.5.3 JOSEPH RAZ

On the positivist side, the work of Joseph Raz (1939–2022), a former student of H. L. A. Hart, represents one of the most influential contemporary contributions to legal philosophy.[28] His book *The Authority of Law: Essays on Law and Morality* (1979) has profoundly shaped modern debates about the nature of law and its relationship to morality.[29]

Raz defends a form of value pluralism and argues that different moral and social values can be incommensurable, meaning they cannot always be ranked by a single standard. Continuing Hart's project, he sought to clarify the concept of legal authority and to explain the sense in which law claims moral authority over its subjects. Raz developed a detailed theory of legal systems, emphasizing the autonomy of law as a normative framework grounded in social facts rather than moral content.

He also explored the broader functions of law in society, the ideal of the Rule of Law, and the role of courts in interpreting and applying legal norms. Finally, Raz examined the moral dimension of legal obedience, asking whether citizens have a moral duty to obey the law and under what conditions they may be justified in disobedience. His analysis situates legal positivism within a sophisticated understanding of authority, responsibility, and moral reasoning in modern legal systems.

2.2.5.4 HISTORICAL POSITIVISM

As explained previously, the 19th-century Historical School of Law developed a more empirical approach to understanding law. Rather than relying on abstract reasoning or logical deduction, it sought to discover the true nature of law through observation, history, and social description.

27 Hart, H.L.A., 2012, *The Concept of Law*, 3rd ed., Clarendon Law Series, OUP Oxford.

28 Another important work in modern legal positivism is Legality by Scott J. Shapiro. Shapiro, Scott J., 2011, *Legality*, The Belknap Press of Harvard University Press. It is one of the most significant books on the question "What is law?" since Ronald Dworkin's Law's Empire (Dworkin, Ronald, 1986, *Law's Empire*, Harvard University Press). In this book, Shapiro offers a clear and original theory of law, showing how legal systems work and why they are necessary. Although Shapiro is a positivist, he discusses natural law and anti-positivist ideas with great attention and respect. His "planning theory of law" explains that laws function like social plans created to organize human behavior and solve problems in a structured way. With this approach, Shapiro gives legal positivism a more practical and human dimension, linking it to everyday moral and social concerns.

29 Raz, Joseph, 2009, *The Authority of Law: Essays on Law and Morality*, Oxford University Press.

This movement, often referred to as historical positivism, viewed law as a product of historical evolution and social experience.

The leading figure of this school was Friedrich Karl von Savigny (1779–1861), one of Germany's most influential jurists. Unlike natural law theorists, Savigny did not believe in a universal human law applicable to all societies. Instead, he argued that every people's law is unique and shaped by their own culture, traditions, and collective consciousness. Law, he said, is closely tied to the Volksgeist, or "spirit of the people." For Savigny, the main source of law was therefore custom, not abstract principles or legislative will.

However, Savigny also recognized that a developed legal system does not arise spontaneously from the people's spirit alone. Both society and law evolve together, becoming increasingly technical as civilizations progress. In his view, law rests on two key elements: a political element, which connects it to the life and spirit of the community, and a technical element, represented by the work of jurists who refine and formalize legal rules. Thus, lawyers play a vital role in transforming customary practices into a coherent and sophisticated legal system.

Another prominent figure of historical positivism was the English jurist and historian Sir Henry Maine[30] (1822–1888). Maine was particularly interested in comparing the historical evolution of English and Roman law. He sought to identify general patterns or "rules" that could explain how legal systems develop over time. In his famous book *Ancient Law* (1861), Maine observed that societies tend to evolve from status to contract, that is, from social relations based on kinship and hierarchy to those founded on individual consent and legal equality. His analysis helped lay the foundations of modern legal anthropology and the sociology of law.

2.2.5.5 DWORKIN: POSITIVISM'S MOST ELOQUENT CRITIC

At the end of the 20th century, Ronald Dworkin (1931–2013), often regarded as America's leading legal philosopher and the most eloquent critic of positivism, published his landmark book *Law's Empire* (1986).[31] This work became one of the most influential contributions to modern legal theory. Dworkin developed a complex and coherent system of ideas about the nature of law, challenging the central assumptions of legal positivism. Most of his objections are based on the argument that moral principles can, and often do, have legal force when they reflect fundamental ideas of justice or fairness. By rejecting the "separability thesis," which claims that law and morality are distinct, Dworkin is often identified as a modern representative of the natural law tradition.

However, Dworkin's theory is not simply a return to classical natural law. He introduces an important distinction between the validity of a legal rule and the meaning of that rule in practice. According to Dworkin, a rule is valid and applicable only if it is consistent with principles of justice, fairness, and due process.[32] He insists that law is not just a system of formal commands

30 Maine's work on less-well-known legal systems, such as the Hindu, the Hebrew, the Welsh, the Anglo-Saxon and the Germanic, is very interesting. This work was influenced by his personal experience in India and the publication of his book *Ancient Law* in 1861 (Books Jungle, 2008).

31 Dworkin, *Law's Empire*.

32 As Coleman and Leiter put it: "Dworkin does not claim that the validity of legal principles depends on their morality, but he does believe that in interpreting the meaning of valid legal rules it is often necessary to consult moral principles." They come to the conclusion that "insofar as Dworkin does not claim that morality is a criterion of legality, he appears to reject one of the classic commitments of natural law." Leiter, Brian and Coleman, Jules L., 2010, "Legal Positivism," in *The Blackwell Companion to Philosophy of Law and Legal Theory*, ed. D. M. Patterson.

but a moral enterprise guided by interpretive reasoning. For him, the law must always be understood as an attempt to present the community's legal practices in their best moral light.

A distinctive feature of Dworkin's philosophy is the central role he gives to the interpreter of law, especially the judge. He argues that it is the judge – rather than the legislator – who plays the key role in shaping the law through interpretation. Each judicial decision is like a new chapter in an ongoing story, forming part of a continuous "chain novel" of legal reasoning. In this way, judges are not mere appliers of rules but active participants in defining what justice means in a given society.

Dworkin's influence extends beyond *Law's Empire* to other foundational works, including *Taking Rights Seriously* (1977) and *The Philosophy of Law* (1977), where he developed his theory of rights and his critique of utilitarianism.[33] His writings continue to shape debates about the relationship between law, morality, and interpretation in contemporary jurisprudence.

2.2.6 Other Contemporary Schools of Legal Thought

Beyond natural law and legal positivism, a wide range of other schools of thought have contributed to the development of modern legal theory. These include legal realism, critical legal studies, post-realism, the legal process school, feminist jurisprudence, law and economics, legal formalism, German legal philosophy, and Marxist theories of law, among others. Although often considered marginal compared to the dominant traditions, these movements have each provided valuable insights into the nature, function, and social role of law.

What unites these diverse approaches is their shared effort to challenge traditional conceptions of law as a purely logical or moral system. Instead, they emphasize the practical, political, and cultural dimensions of legal decision-making. In particular, legal realism, critical legal studies, and post-realism deserve special attention, as they significantly influenced 20th-century legal thought by shifting the focus from abstract theory to the realities of how law is actually applied and experienced in society.

2.2.6.1 LEGAL REALISM

Legal realism emerged as an intellectual movement in the United States during the 1920s and 1930s, bringing together influential scholars and jurists such as Karl Llewellyn, Jerome Frank, and Hessel Yntema. Although it remains a minor school of thought in most Civil Law countries, it has had a profound and lasting influence on American legal thought.

Legal realism challenged the idea that judges merely apply legal rules mechanically to reach objective results. Instead, it emphasized the active role of judges in shaping the law through their decisions. Realists focused on what courts actually do in practice rather than on what the law says in theory. They argued that judicial decisions are influenced not only by legal rules but also by social, psychological, and personal factors.

In this view, judges tend to be more "fact-responsive" than "rule-responsive": they decide cases based on how the facts appear to them and on their own sense of justice or fairness, rather than by rigidly following abstract legal principles.[34] Legal realism thus shifted attention from

33 Dworkin, Ronald, 1977, *Taking Rights Seriously*, Harvard University Press, Cambridge, MA. And Dworkin, Ronald, 1977, *The Philosophy of Law* (Oxford Readings in Philosophy), New York: Oxford University Press.

34 Leiter, Brian, 1999, "Positivism, Formalism, Realism," *Columbia Law Review*, vol. 99, p. v.

formal legal reasoning to the real-world behavior of judges and the social effects of their rulings, paving the way for later movements such as critical legal studies and socio-legal research.

2.2.6.2 CRITICAL LEGAL STUDIES

The movement of Critical Legal Studies (often abbreviated as CLS) emerged in the United States during the 1970s as a radical intellectual current challenging both traditional legal scholarship and mainstream liberal thought. It developed as a continuation of legal realism, but went further by questioning not only how judges decide cases, but also how the entire legal system serves to maintain existing structures of social and economic power.

Critical Legal Studies drew inspiration from several sources, including legal realism, Marxist social theory, and structuralist or post-structuralist philosophy, particularly the works of Michel Foucault and Jacques Derrida. These influences led CLS scholars to view law not as a neutral or objective system, but as a tool that reflects and reinforces political, economic, and ideological interests. In their view, legal doctrines often appear coherent and rational, but in practice, they conceal contradictions and serve to legitimize inequality and domination.

Many of the leading figures of the movement, such as Duncan Kennedy,[35] Roberto Unger, and Mark Tushnet, were associated with the left-wing student movements of the 1960s and 1970s. They criticized what they called the "liberal rights discourse," arguing that individual rights and formal equality often fail to address deeper social injustices. For example, they claimed that legal rights, while appearing to protect freedom, can also reinforce hierarchies of class, race, and gender by maintaining the status quo.

The Critical Legal Studies movement thus redefined the study of law as a form of social critique. Its scholars emphasized that law is inseparable from politics, power, and ideology, and that genuine legal reform requires confronting the hidden biases and structural inequalities embedded within legal institutions. Though its influence declined in the 1990s, CLS left a lasting impact on contemporary legal theory, inspiring later movements such as feminist jurisprudence, critical race theory, and law and society studies.

2.2.6.3 POST-REALISM

Post-realism and the legal process movement, which developed between the 1970s and the late 1980s, marked a significant turning point in American legal thought. Building on the insights of legal realism, these approaches accepted that law is not purely objective or mechanical, but they sought to provide a more constructive framework for understanding how legal institutions actually function. While legal realism had emphasized the unpredictability of judicial decisions and the influence of personal and social factors, post-realism aimed to explore how law could still operate as a coherent system within a democratic society despite these uncertainties.

The legal process school, associated with two Harvard Law Professors in the late 1950s – Henry Hart (1904–1969) and Albert Sacks (1920–1991) – argued that the legitimacy of law depends not so much on its substantive outcomes as on the *processes* through which legal decisions are made.[36] According to this view, if legal procedures are fair, transparent, and participa-

35 Some of his most influential works are *Form and Substance in Private Law Adjudication*, 89 Harv. L. Rev. 1685 (1976), *First Year Law Teaching as Political Action*, 1 Law and Social Problems 47 (1980), *The Critique of Rights in Critical Legal Studies*, in Brown and Halley, eds., *Left Legalism/Left Critique* (Duke University Press 2002).

36 Barzun, C. L., 2013, "The Forgotten Foundations of Hart and Sacks," *Virginia Law Review*, vol. 99, no. 1, pp. 1–67.

tory, the resulting decisions can be accepted as legitimate even when people disagree about their moral correctness. This approach shifted attention from the content of law to the *institutional roles* of lawmakers, judges, and administrators to how these actors interact within a broader system governed by reasoned deliberation.

However, post-realists and legal process theorists also emphasized the political nature of law. They rejected the idea that law could ever be completely neutral or detached from social values. Every legal decision, they argued, involves choices that reflect particular political, moral, or economic priorities. In this sense, law is an ongoing process of negotiation between competing interests rather than a fixed set of rules. By highlighting this dimension, the post-realist and legal process movements deepened the understanding of law as a dynamic, interpretive, and political practice – one that constantly evolves alongside the society it seeks to regulate.

2.2.7 Law and Religion's Interplay

Throughout history, law and religion have maintained a close and complex relationship. In many early societies, legal norms were inseparable from divine commandments, and justice was understood as an expression of sacred order. Over time, however, law gradually sought to free itself from religious authority, developing as an autonomous system grounded in human reason and political legitimacy.

This discussion examines two key dimensions of that evolution: first, the emancipation of law from religion, which marked the rise of secular legal systems in the modern world; and second, the continuing cross-cultural dialogue between theological and secular legal thought, which remains central to understanding how diverse societies reconcile faith and law today.

2.2.7.1 LAW'S EMANCIPATION FROM RELIGION

Law and religion are distinct but closely related spheres of social life. Historically, law was often subordinated to religion, with divine commandments serving as the ultimate source of legal authority. In Western societies, the gradual separation between theology and legality was a long and complex process, marked by the growing autonomy of human-made legal rules from religious prescriptions.

This process of emancipation was strongly influenced by the political thought of writers such as Niccolò Machiavelli, Jean Bodin, and Thomas Hobbes, who all argued for the supremacy of state authority over religious power. Their ideas laid the groundwork for modern secularism and for the development of legal positivism. According to this theory, the validity of law depends not on its moral or religious content but on its origin in legitimate political authority. From a positivist perspective, law is defined as the command of a sovereign backed by the power to enforce it, rather than as a reflection of divine or moral order.

2.2.7.2 CROSS-CULTURAL DIALOGUE IN THEOLOGICAL AND SECULAR LEGAL THINKING

Although law has largely freed itself from religious prescriptions, a complete separation between the two has never been fully achieved. As the French legal scholar Jean Carbonnier observed, religion continues to influence law both directly and indirectly, often through the mediation of dominant moral values within a society. In many cultures, religion still provides the ethical framework that legitimizes political authority and shapes the creation of legal norms.

In today's globalized world, this relationship has become even more complex. The coexistence of secular and religious legal systems gives rise to a constant dialogue – and sometimes tension – between different sources of legitimacy. In certain contexts, religious norms continue to play a role within state legal systems, either through personal status laws or through the recognition of foreign legal principles. For instance, judges in France and other Western countries are occasionally required to consider questions rooted in religious traditions, such as the recognition of polygamous marriages contracted abroad. These examples illustrate that, despite the progress of secularization, religion remains a powerful and enduring force in shaping the moral and cultural dimensions of law.

3 Purposes and Features of Law

It is difficult, and perhaps impossible, to find a single definition of law that everyone would accept. Nevertheless, having a pragmatic definition is useful because it helps us understand what law does and how it operates in society. Even though different cultures and legal traditions have developed their own ways of thinking about law, most agree on a few essential points. Law exists to maintain social order and to promote a shared idea of justice. It does this through general and organized rules that are binding on everyone and that can be enforced by authority. These rules are what we call legal norms.

From this perspective, we can define law, in a simple and practical way, as a system of binding general norms created to preserve order and promote justice within a community. This means that law is not only a collection of commands or prohibitions issued by those in power, but also a framework that expresses a society's values, helps solve disputes, and guides people in living together peacefully. Although any definition of law can be debated, adopting a pragmatic and guiding definition gives us a clear starting point for exploring the meaning and purpose of law in human societies.

3.1 Exploring the Various Purposes of Law

The purposes of law are diverse and deeply connected to the organization of society. Laws are created to achieve specific goals, such as maintaining order, resolving conflicts, and promoting justice. As the French poet and thinker Paul Valéry once observed, "law is language in action," reminding us that law is not static but constantly applied and interpreted in real life. Aristotle also associated law with order, seeing it as the foundation of stability within the community. More recently, scholars such as Brian Tamanaha and John Rawls have stressed that law should also protect individual rights and promote fairness among citizens.

However, understanding the true purpose of law raises important questions about interpretation. Should we focus only on the literal meaning of legal texts to understand what lawmakers intended, or should we also consider the broader goals that laws are meant to serve? This question illustrates the complexity of legal interpretation and the importance of examining both the language of the law and its underlying social and moral objectives.

3.1.1 Laws Are Enacted to Achieve Some Goals

Most legal scholars agree that laws are not created without purpose. In principle, both legislators and judges establish rules to achieve specific goals rather than for their own sake. However, there is far less agreement on what these goals actually are. Should law serve individual interests or collective well-being? Is its main objective the public good or the protection of private rights? Should we understand law through a utilitarian and hedonistic perspective, which seeks to maximize happiness, or rather through the idea of social harmony and moral order? These questions reveal the diversity – and sometimes the conflict – of views about the true purposes of law.

Since Antiquity, one of the most frequently stated aims of law has been the pursuit of justice. Yet even this apparently simple idea raises major theoretical difficulties. Although many would agree that the law should promote justice, there is no consensus on what justice actually means. Should the law aim to ensure individual justice between persons, or social justice among groups? Should it prioritize commutative justice, which concerns fair exchanges between individuals, or distributive justice, which focuses on the fair allocation of resources within society? Once again, we find ourselves caught in a definitional dilemma: the more we try to define the purpose of law, the more complex and contested the concept becomes.

3.1.2 "Law Is Language in Action" (Paul Valéry)

The idea that law mediates between politics and ethics is not new. Julien Freund (1921–1993) expressed it as early as 1965 in *L'essence du politique*,[37] though his analysis now belongs to a different intellectual context. Yet the core intuition remains relevant. Contemporary thinkers such as Jürgen Habermas (*Between Facts and Norms*, 1992)[38] and Norberto Bobbio[39] (*L'età dei diritti*, 1990) have reformulated it in modern terms, portraying law as a communicative process that balances political power with moral principles in democratic societies.

Law serves a relational purpose: it places itself between individuals and groups, acting as a bridge that connects people and regulates their interactions. It stands as the hyphen that links society together, translating moral expectations and political power into shared rules of conduct. Through this mediating role, law transforms conflict into dialogue and turns competing interests into structured coexistence.

While this view captures an essential truth about law's relational character, it can be developed further. Law does not merely mediate between politics and ethics; it also operates at the intersection of multiple and often opposing values. It constantly seeks to reconcile what is *just* with what is *reasonable*, what is *individual* with what is *social*, and what arises from *consensus* with what stems from *conflict*. Law, therefore, is not a static set of rules but a living process of negotiation between principles that might otherwise remain irreconcilable.

From this perspective, law is best understood as a dynamic act of communication – the deliberate use of language to shape relationships and organize life in common. As Paul Valéry aptly put it, "law is language in action." It is through words that law binds society together, not only prescribing behavior but also giving meaning and form to human coexistence.

37 Freund, Julien, 1965, *L'essence* du *politique*, Sirey. Julien Freund was a French philosopher, sociologist, and member of the Resistance during World War II. A student of Raymond Aron, he is best known for his work *L'essence du politique* (1965), in which he explored the fundamental nature of the political realm and its relationship with other spheres of human activity, such as morality and law. Freund argued that law stands at the crossroads between politics and ethics, mediating their tensions and translating moral values into institutional forms.

38 Jürgen Habermas (born 1929 in Düsseldorf) is a German philosopher and sociologist, one of the most influential thinkers of our time. A leading member of the Frankfurt School, he combines ideas from Marxism, pragmatism, psychology, and sociology. Habermas believes that modern societies must find unity through open discussion and mutual understanding. In his book *Between Facts and Norms* (1992), he explains that law connects political power and moral values, acting as a bridge between politics and ethics through communication and dialogue.

39 Norberto Bobbio (1909–2004) was an Italian philosopher, jurist, and political thinker, widely known for his work in political and legal philosophy. He taught at several Italian universities, including Turin and Padua, and served as a senator for life. Bobbio focused on the relationship between democracy, human rights, and the Rule of Law. He argued that true democracy requires not only political participation but also the effective protection of human rights and the pursuit of peace through International Law. His vision of citizenship was deeply cosmopolitan, seeing individuals as members of a global community bound by shared legal and moral principles.

3.1.3 The Fundamental Function of Law Is to Maintain Social Order

Law serves several essential purposes within society, but one of its most fundamental functions is to maintain social order. By setting clear rules of conduct and providing mechanisms for resolving conflicts, law ensures stability and coexistence among individuals and groups. Thinkers from Aristotle to modern theorists have emphasized that without law, chaos and injustice would prevail. The following discussions explore three key dimensions of this idea: law as order, law as a social necessity, and law as a means to achieve justice.

3.1.3.1 LAW IS ORDER (ARISTOTLE)

We have rules to secure peaceful and predictable relationships between people, ensuring that social life remains stable and organized. Law functions as a framework within which individuals can act freely while respecting the rights and safety of others. In this sense, it serves as both a guide and a constraint on human behavior – a mechanism that channels individual freedom into forms compatible with collective life.

At its most basic level, law can be understood as an organized system of coercion, one that sets clear boundaries for what is permitted and what is prohibited. These boundaries are not meant to eliminate freedom, but rather to make freedom possible within an ordered community. As Aristotle famously stated, "Law is order," meaning that it transforms the natural chaos of human desires and conflicts into a structured coexistence.

Without law, societies would descend into disorder, as personal interests and passions would prevail over shared norms. Thus, law acts as a stabilizing force – a rational structure that organizes social life, protects individuals from arbitrary power, and provides the conditions for justice to emerge.

3.1.3.2 LAW IS A SOCIAL NECESSITY

Human societies cannot exist without order, for without a minimum level of organization and stability, collective life would quickly disintegrate into conflict and uncertainty. Order provides predictability – a shared understanding of what is expected and what is forbidden – allowing individuals to cooperate, trade, and coexist peacefully. From the smallest tribe to the most complex modern state, every human community has developed rules to regulate behavior and settle disputes.

Since order cannot be maintained without some form of law, it follows that all societies, regardless of time or culture, possess legal systems – whether written or unwritten, formal or customary. Law, in this sense, is not merely a political creation but a social necessity. It emerges from the basic need to prevent chaos and ensure coexistence.

Political communities, therefore, impose law as a matter of necessity, not choice. Individuals agree, implicitly or explicitly, to live under a system of norms that constrains certain behaviors in exchange for the benefits of collective security and cooperation. In this way, law functions as the condition of possibility for social life itself – the invisible structure that holds communities together and allows them to endure across generations.

3.1.3.3 LAW AIMS AT JUSTICE OR RIGHT

Law, nevertheless, is not merely about maintaining order. Its deeper purpose is to order society according to an underlying idea of justice or right. As the legal philosopher Brian Tamanaha points out, "A correct concept of law must recognize that law is imbued with justice and right."

This connection between law and justice regained prominence in the mid-20th century, particularly in reaction to the atrocities of Nazi and Communist regimes, whose laws – though formally valid – were morally abhorrent.[40] These experiences reinforced the conviction that rules which fundamentally violate fairness and human dignity do not deserve to be called "law" in the true sense.

If law is to pursue justice, it must rest on the principles of liberty and equality. Yet, defining justice has always been one of the most debated questions in philosophy. The American philosopher John Rawls offered one of the most influential modern accounts of justice in his book *A Theory of Justice* (1971). For Rawls, justice can be discovered through a thought experiment involving the "original position" and the "veil of ignorance."

In the original position, individuals are asked to design the basic rules and institutions of their society. However, they must do so behind a veil of ignorance – meaning they do not know their future social status, wealth, gender, or abilities. This ensures impartiality, as decisions are made without bias or self-interest. The reasoning echoes Immanuel Kant's moral philosophy, particularly his categorical imperative: one should act only according to maxims that one would wish to become universal laws.[41]

Through this process, Rawls concludes that rational individuals would agree on two fundamental principles of justice: the principle of liberty (each person has an equal right to basic freedoms) and the principle of equality (social and economic inequalities are acceptable only if they benefit the least advantaged). To illustrate his idea, Rawls uses a simple metaphor: When two children must share a cake, the fairest solution is that one cuts the cake while the other chooses the slice.[42]

In short, Rawls defines justice as fairness. Law, if it truly aims to achieve justice, must therefore be designed and applied in a way that secures both liberty and equality – ensuring that order serves not power, but the moral dignity of all.

3.2 Features of Law: Binding and Systemic

Law possesses several essential characteristics that set it apart from other forms of social regulation. First, it is binding in nature and operates within an organized institutional framework, distinguishing it from moral, religious, or customary norms that rely mainly on social pressure. Legal institutions, such as courts and legislatures, give law its legitimacy, enforceability, and authority.

Second, law functions as a system, composed of interconnected rules and principles that together form a coherent legal order. This system provides predictability and consistency while also recognizing that every legal order has its own internal limits and imperfections. Understanding how a legal order differs from the broader concept of state helps clarify law's specific role in governance – it is both a tool of power and a framework that constrains power.

Finally, legal norms have their own internal structure and purpose. They can be analyzed according to their type (whether constitutional, criminal, civil, etc.), their rule-based nature, and their essence, which lies in balancing authority with fairness. Validity and justice remain central to this balance: for law to be respected, it must not only be formally valid but also perceived as fair. In this sense, law is both a technical system and a moral enterprise aimed at ensuring justice within an ordered society.

40 Tamanaha, *Law*.
41 Kant, Immanuel, 1785, *Grounding for the Metaphysics of Morals*.
42 See Rawls, John, 1971, *A Theory of Justice*, The Belknap Press of Harvard University Press.

3.2.1 Law Is Binding

One of the most distinctive features of law is its binding force. Unlike moral or social norms, which rely on voluntary compliance or social pressure, legal norms are backed by institutional authority and the possibility of coercion. Understanding why and how law obliges individuals to obey requires examining the difference between social and legal norms, as well as exploring institutional theories that explain the legitimacy and authority of legal systems.

3.2.1.1 SOCIAL NORMS VS. LEGAL NORMS

Every society is structured around a set of norms – shared rules of behavior that shape how individuals interact and coexist. These social norms emerge naturally within communities, reflecting collective values, traditions, and expectations. They govern everyday behavior: how people dress, speak, show respect, or fulfill their roles in family and community life. Such norms are generally upheld through social approval or disapproval rather than formal sanctions. In other words, people comply with them because they seek social acceptance, not because they fear punishment.

However, not all norms are legal norms. The key distinction lies in the binding and coercive nature of law. Legal norms are not merely recommendations or customs; they are obligatory and enforceable through the authority of the state. Whereas social norms depend on moral persuasion or peer pressure, legal norms rely on institutions such as courts, police, and administrative bodies that ensure compliance and impose penalties for violations.

This organized coercion is what gives law its unique authority. It transforms moral or social expectations into formal obligations backed by sanctions. Yet, the legitimacy of this coercion does not rest solely on fear; it is also grounded in the idea that law expresses the collective will and serves the public good. Thus, law distinguishes itself from other social rules by combining normativity and enforceability – it both prescribes behavior and guarantees its observance through institutional power.[43]

In every society, people follow both social and legal norms, but these two kinds of rules differ in nature and in the way they are enforced. Social norms are informal expectations that guide everyday behavior and ensure smooth interaction within a community. They reflect culture, manners, and shared values rather than formal laws. For instance, in Japan, bowing when greeting someone is a strong social convention that shows respect. In South Korea, removing one's shoes before entering a home is a customary act of politeness. In many Arab countries, offering coffee or tea to guests is part of the tradition of hospitality – refusing it might seem rude but carries no legal consequence. Similarly, in the United States, people are expected to stand in line and wait their turn, while in France, leaving a tip in a restaurant is a social gesture of appreciation rather than a legal duty. These unwritten rules help maintain harmony and mutual respect but rely on social approval or disapproval rather than state enforcement.

Legal norms, on the other hand, are formal rules created and enforced by public authorities. They are binding and backed by sanctions that ensure compliance. Paying income tax, for example, is a legal obligation in most countries, and failure to do so can lead to fines or imprisonment. Driving regulations, such as the requirement to wear a seatbelt or drive on a specific side of the road, are also legal norms that protect public safety. In Canada, anti-discrimination laws prohibit unequal treatment in employment or housing based on gender, race, or religion, while in India,

43 Kelsen, Hans, 1942, "Law as a Specific Social Technique," *The University of Chicago Law Review*, vol. 9, pp. 75–97.

child marriage is banned and punishable by law. Some legal norms can even reflect cultural priorities – in Singapore, for instance, the sale and chewing of gum in public is restricted to preserve cleanliness and order.

In short, social norms express what a community expects from its members in terms of courtesy and behavior, while legal norms define what the State requires to preserve order, justice, and the common good. Both are essential: social norms maintain cohesion through shared values, and legal norms secure peace through authority and enforceability.

3.2.1.2 THE INSTITUTIONAL THEORIES OF LAW

Some scholars argue that law should not be seen as distinct from other forms of social regulation. According to this view, known as the institutional theory of law, legal norms are simply one type among many social norms that shape human behavior. Law, in this perspective, would represent the total complex of social rules, customs, and practices through which societies regulate themselves. It would not be an isolated or superior system but rather part of the broader social fabric that includes moral, religious, and cultural norms.[44]

However, this approach raises important objections. We do not fully share the idea that law can be reduced to social norms, since what distinguishes law is its immediate and organized coercive power. For example, shaking hands after a tennis match is a social norm, reflecting courtesy and sportsmanship, but it cannot be considered a legal norm, because players cannot be legally compelled to do so. This distinction reveals that law operates through institutions capable of enforcing compliance, whereas social norms rely on moral pressure or community expectations.

Social norms can arise from many sources – religion, morality, tradition, fashion – and these normative systems often overlap. In everyday life, individuals act in ways that simultaneously conform to moral, legal, and social expectations. Yet, legality cannot be reduced to any of these other regimes. Law forms a specific category of norms: those backed by the organized power of sanctioning. While violating a social norm might lead to shame, exclusion, or disapproval, breaking a legal rule leads to formal, institutional consequences imposed by recognized authorities, such as courts or administrative bodies.

Legal norms typically prescribe or prohibit specific behaviors, but they also play a creative and distributive role. They can allocate resources, establish rights, or encourage desirable conduct through incentives. For instance, laws may provide subsidies to support certain industries or guarantee citizens access to healthcare and social security. In all such cases, the defining element remains the same: every legal norm carries an enforceable sanction that ensures its observance through the authority of the state.

3.2.2 Law as Systemic

Law functions as a coherent and organized system, composed of interrelated elements that together form what we call a legal order. At its core, this system rests on three essential components. First, there are legal norms, the general rules that prescribe what is permitted, prohibited, or required. Second, there are individuals or entities endowed with legal personality, meaning

44 MacCormick, N., and Ota Weinberger, 1986, *An Institutional Theory of Law: New Approaches to Legal Positivism*, Law and Philosophy Library, (3).

they hold rights and obligations under the law. Third, there are courts and judicial institutions, which interpret and apply legal norms to resolve disputes and ensure justice.

These three components are inseparable and constantly interact. Legal norms would have no meaning without individuals to whom they apply, and rights would be empty without institutions capable of protecting or enforcing them. Likewise, courts could not function without a body of norms to interpret or subjects to whom these norms relate. Together, these elements form a dynamic system through which law organizes social life, defines responsibilities, and guarantees justice within a community.

3.2.2.1 THE THREE KEY FEATURES OF LEGAL ORDERS

In any legal system, three key components work together to maintain order and ensure justice: binding legal norms, individuals who hold rights and obligations through legal personality, and courts that enforce those norms and settle disputes. Legal rules are defined by their binding nature – they impose duties and confer rights that can be enforced through institutional mechanisms. This raises an enduring question in legal theory: are laws binding because they are enforceable by judges, or are they enforceable because they are binding? Regardless of how this relationship is understood, it is clear that without enforcement, a rule would lose much of its legal force. The different categories of legal norms and their sources will be explored in later sections.

Each individual within a legal system possesses what are known as subjective rights – personal and financial rights that they may claim or defend in their relations with others. These rights exist because of a concept central to law: legal personality. As Bryant Smith observed in his 1928 article in the *Yale Law Journal*, "To be a legal person is to be the subject of rights and duties. To confer legal rights or to impose legal duties, therefore, is to confer legal personality."[45] Legal personality thus defines who can act, claim, or be held accountable within a legal system.

Courts, meanwhile, are the institutions responsible for interpreting and applying the law. As defined by *Black's Law Dictionary*, a court is "a governmental body consisting of one or more judges who sit to adjudicate disputes and administer justice." Judges identify the relevant legal norms, interpret them, and render decisions accordingly. Their interpretation is subject to the authority of higher courts – particularly the Supreme Court – which ensures consistency and coherence within the legal order. The reasoning process and techniques judges use in applying and interpreting legal norms are known as statutory interpretation, a topic further discussed in Chapter 6 – *Civil Procedure: The Judiciary and the Unfolding of Civil Procedure.*

3.2.2.2 THE LIMITS OF INSTITUTIONALISM

The study of legal systems has long fascinated scholars and given rise to different theoretical approaches. Among them, institutionalism emerged as an anti-formalist reaction to the limitations of traditional legal positivism, which focused too narrowly on written norms and state authority. Institutionalism seeks to broaden the understanding of law by emphasizing its social foundations and its existence within organized human communities. The classic institutionalist school is generally associated with two major figures of the early 20th century: the Italian jurist Santi Romano and the French jurist Maurice Hauriou. Santi Romano[46] developed a distinctive theory

45 Smith, Bryant, 1928, "Legal Personality," *Yale Law Journal*, vol. 37, no. 3.

46 Santi Romano's views have been diffused in English legal literature thanks to the works of Julius Stone in the 1960s. Prior to this, Romano's *Ordinamento* had only been translated into Spanish, German and French. Legal systems' and

of institutionalism in his 1917 work *L'ordinamento giuridico* (*The Legal Order*).[47] His doctrine rests on two main ideas: first, that every legal order is itself an institution, and second, that institutions are organized social forms arising spontaneously wherever social relations exist. According to Romano, law is not simply created by the legislator; rather, it grows organically from preexisting social practices and relations. As he put it, "Law is never the commencement of law: it is rather an accretion that builds on top of preexistent law or else a modification of that law."

In short, Santi Romano believed that law is not just made by governments but grows naturally from the way people live and organize together in society. For example, if children in a playground create their own rules for taking turns on the slide and everyone follows them, Santi Romano would say that this is also a kind of law – it comes from the group's shared agreement, not from the government. A more complex example would be a professional sports league, like FIFA in football. FIFA creates and enforces its own rules for how the game is played, how players and teams are disciplined, and how disputes are resolved through internal tribunals. These rules are not made by any government, yet they are binding on all members of the organization. According to Santi Romano, FIFA itself forms a *legal order* – an institution that produces and applies its own law within a specific social community. This view challenges the positivist belief that law originates exclusively from the State through formal statutes.

To fully grasp Romano's theory, it is useful to contrast legal institutionalism[48] with legal normativism, particularly as developed by Hans Kelsen. Although Romano and Kelsen were contemporaries, their conceptions of law diverged sharply. Kelsen saw law as a system of norms – a hierarchical structure in which each rule derives its validity from a higher rule, culminating in a basic norm (Grundnorm). Romano, by contrast, conceived of law as something broader and more organic. For him, a legal order is not merely a collection of norms but a living institution – a unified organization that expresses and maintains social order.

Romano argued that law, institution, and legal order are synonymous. Legal phenomena exist wherever organized human activity takes place – not only within the State but in every social entity that exhibits structure and continuity. Families, schools, corporations, trade unions, and associations all embody their own forms of law. In this sense, law transcends the State, and the State's recognition is not what determines the existence of a legal order. Even private or informal groups can generate their own legal norms through internal decision-making or dispute resolution processes. For example, a factory or a private club may establish binding internal rules and procedures that function as a genuine legal order within its sphere.

Furthermore, Romano maintained that legal orders could exist even without preestablished norms. When judges resolve disputes in the absence of clear rules, they create law through their decisions. Thus, for Romano, the Judiciary – as the institution that interprets and applies justice – is central to the very existence of law. One might object, however, that even when norms arise from judicial decisions, they eventually become part of a system of rules, reaffirming that norms remain a fundamental component of legality.

---

lawyers' Reasonings, Human Law and Human Justice, Social Dimensions of law and Justice (London, Steven and Sons, 1964–1965–1966). The third volume in particular contains a summary of S. Romano's doctrine incorporated in developments on institutionalism.

47 Romano, Santi, 2018, *The Legal Order*, 1st ed., Routledge. This is the first English translation of Santi Romano's classic work, *L'ordinamento giuridico* (*The Legal Order*), first published in 1917 (Part 1) and 1918 (Part 2), with a second edition in 1946.

48 Beyond Santi Romano, institutionalism includes the writings of authors such as Georges Renard and Maurice Hauriou.

By asserting that law can exist independently of the State, Romano broke with one of the core dogmas of legal positivism: the idea that all law derives from a single, unified, state-based source. In Romano's view, law is a social institution that may take many forms, both public and private. It emerges wherever human beings organize themselves collectively, creating order through rules, authority, and shared purposes.

3.2.2.3 THE DIFFERENCES BETWEEN A STATE AND A LEGAL ORDER

Every State can be described as a legal order because it includes the three fundamental elements of any legal system: legal norms, individuals with rights and obligations, and courts or tribunals that apply these norms to resolve disputes. However, a State is more than just a legal system – it is also a political organization, established through a constitution that defines both the political and legal framework for an entire territory. Legally speaking, the State has what is known as legal personality, meaning it can act as a legal subject. Yet it is an abstract entity: unlike a natural person, it is not a living human being but a legal construct.

A State typically comprises three main elements that correspond to those of any legal order: a defined territory within recognized boundaries, an organized political authority (the government), and a population or nation. These features are primarily political rather than legal, but they remain essential to the State's existence. Likewise, every legal system has territorial limits, since its rules apply only within certain boundaries. This territorial aspect also characterizes international legal systems, which are usually established through treaties between states.

A clear example of an international legal order is the 1982 United Nations Convention on the Law of the Sea (UNCLOS), also known as the Montego Bay Convention. This treaty created a comprehensive legal framework governing the use of the world's oceans. It sets out detailed rules and principles, such as the freedom of navigation, peaceful use of the seas, equitable exploitation of resources, and protection of the marine environment. The Convention has been signed by around 160 states, and about 60 of them have accepted the compulsory jurisdiction of the International Tribunal for the Law of the Sea (ITLOS), which was established under the Convention. Based in Hamburg and composed of 21 elected judges, the Tribunal settles disputes arising from the interpretation or application of the treaty. UNCLOS, therefore, meets all the criteria of a legal order: it has legal norms, legal subjects, and judicial institutions.

Other entities besides states may also constitute legal orders. Early human societies, tribes, international organizations, and even political entities like the European Union can be considered legal systems because they are founded on legal rules, recognize rights and duties, and possess mechanisms for resolving disputes. Before the Treaty of Lisbon granted the EU formal legal personality, it already functioned as a distinct legal order with its own institutions and binding normative framework.

Finally, the relationship between states and legal systems raises an important question: do states create legal orders, or are states themselves created by law? On one hand, states establish legal systems through their constitutions and legislation; on the other hand, a state's very existence is defined and structured by legal norms. This mutual dependency shows the close and inseparable connection between law and politics. Law gives form and legitimacy to political power, while politics continuously shapes the creation, interpretation, and evolution of law.

3.2.3 The main features of legal norms

It is important to note from the outset that the concept of "legal norm" is an extremely abstract subject and can reach a very high level of theoretical complexity in legal scholarship. The greatest jurists – from Kelsen to Bobbio – have devoted entire volumes to it, because the notion is subtle and sophisticated. Yet great ideas often begin simply, and good pedagogy requires starting with what is clear and concrete before moving toward the more abstract.

For this reason, we will use very simple examples and formulate the ideas in the most accessible way possible. The aim is not to oversimplify the theory to the point of distorting it, but to enable any reader to enter gradually into the logic of law, with explanations that are clear, pedagogical, and approachable, before turning to more technical developments.

3.2.3.1 DEFINITION AND SPECIFICITY OF THE LEGAL NORM

To put it simply, a legal norm is a rule that tells people what they must do, must not do, may do, or are allowed to do. For example, a law that says "You must go to school until you are 16" makes something obligatory. A rule that says "You must not steal" makes something forbidden. A rule that says "You may choose your job when you turn 18" makes something permitted. And a rule that says "The mayor can sign new local regulations" gives someone power or authority to act.

To be a real legal norm, such a rule must come from someone who has the right to make it (like a parliament or a court) and be part of a legal system that enforces it (for example, by police or judges). Moral rules, like "You should help your friends," or social habits, like "You should say thank you," are also norms, but they are not legal ones because no court can punish you if you don't follow them. Legal norms belong to a system where rules are recognized, applied, and, if needed, enforced.

3.2.3.2 THE IDEA OF A HIERARCHICAL ORDER

Law is not a heap of isolated rules but an ordered hierarchy in which each norm derives legitimacy from another. Belonging to such an order implies a plurality of interacting norms, an organization by rank or authority, and unity around a common foundation of validity. A norm is legal only insofar as it inhabits this structured order.

To understand this, simple examples help.

First, rules interact. Imagine a small town: a local rule may say that *shops must close at 10 p.m.*, but this rule only exists because a national law authorizes towns to regulate shop hours. And that national law is valid because the constitution allows parliament to legislate on commercial matters. None of these rules "floats" alone; each depends on another.

Second, rules are organized by rank. If a town made a rule allowing shops to stay open all night, but a national statute sets the maximum closing time at 10 p.m., the local rule would be invalid. Why? Because national statutes rank higher than municipal by-laws. If a statute contradicts the constitution – say, a law that restricts freedom of speech without justification – courts may strike it down because the constitution ranks above statutes. The hierarchy determines which rule prevails.

Third, unity. All these norms connect back to a common foundation: the constitution (or the basic rules that function as the constitution in unwritten systems). This is why laws made in open defiance of constitutional procedures or values cannot be considered valid in the legal order – they break the chain of validity that gives unity to the entire system.

Taken together, these simple examples show why a rule becomes *legal* only when it is part of this organized structure. A command shouted by a stranger, or even a well-intentioned recommendation, is not law: it has no place in the hierarchy. A rule is legal only when it fits into this chain of authorization that links lower rules to higher ones, all the way up to the fundamental norms of the system.

Thus, validity is defined from within the legal system. A rule is binding if it is produced by the right actor, follows the right procedure and is in conformity with higher norms. Judges, by interpreting and applying norms, stabilize their meaning and confirm their juridical existence. Moral precepts and social conventions may guide conduct powerfully, but they are not law unless received into the hierarchy and backed by institutional enforcement.

In brief, a legal norm is a binding prescription whose authority comes from its place in a hierarchical, coherent, and dynamic order. It is obligatory because it is valid; valid because produced under authorized procedures and consistent with superior norms; and juridical because it belongs to an institutional system of recognition and enforcement.

3.2.3.3 A LEGAL NORM MUST BE FAIR AND JUST

We defend the idea that only a just rule deserves to be called "law" in a meaningful sense. This position is, of course, debated within legal theory. Yet several reasons support it. First, law derives its legitimacy from justice: a rule that is profoundly unjust may command obedience through force, but it no longer commands respect, and without respect, its legal authority collapses. Second, the fundamental purpose of law is to protect individuals and maintain order fairly; a rule that harms, discriminates, or arbitrarily restricts rights contradicts the very mission of law and thereby ceases to function as law. Third, if justice is removed from the concept of law, nothing prevents oppressive or abusive measures from being labelled "law," thereby erasing the distinction between legality and domination.

Many positivists argue that law is simply whatever the State enacts and enforces, regardless of moral content. Yet we consider that the concept of law cannot be reduced to a mere apparatus of state coercion. As several theorists have suggested, a genuine concept of law must contain an element of justice or right.[49]

It is true that individuals and cultures may hold different visions of what justice requires. It is often said that Napoleon, during the drafting of the French Civil Code of 1804, repeatedly asked a set of simple but profound questions before adopting or modifying a provision: What was there before? What is there now? Is this useful? Is this just? These questions show a conviction that law cannot be separated from considerations of justice and purpose.

As Amartya Sen – an Indian economist and philosopher, a leading authority on poverty and development, recipient of the 1998 Nobel Prize in Economics for "his contribution to welfare economics," and currently a professor at Harvard University – famously observed, one of the defining features of justice is precisely its plurality: we may share a strong sense that something is unjust, yet disagree on which particular reason best explains that injustice. This relativity does not weaken the link between justice and legality. On the contrary, it highlights why legal systems must remain attentive to fairness, coherence, and human dignity if they are to retain legitimacy.

In short, even if conceptions of justice vary, the aspiration toward justice remains an essential component of the very idea of law. Without it, legality risks becoming nothing more than organized force – effective perhaps, but no longer truly lawful.

4 What Forms Does Law Take?

Law appears through a series of recognizable forms known as sources of law. In analyzing a legal norm, we distinguish its author (parliament, the government, or an administrative authority),

49 Bodenheimer, Edgar, 1940, "Power and Law: A Study of the Concept of Law," *Ethics*, vol. 50, no. 2, pp. 127–143.

its type (constitutional provision, statute, or regulation), and its content (what it prescribes, prohibits, or permits).

This section introduces the sources of law, meaning the authorities and processes through which legal norms are created. Most legal systems distinguish between formal sources – such as constitutions, statutes, regulations, and treaties – and informal sources, including custom, general principles, equity, case law, scholarly writings, and soft law.

This discussion also raises fundamental questions: How do we recognize law when we encounter it? What does it look like in practice? And what criteria allow us to identify a rule as legally valid? Understanding these forms is essential for determining how a legal system recognizes and gives authority to its norms.

4.1 Sources of Law

This part examines the sources of law – that is, who produces each category of legal norms and by virtue of what authority. Legal systems recognize several forms through which law manifests. Formal sources include constitutions, statutes, regulations, and treaties. Informal sources include custom, general principles, equity, case law (depending on the legal tradition), scholarly writings, contracts, and soft law. Contracts produce binding effects between the parties but do not constitute an autonomous source of law for the legal order as a whole.

Although each legal system has its own catalogue of sources, the influence of globalization and the convergence of legal techniques have led most countries to recognize very similar forms of law. What follows provides a clear and accessible overview of these sources, accompanied by simple and concrete illustrations from different regions of the world.

4.1.1 Formal Sources of Law

Formal sources are authoritative instruments enacted or validated by public institutions. They are binding and form the backbone of any legal order. In most legal systems, four main categories of formal sources can be identified: the Constitution, which stands at the top of the hierarchy of norms; statutes, enacted by the legislative branch; regulations, adopted by administrative authorities under delegated power; and treaties or international conventions, which bind states at the international level and may also form part of domestic law.

4.1.1.1 THE CONSTITUTION

A constitution is the fundamental law of a State. It establishes the main institutions, distributes political powers, protects fundamental rights, and sets the conditions under which all lower norms are created and applied. Because it stands at the top of the hierarchy of norms, every statute, regulation, and governmental act must conform to it.

Constitutions may be written, as in South Africa, whose 1996 Constitution enshrines an extensive bill of rights and created a powerful Constitutional Court, or unwritten, as in the United Kingdom, where constitutional rules derive from statutes, case law, and long-standing conventions rather than from a single codified document.

The role, structure, and authority of constitutions – as well as the mechanisms through which courts ensure their supremacy – will be examined in depth in Chapter 5: *Constitutionalism and Judicial Review.*

4.1.1.2 STATUTES

Statutes are laws enacted by a legislative body. They express the will of parliament or congress and constitute one of the primary sources of law in most legal systems. Once adopted through the proper legislative procedure and promulgated by the competent authority, statutes become binding rules that apply to all individuals and institutions within the State. They may establish new rights or obligations, regulate social and economic activities, create offences and penalties, or organize public institutions. Statutes can take many forms – general codes, detailed legislative acts, or specific amendments – and their interpretation and application are central to the daily work of courts and public authorities.

The terminology varies across legal systems, where statutes may be referred to as *Acts*, *legislation*, *laws*, *codes*, or *parliamentary enactments*, depending on national traditions. In the United Kingdom and other Commonwealth countries, they are known as Acts of Parliament, while in federal systems, such as the United States or Germany, they may be called federal laws. More technical expressions – such as *legislative acts*, *parliamentary acts*, or *statutory provisions* – are also common in legal scholarship.

This diversity does not exist in all legal traditions. In French law, for example, a single term – la loi – is used to designate what English-speaking systems would call Acts, statutes, or parliamentary enactments, while la législation refers more broadly to the entire body of legislative norms. English-speaking systems, by contrast, employ a wider range of terms to describe legislative instruments.

Statutes may also be classified according to their function:

Codifying statutes restate an entire field of law, as with the French Civil Code of 1804 or the Japanese Civil Code of 1896.

Consolidating statutes gather dispersed rules into a single act, such as India's Companies Act 2013, which reorganized earlier corporate legislation.

Disabling statutes restrict or remove rights, as illustrated by France's 2010 law prohibiting the concealment of the face in public spaces.

Mandatory statutes impose obligations, for example, compulsory education laws in Germany or the United States.

Organic statutes regulate essential constitutional procedures, such as Spain's Organic Laws governing elections.

Severable statutes remain valid even when certain provisions are struck down, as seen in decisions of the Colombian Constitutional Court, which often preserves most of a statute while invalidating specific articles.

Penal statutes define offences and penalties, such as the Canadian Criminal Code or Nigeria's Criminal Code Act.

Together, these various forms of statutes illustrate the diversity of legislative techniques and the central role that legislation plays in shaping the structure, functioning, and evolution of any legal order.

4.1.1.3 REGULATIONS

Regulations are norms issued by administrative or sub-national authorities under delegated legislative power. They provide the technical detail necessary to apply statutes and ensure their effective implementation in everyday situations. Regulations translate legislative intent into concrete rules, procedures, and standards, allowing the administration to adapt the law to practical needs and evolving circumstances.

Examples vary across legal systems. In Brazil, environmental regulations adopted by IBAMA – the *Instituto Brasileiro do Meio Ambiente e dos Recursos Naturais Renováveis*, the federal agency responsible for environmental protection and the enforcement of national environmental policy – complement statutory protections by setting detailed requirements for activities such as environmental licensing, conservation measures, and environmental impact assessments. IBAMA's regulations specify, for instance, the technical conditions under which a company may operate in sensitive areas, the procedures for evaluating ecological risks, and the compliance standards required to protect biodiversity and natural resources. In Australia, immigration regulations specify the procedures and conditions for visas under the Migration Act, including the evidentiary requirements and administrative steps applicants must follow.

In France, regulations take several forms, including décrets and arrêtés. For instance, a *décret d'application* may specify how a newly adopted statute on public health is to be enforced, while an *arrêté préfectoral* can regulate matters such as local traffic restrictions, opening hours of establishments, or measures related to public safety. Similarly, ministerial orders (*arrêtés ministériels*) often provide technical rules – such as safety standards for buildings or detailed requirements for educational programs – that give practical effect to national legislation.

Through these instruments, regulations ensure that statutory norms are precise, operational, and responsive to administrative realities.

4.1.1.4 TREATIES OR INTERNATIONAL CONVENTIONS

Treaties are binding agreements between states and constitute one of the primary sources of International Law. They formalize commitments in fields such as human rights, trade, security, and environmental protection. After ratification, treaties may also become part of domestic law, but this depends on the constitutional structure of each state.

In monist systems, such as the Netherlands or France, ratified treaties automatically form part of domestic law and may even prevail over conflicting statutes. In dualist systems, such as the United Kingdom or India, treaties have no internal effect unless they are incorporated through specific implementing legislation. This difference illustrates the variety of constitutional approaches to the relationship between international and domestic law.

Examples include the Paris Agreement on climate change, which sets global emission-reduction goals, and the African Charter on Human and Peoples' Rights, which codifies fundamental rights and obligations across Africa.

The nature, formation, and domestic effects of treaties will be examined in greater depth in Chapter 9: *What Is International Law and How Is It Made?*

4.1.2 Informal Sources of Law

Informal sources do not derive from formal enactment. They may be unwritten, flexible, or persuasive. Despite their informal nature, they guide judges, fill gaps, and influence the development of the law. These informal sources typically include customary law, general principles of law, equity, prior judicial decisions, doctrinal writings, contracts, religion, and soft law, each of which contributes in a different way to shaping legal reasoning and complementing the formal sources of the legal order.

4.1.2.1 CUSTOMARY LAW

Customary law arises from long-standing and consistent practice accompanied by a shared belief that such practice is legally required. In International Law, many fundamental rules emerged through custom rather than through treaties – for example, the principle that pirates are *hostis humani generis* ("enemies of all mankind"), which allows any state to prosecute acts of piracy regardless of where they occur.

Customary law also plays a central role in numerous domestic legal systems. In many African countries, such as Ghana, Kenya, or Botswana, customary rules governing family relations, inheritance, or land tenure coexist alongside statutory law and are recognised by national courts, provided they do not conflict with constitutional principles. Similar forms of customary or indigenous law can be found in other regions, including the Pacific Islands and parts of South Asia.

The formation, authority, and interaction of customary law with treaties and domestic legal systems will also be examined in Chapter 9: *What Is International Law and How Is It Made?*

4.1.2.2 GENERAL PRINCIPLES OF LAW

General principles are fundamental ideas such as good faith, equality, proportionality, or due process. They express the core values of a legal system and guide judges when legislation is silent, incomplete, or ambiguous. Because they reflect widely accepted standards of fairness and reason, judges use them to interpret statutes, resolve conflicts between rules, and preserve the coherence of the legal order.

These principles play an important role in many legal traditions. In the European Union, the Court of Justice often applies the principle of proportionality to determine whether national or EU measures impose unnecessary or excessive restrictions. In the Inter-American human rights system, the Inter-American Court regularly applies principles such as good faith, equality, and reasonableness to assess state behaviour and fill gaps when treaties do not provide a clear answer.

Domestic courts also rely on general principles. Many civil law countries treat good faith as a basic rule in contract interpretation, while common law courts use principles such as natural justice or due process to ensure fairness in administrative and judicial procedures.

Through these various functions, general principles help maintain the unity and fairness of the legal system and ensure that the law reflects the fundamental values on which it is built.

4.1.2.3 EQUITY

Equity refers to fairness and allows judges to soften the rigidity of strict legal rules. Historically, it developed in England as a parallel system to the Common Law, offering remedies when the ordinary courts could not provide justice. Equity introduced flexible principles – such as trust, injunction, and specific performance – that balanced the sometimes harsh outcomes produced by rigid legal procedures.

Today, equity continues to play a role when the strict application of the law would lead to an unfair result. For example, Indian courts may grant equitable relief in contract disputes when the literal terms of the agreement would produce injustice.

In France, although equity is not an autonomous source of law, courts sometimes award compensation *ex aequo et bono*, meaning "according to what is fair and good." This expression refers to decisions in which the judge adjusts the outcome to achieve fairness when the strict application of legal rules would produce an unjust result. For example, in co-ownership cases where one owner has invested disproportionately in the common property, courts may grant compensation based on equitable considerations rather than on the exact letter of the law. In everyday legal commentary, one often hears that a judge has *statué en équité* – the judge decided the case on the basis of equity – to describe such decisions that prioritize fairness over strict legality.

The origins, methods, and continuing influence of equity – especially within the Common Law tradition – will be examined more closely in Chapter 3: *The Common Law Tradition.*

4.1.2.4 PRIOR DECISIONS OF COURTS (CASE LAW)

The authority of case law varies across legal traditions. In Common Law systems such as the United Kingdom, Canada, or Kenya, judicial precedents are binding: courts must follow earlier decisions of higher courts when the same legal issue arises. This doctrine – known as *stare decisis* – promotes stability, consistency, and predictability in the law. When a higher court clarifies a rule, that interpretation becomes part of the law itself and must be applied by lower courts.

In Civil Law jurisdictions such as France, Mexico, or many European and Latin American countries, case law does not have formally binding force. Instead, it is considered persuasive: judges are not legally required to follow previous decisions, but they often do so in practice to maintain coherence and uniformity. Over time, repeated decisions on the same issue form what French doctrine calls *jurisprudence constante*, a stable line of authority that carries considerable weight even without being strictly binding.

Famous judicial decisions illustrate the different roles played by precedent. In the United States, the Supreme Court's decision in *Brown v. Board of Education* (1954) fundamentally reshaped constitutional law by declaring racial segregation in public schools unconstitutional; lower courts were bound to apply this new interpretation under the doctrine of precedent. By contrast, in France, the *Cour de cassation* often gradually constructs solutions through a series of consistent rulings. Although these decisions are not binding in a formal sense, they strongly influence judges, lawyers, and legislators and contribute significantly to the evolution of the law.

Through these different mechanisms, case law participates – whether formally or informally – in shaping the legal order and ensuring coherence within each legal tradition.

4.1.2.5 DOCTRINAL WRITINGS

Legal scholarship influences both courts and legislators. Although doctrinal writings are not binding, they help clarify legal concepts, guide interpretation, and often inspire legislative reform. Scholars analyse the coherence of legal rules, propose solutions to unresolved issues, and provide theoretical frameworks that judges and lawmakers frequently rely on when shaping the law.

This influence is visible across many legal traditions. In Germany, Robert Alexy (born in 1945) – a leading jurist and legal philosopher, professor at the University of Kiel, and member of the Göttingen Academy of Sciences – has profoundly shaped constitutional reasoning through his *Theory of Fundamental Rights*, which provides a structured method for balancing rights and applying proportionality, widely used by constitutional courts.

In Latin America, Roberto Gargarella (born in 1962) plays a major role in contemporary constitutional thought. His work on democratic participation, social rights, and constitutional design has guided many courts in interpreting rights and evaluating state obligations.

France also offers key examples of doctrinal influence. Michel Troper (born in 1938) has significantly shaped constitutional interpretation and separation-of-powers theory. Denis Mazeaud (born in 1956) is frequently cited in matters of contract and tort law, especially for his work on good faith and civil liability. And Jean Carbonnier (1908–2003) – a central figure of French civil law and a pioneer of the sociology of law – has shaped entire branches of French private law; his work continues to inform judicial reasoning and legislative reforms today.

In the common law world, Ronald Dworkin (1931–2013) profoundly influenced legal philosophy and constitutional theory through his defence of rights as principles and his vision of law as integrity. Cass R. Sunstein (born in 1954) has shaped debates on behavioural regulation and constitutional interpretation, while Mark Tushnet (born in 1945) is a leading voice in comparative constitutional law, known for his work on judicial review and constitutional design.

African and Asian scholars also make significant contributions. In Kenya, Yash Pal Ghai (born in 1938) has profoundly influenced constitutional design and human rights jurisprudence, especially through his work on participatory constitutionalism in East Africa and the Pacific. In India, Upendra Baxi (born in 1938) has reshaped thinking on social justice, human rights, and the role of courts in protecting vulnerable groups, becoming a major reference in both Indian and global constitutional scholarship. One may also cite Amartya Sen (born in 1933), an Indian American economist and philosopher, whose work on justice, capabilities, and human development continues to influence legal reasoning in constitutional and human rights law.

Through these contributions, modern doctrinal writings play a crucial role in the development of the law. They offer intellectual guidance that helps legal systems adapt to new social, economic, and technological challenges, and provide the analytical tools and theoretical frameworks that courts and legislators rely on to interpret, apply, and reform legal norms.

4.1.2.6 CONTRACTS

Contracts are binding agreements between parties and allow private individuals, companies, or public entities to organise and regulate their relationships. They play a central role in daily economic and social life by creating obligations, transferring goods or services, and allocating risks. However, contracts are not an autonomous source of law for the legal order: their validity and enforceability depend on pre-existing legal norms governing capacity, consent, form, object, and public policy. A contract can therefore produce legal effects only if it complies with these underlying legal requirements.

Contracts operate within a broad range of legal systems. In Japan, employment contracts are strictly regulated by labour legislation, which sets mandatory standards for working hours, wages, safety, and fair treatment. In the United Arab Emirates, commercial leases must comply with statutory provisions on registration, duration, renewal, and tenant protections. In France, contracts must respect public order (*ordre public*) and good faith, while in South Africa, the constitutional requirement of fairness can limit contractual freedom in certain contexts.

Thus, while contracts are essential instruments of private autonomy, they create binding obligations only to the extent that they conform to statutory and constitutional norms. Their power to regulate private relations is significant, but always exercised within the boundaries established by the legal system.

4.1.2.7 RELIGION

In some legal systems, religion functions as a formal source of law, while in others it acts only as a cultural or moral influence. In Saudi Arabia, for example, Sharia is the primary source of legislation, and courts apply religious principles directly when resolving disputes. In Israel, religious authority is more limited but still significant: rabbinical courts have jurisdiction over key areas of family law, including marriage and divorce.

In contrast, in countries such as France or Brazil, religion is not a formal source of law. The legal system is based on secular principles, and legislation is adopted independently of religious authority. Nonetheless, religious ideas may influence public debate and shape discussions on issues such as marriage, family, medical ethics, or bioethics.

Overall, the role of religion varies widely across legal traditions, ranging from direct legal authority to broader social influence.

4.1.2.8 SOFT LAW

Soft law refers to non-binding instruments that nonetheless have legal or practical significance, such as guidelines, recommendations, declarations, or codes of conduct. Although they do not create enforceable obligations, they influence behaviour, guide institutional practice, and often prepare the ground for future binding rules. Soft law can therefore play an important role in shaping expectations, setting standards, and promoting convergence between legal systems.

Examples include the UN Guiding Principles on Business and Human Rights, which, despite being non-binding, are widely used by courts, companies, and governments to assess corporate responsibility. The OECD Guidelines for Multinational Enterprises also shape state expectations and corporate behavior, even though they are not legally enforceable. A classic illustration is the Universal Declaration of Human Rights (1948): initially adopted as a non-binding declaration, it gradually inspired numerous treaties, constitutional provisions, and judicial decisions, showing how soft law can evolve into hard law over time.

Conclusion

Thinking about the connection between law and poetry, as described by the American lawyer, poet, and writer Archibald MacLeish (1892–1982) and echoed by Ronald Dworkin's idea that "we live in and by the law,"[50] helps us see that law is more than a set of rules. Law gives structure to human life, reduces confusion, and helps society work. At the same time, it offers opportunities, protection, and dignity.

Describing the relationship between law and poetry, Archibald MacLeish once elegantly wrote the following words on law:

> The business of law is to make sense of the confusion of what we call human life – to reduce it to order but at the same time to give it possibility, scope, even dignity. But what, then, is the business of poetry? Precisely to make sense of the chaos of our lives. To create the understanding of our lives. To compose an order which the bewildered, angry heart can recognize. To imagine man.[51]

In this sense, law is not only a system of constraints but also a bond and a beam of hope.

Human societies, however, do not exist outside of history. Law always reflects the time in which it is created and applied. As the old idea *Curia tempora, eius jus* (To each age, its law) suggests, the courts and the law are shaped by their historical moment.

50 Ronald Dworking described law as follows: "We live in and by the law. It makes us what we are: citizens and employees and doctors and spouses and people who own things. It is sword, shield, and menace: we insist on our wage, or refuse to pay our rent, or are forced to forfeit penalties, or are locked up in jail, all in the name of what our abstract and ethereal sovereign, the law, has decreed. And we argue about what it has decreed, even when the books that are supposed to record its commands and directions are silent; we act then as if law had muttered its doom, too low to be heard distinctly. We are subjects of law's empire, liegemen to its methods and ideals, bound in spirit while we debate what we must therefore do." Dworkin, Ronald, 1986, *Law's Empire*, Harvard University Press.

51 MacLeish, Archibald, 1972, "Apoligia," *Harvard Law Review*, vol. 85, pp. 1505, 1508–1509.

In our globalized world, law plays a central and increasingly complex role. Legal rules now operate not only within states, but also across borders, through international treaties, regional organizations, international courts, and global regulatory standards. Issues such as climate change, digital technologies, migration, or global trade require legal responses that go beyond the traditional nation-state.[52]

As a result, modern legal systems are more connected, more interdependent, and more layered than ever before. Domestic law, International Law, and transnational norms interact constantly. This does not replace national legal orders, but it transforms how they function and how they relate to one another.

Our understanding of law must therefore adapt. It must take into account this new context while remaining guided by the core values that give law its legitimacy: fairness, coherence, and respect for human dignity. Studying law today means understanding how legal systems can respond to global challenges without losing their essential purpose.

Ultimately, law continues to be a collective project that societies build together. It helps us organize life, resolve conflicts, and imagine a more just future. And in this way, law remains – like poetry – a way to create meaning and to sustain hope.

Selected Bibliography

Domingo, Rafael, 2010, *The New Global Law*, Cambridge University Press, 238 pages.

García Ruales, J., Hovden, K., Kopnina, H., Robertson, C. D., & Schoukens, H., (Eds.), 2024, *Rights of Nature in Europe: Encounters and Visions*, Routledge, 396 pages.

Harris, Phil, 2007, *An Introduction to Law* (7th ed.), Cambridge University Press, 534 pages.

Morgan, Bronwen, & Yeung, Karen, 2007, *An Introduction to Law and Regulation* (Text and Materials), Cambridge University Press, 372 pages.

Patterson, Dennis, 2010, *A Companion to Philosophy of Law and Legal Theory*, Wiley-Blackwell, 700 pages.

Romano, Santi, 2018, *The Legal Order* (1st ed.), Routledge, 220 pages.

Sandel, Michael J., 2010, *Justice: What's the Right Thing to Do?* Macmillan, 320 pages.

Sen, Amartya, 2009, *The Idea of Justice*, Cambridge, MA: The Belknap Press of Harvard University Press, 496 pages.

Shapiro, Scott J., 2011, *Legality*, Cambridge, MA: The Belknap Press of Harvard University Press, 488 pages.

Tamanaha, Brian Z, 2006, *Law as a Means to an End: Threat to the Rule of Law*, New York: Cambridge University Press, 294 pages.

Tamanaha, Brian Z., 2008 January, *Law*, Legal Studies Research Paper Series, paper #08-0095.

Tusseau, Guillaume, 2011, *Jérémy Bentham, La Guerre des Mots*, Dalloz-Sirey, 188 pages.

Tusseau, Guillaume, 2014, *The Legal Philosophy and Influence of Jeremy Bentham: Essays on 'Of the Limits of the Penal Branch of Jurisprudence'*. Routledge, 434 pages.

Twining, William, and Miers, David, 2010, *How to Do Things with Rules*, Cambridge University Press, 426 pages.

Von Daniels, Detlef, 2016, *The Concept of Law from a Transnational Perspective* (1st ed.), Routledge, 236 pages.

Wacks, Raymond, 2020, *Understanding Jurisprudence: An Introduction to Legal Theory*, Oxford: Oxford University Press, 432 pages.

Wacks, Raymond. 2023, *Law: A Very Short Introduction* (3rd ed.), Paperback, Oxford University Press, 192 pages.

Wade, Mansell, Meteyard, Belinda, & Thomson, Alan, 2015, *A Critical Introduction to Law* (4th ed.), Routledge, 220 pages.

52 Teubner, Gunther, 1997, "Global Bukowina: Legal Pluralism in the World Society," in *Global Law Without a State*, ed. Gunther Teubner, Dartmouth Publishing, Aldershot.

2 The Historical Development of Law and Justice

French justice can no longer be a justice that kills.
Robert Badinter
French National Assembly, 17 September 1981

The legal tradition relates the legal system to the culture of which it is a partial expression. It puts the legal system into cultural perspective.
John Henry Merryman
(The Civil Law tradition, 1985)

Law and justice are universal and enduring values, but their expression has evolved over time through the history of human societies. From the earliest written codes of the ancient world to the rise of international and global law, legal thought has developed through a continuous interaction between social needs, political structures, and moral or religious beliefs. Studying the historical development of law helps us understand how different civilizations have sought to define justice, preserve order, and express their collective values through legal norms. Law has influenced cultures as much as cultures have influenced law, in a dynamic interplay that continues to shape the foundations of justice today.

Throughout history, legal systems have emerged as reflections of the societies to which they belong. In ancient Mesopotamia, Egypt, and Greece, as well as in enduring traditions such as those of India and the Islamic world, law has been deeply intertwined with philosophy, theology, and power. The European experience, from the Middle Ages to the modern codifications of the 19th century, marked the gradual separation of law from religion and the rise of legal rationality. The 20th century, in turn, witnessed the internationalization of law and the growing search for universal legal principles capable of addressing global challenges.

From the ancient principle of "an eye for an eye" to modern conceptions of justice rooted in human rights and dignity, the history of law reflects a profound moral and philosophical transformation. What was once seen as justice through vengeance has gradually evolved toward justice grounded in restraint, proportionality, and compassion.

The progressive abolition of the death penalty in many countries, including France, where Robert Badinter (1928–2024) – a lawyer, humanist, former Minister of Justice, and later President of the Constitutional Council – embodied this ideal, illustrates how societies reinterpret justice as they evolve. Across time and cultures, this transformation reveals law's deeper purpose: not merely to punish, but to uphold humanity itself.

Badinter's entry into the Panthéon in October 2025 – a national monument in Paris where France honours those who have greatly contributed to its values and history, bearing on its

DOI: 10.4324/9781003393047-4

façade the words *To Great Men, The Grateful Nation,* now understood to include women and men alike – stands as a tribute to a life devoted to the defence of human dignity and to the conviction that justice must serve humanity rather than vengeance.

This chapter offers both a historical and analytical exploration of these developments. It provides a chronological overview of major legal conceptions from antiquity to the rise of international and global law (section 1), then explains the main frameworks used to classify legal systems and examines the cultural foundations of each (section 2). It also discusses the importance of comparing different legal systems and traditions to better understand their diversity and convergence (section 3), before tracing the origins and development of the legal family approach, from early classifications to contemporary global perspectives (section 4).

Beyond its historical narrative, this chapter also offers a map of the world's legal systems and traditions – a framework for reading and understanding today's complex legal landscape. By following the long path of law through history, we gain a clearer view of how societies have sought justice, and how law continues to evolve as a living expression of humanity's search for order and fairness.

1 Historical Perspectives on Law and Justice

To understand law and justice, we must look back through the long story of human civilization. Across time and place, societies have created laws that reflect their beliefs, values, and social needs.[1] This section explores those historical roots, revealing how ideas of justice have been shaped – and reshaped – through the centuries.

1.1 Different Interpretations of Law and Justice Through Time and Across Cultures

Looking at how different societies and historical periods have understood justice and law provides a richer perspective than simply listing statutes and codes. It helps us see law as part of a wider human story, one that connects cultural values, moral thought, and the constant search for justice across civilizations.

1.1.1 Far Ancient Law

Ancient legal traditions provide valuable insights into how early civilizations conceived justice and social order. In Egypt, for instance, law was already organized around 3000 BC, and sources suggest the existence of a Civil Code, possibly divided into 12 books. Egyptian legal practice reflected principles such as tradition, social harmony, and impartiality, which are surprisingly close to modern ideas of fairness and equity. Law in Egypt was deeply associated with the concept of *Ma'at*, representing truth, balance, and justice, and the pharaoh was regarded as its guardian.

In Mesopotamia, legal development took a more technical and casuistic form. Around 2200 BC, the Sumerian ruler Ur-Nammu promulgated one of the earliest known codes of law, structured according to conditional formulas: "If A occurs, then B shall follow." This logical pattern, still used in modern legal drafting, demonstrates the ancient roots of systematic legal reasoning.

A few centuries later, around 1760 BC, King Hammurabi of Babylon ordered the codification of a comprehensive set of legal norms, carved into stone stelae and publicly displayed

1 See Doe, Norman and Sandberg, Russell (eds.), 2016, *Law and History*, 1st ed., Routledge.

throughout his kingdom. The *Code of Hammurabi* is particularly notable for its reliance on the principle of *lex talionis* – the law of retaliation – expressed in the formula "if a man destroys the eye of another man, they shall destroy his eye." This notion of justice through strict equivalence, often summarized as "an eye for an eye, a tooth for a tooth," illustrates how ancient societies understood balance and retribution. While modern legal systems have long abandoned this principle, its existence reminds us of the historical relativity of our own conceptions of justice and punishment.

The Hebrew tradition, dating from around 1280 BC, presents another major step in the evolution of law. The *Old Testament* links law directly with morality, viewing both as divine commands revealed to Moses on Mount Sinai in the form of the Ten Commandments.[2] These commandments were transmitted to the Israelites and became a moral and legal foundation for later Jewish, Christian, and, indirectly, Islamic traditions. In this conception, law and ethics were inseparable, and justice was understood as obedience to divine order.

1.1.2 Law in Ancient Greece

The conception of law in Ancient Greece is largely rooted in the works of its major philosophers. As mentioned earlier, the question "What is law?" was first posed by Socrates in one of Plato's dialogues (*Minos*). Interestingly, the Greek language of classical Athens did not have a specific term for "law" in the abstract sense, yet this absence did not prevent Greece from producing major political and legal innovations, including the birth of democracy.[3]

Plato's understanding of justice as *harmony* is particularly significant. In *The Republic* (Book IV, 434c–443b), he argues that justice applies both to the individual and to the State, viewing it as a balanced relationship between their different parts. For Plato, justice means that each part

2 The Ten Commandments (Exodus 20:2–17 NKJV):

1. I am the Lord your God, who brought you out of the land of Egypt, out of the house of bondage. You shall have no other gods before Me.
2. You shall not make for yourself a carved image, or any likeness of anything that is in heaven above, or that is in the earth beneath, or that is in the water under the earth; you shall not bow down to them nor serve them. For I, the Lord your God, am a jealous God, visiting the iniquity of the fathers on the children to the third and fourth generations of those who hate Me, but showing mercy to thousands, to those who love Me and keep My Commandments.
3. You shall not take the name of the Lord your God in vain, for the Lord will not hold him guiltless who takes His name in vain.
4. Remember the Sabbath day, to keep it holy. Six days you shall labor and do all your work, but the seventh day is the Sabbath of the Lord your God. In it you shall do no work: you, nor your son, nor your daughter, nor your male servant, nor your female servant, nor your cattle, nor your stranger who is within your gates. For in six days the Lord made the heavens and the earth, the sea, and all that is in them, and rested the seventh day. Therefore the Lord blessed the Sabbath day and hallowed it.
5. Honor your father and your mother, that your days may be long upon the land which the Lord your God is giving you.
6. You shall not murder.
7. You shall not commit adultery.
8. You shall not steal.
9. You shall not bear false witness against your neighbor.
10. You shall not covet your neighbor's house; you shall not covet your neighbor's wife, nor his male servant, nor his female servant, nor his ox, nor his donkey, nor anything that is your neighbor's.

3 Solon's Constitution in particular provided all citizens with political representation and judicial access. The citizens further had the power to elect their representatives which were accountable to them.

performs its proper function without interfering with the others – hence his famous claim that "justice is harmony" and that "justice is doing one's own job." A just person, therefore, is one who occupies the place best suited to his abilities, performs his role with excellence, and gives in proportion to what he receives. In the same way, a just State is one in which every class and institution fulfils its proper purpose, contributing to the harmony of the whole.

1.1.3 The Hindu Legal Tradition

In the Hindu tradition, the giver of laws is known as Manu (around 200 BC).[4] According to legend, Manu was a wise king who was forewarned of a great flood by a fish – an incarnation of the god Vishnu. He built a boat, saved his family, animals, and seeds of every species, and repopulated the Earth after the waters subsided. This mythic account, which closely parallels the Biblical story of Noah and the Mesopotamian flood narrative, situates Manu as both the progenitor of humankind and the archetypal lawgiver.

The Laws of Manu (*Manu Smṛti*), one of the foundational texts of ancient Hindu law, sets out not only legal rules but also moral and social duties (*dharma*) intended to maintain the balance and harmony of the world. The text – which is officially known as Manava-dharma-shastra – reflects a conception of justice rooted in cosmic order and moral reciprocity. A well-known passage proclaims: "Justice, being violated, destroys; justice, being preserved, preserves: therefore justice must not be violated, lest violated justice destroy us" (*Laws of Manu*, Chapter VIII).

This illustrates the idea that justice is a sustaining cosmic force: to preserve it is to preserve life itself. At the same time, the *Manu Smṛti* also contains prescriptions that reflect the hierarchical and patriarchal structure of its time. For instance:

> It is the nature of women to seduce men in this world; for that reason the wise are never unguarded in the company of females.
>
> (*Manu Smṛti*, Chapter II)

Such passages reveal how ancient law reflected the gender hierarchies and social norms of its time. They must therefore be read as historical documents – valuable for understanding the evolution of legal and ethical thought, yet clearly shaped by the inequalities of their cultural context.

1.1.4 Roman Law

Roman law was deeply influenced by Greek philosophy, yet it reached a level of development that represented an unprecedented achievement in the ancient world. The sophistication of Roman legal thought resulted from the intellectual work of jurists, magistrates, and statesmen who systematically analyzed and refined legal principles. Rome thus gave birth to legal theory as a distinct and disciplined study of law.[5]

A decisive moment in this evolution came under the reign of Emperor Justinian (482–565 AD), when Roman law underwent a vast process of codification. Justinian ordered the

4 See Davis, Donald R. Jr., 2018, *Hindu Law: A New History of Dharmaśāstra*, Oxford University Press.
5 Villey, Michel, 2012, *Le droit romain*, PUF, pp. 36–52.

compilation of all existing imperial enactments and juristic writings into a single, coherent body of law known as the *Corpus Iuris Civilis*. This monumental work comprised four parts:

(a) the *Codex Iustinianus*, a collection of imperial constitutions dating back to Emperor Hadrian;
(b) the *Digesta* or *Pandectae*, an anthology of extracts from classical Roman jurists;
(c) the *Institutiones*, a legal textbook for students, summarizing the main principles of Roman law; and
(d) the *Novellae Constitutiones*, which contained the new laws enacted during Justinian's reign.

These four parts were given the full force of law and became the only authoritative legal source within the Byzantine Empire. The *Corpus Iuris Civilis* became the foundational text of European legal education and the model on which all later Civil Law systems and modern legal codes were built. Its influence, however, extended well beyond the Civil Law tradition, leaving a lasting mark on the development of the Common Law as well. For this reason, Justinian remains one of the most influential figures in the history of Western law.

1.1.5 Islamic Law and Sharia

Muhammad (570–632 AD), the prophet and founder of Islam, introduced a conception of law and justice that remains essential to a global and transsystemic understanding of legal history. As both a spiritual and political leader, Muhammad laid the foundations of Sharia law, which continues to regulate many aspects of social and personal life in Islamic societies.

The primary sources of Sharia are the Qur'ān (the revealed word of God), the Hadith (the sayings and actions of the Prophet), and the Ijmaʿ and Qiyās (scholarly consensus and analogical reasoning). In addition, fatwas, or legal opinions issued by qualified jurists (*muftis*), contribute to the practical interpretation and application of Islamic law.

Over time, distinct schools of jurisprudence (*madhāhib*) developed within Sunni Islam, each offering its own interpretive methodology: the Hanafi school, known for its flexibility and openness to reason; the Maliki school, which emphasizes the practices of the people of Medina; the Shafiʿi school, which systematized legal reasoning; and the Hanbali school, the most textually conservative, which remains influential in countries such as Saudi Arabia.

The existence of these parallel schools illustrates how, across civilizations, diverse legal traditions have evolved independently, each grounded in its own moral, cultural, and theological foundations.

1.1.6 European Conception of Law From the Middle Ages to the 19th Century

At the same time, on the western part of the European continent, Roman law gradually declined during the early Middle Ages. It was rediscovered around the 11th century through the work of medieval legal scholars known as the *glossators*, who studied, interpreted, and taught the Justinianic texts in the universities of Bologna and elsewhere. The Roman legal corpus was thus revived and adapted to new social and political contexts. England, however, followed a different path: instead of receiving Roman law, the King's judges developed a distinct body of judicial precedents, which became known as the Common Law.

During the same period, across continental Europe, commercial practice gave rise to a transnational law of merchants, or *Lex Mercatoria*. This body of customary rules was developed by traders themselves to facilitate commerce through shared principles of fairness, reliability, and uniform standards. The *Lex Mercatoria* can be seen as a historical precursor to modern efforts at legal harmonization, such as those undertaken within the European Union, particularly in the field of the common market.

With the rise of nationalism in the 18th and 19th centuries, the *Lex Mercatoria* – along with some of its key principles, including freedom of contract and alienability of property – was absorbed and codified into national legal systems. The most influential examples of this codification were the French Napoleonic Code (1804) and the German Civil Code (Bürgerliches Gesetzbuch, 1896), which became models for modern Civil Law systems around the world.

1.1.7 The Emergence of International Law

Law has continually adapted to the evolution of the international community. Globalization created a worldwide commercial space and fostered the growth of International Law. Increasing interaction among peoples, cultures, and economies has led to a convergence of international and, to some extent, national norms. This raises the question of whether we are witnessing the emergence of a genuine "global law."

Historically, International Law developed in two main areas: commerce and war. In the commercial sphere, the *Lex Mercatoria* – the law of merchants – emerged in medieval Europe from the customs and practices of traders, particularly within the Hanseatic League.[6] It formed a transnational legal system, independent of states, to facilitate trade across borders. The *Lex Mercatoria* can be viewed as a precursor to modern efforts toward legal harmonization, such as those undertaken in the European Union.

In parallel, the growing intensity of international conflicts gave rise to a law of war and peace. Once seen as an act of sovereignty, war became increasingly condemned with the rise of destructive technology. The world wars of the 20th century reinforced the conviction that war violates the laws of humanity. International Law thus sought both to prohibit war (*jus ad bellum*) and to regulate it (*jus in bello*), leading to the paradox of a system that forbids war yet codifies rules for its conduct. The *Law of The Hague* (1899 and 1907) governs warfare and peace, while the *Law of Geneva* (beginning with the 1864 Convention) protects victims of conflict.

Major institutional milestones followed: the creation of the Permanent Court of International Justice in 1920; the United Nations Charter in 1945, which prohibits the use of force (Article 2§4) and promotes peaceful settlement of disputes (Article 33); and the establishment of the International Court of Justice in 1946. From the mid-20th century onward, International Law expanded rapidly, covering nearly all fields of international relations. As the French diplomat and scholar Maxime Lefèbvre observed, the proliferation of treaties reflects the world's search for legal stability amid growing interdependence.[7]

Modern International Law has become more technical, encompassing areas such as trade, environmental protection, development, arms control, and scientific cooperation. Specialized regimes have emerged, including the Law of the Sea (1958 Geneva and 1982 Montego Bay Conventions), air law (1944 Chicago Convention), and space law (1967 Outer Space Treaty).

6 Goldman, Berthold, 1964, "Frontières du droit et lex mercatoria," *Archives de philosophie du droit*, p. 177. See also de Ly, Filip, 1992, *International Business Law and Lex Mercatoria*, North Holland, spéc. p. 207 s.; and Gaillard, Emmanuel, 1995, "Trente ans de Lex Mercatoria: Pour une application sélective de la méthode des principes généraux du droit," *Journal du droit international*, 122e année, no. 1.

7 Lefebvre, Maxime, 2013, *Le Jeu du Droit et de la Puissance*, 4e éd., PUF.

The protection of human rights has also produced a vast and evolving body of norms. In addition to treaties, non-binding instruments such as recommendations, codes of conduct, and declarations – collectively known as soft law – now play an increasingly important role.

At the same time, International Law remains an instrument of power. Despite the partial erosion of sovereignty, states continue to use law as a diplomatic and economic tool. Many states pursue external legal policies, shaping international norms and promoting their legal systems for strategic or commercial advantage.[8] This diplomacy of law is visible throughout history – from the Napoleonic export of the French Civil Code to modern contractual asymmetries, where dominant parties impose their own law or costly arbitration mechanisms.

Ultimately, law functions as a strategic asset in global competition. A country unable to promote its legal system risks losing economic and political influence. Preserving legal identity while engaging in a globalized world remains one of the central challenges of modern international relations.

1.2 Towards a Global Law Framework?

This section examines how the idea of Global Law has emerged and how it operates today. It first explores the main theoretical approaches that challenge traditional, state-centered conceptions of law and seek to explain the rise of legal norms produced beyond the nation-state. It then turns to the contemporary landscape, mapping the diverse networks, institutions, and normative orders that increasingly shape legal governance across the world.

1.2.1 Understanding the Emergence of Global Law

Several scholars have reflected deeply on the contemporary evolution of law and sought to describe its transformation in today's multi-polar world. Among the earliest and most influential is Günther Teubner, a German legal scholar and sociologist, whose 1996 book *Global Law Without a State* examines the rise of legal pluralism within an emerging world society.[9] Teubner argues that globalization has produced a "decentred law-making process" that operates in multiple social sectors independently of nation-states. According to him, "technical standardization, professional rule production, human rights, intra-organizational regulation in multinational enterprises, contracting, arbitration and other institutions of *Lex Mercatoria* are forms of rule by private governments, claiming worldwide validity independently of the law of nation-states."[10] These forms of norm creation, he observes, arise not through formal legislative acts but through "paradoxical acts of self-validation."

This raises the question of what qualifies as *law*. Under traditional doctrine, the *Lex Mercatoria* and other forms of private rule-making are not considered law, since they lack formal recognition from state-based legal systems. They may be professional norms, customs, contractual practices, or social rules, but they do not constitute *law* in the classical sense. Teubner contends, however, that globalization challenges this framework and produces a new type of law – one that lacks legislation, constitution, or political hierarchy. In this "heterarchical" model, new forms of rule production emerge at the periphery of the legal system, in close interaction with

8 La Charrière, Guy de, 1983, "La Politique Juridique Extérieure," *Politique étrangère*, no. 4, 48ᵉ année, pp. 1000–1002.
9 Teubner, Gunther, 1996, *Global Law Without a State*, Dartmouth Publishing Co Ltd.
10 Teubner, *Global Law Without a State*.

social processes.[11] For Teubner, many kinds of private rule-making at the global level have in fact acquired a highly *public* character, as they shape the behavior of states, corporations, and individuals alike.

Building on these ideas, other scholars have sought to conceptualize this transformation through the notion of Global Law. Mikhail Xifaras, a Professor of Public Law at Sciences Po University, where he teaches legal philosophy, property, and jurisprudence, has written a foundational article on the subject, describing the emergence of a new theoretical context that changes how we think about law.[12] He observes that "whether we regret it or rejoice, we must begin by defining its outlines. It is a political question: one may or may not like one's time, want to resist it, subvert it, or embrace it, but in any case one must strive to understand it."[13] For Xifaras, *Global Law* represents a theoretical framework that succeeds the general theories of the State characteristic of continental legal culture, particularly of Germanic inspiration.[14]

Yet, despite its apparent simplicity, *Global Law* is a complex and elusive concept. It encompasses global, transnational, and national legal phenomena that interact in fluid, overlapping, and sometimes contradictory ways. Xifaras cautions that the term "Global Law" is confusing and heavily loaded with ideological assumptions. Like the word "State" before it was scientifically defined, *Global Law* serves as a "catch-all" expression that refers to highly diverse and heterogeneous legal realities.[15]

1.2.2 Mapping Today's Global Legal Landscape

Another major theorist, William Twining (1934–2025), was a British legal scholar and Quain Professor of Jurisprudence Emeritus at University College London, known for his pioneering work on global and comparative legal theory. Twining adopted a more pragmatic definition. For him, "global" refers to legal regimes or organizations whose scope of activity transcends national boundaries. Examples include international trade arbitration, the Lex Mercatoria, humanitarian law, dialogues between constitutional courts, as well as global institutions such as the World Bank, IFRS standards, the Catholic Church, the International Olympic Committee, FIFA, or International Law firms such as Baker McKenzie. According to Twining, whether these regimes or networks qualify as *legal orders* depends on the criteria one uses to define law in a given context. Nevertheless, they all represent global legal phenomena – that is, normative systems operating on a worldwide scale.[16]

Giuliana Ziccardi Capaldo, Emeritus Professor of International Law at the University of Salerno in Italy, is internationally recognized as a leading scholar and pioneer in the study of global law and the concept of a global community. She offers a distinct perspective, linking *Global Law* to the gradual erosion of state sovereignty and the emergence of a new international power structure. In her view, "the erosion of states' sovereignty is giving way to a global community and a new international power structure based on multilateral decision-making processes aimed at protecting fundamental interests and global values."[17] These developments,

11 Teubner, *Global Law Without a State*.
12 Xifaras, Mikhail, 2012, "Après les théories générales de l'État: le droit global?," *Jus Politicum*, no. 8, p. 1.
13 Xifaras, *Après les théories générales de l'État*.
14 Xifaras, *Après les théories générales de l'État*, p. 3.
15 Xifaras, *Après les théories générales de l'État*, p. 4.
16 Twining, W., 2009, *General Jurisprudence: Understanding Law from a Global Perspective*, Cambridge University Press, pp. 14–15.
17 Capaldo, Giuliana Ziccardi, August 10, 2015, "What Is Global Law?," *OUPblog*.

she argues, raise key questions: does this global community generate new norms distinct from traditional inter-state law, and if so, do these norms form a coherent legal system that can be described as *Global Law*?

In 2015, the University of Edinburgh Legal Theory Group organized a seminar entitled *The Concept of Global Law*, which sought to clarify these questions. Participants debated whether genuinely global legal rules exist, whether they constitute a legal system, and what their sources might be.[18]

At that seminar, Jorge Fabra, then a doctoral researcher in the philosophy of law at McMaster University (now Associate Professor at the University at Buffalo School of Law, State University of New York), analyzed the main conceptions of *Global Law* proposed by Twining, Teubner, and Neil Walker, before suggesting his own framework.

Fabra distinguishes between three related phenomena: (a) Global legal norms – norms that belong to no single jurisdiction but arise from interactions among different legal orders, characteristic of law in the era of globalization; (b) Global legal orders – organized sets of norms, such as *lex mercatoria, lex digitalis*, or *lex sportiva;* (c) Fundamental norms of the international community – principles that underpin International Law and express ideals of global governance.

Fabra argues that these norms share two distinctive moral features: they cannot be annulled or overridden by any single legal system – they are *inescapable* – and they claim authority over global issues, aiming to fulfil the requirements of global justice.[19]

In response, Neil Walker, Professor of Public Law at the University of Edinburgh, agreed that global law is not merely an aspiration but a present reality in formation. By describing global law as "intimated," Walker suggests that it already exists in practice, even if its contours are still being defined.[20]

Across this literature, the authors share the challenge of describing a phenomenon that appears both familiar and unprecedented. For Xifaras, *Global Law* does not designate a unified or superior legal order that exists above nation-states.[21] It refers instead to a web of supra- and transnational legal phenomena – regional, national, and local legal systems (such as the European Union or Mercosur), subnational entities (federal states, cities, regions), and cross-cutting networks (religious communities, diasporas, linguistic groups, or global industries) whose interactions have become too dense to separate clearly.[22] He argues that "planetary legal phenomena must be understood through the articulation of these different spaces."[23]

Ziccardi Capaldo offers a vivid metaphor to illustrate this idea. She envisions the global legal system as "a web made up of filaments – resilient, flexible, and elastic – arranged in concentric circles linked by threads, evoking the symbolism of weaving." This "communal spider web," she suggests, best represents the legal system of a complex, multipolar society. In this framework, *Global Law* is elastic enough to integrate the diverse elements of different legal orders into a unified but flexible structure, preserving diversity while maintaining coherence.[24]

18 Cornell, Harriet, 2015, "The Concept of Global Law: What Is It and What Are the Rules?," *Global Justice Blog*, Global Justice Academy and Global Development Academy, University of Edinburgh. Available at: http://www.globaljusticeblog.ed.ac.uk/2015/10/01/globallaw-011015/.

19 Zarbiyev, Farshad, 2023, "Jurisprudence in a Globalized World," review of *Jurisprudence in a Globalized World*, ed. Jorge Luis Fabra-Zamora, Edward Elgar, Cheltenham.

20 Zarbiyev, *Jurisprudence in a Globalized World*.

21 Xifaras, *Après les théories générales de l'État*, p. 5.

22 Xifaras, *Après les théories générales de l'État*.

23 Xifaras, *Après les théories générales de l'État*.

24 Capaldo, *Après les théories générales de l'État*.

In summary, the notion of *Global Law* does not describe a universal and uniform system of norms but rather the networks of interdependence and interconnection that link diverse legal orders. It reflects a world in which law operates across multiple levels – global, regional, national, and local – forming an intricate web of overlapping and interacting norms that shape the governance of an increasingly interconnected planet.

According to Xifaras, *Global Law* represents "the culmination of a historical process of globalization of Western legalism – the triumph of civilization, the triumph of the Civil Law empire."[25] He describes this process in terms of civilization, Westernization, modernization, or even juridicization, which he considers to be closely related expressions of the same phenomenon.

This process describes how non-Western societies have been encouraged – or compelled – to adopt Western rules, procedures, institutions, categories, and modes of legal reasoning, thereby reshaping their individual and collective identities according to the lexicon of Western legal thought and jurisprudence. Xifaras highlights "the formidable symbolic violence suffered by societies now forced to define and understand themselves in the syntax and terms of a language previously unknown to them: that of Western juridism."[26]

2 Parent Legal Families, Systems, and Traditions

Depending on how one defines a legal system, there are more than 40 distinct legal systems in the world today. In practice, however, most of them derive – directly or indirectly – from two major legal families: the Civil Law and the Common Law. A third category must also be recognized: the religious legal systems, which are sufficiently distinct in their sources and operation to warrant separate consideration. Accordingly, most scholars classify the world's legal orders within these three principal families or traditions.

2.1 Parent Legal Families and Legal Systems

A legal system refers to the organized structure of rules, courts, and institutions through which justice is administered in a given State or territory. It is the set of rules and institutions established to create, interpret, and enforce law within a specific national or regional context. For example, France has its own legal system based on written codes, while the United States has one based on judicial precedent.

Parent legal families, by contrast, are broader categories that group together several national legal systems that share common origins, ideas, or methods. For instance, both France and Germany belong to the *Civil Law family*, while England and the United States belong to the *Common Law family*.

The main difference between a legal system and a parent legal family is their scope. A legal system concerns the specific rules and institutions of one country, while a parent legal family describes a group of systems that have developed from similar historical and philosophical foundations. In comparative law, studying these families helps scholars understand how different legal systems resemble or differ from one another. This part aims to explain these two perspectives – the narrow view of individual legal systems and the broader view of parent legal families.

25 Xifaras, *Après les théories générales de l'État*, p. 6.
26 Xifaras, *Après les théories générales de l'État*.

2.1.1 Narrow Definition of Legal Systems

In the narrow sense, a legal system can be defined as the legal rules and institutions of a country. This definition corresponds closely to that of a legal order, though the two concepts are not identical. As developed by Santi Romano in his seminal work *L'Ordinamento giuridico* (1918), a legal order consists of three fundamental elements: legal norms, subjects of rights, and institutions – particularly courts – empowered to apply these norms and resolve disputes.

For example, the French legal system includes codified laws such as the *Code civil*, courts such as the *Cour de cassation*, and citizens or legal entities who are subjects of rights and obligations. Similarly, the English legal system is based on parliamentary statutes, Common Law principles developed by judges, and a network of courts such as the High Court and the Court of Appeal.

While these elements also constitute the foundation of a legal system, the two notions differ in dynamism. A legal order may be seen as a more static concept, emphasizing the structural existence of law, whereas a legal system implies movement and interaction. It is a legal order in motion – a dynamic process that evolves through case law, political developments, and the continuous interaction between legal actors and society. For instance, the legal system of the United States changes over time through Supreme Court decisions, legislative reforms, and social movements that influence the interpretation and application of law.

2.1.2 Broad Definition of Legal Systems: Parent Legal Families

In the broader sense, George Winterton (1946–2008) – who was an Australian Professor of Constitutional Law at the University of Sydney – defines a legal system as the juristic philosophy and techniques shared by a number of nations with broadly similar legal systems.[27] This broader meaning corresponds to what is usually termed a parent legal family, such as the Common Law family or the Civil Law family.

Referring to the major legal systems of the world, therefore, means referring to these major parent legal families: the Common Law, the Civil Law, and the religious legal systems. During the second half of the 20th century, a fourth group – the socialist legal family – was often included. However, this category has lost relevance since the fall of the Soviet Union in the 1990s and the transformation of socialist legal systems.[28]

The theory of legal families proposes grouping legal institutions, jurisdictions, or entire systems that share comparable characteristics under a common conceptual framework. This approach facilitates comparative analysis by identifying structural and cultural affinities among the world's diverse legal traditions.

For example, England, the United States, Canada, and Australia all belong to the Common Law family, which is characterized by judge-made law and reliance on judicial precedent. France, Germany, Italy, and Spain, on the other hand, are part of the Civil Law family, where law is primarily codified in comprehensive statutes such as the *Code civil* or the *Bürgerliches Gesetzbuch*. Religious legal systems include, for instance, Islamic law based on the *Sharia*, Jewish law derived from the *Torah* and the *Talmud*, and Hindu law inspired by the *Dharmaśāstra*. Socialist legal systems, such as those formerly found in the Soviet Union, China, or Cuba,

27 Winterton, George, 1975, "Comparative Law Teaching," *The American Journal of Comparative Law*, vol. 23, no. 1, pp. 69–118.

28 Cf. Peter de Cruz's Comparative Law in a Changing World for descriptions of socialistic laws.

emphasized state ownership of property and the subordination of individual rights to collective interests.

These examples show how the theory of legal families helps to organize and understand the world's legal diversity by grouping systems that share common historical origins, methods of reasoning, and sources of law.

2.1.3 *Identifying the Juristic Style of a Legal System or Parent Legal Family*

Peter de Cruz[29] – a Professor of Comparative Law at Liverpool John Moores University – provides an overview of the various criteria used to classify and compare legal systems. These include historical background, race, language, culture, substantive content of the law, ideology, conception of justice, legal technique, and juristic style. De Cruz notes that there is considerable academic debate over which of these criteria are most relevant for identifying, classifying, and comparing legal systems within the same parent legal family.

Konrad Zweigert (1911–1996)[30] and Hein Kötz,[31] in particular, propose that the juristic style of a legal system can be inferred from the articulation of five elements: mode of development, mode of legal reasoning, distinctive institutions, preferred legal sources, and predominant ideology. These dimensions define the intellectual and functional style of a legal system and form the basis for distinguishing among parent legal families.

The Common Law system, historically rooted in England, is based primarily on judge-made law developed through judicial decisions. It emerged from the activity of royal courts that resolved disputes according to custom and precedent. The authority of prior decisions, or *stare decisis*, remains a cornerstone of Common Law reasoning. In contrast, the Civil Law system, derived from Roman law, is characterized by comprehensive codification. Legal rules are systematically organized in codes and statutes enacted by legislatures. A sharp distinction is maintained between public and private law, and judges apply the law deductively to specific cases.

In terms of legal reasoning, Common Law adopts a pragmatic, inductive approach. Judges analyze concrete facts and derive principles from case outcomes. Civil Law, on the other hand, favors a more theoretical and deductive approach, as judges apply general legal principles to particular situations based on codified norms.

Distinctive institutions in the Common Law tradition include trusts, torts, consideration (as a condition of contract formation), and estoppel. Civil Law systems, by contrast, recognize institutions such as direct action, oblique action, abuse of rights, and unjust enrichment, as well as concepts like abstract legal acts and creditor–debtor relationships.

Regarding sources of law, Common Law relies primarily on judicial precedent, with legislation used mainly to consolidate or clarify existing principles. Civil Law, however, considers statutes and codes as the main sources of law, while judicial decisions and doctrine serve as persuasive or secondary authorities.

Ideologically, both systems are grounded in liberal principles, emphasizing individual rights and the Rule of Law. Yet their methods and structures reflect different conceptions of legal reasoning and authority.

29 De Cruz, *Comparative Law in a Changing World.*

30 Konrad Zweigert was a German jurist and former Director of the Max Planck Institute for Comparative and International Private Law in Hamburg. He became a professor at the University of Tübingen in 1955.

31 Hein Kötz is a German jurist and former Director of the Max Planck Institute for Comparative and International Private Law in Hamburg. He also served as President of Bucerius Law School and Vice President of the German Research Foundation (Deutsche Forschungsgemeinschaft, DFG).

While legal families group systems with shared features, significant differences remain within each family. For example, the French and German Civil Law systems differ in structure and doctrine, but their shared historical origins, methods, and institutions justify their inclusion within the broader Civil Law family.

Comparative lawyers have long sought to classify the world's legal systems according to shared traits. Depending on the chosen criteria, scholars have identified anywhere from a few to more than 100 distinct legal families. However, most contemporary systems derive from three great legal traditions: the Civil Law family, the Common Law family, and the religious or traditional legal systems.

The global expansion of civil and Common Law through colonization, legal transplants, and modernization has profoundly shaped many non-Western legal systems. Japanese law, for example, has been strongly influenced by the Civil Law tradition, particularly the German and French models.

2.2 Legal Traditions

To understand what a legal tradition is, one must first recognize the close connection between law, history, and culture. Legal traditions are not simply collections of rules or procedures; they represent comprehensive systems that reflect the historical experiences and cultural values of a society. Over time, these traditions evolve in response to historical events, social norms, philosophical ideas, and cultural practices. Studying a legal tradition, therefore, means examining how law both influences and is influenced by the history, beliefs, and identity of the society in which it develops.

2.2.1 Definition of a Legal Tradition

John Henry Merryman (1920–2015), who was the Nelson Bowman Sweitzer and Marie B. Sweitzer Professor of Comparative Law Emeritus at Stanford University, emphasized that a legal tradition encompasses far more than the rules governing contracts, marriage, torts, crimes, or corporations. According to Merryman, it embodies "deeply rooted, historically conditioned attitudes about the nature of law, its societal role, political ideology, the structure and functioning of legal systems, and the processes of lawmaking, application, study, refinement, and education."[32]

For Merryman, the concept of legal tradition places the legal system within its broader cultural context. Every community, region, or political organization develops its own particular understanding of law shaped by history, culture, and collective experience. The interaction between a people's historical background and their cultural outlook gives rise to a distinct legal identity, producing the unique atmosphere and character of each legal system. Beyond these cultural foundations, a legal tradition also influences how lawyers think and reason. It shapes methods of interpretation, the authority accorded to judicial decisions or legislation, and the very vocabulary used to describe legal concepts. Two systems may share similar rules yet differ profoundly in their underlying legal culture, for example, in their trust in judges, their preference for abstract principles or detailed codes, or their understanding of the relationship between law and morality. A legal tradition, therefore, operates as an intellectual framework: it guides how legal actors perceive problems, formulate solutions, and justify decisions, ensuring the continuity and identity of a legal system across generations.

32 Merryman, J.H., 1985, *The Civil Law Tradition: An Introduction to the Legal Systems of Western Europe and Latin America*, 2nd ed., Stanford University Press, Stanford, CA, pp. 19–25.

2.2.2 *Examples of Major Legal Traditions*

The Civil Law tradition represents a distinct juristic style that developed from the Romano-Germanic legal heritage. The so-called Civil Law world has given rise to several particular legal traditions, among which the French and German traditions are the most influential. Both belong to the broader Civil Law family and share a common origin in the medieval reception of Roman law, particularly the compilations of Emperor Justinian. They also share a strong commitment to codification as their preferred method of lawmaking, with written codes and enacted statutes serving as their primary sources of law.

Despite these similarities, French and German law differ significantly in their underlying conceptions of law. French legal thought has been influenced by the School of Natural Law, while German legal philosophy was shaped by the Historical School of Law. In France, a strict distinction exists between Private Law and Public Law, each forming a separate branch of law with its own courts, doctrines, and commentaries. The French legal tradition relies on a deductive method of reasoning, drawing from general principles to derive specific rules and solutions.

The German legal tradition, though also rooted in Roman law, took on its modern form in the 19th century with the rise of the Pandectist movement. This school promoted a systematic and dogmatic study of Roman legal material, emphasizing coherence, precision, and abstraction. As a result, German legal reasoning is highly conceptual and theoretical, and the style of German codes differs from the French in tone, structure, and level of detail.

By contrast, English law – though influenced by Roman law during the late 19th century – remains largely shaped by its Common Law tradition. It relies primarily on judicial decisions and the doctrine of precedent (*stare decisis*) rather than on codified statutes. English legal reasoning is inductive rather than deductive: judges derive general principles from specific cases rather than applying abstract rules to particular facts. Although globalization has encouraged the codification of certain areas, English Common Law continues to function mainly as a system founded on case law and judicial interpretation.

Beyond the Civil and Common Law traditions, other major legal traditions also play a central role in shaping the global legal landscape. The Islamic legal tradition, grounded in the Qur'an, the Sunnah, and classical jurisprudence (Fiqh), combines religious norms with interpretive methods developed over centuries, producing a sophisticated legal science that continues to inform contemporary legal reforms in regions such as the Middle East, North Africa, and South Asia. Similarly, African customary legal traditions, rooted in communal values, oral practices, and consensus-based dispute resolution, remain influential across the African continent, often coexisting with statutory and constitutional law within pluralistic legal systems. These traditions illustrate that the world's legal diversity cannot be reduced to the Civil Law and Common Law families alone; it encompasses distinct worldviews, sources of authority, and modes of reasoning that enrich our understanding of law as a global and plural phenomenon.

3 The Significance of Studying Other Legal Systems and Traditions

Exploring the legal systems and traditions of different societies is essential in today's interconnected world. Understanding how other legal systems function broadens our perspective on law, justice, and governance, revealing both the diversity and the shared foundations of human legal experience. This discussion explains why it is important to study law beyond one's own jurisdiction and discusses the value of comparative legal analysis in promoting cross-cultural understanding, legal innovation, and more effective international cooperation.

3.1 Preliminary Question: Is Comparative Law Truly Law?

The question of whether comparative law should be regarded as an independent field of study or simply as a method of legal analysis is central to understanding legal diversity in a world composed of multiple legal systems. This part examines the nature and purpose of comparative law, exploring its role in identifying both the differences and the common principles that shape legal thought across jurisdictions.

3.1.1 Is Comparative Law a Subject or a Method?

Is comparative law fundamentally a field of study or a methodological approach?[33] This question is central to understanding the complexity of legal systems in a world marked by diverse legal orders. It also serves as a foundation for classifying and comparing the major parent legal families.

The classification of comparative law has long sparked debate among legal scholars, much like the ongoing discussion about the very definition of law itself – a concept that shifts depending on philosophical perspective, whether the emphasis lies on justice, social order, or broader societal aims. As discussed in the first chapter of this book, the essence of law remains difficult to define and is closely tied to how one interprets its ultimate purpose. If law is seen primarily as a means of achieving justice, ensuring order, or fulfilling other social objectives, then these differing perspectives will influence how it is understood and applied.

In the same way, questioning the nature of comparative law raises several contentious issues. What is its true purpose? Does it rest on established principles? Should it be treated as a distinct branch of law – like criminal law, property law, or competition law – or rather as a method used to study and evaluate legal systems? What are its defining elements, and how did it develop? These questions continue to shape academic inquiry into whether comparative law operates as an autonomous discipline or functions primarily as a methodological framework for examining, contrasting, and understanding legal systems across jurisdictions and traditions.

3.1.2 Understanding Comparative Law as a Method

Comparatists such as Peter de Cruz argue that comparative law does not possess a central body of substantive rules and therefore cannot be regarded as a distinct legal branch like criminal law or property law. As he notes, "law does not have a core content of subject areas and does not denote a distinct branch of substantive law."[34] Consistent with this view, the present study adopts the position that comparative law lacks a defined substantive content and should not be treated as an autonomous field of law.

Other comparatists, including Zweigert and Kötz, contend that comparative law is primarily an intellectual activity in which law itself is the object of study and comparison serves as the central method. As they explain, it is "an intellectual activity with law as its object and comparison as its process."[35] In this sense, comparative law is best understood as a methodological framework for classifying and analyzing legal systems. It is an academic pursuit dedicated to the systematic examination of similarities and differences among legal traditions, aimed at identifying underlying principles and patterns that transcend national boundaries.

33 See de Cruz, Peter, 2007, *Comparative Law in a Changing World*, 3rd ed., Routledge-Cavendish.

34 De Cruz, *Comparative Law in a Changing World*.

35 See Zweigert and Kötz, *Comparative Law in a Changing World*, p. 2.

3.2 The Goals of Classification and Comparison

Understanding why different legal systems are grouped into major parent legal families is a fundamental question in comparative law. This part examines the main reasons for such classification and discusses its significance for comparative legal analysis, highlighting how it helps organize legal diversity, identify common roots, and facilitate dialogue between different legal traditions.

3.2.1 Purpose of Classifying Legal Systems Into Parent Legal Families

The classification of legal systems into major parent legal families provides a structured and coherent framework for comparative analysis. By grouping legal systems according to their shared characteristics, origins, and modes of reasoning, scholars and practitioners can systematically examine the similarities and differences among them. This organization allows for a clearer understanding of how legal ideas have developed and spread across regions and cultures.

Classifying legal systems also facilitates communication and cooperation in a globally interdependent context. It provides a common vocabulary for discussing legal principles and institutions, helping comparatists, legislators, and judges engage in cross-border dialogue. In this way, the classification of legal families does not merely serve a descriptive purpose – it creates a conceptual blueprint for comparative studies that transcend national boundaries and illuminate the broader structure of global legal diversity.

One may still ask: Why classify legal systems at all? Why not simply focus on the study of one's own legal system or tradition?[36] The answer lies in the recognition that no legal system operates in isolation. Law evolves through contact, exchange, and adaptation, and understanding this process requires looking beyond one's own jurisdiction. Comparative analysis thus helps uncover the underlying logic and values shared – or contrasted – across different legal cultures.

3.2.2 Importance of Studying Other Legal Cultures

Examining legal cultures beyond one's own provides insights that cannot be obtained through the study of a single legal system. As Ehrmann observed, analyzing a range of legal traditions helps reveal what in law is contingent rather than essential, what endures across time, and the moral or philosophical assumptions that underpin legal rules. Comparative study, therefore, deepens our understanding of both the universality and the cultural specificity of law.

Throughout history, the study of foreign legal systems has inspired legal reform and innovation. The ancient Greeks and Romans, for instance, drew from external sources of law to refine their own legislation. In modern times, institutions such as the American Law Institute continue this practice through systematic comparative research aimed at improving legal coherence and consistency.

The exchange and adaptation of legal concepts between systems also illustrate how comparative law drives legal development. A notable example is the influence of the French *Code de commerce* on Prussian company law, demonstrating how one jurisdiction's solutions can inform and shape another's legal evolution.

In practical terms, comparative law serves multiple functions. It helps fill gaps in domestic legislation and case law, offers alternative approaches to solving legal problems, and clarifies

36 Frankenberg, Günter, 1985, "Critical Comparisons: Re-thinking Comparative Law," *Harvard International Law Journal*, vol. 26, p. 411.

the context and origins of transplanted rules. Beyond academia, it has become indispensable for practitioners who operate across jurisdictions, particularly in international business, trade, and arbitration.

Ultimately, studying other legal cultures allows us to see our own system more clearly by highlighting what is often taken for granted.

As Heinrich Ehrmann (1908–1994) – a German-American political scientist and jurist known for his contributions to comparative law and legal culture studies – explained:

> Only the analysis of a variety of legal cultures will recognize what is accidental rather than necessary, what is permanent rather than changeable in legal norms and legal agencies, and what characterizes the beliefs underlying both. The law of a single culture will take for granted the ethical theory on which it is grounded.[37]

Comparative study thus fosters intellectual humility and a broader understanding of law as a living, evolving phenomenon shaped by the interaction of societies, values, and ideas.

3.3 Understanding Law in a Globalized and Interconnected World

As noted in Section 1, the globalization that accelerated from the late 20th century onward has profoundly transformed the study of law. Comparative law has become indispensable for understanding how legal systems interact and evolve within an interconnected world. Simple comparisons or classifications are no longer adequate; a coherent and transsystemic approach is now necessary to grasp the global dimensions of law.

This section adopts such an approach, examining major legal trends and patterns that extend beyond individual legal families. Although the discussion often refers to the Civil Law and Common Law traditions for analytical clarity, the perspective remains global and inclusive, reflecting the diversity and interdependence of today's legal world.

3.3.1 Moving Beyond Traditional Comparative Methodology

Traditional comparative law, focused on contrasting major legal families such as the Common Law and Civil Law, has long provided a valuable foundation for understanding legal diversity. Yet, in the context of globalization, this approach proves increasingly limited. A broader, more global and transsystemic perspective is now required – one that seeks not only to compare legal systems but also to identify wider patterns and underlying principles that transcend cultural, regional, and linguistic boundaries. Such an approach more accurately reflects the realities of an interconnected legal world and provides insights that remain relevant in a multicultural and international context.

This broader perspective also acknowledges that legal ideas today circulate more freely than ever before. Norms, doctrines, and judicial practices circulate across borders through trade, technology, and international cooperation, giving rise to hybrid forms of law that defy traditional classifications. Understanding these global interactions is therefore essential to grasp how law evolves as a shared human enterprise rather than as a collection of isolated national systems.

The emerging concept of Global Law and recent developments in legal theory – particularly in comparative legal studies – make it increasingly necessary to adopt a transsystemic and

37 Ehrmann, Henry Walter, 1976, *Comparative Legal Cultures*, Prentice-Hall.

global approach to law, either in place of or alongside traditional introductions to law that remain confined to national, supranational, or international frameworks.

Understanding contemporary legal transformation requires that legal theory move beyond national frameworks and traditional "cultural areas" such as the Common Law, Europe, Africa, or Asia. A new intellectual field has emerged – known as Global Legal Studies – which seeks to analyze law as a worldwide phenomenon rather than as a geographically bounded one. Global Legal Studies broadens the scope of jurisprudence, diversifies its objects of inquiry, and opens new avenues for research by integrating insights from the social sciences, thereby fostering a renewed and truly global vision of law.

3.3.2 Towards a Global and Transnational Perspective on Law

Law is no longer only the expression of state sovereignty but increasingly the outcome of cooperation among states, international institutions, and private actors. Organizations such as the European Union, the World Trade Organization, and international courts show how legal norms are negotiated and applied across jurisdictions. Global issues like climate change, data protection, and human rights further demonstrate the need for legal thinking that transcends national boundaries and reflects our collective pursuit of justice, order, and coexistence in a connected world.

In today's globalized world, studying law only within national borders has become insufficient. Legal systems such as French or American law can no longer be understood fully without considering the wider context of global interdependence, where people, goods, ideas, and technologies constantly cross frontiers. What is needed is a global and transsystemic perspective – an approach that views law as an interconnected whole, extending beyond the limits of individual jurisdictions.

This perspective breaks down traditional divisions between legal traditions and highlights how legal rules, institutions, and practices interact across borders. Law today operates as a global structure that influences societies far beyond the authority of any single state. In a world where norms and practices circulate through trade, migration, and digital networks, studying law in isolation makes little sense. A global and transnational approach offers a more accurate understanding of how legal systems evolve and influence one another in shaping modern governance.

This shift is reflected in the evolution of contemporary legal education. Over the past few decades, transsystemic and global legal education has gained prominence. New Global Law reviews, international research workshops, and law schools adopting global curricula have emerged. Notably, in 1999, McGill University's Faculty of Law in Canada implemented a pioneering transsystemic model of legal education. Building on its longstanding bijural tradition, McGill recognized that "in a world of borderless human interaction, a localized legal education is insufficient." Its program enables students to develop a cosmopolitan understanding of law that transcends specific jurisdictions and traditions.

Given this evolution, a clear distinction emerges between an introduction to International Law – focused on relations between states – and an internationally oriented introduction to law, which examines law as a common human framework linking national, regional, and transnational systems. Accordingly, an international introduction to law ought to be an introduction conceived for a global audience, beyond national frameworks.

4 Origins and Development of the Legal Family Approach

Understanding the origins and evolution of the legal family approach is essential to grasping how comparative law classifies and interprets the world's diversity of legal systems. This approach groups legal systems into families according to shared features, historical development, and underlying legal philosophies. Over time, it has shaped the way scholars analyze similarities and differences among legal traditions. This section traces the major milestones in the emergence of the legal family theory and discusses the main criticisms directed at its assumptions and methods.

4.1 Key Milestones in the Development of the Legal Family Approach

The concept of legal families has undergone considerable evolution, shaped by the contributions of numerous scholars and pivotal developments in comparative legal thought. Tracing these milestones helps to understand how legal systems have been grouped, compared, and analyzed over time. This section presents the major stages in the formation of the legal family approach, emphasizing the key academic contributions and historical moments that have influenced the study and classification of legal systems worldwide.

4.1.1 1900: The First International Congress of Comparative Law in Paris

The first International Congress of Comparative Law, held in Paris in 1900, brought together mainly European experts, which naturally limited the scope of discussion and centered the debates on enacted legislation – the principal source of law in the Civil Law tradition. Nevertheless, the congress marked a crucial turning point: it sparked a growing interest in the systematic study of foreign legal systems and laid the foundation for future comparative research. Throughout the 20th century, this momentum led scholars to develop various classifications of the world's legal systems, aiming to identify, map, and explain the diversity of legal traditions across different regions of the globe.

It also marked the beginning of comparative law as an autonomous academic discipline, fostering international dialogue among jurists and laying the groundwork for a systematic study of legal diversity across nations.

4.1.2 1905: Esmein's Identification of Five Major Legal Families

In 1905, the French jurist and historian of Civil Law and canon law Adhémar Esmein (1848–1913) proposed one of the earliest systematic classifications of the world's legal systems, identifying five major families of law: the Romanistic, Germanic, Anglo-Saxon, Slavic, and Islamic traditions.[38] His typology reflected the intellectual climate of his time, when European legal scholarship sought to organize and compare legal systems based on their historical roots and structural characteristics. Esmein's work was pioneering, as it introduced a comparative framework that transcended national boundaries and emphasized the shared heritage of certain legal traditions.

Although limited in geographic scope and shaped by a distinctly Eurocentric perspective, Esmein's classification laid the groundwork for future comparative studies. It provided an early model for understanding law as a plural phenomenon shaped by culture, history, and religion. Later in the 20th century, other scholars expanded and refined this approach, incorporating additional criteria such as ideology, legal reasoning, and institutional structure. Their contributions

38 Esmein, Adhémar, 1905, "Le droit comparé et l'enseignement du droit," in *Congrès international de droit compare: Procès-verbaux des séances et documents*, vol. 1, pp. 445, 451, noted in Zweigert and Kötz, pp. 57–58.

would progressively transform Esmein's initial taxonomy into a more sophisticated and inclusive theory of legal families, better suited to a world of increasing globalization and legal interconnection.

4.1.3 1977: Zweigert and Kötz's Identification of Eight Major Legal Families

In 1977, the two German comparatists Konrad Zweigert and Hein Kötz advanced the study of comparative law by offering a more comprehensive and systematic classification of the world's legal systems. Building on a broader set of criteria – including historical development, legal reasoning, distinctive institutions, preferred sources of law, and prevailing ideology – they identified eight major legal families: Romanistic, Germanic, Nordic, Common Law, Socialist, Far Eastern (including China and Japan), Islamic, and Hindu systems.[39]

Their approach represented a significant step forward from earlier classifications such as Esmein's because it combined historical insight with analytical rigor and incorporated non-European traditions more fully into the comparative framework. By emphasizing juristic style rather than geography or culture, Zweigert and Kötz contributed to a more objective and methodologically refined understanding of legal diversity. Their typology became one of the most influential in comparative legal scholarship, providing a lasting reference for the study of how different legal systems evolve, interact, and influence one another in a cross-border environment.

4.1.4 1978: David and Brierley's Classification of Major Legal Systems Into Four Great Families

In 1978, René David[40] and John Brierley[41] further refined the comparative study of legal systems by proposing a new classification based on two fundamental criteria: ideology and legal technique. Using this analytical framework, they grouped the world's legal systems into four major families: the Romano-Germanic, the Common Law, the Socialist, and the Philosophical-Religious family. The latter encompassed Islamic, Hindu, and Jewish law, as well as the traditional legal systems of the Far East, Africa, and Madagascar.[42]

David and Brierley's approach marked a turning point in comparative legal thought by integrating both structural and ideological dimensions into the analysis of legal systems. Their work moved beyond purely historical or geographical categorizations, emphasizing the influence of philosophical and cultural values on the formation of legal norms. Although the Socialist legal family has largely lost its relevance following the decline of Marxist ideology and the dissolution of the Soviet Union, David and Brierley's classification remains widely cited. It continues to offer a coherent and enduring framework for understanding the world's major legal traditions and their interrelations.

39 Zweigert, Konrad and Kötz, Hein, 1998, *An Introduction to Comparative Law*, 3rd ed., Oxford University Press, Oxford.

40 René David (1906–1990), was a French jurist and scholar and one of the leading figures in the field of comparative law during the second half of the 20th century. Between 1929 and 1939, David taught at the University of Grenoble. After serving in the French army during the Second World War, he became Professor of Comparative Law at the University of Paris (1945–1968) and later at the University of Aix-en-Provence (1968–1976).

41 John E.C. Brierley (1936–2001), former Professor and Dean of Law at McGill University, was an internationally recognized scholar in comparative law and Canada's foremost authority on arbitration.

42 David, René and Brierley, John E. C., 1985, *Major Legal Systems in the World Today*, Sweet & Maxwell.

4.1.5 Van 1998: Van Hoecke and Warrington's New Approach

In 1998, Mark Van Hoecke, Professor of Law and Dean of the Faculty of Law at the Katholieke Universiteit Brussel and Co-Director of the European Academy of Legal Theory, together with Mark Warrington, then a doctoral researcher at the same university, introduced a new model for classifying legal systems that moved beyond purely historical or structural comparisons.[43]

Their approach combined both cultural and legal elements, emphasizing the deep interconnection between law and the broader social, moral, and intellectual contexts in which it operates. They proposed an initial macro-division into four large cultural families – African, Asian, Islamic, and Western – each encompassing multiple sub-groups defined by distinct legal and philosophical characteristics.

Within these overarching categories, Van Hoecke and Warrington identified several criteria for differentiation, such as prevailing ideologies, conceptions of justice and law, theories of legal sources, argumentation, and legitimacy. This framework marked an important evolution in comparative law by integrating insights from legal theory, philosophy, and cultural studies. Rather than viewing legal systems as isolated entities, their model emphasized the diversity of world legal cultures and the complex ways in which social and cultural values shape the understanding and application of law across civilizations.

4.1.6 2004: Örücü's Family Tree Approach

In 2004, Esin Örücü (1940–2023) – a professor of Comparative Law at the University of Glasgow and at Erasmus School of Law[44] – introduced what she called the "family trees" approach,[45] representing a renewed attempt to classify legal families in a more nuanced and inclusive way. She questioned whether, in an increasingly globalized world, it remained adequate to divide legal systems merely into the broad categories of "Civil Law" and "Common Law," while treating all other systems as derivatives of these traditions. As an alternative, she proposed the metaphor of a family tree, within which legal systems could be classified according to their constituent elements and degrees of relatedness.[46]

Örücü argued that all legal systems are inherently mixed, overlapping, and intertwining.[47] She suggested that they could be grouped according to the *proportionate mixture of their ingredients*, applying what she termed the "predominance principle."[48] Her approach, centered on the concept of "mixidness," provided a detailed framework for understanding the hybrid nature and composition of numerous legal systems across the world.

43 Van Hoecke, Mark and Warrington, Mark, 1998, "Legal Cultures, Legal Paradigms and Legal Doctrine: Towards a New Model for Comparative Law," *International and Comparative Law Quarterly*, vol. 47, pp. 495–536.

44 A leading figure in comparative legal studies, Professor Örücü's research profoundly influenced the understanding of mixed and plural legal systems. Her outstanding contributions were recognized internationally, notably when the International Academy of Comparative Law named her one of the *Five Great Comparatists* in 2022. She is remembered as a pioneering scholar, an inspiring teacher, and a dedicated member of the global academic community.

45 Örücü, Esin, 2004, "Family Trees for Legal Systems: Towards a Contemporary Approach," in *Epistemology and Methodology of Comparative Law*, ed. Mark Van Hoecke, Hart Publishing, Oxford, pp. 359–375.

46 Örücü, Esin, 2008, "What Is a Mixed Legal System: Exclusion or Expansion?," *Electronic Journal of Comparative Law*, vol. 12, no. 1, p. 1.

47 Örücü, *What Is a Mixed Legal System*, p. 9.

48 Örücü, *What Is a Mixed Legal System*, p. 5.

Since 2004, several scholars have built upon Örücü's insights, refining and expanding the legal family approach through new conceptual tools and comparative methodologies that better reflect the complexity of contemporary legal pluralism.

4.1.7 2007: Glenn's Legal Traditions of the World

H. Patrick Glenn's influential work *Legal Traditions of the World* – which received the Grand Prize of the International Academy of Comparative Law – redefined how comparative scholars understand legal traditions.[49] Instead of viewing them as rigid and isolated categories, Glenn (1940–2014) – who held the Peter M. Laing Chair at McGill University's Faculty of Law and specialized in comparative law, private International Law, and civil procedure – described legal traditions as fluid, interconnected, and constantly evolving systems. He emphasized the importance of legal pluralism and the constant interaction between traditions, rejecting the idea of clear-cut divisions among them. Glenn examined national laws within a broader framework of major legal traditions, including chthonic (or indigenous) law, Talmudic law, Civil Law, Islamic law, Common Law, Hindu law, and Confucian law. Each was analyzed not only in terms of its institutions and doctrines but also through its founding principles, interpretive methods, capacity for change, and patterns of interaction with other traditions.

Glenn's approach transformed comparative law by promoting an inclusive and dynamic understanding of legal coexistence. He argued that legal traditions are not inherently in conflict but are capable of dialogue and mutual enrichment. This perspective challenged the classical dichotomy between "Western" and "non-Western" law, inviting scholars to appreciate the global legal landscape as an interdependent network of traditions. His vision continues to inspire contemporary research on legal pluralism, transnational law, and the evolution of global legal consciousness.

4.1.8 2010: Capra and Mattei's Ecological Approach

Fritjof Capra[50] and Ugo Mattei,[51] recipients of the IBPA Benjamin Franklin Award in Politics and Current Events, developed a groundbreaking framework that bridges law, ecology, and systems theory. In their collaborative work, they argue that the legal crisis of our time is inseparable from the ecological crisis facing the planet.[52] The two scholars propose an ecological approach to law, calling for a shift away from the mechanistic and anthropocentric worldview that has dominated Western legal thought since the Enlightenment. Their new approach emerged from years of dialogue together, including two joint seminars on "The Laws of Nature and the Nature of Law" held at Hastings College. Their work was the first to present jurisprudence – the theory and philosophy of law – as an intellectual discipline whose historical development and conceptual structure reveal striking parallels with those of the natural sciences.

Their approach invites a reconceptualization of law as an integral part of the Earth's living systems, emphasizing interdependence, balance, and sustainability. Capra and Mattei advocate

49 Glenn, H. Patrick, 2014, *Legal Traditions of the World: Sustainable Diversity in Law*, 5th ed., Oxford University Press.

50 Fritjof Capra is an Austrian-born American physicist best known for his book *The Tao of Physics* (1975), which explored connections between modern physics and Eastern mysticism. He later turned his focus to ecology and systems theory, founding the Center for Ecoliteracy in Berkeley, California.

51 Ugo Mattei is a Professor of Law at Hastings College of the Law, San Francisco, and at the University of Turin, Italy.

52 Capra, Fritjof and Mattei, Ugo, 2015, *The Ecology of Law: Toward a Legal System in Tune with Nature and Community*, Berrett-Koehler Publishers.

moving beyond the notion of law as a tool of human control over nature, toward a model that recognizes the intrinsic value of ecosystems and the need for harmony between human societies and the natural world.

In comparative terms, they extend this ecological perspective to the study of legal systems, highlighting the diversity of legal cultures and the dynamic interactions between them. Legal systems, in their view, must be understood within their broader social, economic, and ecological contexts. This vision challenges the hierarchical and reductionist paradigms of classical comparative law, proposing instead a pluralistic, adaptive, and interconnected model that mirrors the complex web of life itself.

Fritjof Capra and Ugo Mattei developed an ecological approach to law that links legal systems, society, and the natural environment, advocating a shift toward a pluralistic and sustainable vision of justice.

4.1.9 2012: Comparative Legal Families Theory by Siems

Mathias Siems, Professor of Commercial Law at Durham University, has played a pivotal role in modernizing the field of comparative law by introducing empirical and interdisciplinary methods to the study of legal systems. Through his *Comparative Legal Families Theory*, Siems integrates both quantitative and qualitative approaches to analyze the relationships, similarities, and divergences among national legal systems. Moving beyond the traditional dichotomy between Civil Law and Common Law, he advocates for a data-driven methodology that employs statistical tools, coding techniques, and expert assessments to classify legal systems with greater nuance and accuracy. This approach allows for the visualization of global legal diversity and the identification of convergence or divergence trends within contemporary legal development.

In his broader research – often conducted in collaboration with scholars such as Mark Fenwick and Stefan Wrbka[53] – Siems also revisits the concept of legal certainty, a cornerstone of modern jurisprudence.[54] He challenges the conventional assumption that legal certainty is inherently higher in Civil Law systems than in Common Law ones, arguing instead that it is a context-dependent and evolving notion shaped by institutional, cultural, and economic factors. His empirical work demonstrates that measuring legal certainty requires more than formal legal analysis; it must also account for how law operates in practice across jurisdictions.[55]

Through his innovative use of quantitative comparative methods and his emphasis on contextual analysis, Siems represents a new generation of comparatists seeking to bridge traditional doctrinal study with the tools of social science. His work underscores the need to understand global legal systems not as static entities defined by historical lineage, but as dynamic, interrelated structures that evolve through continuous interaction, adaptation, and reform.

53 Mark Fenwick is Professor of Law at Kyushu University (Japan), specializing in comparative and regulatory law. Stefan Wrbka is Associate Professor at Kyushu University and Senior Research Fellow at EUIJ-Kyushu, focusing on comparative private law and consumer protection.

54 Fenwick, Mark, Siems, Mathias and Wrbka, Stefan (eds.), 2017, "The Shifting Meaning of Legal Certainty in Comparative and Transnational Law," in *The Shifting Meaning of Legal Certainty in Comparative and Transnational Law*, Hart Publishing, Oxford, pp. 115–134. Available at: https://ssrn.com/abstract=3007094.

55 Siems, Mathias, 2022, *Comparative Law*, 3rd ed., Cambridge University Press, Cambridge.

4.1.10 2018: The Global South Perspective

Recent scholarship has increasingly sought to integrate perspectives from the Global South[56] into the study of comparative law. This shift underscores the need to understand legal systems in developing and post-colonial contexts, acknowledging how colonial legacies continue to shape contemporary legal and constitutional frameworks.

A key contribution to this evolving discourse is *The Global South and Comparative Constitutional Law*,[57] edited by Philipp Dann, Michael Riegner, and Maxim Bönnemann. This volume addresses the transformation of Comparative Constitutional Law by foregrounding voices and experiences from the Global South. It fills a notable gap in existing literature by synthesizing ongoing debates and offering conceptual guidance in this rapidly developing field.

The work examines a range of constitutional models that move beyond the traditional Western liberal paradigm, encompassing transformative, authoritarian, and hybrid constitutionalisms found across Africa, Asia, and Latin America. In doing so, it challenges the dominance of Euro-American perspectives in constitutional scholarship and advocates for a genuinely pluralistic understanding of constitutionalism. By tracing how constitutional ideas travel, adapt, and interact with local realities, the book contributes to broader reflections on modernity, justice, and democracy within a world more connected than ever before.

Examples of such constitutional innovation can be found across the Global South. South Africa's post-apartheid Constitution of 1996, for instance, embodies a transformative vision that seeks not only to guarantee fundamental rights but also to redress historical inequalities through socio-economic justice. In Latin America, the Constitutions of Bolivia (2009) and Ecuador (2008) introduce the concept of *plurinationalism* and the recognition of indigenous legal orders, blending Western constitutional principles with indigenous cosmologies.[58] Similarly, India's constitutional jurisprudence reflects a complex synthesis of British colonial heritage and deeply rooted local traditions, producing a unique model of democratic constitutionalism. These examples illustrate how the Global South contributes original and dynamic approaches to constitutional design, enriching comparative constitutional law with diverse perspectives and experiences.

4.2 Criticisms of the Legal Family Approach

The classification of legal systems into major legal families – such as Civil Law and Common Law – has long been a foundational framework in comparative law. Yet this approach is not without limitations. Scholars have raised several criticisms of the legal family model, questioning its capacity to capture the complexity and diversity of global legal traditions. This subsection examines these critiques in detail, focusing on two central issues: cultural bias and exclusion, and the neglect of religious and philosophical diversity.

56 Countries primarily located in Africa, Latin America, Asia and parts of Oceania (excluding Australia and New Zealand) that share historical experiences of political influence, economic dependency and structural inequality in relation to the industrialized nations of the Global North. The *Global South* represents not just a geographic grouping but also a political and intellectual movement aimed at rebalancing global narratives and structures of power.

57 Dann, Philipp, Riegner, Michael and Bönnemann, Maxim (eds.), 2020, *The Global South and Comparative Constitutional Law*, Oxford Comparative Constitutionalism, Oxford University Press, Oxford. Online edition: Oxford Academic, 19 November 2020. https://doi.org/10.1093/oso/9780198850403.001.0001. Accessed 10 July 2024.

58 Lupien, Pascal, 2011, "The Incorporation of Indigenous Concepts of Plurinationality into the New Constitutions of Ecuador and Bolivia," *Democratization*, vol. 18, no. 3, pp. 774–796.

4.2.1 Cultural Bias and Exclusion

One of the main criticisms of the legal family approach lies in its underlying cultural bias. The traditional division between Civil Law and Common Law is largely derived from Western legal traditions, which tends to marginalize or overlook non-Western systems. This Eurocentric framework fails to reflect the true diversity of legal cultures around the world.

For instance, the legal systems of Indonesia and Malaysia combine elements of Islamic law, customary law, and Civil Law inherited from colonial powers, making them difficult to categorize within the simple Civil Law–Common Law divide. Similarly, Japan's legal system blends Western codification with indigenous practices and Confucian influences, illustrating how hybrid systems challenge rigid classifications. In Africa, many countries such as Nigeria and South Africa operate under plural legal orders, where customary law coexists with modern statutory and constitutional frameworks.

By forcing such systems into predefined Western categories, comparative law risks simplifying complex realities and ignoring valuable local perspectives. Moreover, this model often neglects legal pluralism – the coexistence of multiple legal orders, such as state law, customary law, and religious law, within a single country – thereby limiting our understanding of how law actually functions in diverse societies.

4.2.2 Ignoring Religious and Philosophical Diversity

Another major critique concerns the inability of the legal family approach to account for the diversity of religious and philosophical conceptions of law and justice. Many legal systems are deeply shaped by religious and moral traditions that do not fit neatly within the Civil Law–Common Law dichotomy. For instance, Islamic law (*Sharia*) governs not only legal rules but also ethical and social conduct, reflecting a holistic vision of justice that differs fundamentally from Western secular models. Similarly, Hindu law in India and customary law traditions in Africa and the Pacific Islands are grounded in communal values, spiritual beliefs, and ancestral authority rather than codified statutes or judicial precedent. By overlooking these alternative foundations, the traditional classification risks reducing complex legal orders to mere variations of Western systems.

Furthermore, modern legal systems are increasingly characterized by hybridization and cross-cultural interaction. Countries such as India, Israel, or Malaysia integrate elements of religious, customary, and Western-derived laws, illustrating the fluid and evolving nature of legal development. This ongoing transformation highlights the need for a more inclusive and dynamic comparative framework – one that recognizes the plurality of legal traditions and the interplay between global influences and local identities.

5 Modern Legal Systems: Interconnections and Mixed Influences

As the harmonization of legal systems continues to bring Civil Law and Common Law traditions increasingly closer, this *summa divisio* has become less relevant today than it was in previous decades. Nevertheless, the Civil Law and Common Law families remain the most influential and widespread legal traditions. Through processes of colonization, globalization, and various forms of legal transplants, they have profoundly shaped the development of contemporary legal systems across the world, with the notable exception of those primarily founded on religious law.

5.1 Örücü's Concept of "Mixidness"

In today's globalized world, legal systems are increasingly incorporating elements from various traditions, including Civil Law, Common Law, and religious or philosophical frameworks. Esin Örücü describes this phenomenon as "mixidness," a term that captures the intricate processes of interaction, adaptation, and hybridization among legal systems in a globally connected environment. This growing interdependence challenges the adequacy of traditional classifications, which often fail to reflect the dynamic and overlapping nature of modern legal orders. Consequently, Comparative Law must adopt a more flexible and nuanced approach to understanding how legal ideas converge, transform, and evolve across cultural and jurisdictional boundaries.

5.1.1 Globalization and Legal Mixidness

All legal systems today are, to varying degrees, mixtures of diverse elements. Globalization has greatly accelerated this process by creating unprecedented levels of connectivity and interdependence among cultures, nations, economies, and legal systems. Over time, the major legal families – Civil Law, Common Law, and religious or philosophical traditions – have converged and interacted across different regions and historical contexts. This convergence has produced numerous combinations and mutual influences, including within legal systems in transition, such as the former socialist jurisdictions of Eastern Europe, exemplified by Poland.

Examples of such *mixidness* can be observed worldwide. South Africa, for instance, combines Roman-Dutch Civil Law foundations with English Common Law influences and customary law, reflecting its colonial and indigenous heritage. Japan and Turkey have drawn heavily from European Civil Law models while adapting them to local cultural and social contexts. In Quebec, a unique blend of French Civil Law and Canadian Common Law coexists within a single federation, while Israel integrates elements of Ottoman, British, Jewish, and religious laws. Similarly, Indonesia and Malaysia incorporate Islamic, customary (adat), and Western legal traditions within their contemporary frameworks. Esin Örücü refers to this phenomenon as "mixidness," capturing the complex blending and hybridization that characterize modern legal orders in an increasingly interconnected world.

5.1.2 Challenges in Classification

Örücü rightly argues that it is unsatisfactory to focus solely on legal systems that exhibit both Civil Law and Common Law influences coexisting or overlapping with their original legal structures. Nor, she contends, is it sufficient to group such systems into a separate "third category." Her criticism rests on three points. First, not all mixed systems combining civil and Common Law elements have been consistently included in this proposed category. Second, there exist numerous other forms of legal combination that cannot be neatly classified within it. Third, and most importantly, she maintains that this is not the appropriate moment to create another rigid and inflexible classification of parent legal families, since the very theory of legal families is itself being re-evaluated.

In practice, most legal systems today draw upon both case law and statutory law (including codes) as sources of authority, though they differ in the relative importance assigned to each. Following Cruz's predominance principle, it remains valid to observe that in Civil Law countries such as France and Germany, codified or enacted law continues to serve as the primary source of law, while case law plays a complementary role in interpretation and application. By contrast, in Common Law jurisdictions such as the United Kingdom and the United States, judicial decisions and precedent remain the dominant sources, even though legislation has increasingly gained importance in fields such as commercial or constitutional law.

Mixed jurisdictions like Quebec, South Africa, and Scotland further illustrate this interplay: they rely on both codified statutes inherited from Civil Law traditions and case law principles derived from Common Law. These examples demonstrate that modern legal systems operate along a continuum rather than within rigid categories, confirming Örücü's and Cruz's view that comparative law must adapt to a world of legal hybridity.

5.2 The Convergence Theory

In contemporary legal scholarship, the Convergence Theory represents a pivotal development that departs from traditional, nation-centered approaches to comparative law. This theory highlights the growing harmonization and unification of legal systems worldwide, a process largely driven by globalization, transnational governance, and international cooperation. As legal norms increasingly transcend national boundaries – through international treaties, regional integration, and the diffusion of global standards – Convergence Theory seeks to explain how distinct legal traditions are gradually aligning in principles, methods, and institutional practices.

5.2.1 Legal Harmonization and Unity

The concept of legal convergence has emerged as a central theme in modern legal studies, marking a shift away from the traditionally nation-centered view of law. Driven by globalization, international cooperation, and the growing interdependence of states, legal convergence exerts profound political, legal, and economic effects worldwide. Even legal systems that were initially resistant to external influence have gradually engaged in processes of harmonization, illustrating the flexible and multifaceted nature of this phenomenon.

Legal convergence may occur organically, through the natural interaction of societies and legal practitioners, or as a centrally coordinated effort led by international and regional institutions.[59] For example, the European Union represents a structured and institutionalized form of convergence, as member states harmonize their domestic laws to align with EU directives and regulations. Similarly, the adoption of international commercial norms, such as the UNIDROIT Principles or the United Nations Convention on Contracts for the International Sale of Goods (CISG), reflects a voluntary but widespread movement toward common legal standards in global trade.

In other regions, convergence takes more informal or hybrid forms. The African Union's legal frameworks and the ASEAN Charter encourage member states to align legislation while respecting national diversity. Even countries such as China and Japan, once characterized by distinctive legal traditions, have incorporated aspects of Western administrative and commercial law to facilitate international cooperation and economic integration. These examples demonstrate that convergence is not a uniform process, but rather a dynamic evolution shaped by dialogue, adaptation, and the shared challenges of an interconnected world.

5.2.2 Equal Authority of Sources

The convergence theory focuses on legal harmonization and the gradual unification of legal systems. It suggests that most legal families around the world are becoming increasingly similar in their use and interpretation of legal sources. Over time, this development may lead to a situation in which statutes and judicial decisions are used with equal weight and authority. This evolution

59 Platsas, Antonios, 2024, "The Concept of Legal Convergence," in *Are Legal Systems Converging or Diverging?: Lessons from Contemporary Crises*, eds. Emilie Ghio and Ricardo Perlingeiro, Springer, pp. 27–44.

is already visible in many jurisdictions, where the traditional distinctions between Civil Law and Common Law methods have become blurred.

In France, for instance, judges and lawyers now rely extensively on jurisprudence, even though the Civil Law tradition historically regarded legislation as the only formal source of law. French courts, particularly the *Cour de cassation* and the *Conseil d'État*, have developed rich bodies of case law that guide future decisions and influence legal reasoning in practice. Similarly, in Germany, judicial interpretations play a vital role in shaping the application of codified principles, demonstrating that precedent has gained de facto authority even within a codified legal system.

Conversely, in Common Law jurisdictions such as the United Kingdom and the United States, legislation has taken on an increasingly important role. Parliamentary and congressional statutes regulate wide areas of social and economic life, from environmental protection to digital privacy, thereby limiting the purely judge-made character of the law. In Canada and Australia, courts frequently refer to both statutory provisions and comparative jurisprudence from Civil Law systems, illustrating the influence of transnational legal dialogue.

At the global level, instruments such as the European Convention on Human Rights and the jurisprudence of the European Court of Human Rights have further promoted convergence by requiring states from different legal traditions to interpret domestic laws in harmony with shared principles of justice and human rights. These examples confirm that convergence is not an abstract theory but a practical reality increasingly observable across modern legal systems.

5.3 The Influence of Ideology on Legal Frameworks

Ideology has always played a decisive role in shaping the foundations, structure, and operation of legal systems. Laws do not emerge in isolation; they reflect the political philosophies, moral values, and social priorities of the societies that produce them. Whether grounded in liberal democracy, socialism, or religious doctrine, each legal system carries the imprint of its guiding ideology. This discussion explores how political and ideological forces influence the development and application of law, focusing first on the interaction between legal and political thought, and then on the contrasting dynamics between secular and religious legal systems and their respective conceptions of justice and social order.

5.3.1 Ideological and Political Interplay

In a world marked by diverse political and ideological traditions, each legal system reflects the values and philosophies that underpin its society. These ideologies form the intellectual foundation upon which laws, institutions, and procedures are constructed, shaping both their internal logic and external orientation.[60] For instance, socialist legal systems emphasize collective welfare, equality, and the pursuit of social justice, crafting laws aimed at redistributing wealth and ensuring state control over key sectors of the economy. By contrast, capitalist legal systems prioritize individual autonomy, private property, and economic liberalism, developing legal frameworks that encourage entrepreneurship, protect contractual freedom, and limit state intervention.

Beyond these broad distinctions, many legal systems embody hybrid models, blending ideological influences in response to social realities and historical legacies. Modern welfare states,

60 Kennedy, Duncan, 1980, "First Year Law Teaching as Political Action," *Law and Social Problems*, vol. 1, p. 47.

for example, integrate elements of both socialist and capitalist ideologies by balancing market freedoms with social protections. Similarly, some postcolonial states have merged Western legal forms with indigenous or religious norms, reflecting an ongoing negotiation between imported and local legal cultures.

Although rooted in Marxist-Leninist ideology, China's legal system, for instance, incorporates market-oriented reforms. Laws promote economic growth and private enterprise, yet remain subordinate to state authority and the Communist Party's leadership – reflecting a hybrid model of socialism and capitalism.

Sweden's legal system integrates capitalist economic principles with strong social welfare protections. Its laws on healthcare, education, and labor rights reflect a balance between market efficiency and social equity, characteristic of Scandinavian social democracy.

The Saudi legal order is based on Islamic Sharia, which governs both public and private life. Legal norms derive from the Qur'an and the Sunnah, blending religion with governance and maintaining a theocratic foundation.

The U.S. legal system prioritizes individual rights, private property, and market freedom. Constitutional protections, such as freedom of speech and due process, underscore its liberal democratic ideology, while commercial law supports free enterprise and competition.

The European Union's legal framework embodies a post-national ideology, emphasizing human rights, democratic governance, and market integration. Its laws illustrate the growing trend toward transnational legal harmonization beyond state sovereignty.

These examples demonstrate how ideology – whether socialist, liberal, religious, or pluralistic – continues to influence how laws are conceived, interpreted, and applied in the 21st century.[61] They illustrate how political ideologies and power dynamics shape the evolution and application of laws.

The relationship between political power and law reveals how legal systems evolve under the influence of dominant ideologies and state structures. Law can serve as both an instrument of governance and a vehicle for social transformation – promoting justice and stability on the one hand, while at times entrenching political or economic hierarchies on the other. Ultimately, understanding this dynamic interplay highlights that law is never static or neutral: it is a living institution shaped by the tension between competing values, the balance of political power, and the dialogue between secular, religious, and cultural forces in an interconnected world.

5.3.2 Secular vs. Religious Legal Systems: Impact on Justice and Order

The nature of the relationship between citizens and political power – whether grounded in secular governance or rooted in religious authority – plays a decisive role in shaping how justice, order, and law are conceived and applied within societies. This framework broadly distinguishes between legal systems shaped by secular ideas and those based on religious beliefs. Such distinctions are essential to understanding the diverse moral foundations and institutional arrangements that define legal orders across the world today.

Secular legal systems typically emerge from Enlightenment principles that emphasize rationality, equality before the law, and the autonomy of human reason over divine command. They are characterized by a clear separation between law and religion, with legitimacy deriving from democratic institutions, codified legislation, and judicial interpretation. Examples include

61 See, for example, Lesaffer, Randall and Arriens, Jan, 2009, *European Legal History: A Cultural and Political Perspective*, Cambridge University Press.

France, where *laïcité* (secularism) underpins the constitutional order; the United States, where the First Amendment guarantees separation between Church and State; and Japan, where post-war legal reforms established a secular legal framework grounded in Western-style codification and constitutionalism.

In contrast, religious legal systems derive their authority from sacred texts and divine revelation, integrating moral and spiritual dimensions into the governance of social and legal life. Islamic *Sharia*, for example, continues to form the foundation of law in countries such as Saudi Arabia and Iran. Similarly, Jewish *Halakha* guides many aspects of personal and family life within religious communities in Israel and the diaspora, while Hindu *Dharmashastra* historically shaped the legal and moral order in South Asia and still influences aspects of personal law in India.

These two orientations are not always mutually exclusive. Many contemporary societies exhibit hybrid or pluralist systems where secular and religious norms coexist, overlap, or influence each other. For instance, in India, secular courts apply religious personal laws in matters such as marriage and inheritance; in Egypt and Pakistan, constitutions combine democratic institutions with Islamic principles; and in the United Kingdom, *Sharia councils* operate informally within a secular legal order to mediate family disputes among Muslim communities.

Sharia councils in the United Kingdom (also known as *Sharia tribunals* or *Muslim arbitration councils*) have operated informally since the early 1980s within the country's secular legal framework. The first, the Islamic Sharia Council (ISC) in Leyton, East London, was founded in 1982 to address matrimonial and family issues among British Muslims in accordance with Islamic law. These councils are non-state, faith-based bodies with no official legal authority; their decisions have no binding force under British law but may carry moral or religious weight within the community. Their primary role is to mediate and arbitrate family matters, particularly religious divorces, and to offer guidance on issues such as inheritance, Sharia-compliant finance, or halal certification. While their rulings may occasionally be recognized under the Arbitration Act 1996 when both parties consent and the outcome does not conflict with national law,[62] they remain entirely separate from the formal judiciary.

Imagine a Muslim woman in London who, though already legally divorced under British law, wishes to obtain a religious divorce (khula) to remarry in accordance with her faith. She turns to a local Sharia council, which examines her request, verifies the dissolution of her *nikah* (Islamic marriage contract), and issues a religious divorce certificate. While this certificate carries no legal force in the UK courts, it enables her to align her religious and civil status, demonstrating how Sharia councils operate as informal mechanisms within the UK's pluralistic legal landscape.

Such mixed systems illustrate that the interaction between faith and reason, divine will and human lawmaking, remains one of the most enduring and complex dynamics in the evolution of global legal thought.

Conclusion

The study of law across time, cultures, and traditions reveals that legal systems are neither static nor isolated constructs. From the earliest conceptions of justice in ancient civilizations

62 The UK Arbitration Act 1996 governs arbitration in England, Wales, and Northern Ireland, allowing parties to resolve disputes outside the courts through binding arbitral decisions. It upholds three core principles: party autonomy, minimal court intervention, and enforceable awards. While some Muslim arbitration tribunals have registered under this Act to handle civil disputes – such as commercial or inheritance cases – on a voluntary basis, most Sharia councils in the UK operate outside its scope. They mainly address religious and family matters, issuing non-binding rulings that hold moral or spiritual, rather than legal, authority.

to the sophisticated transnational frameworks of the modern era, law has continually evolved in response to shifting social, political, and moral contexts. Each historical period and cultural tradition – Greek rationalism, Roman pragmatism, Islamic and Hindu spirituality, European codification, and the emergence of International Law – has contributed to the complex mosaic of legal thought that shapes our contemporary world.

The classification of legal systems into parent families such as Civil Law, Common Law, and religious or philosophical systems has long served as a foundation for comparative analysis. Yet, as modern scholarship shows, this framework has inherent limitations. The works of David, Brierley, Zweigert, Kötz, Glenn, and Örücü reveal that traditional distinctions often obscure the fluid, plural, and interconnected nature of today's legal orders. The global circulation of legal ideas, the influence of the Global South, and the growing recognition of legal pluralism all point to the inadequacy of rigid typologies.

In the contemporary context, phenomena such as *mixidness* and *convergence* illustrate how legal systems increasingly interact, borrow, and adapt across borders. Globalization, technological development, and supranational institutions have created new spaces for harmonization and dialogue between different legal traditions. At the same time, ideological and philosophical foundations – whether secular, religious, liberal, or socialist – continue to shape the identity and orientation of national legal frameworks, demonstrating that law remains deeply intertwined with the values and power structures of each society.

Ultimately, the evolution from isolated legal families toward an interconnected global legal landscape reflects a broader movement from diversity to dialogue. Modern comparative law must therefore move beyond mere classification and engage in a deeper understanding of how legal ideas coexist, influence, and transform one another. In a world defined by interdependence, the study of comparative and global law is not only an academic pursuit but also a practical necessity for ensuring justice, coherence, and mutual understanding in the governance of an increasingly unified yet plural world.

Selected Bibliography

David, René, & Brierley, John E. C., 1985, *Major Legal Systems in the World Today*, Sweet & Maxwell.

De Cruz, Peter, 2007, *Comparative Law in a Changing World* (3rd ed.), Routledge-Cavendish, 544 pages.

Doe, Norman, & Sandberg, Russell, (Eds.), 2016, *Law and History* (1st ed.), Routledge, 1490 pages.

Domingo, Rafael, 2010, *The New Global Law*, Cambridge University Press, 238 pages.

Donlan, Sean Patrick, & Mair, Jane, (Eds.), 2020, *Comparative Law: Mixes, Movements, and Metaphors* (1st ed.), Routledge, 196 pages.

Glenn, H. Patrick, 2014, *Legal Traditions of the World: Sustainable Diversity in Law* (5th ed.), Oxford University Press, 456 pages.

Musson, Anthony, & Stebbings, Chantal, 2012, *Making Legal History: Approaches and Methodology*, Cambridge University Press.

Örücü, Esin, 2004, Family Trees for Legal Systems: Towards a Contemporary Approach, Chapter 18 in van Hoecke, M. (Ed.), *Epistemology and Methodology of Comparative Law*, Oxford: Hart Publishing, pp. 359–375.

Örücü, Esin, May 2008, What Is a Mixed Legal System: Exclusion or Expansion? *Electronic Journal of Comparative Law*, 12(1). http://www.ejcl.org/121/art121-15.pdf

Ragone, Sabrina, & Smorto, Guido, 2023, *Comparative Law: A Very Short Introduction*, Oxford University Press, 176 pages.

Siems, Mathias, 2022, *Comparative Law* (3rd ed.), Cambridge University Press, 590 pages.

Twining, William, 2009, *General Jurisprudence: Understanding Law from a Global Perspective*, Cambridge University Press.

3 The Civil Law Tradition

People will forget about my victories.
What will live forever is my Civil Code.
Napoleon Bonaparte

Civil Law, also known as Romano-Germanic law, forms the foundation of most legal systems in continental Europe. It developed through the interaction of Roman, Germanic, ecclesiastical, feudal, commercial, and customary laws, evolving into a coherent and codified legal tradition. Over time, it has influenced regions far beyond Europe, including Latin America, parts of Asia, and Africa. This chapter examines the origins, structure, and worldwide impact of Civil Law, while distinguishing it from the Common Law systems of Anglo-American countries.

The first section, *Origins of Civil Law*, explores the development of Civil Law from its ancient roots, focusing on the influence of Greece and Rome. It analyzes the philosophical foundations of early law, the role of the praetors and judges, and the emergence of the distinction between public and Private Law. It also traces the key phases of Roman law, from its foundation to Justinian's codification and its revival in medieval Europe.

The second section, *Codification and Global Spread of Civil Law*, examines how Civil Law evolved into comprehensive codes and how these codes were disseminated around the world. It discusses the process and purpose of codification, the impact of the Napoleonic Code, and the adaptation of Civil Law in various regions – from Latin America and Africa to the Near East and the Far East. The section also considers the reasons for the global predominance of Civil Law over Common Law.

The third section, *Exemplifying Main Features of Civil Law Systems: French and German Archetypal Models*, presents two key systems that exemplify the Civil Law tradition. It outlines their court structures, law-making processes, and hierarchies of norms, and provides an overview of their most significant judicial decisions. Through case analyses, this section highlights how fundamental principles of Civil Law operate in practice and how these two models continue to influence other jurisdictions worldwide.

1 Origins of Civil Law

Dealing with the Civil Law tradition inevitably leads back to Rome, founded in 753 BC. Rome's early political organization was a monarchy, later replaced by the Republic, and ultimately transformed into the Empire. This Empire, as history records, endured for centuries before its

DOI: 10.4324/9781003393047-5

decline and fall. Although earlier legal systems lacked the sophistication and structure of Roman law, they exerted a significant influence on its formation and contributed to its development.[1]

1.1 Influence of Ancient Greece

The influence of Ancient Greece on the development of Roman law – and, by extension, on the entire Western legal tradition – cannot be overstated. Although Greek city-states placed relatively little emphasis on codified law, Greek philosophy and culture profoundly shaped the intellectual and legal foundations of Rome.[2] This discussion examines the philosophical principles established by the Greeks and their impact on Roman legal thought, as well as the early Roman legal system that emerged from these influences.[3]

1.1.1 Philosophical Foundations

As explained in Chapter 1, the Greek legal system placed greater emphasis on philosophy – particularly on the nature of law and justice – than on the laws themselves. While the city-states had their own legal rules, the systematic study or "science" of law held little importance. Nevertheless, Greek culture profoundly influenced Roman law, especially through its philosophy and art. After the Roman conquest of Greece in the 2nd century BC, Greek ideas were gradually absorbed and integrated into Roman civilization. Despite being a conquered nation, Greece exercised a remarkable intellectual and cultural influence on Rome, shaping its thought, its institutions, and even the formation of its legal scholarship.

This influence created the intellectual environment in which Roman jurists later developed a far more technical and structured legal system. Greek thought provided questions and concepts, Roman practice supplied methods and solutions, and together they paved the way for classical Roman law.

1.1.2 Early Roman Legal System

The early Roman legal system was initially grounded in customary law – rules and practices transmitted orally through generations rather than codified in writing. These customs were widely known and observed by the Roman people and enforced by local leaders or tribal chiefs.[4] The origins of these early laws are often attributed to Romulus, the legendary founder and first king of Rome, or to his successors. Romulus is said to have established the fundamental social and legal norms of early Roman society, particularly in areas such as agriculture, family relations, and dispute resolution through established traditions. These early customs reflected the practical needs of a small, rural community and were closely tied to social life, religion, and family structures. They were simple, flexible, and adapted to the everyday realities of the Roman people.

As Rome expanded and its society became more complex, these unwritten customs gradually evolved into written law. A growing population, increasing diversity, economic exchanges, and

1 See du Plessis, Paul, 2012, *Studying Roman Law*, Bloomsbury Academic.

2 See Watson, Alan, 2008, *The Spirit of Roman Law*, University of Georgia Press.

3 Watson, Alan, 1991, *Roman Law and Comparative Law*, University of Georgia Press.

4 For more information on Roman foundations of the civil law: see Domingo, Rafael, 2018, *Roman Law: An Introduction*, Routledge; and Zimmermann, Reinhard, 1996, *The Law of Obligations: Roman Foundations of the Civilian Tradition*, Oxford University Press.

the emergence of new social classes made it necessary to clarify and fix the law in a more stable and accessible form. Moreover, the exclusivity of the patrician elite in interpreting custom created tensions and demands for greater legal transparency. This transformation culminated in the creation of the Twelve Tables, which codified and systematized existing practices, representing a decisive step in the formal development of Roman law.[5] For the first time, the law became a public and written reference accessible to all citizens, marking the beginning of Rome's long journey toward a structured and sophisticated legal system.

1.2 The Praetorian System

The Praetorian system in early Roman law represented a distinctive method of resolving disputes between private individuals. It began with a preliminary hearing before the *praetor*, a state official responsible for defining the legal issues at stake and framing the terms of the case. The actual judgment, however, was rendered by a private citizen known as the *iudex*, selected by the parties involved. This section examines the respective roles of the *praetor* and the *iudex*, and traces the evolution and influence of this system on the development of Roman and later Civil Law traditions.[6]

1.2.1 Role of The Praetor and the Iudex

An original mechanism for resolving disputes between private individuals existed in early Roman law. When a disagreement arose, a preliminary hearing was held before a *praetor*, a state official who belonged to a group of magistrates elected annually.[7] The purpose of this initial stage was to identify and define the issues in dispute. The case was then referred to a specific judge, the *iudex*, who was essentially a private citizen chosen by the parties.

The *iudex* was empowered by the *praetor* to render a binding judgment. This procedure bears some resemblance to modern arbitration, discussed in the final chapter of this textbook. The *iudices* were lay judges responsible for assessing the facts of the case, while the *praetors* were magistrates responsible for guiding the *iudex* on matters of procedure, legal issues, and available remedies. The *praetor's* authority largely derived from his control over the remedies accessible to plaintiffs. Although neither the *praetor* nor the *iudex* were professional jurists, their decisions were final and not subject to appeal.

The Latin maxim *De minimis non curat praetor* – "the praetor does not concern himself with trifles" – reflects the central role of this judicial officer, who exercised broad discretion in organizing and managing trials while focusing on matters of real significance.

1.2.2 Evolution and Impact

Until 337 BC, the office of *praetor* was reserved exclusively for members of the patrician class, a restriction that caused considerable resentment among the plebeians. Roman citizens were divided into two main social groups: the patricians, families of noble birth, and the plebeians, the

5 See Tellegen-Couperus, Olga and McNab, Shelia, 1993, *A Short History of Roman Law*, Routledge.

6 Nasti, Fara and Schiavone, Aldo, 2021, *Jurists and Legal Science in the History of Roman Law*, Routledge.

7 The Latin word *praetor* probably comes from *prae*, which means "before", and *it*, which means "gone" ("one who goes before").

common people. In 337 BC, eligibility for the *praetura* was finally extended to the plebeians, and Quintus Publius Philo became the first plebeian *praetor*.[8]

The dynamics of Roman legal proceedings were particularly noteworthy. The Latin maxim *De minimis non curat praetor* illustrates that the broad authority granted to the *praetor* to organize and oversee trials was not meant to be invoked for trivial disputes. In other words, Roman officials were expected to focus on matters of genuine legal importance rather than insignificant issues.

Although *praetors* were not bound by precedent and could decide cases freely without reference to previous rulings, a certain practice of continuity gradually emerged. Successful formulas and expressions developed in earlier cases were often reused as models for later ones. These formulas were recorded by the *praetor's* clerk and made available to the public, thereby creating a rudimentary and informal form of case reference.

This continuity shows that, despite the absence of a formal doctrine of precedent, Roman legal practice contained elements that foreshadowed certain features of the Common Law tradition. Nonetheless, the principle of judicial precedent effectively disappeared with the reforms of Emperor Justinian and the codification of the *Corpus Juris Civilis*, which enshrined the maxim *Non exemplis sed legibus judicandum est* – judgments should not be rendered in accordance with examples but in accordance with the law.

This maxim – cases must be judged according to laws, not precedents – reflects the core idea of the Civil Law tradition. In Civil Law systems, judges apply written laws and codes as their main source of authority while previous court decisions serve only as guidance. In contrast, Common Law systems follow the doctrine of precedent and the rule of *stare decisis*, where judges are bound by earlier decisions. This difference shows that Civil Law is based on legislation, whereas Common Law develops through judicial decisions.

1.3 Public Law vs. Private Law: A New Dichotomy

Roman civilization made a major contribution to legal history by developing a sophisticated system of Private Law, distinct from Public Law.[9] While Ancient Greece was mainly concerned with the relationship between citizens and the State, Rome established rules governing private relations between individuals. This distinction between public and Private Law has had a lasting impact on modern legal systems, especially those belonging to the Civil Law tradition.

1.3.1 Development of Private Law

As explained earlier, unlike Ancient Greece – where law primarily focused on the relationship between citizens and the State – Roman civilization pioneered the development of a sophisticated body of Private Law.[10] This marked the first clear distinction between Public Law, influenced by Greek thought, and Private Law. That distinction has profoundly shaped and structured legal and judicial systems in the Civil Law world.

8 According to Titus Livius Livy (59BC-AD17) *The History of Rome*, (Books I – VIII). Livy began drafting his masterpiece from the age of 30 to 70 when he died. The History of Rome was made of 142 books (of which 35 survived).

9 du Plessis, Paul, 2020, *Borkowski's Textbook on Roman Law*, Oxford University Press, Oxford. Available at: https://www.oxfordlawtrove.com/view/10.1093/he/9780198848011.001.0001/he-9780198848011.

10 See Watson, Alan, 2008, *The Spirit of Roman Law*, University of Georgia Press.

Roman Private Law was secular in nature, detached from any religious foundation, and grounded in human reason and rationality as developed by jurists. Since there were no professional legal advisers, lay judges (*iudices*) and *praetors* often sought guidance from a select group of aristocrats who were deeply interested in the study of law and specialized in giving legal opinions – the *jurists*. Before the emergence of these jurists, priests had fulfilled the role of legal experts.

The *jurists* had no true equivalent in modern society. They were neither judges nor advocates, but wealthy patricians devoted to studying, writing, and teaching law. Their motivation was not financial gain but rather the pursuit of honor and prestige in a society that greatly valued legal knowledge. These legal scholars developed an extensive and sophisticated body of Private Law governing relationships between citizens. They produced a vast corpus of juristic literature, including answers to legal questions, commentaries on statutes, and analytical observations. Although much of this work has been lost, many excerpts survived because they were incorporated into Justinian's *Corpus Iuris Civilis*.

The Emperor Theodosius II later recognized the authority of several leading jurists whose doctrines judges were required to follow under what became known as the *Law of Citations*. Among these eminent figures were Gaius (AD 130–180), Papinian, Ulpian, Modestinus, and Paulus. Their writings profoundly influenced the late Roman Empire, establishing a scholarly legal tradition that was transmitted through generations. Interestingly, their case-based reasoning shows certain parallels with English Common Law methods, as the jurists often reasoned from individual disputes rather than relying solely on abstract principles.

1.3.2 The Twelve Tables and Roman Legal Distinctions

The jurists worked with the earliest known source of Roman law, an ancient code called the Twelve Tables, dating from around 450 BC. Customary law was therefore not their only reference. The Twelve Tables were mainly composed of Latin customs with some borrowings from Greek law. They were not a complete code but rather a collection of basic rules meant to organize social life in early Rome.

As Ellen Goodman – an Australian legal scholar and author of *The Origins of the Western Legal Tradition: From Thales to the Tudors* – notes, no original copy of the Twelve Tables has survived. She argues that what we know comes from later quotations and paraphrases by Roman jurists.[11] The provisions of the Twelve Tables dealt mainly with Private Law, including court procedures, family law, inheritance, property, and contracts, but they also covered religious, criminal, and public matters. Writing the law down gave the plebeians access to legal norms and helped protect them from abuses by patricians. Goodman explains that the Twelve Tables probably represented an effort to codify the full rights and duties of Roman citizens. For more than 1,000 years, it remained Rome's only attempt at codification.

Roman jurists later distinguished between the *ius civile* and the *ius gentium*. The *ius civile* was the body of written and customary rules based on the Twelve Tables, applying only to Roman citizens. The *ius gentium*, or "law of nations," developed to regulate relations between Romans and foreigners and can be seen as an early form of International Law.

The Roman legal system deeply influenced the development of law in Western civilization and beyond, providing the foundation for the main civil codes of continental Europe and for

11 Goodman, Ellen, 1995, *The origins of the Western legal Tradition, from Thales to the Tudors*, Federation Press.

many derivative systems in Latin America, Africa, and Asia – even in countries that were never under Roman rule.

A Civil Law system is generally defined as one whose rules derive directly or indirectly from Roman law. The term "civil" comes from *ius civile*, the law governing relations between citizens. Most Civil Law countries today descend from earlier Civil Law jurisdictions through codification and colonization. If we were to map them, most would be found in regions formerly colonized by France, Spain, or Portugal. Napoleon played an essential role in spreading the Civil Law tradition. By contrast, the Common Law system developed independently and was not based on Roman Private Law.

1.4 Phases of Roman Law in World History

Historians of law generally distinguish two main periods in the development of Roman law. The first extends from the foundation of Rome in 753 BC to the codification of Justinian's *Corpus Iuris Civilis* around 550 AD. The second period corresponds to the revival of Roman law during the late 11th century, when scholars at Italian universities rediscovered and began to study the *Corpus Iuris Civilis*, marking the beginning of a renewed influence of Roman legal thought across Europe.

1.4.1 From the Foundation of Rome to Justinian's Codification (753 BC – 550 AD)

As explained in Chapter 2, Roman law underwent a major process of codification during the reign of Emperor Justinian, ruler of the Eastern Roman Empire. It is important to note that the development of Roman law took different paths after Emperor Theodosius I divided the Empire into East and West in 395 AD. Although the Western Roman Empire collapsed in 476 AD, Roman law continued to flourish in the East, where it remained in force until the fall of Constantinople in 1453.

Following the decline of the Western Empire in the late 5th century, centralized political authority disintegrated. The papacy gradually emerged as the main institutional power and developed a theory of governance inspired by Roman concepts, including that of *principatus*. However, Roman law and Canon law differed fundamentally: under Roman law, authority was believed to derive from the people, whereas under Canon law, it was seen as coming from God.

At the same time, several Germanic kings helped preserve and spread Roman legal principles in the West through their own legal compilations. The *Brevarium Alarici*, issued by the Visigothic King Alaric II[12] in 506, incorporated doctrinal writings and other Roman legal sources. Similar compilations appeared in the *Edictum Theodorici*, attributed to Theodoric the Great,[13]

12 Alaric II (458–507), king of the Visigoths, succeeded his father Euric on December 28, 484. He married Theodegotha, daughter of Theodoric, the Ostrogothic king of Italy. His reign covered regions including Aquitaine, Languedoc, Roussillon, and parts of western Spain. Like his father, Alaric was an Arian Christian but reduced the persecution of Catholics and permitted the Catholic council at Agde in 506. To create a legal code for his Roman subjects, he commissioned an abstract of Roman laws and imperial decrees. This influential code, issued in 506, is known as the Lex Romana Visigothorum or Breviary of Alaric. Alaric attempted to uphold his father's treaty with the Franks, but Clovis, the Frankish king, used the Visigoths' Arianism as a reason for war. In 507, the Visigoths were defeated at the Battle of Vouillé in Poitou.

13 Theodoric, Late Latin Theodoricus, byname Theodoric The Great (454–526), king of the Ostrogoths (from 471), who invaded Italy in 488 and completed the conquest of virtually the entire peninsula and Sicily by 493, making himself king of Italy (493–526) and establishing his capital at Ravenna.

and in the *Lex Romana Burgundionum*, promulgated by King Gundobad.[14] These texts reflected the enduring legacy of Roman legal culture even in post-imperial Europe.

1.4.2 Revival of Roman Law in the Late 11th Century

The second period in the development of Roman law corresponds to its revival in the late 11th century within Italian universities, particularly the University of Bologna. This renewed study of Roman law spread across Europe and profoundly influenced the formation of major European legal systems. This "second life" of Roman law lasted until the 19th century, the era of great codifications in Europe.[15]

The revival can be traced to the earliest lectures delivered by Irnerius on the *Digesta* at the University of Bologna, widely regarded as the first European university. Academic communities emerged in northern Italy to read, interpret, and teach Roman law. Bologna became an international center of legal learning, attracting more than 10,000 students. Other universities soon followed, including Paris, Salamanca, Oxford, and Cambridge. These law schools focused on ancient legal texts and trained students who later assumed key roles in government, the Church, and public administration. The knowledge they acquired – rooted in Roman legal sources – spread across Europe and interacted with local customary laws, either through interpretation or harmonization. This process of diffusion became known as the *reception of Roman law*.

Several factors explain the revival of Roman law during this period. First, in a society still fragmented by feudal structures, there was a growing need for political and legal unity. Second, the rise of commerce and trade called for a coherent legal framework to support economic life. Third, the *Corpus Juris Civilis* carried the prestige of Emperor Justinian, viewed as a sacred figure of Roman authority. Finally, the rational and systematic character of Roman law itself contributed greatly to its enduring success and appeal.

2 Codification and Global Spread of Civil Law

Civil Law has long been the dominant legal tradition in Europe, Central and South America,[16] parts of Africa and Asia, and even in certain regions of the common-law world,[17] such as

14 Gundobad, also called Gundibald (died 516), barbarian general during the last days of the Roman Empire in the west, and king of the Burgundians (*c.* 474–516).

15 In an article published in 1967, Joseph Dainow compared the Civil Law and the Common Law, with a particular focus on the history and development of the Civil Law. He described the evolution of the Civil Law further to Justinian's era very well. As he put it, "During the ensuing centuries and in the Middle Ages, the Roman law was eclipsed in many parts of Europe. However it reappeared at different times and in various ways, it was modified and reinterpreted, and by the eighteenth and nineteenth centuries it had acquired the profound appreciation of European jurists and scholars. Roman law was at one of the peaks of its prestige when the several political unifications of Western Europe led to the unification of the Private Law in the national movements of codification, especially in France and in Germany. The essential characteristics of these legislative codifications fixed the basis and determined the nature of the legal systems of which they were the expression." Dainow, Joseph, 1967, "The Civil Law and the Common Law: Some Points of Comparison," *American Journal of Comparative Law*, vol. 15.

16 Merryman, John Henry, 2007, *The Civil Law Tradition: An Introduction to the Legal Systems of Europe and Latin America*, 3rd revised ed., Stanford University Press.

17 Refer to Fairgrieve, Duncan, 2007, *The Influence of the French Civil Code on the Common Law and Beyond*, British Institute of International & Comparative Law.

Quebec,[18] Puerto Rico, Louisiana,[19] Mauritius, the Philippines, Saint Lucia, and Scotland.[20] As Örücü's "family tree" of legal systems illustrates, many of these are mixed jurisdictions – hybrids that combine elements of civil and Common Law – yet they remain strongly influenced by the Civil Law tradition.

The Civil Law is as diverse as the regions where it has developed and become the governing law.[21] Still, certain patterns and common tendencies can be identified. From the 12th to the 19th century, the growth of Civil Law was firmly grounded in Roman law. The great movement toward codification, increasingly independent from its Roman origins, culminated in the adoption of the French *Code civil* in 1804.[22] This event marked a turning point, as it launched a vast wave of legal transplantation across the world. Many countries adopted, adapted, or directly copied the Napoleonic Code, a process driven both by France's conquests and by its intellectual and political prestige during the 19th century.[23]

Soon after the French Code came the Austrian Civil Code, followed by the Spanish Code of 1889, the German *Bürgerliches Gesetzbuch* of 1898,[24] and the Greek Civil Code of 1942. Codification thus became a defining feature of Civil Law systems, though not their essential criterion. For instance, Greece remained a Civil Law jurisdiction applying an uncodified form of Roman law until 1942. Ultimately, the Civil Law's deepest roots lie in the enduring legacy of Roman legal thought.

2.1 The Codification Process

Codification is a key element of legal systems, especially in the Civil Law tradition. It means bringing together and organizing legal rules that govern specific areas of law into a single, clear, and consistent text. This section looks at the purpose and scope of codification as well as its structure and historical background.

2.1.1 Purpose and Scope of Codification

A code is a statute, meaning it is a form of written law enacted by a legislature. Codification seeks to be comprehensive by gathering all the legal rules that govern a specific area of law into a single, organized text. Codes can cover any branch of law, such as civil, commercial, criminal, or procedural law. The purpose of a code is not only to consolidate the law but also to present it in a clear, coherent, and accessible form, allowing citizens, judges, and lawyers to find the relevant rules without needing to consult scattered or contradictory sources. Codification also brings stability by fixing the law in writing while still allowing future reforms.

18 Jobin, Pierre-Gabriel, 1992, "L'influence de la doctrine française sur le droit civil québécois," *Revue internationale de droit comparé*, vol. 44, p. 381.

19 Dainow, Joseph, 1954, "Le droit civil de la Louisiane," *Revue internationale de droit comparé*, vol. 6, p. 19.

20 See Palmer, Vernon V. and Reid, Elspeth, 2009, *Mixed Jurisdictions Compared: Private Law in Louisiana and Scotland*, Edinburgh University Press.

21 As James G. Apple and Robert P. Deyling explain, "each civil-law country has developed its own distinct legal system that draws on the rich history of the Civil Law, and it is not possible to discuss . . . such variations in detail." Apple, James G. and Deyling, Robert P., 1995, *A Primer on the Civil Law System*, Federal Judicial Center, Washington, DC.

22 Amos, 1928, "The Code Napoleon and the Modern World," *Journal of Comparative Legislation*, vol. 10, p. 22.

23 Refer to Spence, George, 2010, *Code Napoleon; Or, the French Civil Code*, Nabu Press.

24 Chabanne, Guy, 1975, "Napoleon, son Code et les Allemands," *Études Lambert*, p. 397.

During the Napoleonic era, five major codes were created: the Civil Code, the Commercial Code, the Penal Code, the Code of Civil Procedure, and the Code of Criminal Procedure. The goal of this project was to make the law accessible to all citizens. The codes were designed to be practical and compact enough for people to keep at home and consult regularly – almost like a companion to the Bible. This idea symbolized the democratization of legal knowledge.

It also reflected the political ambition of the time: to unify the nation by replacing the complex patchwork of local customs and privileges with a single, rational body of law applicable to all. Even today, the small red *Code civil* published by Dalloz remains a familiar and iconic object for most French people.

2.1.2 Systematic Nature and Historical Roots

In the Civil Law tradition, which is based on Roman law, codes are also systematic. This means they are organized in a clear and logical way. A systematic code arranges legal rules according to coherent concepts and categories. For example, the French Civil Code is divided into three main parts: the law of persons, the law of property, and the law of obligations. The structure of codes may differ from one country to another, but both the French and German codes share the same goal: to make it possible to locate, through logic and reasoning, the part of the code relevant to a given case.

This technique of systematization has deep roots in the Roman legal tradition. Over the centuries, Roman law became increasingly organized, especially through the work of jurists such as Gaius and the codification efforts of Emperor Justinian. Their work turned Roman law into a structured and coherent body of norms, laying the foundation for later codifications.

There is also a close link between codification and the Enlightenment. Enlightened thinkers believed that a just and rational society should be governed by clear and accessible laws. Codification reflected this ideal: the law had to be understandable, logically arranged, and based on reason.

2.2 Colonial Expansion and Spread of the Civil Code

The spread of Civil Law beyond Europe is closely linked to colonial expansion and the global influence of European powers, particularly France and later Germany. Through conquest, trade, and diplomacy, Civil Codes were introduced to vast regions of the world, where they were often adapted to local contexts. This section examines how the Civil Law tradition extended its reach across different continents – from Latin America and Africa to the Near East and the Far East – tracing both the diffusion of the Napoleonic Code and the influence of the German Civil Code. It also explores the reasons why Civil Law ultimately became the most widespread legal system in the world.

2.2.1 Napoleonic Empire

When Napoleon conquered new territories, he, like the Spanish and Portuguese conquerors before him, brought his legal codes with him. These codes served as instruments of both governance and cultural influence, exporting the French legal model across Europe and beyond. All these European codes were deeply rooted in Roman law, yet Napoleon's *Code civil* stood out for its clarity, accessibility, and universal ambition. It sought to replace the patchwork of local customs with a coherent and rational legal framework that could apply equally to all citizens, regardless of status or region.

As most South and Central American countries gained independence in the early 19th century after long and violent struggles, their new governments looked for legal models that symbolized modernity and equality. Rather than return to the fragmented and colonial systems of Spain and Portugal, they chose to draw inspiration directly from the French *Code civil*. This decision marked a shift from dependence on former colonial powers to an embrace of French legal rationalism. As a result, Latin America became not only a region influenced by Roman law but also a major area shaped by the French experience of codification.

Napoleon himself was aware of the enduring nature of this achievement. Confident that his political and military victories would fade with time, he is often quoted as having said, "People will forget about my victories. What will live forever is my Civil Code."

2.2.2 Latin American Civil Codes

Within Latin American legal systems, Zweigert and Kötz distinguish several groups of civil codes. The first includes those that are particularly close to the French Code civil, often being direct translations of it, such as the codes of Haiti (1825), Bolivia (1830), and the Dominican Republic (1845/1884). A second and more original group is represented by the Civil Codes of Chile (1855) and Argentina (1869), which, although inspired by French law, show significant independence and creativity.[25]

In Chile, the codification process was led by the Venezuelan jurist Andrés Bello, who worked for more than 20 years on drafting the code. His work drew from major Roman sources, Spanish law (including the Código de Las Siete Partidas), the French Code civil, other European codes such as those of Prussia and Austria, and the writings of Spanish and French jurists. Once enacted, the Chilean Civil Code was adopted in Ecuador in 1860 and in Colombia in 1873 and influenced later codifications in Venezuela (around 1860) and Uruguay (around 1870).

In Argentina, the codification process was led by jurist Dalmacio Vélez Sársfield. The Argentinian Civil Code of 1869, later adopted in Paraguay (1876), combined elements of Spanish, French, and Chilean law. The Brazilian jurist Teixeira de Freitas also influenced the drafting of the Argentinian code through his own work on Brazilian codification.[26]

2.2.3 Civil Codes in Africa

Many African countries adopted Civil Codes as a result of their colonial past.[27] Former French and Belgian colonies such as Côte d'Ivoire, Senegal, and Burundi have Civil Codes based largely

25 Zweigert, Konrad and Kötz, Hein, 1998, *An Introduction to Comparative Law*, 3rd ed., Oxford University Press, Oxford.

26 See Merryman, John Henry, 2007, *The Civil Law Tradition: An Introduction to the Legal Systems of Europe and Latin America*, 3rd revised ed., Stanford University Press, Stanford, CA.

27 It is important to note that during colonial times, the French Civil Code did not apply to everyone in the French territories. It primarily governed French citizens who had relocated to the colonies. Although natives of African origin were granted French citizenship under Article 80 of the 1946 French Constitution (Fourth Republic), they retained a specific local status. As such, they were subject to African customary laws or Islamic law if they were Muslim. This led to a bifurcation in substantive law, which was mirrored in the dual court system of the former French African colonies. African natives were subject to a specific native court system, presided over by tribal dignitaries, and Islamic judges supervised by French colonial officials. In contrast, French citizens had their own court system, which was integrated into the French dualist court system, divided between Private Law courts and administrative courts. Appeals could be made to the Cour de cassation or the Conseil d'Etat in Paris, depending on the case. French law always allowed African natives the option to choose French law over native law. After decolonization, the newly

on the French or Belgian models.[28] These codes were introduced during the colonial period to ensure administrative uniformity and legal control, often replacing or marginalizing customary and religious norms that had governed local communities for centuries. After independence, many states retained these codes because they provided an established legal framework, even though they were colonial in origin.

Over time, however, several African countries have reformed or adapted their Civil Codes to reflect national identity, social change, and local realities. For instance, Senegal's *Code des obligations civiles et commerciales* (1960) closely follows the French *Code civil* but includes provisions adapted to African business practices. Côte d'Ivoire, while maintaining a French-inspired code, has revised its family and property laws to better align with local customs and gender equality principles. Similarly, in Burundi, the Civil Code – originally influenced by Belgian law – was revised in 2018 to modernize its provisions on marriage, inheritance, and land tenure.

Contemporary African legal systems thus remain a mix of inherited Civil Law structures and indigenous or customary law. This coexistence often produces a form of *legal pluralism*, where statutory Civil Codes operate alongside traditional mechanisms of dispute resolution. Customary courts continue to play an important role in resolving personal and community disputes.

In Ghana, for example, traditional authorities – chiefs and their councils – play a vital role in land administration, family and inheritance disputes, and community conflict resolution. Under Ghana's 1992 Constitution, the *chieftaincy institution* is formally recognized and protected, with the National and Regional Houses of Chiefs serving as part of the governance framework. Chiefs act as custodians of customary law and local lands, resolving disputes through traditional norms that remain culturally legitimate and widely respected. No development project in rural Ghana typically proceeds without consultation with the local chief, reflecting the enduring power of traditional governance alongside statutory Civil Law.[29]

Similarly, in Niger and Mali, local customary tribunals decide inheritance and matrimonial disputes, while civil courts adjudicate commercial, contractual, and administrative cases. This coexistence of modern codes and traditional norms illustrates the hybrid nature of African legal systems. The Civil Law tradition, although rooted in colonial history, has evolved into a pluralistic model that integrates statutory codification with indigenous concepts of justice.

Africa's legal landscape is remarkably diverse and cannot be oversimplified; while some countries have advanced reforms and successfully integrated civil and customary law, others continue to evolve at their own pace, reflecting the continent's rich plurality of legal traditions and social realities.

2.2.4 Civil Codes in the Near East

The French codification experience also had a strong influence in the Near East, particularly in countries that were once part of the Ottoman Empire, such as Turkey, Egypt, Syria, and

formed African states abolished the dual court system but continued to apply French law, alongside local customary rules and Islamic law in matters of family and inheritance.

28 See Zweigert and Kötz, *An Introduction to Comparative Law*. It should be noted, however, that the French Code civil was automatically transplanted in Belgium, where it came into force in 1804, further to the incorporation of the Belgian territories into the French Empire (which were previously governed by Austria) by the Peace of Campo Formio in 1797.

29 See Mahama, Ibrahim, 2009, "Local Government and Traditional Authorities in Ghana: Towards a More Productive Relationship," *Commonwealth Journal of Local Governance*, no. 4.

Lebanon.[30] Some Islamic countries, such as Egypt, adopted codified Civil Law while maintaining religious jurisdiction over family and inheritance matters. As Zweigert and Kötz point out, the Egyptian Civil Code is silent on these subjects, which remain governed by religious law.

They further note that since 1949, the Egyptian Civil Code has been adopted or adapted by many Arab states, including Iraq (1951), Libya (1953), Qatar (1971), Sudan (1971), Somalia (1973), Algeria (1975), Jordan (1976), and Kuwait (1980). Some of these countries, particularly Iraq and Jordan, incorporated more elements of Islamic law, though the long-term impact of this remains uncertain.[31]

The influence of the Egyptian Civil Code went beyond its textual adoption and became a model for legal modernization across the Arab world. Drafted under the guidance of the eminent jurist Abd El-Razzak El-Sanhouri (1895–1971), the code aimed to reconcile Western legal rationality with Islamic legal principles, thereby creating a uniquely hybrid system. This synthesis allowed states with strong religious and cultural traditions to modernize their legal frameworks without severing ties to their historical and moral foundations. As a result, the Egyptian Civil Code came to embody a bridge between the Civil Law and Sharia-based systems, offering a flexible and adaptable model suited to the diverse social and political contexts of the Near East.

2.2.5 French Influence in Maghreb Countries

The states of the Maghreb – Morocco, Algeria, and Tunisia – came under French political influence and control in the 19th century, and their modern legal systems bear the imprint of this historical connection. In Algeria, the Napoleonic Civil and Commercial Codes were officially introduced in the 1830s and applied directly to French settlers, while indigenous populations were governed by Islamic and customary law.[32] After independence, Algeria retained much of the French-inspired structure, including its civil, commercial, and administrative courts, while progressively nationalizing its legislation through local reforms.

In Tunisia and Morocco, the French codes were gradually adapted to local realities through protectorate-era legislation. Tunisia adopted its own *Code des obligations et des contrats* in 1906, directly modelled on the French *Code civil*, but infused with Islamic legal concepts, particularly in matters of good faith and contractual fairness. Morocco followed a similar path, modernizing its legal framework through French-style codes while preserving Islamic law in personal status matters.

Across the Maghreb, family and inheritance law continued to be governed by Islamic principles and were only codified after independence – in the 1956 Tunisian *Code du statut personnel*,[33] the 1959 Moroccan *Moudawana*, and the 1984 Algerian *Code de la famille*. These

30 The Ottoman Empire was established by Turkish tribes in Anatolia. It was one of the world's most powerful states during the 15th and 16th centuries, lasting for over 600 years until its dissolution in 1922, when it was replaced by the Turkish Republic and various successor states in southeastern Europe and the Middle East. At its peak, the empire encompassed most of southeastern Europe up to the gates of Vienna, including present-day Hungary, Serbia, Bosnia, Romania, Greece, and Ukraine; Iraq, Syria, Israel, and Egypt; North Africa up to Algeria; and most of the Arabian Peninsula. The term "Ottoman" is derived from Osman (Arabic: Uthmān), the nomadic Turkmen chief who founded the dynasty and the empire. Shaw, Stanford Jay and Yapp, Malcolm Edward, 2024, "Ottoman Empire," *Encyclopedia Britannica*, 13 July, https://www.britannica.com/place/Ottoman-Empire. Accessed 15 July 2024.

31 Zweigert and Kötz, *An Introduction to Comparative Law*, p. 111.

32 See de Cruz, Peter, 2009, *Comparative Law in a Changing World*, 3rd ed., Routledge-Cavendish.

33 The Tunisian *Code du statut personnel* is a set of progressive Tunisian laws enacted on August 13, 1956, by *beylical decree* and brought into force on January 1, 1957. It was one of the most pioneering legal reforms in the Arab and Muslim world. It sought to establish greater equality between men and women in several key areas of family

reforms illustrate how Maghreb countries blended the French Civil Law tradition with their own religious and cultural heritage, producing hybrid legal systems that remain among the most dynamic in the Arab world today.

2.2.6 Civil Codes in North America

In North America, the French legal tradition remains alive in two territories: Louisiana and Quebec.[34] Both are parts of federal states dominated by the Common Law – the United States and Canada – but have preserved their Civil Law heritage. These regions illustrate how mixed legal systems can coexist and have inspired comparative research on transsystemic law. They show that legal traditions are not fixed by geography alone but may persist through institutions, culture, and political choices.

French law was introduced in Louisiana at the end of the 17th century when it became a French colony.[35] After its admission to the United States in 1812, the Louisiana Legislature ordered the creation of a Civil Code based on the French Code civil, with adaptations to local needs.[36] Although Louisiana participates fully in the American legal and judicial system, its private law remains largely civilian in structure, particularly in areas such as obligations, property, and successions. This blend of French foundations and American influences makes Louisiana a unique example of legal hybridization.

In Quebec, French legal influence began with colonization and continued even after France's defeat by England in 1763. The English authorities allowed the French colonists to retain their customary law, notably the Coutume de Paris introduced by Samuel de Champlain in 1608. The first Code civil du Bas-Canada, enacted in 1866,[37] was modeled on the French Code civil but included provisions on commercial transactions. It was replaced in 1994 by the modern Code civil du Québec, prepared under the leadership of Professor Paul-André Crépeau.[38] This reform modernized Quebec's private law while reaffirming its Civil Law identity within a predominantly Common Law federation.

---

life. It abolished polygamy, required mutual consent for marriage, introduced judicial divorce instead of unilateral repudiation (*talaq*), and strengthened women's rights in matters of custody and inheritance. The code also raised the legal age of marriage and gave women legal capacity in their own right, meaning they could marry, work, and manage property without male guardianship. Drafted under the leadership of President Habib Bourguiba shortly after Tunisia's independence, the code became a cornerstone of the modern Tunisian State and a symbol of its secular and reformist orientation. It marked a significant departure from traditional interpretations of Islamic law, showing that social reform and respect for religious principles could coexist within a modern legal framework.

34 Baudoin, Jean-Louis, 1974, "The Impact of the Common Law on the Civilian Systems of Louisiana and Quebec," in *The Role of Judicial Decisions and Doctrine in Civil Law and Mixed Jurisdictions*, ed. Joseph Dainow, I. See also Fairgrieve, Duncan, 2007, *The Influence of the French Civil Code on the Common Law and Beyond*, British Institute of International & Comparative Law.

35 Barham, William, 1973, "A Renaissance of the Civilian Tradition in Louisiana," *Louisiana Law Review*, vol. 33, p. 357.

36 The aim of such code was to codify the existing law.

37 "Bas Canada," or Lower Canada, is the historical name for the region in Canada now known as Quebec. This region was referred to as Lower Canada from 1791 until 1841, after which it was renamed Canada East following the Act of Union of 1841. Krueger, Ralph R., Nicholson, Norman L., Morton, William Lewis, Hall, Roger D. and Bercuson, David J., 2024, "Canada," *Encyclopedia Britannica*. Available at: https://www.britannica.com/place/Canada. Accessed 15 July 2024.

38 Book One – The law of persons (1987), Book Two – Family law (1981), Book Three – The law of successions (1987), Book Four – The law of property (1987).

Both the Louisiana and Quebec codes contain elements of interaction with the Common Law.[39] However, their ability to survive in the long term depends on social and cultural factors. Civil Law may have stronger roots in Quebec, where French language and culture are central to identity, than in Louisiana, where French influence has declined. These two examples, therefore, illustrate that the endurance of a legal tradition is closely linked not only to legal texts but also to community identity and cultural continuity.

2.2.7 Influence of the German Civil Code

Germany had relatively few colonies, but its Civil Code (*Bürgerliches Gesetzbuch* or BGB), which entered into force in 1900, soon gained a strong reputation for its technical precision, systematic organization, and conceptual rigor. It represented the culmination of 19th-century legal scholarship, especially the *Pandectist* school, which sought to create a logical and comprehensive structure for Private Law based on Roman legal science. The BGB's abstract language and layered hierarchy of general principles and specific rules made it one of the most sophisticated legal instruments of its time.

Although the German model was not as widely exported as the French Code civil, it exercised considerable influence on later codifications in Europe and beyond. Japan, for instance, used the BGB as the main source for its 1896 Civil Code, while countries such as Greece, Turkey, and several Central and Eastern European states drew heavily on German doctrine when drafting their own laws. The BGB also inspired parts of Latin American and East Asian legislation, particularly in areas such as contract and property law.

Its limited global spread is explained by two main factors. First, the German Code's complexity and high level of abstraction made it difficult to adapt to societies with different legal traditions and less developed legal education systems. Second, by the time it was promulgated, most Civil Law jurisdictions outside the common-law world had already adopted French-inspired codes, leaving little room for a competing model. Nevertheless, the BGB's methodological influence – its insistence on systematic reasoning and conceptual clarity – continues to shape legal thought in many jurisdictions to this day.

2.2.8 Civil Codes in the Far East

In the Far East, several countries adopted Civil Codes influenced by the German model. Thailand and China[40] enacted Civil Codes between 1925 and 1930, reserving family and inheritance law for local customs. Japan adopted a Civil Code in 1896, following major reforms after the Meiji Restoration of 1868.[41]

The first Japanese Civil Code, drafted by French jurist Gustave-Émile Boissonade, was influenced by French law but later revised under German influence to accommodate traditional

39 As Zweigert and Kötz put it, both territories are "fascinating models of a symbiosis of Civil Law and Common Law, and show that a political unit may comprise states of different legal traditions, even when those legal traditions are as different as those of Rome and Westminster." Zweigert and Kötz, *An Introduction to Comparative Law*, p. 118.

40 Such codes were revoked by Socialist law with the rise of the Communist regime in China.

41 See Kitagawa, Zentaro and Riesenhuber, Karl, 2007, *The Identity of German and Japanese Civil Law in Comparative Perspectives: Die Identität des deutschen und des japanischen Zivilrechts in vergleichender Betrachtung*, de Gruyter Verlags-GmbH.

Japanese values, particularly in family and succession law.[42] The final version, promulgated in 1896 and in force since 1898, consists of five books and has undergone reforms, especially after World War II, to align with modern Civil Law principles.

The German Civil Code also influenced other regions, including Eastern and Southeastern Europe. Hungary drafted a Civil Code based on the BGB after gaining partial independence from the Austro-Hungarian Empire. German influence was also strong in the Baltic states, Czechoslovakia, and Yugoslavia. In Turkey, the Civil Code was largely modeled on the German one, and the Greek Civil Code of the 1940s also followed the BGB's structure and logic.

In short, these examples show that Civil Codes have travelled widely – sometimes through conquest, sometimes through voluntary adoption or imitation.

2.2.9 Reasons for the Global Prevalence of Civil Law Over Common Law

Codification has made Civil Law far more widespread than Common Law. The Common Law, by contrast, travels with greater difficulty because it relies heavily on judicial decisions rather than on systematic codification. Translating and transplanting the Common Law would require not only statutes but also countless court judgments, which makes it less adaptable to foreign contexts.

The appeal of Civil Law lies in its apparent simplicity and systematization, which make it more exportable. Yet, even the most comprehensive code remains only a written text. Its application depends on judicial interpretation, which brings flexibility and subjectivity to the system. Thus, while Civil Law aspires to coherence and self-containment, in practice it remains open and dynamic, shaped by those who interpret and apply it.

Moreover, the global predominance of Civil Law also reflects broader historical, political, and cultural factors. The rise of European colonial empires during the 19th century, especially those of France, Spain, and Portugal, played a decisive role in disseminating Civil Law systems across Latin America, Africa, and parts of Asia. Later, the appeal of codification as a symbol of modernity, rational governance, and equality before the law encouraged newly independent states to adopt Civil Law models as part of their nation-building efforts. Today, while Common Law remains influential in former British territories, the Civil Law's emphasis on clarity, accessibility, and systematic reasoning has ensured its continued influence and adaptability in an increasingly interconnected world.

3 Exemplifying Main Features of Civil Law Systems: French and German Archetypal Models

This section explores the distinctive features of the French and German legal systems, both of which serve as archetypal models within the Civil Law tradition. The French legal system is deeply rooted in Roman legal principles, and anyone studying its operation can easily recognize the influence of Roman thought in its structure, terminology, and reasoning. Likewise, the German legal system has drawn extensively from Roman law, particularly through its systematic organization and abstract conceptualism. Together, these two systems illustrate how a shared Roman foundation can evolve into distinct yet complementary legal cultures.

42 Ishimoto, Tatsukichi, 1954, "L'influence du Code civil français sur le droit civil japonais," *Revue internationale de droit comparé*, vol. 6, p. 744.

In this section, we move from the general framework to a more concrete analysis by examining several judicial decisions. The aim is to show that while Civil Law originates from Roman law and is typically codified, it cannot be reduced merely to written statutes or ancient precedents. Instead, Civil Law is a living system that combines codification with judicial interpretation, balancing structure and flexibility. To illustrate this, we will study two comparative cases that address the issue of joint and several liability. Through these cases, we will see how French and German courts, each faithful to their own legal traditions, approach a similar legal problem in distinct yet equally reasoned ways.[43]

3.1 Main Features of the French Legal System

The French legal system is a quintessential example of the Civil Law tradition, deeply rooted in Roman law principles and shaped by centuries of codification.[44] It is defined by a clear separation between public and Private Law, a systematic organization of legal sources, and a strong reliance on written legislation as the primary expression of legal authority. The system seeks coherence and predictability through its hierarchical structure, where laws derive their legitimacy from the constitution and must conform to established norms. Furthermore, the legislative process in France is detailed and formalized, reflecting the central role of parliament and the Executive in lawmaking. The following subsections examine these features more closely, focusing on the organization of the courts, the hierarchy of legal norms, the stages of law-making, and the institutional role of the President in safeguarding the independence and integrity of the Judiciary.

3.1.1 Court Structure and Hierarchy

The French legal system is founded on the Roman distinction between Public Law and Private Law, a division that remains essential to its structure and operation. Public Law governs the relationships between individuals and the State, encompassing constitutional, administrative, and criminal law. Its primary function is to regulate how state institutions exercise power and interact with citizens. Private Law, by contrast, regulates relationships between private individuals or entities and includes areas such as contracts, property, family, and commercial law. Its main objective is to protect individual rights and ensure fairness in private dealings.[45]

This distinction is reflected in the organization of the French Judiciary. Public Law matters are heard by administrative courts, culminating in the *Conseil d'État* (Council of State), the highest administrative court. The *Conseil d'État* reviews the legality of executive actions, adjudicates disputes involving public administration and public contracts, and serves as a legal adviser to the government.[46] Private Law disputes, on the other hand, are handled by judicial courts, with the *Cour de cassation* (Court of Cassation) at the top of this hierarchy. The *Cour de cassation* acts as the supreme appellate court for civil and criminal cases, ensuring the uniform interpretation and application of the law throughout the country.

43 Federal Judicial Center, n.d., *A Primer on the Civil-Law System*, Federal Judicial Center. Available at: https://www.fjc.gov/library/fjc_catalog.nsf/0/a18d33fc1e8f0eb085256ca30067c10b?OpenDocument. Accessed 14 July 2024.

44 Brown, L. Neville, 1959, "The French Legal System: An Introduction to Civil Law Systems (review of René David and Henry P. De Vries, The French Legal System, Oceana Publications, 1958)," *The Cambridge Law Journal*, vol. 17, no. 1, pp. 132–134.

45 Steiner, Eva, 2018, *French Law: A Comparative Approach*, Oxford University Press.

46 Bell, John and Lichère, Frédéric, 2022, *Contemporary French Administrative Law*, Cambridge University Press.

Above these jurisdictions stands the *Conseil constitutionnel* (Constitutional Council), which safeguards the supremacy of the French Constitution. It reviews the constitutionality of legislation before its promulgation and can strike down laws found to be unconstitutional.

Finally, French courts operate within the broader framework of the European Union legal order. Judges in France must apply both national and EU law, ensuring consistency between the two. They may refer questions of interpretation to the Court of Justice of the European Union (CJEU), whose rulings are binding. This integration reinforces the dialogue between French and European law, contributing to the harmonization of legal standards across the European Union while preserving the distinctive features of the French Civil Law tradition.

3.1.2 Hierarchy of Norms

The French legal order is organized according to a precise and well-defined hierarchy of norms designed to ensure consistency and legal certainty.[47] At its foundation lies statutory law, centered on the five Napoleonic codes, which remain the cornerstone of French legislation. These codes comprehensively regulate the main areas of law. The *Code civil* (Civil Code) governs personal status, family relations, property, contracts, and obligations; the *Code de commerce* (Commercial Code) regulates business activities, corporate law, and commercial transactions; the *Code pénal* (Penal Code) defines criminal offenses and penalties; the *Code de procédure pénale* (Code of Criminal Procedure) establishes the procedures for criminal trials and safeguards the rights of the accused; and the *Code de procédure civile* (Code of Civil Procedure) governs civil litigation, outlining procedural rules, evidence, and the enforcement of judgments. Together, these codes form the structural backbone of the French legal system.

Although codification is the defining feature of French law, other sources also play a significant role. Doctrinal writings by legal scholars (*la doctrine*) and judicial decisions (*la jurisprudence*) serve as important interpretive tools that complement statutory law. This approach has deep roots in Roman legal tradition, where the opinions of jurists profoundly influenced the development and interpretation of the law. French jurists continue this tradition, providing authoritative commentaries that shape legal reasoning and guide both courts and lawmakers.

Similarly, the Roman *praetor–iudex* system, in which magistrates and judges collaborated to interpret and apply the law, can be seen as an early model for the French judicial function. In modern France, court decisions contribute to the evolution of *jurisprudence*, ensuring that codified law remains adaptable to new circumstances. While case law does not carry binding precedent in the same way as in Common Law systems, the decisions of higher courts, especially the *Cour de cassation* and the *Conseil d'État*, hold considerable persuasive authority.

In this way, the French legal system achieves a balance between the stability of codified law and the adaptability provided by judicial interpretation and scholarly analysis. This equilibrium allows the French legal order to remain both coherent and dynamic, continuously evolving in response to social, economic, and cultural change.

3.1.3 Law-Making Process

In the French legal system, as in most democratic regimes, the power to make laws lies with the Legislative branch, and the process is designed to ensure transparency, debate, and balance

47 Bell, John, 2008, "Introduction: The Spirit of French Law," in *Principles of French Law*, 2nd ed., Oxford University Press, Oxford. Online edition: Oxford Academic, 22 March 2012. Accessed 14 July 2024.

among institutions. Law-making typically begins with a *projet de loi* (bill) proposed by the government or a *proposition de loi* introduced by members of parliament. Government bills are first examined by the *Conseil d'État*, which reviews their legality and coherence with existing legislation before they are formally submitted to parliament.

The French Parliament is composed of two chambers: the National Assembly (*Assemblée nationale*) and the Senate (*Sénat*). The National Assembly, whose members are directly elected by the people, represents popular sovereignty, while the Senate, elected by an electoral college, represents local and territorial interests. Both chambers debate, amend, and vote on the text of a bill. If disagreements arise, a joint committee (*commission mixte paritaire*) may be convened to reach a compromise. Ultimately, the National Assembly has the final word if consensus cannot be achieved.

Once a bill is passed by parliament, it is sent to the President of the Republic for promulgation. The President's signature formalizes the adoption of the law, although the President may request a new parliamentary reading if further consideration seems necessary. After promulgation, the law must be published in the *Journal officiel de la République française* (Official Journal of the French Republic), which ensures its accessibility and entry into force.

This methodical process illustrates the French commitment to democratic legitimacy, institutional balance, and the Rule of Law. It ensures that each statute is the result of deliberation, scrutiny, and accountability, reflecting both the will of the people and the safeguards of the constitutional framework.

3.1.4 Role of the President

The President of the Republic serves as the guarantor of the independence of the Judicial Authority, a responsibility that reflects the democratic principle of the Separation of Powers. This principle ensures that the Judiciary remains autonomous from the Executive and Legislative branches, preserving the balance essential to a functioning democracy and protecting citizens from abuses of power.

A historical parallel can be drawn – albeit symbolically – between the French President and the Roman Emperor, both seen as ultimate sources of justice within their respective systems. While the French Republic has long departed from imperial authority, the President retains certain prerogatives that recall this legacy. Article 17 of the French Constitution grants the President the power to issue individual pardons, a modern expression of the clemency once exercised by monarchs and emperors.

The President's role in judicial matters is not absolute but operates in coordination with independent institutions. The *Conseil supérieur de la magistrature* (High Council of the Judiciary) assists in safeguarding the integrity and impartiality of the Judiciary. This body oversees the appointment, promotion, and discipline of judges, ensuring that decisions are guided by merit and independence rather than political influence.

A further guarantee of judicial independence lies in the irremovability of judges, meaning they cannot be dismissed or reassigned without their consent except under exceptional circumstances. This safeguard protects them from external pressure and allows them to rule according to the law and their conscience.

Through this framework – anchored in constitutional guarantees, institutional oversight, and professional security – the French Judiciary maintains both its autonomy and accountability. The President's constitutional role as guarantor, supported by the High Council of the Judiciary, thus embodies a delicate balance between symbolic authority and the practical preservation of judicial independence in the modern Republic.

3.2 Landmark French Court Decisions

In the evolution of the French legal system, certain judicial decisions have played a decisive role in shaping the contours of modern law. These landmark rulings, delivered by the *Cour de cassation* – France's highest court for civil and criminal matters – have clarified key legal principles, refined the interpretation of statutory provisions, and guided lower courts in their application of the law. Through these judgments, French jurisprudence has demonstrated its dynamic capacity to adapt codified law to new social and economic realities.

This section focuses on two emblematic decisions that have had a lasting influence on the development of French Private Law. The first concerns contractual obligations and the limits of liability in contractual relationships; the second deals with tort liability and the emergence of the principle of strict liability in cases involving damage caused by things under one's control. Together, these cases illustrate how judicial reasoning complements codified law in maintaining coherence, equity, and adaptability within the French Civil Law tradition.

3.2.1 *The* Litzinger v. Kintzler *Case of 1957*

The 1957 case of *Litzinger v. Kintzler* is one of the first cases French law students encounter in their studies, as it provides an instructive example of both French legal reasoning and the distinctive style of judicial writing in France.

> LITZINGER v. KINTZLER, Court of Cassation (Civil Chamber, 2d Division), Decision of June 5, 1957, 1957 D.S. Jur, 493.
>
> The Court:
>
> For the sole reason as to all parts of each of the two pourvois:-
>
> Whereas it follows from the appealed decision, affirming the decision of the lower court (Dijon, March 3, 1954), that on January 6, 1952, Nicolas, Roger, Cudel, Litzinger, Chauffaut Paul, Chauffaut Jean, and Thiriet had been hunting deer and that Kintzler was a member of the party, that about 4 o'clock the hunting activity had ceased and, that, while the latter had withdrawn from the hunt in order to get back to his home, the other seven hunters agreed upon the firing of a salute to celebrate the end of the hunt, and that Kintzler, being close by, was hit by a shot in his right eye which inflicted upon him an injury depriving him almost completely of the use of that organ; and that it has been stated by one of them that the seven members fired simultaneously, and, according to another of them, the shots went off "like the burst of a machine gun";-Whereas, on the action against these hunters brought by the victim on the double ground of the articles 1382 and 1384, subsec. 1, civil code, the Court of Appeals laid down, finding them liable jointly and severally, that "the real cause of the accident was the concerted action of the seven hunters engaging in a shooting which did not constitute a normal part of the hunt, under circumstances demonstrating negligence and carelessness imputable to all of them";-Whereas, this joint and several liability of these seven defendants has been established sufficiently and justly, and that it is in no way necessary, for the purpose of supporting evidence, to identify from them the originator of the shot which caused the damage; that, indeed, several persons, by engaging themselves in a concerted action, or acting spontaneously under mutual excitement, may involve themselves in a manifestation for which each ought to carry the liability for consequential damage, whether the damage is the effect of a single act in which all have taken part, or of a number of connected acts so coherent as to their concept and performance that they cannot be separated one from another; -Whereas, because of their superfluous character, it is irrelevant that the other reasons, based upon the alleged

liability at law for a person with a thing under his guard, are erroneous and open to proper criticism of the pourvois, since all the same the appealed decision is legally justified.

For these reasons, reject the "pourvois".

The case concerns a group of hunters who went on a hunting trip during which one member of the group was accidentally shot. It was clear that one of the hunters caused the injury, but it was impossible to determine who. The central question was therefore how to assign liability when the person directly responsible for the harm cannot be identified.

This problem of uncertainty raises important issues about fairness, causation, and risk distribution. The French Supreme Court (*Cour de cassation*) resolved it by holding that all hunters were jointly and severally liable (*responsabilité solidaire*). This meant that each member of the group was legally responsible for the full extent of the damage, and the injured party could seek full compensation from any one of them. The liable hunter could then, in theory, seek contribution from the others. The Court justified its decision under Articles 1382 and 1383 of the Civil Code (now Articles 1240 and 1241), which establish general liability for fault. The judgment explicitly declined to rely on Article 1384, which governs liability for the acts of others or for things under one's control, stating that it was unnecessary to apply that provision since liability had already been established under the first two articles.[48]

The reasoning of the Court, however, is not fully explained in the text of the decision, which is extremely concise. Typical of French Supreme Court judgments, it consists of one long, grammatically continuous sentence built around a series of clauses introduced by the word "attendu que" ("whereas"). This traditional style gives the decision the appearance of a strict logical demonstration: a sequence of brief, factual, and legal propositions leading inevitably to a single conclusion. The goal of this format is to make the judgment appear as a necessary and objective deduction from the law, rather than the result of judicial choice or interpretation.

This stylistic approach has deep historical roots. During the French Revolution, judges were seen as reactionary and politically suspect. Many were executed, and judicial discretion was viewed with mistrust. To prevent judges from being perceived as lawmakers, the post-revolutionary system emphasized that they were only to apply the law, not create it. This is why French judicial decisions are designed to appear purely deductive, as if the outcome were contained within the Civil Code itself and merely revealed through logical reasoning.

In reality, the reasoning behind *Litzinger v. Kintzler* seems to reflect policy and fairness considerations as much as formal legal logic. The Court likely considered that it would be unjust for an innocent victim to go uncompensated simply because it was impossible to prove which of the hunters fired the fatal shot. By imposing collective liability, the Court ensured that the loss would be borne by those who together created the risk, rather than by the victim. This reasoning, though implicit, aligns with the broader principles of equity and social responsibility that underlie French tort law.

The decision also illustrates the French conception of judicial reasoning. While formally grounded in the Civil Code, the judgment reveals how courts can use codified principles flexibly

48 Article 1382: Any act of a person that causes damage to another obliges the person by whose fault it occurred to compensate for the damage.

Article 1383: Everyone is liable for the damage they cause not only by their intentional act but also by their negligent conduct or imprudence.

Article 1384 (1): A person is liable not only for the damage they cause by their own act but also for the damage caused by the acts of persons for whom they are responsible or by things which are in their custody.

to achieve justice in complex factual situations. French judges traditionally present their conclusions as if they were preordained by the law, yet their work often involves balancing competing interests and adapting the law to unforeseen circumstances. The decision in *Litzinger v. Kintzler* demonstrates this dynamic: it upholds the principle of liability for fault while ensuring that fairness and social policy guide the outcome.

Ultimately, this case remains a cornerstone of French legal education because it exemplifies not only the substance of French tort law but also the method and philosophy of French judicial decision-making. It shows how courts, even within a codified system, interpret general legal provisions to address real-world problems while maintaining the appearance of strict logical deduction and fidelity to the text of the law.

3.2.2 The Jand'heur Case of 1930

The 1930 decision in *Jand'heur v. Les Galeries Belfortaises* is another landmark case that French law students study early in their education, as it perfectly illustrates the evolution of judicial reasoning in France and the unique, formal style of the *Cour de cassation's* judgments.

> JAND'HEUR v. LES GALERIES BELFORTAISES, Court of cassation, Full bench, Feb. 13, 1930, 1930 D.P.I. 57.
>
> [Plaintiff's daughter had been hit and badly injured by a truck belonging to defendant while crossing a street. Plaintiff sued and the trial court held that, pursuant to the first paragraph of Article 1384, the person in control of a thing was responsible for the harm caused by it without a need to show fault. The intermediate appellate court reversed on the grounds that the first paragraph of Article 1384 could not be applied since the truck had been operated by a human agent and thus plaintiff's only remedy was to show fault under Article 1382. The Cour de cassation's civil panel agreed with the court of first instance and remanded to an intermediate appellate court, which, in line with the then prevailing opinion insisted that Article 1384 could not be applicable in a case like this. There was thus a new appeal to the Cour de cassation. Under the then prevailing procedure, the case was referred to the full bench (Chambres réunies) which rendered this opinion.]
>
> The Court:
>
> Whereas the presumption of liability established by the first paragraph of Article 1384 of the Civil Code against the person having an inanimate object that has caused harm to another under his control can be rebutted only by proof of an unavoidable and unforeseeable event [cas fortuit] or of an Act of God or of an external event for which the person in control is not responsible and whereas it is not sufficient [for the person in control of the thing] to show that he has committed no fault or that the cause of the harm-causing incident has remained unknown;
>
> Whereas on April 22, 1925, a truck belonging to the Galeries Belfortaises company hit and injured the minor Lise Jand'heur; and whereas the decision under review has refused to apply the above-mentioned provision on the grounds that the fact that the accident was caused by an automobile that was in motion, steered and operated by a human being, did not, since there was no evidence that it was due to a defect of the automobile, amount to damage done by a thing within the meaning of Article 1384, paragraph 1, so that the victim, in order to obtain compensation, had to show some fault on the part of the driver;
>
> But whereas for the applicability of the presumption [of fault] which it provides, the law [i.e., Article 1384, para. 1] does not make any distinction depending on whether the thing that caused the damage was or was not operated by a human being; whereas it is not

necessary that the thing suffer from an inherent defect likely to cause the harm as Article 1384 bases liability on the control of the thing and not on the thing as such;

Whence it follows that in ruling as it did, the decision under review has reversed the burden of proof and violated the statutory provision mentioned above;

For these reasons, reverses . . . and remands . . . .

In this case, the facts are as follows: a young girl was injured by a truck owned by a department store, and her mother brought a lawsuit on her behalf. The main difficulty was that the plaintiff could not prove negligence on the part of the truck driver. Under normal circumstances, Articles 1382 and 1383 of the Civil Code would apply, as they establish liability based on fault. However, these articles were inapplicable because they presuppose the existence of proven negligent behavior, which was lacking in this case.

In a landmark decision, the French Supreme Court decided to rely on Article 1384 of the Civil Code, which states: "A person is liable not only for the damages he causes by his own act but also for that which is caused by the acts of persons for whom he is responsible or by the things which are in his custody." This article had long been viewed as an introductory provision leading to Articles 1385 and 1386, which concern liability for animals and building collapses, respectively. These provisions reflected the social and economic realities of early 19th-century rural France, when the Code was enacted in 1804, a period when injuries were mainly caused by animals or unsafe buildings.

By 1930, France had become an industrial society, and the circumstances had changed dramatically. Accidents increasingly involved machines, vehicles, and other man-made objects not covered by Articles 1385 and 1386. In this modern context, it seemed unjust to require an innocent victim, such as the injured girl, to prove the fault of the person controlling the object that caused the damage. To address this gap, the Court reinterpreted Article 1384 and introduced a presumption of fault against the "guardian" of any physical object that causes harm. This presumption could only be rebutted by proving *force majeure* – that is, an Act of God, an unavoidable, unforeseeable, and external event beyond human control.

Force majeure covers both natural events, such as floods, earthquakes, or hurricanes, and human actions, such as wars, riots, or strikes. The Court's reasoning, though not explicitly stated in the decision, reflects a policy choice aimed at fairness and social responsibility. In an industrialized society, those who introduce potentially dangerous objects – such as vehicles or machinery – into public life should bear responsibility for the risks those objects create. This shift in reasoning effectively transferred the burden of proof from the victim to the person responsible for the harmful object. Rather than requiring the injured party to prove fault, the Court placed the onus on the guardian to prove that the damage resulted from circumstances beyond their control.

This judicial development marked a turning point in French tort law. It demonstrated how courts could adapt the Civil Code to meet the needs of a changing society, even without formal legislative intervention. The decision, written in the Court's traditional single-sentence style composed of a series of "whereas" clauses (*attendus*), exemplifies how French judgments aim to present legal reasoning as a direct, logical deduction from the Code, rather than as judicial creativity. Nevertheless, this case clearly shows that the Judiciary played an active role in shaping the law by expanding the meaning of Article 1384.

For those seeking to understand the reasoning behind such decisions, it is important to note that each case considered by the *Cour de cassation* is accompanied by an internal opinion written by a member of the Court, known as the *rapporteur*. This opinion advises how the case should be decided and often provides a detailed explanation of the legal and policy considerations behind the ruling. While these opinions are not part of the published judgment, they are valuable sources for legal researchers who wish to uncover the underlying rationale and interpretive process behind the Court's decisions.

From a constitutional perspective, the language of the French Civil Code was flexible enough to allow this reinterpretation without violating the principle of Separation of Powers. If the Code had been drafted more rigidly, only parliament could have introduced such a change through legislation.[49] To address such situations, many modern Civil Codes include *directory provisions* – clauses that guide judges on how to proceed when the law is silent or ambiguous.

For example, the Iraqi Civil Code allows judges to refer to the Civil Codes of other Muslim countries if the Iraqi Code offers no solution. Similarly, the Swiss Civil Code explicitly authorizes judges to decide cases based on principles of justice and equity when the Code is silent. Some codes also instruct judges to consult custom or prevailing social practices to resolve gaps in the law. These provisions broaden judicial discretion while maintaining respect for legislative authority, ensuring that when judges look beyond the Code, they do so under its guidance and within its framework.

This case illustrates the capacity of Civil Law systems to evolve through interpretation, balancing the authority of the written law with the need for fairness in modern contexts. The Court's decision under Article 1384 transformed French tort law by establishing a presumption of responsibility in line with contemporary social and industrial realities, while remaining formally faithful to the Civil Code's structure and spirit.

3.3 *Main Features of the German Legal System*

The German legal system is distinguished by its systematic organization and clearly articulated legal principles, which together ensure coherence and predictability in the administration of justice. This part offers an overview of the fundamental components that shape the German legal framework, including its formal sources of law, federal structure, political organization, legislative process, mechanisms of judicial review, and the hierarchy of its courts. Familiarity with these core features is essential to understanding how law is created, interpreted, and applied within the German context, and how this system upholds both legal certainty and democratic accountability.

3.3.1 *Formal Sources of Law*

The German legal system rests on a combination of formal and unwritten sources of law, forming a coherent and highly developed legal framework.[50] The primary formal sources include the Constitution (*Grundgesetz*, or Basic Law of 1949), international treaties, statutes, and

49 The Legislature has the right to amend the code. A code is a statute. A code is ambitious, a code is comprehensive, it is systematic, but it's still a law. And the French Civil Code has been amended hundreds of times. So the French legal system still has the 1800 code, as amended. In other words, particular provisions of the French Civil Code have been amended. But it still is the French Civil Code.

Generally speaking, laws are not retroactive. So the law will not apply to a case that arose before the law was adopted. Most legal systems say the law is not retroactive, even Civil Law.

50 Schmidt, Folke, 1965, "The German Abstract Approach to Law: Comments on the System of the *Bürgerliches Gesetzbuch*," *Scandinavian Studies in Law*, vol. 9, p. 131.

subordinate regulations or bylaws (*Satzungen* and *Ordnungen*).[51] The *Grundgesetz* stands at the top of the legal hierarchy, defining the structure of the State, safeguarding fundamental rights, and establishing the principles of democracy and the Rule of Law. International treaties to which Germany is a party are incorporated into domestic law and influence both legislation and judicial interpretation. Statutes enacted by the federal or state parliaments regulate public, private, and administrative matters, while regulations and bylaws provide the detailed mechanisms necessary for implementing these statutes.

Alongside these formal sources, unwritten sources of law continue to play an important role. These include general legal principles such as fairness, good faith, and proportionality, which guide judicial interpretation and ensure justice in individual cases. Customary law, rooted in long-standing practices and social norms, is recognized when it reflects consistent and accepted behavior within a community. Case law, while not binding in the same way as in Common Law systems, contributes significantly to legal development, as decisions of higher courts are highly persuasive and promote uniformity in interpretation.

At the heart of the German legal order lies the *Bürgerliches Gesetzbuch* (BGB), or German Civil Code, often described as the "legal Bible" of German jurists. Enacted in 1900, the BGB is a monumental codification of Private Law that governs relations between individuals, addressing contracts, property, family, inheritance, and obligations. Its systematic organization and conceptual precision reflect the intellectual rigor of German legal scholarship, particularly the *Pandectist* tradition, which sought to structure law through abstract, logical principles derived from Roman law.

This systematic method, which pervades all areas of German law, ensures clarity, predictability, and fairness in legal reasoning. The interplay between codified norms and unwritten principles allows German law to maintain both stability and adaptability, combining strict legal formalism with flexibility in interpretation.[52] Understanding this balance – between formal authority and interpretive discretion – reveals the core of the German legal philosophy: a commitment to coherence, rationality, and justice within a meticulously ordered legal system.

3.3.2 Federal Structure and Political Organization

Germany's legal and judicial organization is closely tied to its federal structure, which defines both the distribution of powers and the operation of its courts. As a federal republic, Germany consists of 16 constituent states known as *Länder*. Each *Land* has its own government, parliament, and constitution, as well as legislative competence in specific areas, but none possesses full sovereignty. All function within the framework of the *Grundgesetz* (Basic Law), which establishes the supremacy of federal authority while preserving regional self-government. This system seeks to balance the unity of the nation with the autonomy of its regions.

Article 31 of the *Grundgesetz* clearly regulates the relationship between federal and state law, stating that "Bundesrecht bricht Landesrecht" (federal law overrides state law). This principle

51 Bylaws are rules or administrative provisions (sometimes referred to as ordinances or regulations) adopted by an association or by a public corporation, foundation, or institution for its internal governance. The power to issue bylaws is essentially derived from Article 28 section 2 of the German Constitution (Federal guarantee of Land Constitutions and of local self-government): "Municipalities must be guaranteed the right to regulate all local affairs on their own responsibility, within the limits prescribed by the laws. Within the limits of their functions designated by a law, associations of municipalities shall also have the right of self-government according to the laws."

52 Refer to Fisher, Howard, 2008, *The German Legal System and Legal Language: A General Survey Together with Notes and German Vocabulary*, Routledge-Cavendish.

ensures legal uniformity throughout the country and prevents regional laws from conflicting with national legislation. It also embodies the cooperative nature of German federalism: both levels of government share responsibilities but adhere to a clear hierarchy of legal norms.

The distribution of legislative powers between the federal and *Länder* levels is central to the system's functioning. The federal government is responsible for matters of national and international importance, such as foreign policy, defense, currency, and immigration. The *Länder*, on the other hand, retain authority over areas more closely related to regional needs, including education, culture, policing, and local administration. In many fields – such as environmental protection, economic regulation, and health policy – legislative competence is shared, requiring coordination and cooperation between both levels of government.

Germany's Judiciary mirrors this dual structure. The country maintains both federal and state court systems, each operating within its designated areas of jurisdiction. At the federal level, specialized courts ensure consistency in national jurisprudence, including the Federal Court of Justice (*Bundesgerichtshof*) for civil and criminal matters, the Federal Administrative Court (*Bundesverwaltungsgericht*), the Federal Fiscal Court (*Bundesfinanzhof*), the Federal Labour Court (*Bundesarbeitsgericht*), and the Federal Social Court (*Bundessozialgericht*). At the state level, regional and local courts handle most cases in the first and second instance, applying both federal and regional laws.

This structure ensures that legal disputes are resolved efficiently, coherently, and in accordance with both federal and regional interests. It reflects Germany's constitutional commitment to a cooperative form of federalism, where uniformity of law coexists with respect for diversity and regional self-determination.

3.3.3 Lawmaking Process

The lawmaking process in Germany is a carefully structured and participatory procedure designed to balance democratic representation, federal interests, and thorough legislative scrutiny. It involves two main bodies: the *Bundestag* (Federal Diet), which represents the German people and serves as the principal legislative chamber, and the *Bundesrat*, which represents the 16 *Länder* (federal states) and ensures that regional perspectives are incorporated into national decision-making.[53]

Legislative initiatives may originate from several sources. Bills can be introduced by members of the Federal Government, the *Bundestag*, or the *Bundesrat*. This arrangement reflects the cooperative nature of German federalism, allowing both national and regional authorities to contribute to the legislative agenda. Government bills are most common and are typically drafted by federal ministries before being submitted to parliament.

Once introduced, a bill goes through a detailed examination process in the *Bundestag*. It is debated in multiple readings, during which members discuss its principles, propose amendments, and analyze its potential impact. The bill is also reviewed by specialized parliamentary committees that provide expert opinions and refine its provisions. This stage ensures that proposed laws are comprehensive, coherent, and aligned with constitutional requirements.

After approval by the *Bundestag*, the bill proceeds to the *Bundesrat*. The *Bundesrat* plays a decisive role, particularly when legislation affects the interests or administrative responsibilities of the *Länder*. It may approve, reject, or propose amendments to the bill. If disagreements

53 For more information, refer to Bumke, Christian and Voßkuhle, Andreas, 2019, *German Constitutional Law: Introduction, Cases, and Principles*, Oxford University Press.

arise between the two chambers, a Mediation Committee (*Vermittlungsausschuss*) – composed of members from both houses – is convened to reach a compromise. This mechanism embodies the cooperative spirit of German federalism, ensuring that both national unity and regional autonomy are preserved.

Once consensus is achieved, the finalized bill is transmitted to the Federal President (*Bundespräsident*) for promulgation. The President's role, while largely formal, includes verifying the constitutionality and procedural regularity of the legislation. After countersignature by the competent government minister and the Federal Chancellor, the President signs the law, officially enacting it.

According to Article 82 of the *Grundgesetz* (Basic Law),[54] promulgated laws must be published in the *Bundesgesetzblatt* (Federal Law Gazette). Unless otherwise specified, they enter into force 14 days after publication. This period allows time for public awareness and administrative implementation.

Overall, the German lawmaking process is marked by its precision, transparency, and inclusiveness. It ensures that every legislative proposal is subjected to rigorous debate and cross-level review, embodying the principles of democratic governance, federal balance, and respect for the Rule of Law.

3.3.4 Judicial Review

The Federal Constitutional Court of Germany (*Bundesverfassungsgericht*), established in 1951 and seated in Karlsruhe, serves as the guardian of the German Constitution (*Grundgesetz*). It plays a central role in protecting constitutional principles and ensuring the supremacy of constitutional law within the federal legal order.[55] The Court's authority is unique: it is the only judicial body in Germany empowered to declare a statute unconstitutional and thus null and void. This exclusive jurisdiction guarantees uniformity in constitutional interpretation and preserves legal certainty throughout the country.

If a lower court believes that a statute conflicts with the Constitution, it cannot invalidate the law on its own initiative. Instead, it must refer the matter to the Federal Constitutional Court for what is known as a *concrete review* (*konkrete Normenkontrolle*). In this process, the lower court identifies the constitutional question, suspends its proceedings, and requests a ruling from the Constitutional Court. The Federal Constitutional Court then examines whether the contested provision violates the *Grundgesetz* and issues a binding judgment. The referring court must then apply the Constitutional Court's decision to the case at hand.

Beyond these case-specific reviews, the Court also conducts *abstract reviews* (*abstrakte Normenkontrolle*). This procedure allows certain political actors – such as the Federal Government, a group of Bundestag members, or a state government – to request a constitutional review of a statute independently of any particular case. The purpose of the abstract review is preventive:

54 Article 82 of Daz Grundgesetz (Promulgation, publication, and entry into force):

(1) Laws enacted in accordance with the provisions of this Basic Law shall, after countersignature, be certified by the Federal President and promulgated in the Federal Law Gazette. Statutory instruments shall be certified by the agency that issues them and, unless a law otherwise provides, shall be promulgated in the Federal Law Gazette.
(2) Every law or statutory instrument shall specify the date on which it shall take effect. In the absence of such a provision, it shall take effect on the fourteenth day after the day on which the Federal Law Gazette containing it was published.

55 Art. 82 GG.

it enables early detection and correction of constitutional defects before they lead to disputes in ordinary courts.

Through these mechanisms, the Federal Constitutional Court ensures both reactive and proactive oversight of the legislative process. Its decisions have far-reaching effects, not only invalidating unconstitutional laws but also shaping political and social life by clarifying the boundaries of governmental authority.

Further discussion of judicial review, including the differences between concrete and abstract control and comparative models in other legal systems, is presented in Chapter 5. There, the procedural framework, historical evolution, and broader implications of constitutional adjudication in Germany are explored in greater detail, highlighting the Court's enduring role as the cornerstone of constitutional democracy.

3.3.5 Court System

The German court system is organized into five main branches of jurisdiction – civil and criminal, administrative, financial, labor, and social – each with its own hierarchical structure. This multi-tiered framework allows for specialization in different areas of law while ensuring consistency and coherence in judicial decisions. In addition to these five branches, Germany also has both federal and regional constitutional courts, with the Federal Constitutional Court (*Bundesverfassungsgericht*) standing at the top of the judicial hierarchy as the ultimate guardian of the Constitution.[56]

The ordinary courts (*ordentliche Gerichte*) handle civil and criminal matters. These include the *Amtsgerichte* (Local Courts) at the first instance, the *Landgerichte* (Regional Courts) as courts of second instance, and the *Oberlandesgerichte* (Higher Regional Courts) for appeals. At the top level is the *Bundesgerichtshof* (Federal Court of Justice), which serves as the highest appellate court for civil and criminal cases.

In administrative matters, the judicial structure consists of three levels: the *Verwaltungsgericht* (Administrative Court) at first instance, the *Oberverwaltungsgericht* or *Verwaltungsgerichtshof* (Higher Administrative Court) at the appellate level, and the *Bundesverwaltungsgericht* (Federal Administrative Court) as the highest authority in this jurisdiction.

Financial disputes are resolved in two tiers: the *Finanzgerichte* (Finance Courts) serve as the first instance, and the *Bundesfinanzhof* (Federal Finance Court) acts as the supreme court for tax and fiscal law.

Labor law cases are heard by the *Arbeitsgerichte* (Labour Courts) at the first instance, the *Landesarbeitsgerichte* (Higher Regional Labour Courts) at the second instance, and the *Bundesarbeitsgericht* (Federal Labour Court) as the highest appellate court.

Social matters, including disputes over social insurance and welfare benefits, are handled by the *Sozialgerichte* (Social Courts), the *Landessozialgerichte* (Higher Regional Social Courts), and finally, the *Bundessozialgericht* (Federal Social Court).

This structure reflects Germany's commitment to judicial specialization, allowing judges to develop expertise in particular branches of law. Yet the system also preserves coherence through shared procedural standards and a consistent approach to judicial review and appeals.

A defining feature of the German Judiciary is its independence. Judges are appointed based on merit, not political affiliation, and enjoy constitutional protection from external influence or arbitrary dismissal. Their independence is further safeguarded by the President of Germany,

56 See Foster, Nigel and Satish, Sulen, 2010, *German Legal System and Laws*, Oxford University Press.

who acts as the guarantor of judicial autonomy under the Basic Law (*Grundgesetz*). This safeguard ensures the Separation of Powers and maintains public confidence in the Judiciary as an impartial arbiter of justice.

Unlike the French model, where Private Law and Public Law are clearly divided into separate jurisdictions, Germany's judicial organization integrates both Civil Law and Public Law within the same coherent framework. This integration promotes unity in legal interpretation and enhances the system's efficiency because it allows courts to address complex legal issues that span multiple areas of law.

The German court system thus embodies the principles of democracy, the Rule of Law, and judicial independence. Its hierarchical and specialized design ensures fair trials, multiple levels of appeal, and a transparent process. By combining specialization with unity, and independence with accountability, Germany's Judiciary stands as a model of integrity, professionalism, and public trust in the administration of justice.

3.4 Landmark German Court Decision

A landmark German court decision is *S.E. v. SCH*, decided by the Supreme Court of Germany (Federal Court of Justice, Civil Chamber, 6th Division) on November 15, 1960. The case addressed the issue of liability in a multi-vehicle accident where it could not be determined which of several drivers had caused the plaintiff's injuries. The central legal question concerned the interpretation and application of Section 830(1)(2) of the *Bürgerliches Gesetzbuch* (German Civil Code), which governs situations in which several individuals may have contributed to a harmful act, but the specific perpetrator cannot be identified.

3.4.1 Case Summary and Excerpt

On the night of December 11, the plaintiff was struck by a truck while attempting to stop it and was thrown onto the highway, where he remained lying injured. Around one o'clock in the morning, he was run over by the defendant, who was driving an American-made automobile. It could not be determined whether other vehicles had also run over the plaintiff before or after the defendant's car. Evidence suggested that another car may have passed the scene shortly thereafter, making it impossible to establish with certainty which vehicle had caused the most severe injuries. As a result of the accident, the plaintiff suffered serious trauma to his right leg, which had to be amputated below the knee.

In the proceedings, the plaintiff acknowledged partial fault for the accident, accepting responsibility for one-fourth of the total damages. He sought recovery from the defendant, claiming compensation as a joint tortfeasor for 75% of his losses. The damages claimed included loss of income, medical and hospital expenses, pain and suffering, and a support pension. The district court found in favor of the plaintiff, holding that he was entitled to 75% compensation for his injuries, to the extent not already covered by national insurance. The defendant's appeal was dismissed, as was his subsequent petition for review, leaving the lower court's decision in place.

This case raised complex questions about causation and liability when multiple potential tortfeasors were involved, and the precise source of the injury could not be determined. It tested the application of Section 830(1)(2) of the German Civil Code, which addresses joint liability in cases where several actors contribute to a harm but the specific cause cannot be established.

S.E. v. SCH. Supreme Court of Germany (Civil Chamber, 6th Division). Decision of November 15, 1960. 33 BGHZ 286 (1961).

On the night of December 11, the plaintiff was struck and thrown onto the highway by a truck which he was trying to stop, and there he remained lying. About one o'clock he was run over and injured by the defendant, who was driving an American automobile. It is not known whether or not the plaintiff was run over by trucks or cars other than that car driven by the defendant. This might have been the case, particularly with one car that passed by soon after the American car. The plaintiff's right leg was seriously broken and injured below the knee, and the lower part of the leg had to be amputated.

The plaintiff, admitting his own liability for one-fourth of the damages received, claims recovery from the defendant as a joint tort-feasor, for loss of income and for doctor and hospital expenses, as well as for the pain and suffering sustained, and also for a support pension. The district court held that the plaintiff was entitled to compensation for 75% of the damage received, insofar as that amount was not made good by national insurance. The appeal of the defendant was unsuccessful as was his action for revision.

From the reasons for the decision:

1. The attacked judgment holds as follows: In any case, the defendant negligently ran over and injured the plaintiff, and he is therefore liable for the damage which he caused, even if the plaintiffs leg had been run over by several other vehicles. The defendant at least caused part of the damage when he drove over the right leg, the fracture of which was the only serious injury which the plaintiff showed. Even if he was not the only one who caused this injury, even if one or several others had driven over the plaintiff's right leg, the defendant is liable by virtue of sec. 830, subsec, 1, para. 2 of the Civil Code. The language of this section embraces incidents where the share of the individual in the damage cannot be ascertained. Therefore, it does not matter any longer whether the defendant was or was not the only one who brought about this serious leg injury.

2. In the oral argument before the Supreme Court, it was asserted that sec. 830, subsec. 1, para. 2 of the Civil Code is not applicable in this situation, because this section requires contemporaneousness of several dangerous acts. It was argued that only in the case of simultaneous dangerous acts do there exist the objective criteria necessary to determine which dangerous act brought about the injury; while in cases in which the acts are consecutive in time, then the later act may not have been dangerous, because the damage may already have been caused by an earlier act.

This interpretation ignores the purpose and scope of sec. 830 1–2. It must be granted, however, that in most litigations the dangerous acts of several wrongdoers have occurred simultaneously or immediately after one other. This happens to be so for the simple reason that generally there is no doubt as to which action caused the damage when the dangerous acts are separated from one another in time. But cases also arise where, despite the time sequence of the dangerous acts, there is doubt as to which acts caused the injury, The fact that the acts follow one upon another will not make sec. 830 1–2 inapplicable as is demonstrated by two cases decided by the Reichsgericht and the Bundesgerichtshof.

(a) Excitement experienced caused the injured party to have a gall-stone attack. During the evening in question, the plaintiff was stirred up and agitated three separate times: once when the plaintiff was informed by a member of the editorial staff of a newspaper that (though untrue) he was beset by grave financial difficulties. Then, again, upon being informed by the editor of another newspaper that they intended to publish this report in their morning edition, and finally by the conduct of the managing director of the latter paper when he refused to have these untrue newspaper reports retracted. Any of these three incidents could have precipitated the gall-stone attack, but it could not be determined which of these traumatic excitements was responsible for the attack.

The Reichsgericht held that sec. 830 1–2 was applicable to this set of facts. The requisites of this section were present when each occurrence had the ability to bring about the injury in accordance with the general rules of causation, and one of them had acted upon the injured party, although it could not be determined which act actually caused the injury. (RGZ 148, 154, 166 with references.)

(b) A house caved in because of lack of care on the part of the roofers, an undertaking involving two men. The one man had made defective concrete rafters and delivered them to the building site. The other had then installed these defective rafters. It could not be determined which act of negligence caused the collapse of the building. The Bundesgerichtshof held that both men were liable under sec. 830 1–2, because of the delivery to the site and building into the house was to be considered one indivisible act in which both men were involved (VII ZR 268/56 March 14, 1957 – LM BGB sec. 830 No. 4)

3. A commentator on the code (Staudinger, Notes 3, 4 and concurring BGB-RGRK Note 9 at sec. 830) suggests that the concept of "participation" in the sense of sec. 830 1–2 exists when someone is run over by one of several in a group of vehicles, such as that of a festival party, but not when the injury is caused by one of several trucks, independent of one another, though using the same street, for in the latter instance we are not dealing with a joint danger but with accidentally consecutive events. If it is then impossible to determine which of the tort-feasors caused the injury, all of the presumptive tort-feasors will be relieved of liability.

The history of the origin of sec. 830 1–2 speaks against the suggested requirement of a joint venture aspect in the subjective sense, namely that the elements of danger shall act jointly and know of one another. Section 714 of the first draft indicates that joint liability exists "when one of the several injuries was not inflicted by the several parties acting together, but the proportions of damages caused by each cannot be determined." This provision was intended to cover the case at hand, where it is impossible to determine which act caused the damage. (Motive II 738.) To make this principle clear, and not for the purpose of making the change in meaning in the second draft (Protokoll II 606), sec. 753 was stated in the following words: "The same applies (i.e. joint liability) when the several parties have not acted together and it is impossible to determine which individual act caused the damage." The provision was given its final form by the Drafting Committee, and evidently at this stage of the preparatory work, when questions of formulations were the issue, the provision that joint ventures or actions were not a necessary requisite was excluded (Bydlinski, "Haftung bei altemativer Kausalitat," Juristische Blatter, Wien 1959, p. 12). In light of this, the Reichsgericht had already pointed out that the concept of "participation" may be intensified by the mutual knowledge of the acts of the other person to the point that there will be an "act committed in common" (sec. 830, subsec. 1, para. 1), and that there may exist a close connection with respect to the place and time even in the absence of such knowledge (RG WarnRspr 1912 No. 387).

4. Thus, neither sec. 830 1–2, nor the practice of the Supreme Court ("Senat"), supports the suggested postulates that the imputable wrongful dangerous acts of several persons have to be contemporary and have an internal relation with one another.

(a) The purpose of 830 1–2 is to overcome the requirement that the injured party prove the cause of his injury, when it is impossible to ascertain which of several possible wrongdoers actually caused the damage, or which of several people, not acting in accord, caused what particular part of the injury (RGZ 121,400,402 f). To attain this goal, in favor of the injured, a presumption as to the cause of the injury is used (cf. Wussow, Unfallhaftpflichtrecht, 6 ed. TZ 299; Bydlinski, "Haftung bei altemativer Kausalitat," Juristische

Blatter, Wien 1959, p. 13). The reason for this presumption is that the recovery for damages caused by more than one person should not turn on whether the injured party can show with certainty what proportion of damage is attributable to each of the wrongdoers (RG WarnRspr 1912 No. 387). This is particularly necessary because the difficulty existing in proving the cause of the injury was created by the wrongful and imputable acts of the parties involved, and for which each of them is responsible.

The injured party's difficulty in presenting the needed evidence can also arise, and need equal protection when the wrongdoers acted one after the other, just as if they had acted jointly (compare the examples given under 2a and b, supra). Granted that a party acting after another party, is capable of a dangerous act only in case the injury was not caused by the earlier act. However, it is just the doubt as to the cause that often remains unresolved, and the purpose of sec. 830 1–2 is specifically to remove this doubt and to put the burden on those persons who committed the wrongful imputable and dangerous acts.

However, it has to be required that the different acts, even if consecutive parts of a course of events, are materially connected with one another with respect to place and time and are also alternative causes of the injury, so that each separate act appears as a part of a unified whole; only if these conditions are met does a "participation" of each wrongdoer in the occurrence of the damage exist. The question of when such a situation actually exists has to be decided in accordance with the practical common sense of every day life (RG WarnRspr 1908 no 633).

With respect to such course of events, it is irrelevant, both from the point of view of the external relations and with regard to the protected interest of the injured person whether he is able to produce evidence, that the different wrongful and imputable acts are as those of the members of a hunting party or a group of automobiles, internally linked with one another. The presence or the absence of an internal link is of no concern, whether on the side of the wrongdoers or on the side of the injured person. This is so because the injured party was harmed by a single injurious act, although it appeared as if there were a relationship with other acts, and the plaintiff's burden of proof will not be decreased because the various doers of dangerous acts were not acting jointly and did not know of one another.

(b) Consequently, this Court ("Senat") does require that the concept of participation shall imply neither that the dangerous acts take place simultaneously, nor that there is a subjective link between the several wrongdoers. Rather the concept of participation is directed toward the situation, where several persons, each acting independently, have committed unlawful acts, where one of these acts has, and each of them could have individually, caused the resulting harm, where, however, it is impossible to determine the real wrongdoer. This is so, provided that there is an actual course of events where, although independent, the events are uniform and interrelated with respect to place and time, and where the injury is within the sphere of this course of events (BGHZ 25, 274 with references). When the defendant in his appeal refers to the decision of the Court BGHZ 30, 203, he is overlooking the fact that in that case it was ascertained which share of the damage that had been caused by each of the wrongdoers and therefore, indeed, it was impossible to argue the application of sec. 830 1–2. Further, in an extensive opinion-VI ZR 55/59-NJW 1960, 862 No.4- this Court has already rejected the restrictive construction that sec. 830 1–2 requires an internal relationship between several wrongdoers.

5. Thus, there is no objection to the finding of the Court of Appeals that an actual participation, both in time and space, occurred when at midnight the plaintiff was bodily injured on the highway where he was struck by several motor vehicles, and at least it is known that the defendant was involved in this injury. Under sec. 830 1–2, the defendant

has been given the duty to prove that the loss of the lower part of the leg could not have been caused by him. The Court of Appeals reached the correct result that the joint liability for damages under 830 1–2 extends to a case, where the proportion of damage caused by each party is not determinable. Since the plaintiff was not able to carry the burden of proof as to who caused the injury, the Court of Appeals did not commit error in holding the defendant, if not liable as an individual according to sec. 823, nevertheless liable under 830 1–2 for the entire damage.

The Court ruled that when multiple defendants act in a manner that could each have caused the injury, and it is impossible to determine who was directly responsible, all participants can be held jointly and severally liable. This interpretation reflects the principle that uncertainty about causation should not deprive the innocent victim of compensation. Instead, the burden of proof effectively shifts to the potential wrongdoers, who must demonstrate that their actions did not cause the harm.

This decision is widely regarded as a cornerstone of German tort law. It illustrates the Judiciary's pragmatic approach to achieving fairness in complex factual circumstances, ensuring that the costs of uncertainty are borne by those who created the risk rather than by the victim.

3.4.2 Court's Reasoning and Legal Principles

The German case presents a more complex picture than the French examples. First, it is significantly longer and more detailed. Whereas French judgments are famously brief and presented in a single, syllogistic sentence, German decisions typically include a full explanation of the reasoning that leads to the Court's conclusion. This difference reflects deeper variations in judicial style and legal culture. Even though both France and Germany belong to the Civil Law family, their courts approach legal reasoning and the presentation of decisions in distinct ways. In Germany, a court cannot merely announce its ruling – it must demonstrate and justify how that ruling follows from the applicable law.

In this case, the German Supreme Court (Federal Court of Justice) justifies its decision primarily through an interpretive analysis of the relevant statutory provisions. The judges examine the purpose (*Zweck*) of the rule contained in Section 830(1)(2) of the Civil Code, asking what the legislature intended to achieve when drafting the provision. To support this reasoning, the Court reviews the legislative history of the Code, including the preparatory debates (*travaux préparatoires*), and refers to prior decisions to illustrate how similar situations had been addressed in the past. This shows that even within a Civil Law system, courts may rely on a combination of sources – the text of the Code, its legislative history, and earlier case law – to reach and justify a conclusion.

The main question before the Court was whether, in a situation where a person is successively struck by several vehicles, the case should be treated in the same way as that of multiple hunters firing simultaneously, as in the French *Litzinger v. Kintzler* case. In other words, the issue was whether joint and several liability should apply when multiple tortfeasors act independently and at different times, but their actions together result in the injury. The German Court answered in the affirmative, holding that all the potential tortfeasors could be held jointly and severally liable. The rationale was that this interpretation best fulfilled the purpose of the Civil Code – to protect the victim and prevent an unjust denial of compensation simply because it was impossible to determine the exact cause of harm.

This decision illustrates that the divide between civil and Common Law systems is sometimes narrower than traditionally assumed. In terms of judicial writing, the contrast between French and German decisions may even be greater than that between German and Anglo-American ones. The French model prioritizes brevity and the appearance of pure logic, while the German model emphasizes detailed justification and analytical transparency. Each has its strengths and weaknesses: the French style appears objective and efficient but can seem opaque, while the German approach is more explicit but may appear dense or overly theoretical. Ultimately, determining which model is "better" depends less on legal theory and more on the values a legal system seeks to promote – clarity and transparency, or authority and simplicity.

Conclusion

The Civil Law tradition stands as one of the most influential and enduring legal systems in the world. Rooted in the intellectual legacy of Roman law and refined through centuries of philosophical reflection, codification, and judicial practice, it has shaped the legal identity of countless nations. From the *Corpus Iuris Civilis* of Justinian to the Napoleonic Code and the German *Bürgerliches Gesetzbuch,* Civil Law has evolved into a coherent, structured, and systematic body of principles that continues to inspire legal reform and modernization across jurisdictions.

This chapter has shown that Civil Law is not merely a European creation but a global phenomenon. Through historical expansion, political influence, trade, and legal emulation, its principles spread far beyond the continent, influencing legal systems in Latin America, Africa, the Middle East, and Asia. Yet, the Civil Law tradition has never been static. It has adapted to local contexts, producing hybrid systems that blend codified law with customary, religious, or Common Law traditions. This adaptability explains its resilience and its continued relevance in a globally interdependent world.

By examining the French and German archetypal models, we have also seen that even within the Civil Law family, diversity thrives. The French system emphasizes clarity, accessibility, and the appearance of logical deduction, whereas the German system is characterized by precision, systematic depth, and conceptual rigor. Each reflects a distinct legal culture and intellectual heritage, yet both share the same goal: to achieve justice through reasoned and predictable rules.

Ultimately, the Civil Law tradition endures because it balances stability with flexibility. Its codes provide a solid foundation, while its courts and scholars continuously reinterpret those codes in light of social, economic, and moral change. Whether applied in Paris, Berlin, Buenos Aires, or Tokyo, Civil Law remains a living system – one that bridges past and present, combining the discipline of Roman legal science with the evolving needs of modern society.

Selected Bibliography

Bell, J., & Lichère, F., 2022, *Contemporary French Administrative Law*, Cambridge University Press.
De Cruz, Peter, 2009, *Comparative Law in a Changing World* (3rd ed.), Routledge Cavendish, 512 pages.
Domingo, Rafael, 2018, *Roman Law: An Introduction*, Routledge, 252 pages.
Fairgrieve, Duncan, 2007, *The Influence of the French Civil Code on the Common Law and Beyond*, British Institute of International & Comparative Law, 400 pages.
Fisher, Howard, 2008, *The German Legal System and Legal Language*, Routledge Cavendish, 352 pages.
Foster, Nigel, Satish Sulen, 2010, *German Legal System and Laws*, Oxford University Press, 752 pages.
Nasti, Fara, Aldo Schiavone, 2021, *Jurists and Legal Science in the History of Roman Law*, Routledge, 318 pages.
Orucu, Esin, & Nelken, D., 2007, *Comparative Law: A Handbook*, Hart Publishing, 450 pages.
Plessis du, Paul, 2010, *Borkowski's Textbook on Roman Law*, Oxford University Press, 500 pages.
Reimann, Mathias, & Zimmermann, Reinhard, 2008, *The Oxford Handbook of Comparative Law*, Oxford University Press, 1456 pages.
Steiner, Eva, 2018, *French Law: A Comparative Approach*, Oxford University Press, 336 pages.

4 The Common Law Tradition

Like cases should be treated alike and dissimilar cases differently, proportionally to their differences.
Aristotle
Nicomachean Ethics

Common Law is a distinct legal system that originated in England during the 12th century, making it more recent than the Civil Law tradition, whose roots go back to ancient Roman law. As previously discussed, the Civil Law tradition developed from Roman legal principles.

To grasp the essence of Common Law, it is essential to understand that it was shaped by two fundamental elements: British history and the English language.[1] Before being a legal system, Common Law can be regarded as a shared linguistic and conceptual framework.[2] The connection between law and language is particularly strong, as legal ideas, concepts, and norms are created, communicated, and transmitted through language. Legal language and ordinary language are closely related, forming a continuum between them. As a result, there exists a deep relationship between the English-speaking world and the Common Law system, since its legal concepts, mechanisms, and theories are all expressed through English.

Although legal traditions differ, the world's legal systems have become increasingly interconnected. While certain cultural and structural differences remain significant, the major legal systems today share many similarities, perhaps more than distinctions. Law continues to address the fundamental challenges of human societies, such as the protection of individual rights, the maintenance of public order, the regulation of economic relations, and the organization of justice. These shared objectives demonstrate the universality of many legal principles. From this perspective, the major legal systems of the world are not as different as they might appear.

This chapter provides a general overview of the main principles of Common Law.

Section 1 examines the origins and historical development of Common Law in England, focusing on its emergence from medieval judicial practices and the creation of a centralized royal court system. It highlights how the principles of precedent and judicial reasoning shaped the Common Law as a distinctive and evolving legal tradition.

Section 2 explores the expansion and global influence of Common Law, particularly through the British Empire and its former colonies. It considers how the system adapted to different

1 See Salomone, Rosemary, 2024, *The Rise of English: Global Politics and the Power of Language*, Oxford University Press.
2 See Bullier, Antoine J., 2023, *La Common Law*, Dalloz.

DOI: 10.4324/9781003393047-6

social, political, and cultural contexts, including in the United States, and how Common Law principles continue to influence legal systems worldwide today.

1 History and Main Features of the Common Law Tradition

This section offers a detailed examination of the history and defining features of the Common Law tradition, one of the most influential legal systems to have originated in England and later spread throughout the world. It traces the evolution of Common Law from its early roots in feudal England, through major historical developments such as the Norman Conquest and the creation of the Royal Courts of Justice, to its present role as a foundational framework for legal reasoning in many jurisdictions.

By analyzing its main characteristics, including the doctrine of precedent and the incorporation of equitable principles, this section highlights how Common Law has developed into a dynamic and adaptable system. It also considers the interactions between this legal tradition and other legal traditions, showing how it has influenced and, in turn, been shaped by them.

The objective is to provide a clear understanding of the structure, operation, and guiding principles of Common Law, as well as its continuing influence on the formulation of legal standards and the administration of justice. This overview underscores the enduring balance between continuity and adaptation that defines the Common Law tradition.

1.1 Origins of Common Law: Foundations in English History

Approximately one-third of the world's population lives under legal systems derived from Common Law. It is one of the oldest and most enduring forms of municipal law applied uniformly across an entire nation, and its influence has extended far beyond England's borders. The essential components of this system shaped what is known today as English Common Law. Yet, what truly distinguishes this tradition from other legal traditions?

Its origins can be traced to feudal England, a period when justice was exercised locally and differed greatly from one region to another. The Norman Conquest of 1066 marked a decisive turning point, as it initiated the process of unifying the administration of justice throughout the kingdom. Over the following centuries, local customs gradually gave way to a more centralized and coherent legal system, culminating in the establishment of the Royal Courts of Justice.

This section examines the evolution of these developments, the interaction between royal and local jurisdictions, and the emergence of Common Law from its early conception, known as *Commune Ley*, to its modern form.[3]

1.1.1 Feudal England: Jurisdictional Justice Differences

Before 1066 and the Norman Conquest, the region of England known as Danelaw was notable for its distinct approach to justice. This northern area, influenced by Danish settlers, derived both its name and many of its legal customs from Scandinavian traditions. Justice in Danelaw was conducted in a local language shaped by Danish influence, and its legal practices differed considerably from those found elsewhere in England.[4]

3 Bullier, *La Common Law*.
4 Bullier, *La Common Law*.

At that time, England had no unified legal system. Justice was largely local, based on the customs and traditions specific to each region. In Danelaw, as in much of the country, disputes were settled by manorial courts – local feudal tribunals presided over by landowners. These courts applied unwritten rules and customary norms that varied from one manor to another, resulting in significant regional disparities.

This fragmented structure meant that the administration of justice lacked consistency across England. The influence of Danish law in Danelaw produced legal practices distinct from the Anglo-Saxon traditions dominant in southern regions. Manorial courts had jurisdiction within their own estates, handling both civil and minor criminal matters, which created a patchwork of local legal systems.

Custom played a central role in this decentralized framework. Local customs were transmitted orally through generations and reflected the social and cultural values of each community. Consequently, what was deemed fair and lawful in one area could differ entirely in another.

This localized administration of justice mirrored the broader feudal organization of medieval England. Landowners exercised substantial authority within their domains, including the power to resolve disputes and enforce justice. The absence of a centralized judicial authority highlighted the diversity of legal traditions and the autonomy of local governance.

In summary, before the Norman Conquest, England's legal landscape consisted of a multitude of local, unwritten customs and feudal courts. Each region, including Danelaw, followed its own methods of administering justice, resulting in a heterogeneous and decentralized legal system that reflected the social and cultural diversity of medieval England.

1.1.2 The Norman Conquest in 1066 and the Unification of Law

After the Norman Conquest in 1066, William of Normandy, who became King of England following his victory at the Battle of Hastings, initiated a deep transformation of the English legal system. He sought to replace the fragmented local customs with a unified royal framework of law.[5] This new system was administered in the Franco-Norman language, which became the language of the royal court and official administration. Consequently, the evolution of English law progressed in parallel with the evolution of its language.

William of Normandy was acutely aware of the challenges of governing a realm marked by linguistic and legal diversity. His new subjects spoke different tongues and followed distinct customs unfamiliar to him. For this reason, the establishment of a unified legal system was neither immediate nor simple; it unfolded gradually over several centuries. Successive rulers of the Anglo-Norman dynasty, including the Plantagenets and later the Tudors, worked to consolidate royal authority and to extend a uniform system of law across the kingdom.

This process required not only the imposition of royal justice but also the assimilation of regional traditions into a coherent national framework. The creation of centralized royal courts represented a decisive shift away from the decentralized feudal justice of pre-conquest England. Over time, these courts developed principles and procedures that became the foundation of the Common Law system, marked by its consistency, adaptability, and reliance on judicial precedent.[6]

5 Lewis, Andrew D. E., Kiralfy, Albert Roland and Glendon, Mary Ann, 2024, "Common Law," *Encyclopedia Britannica*, 19 May. Available at: https://www.britannica.com/topic/common-law. Accessed 18 July 2024.

6 Lewis, Kiralfy and Glendon, "Common Law."

The close link between law and language during this period illustrates the deep and lasting influence of the Norman Conquest on English legal development.[7] The gradual emergence of a unified legal order laid the groundwork for the enduring institutions and principles that define the modern Common Law tradition.

1.1.3 Gradual Unification of Justice in England

William of Normandy, the new King of England, consolidated his authority over the administration of justice by appointing his own royal officials, known as itinerant commissioners. These officials were tasked with overseeing the collection of taxes and administering justice in the name of the King. They held regular judicial sessions, known as *Assizes*, to deal with serious criminal matters, while local lords continued to adjudicate minor disputes within their own territories.

Over time, the responsibilities of the itinerant commissioners expanded to include civil cases, which contributed to the formation of a more coherent and uniform legal framework across the realm. By drawing upon effective practices and judicial decisions from different regions, a unified system of law – later called *Common Law* – gradually emerged. This system integrated local customs with case-based reasoning, ensuring that judicial decisions and legal rules were applied consistently throughout England.

This evolution allowed the most effective local customs and principles, regardless of their regional origin, to gain national authority. The establishment of Common Law thus represented the creation of a comprehensive legal system grounded in both customary practice and judicial precedent, providing England with a stable and cohesive foundation for the administration of justice.[8]

1.1.4 Establishment of the Royal Courts of Justice

In the years following the Norman Conquest, King Henry II played a decisive role in consolidating royal justice by establishing a centralized court system known as the *Royal Courts of Justice*. Located in Westminster and staffed by professional judges appointed by the Crown, these courts became the cornerstone of England's unified legal framework. Under this new system, only the Royal Courts possessed jurisdiction over serious criminal matters and disputes concerning the ownership of freehold property – land held in permanent and absolute ownership, freely transferable at the owner's will.

Local lords, however, continued to exercise limited judicial authority within their domains. They handled minor disputes involving their tenants, known as *villeins* – feudal dependents bound to their lord or manor in exchange for land and services. This division of jurisdiction ensured that the most significant cases were brought under direct royal supervision, reinforcing the authority of the Crown and promoting uniformity in the administration of justice.

The Royal Courts of Justice at Westminster consisted of three principal tribunals. The *Court of Common Pleas* was responsible for adjudicating disputes between private individuals. The *Court of Exchequer* dealt primarily with financial matters, particularly those concerning taxation and royal revenues. The *Court of King's (or Queen's) Bench* heard cases of special concern to the monarch, including those involving public order or the interests of the state. Together,

7 Lewis, Kiralfy and Glendon, "Common Law."
8 Lewis, Kiralfy and Glendon, "Common Law."

these courts laid the institutional foundations of the Common Law system, ensuring consistency and centralization in English legal practice.

1.1.5 Dynamics Between Royal and Local Courts

As the Royal Courts expanded their authority and influence, the local courts gradually lost their significance and eventually disappeared. The different regions of England were progressively brought under the control of a centralized legal, judicial, and political structure directed by the Royal Courts. This transition required conformity with the standardized procedures of Common Law and the organization of the royal judicial system. Royal justices circulated throughout the kingdom, heard disputes, and applied the same forms of writs and procedures wherever they went. Their judgments, recorded and studied in London, were then used as reference points in later cases, reinforcing uniformity. Over time, this process reduced the autonomy of local courts and diminished the role of local customs in the administration of justice.

As a result, the multitude of local Anglo-Saxon customs and practices that had previously governed justice were absorbed into a unified national framework. Customs that continued to be used had to be presented before royal judges, who accepted, adapted, or rejected them according to emerging Common Law principles. Local variation, therefore, survived only to the extent that it could be integrated into the royal system. What had once been a collection of regional legal traditions evolved into a single, coherent system of law that applied consistently throughout England. This consolidation marked a decisive moment in English legal history: it strengthened the authority of the Crown, created a professional judiciary, and laid the foundations of precedent-based reasoning. By the end of the medieval period, the Common Law had become the dominant legal tradition of the realm, shaping English justice for centuries to come.

1.1.6 Birth of Common Law: From COMMUNE LEY *to Modern Interpretations*

It took approximately three centuries for the Normans, following their conquest of England, to unify the numerous local customs and establish a system of law common to the entire kingdom, administered by the Royal Courts. This body of law, which gradually superseded and replaced the diverse regional practices, came to be known as the *Commune Ley* – that is, the *Common Law*.[9] Its formation was not the result of a single reform, but of a long historical process in which royal authority expanded, royal judges travelled throughout the country, and legal procedures became increasingly standardized. Over successive generations, these developments reduced local variation and created a shared legal vocabulary for the whole kingdom. It represented a legal order that applied uniformly across England, ensuring coherence, stability, and the authority of royal justice throughout the realm. The emergence of the Common Law thus marked a major step in the construction of a unified English state and laid the foundations of a legal tradition that would later spread across much of the world.

1.1.7 Exploring the Varied Meanings of Common Law

It is now necessary to examine the expression *Common Law*, as it is used in several distinct but related senses. The term may refer to (a) the historical *commune ley*, meaning the body of law that became common to all of England following the unification of local customs under royal

9 From Norman-French.

authority; (b) the body of law developed through judicial decisions and interpretations (also known as case law or judge-made law), as opposed to legislation enacted by parliament or constitutional provisions; (c) the body of law distinguished from *Equity*, a complementary system designed to provide remedies where the strict application of Common Law proved inadequate (this concept will be explained in what follows); (d) the English legal system as a whole, in contrast to the Civil Law systems derived from Roman law.

Each of these meanings reflects a particular aspect of Common Law's evolution and application, illustrating both its historical origins and its continuing role as a dynamic and influential legal tradition. Understanding these different uses is essential, for they reveal how the term Common Law has expanded over time – from describing a unified body of rules within medieval England to designating an entire family of legal systems that now spans multiple continents.

1.2 Equity: Its Emergence and Role as a Common Law Complement

The Common Law system, despite its strengths, presented several limitations. Its remedies were largely restricted to financial compensation, or *damages*, which were not always adequate or appropriate to resolve certain disputes. For example, the Royal Courts lacked the power to compel a person to perform a specific act or to prevent them from engaging in particular conduct.

Moreover, the procedure for bringing a case before the Royal Courts was complex, time-consuming, and costly. A claimant was required to obtain an official *writ* – a formal order issued by the court – from the office of the Lord Chancellor. Each writ corresponded to a specific cause of action, and if no suitable writ existed for a given situation, the case could not proceed. This rigidity often left litigants without a remedy, even when they had suffered a genuine wrong.[10]

As a result, many subjects grew dissatisfied with the limitations of Common Law and sought alternative avenues for justice. Petitioners began addressing the King directly, requesting that he decide their cases on the basis of conscience and fairness rather than strict legal formality. The King, advised by his Council and guided by moral and equitable principles, responded to these appeals according to his own sense of justice. This practice gave rise to the concept of *Equity*, in which the source of justice was the King's conscience. Equity aimed to provide fair and flexible remedies where the rigid procedures of Common Law failed to deliver adequate relief.

1.2.1 Equity's Function as a Corrective Mechanism to Common Law

The King eventually delegated the responsibility of handling petitions based on fairness to his Chancellor, who was already in charge of administering the writ system for the Royal Courts of Common Law. Acting as the *Keeper of the King's Conscience*, the Chancellor began to hear cases guided by the same equitable principles that the King himself would have applied. Over time, this practice led to the formation of a distinct body of rules and doctrines – known as *equitable principles* – intended to remedy the deficiencies of the Common Law. Many of these deficiencies arose because the Common Law relied on rigid writs, limited forms of action, and remedies that were often inadequate for the complex disputes of a growing society. The Chancellor's court, by contrast, focused on fairness, flexibility, and the protection of conscience. This emerging system, called *Equity*, introduced new rights and remedies that became highly valued by those seeking justice beyond the limits of formal legal procedure.[11]

10 See Gillespie, Alisdair and Weare, Siobhan, 2023, *The English Legal System*, 9th ed., Oxford University Press.
11 Gillespie and Weare, *The English Legal System*.

Equity's development ultimately gave England a dual judicial structure – Common Law courts and Chancery courts – whose interaction shaped the evolution of English law and added an essential layer of moral reasoning and discretionary justice to the legal system.

1.2.2 Historical Significance of the Court of Chancery

The importance of Equity grew steadily, and by the late 15th century, the Lord Chancellor had established a separate court known as the *Court of Chancery*, or *Court of Equity*. Three main features characterized this development. First, the Court of Chancery operated independently from the three Common Law courts. Second, proceedings before the Court of Chancery did not require a writ, which made access to justice more affordable, efficient, and adaptable than in the Common Law courts. Third, the Lord Chancellor decided cases according to principles of natural justice and fairness, giving concrete expression to the spirit of equity. This approach enabled the court to provide remedies that the Common Law could not offer, such as injunctions, specific performance, and fiduciary duties –tools that proved increasingly useful in commercial, property, and family disputes.

Through these innovations, the Court of Chancery became an essential complement to the Common Law, ensuring that the pursuit of justice could extend beyond rigid legal formalism to embrace moral and equitable considerations. Over time, this dual system allowed English law to balance certainty with flexibility, demonstrating how legal institutions can evolve to meet the needs of a changing society.

1.2.3 Principles Underpinning Equity

Equity focuses on the intention behind actions rather than on their formal expression. It seeks to achieve fairness by considering the substance of a matter rather than its strict legal form. Over time, a number of guiding principles, or *maxims of equity*, have developed to express the spirit and application of equitable reasoning. The most commonly cited maxims are as follows:[12]

He who comes to equity must come with clean hands. Equity is not available to a party whose conduct in relation to the dispute has been dishonest, unfair, or otherwise improper.

One who seeks equity must do equity. A person requesting equitable relief must themselves act fairly and fulfil any corresponding obligations – an extension of the "clean hands" principle.

Delay defeats equity. Equity will not assist a claimant who has unreasonably delayed in seeking relief.

Equity is a shield, not a sword. Equity may be used to defend a person's rights or prevent injustice, but it cannot be used to initiate an independent cause of action.

Equity will not suffer a wrong to be without a remedy. Where the strict application of law offers no solution, equity ensures that a remedy is available to address injustice.

Equity follows the law. Equity respects legal rules and will not grant remedies that contradict established law; it supplements rather than replaces it.

Equity will not assist a volunteer. Equity does not intervene to enforce promises or transactions where the claimant has provided no consideration.

Equity will not allow a trust to fail for want of a trustee. If no trustee is appointed, the person holding title to the property will be treated as the trustee, or the court may appoint one to ensure the trust operates effectively.

12 See Finch, Emily and Fafinski, Stefan, 2021, *Legal Skills*, 8th ed., Oxford University Press.

Equality is equity. When property or benefits are to be distributed, and no specific division is stated, equity presumes that they should be shared equally.

Together, these maxims form the ethical and procedural foundation of Equity, reflecting its central aim: to temper the rigidity of Common Law by promoting fairness, good faith, and justice in each individual case.

1.2.4 The Scope and Rights Within Equity

The development of equitable principles gave rise to several important equitable rights, which offered remedies and protections that the Common Law could not provide. These rights addressed specific shortcomings of the traditional legal system and introduced mechanisms to ensure fairness in legal and contractual relationships.

One of the most significant contributions of Equity was the protection of beneficiaries under trusts. Equity allowed beneficiaries to enforce the terms of a trust and to hold trustees accountable for their actions. Trustees were thus required to manage trust property responsibly, honestly, and in accordance with the trust's purpose.

Equity also created the *right of redemption*, which protected borrowers in mortgage transactions. Under this principle, a borrower retained the right to reclaim mortgaged property even after the repayment deadline, provided that the debt and any associated costs were paid in full. This equitable right prevented lenders from exploiting the strict rules of Common Law, which would otherwise have allowed them to seize property unfairly.

In addition, Equity introduced remedies such as *specific performance*, which compelled a party to perform their contractual obligations, and *injunctions*, which could prohibit or require certain actions. These remedies were particularly valuable in situations where monetary compensation was insufficient to achieve justice.

Through these innovations, Equity transformed the administration of justice by correcting the rigidity of Common Law. It established a more flexible and humane system that prioritized fairness and moral responsibility. The coexistence of Common Law and Equity thus created a more balanced and comprehensive legal framework, ensuring that legal outcomes aligned more closely with principles of justice and good conscience.[13]

1.2.5 Introduction of New Remedial Measures in Equity

Equity introduced a range of remedies, known as *equitable remedies*, which remain available today and are granted at the discretion of the court. These remedies aim to achieve fairness in situations where monetary compensation is inadequate. The three principal types of equitable remedies are *injunctions*, *specific performance*, and *rescission or rectification*.[14]

Injunctions are court orders requiring a person either to perform a particular act or to refrain from doing something. Failure to comply with an injunction may result in a finding of contempt of court, which can lead to imprisonment. Injunctions are particularly important where damages would not provide sufficient relief. There are three main types:

13 Finch and Fafinski, *Legal Skills*.

14 Finch and Fafinski, *Legal Skills*. See also Rutherford, Helen, Kotecha, Birju and Macfarlane, Angela, 2024, *English Legal System*, 6th ed., Oxford University Press.

Mandatory injunctions compel an individual to take a specific action. For instance, a court may order a person to remove overhanging branches, repair property damage, or clear waste they have deposited.

Prohibitory injunctions prevent an individual from performing a certain act. For example, a court may prohibit someone from harassing another person, require them to keep a specified distance, or stop them from contacting the claimant. Such injunctions are especially valuable where money cannot adequately prevent harm, as in cases involving personal safety or environmental protection.

Interim injunctions are temporary orders designed to preserve the status quo until the final resolution of a case. A well-known example is the *Mareva injunction*, which prevents a defendant from disposing of assets before trial, ensuring that potential financial claims remain enforceable.

Specific performance is an equitable order compelling a party to carry out their contractual obligations. This remedy is usually granted when damages would not sufficiently compensate the injured party. It is often applied in real estate transactions, where the court may require a seller to transfer property as agreed, recognizing that land is unique and cannot be replaced by money.

Rescission allows a contract to be cancelled, restoring the parties to their original positions as if the contract had never existed. This remedy is appropriate where a contract was formed under mistake, misrepresentation, or lack of ownership. For example, if a person sells a property they do not actually own, rescission would nullify the sale.

Rectification enables the correction of a written document so that it reflects the true intentions of the parties. For instance, if a contract for the sale of a sailboat mistakenly omits that the sale includes the berth, the court may amend the written agreement to correspond with the parties' actual understanding.

Through these remedies, Equity continues to play a vital role in ensuring justice and fairness, complementing the Common Law by offering flexible and tailored solutions where strict legal rules might otherwise produce unjust outcomes.

1.3 Interaction and Competition Between Common Law and Equity

The English legal system evolved through the coexistence of two distinct but complementary bodies of law: *Common Law* and *Equity*. Each developed its own courts, procedures, and forms of relief, serving different functions within the broader system of justice. Common Law provided the foundation of legal order and uniformity, but it was often rigid and limited, offering primarily monetary compensation. Equity arose to mitigate these shortcomings, introducing flexibility, moral reasoning, and remedies based on fairness and conscience. The interaction and occasional conflict between these two systems played a decisive role in shaping modern English law.

1.3.1 Interplay and Conflict: Equity's Influence on Common Law

Common Law and Equity operated side by side for several centuries, each within its own institutional and procedural framework. The *Court of Chancery* (or *Court of Equity*), presided over by the Lord Chancellor, functioned independently of the three principal royal courts of Common Law – the *Court of Common Pleas*, the *Court of Exchequer*, and the *Court of King's Bench*.

Each system addressed different needs: Common Law enforced established legal rights, while Equity intervened to provide remedies where strict legal rules produced unfair results.[15]

The Court of Equity was created to deliver justice in situations where Common Law was inadequate. While Common Law courts could only award damages, Equity could order *specific performance*, compelling a party to fulfil contractual obligations, or grant *injunctions*, requiring individuals to act or refrain from certain conduct. These remedies made Equity particularly effective in cases where monetary compensation could not ensure fairness.

Equity also introduced a more accessible and flexible procedure. The formalism of Common Law – where initiating a case required a specific writ – was replaced in the Chancery by petitions founded on fairness and conscience. This procedural adaptability allowed Equity to focus on the substance of disputes rather than their technical form, achieving more individualized and morally guided outcomes.

Nevertheless, the coexistence of two parallel systems frequently led to tension. A judgment obtained in a Common Law court could, in some cases, be countered by an equitable order in the Court of Chancery. For instance, a plaintiff might win a case under the strict rules of law, only for Equity to intervene and restrain the enforcement of that judgment if it was deemed unconscionable. Such conflicts created uncertainty and procedural complexity, as litigants could pursue remedies in different jurisdictions with potentially contradictory outcomes.

These tensions ultimately prompted reform in the 19th century, leading to the fusion of Common Law and Equity into a unified system – a development that would profoundly shape the modern administration of justice.

1.3.2 The Earl of Oxford's Case *(1615)*

The growing complexity of maintaining two parallel systems of justice – Common Law and Equity – eventually required the establishment of clear rules to resolve conflicts between them. This necessity was underscored by the *Earl of Oxford's Case* (1615), a landmark decision that defined the relationship between the two systems.[16]

In this case, a dispute arose between the Chief Justice of the Common Law courts and the Lord Chancellor. The Chief Justice contended that the Court of Equity, presided over by the Lord Chancellor on behalf of the King, had no authority to interfere once a Common Law court had rendered a decision. The Lord Chancellor, however, maintained that Equity possessed the power to intervene and set aside unjust rulings issued by the Common Law courts.

King James I ultimately resolved this conflict by declaring that, "where Common Law and Equity are in conflict, Equity shall prevail." This decision established the principle of Equity's supremacy over Common Law in cases of inconsistency, thereby formalizing a hierarchical relationship between the two systems. It meant that even when a Common Law judgment had been issued, the Court of Equity could intervene to ensure that justice and fairness were upheld.

The principle laid down in the *Earl of Oxford's Case* remains embedded in English law. It is reflected in section 49 of the *Supreme Court Act 1981*, which states:

> Subject to the provisions of this or any other Act, every court exercising jurisdiction in England or Wales in any civil cause or matter shall continue to administer law and equity on

15 See Finch and Fafinski, *Legal Skills*.

16 See "Earl of Oxford's Case," *Oxford Reference*. Available at: https://www.oxfordreference.com/view/10.1093/oi/authority.20110803095738846. Accessed 18 July 2024.

the basis that, wherever there is any conflict or variance between the rules of equity and the rules of the Common Law with reference to the same matter, the rules of equity shall prevail.

This doctrine ensured that Equity's emphasis on fairness and moral conscience would guide the interpretation and application of law. While the coexistence of Common Law and Equity created a more comprehensive and nuanced legal framework, it also introduced challenges in maintaining coherence and consistency. The gradual reconciliation and eventual integration of the two systems played a decisive role in the formation of modern English law, striking a balance between the certainty of legal rules and the flexibility of equitable justice.

1.3.3 The Emergence of the Rule of Law Through Equity and Common Law

The supremacy of Equity over Common Law introduced a hierarchy of legal norms long before Hans Kelsen's formal theory of normative hierarchy. Equitable principles, grounded in notions of natural justice and moral fairness, were regarded as superior to the rigid rules of Common Law. This early recognition of a hierarchy between different sources of law represented a significant step toward the development of the modern *Rule of Law*.[17]

Equity ensured that judicial decisions took into account considerations of fairness, conscience, and justice, rather than relying solely on procedural or formal rules. The coexistence of Common Law and Equity thus created a more balanced and adaptable legal framework, capable of addressing complex issues and protecting individual rights more effectively. Over time, the interplay between the two systems established a legal order in which norms were not merely applied mechanically but evaluated in light of higher principles of justice.

This hierarchical vision of legal reasoning profoundly influenced the evolution of major legal systems across the world. The integration of equitable principles into formal law contributed to the creation of more coherent, fair, and responsive legal institutions. It can also be seen as an early manifestation of the broader movement toward *legal convergence*, in which distinct legal traditions increasingly share common standards and values – particularly those emphasizing fairness, human dignity, and the pursuit of justice.

1.4 Unified Court System: Merging Common Law and Equity

The evolution of the English legal system ultimately led to the merging of Common Law and Equity into a single, unified court system.[18] This reform sought to resolve the practical difficulties and inconsistencies created by the coexistence of two separate jurisdictions. By integrating the two bodies of law, the reformers aimed to simplify judicial procedures, eliminate duplication, and ensure that litigants no longer had to choose between courts of law and courts of equity.

The unified system combined the strengths of both traditions: the consistency and precedent-based reasoning of Common Law with the flexibility and fairness of Equity. This integration produced a more coherent and efficient framework for the administration of justice, ensuring that courts could apply both legal and equitable principles within a single proceeding. It marked

17 For more information refer to Gillespie, Alisdair and Weare, Siobhan, 2023, *The English Legal System*, 9th ed., Oxford University Press.

18 Lewis, Kiralfy and Glendon, 2024, "Common Law," *Encyclopedia Britannica*, 19 May. Available at: https://www.britannica.com/topic/common-law. Accessed 18 July 2024.

a decisive step toward modernizing the English legal system and laid the groundwork for the balanced and adaptable legal order that exists today.

1.4.1 Challenges of Overlapping Jurisdictions Between Equity and Common Law

Equity evolved into a distinct legal system operating within the broader legal framework of England and Wales. It developed its own set of principles (known as equitable norms), its own subjects (the King's or Queen's subjects), and its own courts (the Court of Equity, or Court of Chancery). In practice, therefore, Equity functioned as an autonomous system of law, parallel to the Common Law.[19]

However, the coexistence of these two systems created confusion and inefficiency. The overlap between Common Law and Equity produced a complex and costly judicial structure. Litigation often became protracted and expensive, as the two systems followed different procedures and provided different remedies. A single dispute could require separate proceedings – one in a Common Law court to obtain monetary damages, and another in the Court of Equity to secure equitable relief such as an injunction or specific performance.

This duplication of actions not only burdened litigants but also hindered the effective administration of justice. The resulting procedural fragmentation underscored the need for reform and ultimately led to the fusion of Common Law and Equity into a single, coherent judicial system.

1.4.2 The 1852 Court of Chancery Procedure Act and the 1858 Chancery Amendment Act

The confusion and inefficiency resulting from the coexistence of Common Law and Equity prompted several important procedural reforms during the mid-19th century. Among the most significant were the *Court of Chancery Procedure Act of 1852* and the *Chancery Amendment Act of 1858*. These reforms expanded the powers of both jurisdictions: the Court of Equity was authorized to award monetary damages, while the Common Law courts were granted the ability to issue equitable remedies such as injunctions, rescission of contracts, and specific performance.[20]

These legislative changes represented a major step toward integrating the two systems. By allowing both sets of courts to provide a complete range of remedies, the reforms eliminated the need for litigants to initiate separate proceedings in different courts for the same dispute. This not only simplified and accelerated the legal process but also reduced its cost and made it more accessible to the public.

The procedural acts of the 1850s thus laid the foundation for a unified judicial structure. They paved the way for the *Judicature Acts of 1873 and 1875*, which formally merged the administration of Common Law and Equity into a single, coherent court system, ensuring that both legal and equitable principles could be applied together in the pursuit of justice.

1.4.3 Judicature Acts of 1873 and 1875: A New Legal Framework

Eventually, the *Supreme Court of Judicature Acts* of 1873 and 1875, commonly referred to as the *Judicature Acts*, merged the administration of Common Law and Equity within a single court system. This reform aimed to eliminate the need for multiple or overlapping legal proceedings

19 Lewis, Kiralfy and Glendon, "Common Law."
20 Lewis, Kiralfy and Glendon, "Common Law."

by allowing the same courts to apply both legal and equitable principles. The unification ensured that justice could be administered more efficiently and coherently, with courts empowered to grant all appropriate remedies – whether legal or equitable – within one comprehensive judicial framework.[21]

The Judicature Act of 1873 provided as follows (part II – Jurisdiction and Law – 24):

> In every civil cause or matter commenced in the High Court of Justice Law and Equity shall be administered by the High Court of Justice and the Court of Appeal respectively according to the rules following.

In other words, the *Judicature Acts* ensured that Equity and Common Law would henceforth be administered within a single, unified court system operating under one set of legal procedures. The Acts, enacted by parliament in 1873 and 1875, fundamentally restructured the English judicial system, replacing the complex hierarchy of medieval courts that had existed since the Middle Ages.

The reform abolished the old higher courts of Common Law – the *Court of Common Pleas*, the *Court of the Exchequer*, and the *Court of King's (or Queen's) Bench* – which had been established and centralized under King Henry II. These courts were merged into a new, integrated structure known as the *Supreme Court of Judicature*, composed of two main divisions: the *High Court of Justice* and the *Court of Appeal*.[22]

The *Judicature Act of 1873* also reaffirmed the principle, previously recognized in the *Earl of Oxford's Case*, that in any conflict between the rules of Common Law and Equity, the latter would prevail. This was explicitly stated in section 25 of the Act, ensuring that fairness, conscience, and justice remained guiding principles in the unified administration of law:

> Generally, in all matters not herein-before mentioned, in which there is any conflict or variance between the rules of equity and the rules of Common Law with reference to same matter, the rules of equity shall prevail.

1.5 Distinctive Elements of the Common Law System

Common Law is a legal system founded on *case law* and the *doctrine of precedent*, in which judicial decisions serve as the primary source of law. It encompasses distinctive legal institutions such as *trusts*, *estoppel*, *agency*, and *torts*, and relies on analogical reasoning to resolve disputes. Within this framework, two main bodies of law – Common Law and Equity – operate together to provide both legal and equitable remedies. Unlike Civil Law systems, Common Law does not draw a strict distinction between public and private law. It is deeply rooted in liberal ideologies, emphasizing individual liberty and fundamental rights and has played a major role in shaping democratic governance and the modern understanding of the *Rule of Law* – a topic further examined in Chapter 5.

21 Lewis, Kiralfy and Glendon, "Common Law."

22 The High Court of Justice was divided into five specialized court divisions, which were based on the old central courts (King's Bench, Common Pleas, Exchequer, and Chancery) with the addition of the new Probate, Divorce, and Admiralty division. Further trimming of the system took place in 1880 when the Common Pleas and Exchequer divisions were abolished. This radical restructuring did much to unify the system and allowed the ending of ancient and time-consuming practices. See the UK Parliament's Official website. Available at: http://www.parliament.uk/about/living-heritage/transformingsociety/laworder/court/overview/judicatureacts. Accessed 18 July 2024.

Although this system does not formally divide public and private law, *administrative tribunals* play a crucial role in Public Law across Common Law jurisdictions.[23] These tribunals adjudicate disputes involving government action and regulatory frameworks, functioning as key institutions for administrative justice. They are found in many Common Law countries, including the United Kingdom, the United States, Canada, Australia, New Zealand, Ireland, Israel, Hong Kong, Singapore, India, and South Africa. Their work contributes to the broader mission of ensuring fairness, accountability, and accessibility within systems of public administration, thereby influencing the global dialogue on justice and equity.

The pragmatic and adaptive nature of Common Law is well expressed by Oliver Wendell Holmes Jr., former Justice of the United States Supreme Court, who observed that "The life of the law has not been logic; it has been experience."[24] This statement encapsulates the experiential and evolutionary character of Common Law, which contrasts with the systematic and codified reasoning typical of Civil Law traditions.

1.5.1 The Doctrine of Precedent: Foundation and Evolution

The doctrine of precedent – often expressed by the Latin maxim *stare decisis* ("to stand by what has been decided") – is one of the pillars of the Common Law tradition. It requires courts to respect prior decisions, thereby promoting legal certainty and equal treatment. The sections that follow explore the historical development of this doctrine, its binding force, and the reasons for its enduring importance.

1.5.1.1 CENTRALIZATION OF ROYAL COURTS AND DEVELOPMENT OF THE *STARE DECISIS* PRINCIPLE

The entire Common Law system was fundamentally shaped by the early centralization of justice carried out by King Henry II, who established the three Royal Courts at Westminster – the *Court of Common Pleas*, the *Court of Exchequer*, and the *Court of King's Bench*. This centralization marked a decisive step in the creation of a unified legal system for England.

As judges from these courts began to travel across the kingdom to hear cases and return to Westminster to report their decisions, they developed a practice of referring to earlier judgments to ensure consistency in the administration of justice. Over time, this practice evolved into the *principle of stare decisis*, which became a defining feature of Common Law.

The term *stare decisis* derives from the Latin expression *stare decisis et non quieta movere*, meaning "stand by things which have been decided and do not disturb settled matters."[25]

In essence, it establishes that courts should follow established precedents in similar cases, thereby promoting stability, predictability, and coherence within the legal system. By encouraging judges to build on earlier decisions, the doctrine also contributed to the development of a sophisticated and cumulative body of case law that continues to shape the Common Law today.

1.5.1.2 *STARE DECISIS* AND THE BINDING FORCE OF PRECEDENT

The principle of *stare decisis* forms the foundation of the doctrine of *binding precedent*. To understand this doctrine fully, it is useful to refer to the general theory of the sources of law,

23 Thomson, Stephen, Groves, Matthew and Weeks, Greg, 2024, *Administrative Tribunals in the Common Law World*, 1st ed., Bloomsbury Publishing.

24 Holmes, Oliver Wendell Jr., 2005, *The Common Law*, The Lawbook Exchange Ltd., New Jersey. Originally published: Boston, Little, Brown and Co., 1881.

25 See Gillespie and Weare, *The English Legal System*.

which distinguishes between legal norms enacted by legislative bodies (*statutory law*) and those created through judicial decisions (*case law*).

Case law may be defined as "the collection of reported cases that form the body of jurisprudence within a given jurisdiction." It consists of legal principles derived from prior judicial decisions, constituting a body of non-statutory rules developed by the courts. In French legal terminology, this body of law is referred to as *jurisprudence*.[26]

Case law rests on two key doctrines: *stare decisis* and *res judicata*. The doctrine of *stare decisis* requires courts to adhere to established precedents – to "stand by what has been decided." The doctrine of *res judicata*, meaning "a matter already judged," prevents the same parties from reopening a case once it has been finally adjudicated and any right of appeal has been exhausted.

Under the doctrine of binding precedent, when a legal issue has been determined in a previous case, judges are obliged to apply the same reasoning and reach the same conclusion in future cases presenting similar facts or legal questions. This principle ensures consistency, predictability, and fairness in the application of the law, reinforcing public confidence in the stability and coherence of the legal system.

1.5.1.3 ORIGINS AND PURPOSE OF THE DOCTRINE OF PRECEDENT

The practice of studying and referring to earlier judicial decisions is ancient, with intellectual origins traceable to Ancient Greece. In *Nicomachean Ethics* (Book V), Aristotle asserted that similar cases should be treated alike and dissimilar cases differently, in proportion to their differences – an idea that underpins the principle of equality before the law. Nevertheless, the specific Anglo-Saxon doctrine of precedent can be traced back to the 13th century.

In England, the systematic recording of judicial decisions began under the reign of King Edward I, around 1290, with the creation of the *Yearbooks*. These records compiled significant judicial rulings and procedural information, serving as valuable references for lawyers and students of law. This initiative marked a turning point in the formalization of tradition, custom, and precedent as the foundations of English law. Over time, the doctrine of precedent evolved into the central model of judicial reasoning in the Common Law system.[27]

In the 18th century, Sir William Blackstone, in his *Commentaries on the Laws of England*,[28] emphasized the necessity of adhering to prior decisions to preserve justice, stability, and consistency within the legal system. He warned that without respect for precedent, the law would fluctuate with each judge's personal opinion. As he wrote:

> For it is an established rule to abide by former precedents, where the same points come again in litigation; as well as to keep the scale of justice even and steady, and not liable to waver with every new judge's opinion; as also because the law in that case being solemnly declared and determined, what before was uncertain, and perhaps indifferent, is now become a permanent rule, which is not in the breast of any subsequent judge to alter or vary from, according

26 See Peter de Cruz, *Comparative Law in a Changing World*, Routledge-Cavendish, 2007.

27 Similarly, Justice James Park, in his opinion to the House of Lords, in 1833, gave a clear and substantive definition of the rule of precedent and of its philosophy. He wrote that "[o]ur Common Law system consists in applying to new combination of circumstances those rules of law which we derive from legal principles and judicial precedents, and for the sake of attaining uniformity, consistency and certainty, we must apply those rules, where they are not plainly unreasonable and inconvenient, to all cases which arise." *Mirehouse v. Rennell* (1833), 1 Cl & Fin 527.

28 Blackstone, Sir William, 1765–1769, *Commentaries on the Laws of England*.

to his private sentiments: he being sworn to determine, not according to his private judgment, but according to known laws and customs of the land.[29]

The doctrine of precedent ensures that the Common Law operates as a rational, consistent, and adaptable system. Precedents act as "rules about rules," providing judges with a framework to apply established principles to new cases. Judges examine earlier decisions to identify relevant precedents, analyze their reasoning, and assess their applicability to avoid misinterpretation. This process enables the Common Law to evolve with societal changes while maintaining continuity.

Although precedents are binding, the system allows flexibility. Judges may distinguish a current case from earlier ones when factual or legal differences justify a new approach. This capacity for adaptation is vital in addressing modern challenges, including those arising from environmental protection, digital technology, or bioethics, where courts extend or refine existing legal principles.

However, the doctrine of precedent also places a heavy responsibility on judges, who must carefully determine which precedents apply and under what conditions. A superficial or mechanical use of precedent risks producing unjust outcomes. When applied thoughtfully, though, the doctrine provides one of the most reliable and coherent methods of judicial reasoning.

Judicial precedent requires that courts follow decisions from higher or equivalent courts within the judicial hierarchy. This ensures that similar facts produce similar rulings, promoting both fairness and predictability. The existence of a supreme appellate body, such as the *Supreme Court of the United Kingdom*, strengthens the operation of this doctrine by providing final authority in interpreting the law and setting binding precedents for all subordinate courts.

1.5.2 Navigating Precedents: Stare Decisis *and* res Judicata

Case law is built upon two fundamental doctrines: the doctrine of precedent, which relies on the principle of *stare decisis*, and the doctrine of *res judicata*. It is crucial to distinguish between these doctrines.[30]

The doctrine of precedent, based on the principle of *stare decisis*, requires that each court follow the decisions of higher or equivalent courts within the judicial hierarchy. When a similar issue arises in future litigation, judges must adhere to previous rulings. This principle ensures consistency and predictability in the application of the law.

Consider, for example, that a judge once decided that when a delivery company leaves a package unattended outside a customer's door without consent, it is responsible if the package is stolen. Later, in another case involving a similar situation, a different judge applied the same reasoning and reached the same conclusion. This basic example illustrates the doctrine of precedent: judges must follow earlier judicial decisions when similar facts arise.

In *Brown v. Board of Education* (1954), several African American families and associations challenged laws that required Black and white children to attend separate schools. They argued that segregation made Black children feel inferior and denied them equal educational opportunities. An earlier U.S. Supreme Court case, *Plessy v. Ferguson* (1896), had allowed racial segregation under the idea of "separate but equal."

The U.S. Supreme Court in *Brown* looked at new evidence showing that segregated schools were never truly equal and harmed children's development. It decided to overturn *Plessy v.*

29 Blackstone, *Commentaries on the Laws of England.*

30 See Gillespie and Weare, *The English Legal System.* See also Rutherford, Kotecha and Macfarlane, *English Legal System.*

Ferguson, ruling that racial segregation in public schools violated the *Equal Protection Clause* of the Fourteenth Amendment.

This case showed how *stare decisis* works in a balanced way: while courts usually follow earlier decisions for stability, they can overturn precedent when it is clearly unjust or out of step with modern values.

On the other hand, *res judicata* means that once a case has been decided and all avenues of appeal have been exhausted, the parties involved cannot reopen the case to settle their dispute again. This finality applies to all types of cases, except in criminal matters. In criminal cases, reopening a case is permissible, but only concerning the facts (not the law), and only if there has been a miscarriage or mismanagement of justice, such as an error in the actual facts of the case.

Imagine a case where two neighbors went to court over a dispute about the exact location of their shared fence. The court decided where the boundary lay, and both parties accepted the judgment. A year later, one neighbor tried to reopen the same dispute, presenting no new facts. The court refused to hear the case, explaining that the matter had already been decided and could not be brought again. This demonstrates the principle of *res judicata*.

In *Federated Department Stores, Inc. v. Moitie* (1981), a group of shoppers sued several department stores for allegedly fixing prices. The court dismissed all the cases, ruling that the shoppers had not shown real financial harm. Five of them appealed, but two others, including Moitie, chose not to. Instead, those two filed new lawsuits in another court, repeating the same claims. The court dismissed the new cases, applying *res judicata* – the rule that a case already decided cannot be brought again. Later, the five shoppers who had appealed won after the Supreme Court changed the legal interpretation of "harm," and Moitie tried to reopen his case, arguing it was unfair to treat him differently. The Supreme Court, however, refused, explaining that because Moitie had not appealed, his case was final. The Court held that *res judicata* barred reopening the case, even if the earlier decision might have been mistaken. This ruling confirmed that final judgments must be respected to preserve judicial efficiency, fairness, and the stability of the legal system.

1.5.3 Precedents, Ratio Decidendi, and Obiter Dictum

In Common Law, judicial precedents are built on the reasoning behind court decisions, but not every part of a judgment carries the same authority. The *binding* element of a decision is called the ratio decidendi – literally, "the reason for the decision." It includes the legal principle, reasoning, and conclusion that were necessary for the outcome of the case. By contrast, any additional observations or comments made by a judge that are not essential to the decision are known as obiter dicta (from Latin, "things said in passing"). Although obiter dicta are not binding, they can still be persuasive, especially when expressed by higher courts such as the U.S. Supreme Court or the UK Supreme Court.

In Civil Law systems, a similar distinction exists between *motifs déterminants* or *motifs essentiels* (comparable to the ratio) and *remarques incidentes* or *commentaires incidents* (similar to obiter dicta). However, the ratio decidendi goes beyond simply identifying the key reasons for a judgment: it formulates a Rule of Law to be applied in future cases. As Sir Buxton LJ explained in *R (Kadhim) v. Brent London Borough Council Housing Benefit Review Board*, the ratio decidendi of a case is any Rule of Law that the judge treats as a necessary step in reaching the decision, forming the legal rule to be followed in later cases:

> While there has been much academic discussion of the proper way of determining the ratio of a case . . . the ratio decidendi of a case is any Rule of Law, expressly or impliedly treated by

> the judge as a necessary step in reaching his conclusion, having regard to the line of reasoning adopted by him. In short, it is the rule to be followed in subsequent cases.[31]

Identifying the ratio is often challenging because judges do not explicitly separate it from obiter dicta in their written opinions. To determine the ratio, one must isolate the *material facts* – those that directly influence the legal outcome – and identify the part of the reasoning that was essential to deciding the case. The ratio may be narrow, tied closely to the facts, or broad, stated in more general legal terms. The higher the level of abstraction, the wider its potential application as precedent.

A well-known example is *Donoghue v. Stevenson* (1932), the "snail in the bottle" case. The House of Lords held that a manufacturer owes a duty of care to the ultimate consumer, establishing the foundation of modern negligence law. Lord Atkin's formulation of the ratio stated that a manufacturer must take reasonable care to avoid acts or omissions likely to injure the consumer:

> My Lords, if your Lordships accept the view that this pleading discloses a relevant cause of action you will be affirming the proposition that by Scots and English law alike a manufacturer of products, which he sells in such a form as to show that he intends them to reach the ultimate consumer in the form in which they left him with no reasonable possibility of intermediate examination, and with the knowledge that the absence of reasonable care in the preparation or putting up of the products will result in an injury to the consumer's life or property, owes a duty to the consumer to take that reasonable care.[32]

This principle has been interpreted broadly in later cases to mean that any person must take reasonable care to avoid foreseeable harm to others.

Ultimately, determining the ratio decidendi requires both legal reasoning and practical experience. Judges themselves shape its meaning and scope, and their interpretations over time define how legal principles evolve. The ratio thus embodies both what the law *is* (*de lege lata*) and what it *ought to be* (*de lege ferenda*), demonstrating the active role of judges in developing the Common Law.

1.5.4 Judicial Adaptability: Distinguishing, Reversal, and Overruling Precedents

Sometimes, a judge may refuse to follow a binding precedent by distinguishing, reversing, or overruling it.[33]

Distinguishing occurs when a court identifies important differences between the facts of the present case and those of an earlier case. Because the situations are not identical or sufficiently similar, the judge decides that the earlier precedent does not apply. This allows the court to reach a different conclusion without rejecting the earlier rule.

Reversing takes place on appeal when a higher court disagrees with the decision of a lower court in the same case. The higher court may overturn, or "reverse," the judgment, replacing it with its own decision. This affects the outcome for the parties involved and establishes a new precedent that lower courts must follow.

31 *R (Kadhim) v. Brent London Borough Council Housing Benefit Review Board* (2001) QB 955.

32 Finch and Fafinski, *Legal Skills*.

33 See Gillespie and Weare, *The English Legal System* and Rutherford, Kotecha. See also Macfarlane, *English Legal System*.

Overruling happens when a higher court decides that a legal rule established in a previous case was wrongly decided. The court sets aside the old precedent and replaces it with a new rule, although this change does not alter the outcome of the original case because of the principle of *res judicata* (the matter has already been judged).

Precedents that merely apply existing law are called declaratory precedents, while cases in which judges must create new legal rules because none previously exist give rise to original precedents. In such cases, judges are required to innovate to prevent a denial of justice and ensure that the law continues to evolve with society.

1.6 Advantages and Disadvantages of Case Law and Variations Across Borders

Case law, a central element of the Common Law tradition, plays a crucial role in judicial decision-making. It ensures that judges apply established legal principles while allowing the law to evolve through experience and interpretation. The use of case law offers significant advantages, such as consistency, predictability, and flexibility, since it enables courts to adapt legal rules to changing social and economic contexts. However, it also presents challenges: the sheer volume and complexity of precedents can make the law difficult to navigate, and conflicting judgments may create uncertainty. This part explores both the advantages and disadvantages of case law, as well as how its application varies across different legal systems.[34]

1.6.1 Advantages of Case Law

Case law promotes consistency and predictability in judicial decisions, as courts generally resolve similar issues in similar ways. This practice ensures rationality and certainty within the legal framework, giving individuals and institutions confidence in how the law will be applied. At the same time, case law remains flexible and adaptable, allowing the legal system to evolve through methods such as distinguishing, reversing, and overruling earlier decisions. These mechanisms enable the law to respond to new social, technological, and economic developments. In this way, precedent operates as both a stabilizing force and a creative tool, guiding judges while allowing them to refine or adjust the law when circumstances require it.

Although the principle of precedent can also be found, to a limited extent, in some Civil Law jurisdictions,[35] it is a defining characteristic of the Common Law tradition. Through its balance of stability and adaptability, case law ensures that the law remains both coherent and responsive – providing clear guidance while evolving naturally as new situations and challenges arise. This dynamic quality explains why the Common Law has been able to endure, expand, and adjust across centuries and across diverse societies.

1.6.2 Disadvantages of Case Law

The advantages of case law can, in certain circumstances, become disadvantages. Because it relies on *stare decisis* and the binding authority of precedent, case law may appear rigid, leaving judges with limited discretion to adapt the law to unique situations. Moreover, judges may

34 Cappalli, Richard B., 1998, "At the Point of Decision: The Common Law's Advantage over the Civil Law," *Temple International and Comparative Law Journal*, vol. 12, p. 88.

35 In the Civil Law systems there exists a form a precedent. Still, these precedents only serve a persuasive role and courts usually treat precedent as some sort of "soft law," as guidelines. It should be noted that Civil Law courts are increasingly expected to take into account former cases when there is sufficient level of consistency in case law.

interpret or apply precedents differently, leading to inconsistent decisions in cases with similar facts. Such inconsistencies can undermine the predictability and stability that the system seeks to achieve. In addition, the vast number of reported cases makes the system increasingly complex, making it difficult for practitioners to identify the most relevant precedents. This complexity can encourage more litigation and slow down the resolution of disputes. It may also lead to uncertainty when courts must reconcile conflicting lines of authority. Therefore, while case law provides coherence and flexibility, it can also give rise to rigidity, interpretative uncertainty, and procedural complexity. Its strengths and weaknesses are thus closely linked: the very mechanisms that allow the Common Law to evolve can also generate challenges that require careful judicial management and ongoing doctrinal clarification.

1.7 Legal Research in Common Law Jurisdictions

In the Common Law tradition, judicial decisions are published in *Law Reports*, which serve as the primary source for identifying precedents. Their Civil Law equivalent would be the *Recueils de jurisprudence*. Lawyers and judges rely on these reports to locate previous decisions relevant to current cases. However, law reports are not exhaustive – they include only a selection of the most important or influential cases, such as those establishing new legal principles or modifying existing rules.

Historically, the earliest British law reports were known as the *Yearbooks*, named because they were compiled annually. Interestingly, these early reports were written in French, reflecting the linguistic influence of William of Normandy, the first Norman King of England. A royal body, the *King's Council of Law Reporting*, was responsible for recording and maintaining these reports.

Today, law reports are published monthly and hold significant authoritative value, as they are carefully edited and approved by the courts before publication. Among the most well-known and widely cited modern series are *The Law Reports*, *The Weekly Law Reports (WLR)*, *The All England Law Reports (All E.R.)*, and *The New Law Journal (N.L.J.)*.[36] These publications continue to play a vital role in preserving the doctrine of precedent and ensuring consistency in the development of the law.

1.7.1 Understanding Case Citations

A citation is the reference to a legal case in abbreviated form. It indicates where a particular case has been published and how it can be located in law reports.[37] Citation styles vary across countries, but here we will focus on the British system.

For example, in the reference (2012) 3 WLR 1645, the year 2012 refers to the *year of publication*, 3 to the *volume number*, WLR to the *series of reports* (*Weekly Law Reports*), and 1645 to the *page number* on which the case begins.

Case citations often include the court abbreviation to show where the case was heard. For instance, *X v. Smith* (2012) 3 WLR 1645 (CA) means that the case *X v. Smith* was decided by the Court of Appeal (CA) and is reported in the *Weekly Law Reports*, 2012, volume 3, starting

36 Some newspapers (like *The Times* in the UK, the *International Herald Tribune* in the U.S., *The Globe* and *The Mail* in Canada) publish report summaries of the most important cases after the hearing.

37 See Finch and Fafinski, *Legal Skills*.

on page 1645. Other common court abbreviations include HL for *House of Lords*, PC for *Privy Council*, and CA for *Court of Appeal*.

With the growth of the Internet, a neutral citation system was introduced in the early 2000s to make judicial decisions easier to find online. Each approved judgment is now given a unique identification number that does not depend on printed law reports. For example, [2012] UKHL 98 refers to the 98th judgment of the *House of Lords of the United Kingdom (UKHL)* in 2012.

A more recent example is *DELTA Merseyside Limited & Anor v. Uber Britannia* Limited [2024] EWCA Civ 802, decided by the *Court of Appeal, Civil Division*, on July 15, 2024. This case originated in the *High Court of Justice, King's Bench Division*, in 2023. The neutral citation [2024] EWCA Civ 802 identifies it as the 802nd judgment issued by the Court of Appeal (Civil Division) in 2024.

The case name shows that two appellants, *DELTA Merseyside Limited* and another party, brought the appeal against the respondent, *Uber Britannia Limited*. The internal tracking numbers CA-2023-001771 and CA-2023-001772 correspond to the official appeal files. The original High Court judgment is cited as [2023] EWHC 1975 (KB) – meaning it was the 1975th case decided by the *King's Bench Division* of the *High Court of Justice* in 2023.

This system ensures that every case can be precisely identified and easily accessed, whether in print or online.

1.7.2 The Role of Case Summaries in Legal Research

Lawyers, students, scholars, and legal practitioners frequently rely on case summaries to gain a quick understanding of judicial decisions. These summaries provide an overview of the essential elements of a case, including the main facts, the legal issue, and the court's ruling. They are particularly useful for research or initial review, allowing readers to grasp the outcome of a case without having to study the entire judgment.

However, caution is necessary when using case summaries. Since they are prepared by third parties, they may not fully capture the court's precise reasoning or the nuances of the judgment. The author's interpretation can introduce bias, omissions, or oversimplifications that distort the meaning of the original decision.

For this reason, consulting the full case transcript is always advisable when a detailed and accurate understanding is required. The complete text of the judgment provides the full legal reasoning, context, and principles applied by the judges, ensuring that the case is properly understood and interpreted.

1.7.3 Finding Legal Cases and Statutes: Evolution of Legal Research Tools From Paper to AI

Traditionally, law students and practitioners conducted legal research using paper resources. Visiting law libraries and becoming familiar with collections of statutes, law reports, and commentaries was an essential skill. To locate a case, researchers relied on its citation to identify the correct series of law reports, year, and volume in which the decision appeared.

The rise of digital legal databases has revolutionized this process, providing instant online access to cases, statutes, and academic commentary.[38] Researchers can now search by party

38 Some well-known legal databases include LexisNexis Butterworths, which offers access to The Law Reports (AC, QB, Ch, Fam), All England Law Reports (All ER CR), Family Court Reporter (FCR), and Tax cases (TC). Another prominent database is Westlaw, covering The Law Reports (AC, QB, Ch, Fam), Weekly Law Reports (WLR),

name, citation, keyword, or combinations of these. However, coverage still varies between platforms, and not all reports are available everywhere.

In recent years, generative AI technologies, such as ChatGPT, have further transformed legal research.[39] These AI tools are increasingly integrated into professional legal databases, offering enhanced speed, precision, and contextual analysis. By processing vast amounts of legal data, AI can summarize judgments, identify relevant precedents, and even suggest arguments or citations. The digitization of legal records has made it easier for AI systems to access and interpret large datasets efficiently.

Nevertheless, the use of generative AI also presents important risks. AI tools can occasionally produce inaccurate or fabricated information – known as "hallucinations." If such errors go unchecked, they can lead to serious professional consequences, including disciplinary action for submitting documents containing incorrect citations or non-existent cases. For this reason, lawyers must exercise caution and use AI solutions developed by reputable legal technology providers familiar with the professional and ethical standards of the legal field.[40]

Selecting an appropriate AI research tool requires careful consideration of data security, accuracy, and reliability. Most modern systems are cloud-based, which makes confidentiality and compliance with data protection laws essential. Trusted platforms such as Westlaw Precision, Lexis+ AI, Paxton AI, Vincent AI, and Copilot offer varying features and subscription models. Understanding each tool's strengths and limitations allows legal professionals to harness the benefits of AI while maintaining accuracy, ethical integrity, and client confidentiality.[41]

2 Global Expansion and Influence of Common Law

Over time, English law was received, transplanted, and voluntarily adopted in many parts of the world, particularly within the territories that once formed the British Empire. As a result, British Common Law came into contact with diverse legal traditions, often coexisting with local customs, indigenous norms, and religious laws. This interaction created *dualist legal systems* in many colonies and dominions, where English legal principles operated alongside traditional or customary systems.

This process profoundly influenced the development of legal and political institutions in regions such as Africa, Australia, Singapore, Malaysia, New Zealand, India, Pakistan, parts of Southeast Asia (including Hong Kong), and North America (with the exception of Mexico and Quebec, which follow Civil Law traditions).[42]

The objective here is not to examine each of these systems in detail, but rather to understand how and why the Common Law tradition succeeded in spreading its core principles and institutions across the globe, shaping modern legal thought and governance far beyond England's borders.

Human Rights Law Reports (HRLR), European Human Rights Reports (EHRR), and Personal Injury and Quantum Reports (PIQR). Additionally, Justis includes access to European Human Rights Reports (EHRR), English Reports (ER), and Industrial Cases Reports (ICR).

39 Black, Nicole, 2024, "Legal Research Tools in the Age of Generative AI," *ABA Journal*, 25 March (online). Available at: https://www.abajournal.com/columns/article/legal-research-tools-in-the-age-of-generative-ai. Accessed 17 July 2024.

40 Black, *Legal Research Tools in the Age of Generative AI.*

41 Black, *Legal Research Tools in the Age of Generative AI.*

42 See de Cruz, *Comparative Law in a Changing World.*

2.1 Common Law's Expansion to Africa

The spread of Common Law to Africa has played a major role in shaping the continent's modern legal systems. Introduced primarily through British colonial influence, Common Law was often merged with existing customary and religious laws, creating hybrid systems that continue to define many African jurisdictions today. This part examines how Common Law principles and institutions were integrated and adapted across Africa, focusing first on South Africa as a key example of legal fusion, before offering a broader overview of how other African nations adopted and modified Common Law practices to fit their social, cultural, and political contexts.

2.1.1 Common Law Practices in South Africa

In the early 19th century, when the British settled in South Africa, English law began to influence and reshape the local legal system, gradually replacing the earlier Dutch-based customs and institutions. New judicial bodies were established, including the Supreme Court, which replaced the old Raad van Justitie. This court was tasked with applying both the existing law of the colony and any new laws introduced under British administration. English law had a particularly strong impact on civil and criminal procedure.

However, because South Africa had been a Dutch colony, its substantive law continued to be based largely on the Romano-Dutch tradition. In the 1820s, English was declared the official language of the courts, and English legal concepts were increasingly adopted, progressively overshadowing the Romano-Dutch system. The accessibility of English law reports, which were regularly consulted by South African Courts, also contributed to this shift. These reports provided valuable guidance for judges and lawyers whenever Romano-Dutch law or local custom offered no clear answer.

English influence deepened further as judges were appointed directly by the British Crown and were often members of the English Bar. Trained in English law and accustomed to English legal reasoning, they naturally relied on English sources and precedents. Meanwhile, Romano-Dutch law was losing vitality, having ceased to develop in the Netherlands and surviving only in a few territories, including South Africa, Sri Lanka, and British Guiana. By the early 20th century, English law had become a dominant source of law in South Africa, shaping much of its legal framework and judicial practice.[43]

2.1.2 Adoption of Common Law Across the African Continent

Common Law has also influenced other parts of the African continent, where it often merged with Civil Law and customary law to form *mixed* or *hybrid legal systems*.[44] In these systems, elements of English Common Law coexist with Roman-Dutch or Civil Law traditions and local customary norms. This blending is particularly evident in countries such as Botswana, Lesotho, Mauritius, Namibia, Eswatini (formerly Swaziland), and Zimbabwe.

Botswana's legal system exemplifies this hybrid model. Rooted in Roman-Dutch law, it has absorbed many features of English Common Law, especially in procedural and criminal

43 De Cruz, *Comparative Law in a Changing World.*

44 Orücü, E., 2008, "What Is a Mixed Legal System: Exclusion or Expansion?," *Electronic Journal of Comparative Law*, vol. 12, no. 1.

matters.[45] The Penal Code, for instance, reflects both traditions, incorporating Common Law notions such as due process and the right to a fair trial. Customary law also retains considerable authority, particularly in family and land disputes, where traditional courts apply local customs.

Lesotho's legal framework similarly combines Roman-Dutch foundations with English Common Law influences. The Constitution of Lesotho embodies this dual character, protecting individual rights in line with Common Law principles while preserving customary law for family and community matters. The *Laws of Lerotholi*, a codification of traditional rules, continue to regulate personal status and domestic relations.[46]

Mauritius presents a distinct example of legal hybridity. Civil Law, based on the French *Code Napoléon*, governs private law matters, while English Common Law shapes criminal and commercial law. For instance, the Mauritian Criminal Code adopts Common Law concepts such as *mens rea* (criminal intent) and *actus reus* (the wrongful act), illustrating the coexistence of both traditions.[47]

Namibia also operates under a mixed system, with Roman-Dutch law as its foundation and English law exerting strong procedural and constitutional influence.[48] The Namibian Constitution enshrines fundamental rights consistent with Common Law values, and customary law remains recognized and applied in local courts, particularly for cases involving marriage, inheritance, and land tenure.

In Eswatini, Roman-Dutch Civil Law and English Common Law are integrated with a robust customary law tradition. Customary law, administered by traditional authorities, operates alongside formal courts, particularly in matters of family, succession, and local disputes. The *Eswatini Courts Act* formalizes this coexistence, allowing traditional courts to handle customary law cases.

Zimbabwe's legal system also reflects the merging of Roman-Dutch and English Common Law.[49] Its statutes, such as the *Criminal Procedure and Evidence Act*, incorporate Common Law doctrines of fairness and due process. Customary law continues to play a major role, especially in rural areas where local courts resolve disputes involving family and inheritance issues according to traditional practices.

Together, these examples demonstrate how English Common Law, when introduced to Africa, adapted to pre-existing legal and cultural contexts. The result was not the replacement of local systems, but rather the creation of hybrid legal frameworks that balance the formal structures of imported law with the social realities and traditions of African communities.

2.2 Common Law Traditions in India and Pakistan: Adaptations and Influences

The legal systems of India and Pakistan have been deeply influenced by the Common Law tradition introduced during British rule, yet each country has developed its own distinct legal

45 See Fombad, Charles Manga, 2021, "Botswana's Legal System and Legal Research," *GlobaLex*, November–December. Available at: https://www.nyulawglobal.org/globalex/Botswana_Legal_System_and_Legal_Research.html. Accessed 17 July 2024.

46 Shale, Itumeleng, 2019, "The Law and Legal Research in Lesotho," *GlobaLex*, July–August. Available at: https://www.nyulawglobal.org/globalex/Lesotho_Legal_Research.html. Accessed 17 July 2024.

47 Gunputh, Rajendra Parsad, 2022, "The Mauritian Legal System and Research," *GlobaLex*, May–June. Available at: https://www.nyulawglobal.org/globalex/Mauritius_Legal_Research.html. Accessed 17 July 2024.

48 Zongwe, Dunia P., 2020, "Researching Namibian Law and the Namibian Legal System," *GlobaLex*, November–December. Available at: https://www.nyulawglobal.org/globalex/Namibia_Legal_Research.html. Accessed 17 July 2024.

49 Pfumorodze, Jimcall and Chitsove, Emma, 2021, "The Law in Zimbabwe," *GlobaLex*, July–August. Available at: https://www.nyulawglobal.org/globalex/Zimbabwe1.html. Accessed 17 July 2024.

identity by blending these inherited structures with local values and norms. In India, British influence led to the establishment of a comprehensive legal framework based on the Rule of Law, judicial precedent, and codified statutes, which continues to underpin the modern legal system. In Pakistan, while many Common Law principles were retained after independence, they were integrated with Islamic jurisprudence to reflect the country's religious and cultural foundations. This section explores how British legal traditions shaped Indian law and how Pakistan's legal system evolved into a unique hybrid model combining Common Law and Islamic principles.[50]

2.2.1 *The Transformation of Indian Law Through British Influence*

India, one of the world's most ancient civilizations, gained independence in the 20th century after a long history of diverse rule – from early Muslim conquests (1000–1025) and the Mughal Empire to Western colonization and British dominion. What distinguishes India from other former colonies is that it established the largest democracy in the world, with a population exceeding one billion, while maintaining a remarkable degree of social, cultural, and religious pluralism. Although the majority of Indians are Hindus, Hindu religious law does not govern the entirety of social life, as India functions under a secular constitutional framework.

The integration of Common Law principles into India's legal system was largely a result of British influence, which began in the late 17th century with the activities of the East India Company in key cities such as Madras, Bombay, and Calcutta. After the Indian Rebellion of 1857, the British Crown assumed direct control of India, dissolving the East India Company's courts and implementing comprehensive legal reforms. These reforms introduced new legislation and codifications that became the foundation of modern Indian law.

Among the most significant were the Indian Penal Code (1860), which consolidated and clarified criminal law, the Indian Evidence Act (1872), which standardized evidentiary rules, the Transfer of Property Act (1882), which regulated property rights and transactions, and the Civil Procedure Code (1908), which established uniform procedures for civil litigation. These enactments reflected the structure and logic of the Common Law system, emphasizing judicial precedent and legal reasoning, while also accommodating India's religious and cultural diversity – particularly in matters of family law, where Hindu and Muslim personal laws continued to apply.[51]

Thus, India's legal system emerged as a sophisticated blend of British Common Law traditions and indigenous legal concepts, forming a unique framework that continues to support the world's largest democracy today.

2.2.2 *Pakistan's Legal Foundation: Common Law and Islamic Jurisprudence*

India's legal system profoundly influenced the formation of Pakistan's legal framework. When Pakistan became an independent Islamic republic in 1947, following its partition from India, it inherited much of the legal structure developed under British colonial rule. This system, rooted in the Common Law of England and Wales, provided the foundation for Pakistan's Judiciary, legislation, and legal institutions. Many procedural rules, court structures, and concepts such as

50 Ahmad, Furqan and Sharma, Daksha, 2017, "Review of *Cases on Muslim Law of India, Pakistan, and Bangladesh* by Alamgir Muhammad Serajuddin," *Journal of the Indian Law Institute*, vol. 59, no. 2, pp. 211–214. Available at: https://www.jstor.org/stable/26826602.

51 "Introduction," 2019, in *The Indian Legal System: An Enquiry*, New Delhi. Online edition: Oxford Academic, 17 April. https://doi.org/10.1093/oso/9780199489879.002.0013. Accessed 18 July 2024.

precedent, judicial review, and constitutional rights were carried over almost intact, ensuring continuity during the transition to statehood.

However, Pakistan's identity as an Islamic republic led to the incorporation of Islamic law (*Sharia*), particularly in areas of private law such as marriage, divorce, inheritance, and family relations. Institutions such as the Federal Shariat Court and the Council of Islamic Ideology were created to ensure that legislation conforms to Islamic principles. Over time, Pakistan has sought to harmonize Common Law principles with Islamic jurisprudence, creating a hybrid legal system that reflects both its colonial heritage and religious values.[52]

This blending of legal traditions demonstrates how Common Law was not merely transplanted but adapted to the social, cultural, and religious realities of the new State. It also shows how legal systems evolve differently even when they share the same origins. The experiences of India and Pakistan thus illustrate two distinct paths of legal evolution – both grounded in the Common Law tradition yet shaped by their own historical and cultural contexts.

2.3 Common Law Systems in Australia and New Zealand

The Common Law systems of Australia and New Zealand share a common origin in English law but have developed in distinctive ways, reflecting each nation's history, society, and legal evolution. In both countries, British colonization introduced the Common Law framework, which initially mirrored that of England. Over time, however, local courts and legislatures adapted these principles to address unique national circumstances, social values, and indigenous rights.

This section first examines the establishment and evolution of Common Law in Australia, focusing on how it was received, applied, and gradually shaped into an independent legal system. It then explores the development of Common Law in New Zealand, emphasizing the country's particular adaptations, including the recognition of Māori customary law and its influence on the broader legal framework. Together, these examples illustrate how Common Law can evolve beyond its English origins while maintaining its essential principles of precedent, judicial reasoning, and the Rule of Law.

2.3.1 Establishment and Evolution of Common Law in Australia

In 1788, New South Wales was founded as a penal colony governed by a British-appointed governor who held extensive administrative and judicial authority. One of the earliest legal questions concerned whether English Common Law applied to convicts and the colony as a whole. This issue was settled by an imperial statute confirming that English law extended to New South Wales and Tasmania, provided it was capable of practical application in the colonial context. By 1828, English law was formally adopted throughout the colonies. As New South Wales gradually gained legislative autonomy, it acquired the power to enact local laws, provided they did not conflict with English statutes, thereby reinforcing the supremacy of English law within the colonial hierarchy.

In 1839, the British Crown expanded the jurisdiction of New South Wales to include New Zealand through letters patent. Subsequently, the English Law Acts of 1858 and 1908 declared that English laws applied to New Zealand, with necessary adaptations to suit local conditions. Over time, however, New Zealand's legal system began to evolve independently. For example,

52 Soofi, Ahmer Bilal, 2019, "Pakistan," in *The Oxford Handbook of International Law in Asia and the Pacific*, eds. Simon Chesterman, Hisashi Owada and Ben Saul, Oxford Handbooks. Online edition: Oxford Academic, 4 October 2019. Accessed 18 July 2024.

in areas such as mining law, New Zealand drew inspiration not only from English law but also from the Australian colony of Victoria. New Zealand courts increasingly consulted American case law as well, reflecting a broader comparative approach to legal development.

By the late 19th century, law reports from both England and the United States were widely available in New Zealand, contributing to the shaping of its Common Law tradition. The country also selectively adopted British legislation and statutes from other Commonwealth jurisdictions, including the Australian colonies of New South Wales, Victoria, South Australia, and Queensland.[53] Through this process, New Zealand developed a distinctive legal identity, rooted in English Common Law yet shaped by local experience and international influence.

2.3.2 Development of Common Law in New Zealand

In 1839, New South Wales expanded its jurisdiction to include New Zealand, marking the beginning of New Zealand's formal legal development under English law. The English Law Acts of 1858 and 1908 confirmed that the laws of England and Wales applied to New Zealand, with necessary adaptations to suit local conditions.[54] Over time, however, New Zealand's legal system began to diverge from that of England. Its legal framework drew influence from the Australian colony of Victoria, particularly in the field of mining law, and New Zealand courts increasingly referred to American legal authorities for guidance. This openness to external sources gave New Zealand a more eclectic legal identity than many other Commonwealth jurisdictions. By the late 19th century, both English and American law reports were readily available in New Zealand, fostering a distinctive blend of legal traditions. This adaptability allowed New Zealand to incorporate and modify laws from Britain and other Common Law jurisdictions, including the Australian colonies. As a result, New Zealand gradually developed a more independent jurisprudence, increasingly shaped by local realities and judicial innovation.

These subsections illustrate how Australia and New Zealand, while grounded in English Common Law, each developed unique legal systems that reflect local needs, external influences, and the capacity of Common Law to evolve across different societies. They also show that legal transplantation is rarely a passive process: when introduced into new environments, Common Law principles adapt, transform, and generate new traditions that may differ significantly from their English origins.

2.4 Hong Kong: A Distinctive Model of Common Law in Southeast Asia

Hong Kong represents a distinctive example of a Common Law system operating within an Asian context. Its legal structure combines traditional English Common Law principles with local adaptations, producing a hybrid framework that reflects both its colonial history and its modern constitutional status. This section examines the legal foundations and constitutional framework of Hong Kong, followed by an analysis of its judicial system and principal sources of law. Through this exploration, it becomes clear how Hong Kong has maintained the core features of the Common Law tradition – such as judicial independence, the Rule of Law, and reliance on precedent – while adapting to its unique political and cultural environment.[55]

53 See Carvan, John, 2010, *Understanding the Australian Legal System*, 6th ed., Law Book Company, Sydney.

54 See also Hinchy, Ron, 2008, *The Australian Legal System*, Pearson Education Australia, Frenchs Forest.

55 See Tai, Benny Y. T., 2011, "Hong Kong: Maintaining a Common Law Legal System in a Non-Western Culture," in *Law and Legal Institutions of Asia: Traditions, Adaptations and Innovations*, eds. Elizabeth A. Black and Gary F. Bell, Cambridge University Press, Cambridge, pp. 62–90.

2.4.1 Legal Foundations and Constitutional Framework of Hong Kong

After the transfer of sovereignty from the United Kingdom to China in 1997, Hong Kong adopted the *Basic Law of the Hong Kong Special Administrative Region (HKSAR)* as its constitutional framework. This document distinguishes Hong Kong's Common Law system from mainland China's Civil Law structure. Under the "One Country, Two Systems" principle, the Basic Law guarantees that Hong Kong will maintain its separate legal and judicial system until 2047 – 50 years after the end of British rule.[56] The Basic Law covers nearly all areas of governance except for foreign affairs and defense, which remain under the jurisdiction of the central government in Beijing. This arrangement preserves Hong Kong's Common Law heritage and ensures a high degree of autonomy in legal and administrative matters.[57]

Hong Kong's legal system remains firmly grounded in the English Common Law tradition. Judicial decisions of the higher courts serve as binding precedents, and under Article 84 of the Basic Law, Hong Kong courts may refer to judgments from other Common Law jurisdictions such as the United Kingdom, Australia, and Canada. The Court of Final Appeal, Hong Kong's highest court, is empowered to invite eminent judges from other Common Law systems to sit on particular cases, reinforcing the city's international legal character.

The sources of law in Hong Kong include the Basic Law, local statutes compiled in the *Laws of Hong Kong*, and judicial precedents. Other sources include treaties and agreements ratified by the legislature, as well as certain elements of Chinese customary law, particularly under section 13 of the *New Territories Ordinance*, which governs property and inheritance disputes in rural areas. Statutory instruments and regulations made by the Chief Executive in Council also form part of the legal framework, ensuring that legislative decisions are implemented effectively.

Overall, Hong Kong's system reflects a remarkable balance between continuity and adaptation – maintaining the integrity of Common Law principles within a unique constitutional arrangement under Chinese sovereignty.

2.4.2 Judicial System and Sources of Law in Hong Kong

Hong Kong's Common Law system remains dynamic and internationally oriented, combining decisions from its own superior courts with precedents from other Common Law jurisdictions, as permitted under Article 84 of the *Basic Law*. This article also allows the invitation of judges from other Common Law regions to sit on the Court of Final Appeal, underscoring the global and cooperative character of Hong Kong's Judiciary. Legal authority in Hong Kong derives from multiple sources: treaties and agreements approved by the Legislative Council, Chinese customary laws – particularly applicable in property and inheritance matters in the New Territories – and statutes compiled in the *Laws of Hong Kong*. The Chief Executive in Council is responsible for enforcing these laws and issuing regulations to ensure proper legislative implementation.

Together, these features illustrate how Hong Kong's legal system operates as a sophisticated and autonomous Common Law jurisdiction within China. It maintains the essential principles of the Common Law tradition – judicial independence, adherence to precedent, and rule-based governance – while functioning within the unique constitutional framework of "One Country, Two Systems."

56 Zhu, Han, 2019, "Beijing's 'Rule of Law' Strategy for Governing Hong Kong: Legalisation without Democratisation?," *China Perspectives*, 2019(1), pp. 23–33. Available at: https://chinaperspectives.revues.org/8686. Accessed 18 July 2024.

57 Zhu, *Beijing's 'Rule of Law' Strategy for Governing Hong Kong.*

2.5 Common Law in North America

The Common Law tradition has played a central role in shaping the legal systems of North America, especially in Canada and the United States. Both countries inherited English Common Law during the colonial period, yet each has adapted it to its own political, social, and constitutional context. Over time, these adaptations have produced two distinct yet related legal systems, each reflecting the principles of precedent, judicial reasoning, and the Rule of Law.

This section offers an overview of the development and practice of Common Law in Canada and the United States, tracing their historical evolution from English roots to modern constitutional democracies. It also highlights the unique characteristics that distinguish each system – such as Canada's bilingual and bijural legal framework and the United States' strong emphasis on judicial review and constitutional interpretation – illustrating how Common Law continues to evolve across different legal and cultural environments.

2.5.1 Overview of Canadian Common Law

In colonial Canada, the British Crown played a central role in establishing the country's legal framework. The *Royal Proclamation of 1763* sought to protect Indigenous territories while promoting the assimilation of the French population. However, British governance soon faced difficulties due to French resistance and growing tensions with the American colonies. James Murray became Canada's first Governor General in 1764, and the *Quebec Act of 1774* extended civil and religious rights to the French, marking a major step toward legal pluralism.[58]

The introduction of Common Law in Canada occurred gradually and varied by region, depending on when local assemblies were established by the British Parliament. Once a local legislature was created, British legislation ceased to apply automatically – except in areas related to sovereignty. For example, Nova Scotia and Newfoundland held their first assemblies in 1758 and 1833, respectively. In 1866, an imperial decree united Vancouver Island and British Columbia under English law, while the provinces of Manitoba, Saskatchewan, Alberta, the Northwest Territories, and Yukon adopted English law in 1870.[59]

Although British colonies in North America could modify aspects of Common Law and domestic legislation, certain imperial laws relating to sovereignty – such as maritime law and citizenship – remained beyond local authority. This principle of *parliamentary sovereignty* guaranteed the continued supremacy of English law across the colonies.

Today, Canada's legal system remains predominantly based on British Common Law, with the notable exception of Quebec, which applies a Civil Law system in private law matters. This coexistence of two legal traditions – Common Law and Civil Law – creates a bijural system that is unique within the Commonwealth and reflects Canada's complex historical and cultural evolution.[60]

2.5.2 The Common Law in the United States

The goal here is not to provide a full description of the American legal system but to explain how Common Law was transplanted and adapted in the United States, and to identify key principles of British Common Law that continue to shape American law today.

58 Oliver, Peter, Macklem, Patrick and Des Rosiers, Nathalie (eds.), 2017, *The Oxford Handbook of the Canadian Constitution*, Oxford Handbooks. Online edition: Oxford Academic, 6 November 2017. Accessed 17 July 2024.

59 Oliver, Macklem and Des Rosiers, *The Oxford Handbook of the Canadian Constitution*.

60 Oliver, Macklem and Des Rosiers, *The Oxford Handbook of the Canadian Constitution*.

Common Law in the United States evolved within a federal framework, combining both federal and state jurisdictions. This federal structure makes the system complex, as legislation and case law can differ significantly between states.[61] Such diversity raises the question of whether an "Anglo-American legal world" truly exists, given how differently the U.S. and the UK have developed.[62] Even terminology diverged: in the U.S., the "High Court" refers to the *Supreme Court*, while in England it denotes a *court of first instance*. Similarly, "judicial review" in the U.S. allows courts to strike down unconstitutional laws, whereas in England it refers to reviewing the legality of administrative actions.

Historically, English law was the foundation of legal development in the American colonies. Early colonial charters – such as those of Massachusetts Bay (1629), Connecticut (1632), and Carolina (1663) – required local laws to conform to English legal standards. The first English settlement was founded in 1607 at Jamestown, Virginia, and appeals from colonial courts could still be heard in England.

The movement toward independence began with the First Continental Congress (1774), which demanded that the *1689 Bill of Rights* apply in the colonies. The *U.S. Constitution of 1787* then established a government based on the sovereignty of the people, the social contract, and the protection of liberty, later reinforced by the *Bill of Rights* (1791). The Constitution introduced mechanisms to limit political power, including checks and balances, federalism, and judicial review. Landmark cases such as *Marbury v. Madison* (1803) and *Fletcher v. Peck* (1810) confirmed the Supreme Court's authority to invalidate unconstitutional legislation and to uphold the supremacy of the Constitution.

By the mid-19th century, the United States had also merged law and equity in many jurisdictions. New York led this reform under David Dudley Field, whose *Field Code of Civil Procedure* (1848) unified civil actions and abolished the strict division between law and equity. Some states, however, still maintain separate courts for these branches.

The U.S. legal system also diverged institutionally from the English model. Judges in the United States are often elected and may be subject to re-election, making them more politically accountable than their English counterparts, who are appointed from experienced barristers. Furthermore, American judges generally come from broader academic backgrounds rather than long-standing courtroom practice.

To promote greater uniformity across states, organizations such as the National Conference of Commissioners on Uniform State Laws (NCCUSL) and the American Law Institute (ALI) were established. The ALI's *Restatements of the Law* have played a key role in clarifying and harmonizing U.S. law. These Restatements compile legal principles and judicial precedents to summarize the Common Law in various fields, including agency, contracts, property, torts, trusts, restitution, judgments, and conflict of laws. The Restatements do not create law but serve as authoritative references that guide courts, scholars, and practitioners, illustrating how the U.S. continues to uphold the spirit of the Common Law through interpretation, adaptation, and innovation.[63]

61 See Calvi, James V. and Coleman, Susan, 2017, *American Law and Legal Systems*, 8th ed., Routledge.

62 See de Cruz, *Comparative Law in a Changing World.*

63 The way a group of Restaters works is under the supervision of a prominent scholar in the field of expertise. The Restaters select a legal principle or rule on a question of law that is uncertain, which, according to them, reflects the Common Law tradition on that particular issue. Restatement is a codification process, but the codes do not have the same legal force as those in Europe because they are not a mere collection of statutes; instead, they represent the opinion of the leading American scholars and have a great influence and authority. This is why there are plenty of American codes, and these are not a binding source of law, but a source of legal reference. Restatements aim at clarifying and consolidating the law. They are useful guides to the law, in particular for foreign lawyers, but there is no guarantee that what is said in the Restatement actually governs a particular area of law.

Conclusion

In conclusion, the essence of Common Law can only be fully understood through its historical and linguistic roots in England. It is not merely a collection of legal rules but a living legal tradition that reflects the history and culture of the English-speaking world. The constant interaction between precedent, judicial reasoning, and social change allows Common Law to remain relevant and effective in delivering justice around the world.

The integration of Common Law into different legal and cultural contexts – such as its combination with Islamic law in Pakistan or its coexistence with Civil Law in Canada – illustrates its adaptability. Similarly, Hong Kong's Common Law system under the "One Country, Two Systems" principle shows its ability to function within a distinct constitutional framework.

Overall, the global spread of Common Law demonstrates its flexibility and resilience. Adapted to diverse societies while maintaining its core principles of justice and fairness, Common Law continues to evolve as one of the world's most dynamic and influential legal traditions.

Selected Bibliography

Calvi, J. V., & Coleman, S., 2017, *American Law and Legal Systems* (8th ed.), Routledge, 430 pages.

Elliott, Mark, & Hughes, Kirsty, 2023, *Common Law Constitutional Rights* (1st ed.), Bloomsbury Publishing, Paperback, 352 pages.

Finch, Emily, & Fafinski, Stefan, 2021, *Legal Skills* (8th ed.), Oxford University Press, 528 pages.

Gillespie, Alisdair, & Weare, Siobhan, 2023, *The English Legal System* (9th ed.), Oxford University Press, 784 pages.

Hudson, John, 2017, *The Formation of the English Common Law: Law and Society in England from King Alfred to Magna Carta* (2nd ed.), Routledge, 252 pages.

Klonoff, Robert H., 2020, *Introduction to the Study of U.S. Law*, West Academic Press, Paperback, 788 pages.

Reimann, Mathias, & Zimmermann, Reinhard, 2008, *The Oxford Handbook of Comparative Law*, Oxford University Press, 1456 pages.

Rutherford, Helen, Kotecha, Birju, & Macfarlane, Angela, 2024, *English Legal System* (6th ed.), Oxford University Press, 760 pages.

Salomone, Rosemary, 2024, *The Rise of English: Global Politics and the Power of Language*, Oxford University Press, 504 pages.

Samuel, Geoffrey, 2014, *A Short Introduction to the Common Law*, Edward Elgar Publishing, 208 pages.

Thomas, Mark, & McGourlay, Claire, 2020, *English Legal System Concentrate: Law Revision and Study Guide* (2nd ed.), Oxford University Press, 304 pages.

Thomson, Stephen, Groves, Matthew, & Weeks, Greg, 2024, *Administrative Tribunals in the Common Law World* (1st ed.), Bloomsbury Publishing, 480 pages.

Zweigert, Konrad, & Kötz, Hein, 2011, *An Introduction to Comparative Law* (3rd ed.), Clarendon Press Oxford, 742 pages.

Part Two

Courts, Constitutions, and Legal Borrowing

5 Constitutionalism and Judicial Review

I do solemnly swear that I will faithfully execute the Office of President of the United States, and will to the best of my ability, preserve, protect and defend the Constitution of the United States.
Oath of Office of the U.S. President
(U.S. Const., Art. II, §1, cl. 8)

An Act voted by Parliament reflects the general will insofar as it respects the Constitution.
Declaration of the French Constitutional Council in the
New Caledonia Act case of August 23, 1985

Constitutionalism lies at the root of modern democracy and is inseparable from politics. Human beings have always lived in groups. Over time, these groups evolved into societies, which in turn established authority and power. Such power was institutionalized within the State, an entity that required the consent of the people. This consent gradually became explicit and subject to periodic renewal. In essence, this is how modern democracy emerged: it presupposes the creation of the State and the establishment of a government – both prerequisites to democracy – as well as the adoption of a constitution that provides its foundation.

A constitution is, by nature, a constituting norm, as the term itself suggests. The word *constitution* derives from the Latin expression *cum status*, meaning "to set, found, or establish something together." Because it constitutes society, the constitution encompasses several dimensions – political, legal, social, and economic.

Günter Frankenberg – a German legal scholar particularly known for his work on comparative constitutionalism, constitutional theory, and critical legal studies – describes a constitution as "law, instrument, and culture." He emphasizes that constitutions are texts deeply embedded in their specific contexts:

> Constitution – like "Nation", "State", "Democracy" and "Sovereignty" – appears as one of the central icons and also one of the most ambiguous ideological structures in the pool of cultural representations of modernity. Constitutions react to the individual and societal need for orientation by offering a language of rights and values, and to the requirement of authoritative decisions by allocating and balancing power within an institutional arrangement. Hence, constitutions are not cages of norms but texts situated in contested fields of ideas and interests, traversed by competing interpretations.[1]

1 Frankenberg, Günter, 2012, "Comparative Constitutional Law," in *The Cambridge Companion to Comparative Law*, eds. Mauro Bussani and Ugo Mattei, Cambridge University Press, Cambridge.

DOI: 10.4324/9781003393047-8

A constitution stands at the intersection of political and legal systems: it both reflects and creates them. Accordingly, this chapter focuses on the legal and political dimensions of constitutions. It explores what a constitution is and its purpose in establishing the foundation of the State, government, and administration. It examines the legal and political definitions of constitutions and the ways they organize, distribute, and limit political power while safeguarding fundamental rights.

This chapter is divided into five main sections, each exploring a central dimension of constitutionalism and its role in shaping modern democracies.

The first section, "What Is a Constitution? What Is It For?," introduces the concept and purpose of constitutions. It explains how a constitution forms the legal and political foundation of the State, the government, and the Administration. This section also clarifies the distinction between legal and political definitions of the constitution, and shows how constitutions distribute, limit, and legitimize political power while ensuring the protection of fundamental rights.

The second section, "Constitutional Supremacy," traces the historical and philosophical roots of the idea that the constitution stands above all other laws. It explores early examples in France and the United States, the influence of natural law and equity, and the emergence of judicial review. Different models of constitutional control – American, British, French, and others – are compared, along with methods of constitutional amendment and contemporary global developments.

The third section, "Compatibility of Judicial Review with Democratic Principles," addresses a long-standing question: can unelected judges legitimately overrule the decisions of elected representatives? This part reviews historical controversies, lessons from totalitarian regimes, and modern perspectives that see judicial review not as a threat to democracy but as one of its essential safeguards.

The fourth section, "The Rule of Law," examines one of the cornerstones of constitutionalism. It explains the difference between formal and substantive conceptions of the Rule of Law, traces its historical development, and identifies its key features – legality, equality before the law, and judicial independence. The section also compares how the Rule of Law operates in various legal traditions around the world, from Canada to Germany, South Africa, China, and Saudi Arabia.

The fifth and final section, "The New Constitutional World Order," looks at the rise of global constitutionalism in the 21st century. It explores how constitutional ideas now extend beyond national borders through International Law, digital governance, and transnational institutions. The section concludes by weighing the advantages and limitations of this emerging global order and its implications for the future of democracy and sovereignty.

1 What Is a Constitution? What Is It For?

Our goal here is to identify the most important and current aspects of the notion of constitution, as an introduction to Constitutional Law. Throughout this chapter, we will approach the subject from a global, transnational, and comparative perspective, highlighting some of the most fascinating and essential themes of modern constitutionalism. These include the complexity of the notion itself, reflected in the diversity of its definitions; the challenge of maintaining constitutional supremacy over all other norms; the variety of judicial review models developed around the world; and, finally, contemporary debates such as popular constitutionalism and global constitutionalism, which illustrate how the idea of the constitution continues to evolve in today's interconnected world.

1.1 The Foundation of the State, the Government, and the Administration

There are two main ways to define a constitution: a legal definition and a political one. The legal definition stems directly from the definition of the State – it views the constitution as the supreme legal framework that organizes public powers and sets the rules governing their relations. The political definition, on the other hand, is rooted in the idea that all human beings are born equal in rights and seek to preserve those rights and their freedom by living together in an organized society.

1.1.1 Legal Definition

To understand the constitution from a legal standpoint, it is the founding instrument that gives the State its existence, structure, and authority – the State's bylaw.

Following Hans Kelsen's theory, scholars distinguish between the material constitution (rules organizing power) and the formal constitution (rules contained in the constitutional text and amendable by special procedures).

1.1.1.1 THE CONSTITUTION AS THE STATE'S BYLAW

The State is an "institutionalized power," wrote the French scholar Georges Burdeau (1905–1988).[2] For a State to exist, it needs a constitution. The State also depends on the consent of the people it governs, as Guillaume Tusseau, professor of Public Law at Sciences Po and member of the *Institut Universitaire de France*, explains.[3]

In law, there are two kinds of persons: physical persons, like you or the authors of this book, and artificial persons, which exist only legally. For example, an international organization can have employees, offices, and a budget, but it is not a real person – you can meet its president, but not the organization itself. You might one day shake the hand of its president, but you will never meet or shake the hand of the organization itself because it is not, physically speaking, a person. Because it is an abstract person that does not exist physically.

The same is true for the State. It is an artificial person that holds political power to organize and manage society. This artificial person exists because of a legal document: the constitution. The constitution is the State's statute – just as by-laws define how a company operates. It sets out how the State, the government, and public institutions are organized and how they function.

The constitution also defines how the country is structured – whether it is unitary, federal, or regional – depending on its history, geography, and politics. Finally, many constitutions also include fundamental rights and principles that go beyond the organization of government.

1.1.1.2 MATERIAL VS. FORMAL CONSTITUTION

This legal definition, which is quite broad, must be refined by a distinction made by most European constitutional scholars between the *material* and the *formal* constitution, a distinction that originates in Hans Kelsen's *Pure Theory of Law*. The *material constitution* refers to the set of rules that govern how political power is distributed and exercised. The *formal constitution*, by contrast, includes all the rules contained in the constitutional document itself, whatever their subject matter, and can only be changed through a special amendment procedure.

2 Burdeau, George, 1980, *Traité de Science Politique*, vol. II.

3 Tusseau, Guillaume, 2022, *Droit constitutionnel et institutions politiques*, 6e éd., Seuil, p. 50.

The two notions overlap but are not identical. The *formal constitution* may include provisions unrelated to the organization of power – for example, Article 2 of the French Constitution declares that "the language of the Republic is French," which has little to do with the exercise of political authority. Conversely, an important rule of the *material constitution* may not appear in the formal text – for instance, in France, the electoral system for parliamentary elections is defined by ordinary law, not by the Constitution. Similarly, the Constitution of Japan includes in its formal text a rule declaring that the national flag and anthem are symbols of the State – this has little to do with how political power is exercised. Conversely, in the United States, the organization of political parties plays a key role in the functioning of government, yet it is not mentioned in the Constitution at all.

This distinction should not be confused with the difference between *written* and *unwritten* constitutions. A written constitution, like that of France or Japan, is a single codified text. An unwritten constitution, like that of the United Kingdom, is not contained in one document but is formed by statutes, conventions, and judicial decisions. Both may include *material* and *formal* aspects.

Understanding these distinctions is crucial: the *material constitution* reveals how power truly operates within a political system, while the *formal constitution* defines the legally binding framework. In the end, the legal definition of a constitution remains neutral: a totalitarian state may have a written constitution, while a democratic state may not. For instance, the USSR had a written constitution, whereas the United Kingdom does not.

1.1.2 Political Definition

A constitution may be described as a form of creation from nothing, where a people brings itself into existence by adopting a constitution, while already assumed to have the authority to do so.

Hence, the almost mystical foundation of constitutional authority, as Jacques Derrida (1930–2004), the French philosopher and founder of deconstruction, observed – rooted in the self-empowerment of the people or the nation – "We the People."[4]

Constitutions are not like ordinary laws or statutes. They are not simply adopted by parliaments; they are proclaimed or solemnly declared, often as sacred texts. In many cases, the founding document invokes divine providence to lend it higher legitimacy and symbolic authority among the hierarchy of norms.

Comparative Constitutional Law shows that "the people" are first elevated as sovereign and then gradually reduced or fragmented through systems of representation, delegation, and the transfer of power from the collective body of citizens to public authorities.

To go beyond a purely formal or positivist view of constitutions, it is useful to consider their relationship with culture. Some comparatists argue that constitutions not only regulate institutions but also reflect and shape a nation's social practices, values, and even its everyday language and literature.[5]

The political definition of a constitution is more substantive than the legal one: it carries content and emphasizes the need to guarantee fundamental rights. It derives from the idea that the

4 Derrida, Jacques, 1990, "Force of the Law: The Mystical Foundation of Authority," *Cardozo Law Review*, vol. 11, p. 919.

5 For example, M. Meltzer analyzes the influence of a Constitution on culture in Secular revelations. See Meltzer, Milton, 2005, *Secular Revelations: The US Constitution and Classical American Literature*, Harvard University Press, Cambridge, MA.

purpose of politics is to preserve human freedom and equality. From this perspective, *the people* are the source of all political power, and all political power must serve to protect everyone's rights. A constitution, in this sense, can only be democratic – because authority comes from the people, not from God – and liberal, because it limits power through a balance of powers and the protection of fundamental rights.

This vision is reflected in the *Declaration of the Rights of Man and of the Citizen* of 1789, which became part of the French Constitution in 1971, when the Constitutional Council incorporated it into the *bloc de constitutionnalité*[6] (constitutionality bloc, Freedom of Association decision, 1971). The Declaration proclaims that "the principle of all sovereignty resides essentially in the nation" (Article 3) and that "a society in which the observance of the law is not assured, nor the separation of powers defined, has no constitution at all" (Article 16).

A constitution also provides an ideological framework that influences culture and identity. The constitutions of Brazil and India, for example, illustrate how legal texts can embody social ideals and aspirations. As Günter Frankenberg writes:

> Whether and to what extent constitutions are integrated in the symbolic everyday depends on their popular appeal, readability and age. Whether or not they capture the people's utopian fancy and the popular desire for authoritative higher-law settlement, unification and orientation remain open questions. Liberal constitutions (United States, France, Germany, or India) usually keep aloof from notions of community and solidarity and make do, in passing, with a generalized "People" or the abstract "Nation", "Union" or "State". By way of contrast, socialist constitutions recast the atomized society of individuals or groups as the "people of all nationalities" or the "alliance of workers and peasants" (China, Vietnam) or "working people" (North Korea). Constitutions of recently united countries tend to imagine the end of ethnic diversity (Weimar Constitution 1919) and a unity above the fractured society of groups or regions as a "democratic society" (Angola 1992, Namibia 1990), or "civil society" (Afghanistan 2004).[7]

As such, constitutions can be "good" or "bad." Democratic constitutions guarantee human rights and limit power; non-democratic ones may merely disguise authoritarianism. Here lies the difference between legality and legitimacy. From a purely legal standpoint, jurists can only acknowledge the existence of any document called a "constitution" regardless of its content. But from a normative or democratic perspective, constitutionalists must challenge so-called constitutions that fail to respect fundamental rights or popular sovereignty.

Alexis de Tocqueville distinguished between two types of constitutions in France: the *political constitution* and the *administrative constitution.* He observed that France survived thanks more to its administrative constitution than to its political one. History proved him right. After the Revolution of 1789, France experienced a series of unstable political constitutions – monarchist, republican, imperial – until the Third Republic stabilized the republican form of government in the 1870s. Even then, it was not until 1958 and the establishment of the Fifth

6 The "constitutionality bloc" refers to the set of constitutional norms that the constitutional court takes into account to examine the constitutionality of statutes. It includes, in particular, the Constitutional text of 1958, the Declaration of the Man and of the Citizen of 1789, the preamble of the Constitution of 1946, and the Charter on the Environment of 2004.

7 Frankenberg, Günter, 2006, "Comparing Constitutions: Ideas, Ideals, and Ideology – Toward a Layered Narrative," *International Journal of Constitutional Law*, vol. 4, no. 3, pp. 439–459.

Republic that France achieved a lasting political regime. Throughout this period, it was the administration and the bureaucracy that ensured continuity of the State and public services despite frequent governmental change.

Thus, the first function of a constitution is to establish the foundation of the State, the government, and the Administration. But it also defines how political power is distributed and limited, ensuring a balance among the branches of government.

1.2 The Constitution Regulates the Allocation, Removal, and Distribution of Political Power

By establishing rules that determine how political power is obtained, exercised, and removed, a constitution provides the legal framework for government and leadership. These rules naturally limit power. When they also define fundamental human rights and are enforced through an independent and impartial system of judicial review, the constitution becomes a true safeguard of those rights. In most systems, this protection is achieved through a balance of powers, which ensures that each branch of the State is limited by the others. Writing fundamental rights into a solemn document and entrusting judges to uphold it helps guarantee that these rights are respected and effectively applied.

1.2.1 Balance of Power

Modern constitutions generally establish three main branches of the State – the Executive, the Legislative, and the judicial – forming what is often called the "trilogy of powers." Constitutional Law then organizes their relationships through the model of the balance of powers, a framework first developed by Montesquieu.

As Montesquieu wrote:

> Political liberty is to be found only in moderate governments; and even in these it is not always found. It exists only when there is no abuse of power. But constant experience shows us that every man invested with power is apt to abuse it, and to carry his authority as far as it will go. Is it not strange, though true, to say that virtue itself has need of limits? To prevent this abuse, it is necessary from the very nature of things that power should be a check to power.[8]

This idea reflects a fundamental political truth later captured by Lord Acton:[9] "Power tends to corrupt, and absolute power corrupts absolutely."[10]

Accordingly, Montesquieu identified three essential functions of government: making laws, enforcing them, and settling disputes. Each function corresponds to one of the three branches of the State. In his model, every branch has the means to limit or "check" the others, ensuring that no single branch dominates. The system is therefore dynamic – each power acts only through interaction with the others, and this interaction maintains equilibrium.

8 Montesquieu, 1748, *The Spirit of Laws*, Book XI, *Of the Laws which establish Political Liberty, with regard to the Constitution.*

9 Lord Acton (1834–1902) was an English historian, Liberal politician, and advocate of individual liberty, best known for his famous warning about the corrupting nature of absolute power.

10 Acton, John Emerich Edward Dalberg (Lord Acton), 1907, "Letter to Bishop Mandell Creighton (April 5, 1887)," in *Historical Essays and Studies*, eds. J. N. Figgis and R. V. Laurence, Macmillan, London.

Most modern democratic constitutions are built on this model of separation and balance of powers. Yet, some scholars question whether this American-inspired model of checks and balances can be effectively applied to supranational organizations, such as the European Union. As discussed in Chapter 11 (*Supranationalism: The European Institution*), the structure of the European institutions follows a unique and complex organization that departs from the traditional Executive–Legislative–judicial scheme.[11]

1.2.2 Protection of Fundamental Rights

Another important way a constitution ensures the protection of human rights is by writing those rights down and incorporating them into a constitutional document. The very act of setting out fundamental rights and duties in writing helps to limit arbitrariness and informal practices that could lead to abuses of power. A written constitution becomes a reference point known to all: citizens can invoke it, and authorities are bound by it. Any violation of its provisions is, therefore, regarded as a breach of the constitution itself.

Until the 18th century, most political organizations – kingdoms, empires, or city-states – were governed by customary constitutional rules rather than written texts. For example, the *Salic Law* of succession, which excluded women from inheriting the French throne, began as an unwritten custom among the Salii, the dominant Frankish tribe, before later being written in Latin. Such customs provided continuity but also left considerable room for interpretation and arbitrariness.

The first written constitutions appeared in the late 18th century, notably the Constitution of Virginia in 1776. This innovation was revolutionary, as it represented a deliberate effort to fix in writing the organization of public powers and the fundamental rights of citizens. Traditionalist thinkers such as Bonald and Joseph de Maistre sharply criticized these developments, arguing that societies should rest on divine and historical foundations rather than human reason or individual consent.

Today, most states have written constitutions, yet there are exceptions. The United Kingdom remains the leading example of a State with an unwritten constitution, or more precisely, a constitution composed of statutes (such as the *Magna Carta*, *Bill of Rights* of 1689, and *Parliament Acts*), judicial precedents, and long-standing conventions. Unlike countries such as France or Germany, where constitutions were often adopted in the wake of revolutions, Britain developed its constitutional order gradually. Its democracy evolved through incremental legal reforms, without the violent political breaks that characterized continental Europe.[12]

By contrast, in younger nations such as the United States, Canada, or Australia, adopting a written constitution was a foundational act of independence. It was a way of affirming sovereignty, defining citizenship, and guaranteeing fundamental rights. The U.S. Constitution of 1787 and the *Bill of Rights* of 1791 became models for constitutional drafting worldwide.

The length and detail of constitutions vary according to each country's history and context. For instance, the South African Constitution of 1996, which spans around 150 pages, reflects a deliberate effort to ensure a comprehensive protection of rights in a nation emerging from

11 Calabresi, Steven G. and Bady, Kevin, 2010, "Is the Separation of Powers Exportable?," *Harvard Journal of Law and Public Policy*, vol. 33, no. 1.

12 Some of the key dates and texts in the United Kingdom's unwritten Constitution are, for example, 1215, the signature of the Magna Carta by King John, which limits the power of the Sovereign; 1689, the Bill of rights; 1707, the Acts of Union of England and Scotland; 1832, the Reform Act which has given the right to vote to the middle classes; 1973, the European Economic Community membership; and 1998, the Human Rights Act.

apartheid. In contrast, the United States Constitution is remarkably brief, relying on interpretation and judicial precedent to adapt over time.

This historical shift from unwritten to written constitutions can be largely attributed to the influence of Enlightenment political philosophy, which emphasized reason, equality, and individual rights as the foundation of legitimate government.[13] The American (1787) and French (1789) revolutions marked turning points in this evolution. The U.S. Constitution and the *French Declaration of the Rights of Man and of the Citizen* both sought to anchor political power in law, not tradition, and to guarantee that governments exist to serve the people, not rule over them.

1.2.3 Judicial Review Preserves the Balance of Powers and Protects Fundamental Rights

As we will see in section 2, which addresses the fundamental question of constitutional supremacy, there must be a form of legal control to ensure that constitutional rules are respected. This control is known as judicial review. It serves a dual function: first, to preserve the balance of powers by preventing any branch of government – Executive, Legislative, or Judicial – from exceeding its authority; and second, to protect fundamental rights by allowing the courts, often the Supreme Court, to strike down any laws or practices that violate constitutional provisions.

This mechanism ensures that the constitution remains the supreme law of the land and that all public authorities remain accountable to it. Judicial review enables judges to assess whether the acts of the legislature and the Executive comply with constitutional norms. For instance, in the landmark American case *Marbury v. Madison* (1803), the U.S. Supreme Court established the principle that "a law repugnant to the Constitution is void." This decision set a precedent for courts to invalidate laws contrary to the Constitution.

Similarly, in *Kesavananda Bharati v. State of Kerala* (1973), the Supreme Court of India held that parliament could not alter the "basic structure" of the Constitution, even through constitutional amendments. In Europe, the German Federal Constitutional Court and the French Constitutional Council perform comparable roles in ensuring that legislation conforms to constitutional principles, particularly the protection of fundamental rights.

Thus, judicial review stands as a cornerstone of constitutionalism: it guarantees the supremacy of the constitution, upholds the Separation of Powers, and safeguards citizens against abuses of authority.

2 Constitutional Supremacy

This section examines the principle of constitutional supremacy, which holds that the constitution is the highest source of law and authority within a State. It begins by tracing the intellectual and historical origins of this idea, from the early notion of the supremacy of natural law to the first examples of constitutional supremacy in France under the Ancien Régime. It then turns to

13 See, for instance, Rousseau's constitutional project for Corsica: "You ask for a plan of government suitable for Corsica. It is asking for more than you think. There are peoples who, do what you may, are incapable of being well governed, for the law has no hold over them, and a government without laws cannot be a good government. I do not say that the Corsican people is in that condition; on the contrary, no people impresses me as being so fortunately disposed by nature to receive a good administration. But even this is not enough, for all things lead to abuses, which are often inevitable; and the abuse of political institutions follows so closely upon their establishment that it is hardly worth while to set them up, only to see them degenerate so rapidly." Bacot, Guillaume, 2002, "Jean-Jacques Rousseau et la procédure législative," *Revue française d'histoire des idées politiques*, no. 15, pp. 45–61.

the evolution of this concept in the Common Law world, with the rise of equity over Common Law and the debates surrounding the Stamp Act of 1765.

A key part of the discussion focuses on the landmark American case *Marbury v. Madison* (1803), which established judicial review as a means of enforcing constitutional supremacy. The section also presents the European perspective through Hans Kelsen's theory of the hierarchy of norms, as well as non-Western approaches that have reinterpreted or challenged the Western model of constitutional supremacy.

We will then compare different systems of judicial review – the American, British, and French models – and examine how these have spread and evolved globally. The discussion includes the role of judicial review in the protection of individual rights, illustrated through the example of abortion. Finally, the section explores constitutional amendment procedures in various countries, including the United States, France, China, and several African and Arab states, showing how the process of constitutional change reflects each nation's political and legal culture.

2.1 Intellectual Roots of Constitutional Supremacy

The idea that some categories of norms stand above others is ancient. Classic examples of normative supremacy can be found in the concept of natural law developed by the Greeks, the fundamental laws of the realm formulated in parts of the Civil Law world, such as France in the 16th century, and the concept of equity in the Common Law tradition. Building on this long intellectual heritage, Hans Kelsen, in the early 20th century, developed his theory of the basic norm (Grundnorm), which organizes the legal system as a hierarchy of norms, with the constitution placed at the top of this normative pyramid.

2.1.1 Supremacy of Natural Law

The historical development of the concept of natural law reveals how the idea emerged that some rules possess greater authority than others and that human law must align with universal principles of justice. In one of Sophocles' tragedies (written around 441 BC), Antigone argues that natural law is superior to state law because it is rooted in human nature.[14] This is the most well-known starting point of the idea that some norms are higher than others.

This play tells the story of Antigone and Ismene, the sisters of two brothers who died fighting each other for the throne and leading opposite sides in the civil war of Thebes: Eteocles and Polyneices. The new ruler of Thebes, Creon, rules that Eteocles will be honored and his body buried in accordance with the holy rites, whereas Polyneices' body will lie unburied on the battlefield in public shame. But Antigone, who wants to bury Polyneices' body, decides to challenge Creon's edict, whereas her sister, Ismene, refuses to help her because she fears the death penalty. As in most Greek tragedies, the synopsis is inextricable. The edict Creon valued so much will remain in vigor, but because he has acted against the gods as Tiresias, the blind prophet told him, he will lose his child Haemon (who is engaged to Antigone) and his wife (Eurydice, Haemon's mother) will die. What Creon has done was improper, and he has upset the gods by keeping a living body underneath the earth – Antigone's body – (Antigone will die by hanging herself and Haemon – Creon's son – by stabbing himself after discovering the body of her fiancée) and leaving the dead body of Polyneices unburied. Keeping a living body

14 Staehler, Tanja, 2007, "Antigone and the Nature of Law," in *Law and Philosophy*, eds. Michael Freeman and Ross Harrison, *Current Legal Issues*, Oxford University Press, Oxford.

underneath the earth or leaving a dead body unburied is contrary to natural law, according to Tiresias and Antigone.

Natural law shows the importance of having higher norms containing higher rules, standards, or values to make sure that all other existing norms in the legal order will comply with the values regarded as fundamental for the survival of society and human dignity (for example, the right to life or the natural right to bury a dead body). But the idea of a hierarchy of norms also has practical aspects, besides morality. Indeed, why would norms be displayed in such a fashion? Why would they need to be ordered, ranked as if they were steps on a ladder?

Another reason to explain why some norms may be regarded as more important is the necessity to maintain order. Hence, the relationship between the hierarchy of norms and the concept of sovereignty. It is common sense that the sovereign, the chief, the ruler's orders must be applied. This is a matter of authority or pure legality. But legitimacy requires that the sovereign's orders comply with natural law and moral principles. Here, again, the distinction between legality and legitimacy is most important. The key idea is that the more the author of the norm is important in terms of sovereignty, the higher its norms will be ranked in the hierarchy. And constitutional supremacy derives from this central idea. The constitution is the primary norm, which is both the statute of the State and the people, i.e., the most important institution and the source of all power in a democracy. Constitutional supremacy is thus closely related to constitutional democracy. Non-democratic governments – such as the People's Republic of China in 1949 when the new Constitution was adopted – give more importance to the ideology of the party and to its leaders than to the constitution itself, no matter what its content may be.

The establishment of supreme judicial bodies to check the constitutionality and legality of norms is not a discovery of modern states. The law of ancient Greece actually distinguished the *nomos* (which could be in some sense compared to current constitutional laws) and the *psephisma* (what would be called at our time regulations).[15] The Greeks introduced the fundamental idea and principle that regulations (psephisma), regardless of their content, should not be in contradiction with the *nomos* either in form or in content. The adoption of an "unconstitutional" *psephisma* had two consequences: first, the member of the legislature who proposed an unconstitutional regulation was criminally responsible; secondly, the *psephisma* that was contrary to the nomos was considered invalid. In their decisions, Athenian judges, although bound by laws and regulations, were not required to apply the regulations if those were inconsistent with the "constitutional" laws.

2.1.2 Early Examples of Constitutional Supremacy in France

During the Middle Ages, the King of France was considered the source of all justice. However, certain norms were recognized as superior to all others and were known as the *fundamental laws of the realm*.[16] These were, in effect, constitutional rules, even though the term was not yet used. They consisted of customary principles that developed gradually over time and defined the status of the crown and the royal domain. Far from being abstract notions, these principles emerged from political practice, dynastic crises, and doctrinal reflections that progressively shaped the constitutional identity of the French monarchy.

15 Harris, Edward M. and Canevaro, Mirko (eds.), 2015, *The Oxford Handbook of Ancient Greek Law*, online ed., Oxford Academic. https://doi.org/10.1093/oxfordhb/9780199599257.001.0001. Accessed 19 July 2024.

16 Carbasse, Jean-Marie, 2024, *Manuel d'introduction historique au droit*, 10e éd., Presses Universitaires de France.

Jurists and political thinkers of the period regarded these fundamental laws as higher than ordinary laws, and even the King was bound by them. If the King violated these norms, his rule would no longer be legitimate and would be considered tyrannical. This idea reflected a medieval conception of sovereignty in which the monarch, although powerful, remained the guardian rather than the owner of the kingdom. Any departure from these superior norms was seen as a breach of the very foundations of royal authority, opening the way to doctrinal resistance and theoretical limitations on absolutism.

Among the main fundamental laws were the inalienability of the royal domain, meaning that the national territory could not be given away or sold, and the principle of male succession, also known as the Salic Law, which excluded women from inheriting the crown. Thinkers such as Jacques-Bénigne Bossuet and Jean Bodin, though defenders of royal absolutism, agreed that these principles stood above the authority of the monarch. They considered them to be part of an untouchable constitutional order, the continuity of which guaranteed the stability of the State. Thus, even the most ardent theorists of monarchical power recognized the existence of limits that the King could not transgress without undermining the legitimacy of his own rule.

Institutions also existed to ensure respect for these higher norms. The sovereign courts and the parliaments played a key role by verifying that the King's acts complied with the fundamental laws, thus exercising an early form of constitutional control within the French monarchy. Through mechanisms such as remonstrances and the requirement of registering royal edicts, these bodies acted as guardians of the legal order, ensuring that royal power remained consistent with the long-established traditions of the realm. Their interventions prefigured, in embryonic form, the later emergence of constitutional review in modern states.

2.1.3 The Supremacy of Equity Over the Common Law

Another example of the intellectual roots of constitutional supremacy, and of the idea of a hierarchy of norms, is the concept of Equity, already discussed in Chapter 4, in relation to the Common Law. Equity developed as a distinct set of principles designed to remedy the rigidity and shortcomings of the Common Law. When the King's subjects were unable to obtain justice before the royal courts, they appealed directly to the King, who decided their cases according to conscience and fairness. This recourse to the sovereign reflected the belief that justice could not be reduced to the mechanical application of rules and that a higher standard of moral reasoning had to guide the legal order.

Over time, these royal interventions gave rise to a body of equitable principles, administered by the Court of Chancery, which provided new rights and remedies. However, as both systems evolved, Common Law and equity often came into conflict because they operated in parallel and sometimes produced inconsistent outcomes. Such contradictions highlighted the need for a coherent hierarchy within the legal system and revealed the limits of a purely pluralistic judicial structure.

This tension led to the historic decision of King James I in 1615, in the Earl of Oxford's Case, where it was declared that "when Common Law and equity conflict, equity shall prevail." This decision clearly established a hierarchy of norms within the English legal system: principles of fairness and natural justice were deemed superior to the strict rules of Common Law. In other words, even when a case had been decided according to Common Law, the Court of Chancery could intervene and overrule the decision to achieve a just outcome. By asserting the primacy of equitable principles, the ruling introduced a form of substantive justice capable of correcting the formalism of the Common Law. Equity thus became an early expression of the idea that higher norms, founded on justice and morality, take precedence over purely technical legal rules. In this respect, the development of equity foreshadowed modern constitutional theories that distinguish between ordinary legislation and superior principles designed to safeguard fundamental values within the legal system.

2.1.4 The Stamp Act of 1765

At the heart of the tensions between the American colonists and the British Government lay a deep conflict over taxation. The inhabitants of the 13 colonies had no direct representatives in the British Parliament, which meant that the British Government could impose taxes on them without their consent. Lacking any formal mechanism to challenge these taxes, many colonists feared that parliament could arbitrarily deprive them of their property through excessive taxation. In response, they adopted the famous slogan "No taxation without representation."

Following the costly Seven Years' War, Britain emerged victorious but heavily indebted. To replenish its treasury, and unwilling to raise taxes further at home, the British Government turned to its North American colonies as a new source of revenue. After the passage of the 1764 Sugar Act, Parliament introduced a new tax on printed materials – the Stamp Act, passed on March 22, 1765, and scheduled to take effect on November 1. The tax, commonly used in Britain, required that all legal documents, newspapers, and other paper goods bear an official stamp showing that the tax had been paid.

Despite attempts by colonial representatives, including Benjamin Franklin, to propose alternative forms of taxation, Parliament refused to compromise. The colonies reacted with growing anger, particularly because the Stamp Act imposed an internal tax – that is, one levied directly within the colonies – and authorized admiralty courts, bypassing local juries, to judge offenders. To many colonists, this represented an encroachment on their rights as English citizens and on the authority of their own colonial assemblies.

Protests quickly spread across the colonies, especially in Boston and New York. Resistance took both institutional and popular forms. Colonial assemblies created Committees of Correspondence to coordinate their actions, while groups such as the Sons and Daughters of Liberty organized demonstrations and intimidation campaigns against stamp collectors, many of whom were forced to resign.[17]

In June 1765, the Massachusetts Assembly issued a circular letter calling for a meeting of colonial representatives. The Stamp Act Congress convened in New York in October 1765, bringing together delegates from nine colonies. The Congress adopted the Declaration of Rights and Grievances, which affirmed that only colonial assemblies had the legitimate power to tax, condemned the use of admiralty courts, and asserted that the colonists enjoyed the same rights as Englishmen – rights that Parliament had violated by taxing them without representation.

The economic impact of boycotts soon hit British merchants hard, prompting reconsideration of the policy. During the debates on repeal, Benjamin Franklin, testifying before Parliament, argued that the colonies objected only to internal taxes, not to external trade duties. Under mounting pressure, Parliament finally repealed the Stamp Act on March 18, 1766 – but on the same day, passed the Declaratory Act, asserting its authority to legislate for the colonies "in all cases whatsoever."

Although the repeal temporarily calmed tensions, the colonial resistance networks created during the Stamp Act crisis – particularly the Committees of Correspondence and systems of

17 The Editors of Encyclopaedia Britannica, 2024, "Stamp Act," *Encyclopaedia Britannica*, 12 June. Available at: https://www.britannica.com/event/Stamp-Act-Great-Britain-1765. Accessed 22 July 2024.

boycott – remained active. They would later be reactivated during future conflicts, such as the Boston Tea Party (1773). The deeper constitutional issue – whether parliament had the right to tax the colonies without representation – remained unresolved and became a central grievance leading to the American Revolution.

The Stamp Act crisis was thus an early step toward the modern idea of constitutional supremacy. For the first time, ordinary citizens collectively challenged the authority of an Act of Parliament as violating what they considered fundamental principles – representation, property rights, and consent to taxation. It marked the beginning of a political culture in which written constitutional principles could be invoked against government power.

This development would later culminate in the landmark case of *Marbury v. Madison* (1803), which formally established the principle of judicial review and enshrined the supremacy of the Constitution within the American legal system.

2.1.5 Marbury v. Madison *(1803)*

The *Marbury v. Madison* case (1803), decided by the Supreme Court of the United States, was a groundbreaking and highly influential moment in Constitutional Law. It was the first time the Supreme Court declared an Act of Congress unconstitutional, thereby giving concrete effect to the principle of constitutional supremacy.[18]

The American Constitution declares itself to be "the supreme law of the land." However, in the late 18th century, when the Constitution was first adopted, the meaning of this clause – the so-called *Supremacy Clause* – was not entirely clear. Although the Constitution had been written and ratified, the precise interpretation of its provisions and the way in which it would be applied in practice were still uncertain.

In *Marbury v. Madison*, the Supreme Court stated that

> because the Constitution is law, it is up to the courts which are the law-interpreting and the law applying institutions of the government, to determine what the Constitution means and to require the other branches of government to adhere to the courts' interpretation.[19]

Chief Justice John Marshall, in his opinion, argued that the Constitution stands above all other acts of government and that the decisions of the Supreme Court are binding on every public authority, including all administrative bodies and lower courts. Through this reasoning, judicial review was established as a fundamental principle of American democracy.

> **Opinion of the Court by Chief Justice Marshall Marbury v. Madison 5 U.S. 137 (1803)**
>
> The Government of the United States has been emphatically termed a government of laws, and not of men. . . .
>
> The powers of the Legislature are defined and limited; and (that) those limits may not be mistaken or forgotten, the Constitution is written. To what purpose are powers limited, and to what purpose is that limitation committed to writing, if these limits may at any time

18 Clinton, Robert, 2002, "Marbury v. Madison, 1 Cranch (5 U.S.) 137 (1803)," in *The Oxford Companion to American Law*, Oxford University Press, retrieved 22 July 2024 from https://www.oxfordreference.com/view/10.1093/acref/9780195088786.001.0001/acref-9780195088786-e-0584.

19 Beeman, Richard (ed.), 2012, *Supreme Court Decisions*, Penguin Books.

be passed by those intended to be restrained? The distinction between a government with limited and unlimited powers is abolished if those limits do not confine the persons on whom they are imposed, and if acts prohibited and acts allowed are of equal obligation. It is a proposition too plain to be contested that the Constitution controls any legislative act repugnant to it, or that the Legislature may alter the Constitution by an ordinary act.

Between these alternatives there is no middle ground. The Constitution is either a superior, paramount law, unchangeable by ordinary means, or it is on a level with ordinary legislative acts, and, like other acts, is alterable when the legislature shall please to alter it.

If the former part of the alternative were true, then a legislative act contrary to the Constitution is not law; if the latter part were true, then written Constitutions are absurd attempts on the part of the people to limit a power in its own nature illimitable.

Certainly all those who have framed written Constitutions contemplate them as forming the fundamental and paramount law of the nation, and consequently the theory of every such government must be that an Act of the Legislature repugnant to the Constitution is void.

This theory is essentially attached to a written Constitution, and is consequently to be considered by this Court as one of the fundamental principles of our society. It is not, therefore, to be lost sight of in the further consideration of this subject.

If an Act of the Legislature repugnant to the Constitution is void, does it, notwithstanding its invalidity, bind the Courts and oblige them to give it effect? Or, in other words, though it is not law, does it constitute a rule as operative as if it was a law? This would be to overthrow in fact what was established in theory, and would seem, at first view, an absurdity too gross to be insisted on. It shall, however, receive a more attentive consideration.

It is emphatically the province and duty of the Judicial Department to say what the law is. Those who apply the rule to particular cases must, of necessity, expound and interpret that rule. If two laws conflict with each other, the Courts must decide on the operation of each.

So, if a law be in opposition to the Constitution, if both the law and the Constitution apply to a particular case, so that the Court must either decide that case conformably to the law, disregarding the Constitution, or conformably to the Constitution, disregarding the law, the Court must determine which of these conflicting rules governs the case. This is of the very essence of judicial duty.

If, then, the Courts are to regard the Constitution, and the Constitution is superior to any ordinary Act of the Legislature, the Constitution, and not such ordinary act, must govern the case to which they both apply.

Those, then, who controvert the principle that the Constitution is to be considered in court as a paramount law are reduced to the necessity of maintaining that courts must close their eyes on the Constitution, and see only the law.

This doctrine would subvert the very foundation of all written Constitutions. It would declare that an act, which, according to the principles and theory of our government, is entirely void, is yet, in practice, completely obligatory. It would declare that, if the Legislature shall do what is expressly forbidden, such act, notwithstanding the express prohibition, is in reality effectual. It would be giving to the Legislature a practical and real omnipotence with the same breath, which professes to restrict their powers within narrow limits. It is prescribing limits, and declaring that those limits may be passed at pleasure.

That it thus reduces to nothing what we have deemed the greatest improvement on political institutions – a written Constitution, would of itself be sufficient, in America

> where written Constitutions have been viewed with so much reverence, for rejecting the construction. But the peculiar expressions of the Constitution of the United States furnish additional arguments in favor of its rejection.
>
> The judicial power of the United States is extended to all cases arising under the Constitution.
>
> Could it be the intention of those who gave this power to say that, in using it, the Constitution should not be looked into? That a case arising under the Constitution should be decided without examining the instrument under which it arises?
>
> This is too extravagant to be maintained.

This opinion by Chief Justice John Marshall established several fundamental principles of American Constitutional Law that continue to strengthen democracy and the Rule of Law in the United States.

First, it affirmed that the United States is a government of laws and not of individuals. This means that everyone, including public officials and institutions, is bound by the law. Such a system prevents the abuse of power and protects citizens' rights and freedoms.

Second, the opinion emphasized the importance of having a written constitution. A written text clearly defines the powers and limits of government, thereby preventing those in authority from exceeding their constitutional boundaries.

Third, Marshall underlined that the Constitution is the supreme law of the land and cannot be altered by ordinary legislative procedures. This ensures that fundamental principles are not easily changed by temporary political majorities.

Fourth, the decision defined the role of the Supreme Court as the final arbiter in cases of conflict between laws. The Court's duty is to ensure that the Constitution always prevails when ordinary legislation contradicts it.

Fifth, Marshall made clear that any law conflicting with the Constitution is invalid. This principle established the Constitution as the highest standard guiding all acts of government.

Finally, the opinion praised the adoption of a written constitution as a major advancement in political organization. It provides a stable and lasting framework that guarantees the continuity and coherence of the legal system.

The case itself arose from a political dispute. In March 1801, just before leaving office, President John Adams made several last-minute judicial appointments in an effort to maintain Federalist influence within the government. Among these appointments was William Marbury, who was named justice of the peace for the District of Columbia. When Thomas Jefferson took office, his Secretary of State, James Madison, refused to deliver Marbury's commission – the formal document confirming his appointment.

Marbury then petitioned the Supreme Court to issue a writ of mandamus (a judicial order compelling a public official to perform a duty) directing Madison to deliver the commission. The central legal question was whether the Judiciary Act of 1789, which authorized such writs, was consistent with the Constitution.

Chief Justice Marshall held that the Judiciary Act of 1789 had conferred powers on the Supreme Court that went beyond those granted by Article III of the Constitution. Therefore, the Act was unconstitutional. The Court ruled that when a law conflicts with the Constitution, the Constitution must prevail.

The decision in *Marbury v. Madison* (1803) thus established the principle of judicial review, giving the Supreme Court the authority to declare acts of Congress void if they are found to be inconsistent with the Constitution. This power, derived from Articles III and VI of the

Constitution, became a cornerstone of American constitutional supremacy and a defining feature of democratic governance.

U.S. Constitution (extracts)
Article III
Section 1.

The judicial power of the United States shall be vested in one Supreme Court, and in such inferior courts as the Congress may from time to time ordain and establish. The judges, both of the supreme and inferior courts, shall hold their offices during good behavior, and shall, at stated times, receive for their services, a compensation, which shall not be diminished during their continuance in office.

Section 2.

The judicial power shall extend to all cases, in law and equity, arising under this Constitution, the laws of the United States, and treaties made, or which shall be made, under their authority; – to all cases affecting ambassadors, other public ministers and consuls; – to all cases of admiralty and maritime jurisdiction; – to controversies to which the United States shall be a party; – to controversies between two or more states; – between a State and citizens of another State; – between citizens of different states; – between citizens of the same State claiming lands under grants of different states, and between a State, or the citizens thereof, and foreign states, citizens or subjects.

In all cases affecting ambassadors, other public ministers and consuls, and those in which a State shall be party, the Supreme Court shall have original jurisdiction. In all the other cases before mentioned, the Supreme Court shall have appellate jurisdiction, both as to law and fact, with such exceptions, and under such regulations as the Congress shall make.

Article VI

(2) This Constitution and the Laws of the United States which shall be made in Pursuance thereof; and all Treaties made, or which shall be made, under the authority of the United States, shall be the supreme Law of the Land; and the Judges in every State shall be bound thereby, anything in the Constitution or Laws of any State to the Contrary notwithstanding.

Judiciary Act of 1789 (extracts)
Section 13.

And be it further enacted, That the Supreme Court shall have exclusive jurisdiction of all controversies of a civil nature, where a State is a party, except between a State and its citizens; and except also between a State and citizens of other states, or aliens, in which latter case it shall have original but not exclusive jurisdiction. And shall have exclusively all such jurisdiction of suits or proceedings against ambassadors, or other public ministers, or their domestics, or domestic servants, as a court of law can have or exercise consistently with the law of nations; and original, but not exclusive jurisdiction of all suits brought by ambassadors, or other public ministers, or in which a consul, or vice consul, shall be a party. And the trial of issues in fact in the Supreme Court, in all actions at law against citizens of the United

States, shall be by jury. The Supreme Court shall also have appellate jurisdiction from the circuit courts and courts of the several states, in the cases herein after specially provided for; and shall have power to issue writs of prohibition to the district courts, when proceeding as courts of admiralty and maritime jurisdiction, and writs of mandamus, in cases warranted by the principles and usages of law, to any courts appointed, or persons holding office, under the authority of the United States.

This was the first time the Supreme Court struck down a law for being contrary to the Constitution. *Marbury v. Madison* thus marked the beginning of what would become known as judicial review. In a sense, the U.S. Supreme Court created the very concept of constitutional review of legislative acts, giving concrete form to the principle of constitutional supremacy – a principle that would later spread throughout the Common Law world and, to some extent, influence Civil Law systems as well.

2.1.6 European Conception of Constitutional Supremacy: The Kelsenian Theory

We shall not describe in detail Hans Kelsen's theory, as many other works already provide extensive analyses of it. For further study of this subject, readers may refer to the bibliography at the end of the chapter. For the sake of clarity and brevity, we will only summarize Kelsen's main ideas concerning constitutional supremacy.

At the beginning of the 20th century, the Austrian jurist Hans Kelsen developed a modern model of the hierarchy of norms. However, his approach was quite different from that of Chief Justice Marshall in *Marbury v. Madison.* Kelsen sought to identify a single point of origin for all legal norms. Unlike Marshall, who grounded his reasoning in political and moral ideas such as the will of the people, Kelsen's reasoning was purely legal. He based his model on the assumption of a *basic norm* from which all other norms derive their validity.

Kelsen's work is rooted in the tradition of legal positivism, which led him to reject natural law theories.[20] He is often regarded as one of the most influential legal philosophers of the 20th century – and his attempts to understand law in its diversity and its unity are valuable for our global understanding of law.[21] His major work, *The Pure Theory of Law* (1934), aimed to build an objective and scientific understanding of law, independent of moral or political considerations.

Kelsen's theory focuses on the relationships between norms within a legal system, seeking to describe how each norm derives its validity from a higher one, up to the basic norm. His approach, inspired by Kant's philosophy, aimed to establish a "pure" science of law by studying its logical structure rather than its moral content. Although one may question whether law can truly be separated from moral or social values, Kelsen's contribution remains essential to understanding the coherence and hierarchy of legal systems.

In this hierarchical model, law is organized like a pyramid: at the top stands the constitution, followed by legislative acts, administrative regulations, and individual decisions. The system is

20 However, we can see that, from a methodological point of view, both positivists and naturalists agree on the necessity to articulate and hierarchize norms. Positive lawyers argue that norms should be hierarchized because they all derive from a basic founding norm, the Constitution, whereas natural lawyers argue that all norms should comply with higher standards of justice and morals (natural law), which ought to be incorporated in the Constitution.

21 Fassbender, Bardo, 2012, "Hans Kelsen (1881–1973)," in *The Oxford Handbook of the History of International Law*, eds. Bardo Fassbender and Anne Peters, online ed., Oxford Academic. https://doi.org/10.1093/law/9780199599752.003.0064. Accessed 23 July 2024.

dynamic, as each level both creates and applies norms, and the role of the judge is central. The judge ensures the compatibility between norms, verifying that lower norms conform to superior ones.

For Kelsen, the constitution forms the foundation of the entire legal order. It is both the source of authority for all public powers and the rule that determines the validity of all other norms. In his view, the constitution defines the structure of the political community and guarantees the unity and stability of the legal system.

To draw a philosophical parallel, one could compare Kelsen's theory to Jean-Paul Sartre's existentialism: for Kelsen, the existence of law precedes its essence. This legal existentialism, however, has been criticized for presenting law as an abstract and autonomous system of norms detached from social reality. Critics argue that law is not a pure logical construction but an expression of the moral and political order of a community.

Nevertheless, Kelsen's model remains one of the most rigorous and influential attempts to explain constitutional supremacy and the internal coherence of legal systems.

2.1.7 Non-Western Perspectives on Constitutional Supremacy

The new constitutional orders established in young Arab democracies raise an important question: how does the non-Western legal world view the Western concept of a constitution and its supremacy?[22] A constitution is generally considered the highest law of a nation, standing above all other laws, statutes, and administrative acts. This idea of a supreme legal norm is central to the notion of constitutional supremacy.

However, in order to ensure this supremacy, certain mechanisms must be in place. First, legal norms must be subject to effective control in relation to the constitution, which is the purpose of judicial review. Second, as will be seen in the next section, procedures for constitutional revision and amendment must be rigid and clearly defined in order to preserve the stability of the constitution. In Western systems, where the concept of constitutional supremacy was first developed, both of these mechanisms are well established.

Today, constitutions exist in most countries around the world. Although constitutionalism was born in the Western world, Constitutional Law has become a universal discipline. This raises several questions: how have non-Western countries appropriated the concept of constitutional supremacy? To what extent do their approaches differ from Western definitions? And how far are they willing to uphold constitutional supremacy within their institutions?

Some non-Western countries place the constitution at the top of their legal hierarchy, reproducing elements of Western models and procedures. Others do not grant the constitution exclusive supremacy, either because other norms are considered higher or because International Law has become the main source of authority in certain areas, such as human rights. Finally, some countries reject the Western constitutional model entirely.

Many non-Western countries have adopted Western-style judicial review to safeguard constitutional supremacy, at least in theory. Different models of review have developed in the Western world to ensure the constitution's rigidity and superiority. Three main models exist: the American, the Austrian, and the mixed systems.

The American model is a decentralized form of judicial review, where any judge may determine the constitutionality of a law once it has entered into force (*a posteriori* review). This

22 Choudhry, Sujit, 2013, "Constitutional Transitions in the Middle East: Introduction," *International Journal of Constitutional Law*, vol. 11, no. 3, pp. 611–614. https://doi.org/10.1093/icon/mot028.

system originated with the case of *Marbury v. Madison* (1803). Non-Western countries that have adopted this model include India, Kenya, Uganda, and Nigeria.

The Austrian model, prevalent in Europe and Civil Law systems, is based on centralized judicial review. In this system, a constitutional court has exclusive authority to determine the constitutionality of legislation, and it may conduct both preventive (*a priori*) and subsequent (*a posteriori*) reviews. This model emerged partly in reaction to the political instability and judicial weakness seen during revolutionary and authoritarian periods. Non-Western countries that have adopted a similar model include Algeria, Azerbaijan, Belarus, Benin, Egypt, Kazakhstan, Kyrgyzstan, Russia, and Ukraine.

The mixed model combines features of both systems. Ordinary courts may rule on constitutional issues, as in Common Law systems, but a special constitutional court retains ultimate authority. This model is used in South Africa, most Latin American states, and several post-socialist countries.

Beyond judicial review, another technique to safeguard constitutional supremacy is the inclusion of an "eternity clause."[23] This mechanism establishes that certain constitutional provisions can never be amended. The best-known example is found in the German Constitution. Article 79(3) of the Basic Law (Grundgesetz) declares that certain fundamental principles – such as human dignity, the Rule of Law, Separation of Powers, and the federal structure of the State – are unalterable.

Article 79
[Amendment of the Basic Law]

(1) This Basic Law may be amended only by a law expressly amending or supplementing its text. In the case of an international treaty regarding a peace settlement, the preparation of a peace settlement, or the phasing out of an occupation regime, or designed to promote the defense of the Federal Republic, it shall be sufficient, for the purpose of making clear that the provisions of this Basic Law do not preclude the conclusion and entry into force of the treaty, to add language to the Basic Law that merely makes this clarification.
(2) Any such law shall be carried by two thirds of the Members of the Bundestag and two thirds of the votes of the Bundesrat.
(3) Amendments to this Basic Law affecting the division of the Federation into Länder, their participation on principle in the legislative process, or the principles laid down in Articles 1 and 20 shall be inadmissible.

Many other constitutions around the world have similar provisions to protect essential features of their political order, such as the form of government, the state religion, or the independence of constitutional courts.[24]

In some countries, constitutions coexist with other supreme norms, particularly in the field of human rights. For example, in South Africa, a Bill of Rights was incorporated into the Constitution and occupies a central, almost superior position within the legal hierarchy. In India, the Judiciary has developed the "basic structure doctrine," holding that certain constitutional

23 Suteu, Silvia, 2021, "Introduction: The Rise of Eternity Clauses in Democratic Constitutionalism," in *Eternity Clauses in Democratic Constitutionalism*, Oxford Comparative Constitutionalism, online ed., Oxford Academic. https://doi.org/10.1093/oso/9780198858867.003.0001. Accessed 23 July 2024.

24 Nearly 35% of the world's constitutions include eternity clauses.

principles – such as the Rule of Law and judicial independence – cannot be amended or abolished, even by constitutional reform.[25]

In many parts of the world, Constitutional Law also interacts with International Law, especially in the area of human rights. Because fundamental rights are often considered universal, there is a growing tendency to rely on international charters and treaties. For instance, in most African states, human rights protection is guaranteed through the African Charter on Human and Peoples' Rights (1981) or the Universal Declaration of Human Rights (1948). Similarly, Article 5 of the Brazilian Constitution explicitly recognizes that constitutional rights include those derived from international treaties ratified by Brazil.

Article 5 of the Brazilian Constitution provides: "The rights and guarantees expressed in this Constitution do not exclude others . . . deriving from the international treaties in which the Federative Republic of Brazil is a party."

Finally, some states have chosen to reject the Western model of constitutional supremacy altogether. A notable example is Saudi Arabia. In the 1960s, King Faysal Bin Abdulaziz Al Saud is reputed to have remarked: "A constitution? What for? The Quran is the oldest and most efficient constitution in the world." The Basic Law of Saudi Arabia, adopted in 1992, functions as a constitutional text but differs substantially in content and form. It is entirely inspired by Islamic law and places the Quran and the Sunnah above any other legal source. Article 1 of the Basic Law explicitly provides that "the Kingdom of Saudi Arabia is a sovereign Arab Islamic state with Islam as its religion; God's Book and the Sunnah of His Prophet . . . are its constitution."

Thus, the supreme norm in Saudi Arabia is the Sharia. All courts – judicial and administrative – are bound by Islamic law, and judges receive religious rather than secular legal training. Their decisions are based on Sharia principles, and punishments for certain offenses (hudud) are prescribed directly by religious law.

These examples show the diversity of approaches to constitutional supremacy across the world. While many non-Western countries have adopted and adapted Western models, others have integrated constitutional principles into their own cultural and religious traditions, and a few have rejected the Western notion of constitutional supremacy entirely.

2.1.8 Different Modes of Judicial Review

Judicial review is a key mechanism for ensuring that public authorities respect the constitution and act within the law. However, the way judicial review operates varies significantly across legal systems. This section begins by outlining its scope and main forms before examining how different countries have developed distinct models of constitutional review.

2.1.8.1 SCOPE, FORMS, AND GROUNDS OF JUDICIAL REVIEW

Judicial review is usually understood as the process of determining whether legislative statutes are compatible with the constitution. However, its scope is broader and also extends to other areas of government activity. Courts may examine whether regulations issued by the Executive or administrative authorities, as well as specific administrative acts, comply with the constitution.

25 Abeyratne, Rishika, 2021, "Global Constitutionalism Reconfigured Through a Regional Lens," *Global Constitutionalism*, vol. 10, no. 2, pp. 331–350. https://doi.org/10.1017/S2045381720000234.

The public bodies whose decisions may be challenged include government ministers and departments,[26] local authorities,[27] and NHS trusts in England, chief constables and prison governors in matters relating to prisoners' rights, maintained schools and their governing bodies, magistrates, coroners, and county courts in England, as well as regulatory or supervisory bodies such as the Care Quality Commission or the Charity Commission. In France, similar control applies to independent administrative authorities and agencies.

Judicial review can therefore be broadly defined as the process by which courts assess the lawfulness of a decision made – or, in some cases, not made – by a public body. It enables a judge to determine whether a public authority has acted within the limits of its legal powers. If it has not, the court can declare the decision unlawful and set it aside.

The methods and effects of judicial review vary considerably across legal systems. In the Common Law world, judicial review is typically decentralized, meaning that any judge may rule on the constitutionality of a law after it has come into force (*a posteriori*, or *ex post*). This diffuse and generalist form of review is characteristic of the United States.

In contrast, in Civil Law systems, judicial review is often centralized and may occur before a law comes into effect (*a priori*, or *ex ante*). This specialized and concentrated model was designed by Hans Kelsen for Austria after World War I and was later adopted by many European and other countries. Some legal systems combine features of both models.

The effects of judicial review also differ from one jurisdiction to another. In some systems, constitutional decisions by the highest court are binding on all legal actors (*erga omnes* effect), as in the United States. In others, judicial decisions bind only the parties involved in the specific case (*inter partes* effect).[28] These two approaches are known as strong-form and weak-form judicial review.

Mark V. Tushnet explains that in the "strong-form" model, courts have general authority to determine the meaning of the constitution, and their interpretations are binding on all branches of government, at least in the short and medium term. However, he notes that these interpretations are

> not absolutely binding, first, because they can be overturned by a constitutional amendment, which in principle could occur quite rapidly (as occurred with the Eleventh Amendment in the U.S.), and second, because they can be rejected as new justices are appointed to the Court and constitutional doctrine changes.[29]

Tushnet also observes that the strong-form model of the U.S. Supreme Court became the reference point for other constitutional courts established after World War II, such as the German Constitutional Court, which he describes as "perhaps the world's leading constitutional court after the U.S. Supreme Court."[30] For many years, he adds, "it seemed that judicial review meant strong-form review."[31]

26 For example, certain decisions of the immigration authorities and of the immigration appellate authority.

27 For example, decisions of local authorities in the exercise of their duties to provide various welfare benefits and special education for children in need of such education.

28 Reimann, Mathias and Zimmermann, Reinhard, 2008, *The Oxford Handbook of Comparative Law*, Oxford University Press.

29 Tushnet, Mark V., 2003, *Alternative Forms of Judicial Review*, Georgetown University Law Center.

30 Tushnet, *Alternative Forms of Judicial Review*.

31 Tushnet, *Alternative Forms of Judicial Review*.

According to Tushnet, the range of possible institutional designs changed when the drafters of Canada's Charter of Rights introduced *weak-form judicial review* in 1982. The Charter's Section 33, known as the *notwithstanding clause*, allows parliament or a provincial legislature to declare that a statute will take effect *notwithstanding* its potential conflict with certain Charter provisions. The purpose of this clause was to give courts a role in constitutional interpretation without making their decisions final or absolute. A legislature that disagreed with a court's interpretation could reenact the invalidated statute, invoking Section 33 to protect it from further judicial challenge.

Tushnet explains that Section 33 has inspired other countries to design innovative forms of judicial review:

> For present purposes, I need to mention only two examples: the New Zealand Bill of Rights and the British Human Rights Act of 1998. The New Zealand Bill of Rights directs the courts to interpret all legislation to make it compatible with the Bill of Rights, but it does not give the courts the power to refrain from enforcing statutes that are, when fairly read, inconsistent with the Bill of Rights.[32]

Judicial review may be invoked on several grounds. A decision can be challenged if the public body lacked the legal authority to make it, or if it exercised its power for an improper purpose (abuse of power). It can also be reviewed if it is irrational or unreasonable, if the procedure followed was unfair or biased, or if the decision breaches an international treaty or a fundamental norm such as the Human Rights Act. Similarly, judicial review may be sought if the decision violates European Union law or if a public authority has failed to comply with one of its legal duties, such as the public sector equality duty.

In sum, judicial review remains an essential instrument for ensuring that public authorities act within the limits of the law, respect constitutional principles, and protect individual rights against abuse of power.

2.1.8.2 AMERICAN MODEL: DIFFUSE, GENERALIST, STRONG-FORM

In the United States, judicial review is performed on a daily basis by first-instance judges as part of their ordinary judicial work. Any judge, when confronted with a constitutional issue, has both the right and the duty to examine whether the law applied to a case is consistent with the Constitution. If one of the parties argues that a statute governing the dispute is unconstitutional, the judge must address that question before resolving the case. If the judge concludes that the challenged law violates the Constitution, the law is simply not applied to that case. Technically, the judge does not annul the statute but sets it aside. However, when the Supreme Court declares a law unconstitutional, its decision is binding on all other courts, and in practice the law becomes inoperative, as though it had been formally repealed.

The United States Constitution does not expressly grant the Judiciary the power of judicial review. This power has instead been inferred from Articles III and VI of the Constitution. Article III vests the judicial power in one Supreme Court and such inferior courts as Congress may establish, and provides that this power "shall extend to all cases, in law and equity, arising under this Constitution." Article VI, known as the Supremacy Clause, declares that the Constitution, federal laws, and treaties made under it "shall be the supreme Law of the Land," and that judges in every State "shall be bound thereby."

32 Tushnet, *Alternative Forms of Judicial Review*.

Article III

The judicial power of the United States, shall be vested in one Supreme Court, and in such inferior courts as the Congress may from time to time ordain and establish. . . . The judicial power shall extend to all cases, in law and equity, arising under this Constitution, the laws of the United States, and treaties made, or which shall be made, under their authority. . . . In all cases affecting ambassadors, other public ministers and consuls, and those in which a State shall be party, the Supreme Court shall have original jurisdiction. In all the other cases before mentioned, the Supreme Court shall have appellate jurisdiction, both as to law and fact, with such exceptions, and under such regulations as the Congress shall make.

Article VI

This Constitution, and the Laws of the United States which shall be made in Pursuance thereof; and all Treaties made, or which shall be made, under the Authority of the United States, shall be the supreme Law of the Land; and the Judges in every State shall be bound thereby, any Thing in the Constitution or Laws of any State to the Contrary notwithstanding. . . . [A]ll executive and judicial Officers, both of the United States and of the several states, shall be bound by Oath or Affirmation, to support this Constitution.

From these provisions, the Supreme Court inferred in *Marbury v. Madison* (1803) that the Judiciary has the authority – and the duty – to determine whether a statute conflicts with the Constitution. This principle rests on the idea that in any case before the courts, judges must apply the law, and when two laws conflict, the higher law, the Constitution, must prevail. The Supreme Court's final appellate jurisdiction gives it ultimate authority to decide constitutional questions, ensuring uniform interpretation throughout the country.

A modern and striking example of judicial review in the United States can be found in the 2012 Supreme Court decision concerning the Patient Protection and Affordable Care Act (ACA), commonly known as Obamacare. The case placed the Supreme Court at the center of national political and constitutional debate. The challenge to the ACA tested the boundaries between the three branches of government – Executive, Legislative, and Judicial – and carried significant political implications for President Obama's administration.[33]

According to Alexandra Hurd, Matthew Bobby, Faina Shalts, and Robert Greenwald from Harvard Law School's Center for Health Law and Policy Innovation, "The ACA is a long and complex piece of legislation, but constitutional challenges levied against it have focused on just a few provisions."[34] These included: (a) the individual mandate, which requires individuals to obtain health insurance, was challenged as exceeding Congress's power to regulate interstate commerce; (b) the expansion of Medicaid, which plaintiffs claimed coerced states into compliance by conditioning federal funding on participation, allegedly infringing states' rights under the Tenth Amendment.

The lower federal courts reached differing conclusions. One upheld the ACA as constitutional, two declined to hear the challenges on procedural grounds, and one ruled that the

33 Blackman, Josh and Barnett, Randy E., 2013, *Unprecedented: The Constitutional Challenge to Obamacare*, PublicAffairs, 1st ed. This book tells the inside story of the Constitutional challenge to Obamacare.

34 Hurd, Amanda, Bobby, Michael, Shalts, Frank and Greenwald, Robert, 2011, *Constitutional Challenges to the Patient Protection and Affordable Care Act: Four Questions for the Supreme Court*, Harvard Law School Center for Health Law and Policy Innovation.

individual mandate was unconstitutional but allowed the remainder of the law to stand. The Supreme Court agreed to hear the case and focused on four central questions.

Firstly, can the individual mandate be justified as an exercise of Congress's power to regulate commerce?
Secondly, if the individual mandate is found unconstitutional, is that provision severable from the rest of the ACA?
Thirdly, does the Medicaid expansion unconstitutionally coerce states, thereby violating the Tenth Amendment?
Finally, is the individual mandate a tax under the Anti-Injunction Act, thus preventing pre-enforcement challenges?

In a narrow 5–4 decision, Chief Justice John Roberts joined the majority to uphold the ACA, reasoning that the individual mandate could be sustained under Congress's power to tax, even though it could not be justified under the Commerce Clause. This decision was both legally and politically significant. It reaffirmed the Court's independence, preserved Congress's ability to address major national issues, and avoided a constitutional confrontation between the Judiciary and the Executive.

Since its enactment, the ACA has faced multiple legal challenges – based on alleged violations of state sovereignty, claims that it improperly originated in the Senate,[35] or arguments that federal subsidies were unlawfully granted through federal exchanges. None of these challenges has succeeded in invalidating key provisions of the Act. By validating the ACA, the Supreme Court also aimed to protect the nation's most important institution and common good: federalism.

Through such cases, the U.S. Supreme Court continues to play a decisive role in defining the boundaries of constitutional power, illustrating how judicial review remains a cornerstone of American constitutional supremacy.

2.1.8.3 JUDICIAL REVIEW IN THE UK: DIFFUSE, GENERALIST, WEAK-FORM

Unlike the United States and other legal systems, the English doctrine of parliamentary sovereignty does not allow the judicial review of Acts of Parliament, also known as "primary legislation," except in a few cases where primary legislation conflicts with European Union law. However, the courts may review and overturn secondary (delegated) legislation or decisions of public authorities whenever they are found to be inconsistent with higher legal norms.

The English court system does not have a separate system of administrative courts to review the actions of public authorities, as is the case in France, Germany, or many other European countries. Instead, government action is subject to the jurisdiction of ordinary Common Law courts, particularly the Administrative Court, which forms part of the Queen's Bench Division of the High Court. Because of the principle of parliamentary sovereignty, which prevents the judicial review of primary legislation, the scope of judicial review in England is limited to administrative decisions and secondary or delegated legislation.

35 The Constitution's "origination clause" requires that all spending bills originate in the House of Representatives. But the Obamacare was first introduced in the Senate by replacing the text of an unrelated bill that came from the House of Representatives.

Lord Diplock (1907–1985)[36] identified three main categories of grounds for judicial review: illegality, irrationality, and procedural impropriety.[37] Illegality occurs when a public body fails to recognize or give effect to the law governing its decision-making power – in other words, when it acts *ultra vires* (beyond its legal authority).[38] Irrationality refers to a decision so unreasonable or absurd that no reasonable decision-maker could have made it. Procedural impropriety concerns failures to observe either statutory procedural requirements or the Common Law principles of natural justice, particularly bias or the denial of a fair hearing.

A specific issue in the United Kingdom concerns the relationship between judicial review and the European Convention on Human Rights (ECHR). A person claiming to be the victim of a violation of Convention rights by a public body may challenge the act in question through judicial review.[39] Under sections 3 and 4 of the Human Rights Act of 1998,[40] the Supreme Court, the Court of Appeal, the High Court, the Judicial Committee, and the Privy Council may issue a "declaration of incompatibility," stating that a particular legislative provision is inconsistent with one or more rights contained in the European Convention on Human Rights.

In reaching their decisions, the courts consider which article of the Convention was breached, how it was breached, whether the interference with the right was prescribed by law, whether it was necessary in a democratic society, or pursued a legitimate aim, and whether it was proportionate to that aim.[41]

Several remedies are available in judicial review proceedings, not only under the Human Rights Act but more generally. These include:

Quashing order: This remedy cancels an unlawful decision made by a public body, rendering it invalid. It is most often granted when an authority has acted *ultra vires*. The court may order the public body to reconsider its decision in accordance with the law, or, in certain cases, make the decision itself.

Prohibiting order: This order prevents a public body from acting beyond its powers. Unlike a quashing order, which addresses past actions, a prohibiting order is preventive and stops an unlawful act before it occurs – for example, preventing a local authority from issuing an unlawful license.

Mandatory order: This order compels a public body to perform a duty required by law. It applies when a public authority has failed to act where it is legally obliged to do so. Non-compliance with a mandatory order may amount to contempt of court. Examples include compelling a local authority to assess a disabled person's needs or to improve prison conditions.

Declaration: A declaration clarifies the legal rights and obligations of the parties without making an enforceable order. It provides judicial guidance but does not compel any action.

36 Lord Diplock (1907–1985) was a prominent British judge and law lord – a senior judge who sat in the House of Lords, the United Kingdom's highest court of appeal until 2009 – whose influential work helped shape modern constitutional and Public Law.

37 *Council for Civil Service Unions v. Minister for Civil Service*, 1985, 1 AC 374 (HL).

38 A decision of a public body can be set aside if it exceeds the powers granted to it by Parliament.

39 Finch, Emily and Fafinski, Stefan, 2021, *Legal Skills*, 8th ed., Oxford University Press.

40 The Human Rights Act of 1998 incorporated the European Convention of Human Rights into domestic law. Its section 3(1) provides as follows: "So far as it is possible to do so, primary legislation and subordinate legislation must be read and given effect in a way which is compatible with the Convention rights."

41 Finch and Fafinski, *Legal Skills*.

Injunction: An injunction orders a public authority to cease acting unlawfully. Unlike a mandatory order, which requires action, an injunction prohibits conduct.

Damages: Compensation is available only in limited circumstances, such as where there has been negligence, breach of statutory duty, or a violation of European Union law or the Human Rights Act. Unlawful action alone is not sufficient to justify damages.

More than one remedy can be requested in a single proceeding, but all remedies are granted at the discretion of the court.

Because of the doctrine of parliamentary sovereignty, the powers of the UK Supreme Court are much more limited than those of other supreme courts, such as the United States Supreme Court. The UK Supreme Court cannot invalidate Acts of Parliament, but it can strike down secondary legislation or administrative decisions found to be *ultra vires*.

Under sections 3 and 4 of the Human Rights Act of 1998, the Supreme Court and certain other courts may issue a declaration of incompatibility when they consider that legislation is inconsistent with the European Convention on Human Rights.[42] A declaration of incompatibility is a judicial statement that a law is incompatible with the UK's obligations under the Human Rights Act, which incorporated the ECHR into domestic law. Such a declaration may apply to either primary or secondary legislation. It does not, however, annul the legislation. If the government accepts the declaration, ministers may invite parliament to amend the law, often using a fast-track procedure.

In the United Kingdom, declarations of incompatibility can be issued by the High Court, the Court of Appeal, the Supreme Court, and the Judicial Committee of the Privy Council. These mechanisms reflect the balance between respect for parliamentary sovereignty and the protection of fundamental rights within the British constitutional framework.

2.1.8.4 FRENCH MODEL: STRONG-FORM, SPECIALIZED, CENTRALIZED EVOLVING TOWARDS DIFFUSE, GENERALIST

France has developed a distinctive form of judicial review of parliamentary acts, quite different from the American model.[43]

Martin Shapiro[44] – an American legal scholar and professor of Comparative Constitutional Law and Judicial Politics – famously noted that "the French Conseil is more like a third, specialized, legislative chamber than like a court."[45]

In the United States, judicial review is not explicitly authorized by the Constitution but has been exercised since *Marbury v. Madison* (1803) as part of central control over government acts. It is decentralized, reactive, and can be initiated by individuals. In contrast, in France, judicial review is explicitly provided for by the Constitution, is centralized within the State, and

42 Section 3(1) of the Human Rights Act of 1998: *So far as it is possible to do so, primary legislation and subordinate legislation must be read and given effect in a way which is compatible with the Convention rights.*

43 Calabresi, Steven Gow, 2021, "The Republic of France," in *The History and Growth of Judicial Review, Volume 2: The G-20 Civil Law Countries*, online ed., Oxford Academic, New York. https://doi.org/10.1093/oso/9780190075736.003.0007. Accessed 23 July 2024.

44 Martin Shapiro is an American legal scholar and professor emeritus at the University of California, Berkeley, School of Law, where he has taught since 1977. A graduate of UCLA (B.A., 1955) and Harvard University (Ph.D., 1961), he is widely recognized for his pioneering work in comparative constitutional law and judicial politics. In 2003, he received the Lifetime Achievement Award from the American Political Science Association's Law and Courts section.

45 See Shapiro, Martin M., 1989, *Judicial Review in France*, Berkeley Law.

can be triggered only by specific political authorities. American courts review statutes *after* they take effect (*a posteriori*), whereas in France, review traditionally occurs *before* promulgation (*a priori*) through a specialized body, the Constitutional Council (*Conseil constitutionnel*).[46]

Created by the Constitution of the Fifth Republic on October 4, 1958, the Constitutional Council is France's highest constitutional authority. Its role is to ensure that the principles and rules of the Constitution are respected. General Charles de Gaulle intentionally designed it to avoid what he called a "government of judges,"[47] fearing excessive judicial activism like that of the U.S. Supreme Court. France's judicial branch, unlike that of the United States, is not unified under a single hierarchy: administrative courts are under the Conseil d'État, while civil and criminal courts fall under the Cour de cassation.

Only a few public authorities can refer a law to the Constitutional Council for review. This makes French judicial review primarily *ex ante*, since it occurs before a law is enacted. The reasoning behind this approach is to avoid legal instability that might result if a law already in force were later declared unconstitutional. However, this system has been criticized for its limits: the unconstitutionality of a statute may only appear once it is applied, and ex ante review tends to politicize constitutional justice by turning constitutional rulings into victories for the opposition.[48]

The Constitutional Council is composed of nine members, each appointed for a nine-year term by the President of the Republic, the President of the National Assembly, and the President of the Senate. Its powers are both judicial and consultative.[49]

Judicial powers now include both *ex ante* and *ex post* review. The *ex post* mechanism was introduced by the constitutional amendment of July 23, 2008. Under Article 61–1 of the Constitution, individuals involved in legal proceedings may raise a "priority preliminary ruling on the issue of constitutionality" (*Question Prioritaire de Constitutionnalité* or QPC), allowing courts to refer a constitutional question to the Constitutional Council if they believe a statutory provision infringes constitutionally guaranteed rights or freedoms.[50] Before 2010, only political authorities could trigger constitutional review, and only before a statute came into force. The

46 Shapiro, *Judicial Review in France*.

47 The expression comes from the French Jurist Edouard Lambert (1866–1947), who influenced American law by studying judicial review using the idea of a "government of judges," to criticize judges for taking power away from the people. See Lambert, Édouard, 1921, *Le Gouvernement des juges et la lutte contre la législation sociale aux États-Unis. L'expérience américaine du contrôle judiciaire de la constitutionnalité des lois*, Giard, Paris.

48 See Shapiro, *Judicial Review in France*. It is noteworthy that the *ex ante* control of constitutionality, like the one existing in France, tends to politicize constitutional justice. Indeed, there is the possibility that constitutional rulings may seem to be a victory of the opposition against the political majority.

49 The Constitutional Council oversees the regularity of the election of the President of the Republic and referenda, the results of which it proclaims. It rules on the regularity of elections of Members of Parliament, and hence their eligibility; it also takes action where a Member of Parliament is in a situation of incompatibility, or is likely to be so.

50 The priority preliminary ruling on the issue of constitutionality was introduced by Article 61-1 of the French Constitution through the constitutional reform of July 23, 2008. Before this reform, it was impossible to challenge the constitutionality of a statute that had already come into force. Under this new mechanism, the Constitutional Council may, upon referral by the *Conseil d'État* or the *Cour de Cassation*, examine whether a legislative provision currently in force infringes constitutionally protected rights and freedoms.

This procedure allows any person involved in legal proceedings to argue that a statutory provision violates rights and freedoms guaranteed by the Constitution. The question must first be raised during the proceedings, and if deemed serious and relevant, it can be referred to the Constitutional Council for a final ruling. Through this reform, individuals gained a new and direct means to ensure the protection of their constitutional rights before the highest constitutional authority.

QPC reform thus opened access to all litigants and made constitutional control more democratic and dynamic.

In addition, the Constitutional Council supervises the regularity of presidential elections and referenda, proclaims their results, and ensures the legality of parliamentary elections. It may also issue opinions to the Head of State concerning the implementation of Article 16 (exceptional powers).

All Council decisions include the applicable texts, legal reasoning, and the final ruling. They are binding on all public authorities and courts and cannot be appealed.

Constitutional review of regulations (as opposed to parliamentary statutes) falls under the jurisdiction of the Conseil d'État, the highest administrative court. The Conseil d'État plays a crucial role in protecting fundamental rights, ensuring the legality of executive action, and maintaining high standards of public governance. It advises the government on legislation, judges disputes between public and private entities, and oversees the network of administrative courts across France.

Until the 2010 reform implementing Article 61–1, France's system of judicial review was highly restrictive – only a small number of political authorities could initiate review, and only before enactment. Today, any individual involved in a legal case may challenge the constitutionality of a statute, making French constitutional justice significantly more accessible and responsive.

2.1.8.5 GLOBAL OVERVIEW AND DIFFUSION OF JUDICIAL REVIEW MODELS

The German-Austrian model of judicial review is one of the most comprehensive systems in the world. In this model, a single constitutional court has exclusive authority to invalidate statutes that conflict with the Constitution. Different forms of referral exist in Germany, including official,[51] diffuse,[52] and judicial referrals.[53] This centralized model was first conceptualized by Hans Kelsen and later adopted in several countries such as Algeria, Azerbaijan, Belarus, Benin, Egypt, Kazakhstan, Kyrgyzstan, Russia, and Ukraine.

The U.S. model of judicial review, by contrast, has been widely transplanted across the globe, particularly in countries influenced by Common Law traditions. Examples include the Dominican Republic (1844), Mexico (1847), Argentina (1860), India (1949), Kenya, Uganda, and Nigeria. Mixed models, combining features of both centralized and decentralized systems, exist in countries like South Africa and in most Latin American and post-socialist states.

Although the United States and England both belong to the Common Law tradition, their approaches to judicial review are fundamentally different. In the U.S., there is a strong, decentralized system in which every judge can assess the constitutionality of laws, while in the UK, courts can only invalidate secondary or delegated legislation, not Acts of Parliament. The absence of a written constitution in the United Kingdom largely explains this difference. Many British Commonwealth countries, such as Canada, Australia, and India, have adopted stronger forms of judicial review inspired by the American model.

51 State official after it has been promulgated: Federal government, land government, or 1/3 of the Bundestag. Abstract Norm Control or Abstract Judicial review.

52 Anybody who claims that their constitutional rights have been violated may ask the constitutional court to look into the violation, but they have to demonstrate that they are actually interested and that they have suffered it, and, even in this case, the court might refuse to hear the case.

53 If any court is called upon to apply a statute, it can ask the federal constitutional court to rule for it. This is a type of concrete norm control.

In the Netherlands, constitutional review of legislation is prohibited, yet courts can void domestic rules that conflict with binding International Law. The country's stable democracy, high level of education, and strong political participation have made a more extensive system of judicial review unnecessary. Parliamentary oversight and civic engagement are viewed as sufficient to ensure constitutional compliance.

Most Civil Law countries in Western Europe – such as Austria, Germany, and Italy – have adopted a centralized model of constitutional review. Unlike the U.S. system, where judicial decisions are based on precedent (*stare decisis*) and have a concrete effect, European constitutional courts issue decisions that have an erga omnes effect (binding on all) and are generally abstract in nature.

France now combines both a priori and a posteriori constitutional review, conducted by the Constitutional Council, though traces of the doctrine of parliamentary sovereignty still appear in some rulings.

In the Asian, African, and Arab worlds, judicial review often reflects fragile democratic systems that have emerged after long periods of authoritarian rule. For example, Jordan, which has a mixed system of civil and religious law, faces serious institutional and normative challenges in judicial review: courts lack independence, constitutional regulation is weak, and rulings of the High Court are not binding. Consequently, judicial review in Jordan remains limited in effectiveness.

Across Africa, diverse legal traditions coexist, often alongside significant constitutional instability. South Africa, which combines Roman-Dutch Civil Law, English Common Law, and customary law, has adopted the European-style centralized model of constitutional review.

In Japan, judicial review was introduced for the first time under the postwar Constitution of 1946. The Supreme Court was granted the power to determine the constitutionality of any law, order, or regulation. Although modeled on the American system, the Japanese Supreme Court has historically shown great restraint. As Norikazu Kawagishi – Professor of Constitutional Law at Waseda University in Tokyo – explains, although its establishment was almost by accident judicial review has profoundly transformed the political process in Japan. Although modeled on the American system, the situation is different from that of the United States, since the Japanese Supreme Court, for some 60 years, has adopted a practice of judicial passivity.[54]

In China, courts do not have the power of constitutional judicial review. Their role is limited to reviewing certain administrative actions. Constitutional review formally exists but is vested in the Standing Committee of the National People's Congress, not in the Judiciary. Recent years, however, have seen renewed discussion about constitutionalism and possible reforms,[55] as noted by Professor Wang Zhenmin,[56] who highlighted ongoing debates about the need for a constitutional court during a 2013 conference at the University of Pennsylvania.[57]

54 Srour, Mark A., 2012, "Restrained Judicial Constitutionalism in Japan: A Reflection of Judicial Culture Rather Than Political Interests," *Zeitschrift für Japanisches Recht / Journal of Japanese Law*, no. 33.

55 Zhang, Qianfan, 2018, "Establishing Judicial Review in China: Impediments and Prospects," in *The Indian Yearbook of Comparative Law 2016*, online ed., ed. Mahendra Pal Singh, Oxford Academic, New Delhi. https://doi.org/10.1093/oso/9780199482139.003.0008. Accessed 23 July 2024.

56 Professor of Law at Tsinghua University, former Dean of the School of Law, and expert on Chinese constitutional and administrative law.

57 *Judicial Review and Constitutionalism in China: A Discussion with Wang Zhenmin, Dean and Professor of Law at Tsinghua University Law School*, University of Pennsylvania, Center for the Study of Contemporary China, May 10, 2013.

Despite the varying degrees of judicial independence and effectiveness across the world, judicial review remains a central mechanism for upholding constitutionalism and protecting individual rights. Even in systems where it functions imperfectly, it represents a crucial step toward strengthening democratic governance and the Rule of Law.

2.1.8.6 JUDICIAL REVIEW AND INDIVIDUAL RIGHTS: THE ABORTION EXAMPLE

Both France and Germany provide interesting examples of how constitutional courts approach the issue of abortion and the protection of individual rights. In the 1970s, both countries adopted statutes decriminalizing abortion, and in both cases, these statutes were subjected to judicial review. In France, the review was carried out by the Constitutional Council (*Conseil constitutionnel*), and in Germany by the Federal Constitutional Court (*Bundesverfassungsgericht*).

In France, the Constitutional Council examined the *Voluntary Interruption of Pregnancy Act* (Decision 74–54 DC, 1975). The statute was challenged for allegedly violating the rights of man, the Constitution, and the European Convention on Human Rights. The Council upheld the constitutionality of the statute, concluding that although it limited individual freedom, it did not violate the essential principles of human rights protected by the Constitution and the 1789 Declaration of the Rights of Man and of the Citizen. However, the Council declined to rule on whether the statute was compatible with the European Convention, since treaties are considered subordinate to the Constitution in France. The Council's reasoning was brief and did not explain in detail why the statute was consistent with constitutional principles – a characteristic feature of the French judicial style.

This case also illustrates the difference between *abstract review*, performed by the Constitutional Council, and *concrete review*, performed by ordinary courts. The Council cannot assess whether a statute complies with an international treaty; that question may only arise when the law is applied in a particular case before ordinary courts. In conclusion, the French Council sustained the constitutionality of the abortion statute, finding no contradiction with the Constitution or the Declaration of the Rights of Man, while leaving the question of treaty compliance to be decided by ordinary courts on a case-by-case basis.

The German Constitutional Court reached a very different conclusion when faced with a similar challenge. In its decision of February 25, 1975, it declared the German abortion statute unconstitutional and invalid.[58] The Court found that abortion violated the constitutional right to life, defining it as an act of killing. This created a fundamental conflict between two constitutional values: the right to life and the right to free development of personality. The Court held that the right to life must prevail, as it occupies a higher position within the constitutional order. It explained that while abortion destroys life, restrictions on abortion merely limit, but do not abolish, personal freedom.

The German case reveals a distinctive feature of German constitutionalism: the State's positive obligation to protect constitutional values. Unlike in systems such as the United States, where the Constitution primarily limits government power, the German Constitution also requires the State to act affirmatively to safeguard fundamental rights, including the protection of life. Many European constitutions share this principle, recognizing that the State has a constitutional duty to promote social welfare and uphold moral values within society.

The U.S. Supreme Court approached the issue differently in *Roe v. Wade* (1973). The case challenged Texas laws that made abortion a crime except to save the life of the mother. The

58 German Constitutional Court, First Senate Decision of 25 February 1975.

plaintiff, "Roe," sought to terminate her pregnancy, while the state of Texas argued that the fetus was a person protected by the Fourteenth Amendment's guarantee of life. The key constitutional question was whether the right to privacy includes a woman's right to choose an abortion.

The Supreme Court held that the constitutional right to privacy, found in the Fourteenth Amendment's concept of personal liberty, was broad enough to encompass a woman's decision to terminate her pregnancy. Although the Constitution does not explicitly mention privacy, the Court recognized it as implicit in the notion of personal liberty. The justices ruled that before viability, the decision to terminate a pregnancy must rest with the woman and her physician, free from state interference. After viability, however, the State could regulate or even prohibit abortion, except when necessary to protect the life of the mother. Because the Texas statute failed to distinguish between early and late abortions, it was deemed overly broad and unconstitutional.[59]

The comparison between these three cases highlights striking differences. In France and Germany, the legal debate centered on the right to life, while in the United States, the constitutional argument focused on the right to privacy. Yet, these cases all show how constitutional courts balance competing rights and how the scope of constitutional protection depends on each country's legal and moral framework.

In 2024, France became the first country in the world to enshrine abortion rights directly into its Constitution, marking a historic development and sending a powerful message of solidarity to women worldwide.

After examining the main modes of judicial review, we can now turn to another key question: how and why can constitutions be amended?

2.1.9 Amending the Constitution

Constitutions are designed to provide stability, but they must also be capable of change. As societies evolve, their constitutional frameworks must adapt to new political, social, and technological realities. Amendment procedures, therefore, play a crucial role in maintaining the relevance and legitimacy of a constitution. This section examines why constitutions need to be amended, how different political systems organize this process, and how amendment mechanisms reflect deeper conceptions of sovereignty and constitutional authority.

2.1.9.1 CONSTITUTIONAL ADAPTATION IN A CHANGING SOCIETY

How and why would a constitution be amended? In other words, what is the relationship between time and Constitutional law? As time passes, societies evolve, and as they do, customs, values, and political practices also change. This evolution naturally creates a need to adapt constitutional frameworks to new realities. A constitution should therefore not be seen as a fixed document established once and for all; rather, it must be capable of change and renewal. In a democracy, the people hold the ultimate constituent power and thus have the right to amend or replace their constitution. No generation can impose its laws on future generations.

This principle was clearly affirmed during the French Revolution. Article 28 of the Declaration of Rights that preceded the Constitution of June 24, 1793, stated that "a people always has the right to revise, amend and change its Constitution. One generation may not subject future generations to its laws." From this perspective, the right to amend the Constitution is a

59 United States Supreme Court, *Roe v. Wade*, Judgment of 22 January 1973.

fundamental right that belongs to the people themselves. A constitution must therefore remain open to revision, as it cannot be immutable or permanent. This is necessary for at least three reasons:

First, every legal text, even the supreme one, reflects a particular historical, social, and political context – one that inevitably changes over time.

Second, even the most carefully drafted constitution may encounter difficulties in practice, requiring clarification or amendment to better fit political and institutional realities.

Third, the evolution of citizens' expectations, along with scientific and technological progress, demands that constitutional provisions become richer and more substantive to address new issues.

The French jurist Georges Vedel (1910–2002) argued that the legitimacy of judicial review derives from the people's right to amend their constitution. Drawing on the thought of Rousseau and other Enlightenment philosophers, Vedel explained that laws were traditionally viewed as the expression of the "general will" of the sovereign people – the *volonté générale* – and therefore could not be subject to external control without violating popular sovereignty. In contrast, Montesquieu's theory of the Separation of Powers emphasized the need for checks and balances between institutions.

According to Vedel, judicial review by constitutional courts is legitimate only if the legislature or the people retain the power to overrule judicial decisions by amending the constitution. Otherwise, ultimate authority would rest with judges rather than with the people. This reasoning highlights a key difference between the American and European constitutional traditions: the American model places greater trust in the Judiciary, while the European model emphasizes the sovereignty of parliament and the nation's representatives.

With these principles in mind, we can now turn to a concise comparative overview of how major modern constitutions around the world may be amended.

2.1.9.2 IN THE UNITED STATES

In the United States, amendments may be proposed by a two-thirds vote of each house of Congress or by a national convention called by Congress at the request of two-thirds of the states (though this method has never been used before). To become part of the Constitution, amendments must be ratified by the legislatures of three-fourths of the states or by conventions in three-fourths of the states (this method has been used only once – to ratify the Twenty-First Amendment repealing Prohibition). Article V of the U.S. Constitution spells out the processes by which amendments can be proposed and ratified.[60]

> **Article V**
>
> The Congress, whenever two thirds of both houses shall deem it necessary, shall propose amendments to this Constitution, or, on the application of the legislatures of two thirds of the several states, shall call a convention for proposing amendments, which, in either case, shall be valid to all intents and purposes, as part of this Constitution, when ratified by the

60 Rogers, James, 2007, "The Other Way to Amend the Constitution: The Article V Constitutional Convention Amendment Process," *Harvard Journal of Law and Public Policy*, vol. 30, no. 3.

legislatures of three fourths of the several states, or by conventions in three fourths thereof, as the one or the other mode of ratification may be proposed by the Congress; provided that no amendment which may be made prior to the year one thousand eight hundred and eight shall in any manner affect the first and fourth clauses in the ninth section of the first article; and that no State, without its consent, shall be deprived of its equal suffrage in the Senate.

The Constitution sets no time limit during which the states must ratify a proposed amendment. But the courts have held that amendments must be ratified within a "reasonable time." Of the thousands of proposals that have been made to amend the Constitution (around 9,000 proposed amendments), only 33 have obtained the necessary two-thirds vote in Congress. Of those 33, only 27 amendments (including the Bill of Rights) have been ratified.[61]

2.1.9.3 IN FRANCE

In France, the President of the Republic, on the recommendation of the Prime Minister, and Members of parliament alike shall have the right to initiate amendments to the Constitution. In addition, proposals to amend the Constitution must pass by the two Houses in identical terms, and such an amendment, as a rule, only takes effect after approval by referendum. Article 89 of the French Constitution spells out the processes by which amendments can be proposed and ratified.

Article 89: ON AMENDMENTS TO THE CONSTITUTION

The President of the Republic, on the recommendation of the Prime Minister, and Members of Parliament alike shall have the right to initiate amendments to the Constitution.

A government or a Private Member's Bill to amend the Constitution must be considered within the time limits set down in the third paragraph of article 42 and be passed by the two Houses in identical terms. The amendment shall take effect after approval by referendum.

However, a government Bill to amend the Constitution shall not be submitted to referendum where the President of the Republic decides to submit it to Parliament convened in Congress; the government Bill to amend the Constitution shall then be approved only if it is passed by a three-fifths majority of the votes cast. The Bureau of the Congress shall be that of the National Assembly.

61 Examples of Amendments to the U.S. Constitution include the Thirteenth Amendment, which declared that "Neither slavery nor involuntary servitude, except as a punishment for crime whereof the party shall have been duly convicted, shall exist within the United States, or any place subject to their jurisdiction." Formally abolishing slavery in the United States, the Thirteenth Amendment was passed by Congress on January 31, 1865, and ratified by the states on December 6, 1865.

The Nineteenth Amendment to the United States Constitution prohibits any United States citizen from being denied the right to vote on the basis of sex: "The right of citizens of the United States to vote shall not be denied or abridged by the United States or by any State on account of sex. Congress shall have power to enforce this article by appropriate legislation." It was ratified on August 18, 1920. The Constitution allows the states to determine the qualifications for voting, and until the 1910s, most states disenfranchised women. The amendment was the culmination of the women's suffrage movement in the United States, which fought at both the state and national levels to achieve the vote. It effectively overruled *Minor v. Happersett*, in which a unanimous Supreme Court ruled that the Fourteenth Amendment did not give women the right to vote.

> No amendment procedure shall be commenced or continued where the integrity of national territory is placed in jeopardy. The republican form of government shall not be the object of any amendment.

A large number of constitutions throughout the world have pre-dispositions that explicitly forbid any change to be made to their fundamental principles. In France, since the 1884 amendment to the Constitution, the republican form of government cannot be amended under any circumstances.

Yet, right after President Albert Lebrun appointed Marshal Pétain as Prime Minister in 1940, the latter began a revision of the Constitution of the discredited Third Republic and established an authoritarian regime now referred to as Vichy France, which collaborated during World War II with the Nazi Regime of Germany. Marshal Pétain formally assumed absolute powers as "Head of State," though he stated at the time, "this is not ancient Rome and I have no wish to be Caesar." This historical example shows how fragile constitutional rules may be when the sky becomes grey and dull.

In 2024, France became the first country to enshrine abortion rights in its Constitution, demonstrating strong support for women's rights worldwide. French lawmakers overwhelmingly approved a constitutional amendment, with a vote of 780 to 72, to protect women's freedom to have abortions.

Amendment to Article 34 of the 1958 Constitution of France

> The Law determines the conditions by which is exercised the freedom of women to have recourse to an abortion, which is guaranteed.

This historic decision has been officially celebrated on March 8, coinciding with International Women's Rights Day. This event underscores France's commitment to women's rights, hoping to serve as an example for other nations, especially with the U.S. Supreme Court's 2022 decision to overturn *Roe v. Wade*.

On June 24, 2022, the U.S. Supreme Court's decision in *Dobbs v. Jackson Women's Health Organization* overturned *Roe v. Wade*, ending 50 years of precedent. This led to a surge in abortion legislation, with nearly 22 million women losing access to abortion in their states within 100 days. In 2022, state legislators introduced 563 restrictive abortion provisions, and 50 became law. Currently, 14 states have near-total abortion bans, and six states have bans from 6 to 20 weeks. These bans disproportionately affect marginalized groups, especially women of color. In response, many states have introduced protective measures, with 369 bills aimed at safeguarding abortion access introduced in 2022, reflecting strong public support for abortion rights.[62]

2.1.9.4 IN CHINA

Article 64 of the People's Republic of China Constitution spells out the processes by which amendments can be proposed and ratified, providing that

> Amendments to the Constitution are to be proposed by the Standing Committee of the National People's Congress or by more than one-fifth of the deputies to the National People's

62 Cohen, David S., Donley, Greer, and Rebouché, Rachel, 2023, "The New Abortion Battleground," *Columbia Law Review*, vol. 123, no. 1.

Congress and adopted by a majority vote of more than two-thirds of all the deputies to the Congress.

The Fifth National People's Congress adopted the current version of the Constitution on December 4, 1982, with further revisions in 1988, 1993, 1999, and 2004. Three previous state Constitutions – those of 1954, 1975, and 1978 – were superseded in turn.

The 1982 Constitution is widely seen as the foundational text of China's reform era. It was designed to restore institutional stability after the Cultural Revolution and to support the country's gradual shift toward a more pragmatic, development-oriented political system. Amendments adopted since then have reflected major policy changes, such as the recognition of the "socialist market economy," the protection of private property, and the inclusion of human rights language. These developments show that constitutional change in China is mainly a political process led by the Communist Party, rather than the outcome of public debate or judicial interpretation. In 2018, a further amendment abolished the two-term limit for the presidency, allowing President Xi Jinping to be elected to an unprecedented third term in 2023 and to stay in office indefinitely. This marked a clear break with the post-Mao commitment to collective leadership and was widely viewed as concentrating power at the highest level of the state.

China's 2018 amendment illustrates how constitutional change can be used to consolidate executive authority, a dynamic also visible in many other regions of the world.

2.1.9.5 AMENDEMENTS TO STAY IN POWER

Since 2000, several African and Latin American countries have witnessed constitutional amendments designed to extend presidential power, often by removing term or age limits. These changes have frequently sparked controversy, political unrest, and, in some cases, regime collapse.

In Comoros, a 2018 referendum strengthened presidential authority, allowing President Azali Assoumani to serve two consecutive terms instead of one. He was re-elected in 2019 amid accusations of electoral fraud.

In Rwanda, a 2015 constitutional revision enabled President Paul Kagame to run for another term in 2017 and potentially remain in power until 2034.

In the Republic of Congo, a 2015 referendum abolished term and age limits, allowing President Denis Sassou-Nguesso to seek a third term, which he secured in 2016.

In Burundi, President Pierre Nkurunziza's decision to run for a third term in 2015 triggered violent protests and a national crisis. A 2018 referendum later extended presidential terms, potentially allowing him to remain in office until 2034, though he chose not to run again.

In Zimbabwe, the 2013 Constitution permitted Robert Mugabe to seek re-election. He won but was forced to resign in 2017 after nearly four decades in power.

In Djibouti, parliament removed term limits in 2010, enabling President Ismaël Omar Guelleh to win additional elections in 2011 and 2016.

In Algeria, the removal of term limits in 2008 allowed President Abdelaziz Bouteflika to remain in office until mass protests forced his resignation in 2019.

In Cameroon, a 2008 constitutional amendment abolished term limits, enabling President Paul Biya to win a seventh term in 2018.

In Uganda, term limits were abolished in 2005, allowing President Yoweri Museveni to be repeatedly re-elected.

In Chad, a 2005 referendum eliminated the two-term limit, extending President Idriss Déby Itno's long rule until his death in 2021.

In Togo, a 2002 constitutional change removed term limits, enabling President Gnassingbé Eyadéma to continue in office until his death. His son, Faure Gnassingbé, succeeded him in 2005 and has since been re-elected.

In Burkina Faso, President Blaise Compaoré's attempt to change the Constitution to extend his rule provoked a popular uprising in 2014 that led to his overthrow.

In Malawi, parliament rejected President Bakili Muluzi's 2002 effort to secure a third term, under strong opposition from civil society and religious groups.

In the Democratic Republic of Congo, President Joseph Kabila's decision to remain in power beyond his constitutional term limit led to years of political tension before opposition leader Félix Tshisekedi took office in 2019.

A similar dynamic occurred in Honduras, where President José Manuel Zelaya's 2009 attempt to amend the Constitution to allow re-election provoked a constitutional crisis and a military-backed coup, despite international mediation efforts.

These examples highlight a recurring pattern: when constitutional mechanisms meant to ensure alternation of power are manipulated or removed, democratic stability weakens. The amendment of constitutions for personal or political continuity often leads to erosion of the Rule of Law, loss of institutional credibility, and, in extreme cases, political violence or regime change.

3 Compatibility of Judicial Review With Democratic Principles

The question of whether judicial review is compatible with democratic principles lies at the heart of constitutional theory. In a democracy, power originates from the people, who express their will through elected representatives. Yet, judicial review grants unelected judges the authority to strike down laws enacted by those representatives. At first glance, this may seem to contradict the very notion of popular sovereignty.

However, the experience of totalitarian regimes demonstrates the dangers of unchecked power. In systems without judicial review, the absence of legal limits on the legislature or the Executive often leads to abuses of authority and the suppression of fundamental rights. Judicial review, therefore, acts as a safeguard against such excesses. It ensures that majority rule operates within the boundaries set by the constitution, protecting the rights and freedoms of individuals and minorities.

Far from opposing democracy, judicial review reinforces it. It embodies the principle that the Rule of Law must prevail over the rule of men and that all branches of government remain subject to the constitution. By guaranteeing the supremacy of constitutional norms and ensuring that the actions of public authorities conform to democratic values, judicial review preserves the balance between popular sovereignty and the protection of rights.

In this sense, judicial review and democracy are not mutually exclusive but complementary. Judicial review prevents arbitrary power, strengthens citizens' trust in institutions, and upholds the moral and legal foundations upon which democratic governance depends.

3.1 Importance of the Question

The relationship between judicial review and democracy raises fundamental questions about the balance between majority rule and the protection of individual rights. Understanding this relationship is essential to grasping how modern democracies reconcile popular sovereignty with constitutional limits.

3.1.1 Controversy in France

The question of whether judicial review is compatible with democratic principles has long been debated. In France, this controversy is deeply rooted in the country's intellectual and political tradition. Influenced by the writings of Jean-Jacques Rousseau, French constitutional thought viewed *la loi* (the law) as the direct expression of the *volonté générale* – the general will of the people. This general will, expressed through the vote of the political majority, was seen as embodying the *intérêt général* (the general good or general interest), and therefore as the ultimate manifestation of popular sovereignty.

From the late 18th century through much of the 20th century, this conception of sovereignty was considered absolute and indivisible. The idea that unelected judges could overturn or even review a law adopted by democratically elected representatives was seen as incompatible with the very notion of democracy. To allow such review would, in the eyes of many, mean subordinating the will of the people to the judgment of a small, unelected elite.

This understanding of democracy was, however, a narrow one – limited to what might be called *electoral democracy*, which focuses primarily on majority rule and the outcome of elections, rather than on the protection of fundamental rights and the Rule of Law. Under this conception, a law could be constitutional merely because it had been enacted by the majority, even if it violated fundamental rights. Judicial review, by contrast, rests on the idea that democracy is not only about majority rule but also about limiting power and safeguarding individual freedoms.

3.1.2 Modern Perspective

Today, this narrow conception of democracy has been largely reconsidered. The focus has shifted from the sole expression of majority rule to the protection of fundamental rights, even against the will of the political majority. Modern democratic theory recognizes that genuine democracy requires more than periodic elections – it demands respect for the Rule of Law and the safeguarding of individual and minority rights. This evolution reflects the understanding that democracy is not merely a mechanism for selecting rulers, but a normative system grounded in principles of justice, equality, and human dignity. Courts, constitutional safeguards, and independent institutions play a crucial role in preventing abuses of power and ensuring that no majority, however large, may undermine the basic rights that constitute the democratic order.

Elections remain an essential feature of democratic life, but they are not, by themselves, sufficient to ensure a just and balanced society. A democracy that merely counts votes without protecting freedoms risks degenerating into the tyranny of the majority. Consequently, contemporary democracies emphasize *substantive democracy* – one that values constitutional limits, judicial oversight, and the protection of fundamental rights as integral to democratic governance. In this way, democracy is conceived not only as the rule of the many, but as a system designed to guarantee that all individuals, including minorities and dissenters, enjoy equal protection and meaningful participation in public life.

3.2 Lessons From Totalitarian Regimes

The 20th century revealed the dangers of unchecked political power. Totalitarian regimes demonstrated how the absence of judicial review can lead to widespread violations of rights and the collapse of democratic institutions.

3.2.1 Nazi Germany

In the aftermath of World War II, democratic thought and constitutional design underwent a major evolution. The experience of Nazi Germany revealed that formal legality and periodic elections were not enough to protect human life and dignity. The Nazi regime, though initially established through electoral means, demonstrated how a State without an independent Judiciary and without judicial review of legislative and executive actions could descend into totalitarianism and mass atrocities.

No one today would consider Hitler's Government a democracy, despite the formal appearance of democratic elections in 1938. This historical tragedy made it clear that democracy must be more than majority rule – it must be a political system that safeguards fundamental rights and human dignity. Such protection is only possible when those rights are enshrined in a supreme legal norm and enforced by independent judges empowered to review and strike down laws or government actions that violate them.

From this realization emerged the modern notion of *constitutional democracy* – a system where electoral legitimacy is complemented by constitutional supremacy and judicial oversight. In this model, democracy is not only about electing representatives but also about ensuring that power remains subject to the Rule of Law and that individual rights remain protected against the excesses of political majorities.

3.2.2 Post-War Realization

The Nazi experience underscored the urgent need for democracies to protect human rights through a supreme legal framework enforced by an independent Judiciary. The unchecked power of the Nazi regime, initially established through seemingly democratic means, demonstrated that electoral democracy alone cannot ensure the protection of individual rights and freedoms. This realization led to a global consensus that democracy must rest not only on the will of the majority but also on the Rule of Law and the safeguarding of fundamental rights.

After World War II, it became clear that elections, while essential, were insufficient to prevent the abuse of power. A true democracy requires institutions capable of limiting government authority and upholding constitutional principles. From this understanding emerged the concept of *constitutional democracy*, in which judicial review became a cornerstone. Judicial review empowers courts to verify the constitutionality of laws and executive acts, ensuring that even democratically elected governments remain subject to legal and moral constraints.

This transformation was crucial for strengthening accountability and maintaining the Separation of Powers. Independent courts became guarantors of justice, capable of preventing the concentration of power and protecting citizens from arbitrary rule. In this framework, the constitution serves as both a legal and moral compass guiding state action.

In conclusion, the post-war evolution of democratic thought placed judicial review at the heart of constitutional democracy. It bridged the gap between popular sovereignty and the protection of human dignity, ensuring that democracy is not only a matter of elections but a continuous commitment to uphold fundamental rights and the Rule of Law.

3.3 Judicial Review as a Democratic Requirement

Judicial review is now widely regarded as a cornerstone of modern democracy. It ensures that political power remains subject to law and that fundamental rights are respected regardless of political majorities.

3.3.1 Compatibility and Necessity

Judicial review is not only compatible with democratic principles – it is essential to their preservation. In a democracy governed by the Rule of Law, judicial review serves as a safeguard ensuring that legislative and executive acts conform to constitutional principles and respect fundamental rights. However, this power is not unlimited: courts must carefully justify their decisions, demonstrating why a given law or governmental act complies or conflicts with the constitution. Judicial review must never reflect the judges' personal views but must remain a neutral instrument for protecting citizens' rights and preventing abuses of power. Its legitimacy rests on rigorous legal reasoning, transparency of decisions, and adherence to constitutional standards rather than political preference.

Modern democracies increasingly embrace a *substantive* conception of democracy – one that values not only majority rule but also the effective protection of individual freedoms and human dignity. Experience has shown that parliaments, even when democratically elected, do not always produce legislation that upholds constitutional or human rights standards. For this reason, most contemporary legal systems entrust independent courts with the power of judicial review. This mechanism ensures that the will of the political majority does not override the basic rights and liberties that form the foundation of a democratic society. In this sense, judicial review strengthens democracy by ensuring that public power remains accountable to higher constitutional norms, thereby securing a stable balance between majority decision-making and the protection of fundamental rights.

3.3.2 The Democratic Difficulty of Judicial Review

The debate over whether judges should have the power to overrule parliaments lies at the heart of what scholars call *the democratic difficulty of judicial review*. This difficulty arises because unelected judges – in the United States, for instance, only nine members of the Supreme Court – have the authority, by a narrow majority, to invalidate acts passed by democratically elected representatives. Such a power raises an important question: can democracy remain legitimate when the Judiciary, rather than the legislature, has the final say on what the law means? Yet, every country that has adopted a written constitution faces this tension between democracy and constitutionalism.

Several approaches have been developed to address this dilemma.

The first approach rejects the idea that courts can invalidate statutes on the ground that it would undermine democratic legitimacy. This is the traditional position in the United Kingdom, based on the principle of parliamentary sovereignty. Since the British Constitution is largely unwritten and founded on conventions, parliament remains the supreme authority, and no court can strike down its legislation.

The second approach is the American model, established in *Marbury v. Madison* (1803). The U.S. Supreme Court held that it is the duty of the Judiciary to apply the law – and if a conflict arises between the Constitution and an Act of Congress, the Constitution must prevail. This model of *decentralized judicial review* allows every court, whether state or federal, to refuse to apply legislation it deems unconstitutional, particularly when it violates the Bill of Rights.

The third approach is an intermediate one, which entrusts a single, specialized body – such as a Constitutional Court – with the exclusive power to review and invalidate unconstitutional laws. This *centralized model*, inspired by Hans Kelsen's theory, has become the most widespread in the world today, as it offers greater consistency, predictability, and institutional stability.

In practice, most countries have recognized that parliamentary majorities cannot always be relied upon to respect human rights or constitutional principles. Therefore, they have introduced mechanisms of judicial control while seeking to avoid giving judges excessive political power.

In conclusion, judicial review remains essential to a modern and substantive conception of democracy – one that prioritizes the protection of fundamental rights over the unrestricted rule of the majority. Far from opposing democracy, judicial review ensures that democratic government operates within the bounds of constitutional justice, preserving both liberty and legitimacy.

4 The Rule of Law

This section serves as a brief introduction to the concept of the Rule of Law – a principle so fundamental that it could easily warrant an entire volume of its own. Since ancient times, thinkers have emphasized its importance: Aristotle famously declared that "the Rule of Law is better than that of any individual." Today, it stands as the cornerstone of all modern democratic states and institutions. It is enshrined in the founding principles of the United Nations, the European Union, and the European Convention on Human Rights. Yet, despite its universal appeal, the degree of adherence to the Rule of Law still varies widely across nations.

The concept itself is complex and multifaceted. It has been interpreted in many ways – from a minimalist definition describing a well-functioning legal system[63] to a more rhetorical use, meaning little more than "Hooray for our side."[64] Lord Bingham[65] proposed a unifying view, defining the Rule of Law as the principle that "all persons and authorities within the State . . . should be bound by and entitled to the benefit of laws publicly and prospectively promulgated and publicly administered in the courts."[66]

In this section, we will clarify the notion of the Rule of Law by examining its various meanings and dimensions. We will distinguish between *formal* and *substantive* conceptions of the Rule of Law, trace its historical development and essential features, and explore how it is understood and applied across different legal systems – from Civil Law and Common Law traditions to mixed, socialist, and religious systems.

4.1 Formal vs. Substantive Conceptions of the Rule of Law

In this part, we will examine the two main conceptions of the Rule of Law: the *formal* and the *substantive* views. The formal conception emphasizes procedure – how laws are made, applied, and enforced – focusing on legality, consistency, and predictability. It is concerned with *rule by law*, ensuring that government action follows established legal processes. The substantive conception, by contrast, goes beyond procedure to consider the moral and ethical quality of laws. It insists that laws must promote justice, equality, and the protection of fundamental rights. By comparing these two perspectives, we can better understand how differing interpretations of the Rule of Law influence the nature of democracy and the protection of individual freedoms.

63 Finnis, John, 1980, *Natural Law and Natural Rights*, Oxford, p. 270.

64 Waldron, Jeremy, 2002, "Is the Rule of Law an Essentially Contested Concept (in Florida)?," *Law & Philosophy*, vol. 21, no. 2, p. 119.

65 Thomas Henry Bingham, Baron Bingham of Cornhill (1933–2010), was a distinguished British judge who successively served as Master of the Rolls, Lord Chief Justice, and Senior Law Lord. Widely admired for his intellect and integrity and was described upon his death as the greatest judge of his generation.

66 Bingham, Lord, 2007, "The Rule of Law," *Cambridge Law Journal*, vol. 66, no. 1, pp. 67–85.

4.1.1 Formal Conception

In legal theory, the Rule of Law is generally divided into two main conceptions: *formal* and *substantive*. The *formal* conception focuses on the structure, source, and procedure of legality, while the *substantive* conception concerns the content of the law, distinguishing between what may be considered "good law" and "bad law."[67]

According to Brian Tamanaha, the formal conception can be understood through three progressive levels: (1) *rule by law*; (2) *formal legality*; and (3) *democracy and legality*. These stages represent an evolution from basic legality toward the foundations of a liberal democratic system. The *substantive* conception builds upon these formal levels, introducing individual rights and moral principles that connect the Rule of Law with democracy, human rights, and good governance.

Although varying in degree and application, a country that embraces a substantive conception of the Rule of Law can generally be said to have adopted the essential values of a liberal democracy.

4.1.1.1 RULE BY LAW

The concept of *rule by law* refers simply to a situation in which governance is conducted through legal mechanisms rather than through the use of force or violence.[68] This conception is foundational but minimalist – it ensures that government action is carried out under and through the law. However, because every modern State, regardless of its political system, uses law as an instrument of governance, *rule by law* can exist even in authoritarian regimes.[69] In such cases, law functions primarily as a tool of government control rather than as a limitation on government power. For instance, China promotes this conception of the Rule of Law to legitimize its legal order in response to international pressure from institutions such as the United Nations and the World Bank, which tend to advocate for more substantive, rights-based conceptions.[70] In practice, this means that the law is used mainly to organize and strengthen State power, not to protect citizens from abuse, and that legality is valued more for its efficiency than for its commitment to individual rights.

4.1.1.2 FORMAL LEGALITY

Lon Fuller, a major 20th-century legal philosopher, identified eight principles of legality that distinguish a legal system from mere command and coercion. These principles are: (1) generality of rules; (2) public promulgation; (3) non-retroactivity; (4) clarity; (5) consistency; (6) feasibility of compliance; (7) stability over time; and (8) congruence between official action and declared rules. While Fuller regarded these as moral principles, they do not concern the morality of law's content but rather its *form* – its capacity to guide behavior. A system that violates these principles, he argued, ceases to be a genuine legal order because its subjects cannot effectively follow or rely upon its rules.

Legal theorists such as Friedrich Hayek and Joseph Raz later reinforced this view, emphasizing the importance of predictability and procedural fairness. Building upon Fuller, Raz added

67 Tamanaha, Brian Z., 2004, *On the Rule of Law: History, Politics, Theory*, Cambridge, p. 92.

68 Loughlin, Martin, 2010, *Foundations of Public Law*, Oxford, p. 123.

69 Tamanaha, *On the Rule of Law*, p. 92.

70 Peerenboom, Randall, 2002, *China's Long March Toward Rule of Law*, Cambridge, p. 6.

that the Rule of Law requires institutional guarantees – an independent Judiciary, open and fair hearings, and a degree of discretion among enforcement authorities – to ensure that legal procedures are followed faithfully.

In this sense, formal legality stands as a safeguard against arbitrary power. Yet it does not guarantee justice. A regime may comply perfectly with the principles of legality and still enact oppressive laws. For instance, during racial segregation in the United States, discriminatory statutes fulfilled Fuller's formal criteria – they were clear, public, stable, and enforceable – yet substantively unjust. Formal legality thus offers procedural predictability but not moral assurance.

4.1.1.3 DEMOCRACY AND LEGALITY

The final stage of the formal conception of the Rule of Law integrates democracy into legal processes. Here, legality gains legitimacy through democratic participation, even though the emphasis remains on procedure rather than substance. Without democracy, legality alone risks being used as a façade for authoritarian rule, as laws may be enacted through undemocratic or illegitimate means.[71]

Philosopher Jürgen Habermas argued that democracy provides legitimacy because it incorporates moral pluralism into lawmaking.[72] In a world where universal truths can no longer be derived from natural law, democracy allows citizens to participate rationally in shaping the norms that govern them. Law, therefore, must be the product of public deliberation and self-determination.

However, critics point out that democracy can still produce instability or "bad laws" shaped by fleeting public passions or populism, particularly in societies without strong democratic traditions.[73] Nevertheless, democracy remains the most effective system for ensuring legitimate governance and aligning legality with collective self-rule. The combination of democracy and formal legality thus strengthens both the legitimacy and fairness of the legal order.

4.1.2 Substantive Conception

The *substantive* conception of the Rule of Law builds upon the formal conception by examining not only *how* laws are made but also *what* they contain. It distinguishes "good law" from "bad law" by reference to liberal democratic values such as self-rule, legal liberty, personal freedom, and Separation of Powers.[74] At this level, the Rule of Law becomes inseparable from the protection of individual rights.[75]

Ronald Dworkin, among others, argued that law must embody moral principles and protect fundamental rights to truly fulfil its purpose. This modern understanding – combining formal

71 Tamanaha, *On the Rule of Law*, p. 99.

72 Habermas, J., 1996, *Between Facts and Norms*, MIT Press.

73 Tamanaha, *On the Rule of Law*, p. 100.

74 Tamanaha, *On the Rule of Law*, p. 35.

75 Ronald Dworkin describes the individual rights conception of the Rule of Law as follows: "Citizens have moral rights and duties with respect to one another, and political rights against the State as a whole. . . . The Rule of Law on this conception is the ideal rule by an accurate public conception of individual rights. It does not distinguish . . . between the Rule of Law and substantive justice; on the contrary it requires, as a part of the ideal of law, that the rule in the rule book capture and enforce moral rights." Dworkin, Ronald, 1980, *Political Judges and the Rule of Law*, British Academy, p. 259.

legality, democracy, and rights – underpins most contemporary references to the Rule of Law, including those of major international organizations.

The United Nations defines the Rule of Law as a system in which all persons and institutions, including the State, are accountable to laws that are publicly promulgated, equally enforced, independently adjudicated, and consistent with international human rights norms.[76] It also requires fairness, equality before the law, participation in decision-making, legal certainty, and transparency.[77]

Similarly, the Venice Commission of the Council of Europe lists six essential elements of the Rule of Law:

(1) Legality, including a transparent and democratic process for enacting laws;
(2) Legal certainty;
(3) Prohibition of arbitrariness;
(4) Access to justice before independent and impartial courts;
(5) Respect for human rights;
(6) Non-discrimination and equality before the law.[78]

This definition illustrates how the substantive conception unites both procedural and moral dimensions of law.

However, this approach faces two major criticisms. The first concerns moral disagreement: in pluralistic societies, defining "moral rights" is highly contested – as seen in debates over abortion, same-sex marriage, or capital punishment in the United States. The second concerns universality: since the substantive Rule of Law is inseparable from democracy, promoting it worldwide implies exporting liberal democratic values, raising questions about cultural and political autonomy.

Despite these challenges, the substantive conception remains the most comprehensive expression of the Rule of Law today – one that aspires not only to govern by law but to ensure that law itself serves justice, equality, and human dignity.

4.2 Historical Background and Key Features of the Rule of Law

The central question of the Rule of Law is this: how can political power both create the law and be limited by the law? In other words, how can a sovereign authority that possesses the power to make legal norms also be constrained by them? The answer lies in the very organization of the political and legal system. Vertically, this limitation is ensured through a hierarchy of norms within the legal order, placing the Constitution at its apex. Horizontally, it is achieved through the balance of powers among the Executive, Legislative, and Judicial branches, each responsible for checking and limiting the others. Thus, law becomes both the instrument and the boundary of political power.

76 United Nations, 2004, "Report of the Secretary-General on the Rule of Law and Transitional Justice in Conflict and Post-Conflict Societies."
77 Bingham, Lord, 2007, "The Rule of Law," *Cambridge Law Journal*, vol. 66, no. 1, p. 76.
78 Venice Commission, "Report on the Rule of Law," p. 10.

4.2.1 Vertical Hierarchy of the Legal Order

The sources of law identified in Chapter 1, "What is Law? What Forms Does Law Take?," do not all hold the same value or authority within a democratic legal order. Some norms have a higher rank than others. When a lower norm conflicts with a higher one, the judge must disregard the lower norm. This structure of legal hierarchy was developed by Hans Kelsen, one of the most influential jurists and legal theorists of the 20th century, who proposed a model that views law as a coherent system of interrelated norms.

In Kelsen's model, the validity of a legal norm depends on the validity of a superior norm. This reasoning continues upward in a logical sequence until it reaches the highest point of the hierarchy: the constitution. At this stage, a question arises: how can the validity of the constitution itself be justified? Kelsen answered this by postulating the existence of a basic norm, or *grundnorm*, whose validity is assumed rather than proven. This hypothesis serves as the logical foundation of the entire legal system.

In his major work, *The Pure Theory of Law* (1934), Kelsen developed a new understanding of law as a "science of norms," aiming to describe law objectively, without reference to politics or morality. Following a Kantian approach, Kelsen sought to identify the universal structures underlying legal systems. He argued that legal norms should be studied as objective entities, focusing on their relationships rather than their content. This raises fundamental questions: can law truly be separated from moral considerations? Can there be universal legal structures applicable to all systems?

Kelsen's theory views the legal order as a dynamic system in which judges play a central role. It is the judge who ensures that lower norms comply with higher ones and who maintains the coherence of the legal order. The constitution, in this model, is not only the founding norm that establishes a political community but also the rule that determines the validity of the entire legal system.

The hierarchy of norms represents a rational and objective conception of law. Kelsen asked how positive law – the law as it exists – can be understood scientifically. He distinguished between what *is* (facts) and what *ought to be* (norms). Legal validity, according to Kelsen, derives not from moral or social considerations but from its conformity with a superior norm. This logical regression culminates in the constitution, whose validity, being unprovable, must simply be assumed. Kelsen acknowledged that this assumption introduces an element of uncertainty, but he considered it a necessary methodological hypothesis.

In this hierarchical structure, norms are arranged in a pyramid. The higher a norm stands, the more general it is, and the fewer such norms exist. At the base are numerous individual norms that apply general rules to specific cases. The constitution – or *Grundgesetz* – provides unity to the entire system. Kelsen distinguished between a static order of norms (concerned with their logical structure) and a dynamic order (concerned with how norms are created and applied).[79]

He identified several levels within the legal order: the fundamental norm, organic laws derived directly from the constitution, ordinary laws, administrative regulations, and individual decisions or rulings. Each lower level derives its validity from the one above. What makes a norm valid is not its content, but the procedure through which it was created in accordance with a superior rule. A legal system, Kelsen argued, cannot be based on facts alone; it must rest on rational, normative foundations.

79 See, for example, Araszkiewicz, Michał and Pleszka, Krzysztof, 2015, *Logic in the Theory and Practice of Lawmaking*, Springer, p. 196.

For example, robbery is prohibited by law not because it is morally wrong, but because a general legal principle – ultimately derived from the constitution – enables the creation of a specific norm forbidding it. Judges interpret and apply such general principles, ensuring that their decisions are consistent with the fundamental norm.

In democratic terms (though Kelsen himself did not develop a democratic theory), the highest norm is the most legitimate one because it is closest to the source of political authority: the people. Constitutions are often adopted through referenda for this reason. The hierarchy of norms thus ensures coherence, stability, and predictability within the legal system, while protecting it from arbitrariness and the abuse of power.

4.2.2 Horizontal Balance of Powers

In October 2009, upon the inauguration of the Supreme Court of the United Kingdom, Lord Phillips of Worth Matravers – the Court's first President – highlighted the significance of establishing a judiciary fully independent from parliament. He stated:

> For the first time, we have a clear Separation of Powers between the legislature, the Judiciary and the Executive in the United Kingdom. This is important. It emphasizes the independence of the Judiciary, clearly separating those who make the law from those who administer it.

The theory of the Separation of Powers is traditionally attributed to Montesquieu, though its roots can be traced back to Aristotle's *Politics*. Aristotle identified three essential components of any political system: the deliberative body (the parliament), the executive authority (the government), and the judicial body (the courts). Montesquieu later refined these ideas in *The Spirit of the Laws* (1748), where he described three powers inherent to every State – the Legislative, the Executive, and the Judiciary – and argued that these powers should be exercised by separate institutions. His central idea was that power can only be restrained by power: if one branch of government becomes dominant, liberty is threatened.

This theory deeply influenced Western political thought. Article 16 of the *Declaration of the Rights of Man and of the Citizen* (1789) affirms that "any society in which rights are not guaranteed, nor the Separation of Powers determined, has no Constitution." Montesquieu's model also inspired the framers of the United States Constitution,[80] where the Separation of Powers is enshrined in Articles I, II, and III, which respectively establish the Legislative, Executive, and judicial branches of government.[81] Each branch has its own powers and checks on the others: for example, the President can veto laws passed by Congress, but Congress can override the veto; the President appoints judges and senior officials, but these appointments require Senate approval; and the Supreme Court can declare laws unconstitutional, while Congress and the States retain the power to amend the Constitution. This system ensures that no single branch can dominate the others.

80 Legend has it that Benjamin Franklin, to illustrate the importance of limiting political power and establishing a balance of powers, had coffee with Thomas Jefferson. Franklin poured boiling hot coffee into a cup, then transferred it into another empty cup, and back and forth between the two cups, cooling it down in the process. He explained to Jefferson, "You see, I have cooled the coffee down. Let's do the same with legislative power. Let's cool down the laws by establishing a balance of powers, so that power can be a check to power."

81 The Legislative (composed of the House of Representatives and the Senate) is set up in Article 1. The Executive (composed of the President, Vice-President, and the Departments of State) is set up in Article 2. The Judicial (composed of the federal courts and the Supreme Court) is set up in Article 3.

The purpose of this separation is to preserve individual liberty and prevent the abuse of power. Montesquieu observed that when Legislative, Executive, and judicial powers are concentrated in the same hands, liberty cannot exist. The Separation of Powers thus guarantees that each branch remains limited by the others and that political authority remains balanced and accountable.

Montesquieu, The Spirit of Laws, Book XI, Chapter 4 (extract)

In every government there are three sorts of power; the legislative; the executive, in respect to things dependent on the law of nations; and the executive, in regard to things that depend on the Civil Law.

By virtue of the first, the prince or magistrate enacts temporary or perpetual laws, and amends or abrogates those that have been already enacted. By the second, he makes peace or war, sends or receives embassies; establishes the public security, and provides against invasions. By the third, he punishes criminals, or determines the disputes that arise between individuals. The latter we shall call the judiciary power, and the other simply the executive power of the State.

The political liberty of the subject is a tranquility of mind, arising from the opinion each person has of his safety. In order to have this liberty, it is requisite the government be so constituted as one man need not be afraid of' another.

When the legislative and executive powers are united in the same person, or in the same body of magistrates, there can be no liberty; because apprehensions may anise, lest the same monarch or senate should enact tyrannical laws, to execute them in a tyrannical manner.

Again, there is no liberty, if the power of judging be not separated from the legislative and executive powers. Were it joined with the legislative, the life and liberty of the subject would be exposed to arbitrary control, for the judge would then be the legislator. Were it joined to the executive power, the judge might behave with all the violence of an oppressor.

There would be an end of every thing were the same man, or the same body, whether of the nobles or of the people to exercise those three powers that of enacting laws, that of executing the public resolutions, and that of judging the crimes or differences of individuals.

Most kingdoms in Europe enjoy a moderate government, because the prince, who is invested with the two first powers, leaves the third to his subjects. In Turkey, where these three powers are united in the sultan's person the subjects groan under the weight of a most frightful oppression.

One branch must stop another in case of abuse. Therefore, the different organs that represent these powers should be separated in order to have balanced institutions that provide individual liberty. The main goal of such a distribution is to protect the individuals against the excesses of an unlimited power, which in the end must walk on the individual's rights and liberty. Power being understood here, as the structural capacity of an actor to impose its will over other social actors.

However, the effectiveness of this theory in practice depends on the political system, the mode of election, and the behavior of institutions. For instance, in France, the introduction of direct universal suffrage for the presidential election in 1962 transformed the functioning of institutions. It gave the President a strong democratic legitimacy, which, combined with a parliamentary majority of the same political orientation, tends to blur the separation between executive and legislative powers. In such situations, the mechanisms designed to ensure balance – such as the motion of censure or the power of dissolution – are rarely used. Similarly, in parliamentary systems dominated by a single majority, such as in the United Kingdom, the Separation of Powers is limited by political discipline.

Opposition parties play a crucial role in maintaining the balance of power. Their ability to counter the majority depends on institutional safeguards. In France, the opposition can refer laws to the Constitutional Council to verify their conformity with the Constitution, table a motion of censure, or question the government directly.[82] In the United Kingdom, the "Leader of the Opposition" and the "Shadow Cabinet" ensure democratic oversight of government actions. In the United States, opposition parties can block presidential initiatives through Congress, maintaining a balance between branches. In contrast, in authoritarian regimes such as North Korea, opposition parties exist only nominally, and in absolute monarchies such as Saudi Arabia, they are entirely absent.

Beyond political institutions, modern democracies recognize new forms of counter-power. The media, often referred to as the "fourth power," plays a crucial role in holding governments accountable.[83] The *Watergate* affair, which led to President Nixon's resignation in 1974, illustrates the impact of investigative journalism. Today, social media – sometimes described as the "fifth power" – has amplified this influence. Online platforms and social media disseminate information instantly and can reveal political scandals or mobilize public opinion,[84] even in countries where traditional media is censored. In China, for instance, access to social networks like Facebook is restricted, demonstrating the government's concern over their potential to challenge state control.[85]

Interest groups and lobbies also test the modern balance of powers. Lobbies seek to influence legislation by representing specific social or economic interests. Their role varies according to political systems.[86] In France, the government may consult lobbies, but participation is not institutionalized. In the European Union, lobby participation in lawmaking is more structured, with expert consultations and an official register of lobbyists. In the United States, lobbying is a central element of political life. For example, organizations such as the National Rifle Association (NRA) have significant influence.[87] In contrast, in neo-corporatist systems like Sweden and Austria, participation in a limited number of official associations is required, reflecting a more regulated form of interest representation.

Religion, the economy, and supranational governance also act as counterbalances to state power.[88] Religious movements can challenge governmental authority when their moral princi-

82 Article 61 of the French Constitution.

83 Kessler, David, 2012, "Les médias sont-ils un pouvoir?," *Pouvoirs*, vol. 143, no. 4, pp. 105–112.

84 In January 2011, during the Arab revolutions, Hosni Mubarak cut the Internet to stop the flow of contestations against its government. It had two major consequences: the international community could still talk about the revolution, but this would not influence the country, and no information about the rebellion could leave Egypt. The internet cut lasted for five days. Mubarak was said to have been condemned by the Egyptian Administrative Court to a fine for "prejudice against the country's economy." Peoples' expression and opinion are thus a strong opposition force. It can either lead to revolutions or simply impact institutions or elections. Nowadays, people and politicians give a lot of importance to opinion polls.

85 In China, the government does not allow Facebook (even if the population still finds ways to access it).

86 Molenat, Xavier, 2006, "Lobbies et groupes de pression," *Sciences humaines*, vol. 177, no. 12, p. 8.

87 Molenat, *Lobbies et groupes de pression*.

88 Olivier Beaud, Professor at the University Panthéon-Assas, writes: "The financial power seems to be powerful enough to impose states to pay their debts. But, on the opposite, banks close to bankruptcy, have also the strength to impose the help of the State. We can interpret this way the several laws taken by states after autumn 2008." Beaud, Olivier, 2012, "La multiplication des pouvoirs," *Pouvoirs*, vol. 143, no. 4, pp. 47–59.

ples conflict with state law, as illustrated by some movements during the Arab Spring. Economic forces, including multinational corporations and financial markets, exert strong pressure on governments, shaping legislation to favor stability or growth.

Finally, political power can be limited through institutional structures such as federalism. In federal states like the United States and Germany, power is divided vertically between the federal government and regional entities, each with its own constitution and institutions. This contrasts with unitary states, where power is concentrated at the national level.[89]

In conclusion, the doctrine of the Separation of Powers remains a cornerstone of democratic theory but has evolved to accommodate new political realities. Modern democracies are not limited to the traditional tripartite model of Executive, Legislative, and judicial powers. They also include horizontal and vertical counter-powers – opposition parties, the media, civil society, lobbies, and supranational institutions – that contribute to maintaining balance and protecting individual freedoms in increasingly complex political systems.

4.2.3 Essential Conditions: Equality Before the Law and Judicial Independence

The Rule of Law can only be valid and meaningful if two fundamental conditions are met: equality of all citizens before the law and the independence of the Judiciary. Without these essential foundations, neither the hierarchy of norms nor the balance of powers can be maintained. If the law does not apply equally to everyone, or if judges lack independence in ensuring its proper application through judicial review, the very structure of legal order and constitutional control collapses. Equality and judicial independence are therefore indispensable for upholding the coherence and legitimacy of the Rule of Law.

4.2.3.1 EQUALITY BEFORE THE LAW

Equality before the law is a fundamental legal principle deeply embedded in the foundations of Common Law, Civil Law, Religious, and Mixed legal systems – though rarely achieved in practice. It affirms that all individuals are entitled to the same legal protection and treatment, regardless of their status, origin, or belief. This principle is enshrined in the constitutions of most nations and recognized as one of the most essential human rights. Countries with vastly different

89 Even in this model, for practical reasons, the State can delegate some of its power to a regional authority. Indeed, different administrative repartitions of powers exist. The first form is the "centralized State." All powers come from a central authority: the government. This form is used in small states with a strong central power, sometimes in the hands of one person. The second form is a decontrated State ("*déconcentré*" in French). The central power sends its representatives to regions. State employees, as the "Préfet," receive their power directly from the State. It is a form of a centralized state; the regional authorities are still under the control of the central power, even if they possess some prerogatives. There is also the so-called "decentralized system" ("décentralisé" in French). Within this framework, the State gives power to small administrative authorities, distinct from the central government, such as towns and regions. These authorities may be elected and exert their own power freely (in the areas given by the State) and the execution of their own decisions. The goal is to better take into account the specificities of each area, especially in a large country, or with several groups of minorities. Decentralization is, as an example, widely found in Africa, where the central power has to coordinate with local traditional chiefs. The last kind of unitary state is a "regionalized state." In this system, the autonomy of regions does not come from the law, but directly from the constitution. It gives them a list of subjects that the national law cannot modify, and, as in Spain (like Catalonia, for instance, and all other Spanish autonomous communities: the CCAA, *comunidad autonoma*), the constitution can also allow regions to determine for themselves their organization and ways of working. This system is thus close to a federal state.

legal traditions – from the United States to France,[90] from China to Brazil, from Cuba to Saudi Arabia – have all affirmed equality as an inherent and inalienable right.

Imagine a simple situation: two drivers cause the same car accident – one is an ordinary citizen, and the other is a powerful politician. If the judge punishes only the ordinary citizen and excuses the politician because of his position, the two individuals are no longer equal before the law. This destroys both the independence of the Judiciary and the very foundation of the Rule of Law, which requires that justice be impartial and applied in the same way to everyone.

Consider another simple example: two business owners are accused of tax evasion. One of them is wealthy and well-connected, while the other runs a small local shop. If the wealthy businessman avoids prosecution thanks to his influence, while the small shop owner is convicted and fined, then equality before the law no longer exists. This kind of injustice undermines public trust in the Judiciary and weakens the Rule of Law itself.

Similarly, imagine a workplace harassment case where a female employee accuses her male supervisor of repeated inappropriate behavior. Both present their versions before the court. If the judge, influenced by cultural stereotypes, assumes that the woman is exaggerating or that the man's behavior is merely "misinterpreted," and dismisses the case without seriously examining the evidence, then the principle of equality before the law is violated.

In this situation, gender bias subtly distorts the judicial process. The woman is denied impartial consideration of her claim, and the man benefits from preconceived notions about credibility and authority. This imbalance not only undermines justice in that individual case but also erodes public confidence in the independence and fairness of the judicial system.

International human rights instruments have also placed equality before the law at their core. Article 7 of the 1948 *Universal Declaration of Human Rights* proclaims: "All are equal before the law and are entitled without any discrimination to equal protection of the law."

In the Common Law tradition, the notion of equality before the law is closely connected to the concept of *due process*, which refers to the fair conduct of legal proceedings in accordance with established rules and principles that protect individual rights. Due process ensures notice, impartiality, and the right to be heard before a competent tribunal having the power to decide the case.[91]

Yet, a paradox lies at the heart of this principle. Although equality before the law calls for fairness and impartiality, many societies continue to discriminate against minorities and vulnerable groups. The challenge lies in determining what equality truly means: equal to whom, and under what standard? The very act of defining equality establishes a norm or model of fairness that may exclude those who do not conform to it. Thus, while the law aspires to be blind and impartial, the societies in which it operates are neither blind nor equal.

Ultimately, equality before the law remains an aspirational legal ideal – an objective to be realized through the vigilance of independent judges who apply the law impartially and strive to ensure that justice is not merely proclaimed, but genuinely achieved.

The imprisonment of former French president Nicolas Sarkozy in October 2025 marked an unprecedented moment in the history of the Fifth Republic. Sentenced to five years in prison for criminal association in connection with alleged Libyan financing of his 2007 campaign, he became the first former head of State to serve time in detention. His incarceration, however, has sparked debate after reports revealed that he receives special treatment – more visits, longer sessions, and exceptional security measures.

90 Article 1 of the French Declaration of The Rights of Man and of the Citizen provides: "Men are born and remain free and equal in rights. Social distinctions may be based only on considerations of the common good."

91 Garner, Bryan A., 1999, *A Dictionary of Basic Law Terms*, Thomson West.

This situation raises a fundamental question about *égalité devant la loi* – equality before the law – a core value of the French Republic since 1789. For some, imprisoning Sarkozy affirms the Rule of Law: no one, not even a former president, is above justice. It demonstrates democratic maturity and the impartiality of French institutions. For others, jailing a former head of State undermines the dignity of the office and the nation, suggesting that punishment should take another form, such as house arrest, out of respect for the institution he once embodied.

Others go even further, questioning the independence of the Judiciary itself. They argue that Sarkozy's conviction reflects a form of political revenge – a trial driven less by law than by the desire of certain magistrates to settle scores with a former president of the Republic.

The Sarkozy case thus captures a deep French paradox – between the passion for equality, which demands blind justice, and the reverence for authority, which sees the presidency as sacred. It leaves an open question: does imprisoning a former president strengthen the Republic by proving that all are equal before the law, or does it weaken it by diminishing the aura of its highest office?

4.2.3.2 JUDICIAL INDEPENDENCE

The judicial branch plays a decisive role in shaping the law. In theory, judges are meant only to apply the law, not to create it. Their task should be limited to identifying the relevant legal rule and applying it to the facts of a case. In practice, however, this is rarely possible. Laws are written in broad and general terms, and judges must interpret them in order to apply them to specific situations. This process involves reconstructing the facts and legally qualifying them, which inevitably grants judges a degree of creative authority. Through interpretation, judges contribute to the evolution of the law – a role reinforced by their duty to render justice even when the law is unclear or silent.[92]

Judicial activity sometimes requires decisions that go against public opinion or political interests. Because courts do not operate on majority rule, judicial independence protects judges from external pressures, whether from the public or from the government. As former Canadian Prime Minister Arthur Meighen observed, judges occupy "a place apart" in society. Though appointed and paid by the State, they must remain free from political or bureaucratic influence once in office.

Several safeguards ensure this independence: administrative autonomy (so that governments cannot assign judges or set hearing dates), security of tenure, and legal immunity, allowing judges to act without fear of reprisal. Yet institutional independence alone is not enough. Individual judges must also appear impartial and objective. They are expected to maintain dignity, neutrality, and restraint – avoiding words or actions that might suggest bias.[93]

Judges must show respect to all participants in court proceedings and recuse themselves from any case involving relatives, friends, or personal interests. Judicial independence, therefore, is not merely a structural safeguard but also a personal ethical obligation, essential to maintaining public confidence in the Rule of Law.

92 Also, as discussed previously, judges possess the power of controlling the conformity of law with the constitution, which puts them at the center of most social-political discussions in most countries.

93 Judges often choose to avoid most forms of community involvement. A judge may undertake community or charitable work but cannot offer legal or investment advice. Judges cannot take part in politics, either as a party member, fundraiser or donor, and many choose to relinquish their right to vote. While judges have been more willing in recent years to make public speeches or agree to media interviews, they refrain from expressing opinions on legal issues that could come before them in a future case. Judges are forbidden from being paid to do anything other than their judicial duties, but can accept appointments to serve on royal commissions, inquiries, and other official investigations.

4.3 Overview of the Rule of Law Around the World

Let us now examine how different legal systems around the world adhere to, or diverge from, the principles of the Rule of Law. To illustrate this diversity, we will consider several representative countries, each reflecting a distinct legal tradition: Canada, a democratic Common Law system; Germany, a democratic Civil Law system; South Africa, a democratic mixed legal system; China, a single-party quasi-socialist system with Asian characteristics; and Saudi Arabia, an absolute monarchical system based on religious law. Through these examples, we can better understand how historical, political, and cultural contexts influence the practical application of the Rule of Law.

4.3.1 The Rule of Law in Common Law Countries: The Example of Canada

Canada's Constitution, like the United Kingdom's, is not contained in a single document. It consists of several instruments, chiefly the Constitution Act, 1867, and the Constitution Act, 1982, together with a set of statutes and orders listed in section 52 of the 1982 Act. As in most Western democracies, the Canadian constitutional order protects both the formal and substantive dimensions of the Rule of Law.[94] The preamble to the Constitution Act, 1982, affirms that Canada is founded on principles that recognize the Rule of Law, and Canadian constitutional practice has evolved alongside modern understandings of equality and rights.

On the formal side, the Constitution Act, 1982, declares the Constitution to be the "supreme law of Canada," ensuring that all other laws must conform to it. The Charter of Rights and Freedoms sets procedural guarantees that guard against arbitrariness and require congruence between legal rules and their administration. The Constitution Act, 1867, also establishes the basic institutional framework of government and separates Legislative, Executive, and judicial functions, providing a stable structure within which public power is exercised and reviewed.

On the substantive side, the Charter supplies a comprehensive catalogue of fundamental protections, including democratic rights, legal rights, equality rights, and freedoms of expression, religion, and association. The Constitution recognizes the rights of Indigenous peoples in section 35 of the 1982 Act, and promotes interprovincial fairness through fiscal and regional provisions (often called "equalization") designed to support comparable public services across the country. Canadian courts enforce these guarantees through judicial review, striking down or reading down legislation that is inconsistent with constitutional norms while also applying the Charter's reasonable-limits clause and the possibility of legislative override in section 33.

In practice, Canada has used this framework to expand and protect individual rights. Notably, parliament enacted the Civil Marriage Act in 2005 to recognize same-sex marriage nationwide, and federal benefit schemes (such as pension legislation) were amended to include same-sex spouses and partners. These developments illustrate how Canada's constitutional architecture integrates formal supremacy and institutional checks with substantive commitments to dignity, equality, and rights.

4.3.2 The Rule of Law in Civil Law Countries: The Example of Germany

The Federal Republic of Germany provides one of the most complete embodiments of the Rule of Law in the modern world. The German notion of *Rechtsstaat* – the State governed by law – emerged in the early 19th century and integrates both the formal and substantive dimensions

94 Canada Constitutional Act of 1982, part I § 2.

of the Rule of Law.[95] Since 1949, the *Grundgesetz* (Basic Law), Germany's Constitution, has served as a model for democratic constitutionalism, combining legal certainty with the protection of human dignity and fundamental rights.[96]

Formally, the Basic Law establishes the supremacy of the Constitution and guarantees the equality of all before the law (Article 3). It also provides for the promulgation and consistency of laws (Articles 145 and 146), and prohibits retroactive criminal legislation. Chapter IX, devoted to the administration of justice, reinforces these principles by ensuring that judicial decisions conform to the law and that courts remain independent. The Basic Law further divides governmental authority among the Executive, Legislative, and judicial branches, creating a robust system of checks and balances. In this way, Germany achieves the highest level of formal legality and democratic organization.

Historically, Germany's commitment to the Rule of Law was profoundly shaped by its experience under totalitarian regimes – first under the Nazi dictatorship and later, in East Germany, under communist rule. As a direct response to these past violations of justice, the framers of the 1949 Constitution placed human dignity at the center of the legal order.[97] Article 1 declares that "human dignity shall be inviolable" and that it is the duty of all state authorities to respect and protect it. This principle, together with the recognition of "inviolable and inalienable human rights," forms the moral foundation of the German constitutional system.

Substantively, the Basic Law enumerates 17 fundamental rights, including freedom of expression, assembly, association, and movement, as well as the rights to petition, citizenship, and the inviolability of the home. These rights are directly enforceable by the courts, particularly by the Federal Constitutional Court (*Bundesverfassungsgericht*), which serves as the guardian of the Constitution and the protector of individual rights.

Germany's Rule of Law commitment also extends beyond its borders. Article 23 of the Basic Law of the Federal Republic of Germany provides for participation in the European Union, emphasizing adherence to "democratic, social, and federal principles, to the Rule of Law, and to a level of protection of basic rights essentially comparable to that guaranteed by this Basic Law." Furthermore, Article 25 establishes a monist approach to International Law, incorporating general rules of International Law directly into the German legal order.

This dual commitment – to domestic constitutionalism and to European and international legal frameworks – illustrates the depth of Germany's adherence to the Rule of Law. The Federal Constitutional Court has consistently upheld Germany's engagement in European integration, as shown in its review of the European Stability Mechanism (ESM) Treaty, where it affirmed the treaty's compatibility with the Basic Law.[98] This balance between national sovereignty and supranational cooperation demonstrates Germany's view that the Rule of Law is not only a national ideal but also a foundation for peace, justice, and stability within the broader international community.

4.3.3 The Rule of Law in Mixed Legal Systems: The Example of South Africa

South Africa is a constitutional democracy that has undergone a remarkable transformation since the end of apartheid. Once defined by institutionalized racial discrimination, the country

95 Tamanaha, *On the Rule of Law*, p. 109.
96 Basic Law of the Federal Republic of Germany.
97 Basic Law of the Federal Republic of Germany.
98 Darnstädt, Thomas, 2012, "Ceding Power: Ruling Shows Court's Weakness in EU Matters," *Spiegel Online International*, 12 September 2012.

has rebuilt its legal and political systems around the principles of equality, justice, and the Rule of Law. The 1996 Constitution formally established South Africa as a democratic state founded on respect for human dignity, human rights, and the supremacy of the Constitution – embodying both the formal and substantive dimensions of the Rule of Law.

Formally, the supremacy of the Rule of Law is explicitly recognized as one of the founding values of the Republic in Chapter 1, Section 1 of the Constitution. The Preamble envisions a "democratic and open society in which government is based on the will of the people and every citizen is equally protected by law."[99] Chapter 8 establishes the independence of the Judiciary, stating that "courts are independent and subject only to the Constitution and the law, which they must apply impartially and without fear, favour or prejudice."[100] These provisions ensure separation of powers, judicial independence, and government accountability.[101] Chapters 14 and 8 further reinforce legal consistency and access to justice, while section 235 recognizes the right to self-determination within the constitutional framework.

Substantively, the Constitution's Bill of Rights, contained in Chapter 2, "enshrines the rights of all people in our country and affirms the democratic values of human dignity, equality, and freedom."[102] The Bill applies to all laws and binds every branch of government as well as all organs of State. It guarantees a wide range of rights, including freedom of expression, religion, movement, and trade, along with socio-economic rights such as access to housing, healthcare, and education. These provisions reflect South Africa's commitment to a broad, inclusive conception of democracy and justice.

The Judiciary has played a central role in upholding these principles. In *South African Litigation Centre and Another v. National Director of Public Prosecutions and Others*, the applicants challenged the failure of South African authorities to investigate alleged crimes under International Law committed in Zimbabwe. The courts ruled that government institutions had a constitutional and international duty to investigate and prosecute such crimes, referencing the Rome Statute of the International Criminal Court and South Africa's domestic ICC Act.[103] The decision reaffirmed the supremacy of the Constitution and the state's obligation to act in accordance with both domestic and international legal commitments.

This case exemplifies South Africa's adherence to the Rule of Law and its commitment to accountability, transparency, and respect for fundamental rights. Despite ongoing social and economic challenges, South Africa's constitutional framework remains a powerful symbol of democratic transformation and a model of how the Rule of Law can serve as a foundation for equality and justice in a post-authoritarian society.

4.3.4 Building the Rule of Law in China

China is a decentralized authoritarian state governed by the Communist Party, where power remains highly centralized despite an increasingly complex legal system. When one looks at official legal documents, China formally satisfies the requirement of rule by law and some criteria of formal legality. Both the Constitution of the Communist Party of China adopted in September

99 Republic of South Africa Constitution, Chapter 3 s4.

100 Republic of South Africa Constitution, Chapter 8.

101 Agrast, Mark David, et al., 2011, *Rule of Law Index 2011*, The World Justice Project, p. 34.

102 Agrast, et al., *Rule of Law Index 2011*, p. 5.

103 *Southern African Litigation Centre and Another v. National Director of Public Prosecutions and Others*, 2012, case no. 77150/09, 8 May 2012.

1982 and the Constitution of the People's Republic of China adopted on December 4, 1982, confirm a government of laws embodying principles such as the supremacy of the law and the equality of all before the law.

The Constitution of the Communist Party of China includes several provisions that formally commit the Party to the principle of rule by law. Notably, Article 3 (4) provides "[t]o conscientiously . . . abide by the laws and regulations of the State in an exemplary way," while Article 31 (7) lays out that

> Party and non-Party cadres strictly observe the law and administrative discipline and the financial and economic statues and personnel regulations of the State and that none of them infringe on the interests of the State and collective or the masses.[104]

In addition, the Constitution of the People's Republic of China, in its Article 4 provides that "[t]he State protects the lawful rights and interests of the minority nationalities and upholds and develops the relationship of equality, unity and mutual assistance among all of China's nationalities," while Article 5 provides that all the State organs shall abide by the Constitution and that "[n]o law or administrative or local rules and regulations shall contravene the constitution."[105]

It is important to note that Article 5 of the 1982 Constitution was later reinforced by Jiang Zemin's policy of "ruling the country in accordance with the law and building a socialist rule-of-law state." This principle, formally incorporated into the Constitution in 1996, marked a significant step in the Chinese Government's official recognition of the Rule of Law as a cornerstone of governance, at least in a formal and ideological sense.[106]

Though China does not meet all the criteria of formal legality, it has made significant efforts to do so. As regards publication of laws, not only are the laws accessible in both print and online formats, but the State has also been active in promulgating law through various forms of media, such as the daily TV program *Today on Law* and various radio shows on citizen rights.[107] In recent years, China is following Unger's prediction that even societies operating under a very narrow conception of the Rule of Law will eventually face the "spill-over" effect by which the previous consciousness and organization will be eroded and subject to change over time.[108] The Party Constitution, for example, has directly referred to the Rule of Law and democracy in its fourth five-year plan in the following terms:

> The Communist Party of China . . . builds a socialist country under the Rule of Law. . . . The Party should encourage the people to act as the masters of the country and take effective measures to protect the people's right to run the affairs of the State and of society and manage economic and cultural undertakings. It should encourage the free airing of views and establish and improve systems and procedures of democratic decision-making and supervision.[109]

Furthermore, on February 28, 2007, the State Council of China issued a White Paper on *China's Efforts and Achievements in Promoting the Rule of Law*.[110] Although one may be rightly

104 Chinese Communist Party Constitution, art. 3 § 4, art. 31 § 7.
105 Constitution of the People's Republic of China, art. 3 and art. 4.
106 Peerenboom, *China's Long March*, p. 6.
107 Peerenboom, *China's Long March*, p. 7.
108 Jones, Carol A. G., 1994, "Capitalism, Globalization and the Rule of Law," *Social & Legal Studies*, vol. 3, p. 206.
109 Chinese Communist Party Constitution, General Program.
110 Xinhua, 2008, "Full Text of White Paper on PRC's Efforts in Promoting Rule of Law," 28 February 2008, Open Source Center, no. CPP20080228968165.

suspicious of China's commitment to the Rule of Law due to the ambiguity of the term, this Chinese recognition of the importance of the concept reveals the effectiveness of international pressure and the necessity for China to obey international norms to be accepted as a legitimate actor on the international scene.

These are good signs of China's Rule of Law transformation, but these alone do not amount to the congruence of what law enshrines and what is acted upon in practice. Legislative and judicial powers are not completely independent due to the veto power of the Party, dissidents are often denied rights provided by the law (as most recently seen with the Chinese artist and political dissident Ai Weiwei), and some Party policies still have power over law.[111] In addition, since at least Deng Xiaoping in 1988, Chinese leadership has been careful to state that China has no intention to adopt a fully Western idea of the Rule of Law.[112]

Substantively, China has been fighting against bribery and embezzlement, especially of high officials closely linked to the government, as a means to increase government accountability and legitimacy. Public accusation has especially been encouraged, as can be seen in the case *The No.2 People's Procuratorate of Beijing Municipality v. Cheng Shaozhi*. This case, tried in first instance on December 20, 2002, and appealed on March 12, 2006, involved a high deputy director of the Administrative Department of Oilfield Exploration & Development of China Petroleum and Chemical Corporation, who was found guilty of accepting bribery. His appeal was rejected by the Higher People's Court of Beijing Municipality based on article 189 of the Criminal Litigation Law of the People's Republic of China, which criminalizes acceptance of bribes and advantage taken by state functionaries.[113] Also, China has taken a tough stance on embezzlement. For instance, in *Chengdu City People's Procuratorate v. Shang Rongduo, etc.*, the Higher People's Court of Sichuan Province confirmed the sentence against Shang (the vice president of Chengdu University of Technology) for embezzlement, ground its decision on Article 382 of the Criminal Law which penalizes state functionaries for embezzlement and advantage taking of their office.[114] These two examples show the increased efforts by the Chinese Government to improve its legitimacy not only to its people, but also to the world by adopting principles of the Rule of Law (if they are not fake trials against political opponents).

China would benefit from adopting a more global and diversified approach to legal development, one that moves beyond the two dominant Western traditions – the Anglo-American Common Law and the continental Civil Law systems. By studying and integrating elements from a variety of legal cultures and civilizations, China could strengthen its own legal framework in ways that reflect both its unique context and universal principles of justice. Drawing from the strengths of established legal systems around the world would enable China to advance a more coherent, credible, and effective version of the Rule of Law suited to its evolving society.[115]

4.3.5 The Rule of Law in Religious Legal Systems: The Example of Saudi Arabia

As the birthplace of the Prophet of Islam Muhammad and of the *Sharia*, Saudi Arabia belongs to the *Hanbali* School of Law and the Wahhabi doctrine of the Islamic religion, which upholds

111 Peerenboom, *China's Long March*, p. 8.

112 Jones, *Capitalism, Globalization and the Rule of Law*, p. 206.

113 Beijing No. 2 Intermediate People's Court, 2003, *The No. 2 People's Procuratorate of Beijing Municipality v. Cheng Shaozhi (Acceptance of Bribes)*, 12 March 2003.

114 Chengdu Intermediate People's Court, 2004, *Chengdu City People's Procuratorate v. Shang Rongduo*, 17 June 2004.

115 Li, Ling, 2017, *Building the Rule of Law in China*, Elsevier.

the strict and conservative interpretation of law and religion. Indeed, it does not recognize non-textual sources of religious law[116], making of Saudi Arabia one of the most traditional Muslim states in the world. Alongside its non-constitutional monarchy and a tribal social structure, the existing legal system (and political situation) is generally very refractive to liberal democratic values.[117] Nonetheless, Saudi Arabia's *Sharia*, the divine law of Islam, applies the rule by law and, to a certain extent, some aspects of the formal Rule of Law.

The supremacy of law is embedded in Islamic law as everyone, including the *Caliph* (the ruler of the Muslim community), must submit to the *Sharia*.[118] Though the *Sharia* is not codified in Saudi Arabia, its main sources, the *Quran* and the exemplary of the Prophet recorded in the *Hadith* (sayings of the prophet), are very much in line with the formal legality criteria of being general, public, prospective, clear, consistent, capable of being followed, stable, and enforced[119]. The *Quran* and the *Hadith* provide clear general rules accessible to all, and these rules have not changed much under the dominant conservative interpretations in Saudi Arabian. Though the content of the rules themselves may be oppressive, which is evident through its discriminatory approach to women for example, the *Sharia* seems compatible with the formal aspects of the Rule of Law.

Even still, Saudi Arabia does not substantively comply with the Rule of Law, for there is a lack of democracy and religious freedom, alongside to severe oppression of women's rights and human rights. Similar to the assertion of an "Asian Value," there are Islamist scholars who see concepts like human rights as incompatible with Islam's own system of rights and duties.[120] One may only hope that, like China, Unger's "spill-over" effect take hold in Saudi Arabia as well. In this respect, it is noteworthy that Saudi Arabia very connected to the Western world and prone to pressure of the international community. For instance, in September 2011, King Abdullah bin Abdulaziz Al Saud decreed women's right to vote and stand for office in municipal elections as of 2015.[121] More generally, the Deputy Foreign Minister of Saudi Arabia, Prince Abdul Aziz bin Abdullah, expressed Saudi Arabia's commitment to the Rule of Law at the meeting on the Rule of Law at the United Nations headquarters in New York in September 2012. He stated that the *Sharia* is compatible with the Rule of Law as it is based on *Consultation, Justice, Equality and Dignity*. These statements and gradual measures suggest a cautious willingness to engage with elements of the global rule-of-law discourse, while maintaining the primacy of Sharia within the Saudi legal and political system.

5 The New Constitutional World Order

In this part, we will discuss the New Constitutional World Order, a term that captures the transformation of constitutionalism in an increasingly interconnected world. This development reflects how national constitutions are no longer isolated but are shaped by global legal norms, international institutions, and transnational judicial dialogue. We will explore the emergence of global constitutionalism, which seeks to establish shared constitutional principles such as

116 Congressional Research Service, "The Islamic Traditions of Wahhabism and Salafiyya," p. 2.
117 Esmaeili, Hossein, 2009, "On a Slow Boat towards the Rule of Law," *Arizona Journal of International and Comparative Law*, p. 4.
118 Emon, Anver M., 2012, *Religious Pluralism and Islamic Law: Dhimmis and Others in the Empire of Law*, Oxford University Press, chapter 5 "Sharīʿa as Rule of Law," pp. 167–222.
119 Esmaeili, *On a Slow Boat towards the Rule of Law*, p. 11.
120 Shah, Nazia A., 2006, "Women's Rights in the Koran," *Human Rights Quarterly*, vol. 28, p. 871.
121 See Anderson, Lisa, 2012, *Saudi Arabia Takes Tiny Steps on Women's Rights*, Trustlaw.

the Rule of Law, human rights, and the Separation of Powers across different legal systems. Furthermore, we will consider the rise of new theoretical approaches that question traditional state-centered models of constitutional law and propose alternative frameworks better suited to globalization. Finally, we will assess both the benefits and the limitations of this evolving order – its ability to foster cooperation, protect fundamental rights, and strengthen democratic governance, while also confronting issues of cultural diversity, national sovereignty, and legitimacy in an increasingly plural world.

5.1 Global Constitutionalism

Global constitutionalism is a broad and interdisciplinary concept that extends beyond the boundaries of Public International Law. It seeks to understand how constitutional principles – such as human rights, the Rule of Law, and the Separation of Powers – operate and interact at both national and international levels. This approach recognizes that in an increasingly interconnected world, legal systems are no longer entirely autonomous, as global norms, international courts, and transnational organizations shape and influence domestic constitutional frameworks.

In this part, we will define global constitutionalism, trace its historical evolution, and examine how it has developed alongside globalization and international governance. We will also analyze its practical impact on domestic legal systems, exploring how international standards and judicial dialogue contribute to reshaping constitutional interpretation, the protection of fundamental rights, and the balance of powers within states.

5.1.1 Definition and Evolution

"Global constitutionalism" is not a concept confined solely to Public International Law. It has been studied and debated across multiple disciplines, including anthropology, history, international relations, environmental studies, philosophy, political theory, sociology, and theology. Each field contributes to understanding how global governance and normative orders evolve. However, in recent decades – amid the growing interconnection between domestic and international spheres – the term has been increasingly adopted by legal scholars. They use it to describe and analyze the transformation of legal systems, where constitutional principles such as human rights, accountability, and the Rule of Law transcend national boundaries and influence global and domestic legal structures alike.

This perspective highlights the emergence of shared legal standards and common institutional practices across different jurisdictions, suggesting that certain constitutional values now operate on a global scale. In this sense, global constitutionalism offers a framework for understanding how national constitutions, international law, and global governance interact and shape one another.

5.1.2 Impact on Domestic Systems

Global constitutionalism refers to the idea that the international community increasingly operates under a set of shared legal and moral principles that function like a "world constitution." It is based on the belief that states and global institutions should be bound by fundamental rules ensuring legality, accountability, and respect for human rights. In this sense, international norms are progressively assuming a role similar to that of constitutional principles in domestic legal orders. They guide and constrain state behavior, influence national legislation, and shape judicial reasoning and enforcement. As a result, global constitutionalism is transforming domestic legal systems by introducing new frameworks of authority, interpretation, and compliance that transcend national borders.

For International Lawyers, global constitutionalism raises two main questions. The first concerns substance: which norms and principles should form the foundation of this emerging global constitution? Candidates often include the Rule of Law, democracy, Separation of Powers, human rights, and respect for state sovereignty. The second question is procedural: by what processes does constitutionalization occur at the global level? Scholars debate whether it emerges through formal treaties and institutions – such as the United Nations, the World Trade Organization, or the International Criminal Court – or through the gradual evolution of customary International Law and judicial practice.

To grasp the complexity of global constitutionalism, it is essential to understand three key dimensions central to constitutional theory itself: the limitation of power, the institutionalization of authority, and the protection of individual rights. These principles, traditionally applied within the framework of the nation-state, now increasingly extend to global governance. The challenge lies in determining whether such constitutionalization of International Law can reconcile the need for effective global cooperation with the preservation of national sovereignty and democratic legitimacy.

5.2 Emerging Schools of Thought

In exploring global constitutionalism, several scholars have challenged the traditional state-centered model of constitutional order, arguing that the foundations of a global constitution should not rest solely on states or intergovernmental institutions. Instead, they propose a vision of global constitutionalism grounded in civil society – a framework shaped by transnational actors, social movements, and global networks that influence international norms and governance. This part examines two major emerging perspectives within this line of thought: the concept of *global civil constitutions*, which emphasizes the role of societal actors and transnational norms in shaping global governance, and *political global constitutionalism*, which focuses on embedding democratic legitimacy, accountability, and participation into the global constitutional process.

5.2.1 Global Civil Constitutions

Günter Teubner,[122] along with Andreas Fischer-Lescano[123] and Philip Allott,[124] rejects the traditional state-centered understanding of constitutionalism and instead promotes the idea of a *global constitutionalism of civil society*.[125] Teubner's theory rests on the notion of *global civil constitutions* – autonomous legal and normative frameworks emerging within different sectors of global society.[126] In his view, constitutionalization no longer occurs only within states but also

122 Günter Teubner is a German legal scholar and sociologist, best known for his works within the field of Social Theory of Law.

123 Andreas Fischer-Lescano is a German legal scholar who held a professorship at the University of Bremen from 2008 to 2022, focusing on Public Law, European law, International Law, legal theory, and legal policy. In 2022, he moved to the University of Kassel, where he now holds the Chair of Transitional Justice.

124 Philip Allott is Professor Emeritus of International Public Law at Cambridge University and a Fellow of Trinity College Cambridge. Allott, Philip, 1990, *Eunomia: New Order for a New World*, Oxford University Press, Oxford.

125 Schwöbel, Christine, 2011, *Global Constitutionalism in International Legal Perspective*, Martinus Nijhoff Publishers.

126 Teubner, Gunther, 2003, "Globale Zivilverfassungen: Alternativen zur staatszentrierten Verfassungstheorie," *Zeitschrift für ausländisches öffentliches Recht und Völkerrecht*, vol. 63, no. 1, pp. 1–28.

within distinct functional systems such as the economy, science, technology, and media. These systems, operating globally and independently, develop their own internal rules and mechanisms of self-regulation.

Building on Niklas Luhmann's sociological theory of systems,[127] Teubner argues that applying the model of the nation-state to the global level is inadequate, as it fails to account for the growing decentralization of politics in world society. He identifies three major trends driving this transformation: digitalization, privatization, and the rise of global networks. To reflect these realities, Teubner dissociates constitutionalism from the State, proposing instead a plurality of civil constitutions that collectively structure global society.

In this framework, constitutionalism becomes a process of *institutionalized self-restraint* – a way for each social subsystem to regulate its own power and prevent domination over others. These global civil constitutions thus serve both to liberate social forces and to impose limits on them through internalized norms and accountability mechanisms. While Teubner's vision carries a degree of idealism, he contends that these developments are already observable in practice, as various global spheres – from digital governance to transnational markets – begin to exhibit quasi-constitutional features of their own.

5.2.2 Political Global Constitutionalism

Like Teubner, Andreas Fischer-Lescano argues that global constitutionalism must be understood primarily as *political global constitutionalism*. For him, this means going beyond the traditional boundaries of Public International Law, which is largely limited to states and intergovernmental institutions. Fischer-Lescano emphasizes the need to include civil society, transnational actors, and global social movements as key participants in shaping constitutional norms at the international level. He envisions a global order where political legitimacy and accountability are grounded not only in states but also in the democratic participation of global civil society.

Philip Allott, in his seminal work *Eunomia*, develops a broader and more philosophical vision for a new global order relevant to global constitutionalism. Although he does not claim that such an order currently exists – or that it is necessarily emerging – Allott insists on the *necessity* of reforming the foundations of the international system. He calls for a rethinking of both the conceptual basis of International Law and the deeper structures of international society. At the core of his vision lies the idea of a *global constitution*, a universal framework of principles and values capable of guiding humanity toward a more just and rational global order. In *Eunomia*, Allott describes his project as an effort to propose a "general theory of society and law which is potentially universal – a theory capable of being the theory acted upon by all participants in international society." His work thus highlights the transformative potential of constitutional thinking at the global level, urging a shift from a system of fragmented state interests to a coherent, value-based international community.[128]

5.2.3 Digital Constitutionalism

Traditionally, Constitutional Law and Political Science have been concerned with how political power is exercised, distributed, and limited within governments. The main purpose of constitutional law has been to organize public power, ensure checks and balances among institutions, and protect individual rights from abuse by the State.

127 Niklas Luhmann (1927–1998) was a German sociologist specializing in administration and social systems.

128 Allott, *Eunomia: New Order for a New World*, preface xix.

However, in the digital age, this traditional understanding of power has changed profoundly. Power is no longer held exclusively by governments but increasingly by private actors – especially large digital platforms and technology corporations. These companies control vast amounts of data, shape access to information, and influence social and political behavior on a global scale. As a result, threats to democracy, freedom, and equality no longer come only from states but also from corporate actors that operate beyond national boundaries and democratic accountability.

This transformation has exposed the limitations of traditional constitutional law, which was designed to regulate state authority, not private global power. In response, scholars and policymakers have begun to explore the concept of *digital constitutionalism* – an emerging framework seeking to apply constitutional principles to the governance of digital technologies and the internet. Digital constitutionalism is not about drafting a single legal constitution but about embedding core values such as transparency, accountability, freedom of expression, privacy, and equality into the global digital environment.[129]

An international conference on digital constitutionalism, for example, might address three main dimensions: the evolution of constitutional principles in the digital sphere; the growing role of private companies in performing functions that were traditionally public; and the protection of fundamental rights in the age of artificial intelligence.[130] Ultimately, digital constitutionalism represents an effort to redefine the relationship between power, law, and rights in a world where digital infrastructures increasingly shape human life and social order.

5.3 Advantages and Limitations

Global constitutionalism carries significant implications for international governance, human rights, and the balance of power between states and global institutions. This part examines both the advantages and the challenges of establishing a global constitutional framework.

5.3.1 Advantages of Global Constitutionalism

Global constitutionalism presents several key advantages for the international community. It envisions a world governed by laws that protect rights, promote democracy, and prevent the concentration of power in the hands of any single State, institution, or corporation. By emphasizing the Rule of Law, the Separation of Powers, and respect for cultural diversity, global constitutionalism supports a more balanced and inclusive political environment.[131] It encourages the development of international institutions that safeguard human rights, promote transparency, and foster participation and dialogue among nations and civil society. This framework contributes to a more stable, accountable, and just global order.

The effects of constitutionalism's globalization can already be observed in various international institutions, particularly the United Nations and its Charter, which functions as a quasi-constitutional document for global governance. The ultimate aim of the global constitutionalist

129 See Tusseau, Guillaume, 2023, *Taking Chaos Seriously: From Analog to Digital Constitutionalism(s)*, Research Paper, Sciences Po Chair Digital, Governance and Sovereignty.

130 Digital Constitutionalism Conference, 2023, University of the Antilles, Guadeloupe Campus, Faculty of Legal and Economic Sciences, Fouillole Campus – Amphitheater Lepointe, 17 November 2023.

131 Lang, Anthony F. Jr., & Wiener, Antje, 2023, "Introduction to the Handbook on Global Constitutionalism: Protecting Rights and Democracy while Binding Power," in *Handbook on Global Constitutionalism*, Edward Elgar Publishing, Cheltenham. https://doi.org/10.4337/9781802200263.00006. Accessed 24 July 2024.

project is to prevent the excessive concentration of power – whether in individual states, international bodies, or private actors – by establishing shared norms and mechanisms of accountability. For this system to function effectively, however, many scholars stress the importance of direct participation by individuals and civil society. Without such inclusion, a global constitution risks being a purely institutional or elitist construction, detached from the people it seeks to represent.

At the same time, global constitutionalism should not be seen in isolation. It exists alongside and often overlaps with other frameworks that seek to organize International Law and governance, such as global administrative law,[132] theories of global governance,[133] and international public policy doctrines. Each of these approaches offers a different response to the same fundamental question: how to ensure legitimacy, accountability, and justice in a world increasingly shaped by interdependence and transnational challenges.

5.3.2 Limitations and Challenges

Despite its advantages, global constitutionalism faces significant challenges. Some forecast a dystopian global order, for the

> global problems of complex interdependence of the global commons, and of international social and economic life, are likely to produce over time an integrative type of world order, but in the form of a dystopia, that is, lacking a nucleus of world order values to serve as a normative lodestar.[134]

Others argue that supranational lawmaking, operating outside traditional checks and balances, risks undermining national sovereignty and constitutional strategies. Many states are reluctant to give up their sovereignty, making it hard to implement a global constitution effectively.

A major issue is also the liberal bias, which oversimplifies international politics by focusing too much on rights and legal frameworks while neglecting deeper political dynamics and democratic participation. This leads to inadequate handling of real challenges and conflicts in global governance.[135]

Historically rooted in Enlightenment ideals and inspired by the American and French revolutions, global constitutionalism promotes principles such as the Rule of Law, Separation of Powers, and the protection of human rights. Yet, its modern expression has increasingly expanded judicial authority, giving judges and legal professionals greater influence over global and domestic policy. This "judicialization" of politics can be seen in institutions such as the

132 This mode of legality was defined as the "mechanisms, principles, practices, and supporting social understandings that promote or otherwise affect the accountability of global administrative bodies, in particular by ensuring they meet adequate standards of transparency, participation, reasoned decision, and legality, and by providing effective review of the rules and decisions they make." Kingsbury, Benedict, Krisch, Nico and Stewart, Richard, 2005, "The Emergence of Global Administrative Law," *Law and Contemporary Problems*, vol. 68, p. 15.

133 In Rosenau's words, "an order that lacks a centralized authority with the capacity to enforce decisions on a global scale." Rosenau, James, 1992, "Governance, Order and Change in World Politics," in *Governance without Government: Order and Change in World Politics*, eds. James Rosenau and Ernst-Otto Czempiel, Cambridge University Press.

134 Falk, Richard A., Johansen, Robert C. and Kim, Samuel S. (eds.), 1993, *The Constitutional Foundations of World Peace*, State University of New York Press, Albany.

135 Volk, Christian, 2012, "Why Global Constitutionalism Does Not Live Up to Its Promises," *Goettingen Journal of International Law*, vol. 4, no. 2, pp. 551–573. https://doi.org/10.3249/1868-1581-4-2-volk.

European Court of Human Rights and the European Union, where states must align their laws with supranational norms. Supporters view this as progress toward democracy and universal justice; critics, however, see the rise of *juristocracy* – the dominance of unelected judges – and the weakening of democratic decision-making.[136]

Finally, concerns have emerged about the growing influence of private and economic interests in shaping judicial and constitutional outcomes. When courts or international institutions become tools for powerful actors, the legitimacy of global constitutionalism is undermined. Combined with examples of democratic backsliding and the politicization of law – as seen in parts of the United States and Europe – these trends reveal the fragile balance between law, democracy, and global governance.[137] Global constitutionalism thus stands at a crossroads: it can either evolve into a framework that truly strengthens global justice, or risk becoming a technocratic order detached from the people it claims to serve.

Conclusion

Mark Tushnet once wrote, "Constitutions lie at the intersection of law and high politics."[138] In today's world, new constitutional paths are emerging at the intersection of law and high politics. One significant development is the rise of Global Constitutionalism, which is creating an interconnected legal world. This concept of connectivity is central to our approach to Law in a World of Multiple Legal Orders. Connectivity in the legal realm occurs through the dialogue of national and international judges, the exportation of legal concepts, and the diffusion of universal standards of the Rule of Law.

Global Constitutionalism brings about fundamental standards such as the balance of power, hierarchy of norms, protection of fundamental liberties, legal and political pluralism, and judicial independence. States are increasingly aware that they must comply with these standards to be fully integrated and accepted into the international community, under the supervision of the United Nations.

However, constitutionalism can have both positive and negative outcomes. At its best, constitutionalism ensures procedural democracy, upheld by constitutional judges and grounded in the Rule of Law. This represents the ideal of constitutionalism. On the other hand, constitutionalism can lead to negative consequences if abused or overly legislated, undermining democracy and representativity.

As will be discussed in Chapter 11 on Supranationalism, the Lisbon Treaty emphasizes the values of the European Union, yet it has resulted in a democratic deficit and public reluctance towards EU institutions. If the constituent body loses its power, constitutionalism can undermine the Rule of Law.

The State has evolved from a purely legal or legislative organization to a constitutional one, facilitated by the dialogue between national and international judges. However, it is crucial to ensure that this evolution does not lead to the concentration of power in an oligarchy. This balance is vital for maintaining the resilience and effectiveness of constitutional norms, especially in times of crisis.

136 See Cliquennois, Gaëtan, Huten, Nicolas and Parau, CrisAna, 2024, *Symposium on Global Constitutionalism and Its Limits*, Castle, Nantes University, 22 March 2024.

137 Cliquennois, *Symposium on Global Constitutionalism and Its Limits*.

138 Tushnet, Mark, 2008, "Comparative Constitutional Law," in *The Oxford Handbook of Comparative Law*, eds. Mathias Reimann and Reinhard Zimmermann, Oxford University Press.

Selected Bibliography

Belov, M., (Ed.), 2023, *Rule of Law in Crisis: Constitutionalism in a State of Flux* (1st ed.). Routledge, 292 pages.

Drinóczi, T., & Bień-Kacała, A., (Eds.), 2021, *Rule of Law, Common Values, and Illiberal Constitutionalism: Poland and Hungary within the European Union* (1st ed.). Routledge, 260 pages.

Frankenberg, G., 2012, *Comparative Constitutional Law, the Cambridge Companion to Comparative Law*, Cambridge University Press, pp. 170–190.

Lang, A. F. Jr., & Wiener, A., 2023, *Handbook on Global Constitutionalism,* Cheltenham, UK: Edward Elgar Publishing, 608 pages.

Lemieux, S. E., & Watkins, D. J., 2018, *Judicial Review and Contemporary Democratic Theory: Power, Domination, and the Courts* (1st ed.), Routledge, 194 pages.

Masterman, R., & Schütze, R., (Eds.), 2019, *The Cambridge Companion to Comparative Constitutional Law*, Cambridge University Press, 652 pages.

McGarry, J., 2017, *Intention, Supremacy and the Theories of Judicial Review* (1st ed.). Routledge, 148 pages.

Postema, G. J., 2023, *Law's Rule: The Nature, Value, and Viability of the Rule of Law*, New York: Oxford University Press, 400 pages.

Sevel, M., 2024, *Routledge Handbook of the Rule of Law* (1st ed.), Routledge, 444 pages.

Toope, S. J., 2023, *A Rule of Law for Our New Age of Anxiety*, Cambridge University Press, 250 pages.

Tusseau, G., 2021a, *Contentieux constitutionnel comparé: Une introduction critique au droit processuel constitutionnel*, LGDJ, 1, 452 pages.

Tusseau, G., 2021b, *Droit constitutionnel et institutions politiques* (6th ed.), Seuil, 1, 208 pages.

6 Civil Procedure

The Judiciary and the Unfolding of Civil Litigation

Be sure of it; give me the ocular proof.
Shakespeare, *Othello* (Act III, Sc 3)

Audi alteram partem
(Hear the other side too)

These two maxims capture the essence of procedural justice: the pursuit of proof and the duty to hear both sides. They remind us that law is not only about what is true, but about how truth is established and fairness ensured through proper procedure.

Here, we begin examining some real activity in law by looking at litigation. This chapter addresses civil procedures, which are crucial because legal systems rely heavily on them. To illustrate the significance and rigidity of procedural rules, consider a rule that states a person must enter a room through the door to be considered present. If someone enters through the window, the law does not recognize their presence in the room, despite them being physically there, because they did not follow the correct procedural rule. Procedure is that crucial. If you do not file in the correct court with jurisdiction over your matter, your case will not be heard. Similarly, if the statute of limitations for an action is five years, filing after six years means you can no longer pursue your claim. It is too late under the law.

This chapter is dedicated to presenting and discussing civil procedure because it is fundamental to litigation. It compares procedural aspects rather than substantive ones, focusing on procedure since procedural law raises litigation-related questions more than any other legal field.

A long-standing debate in the Western world concerns whether there is a significant difference in how trials are conducted in Civil Law versus Common Law systems. Section 1 addresses this debate. Section 2 describes the structure of courts and judicial organization. Section 3 provides a comparative overview of civil procedures. Section 4 discusses the convergence and transnational rules of civil procedure developed by UNIDROIT and the American Law Institute. Section 5 covers the right to a fair trial, a fundamental principle of litigation. Section 6 deals with the legal burden of proof. The final section, Section 7, explains the basics of lawyering and legal reasoning.

By the end of this chapter, you will have a comprehensive overview of the entire procedural framework, giving you the basis needed to understand how litigation operates in most legal systems worldwide.

DOI: 10.4324/9781003393047-9

1 The Conduct of Trials in Civil Law and Common Law Systems

In this section, we delve into the ways trials are conducted in Civil Law and Common Law systems, focusing on procedural aspects rather than substantive law. By comparing the German and American systems, we highlight significant differences and potential areas of convergence. Through examining influential articles and academic debates, we aim to provide a comprehensive understanding of civil procedure's role in litigation and the ongoing evolution of judicial practices.

1.1 The German Advantage in Civil Procedure

In the 1980s, an American Professor of Law, Professor John H. Langbein,[1] generated a lot of controversy with an article which seemed merely unpatriotic, entitled *The German Advantage in Civil Procedure*.[2]

Langbein was highly critical of American litigation – and deliberately so. At the time, he intended to be provocative. In Comparative Law, there is always a risk of caricature, an exaggerated portrayal of a legal system for the purpose of making a point or emphasizing existing differences. Langbein adopted the view that he could make his argument most effectively by being especially, perhaps overly, critical of the American system, while presenting a somewhat idealized picture of the German system, which he considered the other paradigm.

1.1.1 Key Differences Between German and Anglo-American Procedures

John H. Langbein wrote in his controversial article:

> My theme is that, by assigning judges rather than lawyers to investigate the facts, the Germans avoid the most troublesome aspects of our practice.[3]
>
> There are two fundamental differences between German and Anglo-American civil procedure, and these differences lead in turn to many others. First, the court rather than the parties' lawyers takes the main responsibility for gathering and sifting evidence, although the lawyers exercise a watchful eye over the court's work. Second, there is no distinction between pretrial and trial, between discovering evidence and presenting it. Trial is not a single continuous event. Rather, the court gathers and evaluates evidence over a series of hearings, as many as the circumstances require.[4]
>
> The episodic character of German civil procedure . . . has other virtues: It lessens tension and theatrics, and it encourages settlement. Countless novels, movies, plays, and broadcast serials attest to the dramatic potential of the Anglo-American trial. The contest between opposing counsel; the potential for surprise witnesses who cannot be rebutted in time; the tricks of adversary examination and cross-examination; the concentration of proof-taking and verdict into a single, continuous proceeding; the unpredictability of

1 John H. Langbein is an American legal scholar who serves as the Sterling Professor emeritus of Law and Legal History at Yale University.

2 Langbein, John H., 1985, "The German Advantage in Civil Procedure," *University of Chicago Law Review*, vol. 52.

3 Langbein, *The German Advantage in Civil Procedure*, p. 1.

4 Langbein, *The German Advantage in Civil Procedure*, p. 2.

> juries and the mysterious opacity of their conclusory verdicts – these attributes of the Anglo-American trial make for good theatre. German civil proceedings have the tone not of the theatre, but of a routine business meeting – serious rather than tense.[5]

Langbein identified two fundamental differences between German and Anglo-American civil procedures. In Germany, the court – rather than the parties' lawyers – bears the primary responsibility for collecting and evaluating evidence. Lawyers play a supervisory role but do not control the process. Unlike in the Anglo-American system, German trials are not single, continuous events. Instead, evidence is gathered and assessed over a series of hearings, which tends to reduce tension and promote settlement. Langbein argued that these features of the German system alleviate many of the problems characteristic of American litigation, such as the theatrical nature of trials and the unpredictability of jury verdicts.

1.1.2 Academic Reactions and Debate

This article, as mentioned, generated an enormous amount of academic debate. Practitioners, however, were largely indifferent – they simply continued to practice as they always had. Academics and legal reformers, by contrast, were deeply engaged in the discussion. The piece provoked a strong reaction among German scholars, who argued, contrary to what one might expect, that Langbein had been entirely uncritical of the German system. At the same time, American commentators contended that he had been far too critical of the American legal system. In total, six or eight major responses were published. This was before the age of blogs and social media; had they existed then, there would undoubtedly have been a flood of commentary.

The intensity of the debate reflected broader concerns about comparative methodology and the challenges of evaluating foreign legal systems without oversimplification. Many scholars emphasized that procedural traditions must be understood within their cultural and institutional contexts, cautioning against assuming that practices successful in one system can be easily transplanted to another. Others welcomed Langbein's work as an opportunity to rethink entrenched assumptions about adversarial litigation and to explore whether inquisitorial elements might offer solutions to persistent problems in American civil justice.

1.2 The Appraisal of the American Judicial System

In 1990, Professor John C. Reitz[6] published an article entitled *Why we probably cannot adopt the German advantage in civil procedure*[7] in response to Professor John H. Langbein's previous article. Reitz's article offered a balanced critique and examination of Langbein's assertions about the superiority of the German system.

1.2.1 Comparison of German and American Judicial Systems

Reitz acknowledged Langbein's observations about the German system, where judges control the order of proof, witness examination, and record creation. This system aims to reduce

5 Langbein, *The German Advantage in Civil Procedure*, p. 4.

6 John C. Reitz is the Edward L. Carmody Professor of Law at the University of Iowa and a leading scholar in comparative and administrative law. Former President of the American Society of Comparative Law, he has taught and lectured widely around the world.

7 Reitz, John C., 1990, "Why We Probably Cannot Adopt the German Advantage in Civil Procedure," *Iowa Law Review*, vol. 75.

litigation costs and enhance testimony quality by minimizing the influence of partisan lawyers. However, Reitz highlighted fundamental differences that prevent the direct adoption of these practices in the American context.

> In 1985, Professor John Langbein published an article entitled "The German Advantage in Civil Procedure", in which he claimed that certain aspects of the modern German . . . system of civil procedure make it superior to American civil procedure. This provocative article sought to acquaint American lawyers with the German system of trial, in which the judges, not the parties' attorneys, have chief responsibility to (1) determine the order of proof, (2) examine the witnesses, (3) create a compact record of the witnesses' testimony by dictating summaries of their testimony, and (4) secure the testimony of experts, if needed. German lawyers and their clients, like their counterparts in our system, are responsible for producing documents in support of the client's claims and identifying for the court the fact witnesses whose testimony they believe will support those claims.
>
> The German system differs from ours, however, by making the judge responsible for and in control of the process of examining both fact and expert witnesses and creating the record based on those examinations. Furthermore, the German system strongly discourages attorneys from having any contact with nonparty witnesses out of court.
>
> Langbein argues that the German system secures two significant procedural advantages: (1) it reduces the cost of litigation, and (2) it enhances the quality of the testimony by reducing the opportunity for partisan lawyers, intentionally or unintentionally, to influence that testimony. According to Langbein, we should, therefore, modify our system of procedure to incorporate these advantages. He notes the recent trend in the United States for judges to become more involved in the pretrial phase in order to prevent discovery abuse, expedite the proceedings, and promote settlement – a trend that has been christened "managerial judging." Langbein views the development toward "managerial judging" critically because the American judicial system lacks most of the control mechanisms placed upon German judges to prevent abuse of judicial power. But he also views the trend toward "managerial judging" as "telling evidence for the proposition that judicial fact-gathering could work well in a system that preserved much of the rest of what we now have in civil procedure."
>
> This essay takes issue with Langbein's claim. I do not question, as others have, the claimed advantages of German civil procedure. My interest lies with Langbein's claim that we could adopt the central aspect of German civil procedure, judicially dominated fact-finding, without changing many other fundamental characteristics of our modern civil procedure. I believe we could not.[8]

In Germany, judges have a significant role in fact-finding and managing evidence, whereas in the U.S., this responsibility primarily lies with the attorneys.

The German system discourages attorneys from interacting with nonparty witnesses outside of court, a practice contrary to American legal traditions.

To illustrate, imagine a commercial dispute in Germany between Müller GmbH and Schneider AG over the late delivery of machinery. In court, the judge decides which witnesses to hear first and personally questions the parties and their employees. The lawyers may suggest questions, but do not control the examination. The judge then dictates a concise summary of

8 Reitz, *Why We Probably Cannot Adopt the German Advantage*, p. 1.

each statement for the official record. By contrast, in a similar case in the United States between *MetroBuild Ltd. v. UrbanStone Developers,* each side's attorneys conduct the questioning themselves. The transcript records every word verbatim, and much of the hearing revolves around strategic objections and attempts to persuade the jury.

Another difference concerns contact with witnesses. In Germany, the lawyers for Müller GmbH would not be allowed to meet privately with Schneider AG's employees before trial, as doing so could be viewed as improper influence. In the U.S., however, BrightTech's lawyers would be expected to interview potential witnesses extensively before trial to prepare their case. Furthermore, while the German judge actively manages the proceedings and might even propose a settlement after hearing preliminary testimony, the American judge would largely remain a neutral referee, intervening only when necessary to rule on objections or instruct the jury. Finally, whereas the German case would likely unfold over several short hearings spread across months, the American case would be tried in one continuous, often dramatic, week-long trial.

1.2.2 Structural Obstacles to Adopting the German Advantage

While Langbein argued that certain features of German civil procedure could be imported into the American system to improve efficiency and accuracy, Reitz emphasized that deep structural differences make such reforms unlikely, if not impossible. The German advantage is not simply a matter of judicial technique; it rests on institutional, cultural, and procedural foundations that have no equivalent in the United States.

First, the role of the judge differs fundamentally in the two systems. German judges are trained from the outset as career professionals whose responsibilities include the active investigation of facts. In contrast, American judges typically emerge from adversarial practice and are expected to remain neutral arbiters rather than inquisitors. Reitz argued that shifting to judge-directed fact-finding would require a complete redefinition of the judicial role in the United States.

Second, the American adversarial tradition assigns primary responsibility for gathering and presenting evidence to the parties' attorneys. This tradition is deeply embedded in legal culture, supported by strong norms of attorney autonomy, extensive pretrial discovery, and the strategic use of evidence. Reitz observed that limiting attorneys' involvement – particularly by restricting out-of-court contact with witnesses, as in Germany – would be incompatible with the assumptions of American litigation.

Third, the jury system constitutes a major barrier to adopting the German model. Because American civil trials often hinge on persuading a lay jury, attorneys play a dominant role in shaping testimony and constructing narratives. German civil justice, by contrast, is designed for professional judges who evaluate evidence directly, making written summaries and episodic hearings both practical and effective.

Finally, Reitz highlighted institutional safeguards present in Germany but absent in the United States. German judges operate under strict hierarchical supervision and procedural constraints that limit the risk of abuse. Without comparable mechanisms, expanding judicial authority in the U.S. could create concerns about unchecked judicial discretion – precisely the opposite of the intended reform.

In light of these differences, Reitz concluded that the German advantage cannot simply be transplanted into the American system. Any meaningful convergence would require profound structural changes to judicial training, legal culture, and procedural norms – changes that extend far beyond technical adjustments to trial practice.

1.3 Managerial Judging: A Path to Convergence

In his article *Why We Probably Cannot Adopt the German Advantage in Civil Procedure,* Professor Reitz deliberately avoids engaging in the debate over whether Professor Langbein's description of the German system is accurate. He acknowledges that numerous scholars agree with Langbein's portrayal, while many others dispute it. Reitz states, in essence: "I will accept everything Professor Langbein says about the German system as accurate, and now I want to ask whether it can be adapted or adopted in our culture." His answer is no. He offers eight to ten cultural considerations to explain why such a reform, however desirable in theory, would not fit within the American context. Reitz concludes that, despite its potential benefits, the German model cannot be transplanted wholesale into the United States. The most realistic prospect, he suggests, lies in a partial convergence – an approach that mitigates the most serious weaknesses of both systems without attempting to erase their fundamental cultural differences.

1.3.1 Concept of Managerial Judging

Reitz notes a growing consensus that the Common Law system – particularly in the United States – is evolving toward what has been termed managerial judging. This development does not involve judges engaging directly in fact-finding, but rather in managing the process through which lawyers gather and present evidence. Judges now play an active supervisory role: they work with lawyers to narrow the issues, streamline the proceedings, and evaluate discovery requests in order to prevent excessive or abusive practices. In this sense, judges manage the litigation but do not conduct it. One may manage a procedure without performing it; to oversee, supervise, and correct excesses is distinct from conducting the trial itself. It is in this distinction – between judicial management and judicial performance – that Reitz identifies a meaningful point of convergence between the German and American systems. This convergence takes the form of managerial judging.

Reitz further explains that this evolution reflects broader pressures within the American legal system: rising litigation costs, increasingly complex disputes, and a growing expectation that courts should facilitate efficient case resolution. Managerial judging allows the judiciary to respond to these challenges without abandoning the adversarial framework that defines American procedure. Although it does not replicate the German model of judge-led fact-finding, it introduces a more structured and interventionist judicial role that incrementally reshapes the dynamics of litigation. For Reitz, this trend signals not a transformation of the Common Law tradition, but a pragmatic adaptation that brings the two systems slightly closer together while preserving their foundational differences.

1.3.2 Practical Implications and Convergence

Reitz argues that managerial judging represents a genuine form of convergence between the Civil Law and Common Law traditions. By adopting this approach, the American system can temper the excesses of adversarial litigation while preserving party autonomy. Conversely, elements of party autonomy can be introduced into Civil Law systems to soften their procedural rigidity.

As Reitz explains, American lawyers and judges increasingly accept the idea that "we want party autonomy – we want the lawyers in the driver's seat, and we will never give that up – but we will accept that the judge may manage the process." Judicial management allows the judge to intervene constructively: for example, to suggest narrowing the issues or to hold a pre-trial conference with counsel to clarify the scope of the dispute. During discovery, the judge may act as a procedural manager, limiting document requests deemed excessive or abusive. This managerial role enables the court to ensure fairness and efficiency without undermining the adversarial structure.

In this sense, managerial judging reduces the excesses of the Common Law system just as greater party autonomy can mitigate the rigidity of the Civil Law model. Reitz concludes that, while the full adoption of the German system in the United States remains impractical, these incremental developments point to a meaningful and sustainable convergence, balancing the strengths and addressing the weaknesses of both legal traditions.

Reitz adds that managerial judging reflects a practical middle ground. It allows American courts to introduce more structure and oversight without abandoning the adversarial framework, and it shows Civil Law systems how limited party participation can make proceedings more flexible. In this way, both traditions borrow useful elements from each other, leading to gradual and realistic forms of convergence rather than radical procedural change.

2 Court Structure and Judicial Organization

The structure and organization of courts vary significantly across different legal systems around the world. This section delves into the hierarchical arrangement of courts, highlighting the distinctions between inferior and superior courts. The vertical organization of courts ensures that decisions can be reviewed and justice can be administered consistently. We will explore the court structures in various legal systems, including those in France, the United Kingdom, the United States, Sharia law countries, the Asia-Pacific region, and authoritarian political systems.

2.1 The Vertical Organization of Courts

The vertical organization of courts is a fundamental principle in most legal systems, ensuring a clear hierarchy where decisions of lower courts can be reviewed by higher courts. This part discusses the distinction between inferior and superior courts and examines specific court structures in different jurisdictions.

2.1.1 Differentiating Inferior and Superior Courts

In Chapter 4, we examined the emergence of the Common Law in the United Kingdom during the Middle Ages. To understand the structure of the court system in the Common Law world, it is essential to recognize a fundamental distinction: the separation between inferior and superior courts. Superior courts, positioned at the top of the judicial hierarchy, hold greater authority, prestige, and influence. Their decisions carry more legal force and precedential value than those of lower courts.

This distinction between inferior and superior courts constitutes a foundational principle of judicial organization. Virtually every legal system operates within a structured hierarchy of courts, distinguishing those of lesser jurisdiction from those of higher authority. This hierarchy determines each court's capacity to shape the law through interpretation and precedent, its power of judicial review, its influence over the Legislative and Executive branches, and the binding effect and legal weight of its rulings.

For example, imagine a dispute over a construction contract. In England, a lower court judge hearing *Stonebridge Builders v. Northfield Homes* must follow a precedent previously set by the Court of Appeal on how to interpret delay clauses in contracts. Even if the judge personally disagrees with that interpretation, they are bound by the higher court's ruling under the doctrine of *stare decisis*.

By contrast, in France, if a similar dispute arises between *Enterprise Durand* and *Société Lemoine*, the trial judge will look to a prior decision of the Cour de cassation on contract interpretation for guidance. However, that decision is not formally binding. The judge may follow it to ensure consistency, but in principle remains free to reason differently if the facts or equities of the case justify it.

This comparison shows how court hierarchies function differently: in the Common Law, higher court decisions are binding rules that secure uniformity; in the Civil Law, they are persuasive authorities that promote coherence while preserving judicial flexibility.

In practice, however, lower courts in Civil Law systems rarely depart from the case law of the supreme courts. A trial court judge in France would hardly go against a precedent of the *Cour de cassation*, knowing that such a decision would almost certainly be overturned on appeal – unless, of course, the higher court were about to change its own precedents. In that sense, both systems ultimately converge: lower courts tend to align their decisions with those of higher courts, whether by formal obligation in the Common Law or by pragmatic anticipation in the Civil Law tradition.

2.1.2 Court Structure in France

In France, the judicial system is divided into inferior and superior courts, each playing a distinct role in administering justice. Inferior courts include the courts of first instance and courts of appeal, both civil and administrative, known as *juridictions du fond*. These courts handle both legal and factual elements of cases. Superior courts consist of the *Cour de Cassation*, which is the Supreme Court for civil matters, the *Conseil d'État*, the Supreme Court for administrative matters, and the *Conseil Constitutionnel*, the Supreme Court for constitutional matters. For example, if a party believes that a Court of Appeal has misapplied the law in a tenancy case,[9] they may lodge an appeal in law before the *Cour de Cassation*, which does not re-examine the facts but checks whether the law was correctly applied.

Civil jurisdictions in France include the Judicial Court and the Proximity Court. The Judicial Court handles a wide range of civil disputes between private individuals, such as issues with rent, consumer matters, banking law, insurance, civil status, name changes, and family issues like divorce, adoption, and inheritance. Some Judicial Courts have a special social division to resolve conflicts between social security funds and users. This division is led by a judge and assisted by two non-professional assessors, one representing employees and the other representing employers and independent workers. The Judicial Court can operate with a panel of three judges or a single judge, particularly in family disputes. Judges are assisted by clerks who authenticate the decisions. In civil matters, the involvement of the public prosecutor depends on the nature of the disputes. There are 164 Judicial Courts in France. For instance, if Anna rents an apartment in Paris and her landlord refuses to return her deposit, she can bring her case before the Judicial Court, which will examine both the factual question of the apartment's condition and the legal question of the landlord's obligation to return the deposit.

The Proximity Court is part of the Judicial Court system and handles everyday civil disputes up to €10,000, including traffic accidents and debt collection. It also exclusively handles

9 A tenancy case is a dispute between a landlord and a tenant about a rented property, such as unpaid rent, repairs, or the return of a security deposit.

neighborhood disputes, such as boundary issues, tree pruning, and easements, as well as rural life matters and funeral-related disputes. The Proximity Court usually has a single judge, and the public prosecutor is not always present at hearings. Parties can appeal decisions from any civil jurisdiction. If they do, the case is reviewed by a Court of Appeal. Judgments for claims of €5,000 or less can only be appealed to the Court of Cassation, not a higher appellate court. There are 125 Proximity Courts in France. For example, if Marc's neighbor's tree roots crack his garden wall and he seeks €2,500 for repairs, his case will be heard by the Proximity Court. If he loses, he cannot appeal on the facts but may appeal to the Cour de Cassation on a point of law.

France also has three main specialized civil courts: the Labor Court, the Commercial Court, and the Rural Leases Court. Each court handles specific types of disputes. The Labor Court (*Conseil de Prud'hommes*) resolves disputes between employees or apprentices and employers. It handles issues related to employment contracts, such as paid leave, salaries, bonuses, and dismissals. Each district has at least one Labor Court. A conciliation attempt is made first, and if it fails, the court makes a decision. The court consists of equal numbers of non-professional judges representing employees and employers, and it is divided into five sections: management, industry, commerce, agriculture, and miscellaneous activities. There are 210 Labor Courts in France. For instance, Sophie, a bakery employee, who believes she was unfairly dismissed and not paid her overtime, can take her case before the Labor Court. After an attempt at conciliation, the dispute will be judged by a parity panel of employee and employer representatives.

The Commercial Court (*Tribunal de Commerce*) handles disputes between merchants or between merchants and individuals, as well as issues related to commercial acts. It also assists businesses in financial distress through procedures like safeguard, judicial recovery, or liquidation. For disputes of €5,000 or less, its decisions are final and only appealable to the Cour de Cassation. Higher claims can be appealed to a Court of Appeal. Judges in the Commercial Court are non-professional and come from the business world, serving voluntarily. Each court has a president, vice-president, and chamber presidents. Disputes are decided by a panel of three judges. There are 134 Commercial Courts in France. For example, if a wholesaler sues a retailer for late delivery, causing lost profits, the Commercial Court will determine whether the delay breached the sales contract and will decide on damages accordingly.

The Rural Leases Court (*Tribunal Paritaire des Baux Ruraux*) deals with disputes between landlords and tenants of rural leases, such as rent disagreements. This court is not permanent and meets as needed. It hears disputes of €5,000 or less in the first and final instance. Higher claims can be appealed. The court is presided over by a judge from the Judicial Court and includes four non-professional assessors, two representing landlords and two representing tenants. Representation by a lawyer is not required. These specialized courts ensure that specific disputes are handled by knowledgeable and representative bodies. For example, if a farmer contests a rent increase imposed by his landowner, the Rural Leases Court, composed of both landlords and tenants, will decide the lawful rent level.

Criminal courts in France judge individuals and legal entities suspected of committing offenses prohibited by law. There are four main types of criminal courts. The Police Court (*Tribunal de Police*) handles minor offenses, or contraventions, committed by adults, such as speeding or property damage. It operates within the Judicial Court, with a single judge and a clerk. The public prosecutor represents society's interests. Penalties include fines and supplementary punishments like driving bans, but not imprisonment. Most cases are resolved without a hearing, except for the most serious offenses. For example, Léa, who was caught driving far above the speed limit, may receive a fine and a temporary driving ban from the Police Court.

The Correctional Court (*Tribunal Correctionnel*) handles intermediate offenses (*délits*), such as theft and serious assault, as well as related minor offenses. It can impose prison sentences up to ten years (20 years for repeat offenders), fines, and alternative penalties like community service. Cases are judged by a panel of three professional judges or a single judge for lesser offenses. Hearings are generally public. For instance, a man who breaks into a store to steal electronics will be tried before the Correctional Court, where the judges determine both his guilt and sentence.

The Departmental Criminal Court (*Cour criminelle départementale*) judges serious crimes punishable by 15 to 20 years of imprisonment, like rape and armed robbery, except in cases of legal recidivism. It consists of five professional judges and usually holds public hearings. Appeals are heard by the Court of Assizes. The Court of Assizes (*Cour d'assises*) handles the most serious crimes, such as murder, rape, and armed robbery, punishable by 15 years to life imprisonment. It comprises three professional judges and a jury of six citizens. The court also tries attempted crimes and complicity in crimes. Hearings can be public or private for sensitive cases. There are special formations for minors, organized crime, or terrorism cases. For example, if someone is accused of homicide, the Court of Assizes, composed of judges and jurors, will decide both on the facts and on the sentence, which could range from 15 years to life imprisonment.

Specialized Interregional Courts (*Juridictions Interrégionales Spécialisées*) handle complex organized crime and financial crimes. They cover areas like drug trafficking, human trafficking, and major financial fraud. These courts manage all aspects of the case, including investigation, prosecution, and judgment. They have advanced investigation tools and operate in eight jurisdictions, including Paris and Lyon. For instance, a large-scale money laundering network operating across several French regions would be prosecuted before a Specialized Interregional Court, given the complexity and financial dimension of the case.

These examples illustrate how the French judicial system ensures that each type of dispute – civil or criminal, minor or major – is handled by the most competent and appropriate jurisdiction.

2.1.3 Court Structure in the United Kingdom

In the United Kingdom, the Government itself recognizes the complexity of its court system:

> Our courts system is complicated and – in places – confusing, because it has developed over 1,000 years rather than being designed from scratch. . . . The courts structure covers England and Wales; the tribunals system covers England, Wales, and in some cases Northern Ireland and Scotland.[10]

All criminal cases start in the Magistrates' Court. For example, if someone is accused of shoplifting or a minor assault, the case will first be heard before local magistrates. More serious cases, such as robbery or murder, are sent to the Crown Court, where a judge and jury decide the verdict. Appeals from the Crown Court go to the Court of Appeal (Criminal Division), and, in exceptional cases, to the UK Supreme Court.

Civil cases usually begin in the County Court. For instance, if a tenant sues a landlord for failing to return a deposit, or if a company claims unpaid invoices, the case will start there. Appeals from the County Court go to the High Court, then to the Court of Appeal, but they may go to different divisions depending on the subject – for example, contract disputes may go to the King's Bench Division, while inheritance or trust disputes go to the Chancery Division.

10 See Courts and Tribunals Judiciary, official website, online. Available at: https://www.judiciary.gov.uk.

The tribunals system operates separately and has its own appeal structure. For example, if someone disagrees with a tax decision or an immigration ruling, they can appeal before a specialized tribunal. Decisions from the Upper Tribunal or the Employment Appeal Tribunal can also be appealed to the Court of Appeal.

The United Kingdom Supreme Court is the highest court in the UK and only hears appeals on important points of law, such as whether a government decision violates constitutional principles. The Court of Appeal is divided into two parts: the Civil Division, which hears appeals from civil courts and tribunals, and the Criminal Division, which reviews convictions or sentences from the Crown Court.

The High Court of England and Wales is divided into several sections. The King's Bench Division deals with a broad range of cases, including administrative law, planning disputes, and personal injury claims. The Chancery Division handles business, property, and inheritance matters – for example, disagreements between shareholders or over intellectual property rights. The Family Division deals with family issues such as divorce, child custody, and cases involving people who lack mental capacity, through the Court of Protection.

The Crown Court hears the most serious criminal cases and appeals from Magistrates' Courts, while the County Court focuses on civil disputes at a local level. The Court of Protection, within the Family Division, manages cases involving vulnerable adults who cannot make legal or financial decisions for themselves. Magistrates' Courts handle less serious criminal cases, some family issues, and small civil matters.

The Upper Tribunal is divided into several chambers, each specializing in a particular area: Administrative Appeals, Tax and Chancery, Immigration and Asylum, and Lands. The First-tier Tribunal, which is the entry level of the system, includes chambers for war pensions, social welfare, education, health, taxation, property, and immigration. For instance, a person denied disability benefits would first appeal to the Social Entitlement Chamber of the First-tier Tribunal, and if unsuccessful, to the Upper Tribunal.

Employment Tribunals deal with conflicts between employers and employees, such as unfair dismissal or discrimination, and appeals are heard by the Employment Appeal Tribunal. Coroners' Courts investigate sudden or unexplained deaths, determining their cause rather than assigning guilt – for example, after a workplace accident or an unexpected death in custody.

Through this system, the UK ensures that each type of case – criminal, civil, administrative, or employment-related – is handled by a specialized and competent court or tribunal.

2.1.4 Court Structure in the United States of America

In the United States, each court system – state or federal – is organized into a hierarchy. The two systems exist side by side, and parties sometimes have the choice of which one to use. Cases begin in trial courts, the first level in the hierarchy, and can work their way up to the highest level. In the federal system, trial courts are called U.S. District Courts. In the state systems, they have different names, such as District Courts, Circuit Courts, Chancery Courts, Small Claims Courts, or Family Courts, depending on the type of case. Trial courts are the only courts where trials actually take place and where juries may be used.

Each U.S. District Court has several judges, depending on the population and the number of cases. For example, the entire state of Massachusetts has just one federal trial court, the U.S. District Court for the District of Massachusetts (D. Mass.), while California, with a much larger population, has four: the Northern (N.D. Cal.), Southern (S.D. Cal.), Eastern (E.D. Cal.), and Central (C.D. Cal.) Districts. A person accused of a federal crime in Los Angeles, for instance, would appear before the U.S. District Court for the Central District of California.

If one of the parties is unhappy with the trial court's decision, they may appeal to a higher court, known as an appellate court. In the federal system and in most states, there are two levels of appellate courts: an intermediate court of appeal and a final court of appeal. The federal intermediate courts are called U.S. Courts of Appeals. The country is divided into 12 geographic regions known as circuits, each with its own Court of Appeals. For example, a business in New York contesting a federal ruling would appeal to the Second Circuit Court of Appeals, while a case from Texas would go to the Fifth Circuit Court of Appeals.

Above the intermediate appellate courts are the highest appellate courts, often called courts of last resort or high courts. At the top of the entire judicial pyramid stands the U.S. Supreme Court, which has authority over cases from the U.S. Courts of Appeals and, in some instances, from the highest courts of the states and territories. It consists of one Chief Justice and eight Associate Justices, appointed by the President and confirmed by the Senate.[11] Unlike lower courts, the Supreme Court chooses which cases it will hear – its jurisdiction is discretionary.

A party dissatisfied with a ruling from a federal appeals court or a state supreme court may petition the Supreme Court for a writ of certiorari, commonly called a "cert." If the justices grant cert, the case will be heard. Out of roughly 10,000 petitions filed each year, only about 150 are accepted. For example, if a constitutional issue arises in a state law – say, a restriction on freedom of speech – the losing party might ask the Supreme Court to review whether that law violates the U.S. Constitution.

From this structure, it becomes clear that the American Judiciary is composed of two parallel systems – state and federal – both ultimately leading up to the Supreme Court. Within each system, as in the United Kingdom and other Common Law countries, lower courts must follow the precedents set by higher courts that can review their decisions. For instance, a California state trial court must follow the rulings of the California Court of Appeal, the California Supreme Court, and the U.S. Supreme Court.

However, the coexistence of federal and state courts can create complications. This is a direct result of federalism, the principle that both the federal government and the individual states have their own laws and judicial systems. States and even their local governments (counties and cities) enact laws in addition to federal ones, and their courts interact in complex ways. For example, someone caught with illegal drugs on a U.S. highway could face both state and federal charges for the same act – since drug possession is a crime under both systems. Similarly, a driver involved in a car accident might simultaneously fall under city traffic laws, state negligence rules, and federal vehicle safety regulations.

This overlapping network illustrates the richness – but also the complexity – of the American judicial system, where two lines of courts coexist and interconnect under a single constitutional framework.

2.1.5 Court Structure in Sharia Law Countries

In religious legal systems, the distinction between inferior and superior courts is also one of the main principles structuring the organization of justice. For example, in Saudi Arabia and other countries that follow Islamic legal systems – meaning systems applying the theory of Islamic law (Sharia), based on the Qur'an and the teachings of the Prophet (Sunnah) – the court

11 The federal Constitution establishes five significant aspects of the federal Judiciary: the Supreme Court, congressional power to create lower federal courts, life tenure and salary protections for all federal judges, the process for nominating, confirming, and removing federal judges, and the boundaries of the jurisdiction of the federal courts.

hierarchy is directly inspired by religious foundations. The entire structure reflects traditional Islamic codes of conduct, as interpreted by Islamic jurists (*fiqh*).

Article 1 of the Saudi Arabian Law of Procedure clearly states:

> Courts shall apply to cases before them provisions of Shari'ah laws, in accordance with the Qur'an and Sunnah of the Prophet (peace be upon him), and laws promulgated by the State that do not conflict with the Qur'an and Sunnah, and their proceedings shall comply with the provisions of this Law.[12]

In other words, any law or decision must align with Islamic principles, and no court can decide in contradiction with them.

In Saudi Arabia, there are four levels of Sharia courts. At the base are Courts of First Instance, which deal with everyday matters such as family disputes, inheritance, or minor commercial issues. For example, if two brothers disagree over the division of their father's estate, the case will first be heard by a local Sharia court applying Quranic inheritance rules. Above them are the Courts of Appeal, which review decisions from lower courts to ensure that judges correctly interpreted and applied Islamic law. At the top stands the Supreme Court, which examines the most serious or complex cases and ensures consistency in the interpretation of Sharia.

Alongside these, the Board of Grievances acts as the highest appellate court for administrative and Public Law cases. It is directly responsible to the King rather than to the judicial branch. For instance, if a citizen challenges a government decision or a contract involving a public authority, the case can ultimately be brought before the Board of Grievances. There are also specialized tribunals, such as those for banking disputes or labor issues, that handle specific types of cases in accordance with Sharia principles.

Despite cultural and historical differences, Civil Law systems, Common Law systems, and religious legal systems share a similar underlying structure: a vertical hierarchy of courts. Whether in Paris, London, or Riyadh, one finds lower courts whose judgments can be reviewed by higher courts. For example, just as a tenant in France can appeal a Judicial Court's decision to a Court of Appeal, or a defendant in the U.S. can appeal a conviction to a higher federal court, a party in a Saudi family dispute can seek review from an appellate Sharia court.

This shared logic illustrates a universal idea: the right to appeal – the ability to ask a higher court to review a lower court's judgment – is recognized by most of the world's legal traditions. Without entering philosophical debates about universal justice, one can say that this right, found across civilizations, faiths, and legal cultures, represents a fundamental principle of fairness deeply embedded in human conceptions of law.

2.1.6 Court Structure in the Asia-Pacific Region: Singapore as a Case Study

In the Asia-Pacific region, several countries have judicial systems built on similar hierarchical models. In Thailand, which follows the Civil Law tradition, the system is organized into courts of first instance, courts of appeal, and a Supreme Court that oversees all 76 provinces. For example, if two neighbors in Bangkok argue over a land boundary, their case would begin in a local court of first instance. If one of them disagrees with the decision, they can appeal to a Court of Appeal, and finally, the case could reach the Supreme Court if further review is needed.

12 Saudi Arabian *Law of Procedure before Sharia Courts*, Royal Decree No. M/21 of 20 Jumada I 1421 (19 August 2000).

Thailand also has specialized courts such as the Central Bankruptcy Court, which handles cases involving companies that cannot pay their debts, and the Central Intellectual Property Court, which deals with trademark or copyright disputes, for example, when one company copies another's logo.

Singapore, on the other hand, follows the Common Law tradition and bases its judicial system on the rule of precedent, meaning that lower courts must follow the decisions of higher ones. Although its system is not identical to those of the United Kingdom or the United States, it shares many similar features. As described by the Singapore Academy of Law, Singapore's judicial system is comprehensive and structured in tiers.[13] The first level consists of the State Courts, formerly called Subordinate Courts, which include the District Courts, Magistrates' Courts, and several specialized courts such as the Family Court, Juvenile Court, Coroner's Court, Small Claims Tribunals, and the Court Mediation Centre. For example, a couple in conflict over child custody would appear before the Family Court, while a customer demanding a refund for a faulty laptop could take the case to the Small Claims Tribunal. The District Courts, Magistrates' Courts, and Small Claims Tribunals handle civil disputes up to $250,000, $60,000, and $10,000, respectively.

The second level is the Supreme Court, which includes the High Court and the Court of Appeal. Both can hear criminal cases and civil claims exceeding $250,000. The Chief Justice, Judges of Appeal, and other judges are appointed by the President on the advice of the Prime Minister. For example, if a company loses a $1 million contract dispute in the High Court, it can appeal to the Court of Appeal for a final decision.

The highest court in Singapore is the permanent Court of Appeal, which reviews civil and criminal appeals from the High Court and the State Courts. Another important body, the Singapore International Commercial Court, is part of the High Court and deals with international and commercial disputes between foreign companies under a written jurisdiction agreement. For instance, if a French company and a Japanese company disagree over a contract signed in Singapore, they may submit their case to this court.

Finally, Singapore has a Constitutional Tribunal within the Supreme Court that addresses questions referred by the Elected President about the interpretation of the Constitution. As in most judicial systems, any party dissatisfied with a decision has the right to appeal to a higher court, ensuring that justice is reviewed and fairly applied at every level.

2.1.7 Court Structure in Authoritarian Political Systems

In authoritarian systems such as those in Russia and China, the leading political party exercises significant control over the legal and political systems. While judicial independence and the right of appeal are formally recognized, these rights often lack practical implementation, meaning they do not guarantee a real and authentic right of appeal.[14]

In China, the judicial system is outlined in Articles 123 to 135 of the 1982 Constitution of the People's Republic of China. This system includes the people's courts, the Supreme People's Court, the people's procuratorates, the Supreme People's Procuratorate, military procuratorates, and other special people's procuratorates. The court system is hierarchical, with the Supreme

13 Singapore Academy of Law, official website, online. Available at: https://www.sal.org.sg.

14 Hence, in cases like the Ukos case fore example, the Defendant used international arbitration to overcome the national court's resistance.

People's Court at the top, followed by the Higher People's Courts, Intermediate People's Courts, and Basic People's Courts at the bottom.

Despite this structured hierarchy, the independence of the Judiciary is compromised by the influence of the Chinese Communist Party (CCP). Judges and court officials are often subject to the directives of the CCP, and decisions can be influenced by political considerations rather than purely legal ones. This undermines the fairness and impartiality of the judicial process. Appeals may be permitted in theory, but in practice, the outcomes are often predetermined or heavily influenced by political pressures, especially in cases that involve sensitive political issues or high-profile figures.

Similarly, in Russia, the Judiciary is formally independent, but in practice, it is often subject to the influence of the Executive branch and the ruling party. The legal framework allows for appeals, but the effectiveness of this right is limited by the lack of true judicial independence. High-profile cases, particularly those involving political opponents or issues of state interest, are frequently handled in ways that align with the interests of the ruling party.

In both countries, the legal system's subordination to political control means that while there are mechanisms for appeal and judicial review, these mechanisms do not function as genuine checks on the government's power. Instead, they often serve to legitimize decisions that have already been made through political channels. As a result, the Rule of Law is weakened, and the Judiciary cannot effectively protect the rights of individuals against state abuse.

Because national courts often lack independence in authoritarian systems, leading defendants in significant cases to seek justice through international arbitration. This was evident in the Yukos case, where the Russian Government accused Yukos Oil Company and its CEO, Mikhail Khodorkovsky, of tax evasion and fraud. The national courts, seen as biased, consistently ruled against Yukos, leading to the company's bankruptcy and seizure of its assets by the State.

Yukos shareholders, doubting the fairness of the Russian Judiciary, turned to international arbitration under the Energy Charter Treaty, which protects foreign investments in the energy sector. The arbitration tribunal in The Hague found that the Russian Government had unlawfully expropriated Yukos's assets for political reasons. In 2014, the tribunal awarded Yukos shareholders $50 billion in damages.

The Yukos case illustrates how International Arbitration can provide a neutral platform for resolving disputes that might be unfairly judged in national courts, offering a path to justice when local systems are compromised by political influence.

2.2 The Horizontal Organization of Courts

The horizontal organization of courts looks at how a country divides its courts by the type of case they handle – for example, civil, criminal, or administrative cases.

It is often described as either monistic or dual. In a monistic system, all types of cases are handled within one unified court system. In a dual system, there are two separate branches of courts – usually one for ordinary cases (civil and criminal) and another for administrative cases involving the government.

For example, the United Kingdom has a monistic system, while France has a dual system with separate administrative courts (like the *Conseil d'État*) and judicial courts.

2.2.1 Monistic Court Systems

The different systems are often described by contrasting the dual court system with the monistic court system. In a monistic system, the same judges and courts deal with both private and administrative cases. In a dual court system, there are two different types of judges and separate sets of courts: one for private disputes between individuals or companies, and another for administrative disputes involving public authorities or government decisions.

For example, France clearly follows a dual court system. If two neighbors argue over a property boundary, their case will be heard by an ordinary civil court. But if a citizen challenges a local mayor's decision to refuse a building permit, the case goes to an administrative court, since it involves a public authority. This separation between the two branches of law dates back to the French Revolution, when the founders wanted to keep the Judiciary from interfering in government administration.

By contrast, Germany also has a dual system but with more categories of courts, including special branches for labor law, social security, and tax matters, each with its own hierarchy.

The United Kingdom, on the other hand, is often described as having a monistic system, since civil and administrative cases are heard within the same court structure. For example, both a contract dispute between two businesses and a challenge to a government decision can ultimately be decided by the High Court. However, this description oversimplifies reality. Historically, the UK developed a form of dualism through the creation of Equity, a separate system of justice managed by the Court of Chancery. For instance, if someone sought fairness rather than strict legal enforcement – such as asking a court to force another party to complete a contract rather than just pay damages – they would go to the Court of Chancery rather than the Common Law courts. This separation between Common Law and equity lasted until the Judicature Acts of 1873–1875 (often simplified to the 1895 reform), which merged the two systems into one unified court structure.

These examples show that the simple contrast between dual and monistic systems is misleading. Most countries have a mix of both traditions, shaped by their history, political values, and institutional evolution.

2.2.2 Dual Court Systems

Dual court systems are based on the idea that administrative authorities, which represent the State, cannot be treated exactly like private individuals. Public Law, including administrative law, aims to protect the common good rather than private interests. Because of this, the State is given special powers that it can exercise only when acting in the public interest. For example, under expropriation laws, the State can take private property to build a road or a hospital, provided that it compensates the owner and that the project serves the public good. Another example is the use of emergency powers when the State restricts certain rights temporarily to protect public safety, such as imposing curfews during a crisis. In these situations, citizens who believe that the administration has overstepped its powers can bring their complaints before special administrative courts, rather than ordinary civil courts.[15]

As the legal scholar John S. Bell explains, the real question is how the notion of "common good" is defined. In the past, it was mostly seen as a political matter, decided within each nation's own institutions. Today, however, international standards of human rights play an increasing role in shaping what governments can legitimately call the common good. For example, a government cannot restrict freedom of speech in the name of public order if that restriction violates international human rights conventions.[16]

15 Bell, John S., 2006, "Comparative Administrative Law," in *The Oxford Handbook of Comparative Law*, eds. Mathias Reimann and Reinhard Zimmermann, Oxford University Press.

16 Bell, *Comparative Administrative Law*.

When comparing court systems, one major difference between legal traditions is how they organize civil and administrative justice. Civil Law countries tend to have several separate systems of courts, while Common Law countries usually have one unified structure. In a Civil Law system, a case that falls within the jurisdiction of one type of court cannot be heard by another.

France illustrates this dual structure clearly. The French system is divided vertically into two branches: administrative courts, which deal with disputes involving public authorities, and judicial courts, which handle private disputes between individuals or companies. For example, if a citizen challenges a mayor's decision to refuse a building permit, the case will go to an administrative court, whereas a conflict between two business partners will be decided by a judicial court. Horizontally, the French judicial system is divided into first instance courts that handle general civil, criminal, and specialized cases, followed by appellate courts, and finally the Cour de cassation, which ensures that the law has been correctly applied.

In Civil Law countries like France, the interpretation of laws has traditionally been left to the legislature rather than the Judiciary. However, as legislation has become more complex and as constitutional principles have gained importance, the need for a body to interpret laws has grown. This led to the establishment of constitutional courts, such as the French Constitutional Council, which ensures that laws comply with constitutional rights.[17]

In contrast, Common Law countries such as the United Kingdom and the United States have integrated court systems where the same courts handle civil, criminal, administrative, and even constitutional matters. A single High Court in the UK, for example, can decide both a contract dispute and a case challenging a government decision. These systems are more unified but also more decentralized. Judges have wide discretion to interpret the law and create precedents through their rulings. This principle, known as stare decisis, meaning "let the decision stand,"[18] requires lower courts to follow the precedents set by higher ones. For example, if the U.S. Supreme Court decides that a particular police practice violates the Constitution, all lower courts in the country must follow that ruling in similar cases.

Thus, while Civil Law systems rely more on codes and institutional separation, and Common Law systems rely more on precedent and judicial independence, both structures aim to balance the protection of individual rights with the pursuit of the common good.

3 Comparative Overview of Civil Procedures

Civil procedures vary greatly from one legal system to another, reflecting different histories, cultures, and ways of thinking about justice. This section compares these systems, showing what makes each one unique. It also explains their main strengths and weaknesses and how they work in practice.

One of the most striking differences among legal traditions concerns the expression of judicial reasoning and disagreement. While all systems share the goal of delivering coherent and reasoned judgments, they diverge in whether and how they reveal internal divisions within a court. This divergence is particularly evident in the treatment of concurring and dissenting opinions. Another important aspect of comparison is how different legal systems handle situations where civil and criminal matters arise from the same set of facts; in other words, how they conjugate the civil and the criminal when they arise out of the same proceeding.

17 The incorporation of supra-national legal standards on fundamental rights and administrative behavior has an influence on the shaping of national standards of judicial review. Bell, *Comparative Administrative Law*, p. 1267.

18 See Chapter 4 – *The Common Law*.

3.1 Concurring or Dissenting Opinions

While all judicial systems aim to deliver reasoned and coherent judgments, they differ in how they express judicial disagreement. Some systems allow judges to write separate opinions, revealing differing views within the same court, while others emphasize the unity of the court's voice. This contrast is particularly visible between Common Law and Civil Law traditions.

3.1.1 The Practice and Impact of Concurring and Dissenting Opinions in Common Law Systems

An opinion is a judge's written explanation of the court's decision. When a case is heard by several judges, such as in most courts of appeal, and all judges agree on the outcome, one judge writes the opinion on behalf of the entire court. If the judges do not all agree, the decision reflects the view of the majority, and one judge from that majority writes the main opinion. Judges who disagree with the reasoning or the result may write separate opinions to explain their own views. A concurring opinion agrees with the final result but relies on different reasoning, while a dissenting opinion disagrees with the result altogether.

In Common Law systems, particularly in the United States, this practice is well established and plays an important role in shaping the law. It allows for open discussion among judges and makes their reasoning transparent to the public and future courts.

Imagine a case where a state law limits online speech to prevent hate messages. The majority of judges might uphold the law, considering it a legitimate measure to protect public safety, while one judge writes a dissenting opinion arguing that the restriction violates the constitutional right to free expression.

Consider another example where a company sues a city after being denied a construction permit. The court may rule in favor of the company, agreeing that the city acted unfairly. However, one judge might write a concurring opinion, agreeing with the outcome but emphasizing environmental concerns as the main reason for the decision.

These examples show how dissenting and concurring opinions enrich legal debate. They preserve alternative viewpoints, help identify weaknesses in existing reasoning, and sometimes guide future changes in the law when courts revisit similar issues.

3.1.2 The Absence of Concurring and Dissenting Opinions in Civil Law Systems

Do concurring or dissenting opinions exist in the French system? No, they do not. French court decisions, like those in most Civil Law countries, never include separate opinions. Unlike in the American system, where judges may openly express disagreement, French judgments are written and presented as if there were only one possible reasoning and one inevitable result.

This approach reflects a belief that the authority of justice depends on unity. If judges were to publish differing opinions, it could give the impression that the law is uncertain or subjective. Even though judges in France debate extensively and sometimes disagree during their deliberations, the final written decision speaks with one single voice. The judges who disagreed are not named, and the public never learns how the vote was divided.

Imagine, for instance, that a case before the Cour de cassation involves a dispute over inheritance between family members. The judges may have disagreed in private over how to interpret the will, but the published decision will not reveal any disagreement or separate reasoning – it will appear unanimous.

Consider another example where the Conseil d'État reviews a government policy on environmental protection. Some judges might think the government acted unlawfully, while others believe it acted within its rights. After deliberation, only one final judgment is issued, expressing the majority's view without identifying individual opinions.

This unity contrasts sharply with the Common Law tradition. In the United States, for example, if a judge strongly disagrees with the majority, he or she may write a dissent, sometimes using vivid or even harsh language to criticize the reasoning of the court. Imagine an American Supreme Court justice writing that "the majority's decision is inconsistent with both reason and the Constitution." Such expressions are unthinkable in the French system, where judicial restraint and institutional unity are seen as essential to preserving the authority and legitimacy of the courts.

3.2 Conjugating the Civil and the Criminal When They Arise Out of the Same Proceeding

Civil and criminal law can sometimes overlap, especially when both types of cases arise from the same facts. This part explores how different legal systems handle these situations. We compare the separate approach used in the United States with the integrated approach in France, highlighting the benefits and challenges of each method.

Imagine a car accident caused by a driver who was speeding while intoxicated. In the United States, the victim could bring a Civil Lawsuit to claim compensation for medical expenses and damages, while the State would file a criminal case to punish the driver for the offense of drunk driving. These two cases would be handled separately by different courts, with separate procedures, judges, and outcomes.

In France, by contrast, both aspects can be dealt with together in the same criminal proceeding. The injured person may join the criminal case as a *partie civile* (civil party) and claim compensation directly before the same court that decides on the criminal responsibility of the driver. This integrated approach avoids the duplication of cases and allows the victim to obtain both justice and compensation within a single trial. However, it also means that the outcome of the civil claim depends on the progress of the criminal case, which can sometimes delay compensation.

3.2.1 Distinctions and Overlaps Between Civil and Criminal Law

There is often confusion between criminal law and Civil Law, so it is important to distinguish them clearly. The police generally have no role in civil litigation. Civil cases typically concern matters such as divorce, contracts, torts, property, or inheritance. The police may be involved only if a criminal offense arises within a civil dispute – for example, if violence occurs during a divorce case, or if a tort, such as theft, also constitutes a crime. In those situations, the same act can lead to both civil and criminal proceedings.

This Chapter focuses mainly on civil litigation, which includes non-criminal disputes such as family law, contractual issues, property rights, inheritance, and compensation for harm caused by others.

In some cases, civil and criminal proceedings can take place at the same time. A well-known example is the O.J. Simpson case in the United States. The O.J. Simpson case involved two separate trials. The criminal trial took place in 1995, and the civil trial followed in 1997. In the criminal trial, Simpson was accused of murdering his ex-wife and her friend but was found not guilty. Later, in a civil trial brought by the victims' families, he was found responsible for their deaths and ordered to pay millions of dollars in damages. This shows how a person can be acquitted in a criminal case but still be held liable in a civil one.

This shows how both types of cases can coexist – criminal law dealing with punishment and Civil Law focusing on compensation. In systems like the United States, these proceedings are separate, whereas in countries like France, they can be combined within a single process.

This situation is possible because criminal law and Civil Law apply different standards of proof and pursue different objectives.

In a criminal trial, the goal is to determine whether the accused committed a crime and should be punished by the State. The prosecution must prove guilt "beyond a reasonable doubt," which is a very high standard. If there is any serious doubt, the defendant must be acquitted. That is what happened in O.J. Simpson's 1995 trial – the jury found that there was not enough certainty to convict him of murder.

In a civil trial, however, the purpose is not to punish but to compensate the victims. The standard of proof is lower: the court decides based on the "preponderance of evidence" – that is, whether it is more likely than not that the defendant is responsible. In Simpson's 1997 civil trial, the jury found that, even if there was some doubt, the evidence showed it was more probable that he caused the victims' deaths, and he was ordered to pay damages.

This can seem absurd or contradictory, because one court declares a person "not guilty," while another holds him "responsible" for the same acts. But legally, it reflects the difference between criminal guilt (which requires near certainty) and civil liability (which is based on probability). The two systems serve different purposes: one protects individuals from wrongful punishment, the other ensures victims receive compensation.

3.2.2 Integrated Proceedings in Civil Law Systems

A situation like the O.J. Simpson case could not happen in France, because the French legal system allows civil and criminal matters arising from the same facts to be handled together within the same proceeding. In France, when a criminal act also causes harm to a victim, that victim can join the criminal case as a *partie civile* (civil party). This means that the same court decides both the criminal responsibility of the accused and the civil compensation for the victim. If the court finds the accused not guilty, the civil claim linked to that criminal offense usually fails as well, since there is no criminal fault on which to base liability.

For example, if someone is accused of assault, the victim can claim damages directly in the criminal trial. If the accused is acquitted because the court finds that the assault did not occur, the victim cannot then start a separate civil case for the same act. This system avoids contradictions between criminal and civil judgments, but it also means that the victim's compensation depends on the outcome of the criminal trial, which can sometimes delay the resolution of the civil aspect.

In France, and in countries that have followed its model, it is considered socially desirable that the victim of a crime can also bring a civil claim arising from the same act. The victim has the right to become a co-plaintiff in the criminal case before the criminal court. For instance, the victim of an assault may join the criminal proceedings against the accused and claim compensation as a *partie civile*. In the United States, by contrast, the same victim would have to file a separate Civil Lawsuit for damages in a different court.

The French approach offers clear advantages. The victim benefits from the police investigation and from the work of the public prosecutor (*ministère public*). The State helps to gather and present the evidence of the crime. However, the victim must still prove and quantify the damages to obtain compensation.

The relationship between civil and criminal proceedings has long raised complex questions. If the civil case is decided first, are its findings binding on the criminal court? If the criminal court rules first, must the civil court follow its conclusions? And if the two cases proceed at different speeds, should the second court be bound by the facts already established by the first? These issues have generated considerable discussion, legal writing, and reforms in many countries.

Tort law deals with civil wrongs between private parties, while criminal law addresses offenses against society. Sometimes, a single act can be both a tort and a crime. For example, a drunk driver who injures another person commits a crime (for endangering public safety) and a tort (for causing harm to another individual). However, not all torts are crimes.

Divorce, for instance, is neither a tort nor a crime – it is a legal process that ends a marriage. Adultery, once criminalized in some countries, is no longer a crime in most jurisdictions, though in a few U.S. states, such as North Carolina, it can still lead to a civil claim for damages. Harassment is often a tort, but in serious cases it can also be a crime. A minor car accident that causes only property damage is a tort, but if it involves drunk driving or reckless behavior, it becomes both a tort and a crime.

Defamation provides another example. In most countries, defamation – known in French as *diffamation* – is a tort, not a crime. It includes libel (written defamation) and slander (spoken defamation). For instance, if a journalist publishes false statements damaging someone's reputation, the person can sue in civil court for damages, but the act is not usually prosecuted as a crime.

Medical or legal malpractice also illustrates the overlap. A doctor whose negligence causes injury commits a tort and may be ordered to compensate the patient. If the negligence causes death, it may also constitute a criminal offense, such as involuntary manslaughter.

Tort law and criminal law are therefore closely connected. Both aim to discourage wrongful behavior: tort law through financial liability and criminal law through punishment. Their goals differ, however – tort law focuses on compensation and deterrence, while criminal law emphasizes punishment and deterrence. Their shared purpose of deterrence explains why these two fields often overlap.

In the United States, civil and criminal cases are usually heard by the same courts but through separate proceedings. In France, they are handled by different chambers within the same court system. For example, the *Cour de cassation* includes a *chambre criminelle* for criminal matters and several *chambres civiles* for civil cases. This structure reflects the dual role of the French Judiciary in addressing both private disputes and public offenses.

3.3 Inquisitorial and Adversarial Procedures

In civil procedure, two main models are frequently discussed: the inquisitorial and the adversarial systems. Although these terms are often used broadly, it is important to grasp their specific meanings and the contexts in which they operate. In his well-known article, Professor Langbein criticizes the adversarial model and praises the inquisitorial approach, particularly as implemented in Germany. This section examines the defining features of both systems, clarifies common misunderstandings, and highlights the areas where they converge and differ.

3.3.1 Definitions and Clarifications

It is often said – though some find the distinction oversimplified – that there are two main models of civil procedure: the inquisitorial and the adversarial systems. These terms appear frequently in discussions of Comparative Law.

In the inquisitorial system, the judge plays a central role in directing the proceedings. The judge is responsible for gathering the facts, questioning witnesses, and compiling a complete case file before applying the law. Lawyers have a more limited role: they may question witnesses only with the judge's permission. Judges also appoint their own expert witnesses, whose opinions often carry greater weight than those of experts hired by the parties.

In the adversarial system, by contrast, the parties and their lawyers control the litigation. They are responsible for collecting evidence, presenting witnesses, and arguing their case. Cross-examination is essential, as it allows each side to challenge the credibility of the other's witnesses. This model relies heavily on the skill and resources of the parties' legal representatives, which can sometimes create inequalities between well-funded and less well-funded litigants.

In his well-known article, Professor Langbein criticized the adversarial system and praised the inquisitorial approach, particularly as practiced in Germany.[19] Germany is often seen as the country whose civil procedure is most strongly characterized by inquisitorial features. It is important to note that this is in reference to civil procedure, not criminal procedure, as the two have distinct rules and goals.

Before examining the details, it is worth clarifying the terminology. The word "inquisitorial" can sound misleading – it does not refer to the historical Inquisition of 15th-century Spain. Many scholars prefer alternative terms such as "investigatory" or "investigative," which better capture the idea of a judge-led inquiry without the historical connotations.

Similarly, the term "adversarial" can also be misunderstood. In truth, even inquisitorial systems contain adversarial elements. Both models are adversarial in the basic sense that civil procedure always involves two opposing parties – the plaintiff and the defendant – who determine the scope of the dispute. The court does not choose the issues; the plaintiff defines the claims and the remedy sought, while the defendant responds and seeks to defeat them.

Nevertheless, in legal literature and practice, "adversarial" is generally used to describe systems like that of the United States, where lawyers drive the proceedings, and "inquisitorial" refers to systems where the judge leads the process. The important point to remember is that "inquisitorial" does not mean "Inquisition-like," and even inquisitorial systems preserve a degree of adversarial structure.

3.3.2 Convergence and Divergence

So now we can use these terms – inquisitorial and adversarial – freely, understanding their limitations. We can also see from three major articles by Professors Damaska,[20] Reitz,[21] and Langbein[22] that, at least in their pure form, the inquisitorial and adversarial systems operate on very different premises. Yet, all three authors acknowledge that there is increasing convergence between them.

As Professor Damaska writes, the traditional contrasts between Common Law and Civil Law have become less significant, overshadowed by new differences that transcend these categories.[23] With modern communication and globalization, legal systems increasingly borrow from one another, creating forms that blend elements of both traditions. Similarly, Professor Reitz notes that both systems are evolving toward convergence, driven by the need to address issues such as procedural delays and judicial efficiency.[24] Professor Langbein adds that the rise of the "managerial judge" in the United States reflects this convergence, as American judges

19 Langbein, *The German Advantage in Civil Procedure*.

20 Damaška, Mirjan, 2010, "The Common Law / Civil Law Divide: Residual Truth of a Misleading Distinction," *Supreme Court Law Review*, vol. 49 (2d), p. 3.

21 Reitz, *Why We Probably Cannot Adopt the German Advantage*, p. 987.

22 Langbein, *The German Advantage in Civil Procedure*, p. 823.

23 Damaška, *The Common Law / Civil Law Divide*.

24 Reitz, *Why We Probably Cannot Adopt the German Advantage*.

are taking a more active role in managing the fact-gathering process, much like their European counterparts.[25]

However, convergence does not mean uniformity. As Damaska, Reitz, and Langbein all emphasize, differences between the systems persist. They may fade over time, but they never disappear entirely. The goal, therefore, is to understand the extent and the reasons for convergence – why certain features evolve in similar ways while others remain distinct. But to understand convergence, one must first understand the differences.

The German system remains the best-known example of a judge-centered model of civil procedure. In this system, the judge is responsible for developing the factual record, known as the dossier. The judge plays an active role in gathering evidence, questioning witnesses, and ensuring that the record is accurate and complete. Justice, in this model, is achieved when the judge, equipped with a comprehensive understanding of the facts, applies the law – usually codified in the civil code – to those facts.

The judge is also the primary questioner during hearings. Lawyers may only ask questions with the judge's permission, and they cannot speak unless the judge allows it. This differs sharply from Common Law practice, where lawyers lead the questioning and judges intervene only to maintain order.

Expert evidence provides another example of this judge-centered approach. Civil judges in Germany, though highly trained in the law, are not experts in fields such as medicine, engineering, or foreign law. To assist them, they select their own experts from official lists. Each court typically maintains a roster of experts in various disciplines – medicine, construction, accounting, and so on – and the judge freely chooses which expert to appoint. Lawyers may also present their own experts, but their influence is generally weaker than that of the court-appointed expert.

This system reflects a broader philosophy: litigation is a matter of public concern. It is seen as a form of public administration, where the judge, as a civil servant, is responsible for ensuring that justice is done. Justice, in this sense, means the correct application of the law to an accurate and complete record of facts.

The American system represents the opposite model. There, judges do not investigate or build the record themselves. Instead, they listen to the evidence presented by the parties, each of whom selects and prepares its own witnesses. These witnesses are literally "for the claimant" or "for the defendant." The idea is that truth emerges from the confrontation between opposing lawyers – the so-called "clash of the advocates." The judge's role is to act as a neutral referee, deciding which side's case is more persuasive.

Because the adversarial system allows lawyers to prepare and coach their witnesses, cross-examination is essential to ensure fairness. Each side has the right to challenge the credibility of the other's witnesses, testing the strength and reliability of their testimony. This is one reason why courtroom trials in the United States lend themselves so well to dramatization – the process is designed as a contest between opposing parties.

One of the main weaknesses of the adversarial system is that it assumes equality between the parties. In reality, success in court often depends on the quality and resources of one's legal representation. Wealthier litigants can afford better lawyers, experts, and preparation. The inquisitorial model, by contrast, seeks to reduce such inequalities by placing more responsibility in the hands of the judge, who conducts the investigation and ensures that both sides are heard.

25 Langbein, *The German Advantage in Civil Procedure*.

Each system has its strengths and weaknesses. The adversarial model values party autonomy, public transparency, and vigorous debate; the inquisitorial model emphasizes judicial responsibility, procedural fairness, and equality of access. The ongoing convergence between the two reflects a shared search for balance between these competing ideals.

3.4 The Jury

The jury plays a vital role in the legal system by determining the facts of a case and applying the law as explained by the judge. Although juries function within an adversarial system, their members are ordinary citizens rather than legal experts. This makes the strict rules of evidence essential to guarantee fairness and to prevent jurors from being influenced by unreliable or prejudicial information.

This section examines the role and impact of the jury in both civil and criminal proceedings. It looks at how jury trials operate in practice, how judges and lawyers interact with juries, and what strategic considerations guide the parties when deciding whether or not to request a jury trial.

3.4.1 Role and Influence of the Jury

In the United States, juries are used in both criminal and civil cases. This is a constitutional right, and a jury will be present unless both parties in a civil case agree otherwise. In serious criminal cases, however, a jury is always required. In the United Kingdom, juries are now used only in criminal cases involving serious offenses such as murder, rape, or major theft; civil juries have been almost entirely abolished, except in rare cases like defamation. In France, juries exist only in criminal cases tried before the *Cour d'assises*, which deals with the most serious crimes. Civil cases are decided solely by professional judges. In most other Civil Law countries, such as Germany, Spain, or Japan, juries are uncommon. Serious cases may be heard by panels of professional judges, sometimes assisted by lay assessors, but not by juries in the Anglo-American sense. In short, juries are central to the American system, limited to criminal law in the United Kingdom and France, and largely absent from the rest of the Civil Law world.

The jury's main function is to determine the facts of the case. It applies the law to those facts, but only as instructed by the judge. The judge explains the relevant legal principles, while the jury focuses on assessing the evidence and deciding what actually happened.

Within the adversarial system, the jury listens to witnesses who have been prepared and questioned by the parties' lawyers. Because jurors are ordinary citizens rather than legal professionals, the legal system imposes strict rules of evidence to protect them from unreliable or misleading information. This explains why, in American and British trials, lawyers frequently raise objections such as "I object!" – challenging a question or a piece of evidence as irrelevant, prejudicial, or unreliable. These rules help ensure that the jury bases its decision only on trustworthy and legally admissible material.

This framework also reflects a fundamental difference between Common Law and Civil Law proceedings. In the Common Law world, the trial is concentrated – a single, continuous "day in court" where all evidence is presented before the jury. It functions almost like a carefully staged performance between opposing lawyers, beginning and ending within a defined time frame. In contrast, Civil Law systems, which are judge-led, proceed through a series of hearings spread out over time.

The concentrated nature of a jury trial is also practical. Because jurors are ordinary citizens, they cannot be expected to return repeatedly for months of intermittent hearings. The trial must therefore be organized so that the jury can attend continuously, usually over a few days or weeks, and reach a decision efficiently.

3.4.2 Jury Selection and Strategic Considerations

The jury is meant to be chosen at random from the general population. Anyone who is a lawful resident can be selected, and serving on a jury is a civic duty. In the United States, juries still exist in both criminal and civil cases. In contrast, the United Kingdom has abolished juries for civil cases – today, they are used only in criminal trials.

In the U.S., the right to a jury trial is guaranteed by the Constitution, specifically the Sixth Amendment. This means that in most cases, either party can request a jury. There will be no jury only if both sides agree to waive that right.

Once a pool of potential jurors is selected at random, the process of jury selection begins. During this stage, lawyers for both sides can question jurors and ask that some be dismissed for specific reasons – for example, if they show bias or have a personal connection to the case. This helps ensure that the final jury is fair and impartial.

If you were a plaintiff – the person bringing a lawsuit – you would probably prefer to have a jury. Plaintiffs often believe that a jury of ordinary citizens will be more sympathetic to their situation. For example, in a personal injury case where someone is suing a company after an accident, the plaintiff's lawyer might prefer a jury, thinking that jurors will identify with the victim.

However, in commercial disputes between two businesses, both sides often agree to skip the jury. They may want a faster and more predictable decision from a professional judge, rather than leaving the outcome to non-specialists. For example, two companies arguing over a contract might agree in writing: "No jury trial." This helps avoid the delays and extra procedures that come with a jury.

In criminal cases, things are different. The use of a jury is a matter of public policy – it cannot be waived simply because the parties agree. Criminal law exists to protect society, not just the individuals involved, so a jury trial is considered essential. Even if both the prosecutor and the accused preferred to have only a judge, the law requires that serious criminal charges be decided by a jury.

3.5 Pre-Trial and Discovery

The pre-trial and discovery phases play a key role in the American legal process, as they largely determine how a case will unfold in court. During these stages, lawyers gather evidence, question witnesses, and exchange information with the opposing side to prepare their arguments. This preparation aims to make the trial more efficient and transparent, but it also makes the process lengthy and costly. This part examines the functions of the pre-trial phase and discovery, their impact on the outcome of cases, and the main criticisms and reform proposals aimed at making the system more balanced and accessible.

3.5.1 Pre-Trial Preparation

In order to create this "day in court," which may last several weeks rather than a single day, lawyers must engage in extensive preparation. A trial in the American system is not a routine bureaucratic procedure – it is a performance, a structured confrontation between two opposing sides. To make this possible, lawyers must prepare every detail in advance to ensure a dynamic and persuasive presentation.

This is why the pre-trial phase is so important. In American law, before the trial begins, there is a period known as pre-trial discovery. During this stage, lawyers gather information and evidence to prevent any unfair surprises during the trial. Each side has the right to obtain documents, request records, and question witnesses before they appear in court. These pre-trial interviews are called depositions.

The discovery process has become one of the defining features of the American legal system. It reflects the idea that a fair and effective trial depends on full access to information, allowing both sides to prepare thoroughly for the courtroom – the stage where the "theater" of justice unfolds.

Because so much of the trial's success depends on what happens before reaching the courtroom, discovery often shapes the entire strategy of the case. Many disputes are even resolved at this stage, once the parties understand the strength of the evidence available to each side. When discovery reveals that one party's position is significantly weaker than initially believed, the incentives to proceed to trial diminish. Conversely, strong documentary or testimonial evidence may encourage the opposing party to settle to avoid the risks and costs of a public trial. In this way, discovery functions not only as a tool for gathering information but also as a mechanism for promoting early resolution. By clarifying the factual landscape, it enables both sides to make more realistic assessments of their chances, often leading to negotiated settlements that spare the court and the parties the burdens of a full trial. The extensive scope of discovery, therefore, explains both the power and the cost of American litigation: while it promotes transparency and fairness, it also requires significant time, resources, and legal expertise.

3.5.2 Discovery Process

Before the trial begins, each lawyer in the American system can request from the opposing side any documents or information that might be relevant to the case. For example, in a lawsuit against a pharmaceutical company, a victim's lawyer might demand access to all studies, reports, and correspondence that led the company to conclude that a drug was safe. The lawyer could also require the company's executives to answer questions under oath in what is called a deposition, or to respond in writing to a list of interrogatories – formal questions submitted before trial.

This process, known as pre-trial discovery, can be extremely extensive and may last months or even years. It often involves reviewing thousands of documents and conducting numerous interviews. For instance, imagine how many files a large bank like Société Générale would have to produce in a case related to Jérôme Kerviel's trading activities – millions of pages of internal reports, emails, and transaction records could all be relevant.

In theory, the judge plays little or no role in discovery. It is primarily an exchange between lawyers, who can object to requests they consider excessive. A common objection is that a request is "overbroad" or a "fishing expedition," meaning that the other side is asking for information without knowing whether it even exists or is relevant.

Discovery is one of the defining features of the American adversarial system, but also one of its most criticized aspects. Scholars like Professor Langbein have pointed out that it generates vast amounts of paperwork and high costs, often lasting months or years. Because discovery is so expensive, it can deepen inequalities between wealthy and less wealthy parties. Many litigants, even those with strong cases, choose to settle simply to avoid the financial burden of continuing the process.

As a result, there is now a growing movement in the United States to reform and limit discovery. Judges are increasingly encouraged to intervene and reject requests that are repetitive, speculative, overly costly, or not directly relevant to the case. This trend reflects an effort to make the system more efficient and fair while maintaining the transparency that discovery was originally designed to promote.

3.6 Goals of a Good Civil Procedural System

This section explores what the goals of a good civil procedural system should be and how different systems strive to meet these goals. It also examines the balance between ensuring fairness and allowing for individual autonomy.

3.6.1 Accuracy and Economy

Let us consider what the goals of a good civil procedural system should be. Imagine that we could design a system of litigation from scratch. What would we want it to achieve? First, it should aim for accuracy, meaning it should help uncover the truth. Second, it should be reasonably affordable, avoiding excessive costs and unnecessary delay. These two goals – accuracy and economy – are at the heart of any fair and efficient justice system. A good system should therefore be capable of finding the truth while being neither too expensive nor too time-consuming.

The question then arises: which of the two main systems – the inquisitorial or the adversarial – is more likely to produce the truth, and which is more economical? Opinions differ. Some argue that the bureaucratic and judge-led nature of the inquisitorial model makes it more efficient and less costly. Others believe that the adversarial system, when it works properly, offers a better chance of uncovering the truth through active debate and confrontation between the parties.

In the Common Law world, the prevailing view is that vigorous adversarial proceedings, where both sides challenge each other's arguments and evidence, are more likely to lead to the truth. However, this belief cannot be definitively proven or disproven. Much depends on personal intuition and on which kind of system one would rather experience – civil or Common Law, inquisitorial or adversarial.

3.6.2 Equality and Autonomy

Equality is another essential goal of any fair legal system. If we aim for equality – absolute or as close as reasonably possible – the adversarial system poses challenges. It relies heavily on the parties' financial means and the quality of their legal representation. Unless there is a strong system of public legal aid that ensures everyone has equal access to resources, the adversarial model tends to favor those who can afford better lawyers and experts. Only with extensive public funding for litigation could such a system approach real equality.

Beyond accuracy, economy, and equality, there is a fourth important value that helps explain the attachment of Common Law systems, particularly the American one, to their procedures. This value is more difficult to name, but it centers on individual autonomy – the idea that each party should have as much freedom as possible to present their case in their own way. The American system reflects a deeply rooted belief in personal initiative and free enterprise. It values the satisfaction that comes from being able to use one's skill, creativity, and strategic choices – through advocacy, cross-examination, or expert testimony – to influence the outcome of a case.

This emphasis on autonomy, however, often conflicts with the principle of equality. The more freedom parties have to control their litigation, the greater the disparity between those with more and fewer resources. The structure of a legal system, therefore, depends on which value it prioritizes: equality of arms or party autonomy. Systems that prioritize equality tend to favor a bureaucratic, judge-centered approach, while those that value individual freedom and initiative prefer the adversarial model, where lawyers and parties drive the process.

Ultimately, it is uncertain whether one system is better at discovering the truth or managing costs. What is clear is that the adversarial model promotes free enterprise and party control, while the inquisitorial model limits this freedom in favor of neutrality and judicial oversight. Each system reflects a different vision of justice – one focused on individual autonomy, the other on fairness and equality.

4 Transnational Rules of Civil Procedure Developed by UNIDROIT and the American Law Institute

The transnational rules of civil procedure are a set of principles jointly developed by UNIDROIT and the American Law Institute (ALI). The ALI is an organization composed of prominent judges, lawyers, and academics in the United States, known for producing influential "Restatements" that clarify and modernize American law. UNIDROIT, based in Rome near the Colosseum, is an international organization whose mission is to harmonize private law across different legal systems worldwide.

These two institutions decided to collaborate on creating a model framework for civil procedure, not as a binding code of rules, but as a set of guiding principles – hence the name *ALI–UNIDROIT Principles of Transnational Civil Procedure*. The project aimed to find common ground between Civil Law and Common Law traditions and to establish standards that could inspire national reforms or apply to cross-border cases.

The work took nearly ten years to complete. The resulting principles appear simple, but they represent a major intellectual achievement – a careful reconciliation of deep procedural differences between legal systems. They reflect a shared commitment to fairness, efficiency, and access to justice, demonstrating that even systems with contrasting traditions can converge toward common values.

4.1 Transnational Rules, UNIDROIT, and the American Law Institute

The transnational rules of civil procedure are a collaborative effort by the American Law Institute (ALI) and the International Institute for the Unification of Private Law (UNIDROIT). These principles aim to harmonize civil litigation processes across different legal systems, bridging the gap between Civil Law and Common Law traditions.

4.1.1 The American Law Institute and UNIDROIT

The American Law Institute is the leading independent organization in the United States producing scholarly work to clarify, modernize, and otherwise improve the law.[26]

> UNIDROIT is the International Institute for the Unification of Private Law. It is an independent intergovernmental Organisation with its seat in the Villa Aldobrandini in Rome. Its purpose is to study needs and methods for modernising, harmonising and co-ordinating private

26 See American Law Institute, official website, online. Available at: https://www.ali.org.

> and in particular commercial law as between states and groups of states and to formulate uniform law instruments, principles and rules to achieve those objectives.[27]

Membership of UNIDROIT is restricted to states acceding to the UNIDROIT Statute. UNIDROIT's 63 member states are drawn from the five continents and represent a variety of different legal, economic, and political systems as well as different cultural backgrounds. Set up in 1926 as an auxiliary organ of the League of Nations, the Institute was, following the demise of the League, re-established in 1940 on the basis of a multilateral agreement, the UNIDROIT Statute.

Together, the American Law Institute and UNIDROIT illustrate how legal development now occurs not only within national boundaries but also through collaborative international efforts. While ALI focuses on guiding and improving U.S. law, UNIDROIT seeks to promote coherence across different legal systems. Their work reflects a broader trend in contemporary law: the increasing need for shared principles and harmonized norms in a world where economic, commercial, and social relationships are increasingly interconnected.

4.1.2 Collaboration and Principles

ALI and UNIDROIT decided to work together to create a model code of civil procedure, but at the level of principles, not detailed rules. That is why their work is called the *ALI/UNIDROIT Principles of Transnational Civil Procedure*. These principles were designed as general standards for resolving transnational commercial disputes, but they can also apply to many other types of civil cases. They may even serve as a foundation for future reforms in national civil procedure systems.

The aim of these principles is not to regulate technical details – such as the exact number of days to respond to a complaint – but to set out the core ideas and fundamental values of a fair and effective civil procedure. Their purpose is to show what the essential features of a sound procedural system should look like. They can therefore inspire national legislatures, guide judges in interpreting their own procedural rules, or provide a procedural framework for arbitration tribunals, where private arbitrators resolve disputes outside state courts. (Arbitration will be discussed in Chapter 12.)

The *ALI/UNIDROIT Principles* were drafted to be clear, concise, and accessible, even compared with national procedural codes. They represent a balanced synthesis between the American adversarial model and the German inquisitorial model, showing how these two traditions can be reconciled at an international level. While their primary goal is to improve transnational dispute resolution, they also reveal broader trends in the evolution of civil litigation – trends that reflect increasing globalization and the gradual convergence of legal systems.

4.2 Jurisdiction Over Parties

Jurisdiction over parties refers to a court's legal power to make decisions that bind specific individuals or entities. It defines whether a court has the authority to summon the parties, hear their case, and issue a judgment that they must respect. In international contexts, this question becomes especially important because it determines whether a court in one country can

27 See International Institute for the Unification of Private Law (UNIDROIT), official website, online. Available at: https://www.unidroit.or.

legitimately exercise authority over a person or company located in another country. Without proper jurisdiction, any judgment rendered may be considered invalid or unenforceable abroad.

4.2.1 Principles of Jurisdiction

Jurisdiction over parties is a key element of international civil procedure, ensuring that disputes are heard in a fair and appropriate forum. Article 2 defines the main principles and limits for determining when a court may exercise jurisdiction.

First, jurisdiction may be based on consent, when the parties have agreed to submit their dispute to a particular court or tribunal. It may also arise from a substantial connection between the forum state and the parties or the facts of the case – for example, when an important part of the events occurred in that state, when the defendant resides or is incorporated there, or when the property at issue is located there.

If no other forum is reasonably available, jurisdiction may exceptionally be exercised on the basis of the defendant's presence or nationality in the forum state, or the presence of the defendant's property, even if the property is unrelated to the dispute. In that case, however, the court's authority is limited to the value of that property.

A court may also issue provisional measures, such as freezing assets or protecting property, even if it lacks full jurisdiction over the main dispute. At the same time, courts should generally decline jurisdiction when the parties have agreed to an exclusive forum elsewhere, or when another court is clearly more appropriate. If the case is already pending before a competent court, the second court should suspend or decline proceedings unless the first forum is unable to ensure a fair and efficient resolution.

Overall, Article 2 seeks to balance fairness, efficiency, and respect for party autonomy. By emphasizing consent, substantial connections, and procedural safeguards, it ensures that jurisdiction is exercised only where there is a legitimate and meaningful link to the dispute, while avoiding parallel or conflicting proceedings.

4.2.2 Challenges and Limitations

There is often great debate about whether the courts of one country can exercise jurisdiction over a person or company from another country. It seems natural to question whether, for example, someone who is neither a French citizen nor a resident of France should be subject to the authority of French courts. No national court has universal jurisdiction – none can rule over everyone in the world. Each country must therefore define, or be guided by international principles defining, the limits of its jurisdiction.

If France were to restrict its courts only to French nationals or residents, that would clearly be too narrow. Imagine an American company operating in France that causes severe pollution in the Loire Valley. Should it escape responsibility simply because it is not French? Obviously not. France must have the right to hold that company accountable before its courts, as its actions directly affected French territory and interests.

At the same time, allowing countries to claim jurisdiction without limits would be equally problematic. It would lead to unfairness, unpredictability, and conflicts between legal systems. Therefore, international law seeks to strike a balance: countries must be able to exercise jurisdiction when there is a real and meaningful link to the case – such as the place where the harmful act occurred – but they must also respect limits to prevent excessive or arbitrary use of power.

This balancing approach reflects a basic requirement of any fair legal system: disputes should be decided by a court that has a genuine connection to the matter. To achieve this, countries rely on objective links such as nationality, residence, the location of assets, or the place where a harmful act occurred. These criteria help ensure that people and companies are not subjected to foreign courts without sufficient justification, while still allowing states to address conduct that has real effects within their territory or on their population.

4.3 Substantial Connection and Adequate Personal Jurisdiction

The concept of substantial connection is crucial in determining whether a court has adequate personal jurisdiction over a party in international litigation. According to Article 2.1.2, a substantial connection exists when there is a significant link between the forum state and the party or the transaction in dispute. This can be established if a major part of the transaction occurred in the forum state, the defendant is a habitual resident, the corporation has its principal place of business there, or the relevant property is located in the forum state.

4.3.1 Substantial Connection

With this background, we can now turn to Article 2.1.2, which defines when a court may exercise jurisdiction. It states that jurisdiction may exist "when there is a substantial connection between the forum state and the party or the transaction or occurrence in dispute." The term *forum* simply refers to the country or place where the court is located.

A substantial connection exists, for example, when an important part of the events took place in that country, when the defendant lives there, when a company is incorporated or has its main office there, or when the property involved in the dispute is located there.

Although this definition sounds clear, it still leaves room for disagreement. Lawyers often argue about what counts as a "substantial" connection. How much activity must occur in the forum state? Is having a small office there enough? What if only part of a contract was performed there? These questions appear in nearly every case involving cross-border disputes.

Nonetheless, there is broad agreement internationally that courts should not claim jurisdiction over non-residents or foreign companies unless a real and meaningful link exists between them and the country where the court sits. This principle – known as *personal jurisdiction* in American law – is essential to fairness and due process in international litigation.

Imagine a French court hearing two different cases. In the first case, a Canadian company sells defective machinery to a French manufacturer, and the equipment causes an accident at a factory in Lyon. Even though the company is based in Canada, the harmful event occurred in France, and the victims are French. There is a substantial connection between the dispute and France, so the French court would likely have jurisdiction. In the second case, a Japanese company signs a contract with a German distributor, and all negotiations, production, and delivery take place outside France. However, the German distributor later sued the company in a French court simply because it had once attended a trade fair in Paris. In this situation, there is no substantial connection between the dispute and France, so the French court would probably decline jurisdiction.

4.3.2 Adequate Personal Jurisdiction

The principle of substantial connection ensures that courts exercise jurisdiction only when there is a meaningful link between the dispute and the forum state. It prevents excessive or arbitrary use of authority by limiting a court's power over non-nationals or non-residents. Although each country defines and applies this idea differently, the underlying rule is universal: a court cannot claim authority over every person in the world. For jurisdiction to be fair and legitimate, there must be a real connection – such as where the events occurred, where the parties are based, or where the property in question is located. This principle is now a cornerstone of international civil procedure and serves as a model standard for ensuring balanced and just jurisdiction.

Imagine two situations that illustrate how the principle of substantial connection works in practice:

In the first example, a Spanish company builds a bridge in Morocco under a contract with the Moroccan Government. During construction, an accident occurs, causing damage in Morocco. The Moroccan courts have jurisdiction because the event and its effects took place on Moroccan territory – a clear and substantial connection exists between the dispute and Morocco.

In the second example, a Brazilian company and an Italian company sign a contract entirely negotiated and performed in South America. Later, the Italian company tries to sue in a French court simply because the Brazilian company once opened a temporary exhibition office in Paris. Since the dispute has no real link with France, the French court would likely refuse to hear the case for lack of substantial connection.

These examples show why the principle is so widely accepted: it provides a rational, predictable basis for determining which court should hear a dispute. By requiring a real link between the case and the forum, it protects individuals and companies from being drawn into distant or unrelated legal proceedings, while still allowing states to address conduct that genuinely affects them. In this way, the principle of substantial connection promotes fairness, reduces conflict between legal systems, and helps ensure that judicial decisions are respected internationally.

4.4 Exclusive Jurisdiction

Exclusive jurisdiction refers to the scenario where the parties involved in a dispute have previously agreed that only a specific tribunal or court has the authority to resolve their dispute. This principle is particularly important in international litigation and is governed by Article 2.4. Its purpose is to give parties certainty and predictability, ensuring that they know in advance which court will decide any future dispute. This helps reduce forum shopping and encourages efficient dispute resolution in cross-border transactions.

4.4.1 Principle of Exclusive Jurisdiction

Article 2.4 introduces an important rule about party autonomy: the ability of parties to choose the court that will resolve their disputes. It provides that a court should normally decline jurisdiction if the parties have already agreed that another tribunal will have exclusive jurisdiction. In other words, even if a court technically has authority over a case, it should not hear it when the parties have previously chosen a different forum.

This principle reflects modern international practice, where businesses and individuals often decide in advance where potential disputes will be resolved. For example, two companies – one from Japan and one from Canada – may include in their contract a clause stating that any disputes will be settled in the courts of Singapore. If one party later brings the case before a Canadian court, that court should ordinarily refuse to hear it, respecting the parties' original agreement.

This rule shows how international law values contractual freedom. The parties are free, within certain legal limits, to choose any court they prefer – even one in a country that has no direct link to the dispute. Of course, there are exceptions established by national laws, especially in areas like consumer protection or employment, where one party might need additional safeguards. But overall, Article 2.4 embodies the modern idea that, in civil and commercial matters, jurisdiction can largely be a matter of agreement.

This flexibility is especially valuable in international commerce, where parties often choose neutral courts or familiar legal systems to minimize uncertainty and avoid potential bias. Such agreements, therefore, promote trust and stability in global business relations.

4.4.2 Autonomy and Exceptions

The general rule is that a court must have a substantial connection to a dispute in order to exercise jurisdiction. However, if the parties have agreed in advance to resolve their dispute in a third country that would not otherwise be competent, they are generally allowed to do so. This reflects the principle of party autonomy, which gives individuals and companies the freedom to choose the forum where their disputes will be heard.

It is important not to confuse the question of jurisdiction with the question of which law will apply. Determining whether a court has the authority to hear a case is different from deciding which country's law the court will use to resolve it. A court may have jurisdiction but still apply foreign law, depending on the case. The discussion here concerns only the choice of forum, not the applicable law, which is a separate issue addressed under conflict of laws.

In summary, exclusive jurisdiction allows parties to agree on a specific forum for their disputes, highlighting the value of autonomy and flexibility in international law, while recognizing that this principle operates within certain statutory limits designed to protect fairness and public interest.

These limits ensure that party autonomy does not lead to abuse, such as forcing a weaker party to litigate in a distant or unsuitable forum. Courts therefore retain the power to set aside unfair or unreasonable jurisdiction clauses in exceptional circumstances.

4.5 **Forum Non Conveniens:** ***The Principle of Inconvenient Forum***

Forum non conveniens is a legal doctrine that allows a court to decline jurisdiction if another court is more appropriate for hearing the case. This principle, originating from Common Law traditions, has been adopted by the ALI/UNIDROIT Principles of Transnational Civil Procedure as outlined in Article 2.5.

Its purpose is to promote fairness and efficiency by ensuring that cases are heard where they can be handled most effectively, with minimal cost and inconvenience to the parties.

4.5.1 The Principle of Forum Non Conveniens

Article 2.5 of the ALI/UNIDROIT Principles introduces an important and pragmatic rule: a court may decline jurisdiction or suspend a proceeding if it is manifestly inappropriate compared to another, more suitable court. In other words, even when a court has a substantial connection and is technically competent, it can still refuse to hear the case if another court is clearly better placed to deal with it.

This principle reflects a practical concern for fairness, efficiency, and convenience. For example, imagine an industrial explosion in India that causes massive damage, with all the evidence, witnesses, and relevant documents located there. The company responsible is based in the United States, so technically, a U.S. court could hear the case. However, since everything connected to the dispute – facts, witnesses, and harm – occurs in India, an Indian court would be the more appropriate forum. This logic was applied in the real-life Bhopal disaster of 1984, when a U.S. court declined jurisdiction, ruling that the case should be tried in India.

This doctrine, known in Common Law as *forum non conveniens*, allows courts to prioritize practicality over strict jurisdictional rules. It emphasizes the importance of ensuring that cases are heard where justice can be most effectively and economically achieved, avoiding unnecessary expense, complexity, or inconvenience.

This approach also reduces the risk of forum shopping, discouraging parties from choosing a court solely because they think it will offer a strategic advantage rather than because it is genuinely suited to the dispute.

4.5.2 Application and Impact

The doctrine of *forum non conveniens* originated in Scotland and literally means "inconvenient forum." It allows a court to decline jurisdiction if another court is clearly more appropriate for hearing the case. This idea contrasts with the traditional Civil Law approach, which values predictability and certainty. In countries like France, the rule has long been that if a court is competent, it must hear the case. The Civil Law mindset favors order and consistency: competence implies obligation.

By contrast, the Common Law approach is more pragmatic. It asks why a court should handle a case that would be better resolved elsewhere. The adoption of *forum non conveniens* in the ALI/UNIDROIT Principles reflects this practical shift in international litigation. It acknowledges that justice is best served when cases are heard where the evidence, witnesses, and interests are most directly involved.

This doctrine brings flexibility to the rigid framework of jurisdiction, allowing courts to balance fairness and efficiency in complex cross-border disputes. It represents a clear victory of Common Law pragmatism over Civil Law formalism and sets the stage for Article 2.6, which introduces a related concept within the Civil Law tradition.

In practice, this flexibility helps courts manage global disputes more effectively and ensures that litigation proceeds in the forum best equipped to deliver a fair and timely resolution.

4.6 Litis pendens: *The Principle of Pending Litigation*

Litis pendens is a legal principle originating from the Civil Law tradition, which is reflected in Article 2.6 of the ALI/UNIDROIT Principles of Transnational Civil Procedure. Its aim is to avoid duplication and conflict by ensuring that only one court handles a dispute at any given time.

4.6.1 The Principle of Litis Pendens

Article 2.6 provides that a court should decline jurisdiction or suspend the proceedings if the same dispute is already pending before another competent court, unless it is clear that the other court will not resolve the matter fairly, efficiently, or within a reasonable time. The purpose of this rule is to prevent duplication, reduce unnecessary costs, and avoid contradictory judgments between different jurisdictions.

For example, imagine a French company sues an American company in a court in Paris over a breach of contract. At the same time, the American company files a similar case in New York concerning the same contract and the same facts. Under Article 2.6, the French court should normally suspend or decline to proceed with its case, recognizing that the dispute is already pending before a competent U.S. court. However, if it appears that the American court is unlikely to handle the matter fairly or promptly – for instance, if there are procedural obstacles or delays – the French court could decide to retain jurisdiction.

This rule reflects a broader commitment to judicial cooperation and efficiency in international litigation, ensuring that disputes are handled once, in the most appropriate and effective forum.

It also encourages courts to respect one another's authority, reinforcing mutual trust between legal systems and reducing unnecessary jurisdictional conflicts.

4.6.2 Application and Impact

The principle of *litis pendens* promotes judicial efficiency and coherence by ensuring that the same dispute is not handled by multiple courts at the same time. The idea that a court should decline jurisdiction when the case is already pending before another competent court originates from the Civil Law tradition. The term *litis pendens* is Latin for "pending litigation." It reflects the notion that once a dispute is being heard somewhere, other courts should refrain from intervening to avoid duplication, confusion, and contradictory judgments.

Together, *forum non conveniens* and *litis pendens* illustrate the two great traditions of procedural law: the pragmatic flexibility of the Common Law and the orderly predictability of the Civil Law. Modern international principles, such as those found in the ALI/UNIDROIT Rules, aim to combine both approaches – drawing from Common Law practicality and Civil Law structure – to create fair, efficient, and balanced systems of transnational justice.

This combined approach helps create a more coherent global procedural framework, reducing delays, lowering litigation costs, and strengthening confidence in international dispute resolution.

4.7 Provisional or Preliminary Relief

In legal proceedings, delays can create serious problems, particularly in cases where swift action is needed to prevent harm or preserve rights. Article 8 of the ALI/UNIDROIT Principles of Transnational Civil Procedure responds to this concern by authorizing courts to grant provisional or preliminary relief. This means that before the final judgment, a court can take temporary measures – such as freezing assets, preserving evidence, or restraining certain actions – to ensure that justice remains effective and that the eventual decision is not rendered meaningless by the passage of time.

For example, if a company fears that its business partner will transfer assets abroad to avoid paying an expected judgment, the court may order those assets to be temporarily frozen. Similarly, if a party risks losing crucial evidence, the court can order that it be secured immediately. These provisional measures are essential tools for protecting parties' rights and maintaining fairness during the course of litigation.

Such relief is especially important in international disputes, where assets can easily move across borders and evidence may be difficult to preserve without swift judicial intervention.

4.7.1 The Need for Provisional Relief

Provisional or preliminary relief is essential in situations where waiting for a final judgment would cause serious harm or make it impossible to obtain effective justice later. Most cases are not urgent, but some clearly are. For example, if someone's copyrighted work is being illegally distributed online, or if a defamatory article is spreading rapidly and damaging a person's reputation, or if there is an immediate threat of physical harm, it would be unreasonable to wait years for a final judgment.

In such cases, a party can ask the court for temporary protection – known as *provisional, preliminary*, or *interim relief*. This allows the court to issue quick, temporary orders to preserve the situation or prevent further harm until the case is fully resolved. Article 8 of the ALI/UNIDROIT Principles of Transnational Civil Procedure gives courts this power, ensuring that justice can be both fair and timely, even before the main trial concludes.

These measures help ensure that neither party gains an unfair advantage from delays and that the integrity of the judicial process is protected throughout the proceedings.

4.7.2 Provisions for Provisional Relief

Article 8 establishes the framework for courts to grant provisional or protective measures when quick action is needed to prevent injustice. It allows a court to intervene temporarily to preserve the ability to grant effective final relief or to maintain the current situation (*status quo*). These measures must always respect the principle of proportionality, meaning that the court's intervention should be no broader or harsher than necessary.

In exceptional and urgent cases, the court can issue provisional relief without notifying the other party – known as *ex parte* relief – if fairness clearly requires it. However, the applicant must disclose all relevant facts honestly, and the affected party must be given the chance to respond as soon as possible.

Finally, to avoid abuse of this procedure, anyone requesting provisional relief may be required to compensate the opposing party if the measure later proves unjustified. The court can also require the applicant to post a bond as security.

Overall, provisional relief is a vital mechanism to ensure that justice remains meaningful in urgent or high-risk situations – such as freezing assets, stopping publication of defamatory material, or preventing destruction of evidence – while still protecting both sides from unfair consequences.

By balancing urgency with procedural safeguards, Article 8 ensures that provisional measures support rather than undermine the fairness of the overall judicial process.

5 The Right to a Fair Trial

The right to a fair trial is one of the cornerstones of any justice system, ensuring that cases are heard impartially, transparently, and with respect for the rights of all parties. It is protected by both national constitutions and international instruments such as Article 6 of the European Convention on Human Rights and Article 14 of the International Covenant on Civil and Political Rights.

5.1 The Notion of Fair Trial

The concept of a fair trial is broad and complex. According to *Black's Law Dictionary*, it is defined as a hearing before an impartial and disinterested tribunal that makes a decision only after proper inquiry. Yet, this definition immediately raises questions about what it truly means to be "impartial" or "disinterested," and what exactly qualifies as a "tribunal."

5.1.1 Definition Challenges

Terms such as "disinterest" and "impartiality" are inherently subjective – what seems neutral to one person may appear biased to another. The definition also leaves open what kind of inquiry is required and how thorough it must be. Moreover, it treats fairness as a purely procedural matter – focusing on how the trial is conducted – without addressing whether the outcome itself is just. These ambiguities show that defining a fair trial cannot rely only on formal procedures; it must also include substantive fairness and respect for fundamental rights.

In other words, procedural guarantees are necessary but not sufficient. A trial may follow every formal rule and still fail to deliver justice if the underlying process does not allow the parties to present their case effectively or if structural inequalities distort the outcome. A meaningful notion of fairness, therefore, requires examining the broader context: whether the parties had equal access to legal representation, whether evidentiary rules allowed the truth to emerge, and whether the decision-maker exercised genuine independence and impartiality.

This means that a fair trial must be evaluated not only by examining the steps followed, but also by considering whether the process genuinely protects the parties' rights and leads to decisions that reflect truth, equality, and justice.

For example, if both parties are given equal time to speak but one cannot afford a lawyer while the other is represented by a powerful legal team, the proceedings may look fair on the surface yet produce an outcome that is fundamentally unbalanced.

5.1.2 Fair Trial as Truth-Seeking

Although expressed over 25 years ago, in a 1998 lecture at the University of Chicago Legal Forum, Judge Danny Boggs – an American lawyer and senior United States Circuit Judge on the U.S. Court of Appeals for the Sixth Circuit – offered a clear and pragmatic view of what constitutes a fair trial. He argued that a fair trial is one that leads to a verdict consistent with an objective truth, emphasizing that the primary purpose of a trial is the search for truth rather than the mere observance of procedure.

He explained that achieving such a fair trial requires several key elements: an impartial and independent decision-maker, an atmosphere that allows for thoughtful deliberation, and a careful distinction between relevant and irrelevant evidence. Each of these factors serves to increase the likelihood that the final verdict will reflect the reality of the facts rather than distortions or bias:

> I think the traditional view is essentially, though not exclusively, a search for the truth. The characteristics set out above – an impartial decision maker, an atmosphere conducive to consideration, with relevant evidence considered and irrelevant evidence excluded – are aimed primarily at improving the chances of arriving at a verdict that accords with some notion of preexisting, objective truth. Of course, if you dispute the notion of objective truth, as some do, this may be problematic; but I will not try to enter into that fray today.[28]

Judge Boggs acknowledged that some might challenge the idea of "objective truth," but maintained that the justice system must at least strive toward it. His reasoning highlights a

28 Boggs, David J., 1998, "The Right to a Fair Trial," *University of Chicago Legal Forum*, vol. 1998, Article 2. Judge Danny J. Boggs is an American lawyer and senior United States Circuit Judge on the U.S. Court of Appeals for the Sixth Circuit. He was appointed to a newly created seat on the court by President Ronald Reagan on January 29, 1986, confirmed by the U.S. Senate on March 3, and received his commission on March 25 of the same year. Judge Boggs served as Chief Judge of the Sixth Circuit from 2003 to 2009. Known for his intellectual rigor and extensive writings on legal theory and judicial reasoning, he has made significant contributions to discussions on procedural justice, particularly through his view that a fair trial should aim to produce a verdict consistent with an objective truth.

foundational belief shared by many legal traditions: that fairness in a trial ultimately depends on its capacity to uncover and affirm the truth.

5.2 Key Texts on the Right to a Fair Trial

Several key international and national instruments have defined and protected the right to a fair trial, each developed in different historical contexts and reflecting evolving conceptions of justice and due process. Together, these texts show how the idea of a fair trial has gradually become a universal legal standard, shared across different legal cultures and traditions.

5.2.1 International Texts

The Universal Declaration of Human Rights (UDHR), adopted in 1948, emphasizes this right in Articles 6, 8, 10, and 11, which highlight the right to legal recognition, effective remedy, fair public hearing, and presumption of innocence. As the first global human rights document, the UDHR played a foundational role in shaping modern understandings of fair trial guarantees.

The International Covenant on Civil and Political Rights (ICCPR), adopted in 1966, further underscores the right to a fair trial in Articles 14 and 16, focusing on equality before courts, fair public hearings, and the right to legal assistance. The ICCPR remains one of the most detailed international sources on fair trial rights, providing a binding framework for more than 170 States.

The European Convention on Human Rights (ECHR), which came into force in 1953, addresses this in Article 6, which guarantees the right to a fair and public hearing and presumption of innocence. Article 6 is one of the most frequently litigated provisions before the European Court of Human Rights, illustrating its central role in European legal practice.

The Inter-American Commission on Human Rights, established in 1959, ensures this right in Article 8, providing for a fair trial with due guarantees and within a reasonable time. This regional text places strong emphasis on procedural guarantees and protection against arbitrary detention, reflecting the political context of Latin America in the mid-20th century.

The African Charter on Human and Peoples' Rights (Banjul Charter), adopted in 1981, outlines the right to appeal, presumption of innocence, and defense rights in Article 7. Unlike other instruments, the African Charter links fair trial rights to broader communal and societal values, illustrating its unique normative approach.

5.2.2 National Texts

Examples of national texts that protect the right to a fair trial include the following. The Sixth Amendment to the U.S. Constitution, ratified in 1791, guarantees a speedy and public trial by an impartial jury, the right to be informed of charges, confront witnesses, and have legal assistance. This amendment remains central to American criminal justice, shaping trial procedures and the rights of defendants in everyday practice.

The Canadian Charter of Rights and Freedoms, enacted in 1982, ensures the right to a fair trial in Sections 7 to 14, particularly in Section 11 (Proceedings in criminal and penal matters). Section 11 outlines specific rights for individuals charged with an offence such as the right to be informed without unreasonable delay of the specific offence, the right to be tried within a reasonable time, the right not to be compelled to be a witness in proceedings against oneself, the right to be presumed innocent until proven guilty in a fair and public hearing by an independent and impartial tribunal. Canadian courts have developed an extensive case law under these provisions, making the Charter one of the strongest constitutional safeguards of fair trial rights worldwide.

The Constitution of South Africa, adopted in 1996, includes the right to a fair trial in Section 34. This section guarantees the right to have any dispute that can be resolved by the application of law decided in a fair public hearing before a court or, where appropriate, another independent and impartial tribunal or forum. South Africa's post-apartheid Constitution is known for its strong commitment to human rights, and Section 34 embodies this transformative vision of justice.

The German Basic Law (Grundgesetz), enacted in 1949, ensures the right to a fair trial in Article 103. This article includes the right to be heard in court, protection against double jeopardy, and the principle of legality in criminal law.

These guarantees reflect Germany's post-war emphasis on the rule of law, judicial independence, and the protection of individual rights against state power.

5.3 The Rights Associated With a Fair Trial

The rights associated with a fair trial in general include the right to a public hearing, before an independent and impartial tribunal, within reasonable time, the presumption of innocence as well as other minimum rights for those charged in particular with criminal offense (including adequate time and facilities to prepare their defense, access to legal representation, right to examine witnesses against them or have them examined, right to the free assistance of an interpreter, etc.).

5.3.1 The Right to a Public Hearing Within a Reasonable Time

Imagine a man named David who is arrested in California on suspicion of fraud. He waits for three days before being brought before a magistrate to be informed of the charges against him. In this situation, David's lawyer would likely argue that his right to a public hearing within a reasonable time has been violated. Under American law, particularly since the *County of Riverside v. McLaughlin* decision,[29] the U.S. Supreme Court has held that "reasonable time" cannot exceed 48 hours, except in cases involving weekends or public holidays.[30]

As regards the right to a public hearing within a reasonable time, a crucial difference between legal systems is that American law focuses mainly on delay before trial – between arrest and first appearance – whereas countries such as Germany, Ireland, and England focus on delays within the trial proceedings themselves. In Common Law jurisdictions like the UK and Ireland, courts have ruled that delays of 12,[31] ten,[32] and even four years[33] in concluding trials constitute a denial of the right to a fair trial. In Germany, a Civil Law jurisdiction, a delay of only six and a half months[34] was found to violate this right in a defamation case. Although this may appear

29 United States Supreme Court, *County of Riverside v. McLaughlin*, 500 U.S. 44 (1991).

30 United States Supreme Court, *Baker v. McCollan*, 443 U.S. 137 (1979).

31 European Court of Human Rights, *T.H. v. Ireland*, Application No. 37868/06, Judgment of 8 December 2011.

32 European Court of Human Rights, *McFarlane v. Ireland*, Application No. 31333/06, Judgment of 10 September 2010.

33 European Court of Human Rights, *Minshall v. United Kingdom*, Application No. 7350/06, Judgment of 20 December 2011.

34 European Court of Human Rights, *Hoffer and Annen v. Germany*, Applications Nos. 397/07 and 2322/07, Judgment of 13 January 2011.

short compared to the Common Law examples, the nature of defamation proceedings justifies the stricter standard.

South Africa, with its mixed legal system, takes a balanced approach. In *Zanner v. Director of Public Prosecutions, Johannesburg,*[35] the court held that delay is not automatically a violation of the right to a fair trial. Instead, it must assess factors such as the length of the delay, the reasons for it, and the extent of prejudice caused to the accused.

A similar balance can be observed in the right to a public hearing. For example, in China, this right can be restricted if the case involves commercial secrets.[36] Likewise, Article 306 of the French Criminal Procedure Code allows hearings to be held in private if a public hearing would endanger public order or morality. Both systems recognize that the right to a public trial is not absolute, though they differ in the reasons justifying its limitation – economic in China, moral and social in France.

5.3.2 Equality of Arms

The right to equality of arms includes, for instance, the right to notice and evidence of all charges against the defendant and the right to freely access, communicate, and have interpreted for the defendant the legal advice of a lawyer.

There appears to be universal agreement amongst all the legal systems examined that the accused should have the right to legal assistance, interpretation of that legal assistance, choice of the lawyer, and the ability to freely consult with the lawyer provided. The only slight variations are as to the time and extent to which legal assistance should be available to the accused.

In France, there is a right to legal representation at trial and during the magistrate's interrogation of the defendant. In Germany, the defendant has both the choice of a lawyer and the opportunity to dismiss the legal counsel should they feel it unsatisfactory for their defense.[37] Furthermore, they have the right of access to a lawyer at any stage of the criminal process. In the Netherlands, the right is limited such that where the consultation with legal counsel will lead to the discovery of a circumstance which the defendant should not discover in the interests of the investigation, or where a particular circumstance creates a strong suspicion that such a communication is being misused to frustrate the investigation, then it is disallowed. This provision appears to be out of line with the spirit of the right to legal advice; nonetheless, it is in keeping with the general respect for the right to legal assistance across all legal systems. In the UK, too, legal assistance has been extended to adjudication proceedings in *Black v. UK.*[38] In the U.S., the Sixth Amendment guarantees a defendant the right to counsel in criminal cases involving possible incarceration. In *Brewer v. Williams,*[39] the Supreme Court held that, similar to French Criminal procedure, the right extends to the initial appearance before a judge when the defendant learns of the charge against him, whether or not the public prosecutor is involved. Similar to the limitation of the rights in the Netherlands, in *Rothgery v. Gillespie Co., Texas,*[40] the Supreme

35 Supreme Court of Appeal of South Africa, *Zanner v. Director of Public Prosecutions, Johannesburg,* Case No. 107/05, [2006] ZASCA 56; 2006 (2) SACR 45 (SCA); [2006] 2 All SA 588 (SCA), Judgment of 3 April 2006.

36 Lubman, Stanley, 2012, "China's Criminal Procedure Law: Good, Bad and Ugly," *China Real Time Report,* Wall Street Journal, 21 March, online. Available at: https://www.wsj.com. Accessed 8 April 2013.

37 Pieck, Hans, 1962, "The Accused's Privilege against Self-Incrimination in the Civil Law," *American Journal of Comparative Law,* vol. 11.

38 European Court of Human Rights, *Black v. United Kingdom,* Application No. 56745/00, Judgment of 16 January 2007.

39 United States Supreme Court, *Brewer v. Williams,* 430 U.S. 387 (1977).

40 United States Supreme Court, *Rothgery v. Gillespie County, Texas,* 554 U.S. 191 (2008).

Court held that statements obtained without counsel present were only inadmissible once the defendant had actually invoked their right to counsel under the Sixth Amendment. Finally, South Africa appears to be the only jurisdiction through its generous interpretation of Article 35 (3) f in *S v. Tandwa and Others*,[41] which guarantees not only the right to legal assistance but also the *quality* of such representation to ensure the trial is fair.

5.3.3 Presumption of Innocence

The presumption of innocence includes the right to an independent and impartial trial, an impartial judge, the right to appeal, and a right against double jeopardy – meaning that no one should be tried or punished twice for the same offense. These guarantees collectively ensure that justice is administered fairly and that the accused is protected from abuse of process.

Whilst all the legal systems seem to converge with regard to all of the rights, what is interesting to note here is the apparent weight one can deduce from the case law that is placed on each of the rights. Overwhelmingly, it is the Common Law systems of Ireland, the UK, and the USA that appear most concerned with the presumption of innocence and an impartial trial, as well as preventing double jeopardy. This phenomenon has been described by commentators as the age-old dichotomy between Civil Law and Common Law, such that the presumption of innocence "epitomized the rivalry between the Civil Law and the Common Law"[42] as it is reflected in the traditional dichotomy between the Latin presumption of guilt and the Anglo-American presumption of innocence. The right can be seen as both a shield to conviction as well as a rule of proof. We will now examine its operation in the Common Law system, where it is most widely invoked.

The case *Hanif and Kahn v. UK*[43] held that where a policeman who knew and had worked with the policeman giving evidence and had convicted the accused of drugs offences previously was sitting on the jury would be an indication of a jury lacking impartiality and the domestic court's rejection of that juror's removal was contrary to the applicant's right to a fair trial under Article 6 of the ECHR.

In the U.S., the case *Sparf and Hansen v. United States*[44] ruled that a defendant is entitled to a jury determination beyond a reasonable doubt of every element of the crime for which he is charged. This right was qualified in *Oregon v. Ice*,[45] which held that the practice of assigning judges rather than juries in states was not in violation of the Sixth Amendment.

In the 2010 European Court of Human Rights Civil Law case *Chesne v. France*,[46] the ECHR ruled that there was no presumption of innocence for the defendant as the trial judge had referred to him while trying his girlfriend as "the girlfriend of one of the main traffickers." And the State's subsequent refusal to change judges was deemed a violation of the right to a fair trial.

Rights against double jeopardy are also protected within the Common Law world. In Ireland, the "victims' initiative" whereby a person will be tried again if crucial evidence emerges was a cause of grave concern as it potentially abridged the right against double jeopardy. The Fifth

41 Supreme Court of Appeal of South Africa, *S v. Tandwa and Others*, 2008 (1) SACR 613 (SCA).

42 Pieck, *The Accused's Privilege against Self-Incrimination*.

43 European Court of Human Rights, *Hanif and Khan v. United Kingdom*, Applications Nos. 52999/08 and 61779/08, Judgment of 20 December 2011.

44 United States Supreme Court, *Sparf and Hansen v. United States*, 156 U.S. 51 (1895).

45 United States Supreme Court, *Oregon v. Ice*, 129 S. Ct. 711 (2009).

46 European Court of Human Rights, *Chesne v. France*, Application No. 29808/06, Judgment of 22 April 2010.

Amendment of the U.S. Constitution provides that no person shall be "subject for the same offense to be twice put in jeopardy of life or limb."

Having established that the right to a fair trial is widely recognized across different legal systems, despite some variations, we can say that there is a shared international understanding of how this right should be protected.

In modern societies, one of the most serious threats to the presumption of innocence no longer comes from the courtroom, but from the media. In high-profile cases, intense media coverage often portrays suspects as guilty before any verdict is reached. When newspapers, television channels, or social media users circulate images of a person in handcuffs, reveal private details of their lives, or discuss their case as if guilt were already established, they shape public opinion in a way that deeply undermines the presumption of innocence.

For example, imagine a well-known business leader accused of corruption. Before the investigation even concludes, headlines describe them as "the architect of a vast fraud scheme." Even if they are later acquitted, their reputation and career are irreparably damaged. The court of public opinion often delivers its "verdict" long before the judicial process has a chance to unfold.

Similarly, in criminal cases involving violence or sexual assault, the accused may face public condemnation and social exclusion based solely on allegations. The balance between the right to inform the public and the right to a fair trial becomes particularly fragile in such contexts. While the media play a vital role in ensuring transparency, they also carry a moral and legal responsibility not to prejudice judicial outcomes or destroy lives through speculation.

Thus, in the age of instant communication and globalized media, protecting the presumption of innocence has become more complex but also more essential. It requires vigilance not only from judges and lawyers but also from journalists, politicians, and the public itself. Justice cannot coexist with a rush to judgment. The true test of a fair legal system – and of a mature democracy – is its ability to preserve fairness and human dignity even under the glare of public scrutiny.

In highly sensitive cases – such as allegations of sexual assault, particularly when they involve public figures – the balance between the presumption of innocence and the recognition of victims' voices becomes one of the most complex and delicate issues in modern justice.

On one hand, it is morally and socially essential that victims' testimonies be heard and taken seriously. For decades, many victims of sexual violence remained silent due to shame, fear, or lack of faith in the judicial system. Movements such as *#MeToo* have played a crucial role in breaking this silence, revealing systemic abuses, and empowering survivors to speak out. Recognizing this voice is therefore a necessary act of justice and dignity.

On the other hand, the presumption of innocence remains a cornerstone of the Rule of Law. It means that no one should be declared guilty until proven so by a competent and impartial court. This is not merely a procedural safeguard – it is a moral principle that protects everyone from arbitrary judgment and social condemnation. When an alleged crime cannot be tried – because it is time-barred, the accused has died, or there is insufficient evidence – the legal system cannot render a verdict. In such situations, public debate often takes the form of a media or moral trial, conducted on television, in newspapers, or on social networks.

While these media trials may seem to offer a form of symbolic justice to victims, they also carry significant risks. They can destroy reputations, stigmatize individuals without proof, and bypass the safeguards of due process. In these cases, society must resist the temptation to replace judicial truth with public opinion.

The challenge for modern democracies is therefore to listen to victims without automatically transforming testimony into condemnation.

This balance may be difficult to maintain, but it is crucial and essential to a fair system of justice. True justice requires protecting both the dignity of victims and the rights of the accused. One cannot exist without the other. Protecting the voice of victims does not mean abandoning the presumption of innocence; both are essential components of a just and humane legal order. Without this balance, societies risk oscillating between silence and vengeance – neither of which is compatible with justice.

6 The Legal Burden of Proof

The burden of proof is the rule that determines which party must prove what they claim in a legal case. In other words, it establishes which party is responsible for proving an assertion made in judicial proceedings, and who must convince the judge that their version of the facts is true.

Imagine a person who sues their neighbour, saying, "He damaged my car." The court will not simply assume it is true – the person making the claim must prove it, for example, by showing a repair invoice, a photograph, or a witness statement. The neighbour, in turn, can present counter-evidence, such as proving he was away that day or that the damage was already there. The judge's role is to weigh both sides' evidence and decide which version is more credible.

In practice, meeting the burden of proof is demanding. It requires collecting evidence, organizing documents, analyzing facts, and presenting them clearly before the court. This is why the burden of proof represents one of the main challenges in any legal process: even a person who is right may lose if they cannot prove their claim. This illustrates a deeper truth about justice: what matters is not only what is said, but what can be proven.

That is why the burden of proof is both a legal and moral safeguard – it protects individuals from being condemned or discredited without evidence.

In everyday life, we often forget this principle. Rumour is the opposite of proof: it spreads easily, requires no evidence, and often harms reputations without any basis in fact.

The law exists precisely to draw a clear line between what is claimed and what is demonstrated. Justice demands more than words – it demands verification.

That is why judges, lawyers, and all participants in a trial must work patiently to collect, analyze, and present evidence.

Sometimes, the law adjusts or even reverses the burden of proof to ensure fairness. For example, in employment law, it is often the employer who must prove that no discrimination took place. In consumer law, the seller must demonstrate that the buyer was properly informed about a product. These presumptions protect individuals who would otherwise struggle to access or present evidence.

The burden of proof is therefore at the core of justice. It connects truth and law, turning arguments into verified facts. Without proof, justice cannot function – because fairness depends not only on what is true, but on what can be shown to be true.

6.1 The Ambivalence of Proof

Proof in the legal context holds a dual nature. It has the power to decisively influence the outcome of a case or be deemed insignificant in the judge's final decision. The management of proof demands meticulous care due to its potential dramatic impact on legal proceedings. Moreover, proof is regarded as a fundamental right, as highlighted by the Latin maxim *idem est non esse et non probari* (not to be and not to be proved are the same thing).

6.1.1 Definition and Importance of Proof

Proof can be defined as the act and obligation of establishing a fact by the use of evidence in order to win before the judge. Its definition is wider than that of evidence, for it includes evidence and any other modes of proving at trial. Twining and Stein indeed note that "the logic of proof is always antecedent to evidentiary rules."[47] The French jurist and sociologist Henri Lévy-Bruhl (1884–1964) described proof as a "mechanism designed to establish a conviction on an unsure point."[48] Encapsulating the idea that *prouver, c'est faire approuver*[49] (proving means obtaining approval).

For example, if a company claims that a supplier delivered defective products, it must prove this with photos, expert reports, or customer complaints – not just by saying it happened. Likewise, if a driver is accused of causing an accident, they can prove the opposite by showing a traffic camera recording or witness testimony. In both cases, the goal of proof is not just to show something happened, but to convince the judge that it did.

These examples illustrate that proof is not a purely technical exercise but a process grounded in persuasion. The party bearing the burden of proof must not only present relevant material but must do so in a manner that satisfies the judge's standard of conviction. In this sense, proof operates at the intersection of factual reconstruction and legal reasoning: it requires assembling reliable information, organizing it coherently, and demonstrating its probative value. Ultimately, the success of proof depends not simply on the existence of evidence but on its capacity to produce judicial belief, thereby transforming uncertainty into a legally recognized fact.

6.1.2 Proof and the Notion of Truth

The question of knowing whether proof is really linked to the notion of truth is highly debated, however. Proof primarily serves as a logical reasoning process, aiming to persuade the judge of a certain aspect or version of the truth. Now, truth is always relative in justice, shaped by the arguments and evidence presented.

Each party in a legal proceeding presents its version of the truth, supported by its interpretation of the evidence, and the judge or jury evaluates these competing narratives to determine which is more convincing and legally sound. The relativity of truth in justice is further influenced by varying standards of proof, such as *beyond a reasonable doubt* in criminal cases or *preponderance of the evidence* in civil cases, which set the level of certainty needed to prove a case. Therefore, while proof and truth are connected in legal contexts, they are distinct. Proof is the means to present a persuasive and credible narrative within legal reasoning and standards.

In this sense, law aspires to reach truth, but only through what can be demonstrated within the constraints of procedure, admissibility, and the burden of proof. The "truth" recognized by a court is therefore an institutional truth: not necessarily a perfect reconstruction of what happened, but the best-supported version that the legal process can validate.

So in law, people try very hard to build justice from the truth, even though it's not always exactly what happened in real life. Justice is like a puzzle – made of the pieces of truth that can be proven.

47 Twining, William and Stein, Alex (eds.), 1992, *Evidence and Proof*, New York University Press.

48 Lévy-Bruhl, Henri, 1963, *La preuve judiciaire*, Marcel Rivière et Cie, p. 15.

49 Lévy-Bruhl, *La preuve judiciaire*.

6.2 The Decisive Nature of the Burden of Proof

The burden of proof is a decisive element in legal proceedings. It determines which party must prove its case, directly impacting the trial's outcome. The party that bears the burden of proof faces significant challenges and responsibilities, influencing the direction and strategy of the litigation.

6.2.1 The Responsibility of the Burden of Proof

The burden of proof dictates that the party responsible must provide sufficient evidence to support their claims. If they fail to do so, they risk losing the case. This responsibility answers the critical questions: Who must prove? Who should provide evidence? Convincing the judge is also much about logical reasoning than merely presenting evidence. The claimant must construct a logical argument that leads the judge to a favorable decision.

Whoever bears the burden of proof holds the keys to legal argumentation; he has the power to reveal new facts or evidence. Yet this requires considerable work and preparation, and it places a substantial risk on his person.

This central role explains why the allocation of the burden of proof is often decisive: it determines which party must take the initiative, gather documentation, identify witnesses, and anticipate objections. It also shapes the strategy of litigation, since the party who bears the burden must meet a specific evidentiary threshold – sometimes very demanding – to prevail. In many cases, the outcome of a dispute depends less on the intrinsic truth of each side's narrative than on which party is legally required to substantiate it. Thus, the burden of proof operates not only as a procedural rule but as a structural mechanism that distributes risks, responsibilities, and strategic opportunities between the parties.

6.2.2 The Power and Risks of Bearing the Burden of Proof

Bearing the burden of proof gives the party the power to introduce new facts and evidence, shaping the legal argument. However, this also requires extensive work and preparation and carries substantial risks. The party must be meticulous and strategic, as their ability to meet this burden can determine the trial's outcome. This raises fundamental questions about litigation: Is the burden of proof a weakness or a source of power? How does the burden's allocation affect the procedure's meaning and fairness?

Seen from one perspective, the burden of proof can appear as a disadvantage because it imposes the heaviest obligations on the party bearing it: they must gather evidence, construct a coherent narrative, anticipate counterarguments, and withstand procedural scrutiny. Failure at any stage may result in losing the case, even when their version of events is closer to the truth. Yet from another perspective, the burden of proof can function as a strategic advantage. The party that bears it controls the initial framing of the dispute, sets the factual and legal agenda, and compels the opponent to respond to the narrative they have established. The allocation of the burden, therefore, influences not only the dynamics of persuasion but also the deeper fairness of the process, since it determines which party must overcome uncertainty and which may capitalize on doubt.

6.3 Comparative Overview of Legal Burden of Proof

The concept of the legal burden of proof varies significantly between Common Law and Civil Law systems. Understanding these differences requires examining the unique approaches each system takes towards the burden of production and the burden of persuasion. This part explores these distinctions and their underlying legal philosophies.

6.3.1 Common Law Systems

In Common Law systems, proof involves two related duties: the burden of production and the burden of persuasion – "the duty of a party to persuade . . . of the truth of certain propositions."[50]

The burden of production, sometimes called "passing the judge," means that a party must present enough evidence to make their claim appear legally credible – what lawyers call a *prima facie* case.

For example, if a tenant sues a landlord for unsafe living conditions, the tenant must first produce some evidence – such as photos of water damage or a health inspection report – to show that the complaint is not unfounded. If the tenant fails to provide any evidence at all, the judge can dismiss the case before it ever reaches trial.

The burden of persuasion, on the other hand, is the duty to convince the judge or jury that the claim is actually true, according to the appropriate legal standard – such as *beyond a reasonable doubt* in criminal cases or *by a preponderance of the evidence* (more likely than not) in civil cases.

For example, in a criminal trial, the prosecution must persuade the jury *beyond a reasonable doubt* that the defendant committed the offense. If any serious doubt remains, the defendant must be acquitted.

This dual burden ensures that both the sufficiency and the credibility of evidence are tested: a case must first be strong enough to proceed, and then convincing enough to win.

6.3.2 Civil Law Systems

In Civil Law, the burden of proof merely refers to the duty to prove allegations and to the doctrine of *actori incumbit probatori.* There is no distinction between the two burdens since both the law and facts are on the judges' side. Yet in both judicial systems, the burden of proof rests on whoever makes allegations. In theory, the court knows the law and does not need to be persuaded, but it is the parties' right to persuade it on issues of law.

The court then makes its own legal examination to come to a conclusion.[51] In both legal systems, the burden of proof lies with the party making allegations. The difference that exists between legal systems as to the interpretation of the legal burden of proof often results from different legal philosophies on the unfolding of the trial.

For example, in a French civil case about a faulty product, the buyer must prove that the defect existed when the item was sold by presenting receipts, expert reports, or photos. The judge will then examine these materials, possibly order an independent expert opinion, and apply the law without needing to be "convinced" by either party's rhetoric.

Similarly, in a German family law case, if a parent claims unpaid child support, they must show bank records or correspondence proving that payments were not made. The judge reviews the documents, checks the legal obligations, and issues a decision based on the facts and applicable law, not on persuasion or performance.

50 Heydon, John D., 1975, *Cases and Materials on Evidence*, Butterworths.

51 Pauwelyn, Joost, 1988, "Evidence, Proof and Persuasion in WTO Dispute Settlement: Who Bears the Burden?," *Journal of International Economic Law*, no. 1.

These examples show how, in Civil Law systems, proof is about demonstration rather than persuasion – the judge actively seeks the truth, using the evidence provided to apply the law objectively.

6.3.3 Common Features of Burden of Proof in Common and Civil Law Systems

The central feature of most legal systems is that whoever asserts must prove. This rule has been coined in the Latin adage *Semper necessitas probandi incumbit ei qui agit* (the necessity of proof always lies with the person who lays charges). *Actori incumbit probatori.* The proof is incumbent on the plaintiff. In French: *La preuve incombe au demandeur*.

As a result, in Criminal cases, the burden of proof is on the side of the prosecution since it is the one asserting.

Conversely, in civil cases, the plaintiff must prove everything to get financial relief. A party that charges another has to prove the grounds on which it lays the charge. The other party will then respond to the evidence that is presented against him if necessary, and a reversal of the burden of proof is said to occur.

The UNIDROIT Principles of Transnational Civil Procedure[52] rule that "each party has the burden to prove all the material facts that are the basis of that party's case" and that "facts are considered proven when the court is reasonably convinced of their truth." Yet those principles admit that a court can draw *adverse inferences* from the evidence that is presented before it. This is why the burden of proof is a risk that the party undertakes to surmount. This risk also limits people's excessive readiness to trial others without sufficient motives.

Once the plaintiff has made his case and completed the burden of proof, the defendant often develops an *affirmative defence* to reduce or defeat the claim brought against him. Generally speaking, the main reason for the burden of proof to shift is when the defendant refuses to admit the proof provided by the claimant. The *reverse-onus provisions* then put the burden of proof on the defendant (shift in the burden of proof). But there exist numerous other reasons for the burden to shift. The first reason derives from the *reus in excipiendo fit* rule (the defendant becomes claimant in exception). Though the claimant bears the burden of proof in most jurisdictions, when the defendant brings out an exception, the burden of proof shifts to him.

In tort law, the burden of proof can also be exceptionally placed upon the defendant. This is often seen. For example, it has been ruled by the House of Lords that the owner of a truck should show that all reasonable care was taken in the maintenance of his engine before its brakes suddenly failed, causing it to fall down a hill and to kill a pedestrian.[53] The burden of proof lies on the defendant rather than on the plaintiff for reasons of efficacy and equity in the trial.

Sometimes the burden of proof simply rests on both parties. For claims regarding wills, for example, both parties will have to prove or disprove the mental competence of the will-drafter.

The burden of proof and shift in the burden of proof are well summed up in Judge Walsh JA's words. In *Currie v. Dempsey* (1967),[54] he stated as a general rule that:

> The burden of proof in establishing a case, lies on a plaintiff if the fact alleged (whether affirmative or negative in form) is an essential element in his cause of action, eg if its existence is a condition precedent to his right to maintain the action. The onus is on the defendant, if the

52 *Uniform Law Review*, 2004–4, Article 21.

53 House of Lords (UK), *Henderson v. Henry E. Jenkins & Sons*, [1970] AC 282.

54 Supreme Court of New South Wales, *Currie v. Dempsey*, (1967) 69 SR (NSW) 116 and 539.

allegation is not a denial of an essential ingredient in the cause of action, but is one which, if established, will constitute a good defence, that is, an "avoidance" of the claim which, prima facie, the plaintiff has.

In conclusion, both Common Law and Civil Law systems share the same fundamental idea: the party who makes an allegation must prove it. This principle ensures fairness and prevents baseless claims. However, the burden of proof can shift during proceedings, depending on the evidence and the parties' arguments. Ultimately, the burden of proof serves as both a test of credibility and a safeguard of justice, ensuring that legal decisions are based on reasoned conviction rather than assumption or accusation.

6.3.4 Major Differences Between Common and Civil Law Systems

The major differences between the two systems – Civil Law and Common Law – stem from the extent of investigative power granted to judges.

In the Common Law world, the main goal is not to help the judge uncover every detail of the truth but rather to ensure that the jury is not misled by weak or unreliable evidence. In other words, the focus is on safeguarding fairness in the process rather than giving the judge a full investigative role. Since the jury is composed of ordinary citizens, strict rules of evidence exist to prevent them from being influenced by doubtful or emotional information. The system prefers to exclude questionable evidence rather than risk an unfair verdict. The goal is to limit arbitrariness.

In contrast, the judge plays a much more active role in the inquiry in Civil Law countries such as France, Germany, or Italy. While in Civil Law systems the court itself participates in gathering materials and finding evidence, in Common Law systems the parties bear this responsibility through the "discovery process." They must locate evidence and identify witnesses themselves. In this sense, Common Law procedures can be described as more partisan:[55] the parties prepare extensively in advance, while in Civil Law countries, hearings are more often spread over time. In Common Law systems, trials usually take place on consecutive days, and the jury ultimately renders the verdict after hearing the case.

As summarized in John Heller and Marcus Dubber's *Handbook of Comparative Law*, in Civil Law systems, "the fact that a circumstance has an exonerating rather than an incriminating effect is not relevant for the criminal process."[56] This distinction reflects the procedural structure typical of Civil Law systems, where proceedings are divided into two distinct phases – investigation and trial – whereas Common Law procedures tend to be shorter and more concentrated.

Mirjan Damaška[57] – an American and Croatian jurist and Sterling Professor Emeritus of Law at Yale Law School – characterizes this distinction as one between "privatized action" in the Common Law tradition, where parties drive the proceedings, and "officialized action" in the Civil Law tradition, where the judge plays an active role in uncovering the truth.

55 When we say the Common Law system can be described as more partisan, we mean that each party plays an active role in presenting its own case, finding evidence, questioning witnesses, and persuading the judge or jury. In other words, it is a party-driven system, where the outcome depends heavily on the skill, preparation, and strategy of the lawyers, rather than on the judge's investigation. By contrast, the Civil Law system is less partisan because the judge leads the investigation and actively seeks the truth instead of relying mainly on the parties to present it.

56 Heller, Kevin Jon and Dubber, Markus Dirk, 2011, *The Handbook of Comparative Criminal Law*, Stanford Law Books.

57 Damaska, *The Common Law/Civil Law Divide*.

However, these contrasts are often captured by the broader opposition between *adversarial* and *inquisitorial* procedures. The Common Law system relies on confrontation between the parties, whereas the Civil Law system relies on judicial inquiry. This fundamental distinction leads to different philosophies regarding the burden of proof.

In conclusion, the main distinction between Common Law and Civil Law lies in the role of the judge and the structure of fact-finding, both in civil and criminal proceedings.

In civil cases – such as disputes over contracts, property, or accidents – Common Law systems like those of the United States or the United Kingdom rely on an adversarial model. The parties themselves are responsible for gathering and presenting evidence, examining witnesses, and convincing the court of their version of the facts. The judge acts primarily as an impartial referee, ensuring fair play and respect for procedural rules, while the jury or the judge decides which argument is stronger.

For example, imagine a car accident in London. The injured driver sues the other driver for damages. Each side hires its own lawyer, presents its own experts, and tries to persuade the court. The judge does not investigate what happened but decides which version of the story is more convincing based on the evidence presented.

In contrast, in Civil Law systems such as France or Germany, the process is more inquisitorial. The judge takes an active role in investigating the facts, questioning witnesses, and gathering evidence. The goal is not to let the best advocate win but to allow the judge to uncover the objective truth through a structured inquiry. If the same car accident happened in Paris, the judge would personally request police reports, order an expert assessment, and question both drivers to establish what really happened.

The same philosophical divide appears in criminal law, though with higher stakes. In Common Law countries, criminal trials are highly adversarial: the prosecution and the defense present their cases before an impartial judge and often a jury, whose role is to determine guilt or innocence. The judge does not investigate but ensures that the trial is fair and that the rights of the accused are protected.

For example, in a theft case in the United States, the prosecutor must prove the defendant's guilt "beyond a reasonable doubt," while the defense lawyer challenges the evidence. The judge supervises the process but does not search for the truth personally.

In Civil Law countries like France, the procedure often begins with an investigating magistrate (juge d'instruction), who leads the inquiry, gathers evidence, and questions the accused before the trial. The same judge or another court later determines guilt based on that investigation.

Both systems aim to achieve justice, but they follow different paths: the Common Law model trusts in the confrontation of opposing parties to reveal the truth, whereas the Civil Law model places its faith in judicial investigation. Each seeks, in its own way, to balance fairness, truth, and procedural efficiency.

6.3.5 Rules of Evidence in Various Legal Systems

In China, both criminal and civil procedure reflect the country's hybrid legal identity, which combines Civil Law traditions with Socialist legal principles. The Criminal Procedure Law of the People's Republic of China (first adopted in 1979 and amended several times, notably in 1996) establishes a state-led process in which the public security organs, people's procuratorates, and people's courts each play a defined role. In criminal cases, the burden of proof lies mainly with the prosecution, while public security organs are responsible for collecting both incriminating and exculpatory evidence. Defense lawyers may present exculpatory proof, but the process remains largely centralized and investigative rather than adversarial. The guiding objective is to maintain public order and ensure that crimes are accurately and promptly ascertained while protecting the innocent.

By contrast, the Civil Procedure Law, which underwent its first major revision in 30 years and came into force on January 1, 2024, reflects a different emphasis. It modernizes China's civil and commercial justice system – especially in cases involving foreign parties – by expanding the jurisdiction of Chinese courts, allowing challenges to jurisdiction, and improving rules for the recognition and enforcement of foreign judgments and arbitral awards. It also introduces faster mechanisms for serving processes and gathering evidence in cross-border disputes.

While criminal procedure remains oriented toward state control and social stability, civil procedure now demonstrates a stronger commitment to fairness, efficiency, and international cooperation. Together, these two frameworks illustrate China's dual legal evolution: a system seeking to uphold public order and justice at home while adapting to the demands of globalization and cross-border legal exchange.

India uses a hybrid system rooted in Common Law. In criminal cases, the prosecution carries the burden to prove guilt "beyond reasonable doubt," so the accused is acquitted unless that standard is met. In civil cases, under the Indian Evidence Act, 1872, the party who asks the court to decide a right or liability must prove the facts they assert – typically on the "preponderance of probabilities" (more likely than not).

Civil litigation concerns private disputes (contracts, property, family, tort). It is governed mainly by the Code of Civil Procedure, 1908. Typical outcomes are compensation, injunctions, or specific performance. Criminal litigation addresses offenses against society (theft, fraud, assault, rape, murder) and is governed by the Bharatiya Nyaya Sanhita, 2023 (replacing the IPC, 1860) and the Code of Criminal Procedure, 1973. Outcomes include fines, probation, or imprisonment.

Procedurally, civil cases start with a complaint and move through pleadings, discovery, possible settlement, trial, and appeal. Criminal cases proceed from a first information report and investigation to a charge-sheet, arraignment, bail, trial, and sentencing. Evidence in civil matters supports or rebuts private claims; in criminal matters, it establishes guilt or creates reasonable doubt. Civil cases often take longer; criminal cases are constrained by the right to a speedy trial.

Both tracks allow appeals (trial court, High Court, Supreme Court, with variations by case type and forum). Some conduct can trigger both civil and criminal proceedings (like fraud or defamation), which run independently because the standards of proof differ.

Jurisdictionally, civil suits begin in courts scaled to the claim's value, while criminal matters start in Magistrates' Courts or Sessions Courts, depending on offense severity. If a shopkeeper in Kerala sues a supplier for 80,000 rupees, the case will likely start in the Munsiff Court. If the disputed amount were 800,000 rupees, it might go to the Civil Judge (Senior Division).

If one party loses and wants to challenge the decision, they can appeal to the District Court, then to the High Court, and ultimately to the Supreme Court.

In International law, the burden of proof should also be borne by the claimant, though International Courts are sometimes even more proactive than Civil Law courts.

The ICJ has the particularity of being very proactive in litigation, besides its consultative function. It bears the burden of proving in virtue of International law whether it has jurisdiction and what the issue will be, even with elements missing from the proceedings. If a party refuses to appear before the judge, for instance, the Court bears the burden to check that "the claim presented before it is well founded in fact and law"[58] and to decide despite the absence of that party. In addition, the Court has to provide evidence as to which national law may apply and why.

58 Article 53 of the Statute of the International Court of Justice.

The Fisheries Jurisdiction case of 1973[59] additionally stated that "the burden of establishing or proving rules of international law cannot be imposed upon any of the Parties, for the law lies within the judicial knowledge of the Court."

The Rome Statute[60] also rules for criminal proceedings in its article 66(2) that the burden is on the prosecutor. However, if a State invokes a tradition which it judges binding for another, it has to prove that there was "a constant and uniform usage practiced by the states in question"[61] as ruled by the Court in the *Colombia v. Peru asylum* case. Consequently, Colombia's claim to apply the customs in the case in point was rejected. It was less severe in the *Fisheries* case opposing Norway to the UK in 1951, where it ruled that the principle had to be proved "generally . . . adopted by the practice of states."[62] "Notorious facts," on the other hand, do not need to be proved. Yet consensus on which facts this notion encompasses is hardly reachable. Since international proceedings are based on a one-stage procedure very similar to that of Civil Law countries, the only burden of proof is that of persuasion.

The World Trade Organization has progressively emerged as an independent legal system, and its rules regarding the burden of proof have strengthened. The question is to know which State will bear the burden of proof. As Joost Pauwelyn – a Professor of International Law at the Graduate Institute of International and Development Studies in Geneva – notices: "Gone are the days when panels were able to adjudicate on a cluster of 'undisputed facts' yielded, without great effort, after two sets of submissions and oral hearings. These days panels are flooded with evidence."[63]

The WTO is nonetheless based on Civil Law and Common Law, which both place the burden of proof on the party bearing a specific claim or defence. More specifically, a State must prove the adverse incidence that the measures taken by another State had on its trade. The WTO Appellate Body has ruled in accordance with he U.S. case *Shirt and Blouses decision*[64] that "If that party aduces evidences sufficient to raise a presumption that what is claimed is true, the burden then shifts to the other party, who will fail unless it adduces sufficient evidence to rebut the presumption." It has recalled later on in the *EC-Hormones* decision[65] that "the initial burden lies on the complaining party, which must establish a primafacie case of inconsistency with a particular provision" and that once this *prima facie* case raised, the burden of proof turned to the defendant which could try to rebut it.

WTO jurisdictions have perpetuated Common Law and Civil Law burden of proof customs to assert itself as a legal system, and so did the European Union.

Because there are no European codes of procedure, the doctrine on the burden of proof principally relies on EU Council directives and on the European Court of Justice (ECJ) case law.

59 International Court of Justice, *Fisheries Jurisdiction (United Kingdom v. Iceland)*, Judgment of 2 February 1973, ICJ Reports 1973.

60 Rome Statute of the International Criminal Court, July 1998.

61 International Court of Justice, *Asylum Case (Colombia v. Peru)*, Judgment of 20 November 1950, ICJ Reports 1950.

62 International Court of Justice, *Fisheries Case (United Kingdom v. Norway)*, Judgment of 18 December 1951, ICJ Reports 1951.

63 Pauwelyn, Joost, 1998, "Evidence, Proof and Persuasion in WTO Dispute Settlement: Who Bears the Burden?," *Journal of International Economic Law*, no. 1.

64 World Trade Organization, Appellate Body Report, *United States – Measure Affecting Imports of Woven Wool Shirts and Blouses from India*, WT/DS33/AB/R, 25 April 1997 (adopted 23 May 1997).

65 World Trade Organization, *European Communities – Measures Concerning Meat and Meat Products (Hormones)*, WT/DS26/29.

For example, the EU Council directive 2000/78 – known as the Employment Equality Directive – which prohibits discrimination on grounds of religion and belief, age, disability, and sexual orientation. This EU Council Directive covers the fields of employment and occupation, vocational training, membership of employer and employee organizations. It sets out minimum requirements. Member states may therefore provide for a higher level of protection against discrimination in national legislation.

Article 10 of the Directive provides that once the claimant has "shown something more than a difference of status, a difference of treatment and detrimental treatment" and once it has been established that the employer wronged equal treatment, the burden of proof is on the respondent to show that he did not breach the principle.

6.4 Evidence Requirements

Evidence is a critical component of legal proceedings, significantly influencing the outcome of a trial and the burden of proof philosophy. It can take various forms, such as oral, written, or forensic evaluations, and its admissibility and weight can vary across legal systems. The process of uncovering and presenting evidence is essential to maintaining the integrity and fairness of the trial.

6.4.1 Types and Admissibility of Evidence

Evidence in legal proceedings can be oral, written, or derived from forensic evaluations. Different legal systems may favor specific types of evidence. For instance, certain forms of evidence, such as illegally obtained audiotapes, are inadmissible regardless of their revelatory nature. The French *Cour de cassation* ruled in 1991 that evidence collected by an employer through spying on an employee could not be used in court.[66] Similarly, in 2009, it ruled that emails and texts intercepted by a wife to prove her husband's infidelity were inadmissible in a divorce case.[67] This underscores the importance of the loyalty of proof, ensuring that evidence is obtained and presented ethically. The principle of loyalty in evidence collection was reinforced by the Cour de Cassation in 2021.[68] The court ruled that using paid third parties to stage transactions and gather evidence of unfair competition is unfair and inadmissible. In this case, the *Rassemblement des opticiens de France* hired "mystery shoppers" to investigate IMD Optic. The court found that this evidence was obtained in a biased and unfair manner, leading to its exclusion from the trial. This decision highlights the need for ethical and lawful evidence gathering in legal proceedings.

The loyalty of proof is thus an essential element of the trial. That is why the United Kingdom reformed its legal system to substitute experts chosen by the parties to inquire with experts named by the judge himself.

6.4.2 Handling Sensitive Evidence and Confessions

More generally, dealing with secrets and the burden of proof can be particularly arduous. In Public Law, for instance, since every element of the trial remains public, the judges need to

66 Cour de cassation (France), Civil Chamber, *Ruling of 20 November 1991*.

67 Cour de cassation (France), Civil Chamber, *Ruling of 17 June 2009*.

68 Cour de cassation (France), Commercial Chamber, *Ruling of 10 November 2021*, Appeal No. 20-14.669.

be very careful as to how the evidence is uncovered, for the politicization of the affair might threaten neutrality and the due process of law.

The Watergate scandal of the Nixon administration in the 1970s in the U.S., for example, or the Bettencourt scandal in France, are examples of major Public Law procedures where evidence proves decisive. State obligations as to the secrecy of proceedings might also slow down the process. In Belgium, for instance, the Council of State has the obligation to hide the truth if it threatens fundamental institutions of the State.

Confessions outside or during trials are another type of tough evidence to handle. The judge indeed needs to ensure that the person who confesses is not subject to physical and psychological pressure. Depending on the moment at which the confession is made during proceedings, he will then take it into account or ignore it. That is why in Talmudic law, "oaths" (to be taken in the sense of revelations) are considered to be a "residuary proof" and are only tolerated when no other type of evidence can be delivered.[69]

Likewise, hearsay and *res gestae* (second-hand statements made more or less spontaneously) are accepted to different extents in the various legal systems. In Great Britain, the Criminal Justice Act of 2003 ruled that hearsay could not be accepted as oral evidence except if "it is in the interests of justice for it to be admissible," if "all the parties . . . agree" and if the person cannot attend, either for he is ill (either mentally or physically), dead, for he lives far away or cannot be found.[70] Exceptions also exist for public documents and statements, and hearsay may be accepted in civil proceedings. On the other hand, the U.S law strictly forbids the use of hearsay as evidence. What a young 3-year-old boy says to his mother about his aggressor, for instance, would not be held as evidence. This leads to questioning the validity of a witness's statement as a way to complete the burden of proof.

6.5 The Status of Witnesses

The role and obligations of witnesses vary significantly between the Common Law and Civil Law systems. These differences influence how testimonies are collected, the rights of the accused, and the overall dynamics of the legal proceedings. This part explores the status of witnesses within these two legal traditions, highlighting key distinctions and practices.

6.5.1 Witnesses in the Common Law System

In the Common Law system, witnesses testify under oath, and a testimony subsequently proved false is perjury. Every witness that is cited by any of the parties during the procedure is forced to testify, be it under incarceration if necessary. However, the accused and his relatives are exempted from this obligation. The accused's right to remain silent is much more important than in Civil Law, and police forces, for instance, are not allowed to question the accused. Minors whose mental development is evaluated as insufficient by the judge can be called to "tell the truth" but not necessarily under oath.[71]

69 Cohn, Haim, 1981, "The Proof in Biblical and Talmudical Law," in *La preuve en droit*, eds. Chaïm Perelman and Paul Foriers, Brussels, Éditions Bruylant.

70 Criminal Justice Act 2003, sections 114–117 (United Kingdom).

71 Ginossar, Shmuel, 1981, "Système anglais de la preuve judiciaire," in *La preuve en droit*, eds. Chaïm Perelman and Paul Foriers, Brussels, Éditions Bruylant.

The witness can be submitted to direct and adverse inquiry (by the party that has cited him as a witness and by the adverse party) since it is to the parties to enquire in the Common Law system. Yet, the judge is a spectator rather than an actor in the debate.

This structure reflects the adversarial nature of Common Law trials, where the truth is expected to emerge from the confrontation between two opposing sides rather than through judicial investigation. Cross-examination is therefore considered a crucial safeguard, designed to test credibility, expose inconsistencies, and reveal motives or biases. Because the judge plays a limited role in questioning witnesses, the effectiveness of the process depends heavily on the skill of the lawyers and the ability of the witness to withstand scrutiny. This dynamic illustrates a central feature of Common Law procedure: the trial is a contest of narratives, and the role of the court is to referee rather than to lead the search for truth.

6.5.2 Witnesses in the Civil Law System

In both the Civil Law and Common Law systems, the accused is never obliged to testify, though he has the right to be heard. The difference is that once given the status of "witness," the accused must tell all the truth and everything that he knows. In the Civil system, on the other hand, the amount of information and truth that an accused gives is variable (principle of unrestricted evaluation of evidence). The principle of unrestricted evaluation of evidence means judges can freely decide if the evidence is credible, accurate, and reliable. Similarly, the accused is not forced to respond to all the questions that are asked (though a confession is taken into account to reconstitute the elements of the crime). However, the Civil Law system does not forbid the cross-examination of a witness by the adverse party. This way of proceeding is often seen in the Italian legal system, for example.

These differences reflect deeper procedural philosophies. In Common Law systems, assigning the status of witness to the accused transforms him into a full participant in the evidentiary process, subject to strict duties of truthfulness and exposure to cross-examination. Civil Law systems adopt a more protective posture: the accused remains primarily an object of inquiry rather than a source of compulsory testimony, and his statements are evaluated according to the judge's holistic appreciation of the case. This flexibility allows the judge to consider psychological, contextual, and circumstantial elements when interpreting the accused's silence or partial cooperation. Moreover, permitting cross-examination in certain Civil Law jurisdictions – such as Italy – illustrates the gradual convergence between adversarial and inquisitorial traditions, blending judicial responsibility for fact-finding with party-driven techniques for testing credibility.

6.6 The Effect of Presumptions on the Legal Burden of Proof

Presumptions play a crucial role in legal proceedings, significantly influencing the burden of proof. They create initial assumptions about certain facts, which can shift the responsibility to the opposing party to produce evidence to the contrary.

For instance, if an email is sent from your account, it is presumed that you sent it, unless you can prove that your account was hacked. Likewise, if a book is missing from a library shelf, it is presumed that a student borrowed it, unless it is later found misplaced elsewhere.

This section examines the different types of presumptions and their impact on the burden of proof in both Common Law and Civil Law systems, showing how these legal shortcuts help courts manage uncertainty while maintaining fairness.

6.6.1 Types and Impact of Presumptions

The first type of presumption that can arise in a case is the presumption of probable cause. For instance, if an accident occurs in the middle of a road, it may be presumed that both drivers swerved onto the wrong side, making it difficult to attribute fault to only one party.[72] In such cases, both may be held jointly liable for damages.

A presumption can also serve as a form of indirect evidence.[73] It is a type of legal reasoning presented in court to establish a fact by relying on related or circumstantial evidence. For example, a party seeking to prove a murder might show that the accused bleached a carpet to remove blood stains, and that the victim bore marks from the same carpet's pattern on their skin. From these clues, the court may presume that the accused killed the victim and tried to conceal the evidence. This form of reasoning – called in French *présomption du fait de l'homme* – allows for contrary proof, but it temporarily shifts the burden of proof to the other party.

As John J. Barcelò – William Nelson Cromwell Emeritus Professor of International and Comparative Law at Cornell Law School – explains, if fact A is proven, and fact B logically derives from it, then fact B is presumed true unless the opposing party successfully rebuts it.[74] This logic operates in both Common Law and Civil Law systems.

Barcelò further illustrates this principle: if the respondent shows that a third party (C) may be responsible, the burden shifts back to the claimant to prove that the respondent remains liable – for example, due to negligence. This dynamic can be seen in the U.S. Supreme Court case *McDonnell Douglas Corp. v. Green* (411 U.S. 792, 1973), involving alleged racial discrimination. The claimant established an initial presumption of discrimination by proving that he was Black, qualified for the position, and that his application was rejected while the job remained open and others with similar qualifications were hired. This created a *prima facie* case, shifting the burden to the employer to offer a legitimate, non-discriminatory explanation.

6.6.2 Legal Presumptions and Their Reversibility

Legal presumptions can sometimes reverse the burden of proof, but they can also be challenged by contrary evidence. In some situations, a legal presumption established by law may even release a party from the duty to prove a fact. For instance, Article 1352 of the French Civil Code states: a legal presumption releases from the burden of proof the person in whose favor it exists (*La présomption légale dispense de toute preuve celui au profit duquel elle existe*). This means that when the law grants someone the benefit of a presumption, that person does not have to prove the fact in question – it is assumed to be true until proven otherwise.

Such presumptions can therefore shift the burden of proof. The person who benefits from the presumption is considered, for example, innocent until evidence is presented to the contrary.

However, some presumptions cannot be challenged at all. These are called irrefutable presumptions (*présomptions irréfragables*), as provided by Article 1350 of the French Civil Code, meaning that no evidence can overturn them. The presumption of innocence – as discussed earlier – is one of these: it is a fundamental guarantee in criminal law, recognized in both Civil Law and Common Law systems.

72 United Kingdom, *Bray v. Palmer*, [1953] 1 WLR 1455.

73 Frison-Roche, Marie-Anne, "Présomption," *Dictionnaire bilingue du droit de la régulation et de la compliance*, online. Available at: https://mafr.fr.

74 Barcelò, John J. III, 2009, "Burden of Proof, Prima Facie Case and Presumption in WTO Dispute Settlement," *Cornell Law Faculty Publications*.

Article 6(2) of the European Convention on Human Rights enshrines this principle, stating: "Everyone charged with a criminal offence shall be presumed innocent until proven guilty according to law."

In practice, according to the UN Human Rights Committee (General Comment No. 13), this means that the burden of proof rests entirely on the prosecution. The accused benefits from the doubt: if any doubt remains, they must be acquitted. Public authorities have a duty not to prejudge the outcome of a trial or to present someone as guilty before conviction.

The presumption of innocence, according to which an accused person is deemed innocent until proven guilty, is a fundamental guarantee in most modern legal systems influenced by European, Anglo-American, and international human rights traditions. However, its existence and practical application vary considerably across jurisdictions. In authoritarian or totalitarian regimes such as North Korea or historically in the Soviet Union, the principle is largely absent or purely nominal, with guilt often presumed once charges are brought. In China, for example, although the Criminal Procedure Law formally recognises the presumption of innocence, the extremely high conviction rate reveals its limited effect in practice. Even in democratic systems, certain administrative, fiscal, or anti-terrorism procedures create rebuttable presumptions that partially shift the burden of proof, thereby weakening the principle. In some religious or customary legal systems, particularly in specific applications of Sharia law, the presumption of innocence is not conceptually central, as evidentiary rules may rely on different notions of proof and responsibility. More generally, even where it is constitutionally guaranteed, the presumption of innocence can be undermined by prosecutorial bias, political pressure, or media influence, illustrating that its strength depends as much on judicial culture and institutional independence as on the written law itself.

Another example of an irrefutable presumption is the principle of *res judicata* (Latin for "a matter already judged"). It means that once a case has been finally decided on its merits, it cannot be litigated again. This principle ensures legal certainty and finality: the decision is considered true and binding, and no new evidence or argument can overturn it. The doctrine of *res judicata* is recognized in many systems, including the U.S. Constitution (Seventh Amendment) and international law under Article 38(1) of the Statute of the International Court of Justice (ICJ).

6.7 The Burden of Proof as a Decisive Element in Trial Procedure

The burden of proof is a fundamental element of trial procedure, determining the success or failure of legal claims. It is a dynamic component of legal strategy, comparable to a tennis ball moving back and forth between the parties, influencing the outcome according to the strength and placement of the evidence presented.

6.7.1 The Burden of Proof: Risk and Right

The burden of proof represents a significant risk for the claimant, since failure to discharge it may result in losing the case. Judges must handle this burden with care so as not to discourage individuals or entities from seeking justice. Yet the burden of proof is not merely a risk – it is also a right: the right to prove and to be proved. This right includes the ability to obtain and present evidence, as protected by Article 10 of the French Civil Code, and the obligation of parties to contribute to the production of evidence that may benefit the opposing side, as provided by Article 11 of the French New Code of Civil Procedure. Together, these provisions ensure the fairness of proceedings and guarantee that each party's claims and arguments are properly examined by the judge.

In this sense, the burden of proof operates as both a procedural safeguard and a substantive guarantee. It empowers litigants to actively participate in the construction of the judicial truth while preventing one party from obstructing access to relevant information. The reciprocal duties established by Articles 10 and 11 reflect a cooperative vision of civil procedure, where the search for truth is a shared responsibility rather than an adversarial contest. By allowing parties to compel the disclosure of documents, request investigative measures, or seek judicial assistance in gathering evidence, the law ensures that the burden of proof does not become an impossible task. Instead, it becomes a structured right that supports equality of arms and reinforces the legitimacy of judicial decision-making.

6.7.2 The Dynamic Nature and Strategic Importance of the Burden of Proof

The burden of proof is inherently dynamic, shifting between the parties as evidence is introduced and assessed. Legal systems have developed rules to manage this tension between risk and right. In criminal proceedings, the burden of proof generally lies with the prosecution, counterbalanced by legal presumptions such as the presumption of innocence, which protect individuals and preserve legal certainty. Ongoing debates concern the standards of proof required for the burden to shift, but its strategic importance is undeniable. The allocation of the burden of proof can determine the outcome of litigation or open new lines of argument, making it a decisive and tactical element in judicial proceedings.

This dynamic character means that the burden of proof operates not as a rigid, one-time assignment, but as a procedural mechanism that evolves throughout the case. As new facts emerge or presumptions come into play, the responsibility to produce further evidence may move from one party to the other. Courts often interpret this shifting burden in light of fairness, proportionality, and the parties' respective abilities to access information. In complex disputes – such as medical liability, environmental harm, or employment discrimination – judges may rely on presumptions or evidentiary adjustments to avoid placing an insurmountable burden on the weaker party. Thus, the burden of proof becomes both a guiding principle and a tool of judicial craftsmanship, shaping the rhythm of litigation and influencing the strategic decisions of counsel.

7 The Practice of Law

This section explores the different aspects of lawyering, including the main legal professions, the basic skills needed for case briefing, and the key terms used in litigation. Understanding these elements is essential for anyone involved in law, from students to experienced professionals.

7.1 The Legal Professions

This part provides an overview of the different roles within the legal profession, including lawyers, judges, paralegals, and other legal practitioners. It examines the responsibilities, qualifications, and career paths associated with each role.

7.1.1 Diverse Roles in the Legal Profession

The legal profession includes many different roles, such as lawyers, judges, notaries, and paralegals, each with its own duties and career path. In France, the legal field also involves civil servants, police officers, political leaders, and court clerks. Lawyers, known as officers of justice, work independently and must follow strict ethical rules. Becoming a lawyer in France requires completing a Master's degree in law, vocational training, and passing the bar exam. French legal training places strong emphasis on both theoretical knowledge and professional ethics. Once admitted to the bar, lawyers must continue their education throughout their careers and are bound by strict codes governing confidentiality, conflicts of interest, and client representation. Notaries, who play a central role in property and family law, follow a different path and act as public officers with the authority to authenticate legal instruments. This division illustrates the structured and state-regulated nature of legal professions in Civil Law systems.

In the United Kingdom and other Common Law countries, the profession is divided into barristers and solicitors. Barristers represent clients in court, while solicitors handle legal advice, document preparation, and other legal matters. Although this distinction has been debated in recent years, it still exists today. Barristers receive specialized training in advocacy and often work as independent practitioners, whereas solicitors typically work in firms and maintain direct contact with clients. Reforms in recent decades have allowed some overlap – solicitors may now obtain rights of audience in higher courts, and barristers may take on more advisory work – yet the two-branch structure remains a defining feature of the British legal tradition.

In the United States, lawyers must complete an undergraduate degree, pass the LSAT, and then attend three years of law school to earn a Juris Doctor (J.D.) degree. Each state has its own bar exam, and passing it is required to practice law in that state. Unlike Civil Law systems, the U.S. does not separate the professions of lawyer and notary. American lawyers therefore perform a broad range of functions – from litigation to negotiation to contract drafting – reflecting the highly versatile nature of the profession. The licensing process is largely decentralized, with each state setting its own requirements, and continuing legal education is typically mandatory after admission to maintain professional competence. This unified model contrasts with the more segmented structure found in Civil Law jurisdictions.

7.1.2 Motivations for Pursuing a Legal Career

Motivations for pursuing a legal career can be very diverse, driven by a range of personal, professional, and societal factors.

One major motivation is the intellectual challenge that a legal career provides. Many individuals are drawn to the law because of the intellectual rigor and complexity it involves. The study and practice of law require critical thinking, analytical skills, and the ability to understand and apply complex legal principles. For example, a student fascinated by constitutional law might pursue a career as a constitutional lawyer, enjoying the challenge of interpreting and applying constitutional principles to modern-day issues.

Another significant motivation is the desire to help others. A significant number of people are motivated by the desire to make a positive impact on society. This can include advocating for marginalized communities, defending the rights of individuals, or working to improve the legal system. For instance, someone passionate about social justice might become a public defender, providing legal representation to those who cannot afford it and ensuring they receive a fair trial.

Financial rewards also play a crucial role in motivating individuals to pursue a legal career. The potential for high earnings can be a strong motivator, especially in fields such as corporate law or intellectual property law. An individual with an interest in business and finance might pursue a career in corporate law, attracted by the lucrative salary and the opportunity to work with major corporations.

Lastly, the prestige and respect associated with the legal profession can be a significant motivator. For many, becoming a lawyer is seen as a way to achieve a high status in society and gain respect. This prestige is often tied to the perception of lawyers as knowledgeable, influential, and ethical professionals, which can be a powerful draw for those seeking recognition and esteem in their careers.

After gaining experience and recognition, lawyers can move from working for organizations to starting their own practices. This independence offers several benefits, including a better work-life balance. Having their own practice allows lawyers to control their careers. They can set their schedules, choose their clients, and decide how to grow professionally and financially. This freedom leads to greater job satisfaction. Starting a private practice gives lawyers the flexibility to shape their careers and reach their goals.

Application essays for law school often reveal the diverse motivations behind choosing a legal career. Some applicants are driven by the desire to work within the framework of rules to make positive changes, as illustrated by a Harvard Law School applicant who participated in an International Mission on Diplomacy program in Australia.

> This past summer I was honored to take part in the International Mission on Diplomacy program in Australia. Along with forty other college students, I visited Canberra, Sydney, and Cairns. We toured government buildings, met public officials, and heard lectures by aboriginal speakers. Learning the rules of Australia's electoral system was interesting, but contemplating how to work within the framework of rules to make positive changes is what really tickled my brain. This eye-opening experience cemented my desire to attend law school and enter the legal profession.[75]

Others aspire to become entertainment lawyers to influence and develop the potential of youth through pop culture. "I firmly believe that there is no better way to influence and develop the potential of youth than with pop culture, and I want to be a part of that process as an entertainment lawyer."[76]

Some students aim to specialize in international law, seeking a career that bridges Eastern and Western legal spheres.

> I consider the legal education as my true academic gateway into a purposeful and self-fulfilling career. I hope, through the legal training offered by your institution, to specialize eventually in the world of international law encompassing both the Eastern and Western spheres in an era that will undoubtedly experience numerous confrontations of global proportions.[77]

7.1.3 Global Perspectives on Legal Education and Profession

The legal profession varies significantly worldwide. In the U.S., the number of lawyers has tripled in the past 40 years, with approximately three lawyers per 1,000 inhabitants today. In China, the legal profession was virtually nonexistent during the Cultural Revolution but has grown to about 130,000 lawyers since the 1980s. However, the profession remains subject to state control and the Chinese Communist Party. Globalization and technological advancements

75 Bazan, Rebecca, 2014, "I Want to Be a Lawyer Because . . .," in *55 Successful Harvard Law School Application Essays*, St. Martin's Press, p. 50.

76 Chang, Stephen, 2014, "I Want to Be a Lawyer Because . . .," in *55 Successful Harvard Law School Application Essays*, St. Martin's Press, p. 53.

77 Chung, Natalie, 2014, "I Want to Be a Lawyer Because . . .," in *55 Successful Harvard Law School Application Essays*, St. Martin's Press, p. 57.

are driving changes in China's legal profession, leading to new business models and the rise of online legal service portals.

Criticisms of legal education exist in various countries. In France, for example, the legal education system has been criticized for being too dogmatic and disconnected from social, economic, and cultural realities. This has sparked debates about how lawyers should be trained and the relevance of legal education to real-world issues.

In the U.S, American lawyers must first graduate from college (four years of university studies) in any field in order to access vocational training. That is a key difference and a real stake when it comes to the question: What is a lawyer, and how should a lawyer be trained? Educational systems vary a lot across the world, and there has been a controversy in France on this issue in recent years.[78]

> Criticisms are now being voiced with regard to legal education in France. . . . Indeed, in the wake of the ministerial decree of March 21, 2007,[79] . . . in a critique altogether reminiscent of the charges levied at the case method in Canada and elsewhere, a number of French jurists have decried the fact that law is portrayed within French law faculties as an autonomous and closed system, unaffected by, among other things, social, economic, historical and cultural considerations. Professor and former Dean Christophe Jamin, in particular, laments the "dogmatic" nature of French legal education that inculcates students, from day one, with the idea that law is not what happens outside of the law school, but rather, is to be found in legal texts and treatises. As the former president of France's Conseil National de Barreaux Thierry Wickers has argued, endorsing Jamin's critique, students are thus presented with a vision of the law as "ordered, systematized, categorized and endowed with its own internal system of values, that completely isolates it from external realities." It is clear that the spirit of Langdell, who believed that the content of the law was to be discovered "in a library and nowhere else", is very much alive in many French law faculties.[80]

After graduating from college, American lawyers must pass a qualifying examination (LSAT – Law School Admission Test), and study three years in a law school in order to obtain a J.D., the degree of *Juris Doctor*. Each state has its own bar, and lawyers may only practice in the State where they are members of the bar. To be admitted to a bar, lawyers have to take the bar exam (in the state where the lawyer intends to have a permanent practice) and pay annual dues to become members of the bar and obtain a license to practice. Professional training as a condition of access was generally abandoned in the late 1960s in favor of the immediate exercise in the workplace (in practice) as an employed lawyer (associate).

The U.S. legal system does not recognize the distinction lawyer/notary that countries in the Civil Law world acknowledge. American lawyers thus manage and deal with both estates and real estate transactions and litigation, as well as legal representation.

78 Jamin, Christophe, 2012, *La Cuisine du droit: l'École de droit de Sciences Po, une expérimentation française*, Lextenso.

79 Under French law, the relevant regulation is the Decree of March 21, 2007, which amended the list of degrees considered equivalent to a law master's degree for admission to the legal profession. *Arrêté du 21 mars 2007 modifiant l'arrêté du 25 novembre 1998 fixant la liste des titres ou diplômes reconnus comme équivalents à la maitrise en droit pour l'exercice de la profession d'avocat*, JO, April 8, 2007, 6609.

80 Conrad, Gillian and Lazare, Jérôme, 2015, "The Lawyer in Context: Toward an Integrated Approach to Legal Education," in *« Démoulages »: du carcan de l'enseignement du droit vers une éducation juridique*, eds. Ruth Sefton-Green, Société de législation comparée, Paris.

Each state has its own legal system inherited from the Common Law, except Louisiana, which has kept the private law of the French Civil Code but inherited Public Law from the Common Law.

By contrast with the United States, where the legal profession has expanded considerably over recent decades, the legal profession in China is not understood in the same traditional sense as in the West. During the Cultural Revolution, there were no lawyers. State lawyers appeared in the 1980s with Zhang Sizhi[81] (1927–2022) – a renowned Chinese lawyer who defended political dissidents and Mao Zedong's widow during the trial of the Gang of Four and General Lin Biao.[82] The profession opened in the 1990s and nowadays counts about 130,000 lawyers. The rights of the defense are not really guaranteed, and the profession remains disorganized, subject to state law, and under the control of the Chinese Communist Party.

However, globalization has a major impact on the legal profession in China, as Dr. Jing Li, who wrote on the legal profession of China in a globalized world, acknowledges:[83]

> The legal profession is undergoing fundamental changes; and this is the case not just in established legal markets. Based on a state-of-the-art sketch, this paper identifies and analyzes the latest innovation initiatives and alternative business models in China's legal profession. It finds that, propelled by market demands and benefiting from technological advancements, the provision of legal services has become highly versatile today, giving rise to various alternative service providers, especially the rapidly rising online legal service portals. Because they are technically not law firms, the exclusivity requirements on lawyer ownership and legal service provision are not applicable to them. In the meantime, the competition for large corporate clients and lucrative business transactions is fierce and will continue to be so, not only within the club of big Chinese corporate law firms, but also between Chinese law firms and international law firms globally.[84]

The legal profession in France, especially in Paris, faces the issue of too many lawyers.[85] This oversaturation leads to intense competition, making it hard for new lawyers to find stable jobs

81 Zhang Sizhi was a prominent Chinese lawyer and human rights advocate, often called "the conscience of Chinese lawyers." Born in 1927 in Henan Province, he first served as a judge before becoming one of the few lawyers in the early People's Republic of China. He gained national attention in 1980 for defending Mao Zedong's widow, Jiang Qing, during the "Gang of Four" trial. Despite being persecuted and sent to a labor camp for 15 years during the Anti-Rightist Campaign, Zhang resumed his legal career in 1979 and went on to defend many political dissidents. Honored with France's Legion of Honour in 2016, he remained active until a stroke in 2014 and passed away in Beijing in 2022 at the age of 94.

82 The trial of the Gang of Four and General Lin Biao took place in China in 1980–1981. It was the first major public trial after Mao Zedong's death. The Gang of Four were four top Communist Party officials, including Jiang Qing, Mao's widow. They were accused of committing serious crimes during the Cultural Revolution (1966–1976), a chaotic period marked by political purges and violence.

Lin Biao, Mao's former deputy, was officially accused of plotting a coup against Mao before dying in a mysterious plane crash in 1971. His case was tried alongside that of the Gang of Four, even though he was already dead. The trial aimed to blame them for the excesses of the Cultural Revolution and to mark the end of Mao's radical era. It was widely seen as both a show trial and a symbol of China's move toward legal order under Deng Xiaoping.

83 Li, Jianfu, 2019, "The Legal Profession of China in a Globalized World: Innovations and New Challenges," *International Journal of the Legal Profession*, vol. 26, nos. 2–3, pp. 217–264.

84 Li, *The Legal Profession of China in a Globalized World.*

85 Ten years ago, the Paris Bar warned of an exponential increase in the number of lawyers, with many calling for restrictions on entry into the profession. According to a report, the number of lawyers in Paris was expected to reach 35,000 by 2020, up from around 25,000. As of December 31, 2020, there were 30,593 lawyers registered with the

and potentially lowering the quality of legal services. The situation is similar to what the medical profession faced in the past with an excess of doctors, followed by a shortage. Paris has seen a significant increase in the number of lawyers, creating a highly competitive market. Many young lawyers struggle to find work, and the high competition can lead to reduced service quality as lawyers take on too many cases or lower their fees.

The medical field previously experienced an oversupply of doctors, leading to underemployment. To address this, the government regulated the number of medical students. However, this regulation eventually resulted in a shortage of doctors, particularly in rural areas.

To address the oversaturation of lawyers, a balanced approach is needed. Law schools can adjust admission rates based on market demand. Incentives could encourage lawyers to practice outside Paris. Regularly track employment trends and service demands to inform policy adjustments. Provide robust programs to help new lawyers transition into the profession effectively. Provide assistance in the career transition of lawyers.

Regulating the number of lawyers in France (and everywhere in the world) is essential to maintain high-quality legal services and ensure career sustainability. By learning from the medical profession, France can find a balance that benefits both lawyers and clients.

7.2 Case Briefing: The Basics of Legal Reasoning

Case briefing is an essential skill in legal study and practice. It involves carefully reading, analyzing, and summarizing judicial decisions to understand how courts apply legal rules to specific facts. Through this process, students and practitioners learn to identify key issues, reasoning, and outcomes in cases. Mastering case briefing helps develop clear legal reasoning, precise argumentation, and a deeper understanding of precedent and judicial interpretation. This section outlines the main methods and principles for effective case briefing.

7.2.1 Fundamentals of Legal Reasoning

Basic legal reasoning involves identifying the applicable law – both statutory and case law – analyzing and synthesizing it, researching the relevant facts, and then applying the law through deduction or analogy. Thinking like a lawyer is one of the most challenging skills for law students to master. It means learning how lawyers reason, construct arguments, and use logic to connect facts with legal principles.

For example, imagine a case where a driver injures a pedestrian while running a red light. A lawyer must first identify the applicable law – such as traffic regulations and civil liability rules. Then, they analyze past court decisions on similar accidents to understand how negligence has been defined and applied. After gathering the facts – witness statements, police reports, and medical evidence – the lawyer compares them with the legal standards of fault and causation. Finally, by using deduction (applying a general rule to specific facts) or analogy (comparing with similar precedents), the lawyer argues whether the driver should be held legally responsible for the pedestrian's injuries.

Paris Bar, in addition to 1,838 honorary lawyers. The number of lawyers at the Paris Bar has increased by an average of approximately 751 per year over the period from 1996 to 2020. However, compared to neighboring countries, the density of lawyers in France remains low: Germany and Italy have three times as many lawyers, and Spain has more than twice as many.

Law schools around the world use various methods to develop these skills, such as debates, discussions of legal doctrines and statutes, and the study of parliamentary materials. Two of the most common practical exercises are briefing and solving cases, as well as reading, analyzing, and summarizing judicial decisions.

As seen in Chapters 3 and 4, understanding how to read a case and how judicial decisions are structured – whether in Civil Law systems, illustrated by the *Jeand'Heur* case, or in Common Law systems, where the *ratio decidendi* plays a central role – is essential. While styles and lengths of judgments differ across systems, both rely on logic and syllogistic reasoning.

In practice, lawyering requires much more than locating the correct legal text and applying it mechanically. A skilled lawyer must use legal tools creatively to find innovative solutions to complex problems. This involves strong reasoning, writing, and debating abilities, as well as the capacity to explore comparative perspectives and foreign legal precedents.

A fundamental distinction in all legal systems is the *summa divisio* between fact and law. This universal dichotomy exists because the law governs facts, and the applicable legal norms always depend on the facts of a given case. Ultimately, legal practice consists of understanding the facts, identifying the relevant legal rules, and applying those rules accurately to resolve real-life disputes.

7.2.2 Methodology for Briefing a Case

To brief a case, it is important to follow a clear and logical method:

(1) Identify and summarize the facts.
(2) Characterize the facts using known legal concepts.
(3) Determine which legal rules apply.
(4) Apply those rules to the facts.
(5) Conclude with the likely outcome.

No legal argument can be properly accepted or rejected without following these steps. For example, imagine that George builds a fence on what he believes is his property. His neighbor, Stéphanie, thinks the fence is actually on her land. She says nothing at first, but later hires a surveyor, who confirms that the fence encroaches on her property. When George refuses to remove it, Stéphanie sues him, asking the court to order the fence's removal and to reimburse her for the surveyor's fees.

The first step is to summarize the facts: George built a fence that may stand on Stéphanie's property, and she is now suing him.

Next, we characterize these facts legally. George's act can be qualified as a "trespass" on another person's land.

Then, we identify the applicable rule. In many legal systems, if a landowner knows about an encroachment and does not object, that silence can be interpreted as consent.

Applying the rule to the facts: George informed Stéphanie before building the fence, and she did not object.

The conclusion, therefore, is that Stéphanie implicitly consented to the fence, and a court would likely decide in George's favor.

This example shows how case briefing allows lawyers to organize their reasoning clearly –from facts to law to conclusion – mirroring the method used by judges in their decisions.

7.2.3 Types of Legal Reasoning

Two basic types of reasoning are used by lawyers: analytical (vertical) and analogical (horizontal). The dominant style of legal reasoning is analytical, particularly in its deductive form.

Analytical reasoning can be either deductive or inductive, both involving the relationship between the general and the particular, but in opposite ways. Deductive reasoning starts with general statements and deduces particular conclusions. It is deductive because it draws a conclusion from two or more premises. It is vertical, or "top-down," in that the outcome is dictated by the starting principles. It follows a logical progression from the general to the particular. A classic example of deductive reasoning is the following syllogism:[86]

Premise 1: All men are mortal.
Premise 2: Socrates is a man.
Conclusion: Socrates is mortal.

Alternatively, the reasoning could be reversed:

Premise 1: All men are mortal.
Premise 2: Socrates is mortal.
Conclusion: Socrates is a man.

However, this second example is less valid because being mortal does not necessarily mean Socrates is a man; he could be any mortal creature.

Other examples of deductive reasoning are the following syllogisms:

Premise 1: All fruits develop from flowers.
Premise 2: An apple develops from a flower.
Conclusion: An apple is a fruit.

Alternatively, the reasoning could also be reversed:

Premise 1: All fruits develop from flowers.
Premise 2: This item develops from a flower.
Conclusion: This item is a fruit.

However, this is fully valid if "developing from flowers" is exclusive to fruits.

Inductive reasoning, on the other hand, uses particular statements to draw a general conclusion. The previous examples do not prove that all men are mortal. To prove this in the face of an adversarial challenge in court, we would have to use inductive reasoning by compiling enough examples of mortal men to conclude confidently that "all men are mortal."

Specific statement 1: Socrates was a man, and he was mortal.
Specific statement 2: Plato was a man, and he was mortal.
Specific statement 3: Aristotle was a man, and he was mortal.
Conclusion: All men are mortal.

86 See George, Tracey E. and Sherry, Suzanna, 2009, *An Introduction to the Study of Law: What Every Law Student Really Needs to Know*, Aspen Publishers.

We say "more-or-less confidently" because inductive reasoning cannot logically prove a conclusion; only deductive reasoning can. As Tracey E. George and Suzanna Sherry claim, the best inductive reasoning can do is build a higher level of confidence in the truth of our general conclusion.[87]

Analogical reasoning differs from deductive reasoning in that it neither uses nor requires universal or general statements. It also differs from inductive reasoning in that it does not seek to draw generally applicable conclusions. Analogical reasoning uses conclusions from specific cases to draw conclusions in similar cases (precedent). As Tracey E. George and Suzanna Sherry – two American Professors of law and experts on judicial behavior – put it, "in other words, it compares apples to oranges, but has nothing to say about fruit."[88] This is why reasoning by analogy is said to be "horizontal" – arguments are drawn from parallel cases rather than from first premises, and conclusions are applied only across cases rather than used to create a generalized statement.

George and Sherry provide the following example to demonstrate using analogical reasoning that Bill Gates is mortal:[89]

Specific statement 1: Socrates was a man, and he was mortal.
Specific statement 2: Plato was a man, and he was mortal.
Specific statement 3: Aristotle was a man, and he was mortal.
Conclusion: Bill Gates is a man, and he is therefore mortal.

Hence, thinking like a lawyer involves sharpening both analytical and analogical reasoning skills and learning to apply them in different specific contexts.

7.3 Essential Legal Terminology in Litigation

Understanding litigation requires familiarity with the legal terms most frequently used in court proceedings. Mastering this vocabulary is essential for anyone studying or practicing law, as it allows for precise communication and a clear understanding of procedural steps, judicial decisions, and legal reasoning. Each term carries a specific meaning within the context of litigation, and using them correctly helps lawyers, judges, and students follow the logic of a case and the arguments of each party.

This final section adopts a vocabulary-oriented approach. It presents and explains the essential terms that constitute the foundation of legal language in both civil and criminal proceedings, illustrating each with clear and concise examples that show their practical application in a legal context.

Admissible: Evidence that may be considered by the judge in civil or criminal cases. For example, the judge ruled that the email was admissible as proof of the contract.

Affidavit: A statement made under oath. Consider, for example, a witness who signs an affidavit confirming what she saw at the scene.

Affirmed: When a court of appeal decides that the lower court's ruling was correct. For example, the Court of Appeal affirmed the trial court's decision to convict.

87 George and Sherry, *An Introduction to the Study of Law*.
88 George and Sherry, *An Introduction to the Study of Law*.
89 George and Sherry, *An Introduction to the Study of Law*.

Alternative Dispute Resolution (ADR): Methods for settling disputes outside of court, such as Mediation or Arbitration. Imagine two companies choosing mediation instead of going to court to save time and cost.

Amicus curiae: Latin for "friend of the court." Advice offered by someone not directly involved in the case. For example, a human rights group may submit an amicus curiae brief in a constitutional case.

Answer: The defendant's written response to a complaint. Consider a defendant who files an answer denying the plaintiff's accusations.

Appeal: A request for a higher court to review a lower court's decision. For example, a losing party may file an appeal to challenge the verdict.

Bench trial: A trial without a jury, decided only by a judge. Imagine a fraud case tried as a bench trial before a single judge.

Brief: A written statement explaining each party's legal arguments. For example, the lawyer submitted a brief outlining her client's position on liability.

Burden of proof: The duty to prove disputed facts. Consider a criminal trial where the prosecution bears the burden of proving guilt.

Case law: Law developed through judicial decisions. For example, lawyers often rely on case law to support their arguments on negligence.

Cause of action: A legal claim or ground for suing. Imagine a tenant filing a cause of action for breach of contract against a landlord.

Class action: A lawsuit brought by one or more people on behalf of a larger group. For example, consumers may file a class action against a company for misleading advertising.

Complaint: The document that starts a lawsuit, explaining the plaintiff's claims. Consider a customer who files a complaint accusing a bank of fraud.

Counsel: Legal advice, or the lawyers involved in a case. For example, the defendant discussed a strategy with his counsel before the hearing.

Court: A government body that resolves legal disputes. Imagine a court ruling in favor of a worker who was unfairly dismissed.

Damages: Money awarded to a plaintiff for loss or injury. For example, the company paid €50,000 in damages for breach of contract.

Defendant: The person or entity against whom a lawsuit is filed. Consider a defendant accused of negligence in a car accident.

Default judgment: A judgment entered when the defendant fails to appear or respond. For example, the plaintiff won by default judgment because the defendant never answered.

Discharge: The release of a debtor from certain debts. Imagine a debtor whose financial obligations are discharged after bankruptcy.

Discovery: The pre-trial process of obtaining evidence. For example, the lawyer requested internal emails from the company during discovery.

Dismissal with prejudice: A final dismissal that prevents the same case from being filed again. Consider a case dismissed with prejudice after the parties reached a settlement.

Due process: The right to a fair and impartial legal procedure. For example, a defendant must be given due process before losing property or liberty.

Equitable: Relating to fairness and remedies based on equity rather than strict law. Imagine a court granting an equitable remedy requiring the return of a painting to its owner.

Evidence: Information used to prove or disprove facts in court. For example, video footage served as key evidence in the theft case.

Injunction: A court order requiring someone to do or stop doing something. Consider a company receiving an injunction to stop polluting a river.

Issue: The disputed legal or factual question in a case. For example, the issue in the case was whether the contract was legally binding.

Judge: The official who presides over a court case. Imagine a judge deciding a dispute between two business partners.

Judgment: The official decision resolving a legal dispute. For example, the court's judgment ordered the tenant to pay the unpaid rent.

Jurisdiction: The authority of a court to hear and decide a case. Consider a court that lacks jurisdiction because the dispute occurred abroad.

Jury: A group of citizens who decide factual questions in a trial. For example, the jury found the defendant not guilty after deliberation.

Lawsuit: A legal action filed by one person against another. Imagine an employee filing a lawsuit against an employer for discrimination.

Litigation: The process of taking legal action through the courts. For example, the company avoided lengthy litigation by settling early.

Mistrial: A trial declared invalid due to a serious error. Consider a mistrial declared after a juror spoke to a witness during the case.

Moot: A case no longer requiring a ruling because the issue no longer exists. For example, the case became moot when the law was repealed.

Motion: A formal request made to a judge during a case. Imagine a lawyer filing a motion to dismiss the charges.

Opinion: The written explanation of a court's decision. For example, the judge's opinion clarified how the law applied to the dispute.

Plaintiff: The person who brings a case to court. Consider a plaintiff suing a hospital for medical negligence.

Pleadings: Written statements outlining each party's claims and defenses. For example, both parties filed their pleadings before the first hearing.

Precedent: A previous court decision used as a guide for future cases. Imagine a judge following precedent from an earlier case on freedom of speech.

Procedure: The rules governing how a lawsuit is conducted. For example, the case was dismissed due to a procedural mistake.

Remand: To send a case back to a lower court for further action. Consider an appellate court remanding a case for a new trial.

Reverse: When a higher court overturns a lower court's decision. For example, the Supreme Court reversed the judgment of the Court of Appeal.

Sanction: A penalty imposed to ensure compliance with laws or rules. Imagine a company receiving sanctions for violating safety standards.

Settlement: An agreement to end a case without a trial. For example, the parties reached a settlement after mediation.

Standard of proof: The level of certainty required to prove a case. Consider that in civil cases, the standard of proof is usually "on the balance of probabilities."

Testimony: Oral evidence given by witnesses in court. For example, the witness's testimony confirmed the defendant's alibi.

Tort: A civil wrong causing harm or injury. Imagine a driver being sued for a tort after causing an accident.

Transactional agreement: A written settlement to end or prevent a lawsuit. For example, two companies signed a transactional agreement to resolve their dispute.

Uphold: When a higher court agrees with a lower court's ruling. Consider an appellate court upholding a lower court's decision on liability.

Venue: The location where a case is tried. For example, the proper venue for the dispute was the Paris Commercial Court.

Verdict: The final decision of a jury or judge. Imagine the jury returning a verdict of not guilty.

Witness: A person who gives evidence in court. For example, the witness described what happened during the robbery.

Writ:[90] A written court order directing someone to act or refrain from acting. Consider a writ of habeas corpus ordering the release of a detained person.

Conclusion

In conclusion, civil procedure provides the essential framework through which justice is administered. It ensures that every case is handled fairly, efficiently, and according to clear and predictable rules. Beyond its technical nature, civil procedure reflects the values of due process and equality before the law, guaranteeing that each party has the opportunity to be heard and to defend their rights.

While this chapter has focused mainly on civil proceedings, comparisons with criminal procedure have enriched the discussion by highlighting the common foundations that underlie all procedural systems – such as fairness, impartiality, and respect for fundamental rights. Understanding these shared principles helps those studying or practicing law see how procedural law operates as a coherent whole, linking form and substance, rights and remedies.

Civil procedure is also a mirror of each legal culture. It reveals how societies conceive of justice, the role of judges, and the balance between individual rights and public order. Whether inquisitorial or adversarial, each procedural model expresses a particular vision of the relationship between the citizen and the State. Comparing these systems broadens one's understanding of law as a living institution that evolves with social, political, and economic change.

Beyond these structural and cultural differences, certain principles remain universal. The right to a fair trial, the independence of the Judiciary, equality of arms, and the possibility for every party to be heard are recognized across all modern legal systems. These shared values transcend national boundaries and form the common foundation of procedural justice, reflecting humanity's collective commitment to fairness and the Rule of Law.

However, these universal principles, though widely acknowledged, are not applied with equal strength everywhere. Their genuine implementation depends largely on the democratic nature of the State and the independence of its institutions. In democratic systems, these principles have real substance, protected by impartial courts, a free legal profession, and transparent procedures. In contrast, within authoritarian regimes, they often remain formal declarations rather than effective guarantees – principles of appearance rather than of practice.

Together, these insights provide a solid foundation for approaching litigation not merely as a sequence of procedural steps, but as a vital process for achieving justice in both national and transnational contexts.

90 Writ of *certiorari*: Order issued by the U.S Supreme Court directing the lower court to transmit records for a case which it will hear on appeal.

Selected Bibliography

Allen, C., Taylor, C., & Nairns, J., 2016, *Practical Guide to Evidence* (5th ed.), Routledge, 526 pages.

The American Law Institute, 2010, *Principles of Transnational Civil Procedure*, Cambridge University Press, 242 pages.

Cryer, R., Robinson, D., & Vasiliev, S., 2019, *An Introduction to International Criminal Law and Procedure* (4th ed.), Cambridge University Press, 640 pages.

Epstein, L., Adl, U., Grendstad, G., & Weinshall, K., (Eds.), 2024, *The Oxford Handbook of Comparative Judicial Behaviour*, Oxford University Press, 1032 pages.

Erichson, H. M., 2017, *Inside Civil Procedure: What Matters and Why* (3rd ed.), Aspen Publishing, 316 pages.

He, X., 2024, *The Judicial System of China*, Oxford University Press, 288 pages.

Hendley, K., & Solomon, P. H. Jr., 2023, *The Judicial System of Russia*, Oxford University Press, 272 pages.

Ingram, J. L., 2022, *Criminal Procedure: Theory and Practice* (3rd ed.), Routledge, 736 pages.

Marcus, R., Rowe, T. Jr., & Gensler, S., 2022, *Gilbert Law Summary on Civil Procedure* (19th ed.), Gilbert, 625 pages.

Mcgourlay, C., Thomas, M., & Gower, S., 2024, *Evidence: Law and Context* (6th ed.), Routledge, 550 pages.

Novak, M., 2024, *The Logic of Legal Argumentation: Multi-Modal Perspectives* (1st ed.), Routledge, 178 pages.

Peté, S., Hulme, D., Du Plessis, M., Palmer, R., Sibanda, O., & Palmer, T., 2017, *Civil Procedure: A Practical Guide* (3rd ed.), Oxford University Press, 704 pages.

Sime, S., 2022, *A Practical Approach to Civil Procedure* (25th ed.), Oxford University Press, 696 pages.

7 When and Why Do Courts Apply the Law of Other Countries?

When a court applies the law of another jurisdiction, it does not abandon its own sovereignty; rather, it acknowledges the interconnectedness of legal systems in a globalized world.
Ernst Rabel (1874–1955)

In a world marked by growing cross-border interactions, legal disputes often extend beyond national borders. As businesses operate internationally and individuals move across countries, legal conflicts involving multiple jurisdictions have become common. The field that deals with these situations is known as Conflict of Laws or Private International Law.

The aim of this chapter is to introduce the main ideas and principles that help courts decide which country's law should apply when a case involves more than one legal system. Although the subject is complex and technical, understanding its foundations is essential for anyone dealing with international contracts, cross-border family issues, or global business relations.

This chapter offers a clear and concise overview rather than an exhaustive treatment of the subject. It seeks to explain the basic concepts, sources, and approaches that structure the discipline, while emphasizing how legal systems strive to balance predictability and flexibility in cross-border decision-making.

The discussion begins with an introduction to the notion of Conflict of Laws and its scope (Section 1), examining the types of matters it encompasses – such as transnational disputes and intergovernmental dimensions – and the principal sources of Private International Law, including treaties and domestic legislation. It then turns to the significance of Conflict of Laws in a globalized world (Section 2), highlighting its growing relevance, addressing common misconceptions, and presenting the key instruments that promote international coherence, such as the Rome I and Rome II Regulations.

Next, Section 3 explores the central question of *Which law applies?* through the so-called *When in Rome* principle. This part explains how courts determine the applicable law, how parties may choose it by agreement, and how such choices interact with international norms. Section 4 introduces the essential terminology and core principles of the field, showing how legal systems seek a balance between certainty and adaptability in the face of global diversity. Finally, Section 5 examines the outcomes of conflict-of-laws reasoning, distinguishing between substantive and procedural rules and considering the limits that mandatory provisions and public policy impose on contractual freedom.

By the end of this chapter, you will have acquired a foundational understanding of how and why courts apply the laws of different countries, and how the principles of Conflict of Laws contribute to maintaining coherence and fairness in the international legal order.

DOI: 10.4324/9781003393047-10

1 Introduction to Conflict of Laws

Conflict of Laws, also known as Private International Law, focuses on legal situations that involve more than one country. It addresses questions that arise when individuals or companies have ties, transactions, or disputes that cross national borders. Its purpose is to determine which country's courts have jurisdiction, which country's law should apply, and how foreign judgments should be recognized or enforced. These rules help provide order and predictability in a world where people travel, trade, and communicate across national boundaries.

1.1 Types of Matters Concerned by Conflict of Laws

This branch of law determines which legal system and which court are competent when several jurisdictions may apply. It plays an essential role in ensuring fairness and consistency in international cases, particularly those linked to family or commercial matters.

The following sections explore two key areas where Conflict of Laws is most relevant: transnational litigation and the intergovernmental dimension of legal conflicts.

1.1.1 Transnational Litigations

Conflict of Laws concerns legal situations involving private individuals that extend beyond national borders. These situations usually arise in family or commercial relationships. Therefore, *Private International Law* – also known as *Conflict of Laws* – mainly governs family and business matters with an international aspect. In simple terms, it addresses transnational legal issues, which often lead to litigation.

For example, consider a marriage between a French and a Spanish citizen: should this marriage be governed by French law or by Spanish law? Since two different nationalities are involved, either country's law could apply.

Conflict of Laws is also connected to the resolution of international disputes, which can involve two main types of conflicts: conflicts of laws and conflicts of jurisdiction.

In such cases, the role of Conflict of Laws is to provide clear methods for identifying the appropriate legal system and the competent court. These rules help avoid contradictory decisions and ensure that cases with international elements are handled consistently and predictably. By establishing which national law governs the relationship and which court should hear the dispute, Conflict of Laws maintains legal coordination between states and protects the rights of individuals engaged in cross-border activities.

1.1.2 A Strong Intergovernmental Dimension

The law of conflicts also has a strong intergovernmental dimension because questions of state sovereignty arise whenever it must be decided which country's law applies or which court has authority to hear a case. International private relationships often involve several legal systems at once. Since there is no single "world law" or "world court," it is essential to understand the rules that determine the applicable law and the competent jurisdiction for each case involving private international relations.

Conflicts of laws must therefore be resolved in space, by choosing between different national laws according to the most relevant links that connect the legal situation to one country rather than another. For instance, in the example of a marriage between a French and a Spanish citizen, the question is whether French or Spanish law should apply.

At this stage, you may wonder what counts as "the most relevant links" when determining the choice of forum and the choice of law. Some common connecting factors include the defendant's place of domicile, the *lex loci delicti* (the place where a tort occurred), the place where a contract was made or performed, or the overall proximity of the situation to a given legal system.

Courts and arbitrators usually evaluate these connecting factors to identify the closest and most genuine connection, in order to apply the law that has the most significant relationship with the case.

Tensions also exist when determining jurisdiction and applicable law, particularly between the competing principles of *forum non conveniens* and *forum necessitatis*. Under the first principle, a court that technically has jurisdiction may still dismiss a case if it believes another court is more appropriate or convenient for the litigation. This is done in the interest of justice. However, if all courts were to reject the case, justice would not be served. To prevent such denials of justice, the principle of *forum necessitatis* allows a court to accept a case when no other forum is available, and the dispute has a sufficient connection with that state. This principle is a fundamental rule of Public International Law because it ensures that access to justice is not denied.

Finally, imagine that the same French–Spanish couple later wishes to divorce. Which court should decide the case – the French or the Spanish one? This is a matter of conflict of jurisdictions, which determines which judge is competent. The rules governing applicable law (Conflict of Laws) and competent courts (conflict of jurisdictions) are distinct. Thus, even if the French court is competent, it may apply Spanish law if French conflict rules require it. Since each country has its own rules on these matters, they can sometimes contradict one another. To reduce such inconsistencies, states seek to harmonize their conflict of laws and jurisdiction rules through international treaties, which have become increasingly important given the rise of parallel proceedings and anti-suit injunctions in global litigation.[1]

1.2 The Sources of Private International Law

Private International Law, also called Conflict of Laws, is based on several sources that guide the resolution of disputes involving more than one country. These sources help determine which law should apply and which court has jurisdiction in international cases. The main sources of Private International Law are international treaties or conventions and national legislation, both of which play a key role in regulating cross-border legal relationships.

1.2.1 International Treaties or Conventions

These sources include both bilateral and multilateral treaties. Many of them are the result of work carried out within international organizations such as the Hague Conference on Private International Law, the Council of Europe, and the United Nations. Some treaties regulate conflicts of laws by defining common rules for all member states. For instance, the Hague Convention of March 14, 1978, on the Law Applicable to Matrimonial Property Regimes sets out rules on which law governs property relations between spouses of different nationalities.

1 Since the mid-19th century, Courts in the Common Law world have developed an international power of injunction, by which they may prohibit a party from suing another party before a court of a foreign country or an arbitral tribunal. The recalcitrant party is liable to a fine or imprisonment for "Contempt of court."

Other treaties address conflicts of jurisdiction. A notable example is the Brussels Convention of September 27, 1968, which was later replaced by Regulation (EC) No. 44/2001 on jurisdiction, recognition, and enforcement of foreign judgments, and subsequently by EU Regulation No. 1215/2012, effective since January 10, 2015.

Some conventions go further by avoiding conflicts of laws altogether through the establishment of substantive rules that apply uniformly. The Vienna Convention of April 11, 1980, on Contracts for the International Sale of Goods (CISG) is one such example.

International case law also plays a role in shaping Private International Law. The International Court of Justice (ICJ)has issued several important decisions, such as the Barcelona Traction case (February 5, 1970)[2] and the ELSI case (July 20, 1989),[3] which address the nationality of corporations, and the Boll case (November 28, 1958)[4] concerning the protection of minors.

In addition, international organizations develop non-binding instruments, such as the UNIDROIT Principles of International Commercial Contracts, which serve as models for legislators and contracting parties. Traders and business communities have also created non-state rules, known as lex mercatoria, including the ICC Incoterms and standards for electronic data exchange.

Within the European Union, several key instruments have been negotiated, including the Brussels Convention of September 28, 1968, on conflicts of jurisdiction and the Rome Convention of June 19, 1980, on the law applicable to contractual obligations. These instruments continue to influence the harmonization of Private International Law in Europe

1.2.2 Domestic Law

In domestic law, Private International Law also relies on national and doctrinal sources. These are mainly case law, since Private International Law is often not fully codified. In France, however, a few provisions of the Civil Code address these matters – for example, Article 3, which concerns conflicts of laws, and Articles 14 and 15, which deal with the jurisdiction of French courts.

Articles 3, 14, and 15 of the French Civil Code

Article 3

Statutes relating to public policy and safety are binding on all those living on the territory. Immovables are governed by French law even when owned by aliens. Statutes relating to the status and capacity of persons govern French persons, even those residing in foreign countries.

Article 14

An alien, even if not residing in France, may be cited before French courts for the performance of obligations contracted by him in France with a French person; he may be called

2 International Court of Justice, *Barcelona Traction, Light and Power Company, Limited (Belgium v. Spain)*, Second Phase, Judgment of 5 February 1970, ICJ Reports 1970.

3 International Court of Justice, *Elettronica Sicula S.p.A. (ELSI) (United States of America v. Italy)*, Judgment of 20 July 1989, ICJ Reports 1989.

4 International Court of Justice, *Guardianship of an Infant (Netherlands v. Sweden)*, Judgment of 28 November 1958, ICJ Reports 1958.

before the courts of France for obligations contracted by him in a foreign country towards French persons.

Article 15

French persons 3may be called before a court of France for obligations contracted by them in a foreign country, even with an alien.

These provisions illustrate how domestic law defines both the reach of French legal authority and the situations in which French courts may exercise jurisdiction. Although limited in number, they play a foundational role in guiding judges when dealing with international elements in private disputes.

2 The Significance of Conflict of Laws

In an increasingly interconnected world, the importance of Conflict of Laws is greater than ever. This field deals with the complex legal questions that emerge when several legal systems overlap, especially in situations involving international connections. In examining the significance of Conflict of Laws, we will look at its role in a globalized society, the multinational nature of today's legal challenges, and some common misunderstandings about this complex area of law.

2.1 The Relevance of Conflict of Laws in a Globalized World

As previously mentioned, Conflict of Laws concerns the application of different national laws in international disputes. It highlights the difficulty of operating in a world with many legal systems, where courts must decide which country's law should govern a particular case.

2.1.1 The Multinational Dimension of Legal Problems

Today, many legal problems extend across borders and involve the laws of several countries. It has become increasingly important for courts to determine which country's law should govern a transnational dispute. Likewise, lawyers must anticipate possible legal conflicts when drafting contracts by asking key questions such as: Which law governs the contract? What determines the rights and obligations of the parties? What remedies are available if one party suffers harm? What constitutes a breach of contract, and how should it be resolved?

Although complex and sometimes difficult to navigate, this field of law is essential in our globalized world. That is why this chapter is devoted entirely to it – to provide a clear and structured understanding. The expression "Conflict of Laws" may sound misleading, but it accurately reflects the challenge of dealing with cases that involve more than one country's legal system.

In earlier times, people rarely encountered legal issues beyond their local jurisdiction, and courts simply applied their own national laws. However, with the rise of international communication, commerce, and mobility, the situation has changed. Courts must now decide when and under what conditions it is appropriate to apply foreign law in cases involving multiple jurisdictions.

While most courts remain national in structure, they increasingly handle international disputes. This evolution has given rise to the specialized discipline of Conflict of Laws, developed precisely to manage the legal complexities of an interconnected world.

2.1.2 *Misconceptions: Conflict Does Not Always Mean Disagreement*

Conflict of laws is the area of legal study that focuses on how courts decide when and under what circumstances to apply the law of another country rather than their own. In France, this field is called *Droit international privé*, and it is a fundamental subject taught in law schools. It is crucial for legal professionals because national laws often differ greatly, and the outcome of a case can depend on which country's law is chosen.

The term "conflict of laws" may seem misleading, as the laws themselves do not always contradict one another. The expression comes from the fact that differences between legal systems can create potential conflicts, making it necessary to determine which law should govern a specific situation.

In practice, conflict of laws operates as a set of coordinating rules that help courts navigate these differences in a predictable and coherent manner. Rather than resolving disputes on the basis of substantive law, it provides a methodological framework for identifying the most appropriate legal system for each case. This ensures legal certainty, prevents forum shopping, and promotes fairness by avoiding arbitrary choices of law. As cross-border interactions increase in family, commercial, and digital contexts, the importance of conflict of laws continues to grow, making it an essential tool for managing the legal effects of globalization.

2.2 *Understanding International Legal Acceptance*

When a country applies the law of another country, it does so through its own legal system, using its own conflict of law rules. In practice, a court applies its national law, which may direct it to use a foreign law in certain cases. This method allows the court to rely on foreign law while still remaining within its own legal framework.

Each country has developed its own set of conflict of law rules. Some, such as Switzerland, have enacted clear statutes specifying which law applies in different circumstances. For example, in contract disputes, Switzerland may apply the law of the country where the contract is to be performed.

In contrast, the United States operates mainly under the Common Law system, where judges create principles through judicial decisions rather than relying on a single statute. In the absence of a federal law governing conflicts of law, courts often refer to *Restatements* –collections of general principles that guide but do not bind them. This difference illustrates the continuing divide between Civil Law systems, which tend to codify conflict rules, and Common Law systems, which develop them through case law.

2.2.1 *The Restatement of Legal Principles*

In the United States, many branches of law – such as torts, contracts, property, and Conflict of Laws – are not codified in statutes but instead form part of the Common Law, which develops through judicial decisions. To bring greater consistency and clarity to these uncodified areas, the American Law Institute (ALI) was established in 1923. Composed of judges, scholars, and legal practitioners, the ALI produces Restatements of the Law, which systematically compile and organize the most widely accepted legal principles from courts across all states.

For instance, if one were working on the *Restatement of Conflict of Laws*, one would analyze the rules applied in all 50 states and create a unified set of principles resembling a Civil Code. Although Restatements are not legally binding, they are highly persuasive. Courts often cite them because they are carefully researched and provide clear and balanced interpretations of the law.[5]

5 See American Law Institute, "Restatements of the Law," online. Available at: https://www.ali.org.

Restatements promote uniformity in legal reasoning, but they do not override the U.S. Constitution, Supreme Court rulings, or federal statutes. Judges are not required to follow them, yet they frequently rely on them as authoritative references.

In summary, Restatements play an important role in the American legal system, particularly in areas that remain uncodified. They serve to consolidate and clarify Common Law principles, offering guidance similar to what statutory codes provide in Civil Law countries such as Switzerland, where conflict of law rules are explicitly written into legislation.

2.2.2 *Common Ground: Shared Conflict Of Laws Rules Across Countries*

You might wonder whether different countries share common rules for resolving conflicts of laws. In fact, many do, especially within regions that have chosen to harmonize their legal systems. A key example of this is found in the Rome I and Rome II regulations, which apply to all European Union member states.

If you come from a non-EU country – such as one in Asia, South America, the United States, or Africa – it may not be immediately clear that such unified rules exist. While the Rome Regulations do not apply outside the EU, they serve as an excellent model of regional cooperation in establishing consistent legal principles for cross-border disputes.

Reading these regulations can be difficult, but doing so is essential to understanding the complex nature of International Law and how different legal systems can work together toward greater harmony.

2.2.2.1 THE ROME I REGULATION: KEY PROVISIONS AND IMPACT

Rome I, also known as the Rome Regulation, is a European Union regulation that unifies the conflict of laws rules of all 27 member states in the area of contracts (contractual obligations).[6]

Article 1(1) of the regulation states:

> This Regulation shall apply, in situations involving a Conflict of Laws, to contractual obligations in civil and commercial matters.

However, it specifically excludes certain areas. It does not apply to revenue, customs, or administrative matters, nor to issues relating to evidence and procedure. It also excludes several other topics, such as obligations arising from matrimonial property regimes, wills and successions, arbitration agreements, jurisdiction agreements, and some insurance contracts.[7]

In practice, this means that the European Union tells its member states: When your national courts handle a contractual dispute that involves more than one country, they must apply the law designated by this regulation, rather than their own national conflict of laws rules.

This approach goes beyond harmonization – it is actually unification. The Rome I Regulation creates a single, uniform set of conflict of laws rules for contracts, ensuring that all courts across the 27 member states apply the same legal principles to determine the applicable law in cross-border contractual matters.

6 Regulation EC n° 593/2008 of the European Parliament and of the Council of June 17, 2008, on the law applicable to contractual obligations.

7 See McParland, Michael, 2015, *The Rome I Regulation on the Law Applicable to Contractual Obligations*, Oxford University Press.

Imagine a situation where a French company signs a sales contract with a German company to deliver goods in Italy. If a dispute arises about the performance of the contract, the court must decide which country's law applies – French, German, or Italian. Under the Rome I Regulation, the court will apply the law chosen by the parties in the contract. If no law is chosen, the Regulation provides rules to identify the applicable law, often the law of the country where the seller has their habitual residence or where the contract is most closely connected.

2.2.2.2 THE ROME II REGULATION: EXPANDING THE LEGAL FRAMEWORK

Another important conflict of laws instrument is Rome II, the European Union regulation that governs conflicts of law in tort cases, also called non-contractual obligations.[8] There are also other EU regulations dealing with conflicts of law in areas such as bankruptcy and matrimonial matters.

According to Article 1(1) of the Rome II Regulation:

> This Regulation shall apply, in situations involving a Conflict of Laws, to non-contractual obligations in civil and commercial matters.

However, it does not apply to certain areas, for example, to revenue, customs, or administrative matters, or to the liability of the state for acts and omissions carried out in the exercise of state authority (*acta iure imperii*). Paragraphs 2 and 3 of Article 1 list additional exclusions.

For the regulation to apply, four key elements must be present: a situation involving a Conflict of Laws (that is, a cross-border element), a civil and commercial matter, a non-contractual obligation, and a non-excluded matter.[9] When these conditions are met, the Rome II Regulation provides the rules that determine which national law applies to non-contractual obligations, promoting greater consistency across all EU member states.

Imagine a Spanish tourist who causes a car accident in Portugal that injures a Portuguese resident. The case involves people from two different countries. Under the Rome II Regulation, the court will generally apply the law of the country where the damage occurred – in this example, Portuguese law – because that is where the harmful event took place.

In short, Rome I applies to cross-border contractual disputes, while Rome II applies to cross-border tort or liability cases.

2.2.3 Harmonizing Principles: Global Consensus on Applicable Law Criteria

Countries can agree on shared principles to determine which nation's law should apply in certain situations. The European Union provides a clear example of this through its regulations, which ensure that, no matter which EU country's court handles a case, the same rules are used to identify the applicable law. This does not mean that all national laws are identical – French contract law still differs from German contract law – but it guarantees that courts across the EU will apply the correct law consistently.

8 Regulation (EC) N° 864/2007 of the European Parliament and of the Council of July 11, 2007, on the law applicable to non-contractual obligations (Rome II).

9 See Dickinson, Andrew A., 2010, *The Rome II Regulation: The Law Applicable to Non-Contractual Obligations*, Oxford University Press.

For example, in a matrimonial case, a Spanish court might apply the law designated by the relevant EU regulation, such as the law of the country where the marriage took place or where the couple lived together. The unification of conflict of laws rules does not make all national laws the same; instead, it provides a common framework that brings predictability to which law will be applied. The diversity of national laws remains, but the process for determining the applicable law becomes uniform.

The European Union's objective was to establish a unified set of conflict of laws rules across its member states. Even though the world remains decentralized, without a single global legal system, this approach helps ensure that similar cases are treated consistently across the EU. By joining the Union, member states accepted these shared rules, even though doing so involved some limitation of their national sovereignty and possible changes to their existing domestic laws.

3 The Question "Which Law?" and the "When in Rome" Principle: Navigating Jurisdiction and Applicable Law

This section examines the key question of determining which law should apply when a case involves more than one jurisdiction. The "When in Rome" principle offers a useful way to approach such situations, helping courts and lawyers identify the most suitable law to apply according to the specific circumstances of each case.

3.1 Determining Applicable Law: The "When in Rome" Principle

Here, we examine the "When in Rome" principle, which holds that the law of the place where an event occurs generally governs its legal consequences. This principle guides courts in determining which country's law should apply in cross-border disputes, ensuring that decisions are grounded in the most relevant legal and geographical context.

3.1.1 Contextual Rules: Location-Based Legal Applicability

The applicable rules depend on where you are at the moment when the law becomes relevant. When no choice of law has been made, or when no specific conflict of laws rule exists, this general principle applies: the law of the place most closely connected to the situation governs it. This is known as the "When in Rome" or "territorial" principle. In other words, the legal matter – whether it concerns a contract, an injury, an inheritance, or a divorce – should be governed by the law of the country with which it has the closest connection.

Determining the law of the country most closely connected to a case is not always easy and must be done on a case-by-case basis. For this reason, states have created regulations and guidelines to help identify, for each major type of legal situation, the most relevant law and its associated connecting factors.

To decide which law applies, a conflict of laws rule is used. This rule is procedural rather than substantive and relies on a criterion of connection – a factual link that best identifies the law most appropriately related to the case. This reflects the "When in Rome" principle.

For example, imagine a French couple traveling in Portugal who are involved in a car accident in Lisbon with a Portuguese driver. Their car is registered in France. Two laws could potentially apply: French law, due to the nationality of the tourists and the car's registration, and Portuguese law, due to the location of the accident and the nationality of the other driver.

The task, then, is to choose between these two laws without arbitrariness, by identifying a connecting factor that can be applied consistently in similar cases. Possible connecting factors include the nationality of the parties, the place where the accident occurred, or the location of vehicle registration.

The purpose of the law on conflicts is to determine which connecting factor is the most appropriate for identifying the law applicable to a given situation. The conflict of laws rule serves as a mechanism for resolving such conflicts and has a unique character because it distributes legislative authority among different legal systems. To achieve this, it must locate and situate the facts of the international case within a specific legal framework.

3.1.2 Practical Examples and Illustrations

In the case of the French tourists who have a car accident in Portugal, the most specific and relevant factor is the place where the accident occurred. This reflects the "When in Rome" principle. The location of the accident is a clear and practical criterion for identifying the applicable law. Nationality and vehicle registration do not help resolve the Conflict of Laws, since the parties involved have different nationalities and their cars are registered in different countries. However, the accident itself happened in only one place – Lisbon, Portugal – which makes Portuguese law the applicable law.

The most relevant factor, therefore, is the place of occurrence of the accident, because the event could not have happened simultaneously in both France and Portugal. The conflict rule can thus be stated as follows: the applicable law is the law of the place where the event occurred. This rule is also reflected in the Hague Convention of May 4, 1971, on the Law Applicable to Traffic Accidents.[10] Article 3 of this Convention states that the applicable law is the internal law of the state where the accident occurred.

In this context, "the place of occurrence of the matter of facts" corresponds to "the place of occurrence of the tort" (*lex loci delicti*). Although "the matter of facts" could refer to different types of events (such as a contract being formed or performed), in this case, it clearly means the place where the accident – the tort – occurred. Other facts may still be considered by the judge, but they do not affect the primary connecting factor here.

Another example helps illustrate how Conflict of Laws operates. Suppose a French woman marries an American man in Paris, where they live. The law applicable to their marriage is the law of the place where the wedding was celebrated, that is, French law. The law governing their matrimonial property regime, in the absence of any specific choice by the couple, is the law of their first residence after the wedding, as stated in Article 4 of the Hague Convention of March 14, 1978, on Matrimonial Property Regimes.

10 See the Hague Convention of May 4, 1971, on the Law Applicable to Traffic Accidents (the "Traffic Accidents Convention") available at: http://www.hcch.net. According to the Hague Conference on Private International Law – which is the world organization for cross-border co-operation in Civil and Commercial matter – traffic accidents are among the most significant sources of non-contractual obligations globally. The increase in cross-border traffic and transport have led to a rise in traffic accidents involving international elements. These accidents are notable for two key reasons: in more than 99% of cases, they are (1) resolved outside the court system, and (2) primarily handled by insurers, often through established international arrangements. To determine liability, the nature and extent of damages, and the applicability of prescription and limitation rules, it is essential to establish the applicable law in advance and with certainty.

In France, some of the main conflict of laws rules are:[11]

- for property, the law of the place where the property is located;
- for legal facts, the law of the place where the facts occurred;
- for divorce, Article 309 of the Civil Code, and since June 21, 2012, the Rome III Regulation (EU Regulation No. 1259/2010 of 20 December 2010).

Article 309 of the French Civil Code provides that divorce and judicial separation are governed by French law:

- when both spouses are French nationals;
- when both spouses have their domicile in France;
- when no foreign law claims to apply, while French courts have jurisdiction over the case.

3.2 Contractual Autonomy: Choosing Governing Law

This subsection explores the principle of contractual autonomy, which allows the parties to a contract to freely choose the law that will govern their agreement. This choice plays an important role in shaping how the contract is interpreted, enforced, and ultimately resolved in the event of a dispute.

3.2.1 The U.S. Restatement and Its Implications

Let us now look at the Restatement, which is quite straightforward. It sets out a soft-law framework that defines how courts determine the law applicable to contractual matters.

Section 186 establishes the main rule: contractual issues are governed by the law chosen by the parties, as explained in Section 187.[12] If the parties do not make a choice, the applicable law

11 For contracts: Article 3 of the Rome Convention on contractual obligations, also known as the autonomy law, applies. Since December 17, 2009, this has been governed by Article 3 of the Rome I Regulation. For matrimonial regimes: Article 3 of the Hague Convention of March 14, 1978, allows a limited choice for spouses. According to Article 4, if the spouses do not specify their choice, the applicable law will be that of their first residence after the wedding, subject to Article 5, which provides for the exceptional application of the law of the spouses' common nationality. In tort: The applicable law is that of the place where the tort occurred, as per Article 4 of Regulation (EC) No. 864/2007 of July 11, 2007, on the law applicable to non-contractual obligations (Rome II).

12 Section 186: Applicable Law

Contractual issues are governed by the law chosen by the parties, in line with Section 187, or, if no choice is made, by the law selected according to Section 188.

Section 187: Law of the State Chosen by the Parties

1. The law of the state selected by the parties will be applied if the issue at hand could have been addressed by an explicit provision in their agreement.
2. The chosen state's law will be applied even if the issue could not have been directly addressed by the agreement, unless: (a) The chosen state has no significant relationship to the parties or the transaction and there is no other reasonable basis for the choice, or (b) Applying the chosen state's law would conflict with a fundamental policy of a state that has a materially greater interest in the issue and which, under Section 188, would be the applicable law if no effective choice had been made.
3. In the absence of a specific intention to the contrary, the reference is to the local law of the chosen state.

is determined under Section 188.[13] In short, Section 186 affirms that parties have the right to select the law that will govern their contract, and the court will apply that law within the limits set out in Section 187.

Section 187 concerns the law of the state chosen by the parties. It provides that the chosen law will be applied if the matter could have been addressed directly in the contract. Even when the issue could not have been explicitly covered, the chosen law will still be applied unless the chosen state has no meaningful connection to the parties or transaction, or applying it would violate a fundamental policy of another state with a stronger interest in the matter. In the absence of any special intent, the reference is to the local law of the chosen state.

If the parties do not select a governing law, Section 188 applies. It states that the applicable law will be that of the state with the most significant relationship to the transaction and the parties. Factors to consider include the place of contracting, negotiation, and performance, the location of the contract's subject matter, and the domicile or place of business of the parties. The weight of each factor depends on its relevance to the specific case. When the negotiation and performance occur in the same country, that country's law will generally govern.

These sections form the foundation of conflict of laws rules for contract cases. Each category of cases – tort, family, property – has its own corresponding rules.

From Section 186 alone, it is clear that parties have wide freedom to choose the governing law for their contracts. Whether this freedom is limited depends on the conflict of laws rules themselves. In practice, when drafting a contract, parties can choose the applicable law without having to predict which court will later hear the case. This is known as the principle of party autonomy (or *autonomie des parties* in French law).

For example, if a French seller and a German buyer agree that their sales contract will be governed by New York law, even though neither party is based there, this choice is valid as long as the matter could have been addressed in their agreement, such as delivery terms or packaging. If a dispute arises, the court will apply New York law, respecting the parties' autonomy.

If no governing law is chosen, the court will apply the law of the state most closely connected to the transaction, as described in Section 188. This approach ensures both contractual freedom and predictability, while maintaining fairness in cases where no explicit choice of law has been made.

Finally, within the European Union, the Rome I and Rome II Regulations have introduced uniform conflict of laws rules to reduce forum shopping and ensure that courts across member states apply consistent criteria for determining the applicable law.

13 Section 188: Law Governing in the Absence of Effective Choice by the Parties

1. The rights and duties concerning a contract issue are determined by the law of the state with the most significant relationship to the transaction and the parties, according to the principle stated in § 6.
2. If the parties do not make an effective choice of law (see Section 187), the contacts to consider for applying §6 include:

   (a) The place of contracting
   (b) The place of contract negotiation
   (c) The place of performance
   (d) The location of the contract's subject matter
   (e) The domicile, residence, nationality, place of incorporation, and place of business of the parties

   These contacts are to be assessed based on their relative significance to the issue.
3. If the place of negotiation and performance are the same state, its local law will usually be applied, unless otherwise specified.

3.2.2 Understanding Contractual Clauses and Legal Boundaries

The principle underlying party autonomy is that parties are generally free to contract about almost anything, and the law looks for exceptions to this freedom rather than the rule itself. For example, if I lend you money and charge an interest rate of 75%, such an agreement would usually be considered invalid in most legal systems. Therefore, the parties could not simply choose the law of a hypothetical country like Ruritania that allows such excessive interest, since this would go beyond the lawful limits of contractual freedom.

Section 187(2) of the Restatement explains that the law chosen by the parties will apply even if the issue could not have been explicitly addressed in their agreement, unless one of two exceptions applies:

(a) the chosen state has no substantial connection to the parties or the transaction, or
(b) applying the chosen law would violate a fundamental policy of another state that has a materially greater interest in the matter and would otherwise provide the applicable law under Section 188.

In other words, if the issue involves something that cannot normally be contracted about, the chosen law will only be accepted if it meets these conditions. Parties are free to choose any law for issues they can legitimately contract on, but for matters where freedom of contract is limited, their choice must have a reasonable connection to the transaction and must not undermine the core legal policies of another, more interested jurisdiction.

This framework shows that while party autonomy is broad, it is not absolute. It is restricted where fundamental principles of justice or public policy are at stake. This limitation is essential to understanding how courts evaluate whether a chosen law can validly govern a contract.

Section 188, on the other hand, deals with situations where no effective choice of law has been made. It provides that the applicable law is that of the state with the most significant relationship to the transaction and the parties. To identify this state, courts consider several connecting factors: the place of contracting, the place of negotiation, the place of performance, the location of the contract's subject matter, and the domicile or nationality of the parties.

These factors are assessed in light of their relevance to the dispute. This flexible approach allows courts to adapt to the specifics of each case, though it may lead to less predictability compared to more rigid systems, such as the one established under the Rome I Regulation in the European Union.

In summary, under the Restatement, parties generally have the freedom to choose the law governing their contract, but this autonomy is limited where fundamental public policies intervene. If the chosen law cannot be applied, or if no law was chosen at all, the court will determine the applicable law by identifying the jurisdiction with the most significant relationship to the transaction, as outlined in Section 188.

Imagine a contract between two companies: a French fashion designer based in Paris and an American retailer based in New York. They sign a contract for the sale of luxury clothing, and they choose the law of a small island nation called "Zandora" – a hypothetical jurisdiction – known for having very relaxed commercial laws.

Under their agreement, if the retailer cancels the order, it must pay a penalty equal to 300% of the contract's total value. When a dispute arises, and the retailer refuses to pay, the designer insists that Zandorian law applies because it allows such a clause.

However, when the case reaches a New York court, the judge examines the situation under Section 187(2) of the Restatement. The court finds that: (a) the chosen state, Zandora, has no substantial connection to either the parties or the transaction (neither company operates or delivers goods there) and (b) applying Zandorian law would violate a fundamental policy of New York, where penalty clauses of this kind are considered unenforceable because they are excessive and contrary to public policy.

As a result, the court refuses to apply Zandorian law. Instead, it applies the law of the state with the most significant relationship to the contract, under Section 188 – in this case, likely New York law, since the retailer is based there and the goods were to be delivered there.

This example illustrates that while the parties are free to choose the governing law, that freedom is limited. The chosen law must have a reasonable connection to the transaction and must not conflict with fundamental public policies of a more interested jurisdiction.

3.2.3 A Quick Guide to Navigating Rome I Regulations

As mentioned earlier, we now turn to the Rome I Regulation, which can be quite detailed. For our purposes, we will focus on its essential points. Adopted by the European Union in 2008, Rome I provides uniform rules for courts across the 27 member states to determine which law applies to cross-border contracts, much like the Restatement does in the United States.

Rather than covering preliminary articles, we will go directly to Article 3, which is central to understanding the Regulation.

Article 3 establishes the principle of freedom of choice. It provides that a contract is governed by the law chosen by the parties, and this choice must be clearly expressed in the contract or clearly demonstrated by its terms or the circumstances of the case. The parties may choose one law for the entire contract or different laws for different parts of it – for example, applying French law to one section and German law to another. This rule gives the parties broad autonomy.

If the parties do not make a choice, Article 4 specifies how the applicable law is determined, depending on the type of contract. For instance: (a) a contract for the sale of goods is governed by the law of the seller's habitual residence; (b) a service contract is governed by the law of the service provider's habitual residence; (c) a contract concerning immovable property (real estate) is governed by the law of the country where the property is located; (d) a short-term private lease (up to six months) is governed by the law of the landlord's habitual residence, provided the tenant is a natural person living in the same country; and (e) A franchise agreement is governed by the law of the franchisee's habitual residence.

Article 4(3) adds flexibility by allowing the law of another country to apply if the contract is more closely connected to that country than to those indicated by the standard rules. Article 4(4) further provides that if the applicable law cannot be determined under the preceding paragraphs, the law of the country most closely connected to the contract will apply.

Most jurisdictions recognize the principle of party autonomy but also impose limits. Article 3(3) of Rome I introduces an important restriction: if all elements of a situation are connected with a country other than the one whose law has been chosen, the choice cannot override the mandatory rules of that other country. In other words, parties cannot avoid the application of mandatory provisions by simply choosing a foreign law that is more favorable to them.

In essence, while parties enjoy significant freedom to select the governing law under Rome I, this freedom is not absolute. When key elements of the contract are tied to a particular country, that country's mandatory laws take precedence. This safeguard ensures fairness and prevents abuse of the freedom of choice principle.

Imagine an Italian company and a Spanish company sign a contract for the sale of industrial equipment to be manufactured in Milan and delivered in Barcelona. In their agreement, they choose Swedish law as the governing law because Sweden has very business-friendly regulations.

Later, a dispute arises over defective goods, and the Spanish buyer takes the matter to a Spanish court. The court examines the situation under Article 3(3) of the Rome I Regulation. It notes that all elements of the situation are connected with Italy and Spain – the seller is Italian, the buyer is Spanish, the goods were produced in Italy, and the delivery took place in Spain.

Because the contract has no real connection to Sweden, and all relevant elements are linked to other EU member states, the court decides that the parties' choice of Swedish law cannot override the mandatory rules of Italian or Spanish law. The court therefore applies Italian law, as the law of the seller's habitual residence under Article 4(1)(a), since it governs contracts for the sale of goods.

This example neatly shows how party autonomy under Article 3 can be limited by Article 3(3) when all the relevant facts point to another country. It also illustrates how Article 4 works when no valid or effective choice of law can be applied.

4 Legal Terminology and Core Principles

Understanding the basic concepts and terminology of Conflict of Laws is essential for dealing with legal disputes that involve more than one country. This section offers an overview of the main terms and explains the key principles that define how courts handle cases with cross-border elements.

4.1 Essential Terminology in Conflict of Laws

Most of the definitions presented in what follows are drawn from the *Glossary of Conflict of Laws* compiled by Professor William Tetley, available on the McGill University Faculty of Law website.[14] By distinguishing Key Conventions and Regulations from Core Concepts and Terminology, this section aims to make it easier for readers to recognize and understand each element separately.

4.1.1 Key Conventions and Regulations

This part introduces the main international conventions and regulations that shape the field of Conflict of Laws. These instruments provide common rules for determining jurisdiction, recognizing and enforcing judgments, and identifying the applicable law in cross-border disputes. Together, they promote legal certainty, cooperation among states, and fairness in international legal proceedings.

Brussels Convention (1968) – Formally known as the *Convention on Jurisdiction and the Enforcement of Judgments in Civil and Commercial Matters*, this treaty was adopted on September 27, 1968, and entered into force on February 1, 1973. It established uniform rules for determining jurisdiction and for recognizing and enforcing judgments among member states of the European Community. Its purpose was to ensure consistency and predictability in cross-border civil and commercial litigation within Europe. As of March 1, 2002, the Convention was replaced – except in Denmark – by the EC Regulation 44/2001.

14 McGill University, Faculty of Law, 2004, *Glossary of Maritime Law Terms*, 2nd ed., online. Available at: https://www.mcgill.ca.

EC Regulation 44/2001 – Officially titled the *Regulation on Jurisdiction and the Recognition and Enforcement of Judgments in Civil and Commercial Matters*, this Regulation was adopted on December 22, 2000. It continued the objectives of the Brussels Convention by providing a unified legal framework across EU member states for jurisdiction and the mutual recognition of judgments. It replaced the 1968 Brussels Convention for all EU countries except Denmark and strengthened legal cooperation within the European judicial area.

Rome Convention (1980) – The *Convention on the Law Applicable to Contractual Obligations*, which entered into force on April 1, 1991, aimed to harmonize rules determining the applicable law for contracts with cross-border elements. It granted parties the freedom to choose the governing law for their contracts and provided rules for identifying the applicable law when no choice was made. The Convention was later replaced by the Rome I Regulation (Regulation No. 593/2008), which updated and unified these principles within the European Union.

New York Convention (1958) – The *Convention on the Recognition and Enforcement of Foreign Arbitral Awards*, signed on June 10, 1958, is one of the most important international treaties in arbitration law. It ensures that arbitration agreements and foreign arbitral awards are recognized and enforceable in the courts of its member states. The Convention plays a crucial role in promoting international commercial arbitration as an effective method of resolving cross-border disputes.

UNCITRAL Model Law (1985) – The *Model Law on International Commercial Arbitration* was adopted by the United Nations Commission on International Trade Law (UNCITRAL) on June 21, 1985. It provides a standardized framework for national laws on international arbitration, encouraging consistency and fairness in arbitral proceedings worldwide. Many countries have incorporated their principles into their domestic legislation.

Hague Conference on Private International Law – Established in 1893, the Hague Conference is an intergovernmental organization dedicated to the progressive unification of Private International Law. It has produced more than 35 conventions covering areas such as family law, civil procedure, international child abduction, and the recognition of foreign judgments. Its goal is to facilitate international cooperation and ensure legal certainty in cross-border relations.

4.1.2 Core Concepts and Terminology

This part introduces the fundamental concepts and terms used in the study of Conflict of Laws. Understanding this vocabulary is essential for analyzing how courts determine applicable laws, jurisdiction, and the recognition of foreign judgments in cross-border disputes. Each definition is accompanied by a simple example to illustrate its practical meaning.

Choice-of-Forum: The rules and principles used to identify the most appropriate court or jurisdiction to hear a case. This may also be called a choice-of-court or choice-of-jurisdiction clause. For example, the same contract states that any dispute will be resolved in Paris courts.

Choice-of-Law: The set of principles and rules used by courts to determine which country's law applies to a legal issue in a cross-border dispute. For example, a French company and a German company sign a contract and choose French law to govern their agreement.

Connecting Factors (Contacts): Specific facts or links that connect a dispute, transaction, or event to a particular legal system or jurisdiction (for example, nationality, place of residence, or location of a contract's performance). For example, a car accident in Italy between a Spanish driver and an Italian driver links the case to Italian law because the accident happened there.

Dépeçage: The technique of applying different laws to different aspects of the same legal dispute, such as using one country's law for contractual issues and another's for tort liability. For example, a contract's validity is judged under English law, but its performance is judged under U.S. law.

Dicey, Albert Venn: A leading English legal scholar known for his major contributions to the study of Conflict of Laws, particularly through his works *Conflict of Laws* and *Introduction to the Study of the Law of the Constitution.*

Domicile: The place where a person has their permanent home or principal establishment and intends to remain or return to when absent. For example, a person works abroad but keeps their main home and family in France; their domicile is in France.

Due Process: A fundamental principle ensuring fairness in legal proceedings and guaranteeing that parties receive proper notice and an opportunity to be heard before a court decision is made. For example, a defendant must be informed of the case and given time to respond before judgment is issued.

Forum: The court or tribunal where a case is brought and decided. The appropriate forum depends on the jurisdictional rules and procedural laws in place. For example, a civil dispute between two French residents is heard before a court in Paris.

Forum Conveniens: principle allowing a court to exercise jurisdiction when it is the most appropriate or convenient forum for resolving the dispute. For example, a Belgian court agrees to hear a dispute because all evidence and witnesses are located in Belgium.

Forum Necessitatis: A principle that allows a court to hear a case when no other forum is available, and there is a sufficient connection between the dispute and the state. For example, a French court hears a dispute between two foreign companies because no other country's court is willing to take the case.

Forum Non Conveniens: A principle allowing a court, even when it has jurisdiction, to decline hearing a case if another forum is clearly more suitable for resolving it. For example, a U.S. court dismisses a case because it should be heard in Canada, where the accident occurred.

Forum Shopping: The practice of choosing a jurisdiction primarily to gain an advantage, often viewed as improper if it avoids the court that would normally be competent. For example, a company files a lawsuit in a country known for higher damage awards to obtain a more favorable result.

Governmental Interest Analysis: A method of determining the applicable law by identifying which state has the strongest policy interest in having its law applied to the dispute. For example, a U.S. court applies California law instead of Texas law because California has a stronger public interest in protecting consumers.

Incoterms 2000: Internationally standardized trade terms published by the International Chamber of Commerce, used to define responsibilities between buyers and sellers in contracts for the sale of goods. For example, a contract specifies "FOB Hamburg," meaning the buyer assumes responsibility once the goods are loaded on the ship in Hamburg.

Jurisdiction: The legal authority of a court to hear and decide a case, as well as the scope of a state's legislative and judicial power. For example, a Spanish court has jurisdiction to hear a case because the defendant resides in Spain.

Jurisdiction Clause: A contractual clause specifying which court or courts have the authority to resolve disputes arising under the agreement. For example, a contract provides that all disputes will be submitted to the courts of London.

Lex Fori: The law of the forum, meaning the domestic law of the court where the case is being heard. For example, a French court applies French procedural law to a dispute even if the contract involves foreign parties.

Lex Loci Contractus: The law of the place where a contract was concluded. For example, a contract signed in Germany is governed by German law.

Lex Loci Damni: The law of the place where the damage or injury occurred. For example, a person injured in Italy sues for damages under Italian law.

Lex Loci Delicti: The law of the place where a tort or wrongful act was committed. For example, a traffic accident in Spain is governed by Spanish tort law.

Lex Loci Solutionis: The law of the place where a contract is to be performed. For example, a contract requiring goods to be delivered in Portugal is governed by Portuguese law.

Lex Maritima: The body of customary maritime law governing navigation and maritime commerce. For example, a dispute over international shipping routes is resolved using established maritime customs.

Lex Mercatoria: The body of customary commercial law developed by merchants in medieval Europe, now reflected in modern international trade practices. For example, two companies use international trade customs, such as ICC Incoterms, to settle their dispute instead of relying on national law.

Mandatory Rules: Legal provisions that cannot be excluded or modified by contract because they serve essential social, economic, or public policy purposes. For example, a contract cannot waive the minimum wage laws of a country.

Most Significant Connection/Most Significant Relationship: A guiding principle under which courts apply the law of the state that has the strongest and most meaningful connection to the facts of the case. For example, in a dispute between a U.S. and a French company, French law applies because the contract was mainly performed in France.

Obiter Dictum: A statement made by a judge in a legal opinion that is not essential to the decision and therefore not binding as precedent, though it may be persuasive. For example, a judge notes that another law might apply in future similar cases, but since it is not central to the current ruling, it remains a non-binding comment.

Proper Law: The law that has the closest and most genuine connection to a case, determining the rights and obligations of the parties. For example, a shipping contract between British companies operating in London is governed by English law.

Properly Applicable Law: The law that most appropriately governs a contract or tort, based on its closest and most real connection to the situation. For example, a cross-border tort involving French and Spanish parties is governed by Spanish law, as the accident occurred there.

Public Order/Public Policy: A principle that allows courts to refuse to apply foreign laws or enforce foreign judgments that would violate the fundamental moral or legal principles of the forum state. For example, a court refuses to recognize a foreign contract involving child labor because it violates public policy.

Recognition of Foreign Judgments: The process by which a court accepts and gives legal effect to a judgment rendered by a court of another country. For example, a French court enforces a valid judgment issued by a German court.

Renvoi: A principle where a court, applying the conflict rules of another state, refers back to the law (or conflict rules) of that state to resolve the conflict. For example, a French court applies Italian law, but Italian conflict rules refer back to French law, so French law is used.

Residence: The place where a person actually lives, which may differ from their domicile if the stay is temporary or lacks an intention to remain. For example, a Brazilian student studying in Germany has her residence in Germany but her domicile in Brazil.

4.2 Balancing Certainty and Flexibility: The Law Market

In legal theory and practice, achieving a balance between certainty and flexibility is essential. Certainty ensures predictability and stability in legal outcomes, while flexibility allows the law to adapt to evolving social and economic realities. This section examines how legal systems maintain this balance and introduces the concept of the law market, where parties strategically choose jurisdictions and laws that best serve their interests.

4.2.1 Striking the Balance: Certainty, Predictability, and Flexibility

A central challenge in Conflict of Laws lies in finding the right balance between certainty and flexibility. Certainty ensures clarity about which law governs a legal situation – such as a contract – and which court has the authority to resolve disputes. Flexibility, on the other hand, allows parties to choose both the applicable law and the forum for resolving potential disagreements.

Private International Law must remain clear, practical, and fair to inspire confidence among litigants and uphold justice. Its core objectives are to protect the parties' legitimate expectations, provide predictability in legal outcomes, and ensure fairness in judicial decisions.

Consistency is especially important when several courts may become involved in the same cross-border dispute. Harmonizing and coordinating outcomes among different legal systems not only promotes justice for the parties but also strengthens mutual trust and cooperation between states within the international legal community.

In this sense, Conflict of Laws functions as a stabilizing mechanism in a fragmented legal landscape. By offering structured solutions to determine jurisdiction and applicable law, it prevents arbitrary results and reduces the risk of contradictory judgments. At the same time, it preserves space for party autonomy and judicial discretion, allowing courts to adapt legal rules to the specific circumstances of each case. This dual function – ensuring order while accommodating diversity – explains why Conflict of Laws is indispensable in modern legal practice, where cross-border interactions are increasingly common.

4.2.2 Exploring the Concept of the Law Market

In their 2009 book *The Law Market*, Erin A. O'Hara and Larry E. Ribstein[15] describe how individuals and companies can effectively "shop" for legal systems just as they shop for products or services. This growing mobility forces governments and states to consider the broader consequences of their legal and regulatory choices.[16]

They illustrate this with the example of a commercial transport operator conducting business between the United States and other countries. Although the U.S. Congress and California's Legislature have enacted regulations for companies operating in California, the operator has structured the business strategically: it is incorporated in Delaware, headquartered in Virginia, registers its ships in the Cook Islands, and holds assets in the Cayman Islands. The company's contracts specify that employee disputes must be litigated in Virginia state courts, while customer disputes go to arbitration in the United Kingdom. This arrangement enables the company to avoid many California and federal rules, including those related to taxation, labor, environmental protection, and antitrust regulation. Faced with this type of jurisdictional flexibility, U.S. and state regulators must act carefully to avoid driving such businesses away entirely.

O'Hara and Ribstein highlight how this legal mobility creates a "market for law," where parties choose jurisdictions that best fit their interests. They note that uncertainty about which law applies can be extremely costly. Judges and litigants must know which law governs a dispute,

15 Erin A. O'Hara is an American legal scholar specializing in Conflict of Laws, law and economics, and contract theory. She has served as a professor and dean at Vanderbilt University Law School, where her work focuses on how individuals and businesses use legal rules across jurisdictions to structure their relationships efficiently. Larry E. Ribstein (1946–2011) was a prominent American law professor at the University of Illinois College of Law. He was widely recognized for his research on business associations, jurisdictional competition, and the economic analysis of law. Ribstein was one of the leading figures in developing the concept of the "law market," examining how parties choose legal systems in a globalized economy.

16 See Ribstein, Larry E. and O'Hara, Erin, 2009, *The Law Market*, Oxford University Press.

and individuals and businesses need that same clarity to plan their affairs. For example, a company negotiating a contract must anticipate whether any provisions might be invalid, and if so, decide whether to adjust the terms, select another applicable law, or abandon the deal altogether. Similarly, individuals making decisions about marriage, divorce, property, wills, or contracts must understand the governing legal framework.

To reduce this uncertainty, O'Hara and Ribstein propose that clear and predictable rules be established to identify the governing law in each category of case. However, they also acknowledge that this solution raises tensions: while governments may be reluctant to allow parties complete freedom in choosing their governing law, in practice, courts frequently respect such contractual choices.

5 Legal Outcomes and Mandatory Regulations

This section explores how legal outcomes are influenced by the interaction between Conflict of Laws rules and mandatory regulations. It highlights the tension between flexibility and strict public policy, showing how these factors affect both the predictability of court decisions and the freedom of parties to choose the law governing their agreements.

5.1 Outcome-Driven Rules in Conflict of Laws

In Conflict of Laws, the resolution of disputes often depends on rules that determine which jurisdiction's law applies to a particular case. Understanding these rules is essential for addressing complex cross-border legal issues. This subsection explores the interaction between substantive and procedural conflict rules, both of which play a key role in shaping how international and interstate disputes are resolved.

5.1.1 Distinguishing Between Substantive and Procedural Conflict Rules

Conflict of laws rules raise an important question: are they substantive or procedural? The answer is that they are a hybrid of both. They are procedural because every court must apply its own conflict of laws rules. For example, if a French court hears a contract case, it will apply French conflict of laws rules, such as the Rome I Regulation. In this sense, the rules belong to the forum's procedure.

However, unlike most procedural rules, conflict of laws rules directly affect the outcome of a case. Ordinary procedural rules – like whether witnesses are cross-examined or whether a jury is used – are usually considered neutral and not outcome-determinative. Conflict of laws rules, on the other hand, determine *which* country's law applies, and since laws differ between countries, this choice can substantially change the result.

For example, imagine a German court dealing with a personal injury case involving a German tourist who was injured in Spain. The court must apply its own conflict of laws rules (the procedural aspect) to decide which country's law governs the claim.

If the German conflict rules point to Spanish law, the case will be judged according to Spanish tort law, which might calculate compensation based on fixed statutory limits. But if the rules instead lead to the application of German law, the victim could receive a higher amount of damages or different types of compensation, such as for emotional suffering.

Although the process of determining which law applies is procedural – since the German court is applying its own conflict rules – it directly influences the outcome. The difference between Spanish and German law could significantly change the amount of compensation, showing that the rule is outcome-determinative.

5.1.2 The Determinative Nature of Legal Choices

The choice of law is what lawyers call "outcome determinative," meaning it directly influences the result of a case. Since the law applied can change the outcome, conflict of laws rules are considered a hybrid – they are procedural because courts apply their own rules to decide which law governs, but they are also substantive because that decision shapes the result.

For example, imagine a dispute between a New York company and a French company over a contract that states French law will apply. When the case comes before a New York court, the judge must first decide whether to honor this choice of law clause. That decision is procedural – it concerns which law to apply – but it also has clear substantive consequences. Applying French law rather than New York law could lead to a different interpretation of the contract, different remedies, and even a different winner.

Thus, while the choice of law operates through procedural mechanisms, it ultimately affects the substance of the case, illustrating why Conflict of Laws occupies a unique position between procedure and substance.

This dual nature explains why courts treat choice-of-law issues with particular care: a seemingly technical determination can reshape the entire litigation. Different legal systems may offer broader or narrower contractual remedies, impose varying limitation periods, or interpret key clauses differently. As a result, parties often devote significant effort to arguing for the application of one legal system over another. Understanding this interplay between procedure and substance is essential for predicting legal outcomes and developing sound litigation strategies in cross-border disputes.

5.2 Mandatory Laws and Public Policy: Limits on Freedom of Contract

In Conflict of Laws, parties usually enjoy considerable freedom to structure their contracts as they wish, but this autonomy is restricted by mandatory rules and public policy considerations. These limitations ensure that agreements comply with fundamental legal norms and protect the broader interests of society. This subsection examines how such constraints operate and explores the tension between striving for uniform legal principles and the diverse ways they are interpreted and applied across different jurisdictions.

5.2.1 Key Limitations on Party Autonomy

Mandatory laws are legal rules that cannot be avoided or modified by agreement. They bind the parties regardless of their contractual choices and ensure compliance with essential legal and public policy standards. For instance, a French court must apply the mandatory rules of a country that has a close connection to the case, even if the parties have chosen French law and the dispute itself has limited links to France.

This principle guarantees that minimum legal protections are upheld and that certain fundamental interests – such as consumer rights, labor standards, or environmental regulations – are not undermined by private agreements. The Rome I Regulation clearly states that such overriding mandatory provisions must always be applied, regardless of the law chosen by the parties, to protect public interests and preserve legal coherence within the European Union.

In practice, this means that party autonomy, although central in conflict of laws, is not absolute. Courts must balance contractual freedom with the need to uphold essential societal values. Mandatory rules, therefore, act as safeguards, ensuring that no agreement can deprive a party of core protections or allow conduct contrary to public policy. They also promote fairness and predictability by signaling in advance which norms will prevail, regardless of the law otherwise applicable to the contract.

5.2.2 Uniformity in Law vs. Divergence in Application

The choice of law may be unified, but the laws themselves remain distinct. This distinction captures the essence of Conflict of Laws and reflects the central theme of *Law in a World of Multiple Legal Orders:* modern legal issues often involve several jurisdictions and the interaction of different national laws. The Rome I Regulation, a key instrument of European Union law, illustrates this principle. Its purpose is not to make all member states' contract laws identical but to harmonize the method used to determine which law governs a cross-border contract dispute.

While creating a single, unified body of substantive contract law for all EU countries might seem appealing, it faces serious challenges. National legal traditions are deeply rooted, and countries like France, with its historic Civil Code, are reluctant to abandon their legal identity for a common European Code. Legal practitioners, too, are often attached to familiar national systems and wary of change. Although uniform regulations have been achieved in certain technical fields – such as aviation safety – replacing entire national legal systems would raise issues of sovereignty, identity, and practicality.

For these reasons, the EU has chosen to harmonize the *choice of law* process instead of the substantive laws themselves. This means that while each member state maintains its own legal rules, all courts in the EU apply the same criteria to determine which country's law governs a given dispute. The result is a more predictable and coherent system for resolving cross-border contract cases. Rome I thus provides a unified legal framework for determining applicable law across Europe while preserving the diversity of national laws – a balanced and pragmatic solution that promotes legal certainty without sacrificing national legal traditions.

5.2.3 Governing Law Choices and Their Connections to Jurisdiction

A contract is generally governed by the law chosen by the parties – a principle known as party autonomy, which forms the cornerstone of the Rome I Regulation. However, this freedom is limited by an important safeguard: if the contract is more closely connected to another country, that country's mandatory laws take precedence over the chosen law.

For example, if parties choose French law for their contract but all key elements – such as the buyer, seller, and goods – are located in Germany, German mandatory rules will apply. This is because certain German laws, like those on consumer protection or contract fairness, cannot be avoided by private agreement. Similarly, if German law prohibits interest rates above 8% and the contract provides for a 10% rate under French law, a French court would still apply the German limit, as mandatory rules override party choice.

The Rome I Regulation also improves predictability by providing default rules for determining the applicable law when the parties have not made a choice. For instance, a sales contract with no chosen law is governed by the law of the seller's habitual residence. However, if the contract is clearly more closely connected to another country – for example, where all deliveries and payments occur – then the law of that country will apply instead.

This approach balances flexibility with fairness, ensuring that the law applied corresponds to the contract's most significant connection. Moreover, Rome I includes specific consumer protection rules: when a consumer contracts with a professional, the Regulation guarantees that the consumer cannot lose the protection of the mandatory laws of their home country, even if another law has been chosen.

5.2.4 Mandatory Rules and Public Policy

Article 9 of the Rome I Regulation allows the court of the forum (the country where legal proceedings take place) to apply its own law if it considers that law to be an overriding mandatory rule. This means that even when a contract is governed by a foreign law, the forum can still apply its own essential rules if they are considered crucial to its legal or social order.[17]

For example, a contract governed by German law might still be subject to certain French mandatory provisions if the dispute is brought before a French court. France may apply its own overriding rules – such as those related to labor protections, commercial restrictions, or consumer safety – because these reflect fundamental national values that cannot be ignored, even in cross-border cases.

Article 21 reinforces this idea by allowing the forum to refuse the application of a foreign law if it is manifestly incompatible with its public policy (*ordre public*). For instance, if applying a foreign law would lead to an outcome that contradicts basic principles of justice or morality in the forum state, the court can reject it.

It is important to distinguish between these two concepts: overriding mandatory rules requires the application of certain domestic laws, while public policy considerations prevent the application of foreign laws that violate essential national principles.

As Monika Pauknerová,[18] a Czech professor of International Law and arbitrator, explains, mandatory rules cannot be waived by agreement and are binding within their legal system. In international cases, additional layers of mandatory rules exist – such as overriding mandatory rules that take precedence regardless of the chosen law. Public policy rules, by contrast, act as a safeguard, ensuring that foreign laws are not applied when they conflict with the forum's core values.

The Rome I Regulation thus seeks to balance certainty and flexibility: it provides a predictable framework for determining the applicable law while allowing exceptions in cases where overriding mandatory rules or public policy demand it. This reflects a distinct European approach, which favors harmonization and legal certainty, in contrast to the American system, which focuses more on applying the law of the state most closely connected to the dispute.

Ultimately, this framework demonstrates the delicate balance that international private law strives to achieve – ensuring both consistency across jurisdictions and respect for national sovereignty and fundamental principles.

Conclusion

In exploring the complexities of Conflict of Laws, it becomes evident that this field does not provide universal solutions, but instead requires a careful balancing of competing interests and principles in a world of multiple legal orders.

This chapter has delved into the nuanced mechanisms and regulations governing the choice of law in various legal contexts. We have examined how the Rome I Regulation attempts to harmonize the choice of law within the European Union, providing a framework that respects party autonomy while acknowledging the necessity of mandatory rules and public policy exceptions. By focusing on the principles of party autonomy and the protection of overriding mandatory rules, the Rome I Regulation seeks to offer a balance between flexibility and certainty in cross-border contract disputes.

17 See Zarra, Gabriele, 2022, "Testing the Distinction Between Public Policy and Overriding Mandatory Rules," in *Imperativeness in Private International Law*, T.M.C. Asser Press, The Hague, online. https://doi.org/10.1007/978-94-6265-499-0_2.

18 Monika Pauknerová is a professor at Charles University in Prague, specializing in Private International Law, European law, and arbitration. She has authored around 150 publications and was elected to the Board of Directors of UNIDROIT in 2013.

The discussion has also highlighted the challenges inherent in applying these rules across multiple jurisdictions. The interplay between overriding mandatory rules and public policy underscores the need for careful consideration of both domestic and international legal principles. This approach reflects a broader philosophical stance within the European legal framework, aiming to achieve a balance between uniformity and respect for national legal traditions.

The practical implications of these principles demonstrate the complexity of navigating a legal landscape where multiple systems intersect. Whether dealing with mandatory rules that transcend borders or public policy considerations that safeguard fundamental values, the resolution of legal disputes often requires a nuanced approach that respects both the letter of the law and the underlying principles of justice.

As we conclude this chapter, it is clear that Conflict of Laws is fundamentally about managing the diverse and sometimes competing legal norms that arise in our increasingly interconnected world. The art of balancing these interests requires not only a deep understanding of legal doctrines but also a sensitivity to the broader implications of legal decisions in a pluralistic legal environment.

Thus, the study of Conflict of Laws remains an essential endeavor for legal professionals, policymakers, and scholars alike, offering insights into how we can effectively navigate and harmonize the complex interplay of multiple legal systems.

Selected Bibliography

Berman, P. S., 2014, *Global Legal Pluralism: A Jurisprudence of Law Beyond Borders*, Cambridge University Press, 358 pages.

Bermann, G. A., 2017, *International Arbitration and Private International Law* (1st ed.), Martinus Nijhoff, 644 pages.

Borchers, P., 2020, *Conflicts in a Nutshell* (5th ed.), West Academic Publishing, 465 pages.

Briggs, A., 2024, *The Conflict of Laws* (5th ed.), Oxford University Press, 480 pages.

Cohen, E. S., 2024, *Power and Pluralism in International Law: Private International Law and Globalization* (1st ed.), Routledge, 220 pages.

Ferrari, F., & Fernández Arroyo, D. P., (Eds.), 2019, *Private International Law: Contemporary Challenges and Continuing Relevance* (Elgar Monographs in Private International Law), Edward Elgar Publishing, 520 pages.

Harding, M., 2014, *Conflict of Laws* (5th ed.), Routledge, 368 pages.

Hatzimihail, N. E., 2021, *Preclassical Conflict of Laws*, Cambridge University Press, 642 pages.

Hay, P., Borchers, P., & Freer, R., 2021, *Conflict of Laws, Private International Law, Cases and Materials* (University Casebook Series) (16th ed.), Foundation Press, 1325 pages.

Muir Watt, H., Bíziková, L., Brandão de Oliveira, A., & Fernández Arroyo, D. P., (Eds.), 2019, *Global Private International Law: Adjudication Without Frontiers* (1st ed.), Edward Elgar Publishing Ltd, 640 pages.

Nafziger, J., Telesetsky, A., & Nanda, V., 2022, *Private International Law: Avoiding and Resolving Conflict of Laws*, Carolina Academic Press, 984 pages.

Peari, S., 2018, *The Foundation of Choice of Law: Choice and Equality*, Oxford University Press, 342 pages.

Roosevelt III, K., 2022, *Conflict of Laws (Concepts and Insights)* (3rd ed.), Foundation Press, 273 pages.

Symeonides, S. C., 2016, *Choice of Law*, Oxford University Press, 840 pages.

Varesis, F., 2024, *Private International Law and Arbitral Jurisdiction* (1st ed.), Routledge, 260 pages.

8 The Transplant Debate

Why can't the laws that guarantee British liberties be adopted elsewhere?
Voltaire, *Letters on the English* (1734)

Legal norms – including laws, concepts, and even methods of legal reasoning – frequently migrate across borders, shaping foreign legal systems and fostering both convergence and the blending of legal traditions. This cross-border movement of legal norms is commonly referred to as *legal transplants*, a term that captures the transnational circulation of legal norms and institutions. Despite numerous historical and contemporary examples, our understanding of how and why legal transplants occur remains limited. While individual cases – such as Napoleon's dissemination of the French Civil Code across conquered territories, or the influence of the German Civil Code on Japan's legal modernization – illustrate the phenomenon, research on the mechanisms, contexts, and long-term effects of legal transplants remains underdeveloped.

In 1748, Montesquieu argued in *L'Esprit des lois* that laws should be tailored to each country's specific context, including its form of government, geography, climate, religion, history, and culture. According to Montesquieu's view, it would be rare for a legal system that works well in one society to be equally suitable for another.

Voltaire, on the other hand, expressed admiration for the British legal system in his 1734 *Lettres philosophiques* (*Letters on the English*).[1] In this text, Voltaire asks, "Why can't the laws that guarantee British liberties be adopted elsewhere?" This question reflects Voltaire's belief that the British system offers greater protection for individual freedoms and rational governance compared to other European regimes at the time.

The 19th and early 20th centuries witnessed widespread legal transplants, particularly through colonization and imperialism, when powerful states imposed their legal systems on the territories they controlled. In many cases, legal norms and institutions were transferred alongside military and political domination, shaping the development of legal systems in colonies and newly formed states.

In the 21st century, the nature of legal transplants has continued to evolve. Rather than being imposed through conquest or colonization, contemporary legal transplants are often facilitated by globalization, international development agencies, trade agreements, and the growing influence of International Law and transnational legal networks. Legal norms now frequently migrate through voluntary reform efforts, global governance institutions, and digital dissemination of laws and jurisprudence. The use of foreign legal models in areas such as constitutional

1 A series of essays written by Voltaire based on his experiences living in Great Britain between 1726 and 1729.

DOI: 10.4324/9781003393047-11

engineering, environmental regulation, data protection, and human rights reflects a more interconnected legal world where legal borrowing is often strategic and collaborative, though still contested.

In this chapter, we examine the ongoing debate surrounding legal transplants and the various factors that shape their success or failure. We begin by defining the concept of legal transplants and related terms such as legal borrowing and cross-fertilization, illustrated through key historical examples (Section 1). Next, we explore the theoretical debate over their legitimacy and effectiveness, which gained prominence following two influential but opposing theories published in 1974 (Section 2). Finally, we assess the core conditions necessary for a legal transplant to operate effectively in a different legal and cultural context, and consider the increasing role that foreign legal precedents play in contemporary judicial reasoning (Section 3).

1 Understanding Legal Transplants: Definitions and Concepts

We can define a legal transplant as the transfer of a rule – not only statutory rules, but also institutions, legal concepts, and structures – from one country, referred to as the donor, to another, referred to as the recipient. This process occurs almost every day in legal practice.

Jörg Fedtke, Professor of Comparative Law at Tulane University, highlights that any area of law may be subject to legal transplants. He writes that "foreign ideas have been copied in most areas of private, administrative, constitutional, social security and even criminal law." He further explains that "the process can involve both single provisions and large portions of a statute. In exceptional cases (such as the French Code civil of 1804), even entire codifications have been taken as models by other countries." According to Fedtke, borrowing tends to be easier in legal areas considered more technical in nature, such as data protection, road traffic regulation, the powers and functions of state officials, and election laws. However, he argues that the outcomes of legal transplants become far less predictable when they involve policy considerations or fundamental values such as human rights.[2]

Countries that develop their formal legal order internally and follow distinct legal traditions are known as origins. Examples include English Common Law, French Civil Law, and German Civil Law. Although this classification is open to debate – since no legal system is entirely pure – it remains a useful pedagogical distinction between origins and transplants.

Transplants, in contrast, are countries that received their formal legal system from external sources. A common example includes most Latin American countries, which inherited Spanish or Portuguese law.

A recurring criticism of legal transplants is that they may not be well-suited to certain communities or cultures. This concern often arises from the belief that legal rules are deeply embedded in specific historical, social, or cultural contexts, and that transplanting them to a different setting may result in incompatibility or failure.

However, Alan Watson – a leading scholar on legal transplants, whose work will be examined further in this chapter – has demonstrated that large-scale and successful borrowing is a common feature of legal history. He argues that borrowing is typically the main driver of legal change and that transplants play a crucial role in the development of legal systems.

Watson also points out that it is entirely normal for a borrowed rule to function differently in its new context compared to its original one. Despite this variation in application, he maintains

2 Oliver, Dawn and Fedtke, Jörg (eds.), 2007, *Human Rights and the Private Sphere: A Comparative Study*, Routledge, London.

that the existence of identical rules across systems contributes to a significantly higher degree of similarity between those legal systems.

1.1 Historical Overview of Legal Transplants

This section gives a historical overview of legal transplants, showing how legal systems and ideas have moved from one place to another over time. We will look at important examples from history to see how laws and institutions have been borrowed and changed to fit new cultures and political situations.

These examples show that legal transplants are not just copies. Instead, they are often adapted to match the needs and values of the country receiving them.

1.1.1 Patterns of Legal Transplants: Waves and Trends

Massive legal transplants often happen in waves. As mentioned earlier, large-scale transfers of legal systems, concepts, and institutions took place during the 19th and early 20th centuries. These transplants were mostly the result of colonization and imperialism, when colonial powers brought their legal systems and courts along with their armies to the territories they controlled.

After World War II, the first "law and development" movement began, led mainly by legal scholars from the United States. This effort introduced new legal codes in countries across Latin America, Africa, and, to a lesser extent, Asia. However, this movement largely failed to achieve its goals.

A second wave of legal transplants started after the collapse of the Soviet Union. Countries in Central and Eastern Europe and the Baltic region – often called transition economies –adopted new constitutions, legal codes, and regulations. These countries followed European legal models, especially in commercial law, to attract foreign investment and to show international investors that their legal systems were reliable and in line with global standards.[3]

These successive waves illustrate that legal transplants are rarely neutral or mechanical: they are shaped by political influence, economic pressures, and broader geopolitical dynamics. Transplants often serve strategic purposes, such as signaling stability, aligning with powerful legal traditions, or facilitating international trade. Yet their success depends on how well the imported rules fit local social, institutional, and cultural realities. When foreign models are adopted without considering these factors, the resulting laws may remain ineffective in practice, highlighting the importance of adaptation rather than simple transplantation.

1.1.2 Key Historical Examples of Legal Transplants

The following historical examples are taken from Alan Watson's *Ius Commune* lectures on European private law, published under the Ius Commune Research School.[4] In these lectures, Watson draws on comparative legal history to demonstrate what legal transplants have accomplished "on a grand scale," as he puts it. Through these examples, he illustrates how the borrowing of legal rules and institutions has played a major role in shaping European legal traditions over time.

3 Berkowitz, Daniel, Pistor, Katharina and Richard, Jean-François, 2003, "The Transplant Effect," *American Journal of Comparative Law*, vol. 51.

4 Watson, Alan, 2000, *Legal Transplants and European Private Law*, Unigraphic, Maastricht, published under the auspices of the Research School Ius Commune (Maastricht University – University of Leuven – University of Utrecht – University of Amsterdam).

1.1.2.1 THE RECEPTION OF ROMAN AND CANON LAW IN WESTERN EUROPE

Watson's first example focuses on the integration of Roman law and canon law in Western Europe. During the 17th century, there was a wide circulation of commentaries and editions of Emperor Justinian's *Institutes*,[5] a foundational Roman legal text. One notable work is *The Institutes of the Civil Law, Written and Unwritten* by Natalis Chamart, published in 1684. This book combines Justinian's Roman legal framework with Belgian customary law, showing that much of Roman law had been adopted in Belgium. Many of the local customs included were themselves transplants from other legal systems.

A similar example is Johannis Voet's 1698 *Commentary on the Digest*, which modernized the legal content but remained largely based on Roman law. As Watson points out, these examples demonstrate how Roman legal ideas were not only preserved but also adapted and integrated into local European legal systems, showing the deep and lasting influence of legal transplants in shaping Western law.

These works reveal that legal borrowing was not a passive process but an active form of legal construction. Jurists selected, reinterpreted, and reshaped Roman principles to address local needs, illustrating how transplanted rules gain new meaning in different contexts. The enduring reliance on Roman law across Europe also highlights its perceived authority and technical sophistication, which made it an attractive source for jurists seeking coherent legal solutions. In this way, Watson shows that the circulation of legal ideas has been a driving force in the historical development of European legal traditions.

1.1.2.2 FEUDAL LAW TRANSPLANTS: A HISTORICAL CASE STUDY

Watson explains that the main driver behind the spread of legal rules in medieval Europe was not official imperial legislation, like the *Corpus Iuris Civilis*, but rather private works. One key example is the *Libri Feudorum* (Books of the Fiefs), a medieval compilation of feudal law composed in the early 12th century by Obertus de Orto,[6] a judge at the imperial court in Milan. Although not an official legal code, this private work spread widely across Western Europe, became attached as an appendix to the *Corpus Iuris Civilis*, and was taught by legal scholars in universities. Its influence shows how legal transplants could occur outside formal legislative channels.

Another important example discussed by Watson is *Principia Iuris Feudalis*, an 18th-century work by G.L. Boehmer. This book provides insight into the sources of German feudal law and the role of transplants in its formation. According to Boehmer, the sources of common German feudal law included the feudal law of the Lombards – received across Germany –universal German feudal customs, and the broader legal traditions of the empire, including Roman and canon law.

Watson notes that although feudal law across the Holy Roman Empire was not identical in every region, it was fundamentally the same in nature. This leads him to a key conclusion: legal transplants make different legal systems more similar, even if not entirely identical. He argues that lawmakers – whether they are legislators, judges, or jurists – often rely heavily on foreign legal ideas when making changes to their own systems.

1.1.2.3 THE EARLY ADOPTION OF THE FRENCH CIVIL CODE IN BELGIUM

Watson explains that when Belgium was taken over by France in 1797, the French Civil Code automatically became law there after it was introduced in 1804. Even when French rule ended,

5 Refer to Chapter 3 – *The Civil Law Tradition*.

6 The famous Bolognese jurist Hugolinus contributed to further versions of this private work in the year 1230.

Belgium continued to use the Civil Code. This surprises Watson, since Belgium had previously been a land with many different local customs. He uses this example to question the idea that legal transplants are impossible. If a country like Belgium could accept and keep a foreign legal code, then clearly legal transplants can work.

For Watson, this continuity demonstrates that the success of a transplant does not depend solely on cultural similarity or political domination, but also on the perceived usefulness and coherence of the imported law. The French Civil Code offered a clear, structured, and modern legal framework that replaced a fragmented system of customs, making it attractive for Belgium to retain. This example shows that transplanted laws can take root when they provide practical advantages, reinforcing Watson's broader argument that legal systems often develop through borrowing rather than internal evolution alone.

1.1.2.4 LEGAL TRANSPLANTS IN TURKEY: A UNIQUE CASE

Watson also discusses Turkey as a special example, using the research of Esin Örücü, a Turkish professor of law. Örücü's work helps explain how Turkey created its modern legal system by choosing parts from different legal traditions rather than copying just one.

Between 1924 and 1930, Turkey adopted laws from several countries based on what seemed most useful. For example, it took Civil Law from Switzerland, commercial law from Germany, and criminal law from Italy. These choices were made based on things like reputation, efficiency, or simply practicality – not because they were forced.

Most scholars, including Watson, believe that Swiss law was chosen for the Turkish Civil Code mainly because Mahmut Esad Bozkurt, the man responsible for writing the code, had studied in Switzerland. His education and trust in the Swiss legal system played a big role in shaping Turkish law. This shows that legal transplants can happen through thoughtful decisions and that personal experience can strongly influence legal change.

The Turkish example illustrates that legal borrowing can be deliberate, selective, and reform-oriented. Rather than importing a single foreign system wholesale, Turkish lawmakers assembled a legal framework that combined what they regarded as the most effective elements of several traditions. This approach highlights the agency of national reformers and shows that legal transplants can serve as tools for rapid modernization. It also supports Watson's broader thesis that the movement of legal rules often depends on individual preferences, intellectual influences, and pragmatic choices rather than on deep cultural or historical affinities.

1.1.2.5 LEGAL TRANSPLANTS IN FORMER SOVIET STATES

The draft of Book 2 of the Armenian Civil Code, which covers the law of obligations, was taken almost directly from the Russian Civil Code and was even written in Russian instead of Armenian. Watson comments on this surprising situation, noting that the Armenian code would only come into force after a legal commentary was published – one that would itself be based on the Russian commentary:

> My understanding is that the code will only come into effect after a commentary is published. The Armenian commentary will be based on the Russian one! How is this possible? Are Russia and Armenia the same place? Have they become the same culture? Or could it be that law can indeed be transplanted?[7]

7 See Watson, Alan, 1993, *Legal Transplants: An Approach to Comparative Law*, University of Georgia Press (first published in 1974).

Watson uses this example to challenge the idea that legal transplants require identical cultures to succeed. Instead, it shows that law can cross borders even when societies differ. This case also illustrates the concept of cross-fertilization, where legal systems interact, borrow from one another, and influence each other's development. It highlights how legal ideas can move between countries, adapt, and become part of a new legal order – even across linguistic and cultural divides.

For Watson, the Armenian example serves as a powerful reminder that legal development is often driven by practical needs, institutional convenience, or historical ties rather than cultural uniformity. Armenia's choice to adopt and rely on Russian legal materials reflects both continuity with its Soviet past and a pragmatic desire for ready-made, functional legal solutions during a period of transition. This demonstrates that legal transplants can take root even in contexts of linguistic mismatch or differing social conditions, reinforcing Watson's broader claim that the circulation of legal rules is a common and effective mechanism for building modern legal systems.

1.1.2.6 INTERNATIONAL SALES OF GOODS: A MODERN LEGAL TRANSPLANT

Watson identifies what he calls "an enormous example of legal transplant" in the international sale of goods.

> It was long felt that transnational mercantile transactions would be greatly helped if there was a uniform contract law that crossed national borders. Thus came into force in 1988 the United Nations Convention on Contracts for the International Sale of Goods. The contract of sale was chosen because it is the most important commercial contract.

He argues: "The Convention when it came into force did not represent the law of any nation state. But since 1988 it has been enacted as law in 54 countries." According to Watson, the need to support transnational business is a key reason behind this particular type of legal transplant. As trade and investment increasingly cross national borders, having a unified and predictable legal framework becomes more important.

All the arguments presented by Watson lead him to the conclusion that creating a single code of private law for the European Union – a European Civil Code – is both possible and beneficial. He believes that the long history of successful legal transplants across different countries and cultures shows that legal rules can be shared and adapted without requiring identical societies. Based on this, Watson argues that "the drafting of such a code would be technically easy, despite political difficulties."[8] In other words, while reaching political agreement might be challenging, writing and implementing a common legal code would not be a major technical obstacle.

A European Civil Code would simplify legal transactions across member states, reduce legal uncertainty, and lower the costs of doing business. Watson sees this as a practical and logical step, made even more feasible by the shared legal traditions and past experiences of legal borrowing within Europe.

1.1.2.7 LEGAL TRANSPLANTS IN SOUTH EAST ASIA

Andrew Harding – a leading scholar in Asian legal studies and comparative constitutional law who has held several prominent academic positions, including serving as the Head of the Law

8 Watson, *Legal Transplants*.

School at SOAS, University of London, and as Director of the Centre for Asian Legal Studies at the National University of Singapore – argues that the concept of a "legal family" does not effectively apply to the South East Asian legal experience. He explains that this is due to the region's complex and layered mix of legal traditions, including Islamic, Chinese, Hindu, indigenous customary, and European norms, all of which are intricately intertwined.[9]

Harding describes South East Asian law as consisting of layers of legal traditions, much like geological strata, where each new layer is added on top of the previous ones without fully replacing them. The foundational layer is made up of Aboriginal or native customs, which are still officially recognized in parts of Malaysia, Indonesia, and the Philippines. Above this base layer are more developed forms of custom, such as Burmese or Malay traditions, which either evolved within the region or were introduced through migration. These various layers continue to shape and influence the region's legal systems, reflecting a deep and ongoing legal pluralism.

> The original or bottom layer of South East Asian law is that now referred to as aboriginal or native custom, still extant and recognized by the official legal system in, for example, the Borneo territories of Malaysia and Indonesia, southern Philippines and Irian Jaya. This is distinct from the developed forms of custom such Burmese or Malay custom, which were either imported with the movement of people or were developed somewhat later. This latter type of custom forms a second layer, which, again, is still extant and important in many contexts.[10]

Harding suggests that South East Asian law does not follow a simple progression from one legal system to another. Instead, it represents an accumulation of different legal cultures built up over time. While these systems have become syncretic – blending elements from various traditions into unified legal frameworks – they still retain a strong foundation in European legal influence, introduced during the colonial period. This blending process illustrates legal pluralism, where multiple legal traditions coexist and influence each other. For Harding, South East Asia stands as a key example of how legal transplants can lead to the development of complex and mixed legal systems.

1.1.2.8 COLONIAL EXPANSION AND THE SPREAD OF THE CIVIL CODE

Chapter 3 examines how colonial expansion and legal reform helped spread Civil Codes around the world, focusing especially on the influence of the French and German models. Civil Codes were not only introduced through conquest, but also adopted voluntarily or through emulation, depending on the needs and circumstances of each country. The chapter presents several examples that show how Civil Law traditions were transplanted, adapted, and blended into various legal systems. As a reminder, we come back to these examples in the context of legal transplants, looking at how they have developed over time, how they were adapted in different countries, and what they reveal about the process of borrowing and shaping foreign legal ideas.

The French Civil Code, also known as the Code Napoléon, was one of the first Civil Codes to spread beyond its country of origin. It was introduced across the territories of the Napoleonic Empire in the early 19th century and continued to influence legal systems long after Napoleon's rule. In Latin America, many countries adopted Civil Codes that were either direct translations

9 Harding, Andrew, 2001, "Comparative Law and Legal Transplantation in South East Asia: Making Sense of the 'Nomic Din'," in *Adapting Legal Cultures*, eds. Johannes Feest and David Nelken, Hart Publishing, Oxford.

10 Harding, *Comparative Law and Legal Transplantation in South East Asia.*

of the French Code or original versions inspired by it. Zweigert and Kötz identified different groups of Latin American codes: some, like those in Haiti, Bolivia, and the Dominican Republic, closely followed the French model; others, such as those of Chile and Argentina, were more independent.

In Chile, the civil code was drafted by Venezuelan jurist Andrés Bello, who used a variety of sources, including Roman law, Spanish law, the French Civil Code, and other European models. The Chilean Civil Code later became a model for other Latin American countries, including Ecuador and Colombia, and influenced legal systems in Venezuela and Uruguay. Similarly, Argentina's Civil Code of 1869, later adopted in Paraguay, was based on Spanish and French law as well as the Chilean code. Brazil's civil code took a different direction and was more strongly influenced by German law.

In Europe, the French Civil Code influenced neighboring countries like Spain, Portugal, and Belgium.[11] In Africa, former French colonies in West and Central Africa adopted Civil Codes based on the French model. These codes were introduced despite the presence of customary, religious, and family laws, which continued to operate alongside the Civil Code.[12]

In the Near East, countries such as Turkey, Egypt, and Lebanon, which had been part of the Ottoman Empire, also incorporated elements of the French Civil Code into their legal systems.[13] In many Islamic countries influenced by Civil Law traditions, family law remained under religious jurisdiction, while civil and economic matters were governed by laws inspired by the French model.

In North America, the French legal tradition remains influential in Louisiana and Quebec, even though both regions are part of federal systems dominated by Common Law. In Quebec, the Civil Law system developed over time into a unique legal structure that blends French roots with local evolution.[14] This effort was led by Professor Paul-André Crépeau (1926–2011), who oversaw the drafting of the modern Code civil du Québec, which remains in force today.[15]

The German Civil Code (BGB), introduced in 1900, also spread beyond Germany, although it was not adopted as widely as the French Code. One reason for this was the code's complexity and the fact that many countries had already embraced the French model by the 19th century. However, German legal influence was strong in parts of Eastern and Southeastern Europe, such as Hungary, Czechoslovakia, and Yugoslavia.

11 The French Code civil was automatically transplanted in Belgium, where it came into force in 1804, to further the incorporation of the Belgian territories into the French Empire (which were previously governed by Austria) by the Peace of Campo Formio in 1797.

12 See Zweigert, Konrad and Kötz, Hein, 1998, *An Introduction to Comparative Law*, 3rd ed., Oxford University Press, Chapter 8 – The Reception of the Code civil.

13 The Ottoman Empire was created by Turkish tribes in Anatolia. One of the most powerful states in the world during the 15th and 16th centuries, it spanned more than 600 years and came to an end only in 1922, when it was replaced by the Turkish Republic and various successor states in southeastern Europe and the Middle East. At its height, the empire included most of southeastern Europe to the gates of Vienna, including modern Hungary, Serbia, Bosnia, Romania, Greece, and Ukraine; Iraq, Syria, Israel, and Egypt; North Africa as far west as Algeria; and most of the Arabian Peninsula. The term Ottoman is a dynastic appellation derived from Osman (Arabic: Uthmān), the nomadic Turkmen chief who founded both the dynasty and the empire. Encyclopædia Britannica, 2012, "Ottoman Empire," online. Available at: https://www.britannica.com. Accessed 29 February 2012.

14 Book One – The law of persons (1987), Book Two – Family law (1981), Book Three – The law of successions (1987), Book Four – The law of property (1987).

15 Professor Paul-André Crépeau was a leading Canadian jurist and scholar of civil and comparative law, best known for directing the reform of the Quebec Civil Code and founding McGill's Centre for Private and Comparative Law.

In Asia, German Civil Law influenced legal development in countries like Thailand and China,[16] especially in areas like commercial and Civil Law. Local customs continued to shape family and inheritance law. Japan offers a detailed example of how Civil Law traditions were adapted. Japan's first Civil Code was adopted in 1890 and drafted by French jurist Gustave-Emil Boissonade, who had earlier written Japan's Criminal Code of 1882. However, the legal community criticized this first code for favoring lawyers trained in the French system over those trained in the Common Law system. As a result, the code was revised, and a new version was adopted in 1896. The new code was strongly influenced by German law and Roman law, reflecting a compromise between foreign models and domestic preferences.

Japan's Commercial Code, adopted in 1899, followed German law more directly. Scholars such as Mark Poe, Kay Shimizu, and Jeannie Simpson, in a 2002 article in the Stanford Journal of East Asian Affairs, explain that Japan's corporate law was modeled on Western legal systems:

> Japanese corporate law has always been modelled after that of Western countries. Japan's first declaration of a corporate code came in 1899, after the Japanese Government commissioned a German scholar named Hermann Roesler to write a draft based on the German code.[17]

The government commissioned German scholar Hermann Roesler to draft Japan's Corporate Code, further solidifying German influence in Japanese economic law.

These examples show how Civil Codes have traveled across regions and legal cultures, often through colonial rule, international influence, or internal legal reform. In some cases, foreign models were adopted almost unchanged; in others, they were adapted to fit local traditions. Legal transplants rarely replaced existing systems entirely; instead, they became part of hybrid legal frameworks. The borrowing of legal rules is an ongoing process shaped by history, politics, and the legal traditions of each country.

1.2 Drivers and Impacts of Legal Norms Migration

What makes legal norms and institutions migrate, and what are the effects? This part explores the reasons behind the movement of legal rules from one system to another, as well as the different outcomes this process can produce. Legal borrowing often responds to practical needs such as modernization, economic development, or the desire to attract foreign investment. Sometimes,

16 Such codes were ruined by Socialist law with the rise of the Communist regime in China.

17 Poe, M., Shimizu, K. and Simpson, J., 2002, "Revising the Japanese Commercial Code: A Summary and Evaluation of the Reform Effort," *Stanford Journal of East Asian Affairs*, vol. 2, Spring. As Mark Poe, Kay Shimizu, and Jeannie Simpson observe in this article, "That code went through several revisions during the first half of the 20th century, but was largely discarded after World War II, in part because the U.S. Occupation forces believed that the nature of Japanese corporations was one of the factors that led to Japanese aggression preceding the war. In its place, Occupation officials encouraged Japan to adopt a more democratic corporate governance structure. The primary architects of the new code were officials in the Supreme Commander for the Allied Powers' (SCAP) Legal Section. In an interesting historical quirk, three of the five officials in charge of drafting the code were trial lawyers from Illinois and graduates of the University of Illinois. As a result, the Japanese Commercial Code closely resembles the Illinois code. Rather than simply imposing the code, SCAP sought the input of Japanese officials, scholars, and business organizations. But although the Americans made several compromises, the final draft of the code that the Diet adopted in May of 1950 was essentially a replica of the Illinois code." As these authors show, commercial law in Japan is thus converging towards an Anglo-American system of corporate governance.

the adoption of foreign laws is encouraged through international pressure or inspired by legal prestige.

The impacts of legal transplants vary. In some cases, they lead to greater harmonization between legal systems, while in others, they create tension or confusion when new norms do not fit easily with existing practices. Legal migration can also trigger competition between systems, as countries reform their laws to keep up with international standards or to gain an economic advantage.

We also look at how legal harmonization can occur both vertically – through international bodies or treaties – and horizontally, as countries borrow from each other directly. Cross-fertilization between Civil Law and Common Law traditions is another important factor, showing how different legal systems can blend and influence one another. Through this interaction, legal systems can evolve in creative and unexpected ways, leading to innovation, reform, and sometimes deeper integration across borders.

1.2.1 The Dynamic Process of Legal Borrowing

Jörg Fedtke – Professor of Comparative Law and Co-Director of the Eason-Weinmann Center for Comparative Law at Tulane University Law School – explains that the process of borrowing legal ideas is dynamic and can take several years to complete. The process of legal transplantation begins with identifying a suitable legal model typically chosen for its perceived effectiveness, prestige, or compatibility with the goals of the borrowing system. Once selected, the model often undergoes adjustments to fit the existing legal framework, institutions, and social context of the receiving country. Even the translation of legal texts can lead to variations, as legal terms may not have exact equivalents in another language or system. After the transplant is introduced, it continues to evolve within its new legal environment. The borrowing system is not required to follow the original interpretation or application of the law. Judges, lawyers, lawmakers, and legal scholars may choose to consider or ignore the case law and academic commentary from the country of origin. Over time, the transplanted rule or institution may develop in a different direction, shaped by local legal culture, needs, and practices. This process highlights the flexible and dynamic nature of legal borrowing.[18]

Thierry Rambaud – Professor of Public Law at Université Paris Cité, legal advisor and academic with strong ties to French and European institutions, and active member of various international legal and academic bodies, including as a visiting scholar and invited professor in Europe, Japan, and the Middle East – explains that the migration of foreign legal norms can occur either directly, through transplants, or indirectly, through cross-fertilization.

Transplants themselves may be imposed or voluntarily adopted. When imposed, they often result from military or political domination, such as through conquest or annexation. In such cases, the dominant state imposes its legal system on the subordinate one, reflecting a dynamic of power, control, and submission. Rambaud recalls that Napoleon himself understood the strategic power of law, claiming that the Civil Code was more effective in extending and consolidating his rule than his greatest military victories.[19]

This logic also applies to historical colonial contexts. In some instances, the colonizing state allowed cooperation and partial integration, where Aboriginal law was incorporated into the

18 Fedtke, Jörg, 2012, "Legal Transplants," in *Elgar Encyclopedia of Comparative Law*, 2nd ed., ed. Jan Smits, Edward Elgar.

19 Rambaud, Thierry, 2014, *Introduction au droit comparé: Les grandes traditions juridiques dans le monde*, Quadrige Manuels, Paris, PUF.

colonial legal system – so long as it did not significantly conflict with the imposed rules. This occurred, for example, in British colonies in Africa and Asia, especially in India. In other cases, indigenous legal systems were fully rejected as too "primitive," as seen in Australia, where Aboriginal law was largely ignored by courts until recent decades.

An article published in 2023 by Elena N. Trikoz and Elena E. Gulyaeva from MGIMO University and the Diplomatic Academy of the Ministry of Foreign Affairs of the Russian Federation examines the communicative function of legal transplants in postcolonial and mixed legal systems. The authors use a variety of metaphors – such as anthropomorphic, communicative, mechanical, and musical – to explain how legal norms and institutions are transferred and reinterpreted across different jurisdictions.[20]

Their study explores the transmission of Civil Codes, the spread of Common Law, and the rise of mixed legal systems. They analyze Alan Watson's positivist view of legal transplants and contrast it with the culturalist perspective in the ongoing debate between transferists and culturalists. Transferists argue that legal rules can be transplanted across cultures with little modification, while culturalists insist that successful legal borrowing requires deep adaptation to local social and cultural contexts. The authors also propose the metaphor of *legal transposition* – borrowing from music – to describe how laws are reinterpreted in dependent or hybrid legal systems. This metaphor highlights the flexible and creative ways in which legal transplants are reshaped when applied in national contexts marked by multiple legal traditions.[21]

1.2.2 Convergence Through Competition: An Unintended Effect

Unintended forms of legal transplants arise directly from the economic dynamics of globalization. In a globalized world, industry, commerce, and finance have become key indicators of state power. Just as firms compete with each other, states engage in inter-territorial competition to attract investment, and legal norms become instruments of that competition.[22] Since investors tend to favor legal environments that offer high returns with minimal risk, many national legal systems have gradually aligned themselves with models of liberal economic law.

Even traditionally state-centered legal systems, such as France's, have shown signs of opening up to Anglo-Saxon influence in areas like corporate law. This trend is visible in many other countries as well. It appears that the Common Law model, with its flexible and case-based structure, better suits the demands of economic globalization than the more rigid Civil Law model. According to Jean-Bernard Auby, a leading professor of Public Law and former chair of the Mutations of Public Action and Public Law at Sciences Po (2006–2016), Common Law systems have an inherent capacity to produce regulations that support economic efficiency,[23] while Civil Law systems tend to place more constraints on economic activity.

The *Doing Business* reports, published annually by the World Bank from 2004 to 2021, ranked countries according to how conducive their legal systems were to the creation and growth of businesses. These reports repeatedly highlighted the more business-friendly nature of Anglo-Saxon legal systems in contrast with Civil Law systems, particularly those in continental Europe.

20 Trikoz, Evgeny N. and Gulyaeva, Elena E., 2023, "The Communicative Function of Legal Transplants in Mixed Legal Systems," *Kutafin Law Review*, vol. 10, no. 3, online. Available at: https://kulawr.msal.ru.

21 Trikoz and Gulyaeva, *The Communicative Function of Legal Transplants*.

22 Matoussi Mohamed, Souad, 2001, "La mise en concurrence des systèmes juridiques nationaux: Réflexions sur l'ambivalence des rapports du droit et de la mondialisation," *Revue internationale de droit économique*, vol. XV, no. 3.

23 Auby, Jean-Bernard, 2010, *La globalisation, le droit et l'État*, LGDJ, Paris.

In practice, this has led to a form of substantive harmonization of national legal systems around the liberal economic model typical of Anglo-Saxon countries. However, this trend should not be mistaken for a general move toward deregulation. Investors also seek strong legal institutions, high-quality judicial systems, reliable administrative processes, and appropriate labor laws. Therefore, harmonization around the liberal model often includes efforts to ensure legal certainty, administrative efficiency, and balanced regulation, rather than simply reducing legal obligations.

1.2.3 Vertical Harmonization: Regional Legal Integration

As we saw, legal borrowing can lead to the harmonization of law. This is one of the main effects of legal transplants. Substantive harmonization of legal norms between systems may result from a vertical and voluntary integration of national legal frameworks through collective regional or international projects. Once again, the economic field is the most visible area of this harmonization. As mentioned earlier, Watson pointed to the international sale of goods as a clear example, with the adoption of the 1988 United Nations Convention on Contracts for the International Sale of Goods (CISG), which acts as a legal transplant on a global scale.

In 1993, 14 African states (now 17) created the Organisation pour l'Harmonisation en Afrique du Droit des Affaires (OHADA), aimed at creating and applying uniform business and commercial laws across member states. These laws are adapted within national systems, allowing for harmonization while respecting domestic legal structures. As most OHADA members are former French colonies, the organization draws heavily from the French legal tradition. This example shows how, indirectly, globalization supports the export of specific legal models.

The European Union also gives considerable importance to the harmonization of its members' legal systems, particularly to strengthen and manage the common market. The direct effect of EU regulations and the binding nature of directives make national legal systems within the Union more open to external influence.[24] In response to globalization, legislative efforts have been launched to speed up legal harmonization. In 2001, the European Commission initiated a project to reduce differences between national contract laws, leading to the creation of the Lando Commission, tasked with exploring common principles. There are also proposals to codify European private law in order to improve legal certainty, support cross-border transactions, and reduce legal costs. This connects to earlier references to Watson's arguments supporting the feasibility and benefits of a European Civil Code.

Similar processes can be observed in other regional organizations, such as MERCOSUR in South America or NAFTA in North America. However, it is important to remember that even though harmonization is often initiated from the top (through international agreements or institutions), its practical implementation must go through national legal systems.[25]

This shows that while national systems are increasingly influenced by global and regional legal standards, they still play a central role. National legal frameworks remain essential for understanding and managing legal harmonization, which is one of the key effects of legal transplants and borrowings.

24 See Chapter 11 – *Supranationalism: The European Union.*
25 See Chapter 10 – *The Interface of International Law and National Law.*

1.2.4 Horizontal Harmonization: Mutual Legal Influences

Alongside the vertical harmonization of legal systems – driven by international organizations, treaties, and regional integration – there is also a process of horizontal harmonization. This occurs when national legal systems influence each other directly, through mutual interaction. These systems come into contact, exchange ideas, and evolve by learning from one another, much like living organisms developing in response to their environment and interactions with others of the same kind.

Globalization has played a key role in encouraging this kind of legal interaction. One important example is the legal transformation of post-Soviet countries. After the collapse of the USSR, and in the context of growing globalization, countries in Eastern Europe began to adopt – or at least adapt – elements of the rule-based legal culture found in continental Civil Law systems.[26] Globalization contributed to the decline of the Socialist legal family, pushing former satellite states toward market economies, constitutional governance, the Rule of Law, and the protection of fundamental rights. As previously discussed, this shift marked the second major wave of legal transplants in the 20th century.

The spread of constitutionalism in this context shows that legal harmonization is not limited to economic law. It can also involve more foundational areas, such as political and human rights norms. The growing openness of post-socialist countries to Western legal and political concepts was a direct result of globalization, which weakened their isolation and exposed them to new legal standards and expectations. In this way, substantive legal harmonization through competition between systems resembles horizontal harmonization, where systems grow closer not through formal agreements but through mutual influence.

Later in this chapter, in section 3, we will look more closely at how judicial cooperation and procedural harmonization encourage convergence between Common Law and Civil Law systems. The global dialogue among judges, through citations, meetings, and joint projects, contributes to the spread of legal ideas and facilitates legal transplants on a worldwide scale.

Another key dimension of modern legal influence is legal diplomacy, sometimes called diplomacy by law.[27] Traditionally, diplomacy has focused on political, economic, and cultural exchanges, while law played a secondary role. Today, however, law is central to economic diplomacy. A country that cannot explain or defend its legal system risks losing credibility and influence in international affairs. This is especially relevant in the context of growing reliance on Alternative Dispute Resolution (ADR) methods – such as Arbitration and Mediation – which are often shaped by Anglo-Saxon legal traditions.

The increasing use of ADR in international contracts, particularly through clauses based on Common Law practices, may reduce the importance of national courts in countries with Civil Law traditions, such as France. Some authors have raised concerns that this trend could contribute to the global dominance of Common Law principles and gradually weaken Civil Law systems.[28]

26 Heydebrand, Wolf, 2001, "From Globalization of Law to Law under Globalization," in *Adapting Legal Cultures*, eds. David Nelken and Johannes Feest, Hart Publishing, Oxford.

27 See Gontier, Jean-Yves, 2023, *La Diplomatie Juridique: Défense et Illustration du Droit Français et du droit Continental dans le Droit Global à travers les exemples de la Médiation et de l'Arbitrage international*, Doctoral thesis in Law, Université Paris-Saclay.

28 Gontier, *Legal Diplomacy*.

To respond to this, some scholars advocate for a more active French legal diplomacy. The goal would not be to dominate the international legal scene but to ensure fair competition among legal systems. By promoting the value of continental law traditions – including clarity, codification, and legal certainty – legal diplomacy can help maintain a diverse and balanced global legal order. Such efforts would support mutual learning between systems and help preserve core legal values, avoiding the concentration of legal influence in a single tradition.[29]

1.2.5 Cross-Fertilization Between Civil Law and Common Law

Civil Law and Common Law systems are increasingly influencing one another through a range of procedural mechanisms and forms of interaction, including legal transplants, borrowing of legal ideas, judicial dialogue, and regional integration, particularly within the framework of the European Union. These ongoing interactions are gradually leading to a convergence of the two traditions, with each adopting features traditionally associated with the other.

One key area of convergence is International Arbitration, which has expanded significantly in recent decades, including arbitrations between states. This growth reflects the strong influence of Anglo-Saxon legal traditions and contributes to the gradual blurring of boundaries between public and private law, especially in Civil Law jurisdictions.

Another development is the growing willingness of judges to refer to foreign court decisions as part of their legal reasoning. While this practice has become more accepted in many Civil Law countries, it remains controversial in some Common Law jurisdictions, particularly the United States – a debate we will explore further in Section 3. In Civil Law systems, there is decreasing resistance to the doctrine of *stare decisis* and the rule of precedent, while Common Law countries are placing more emphasis on codification, often through the use of restatements or formal summaries of judicial principles.

Globalization continues to accelerate this procedural convergence. A clear example is the incorporation of the European Convention on Human Rights into the United Kingdom's domestic law through the 1998 Human Rights Act. This legislation significantly reshaped the UK's legal culture by introducing a rights-based framework that has influenced court decisions and judicial reasoning.

In a 2002 decision (*Regina v. Secretary of State for the Home Department*), Chief Justice Lord Woolf highlighted the importance of legal principles over excessive reliance on case citation, signaling a shift in emphasis within the Common Law tradition.

In summary, while Civil and Common Law systems are gradually adopting features from one another – creating new procedural and institutional overlaps – important differences remain, especially in areas such as the structure and organization of the Judiciary. Nonetheless, the trend toward convergence reflects the broader influence of globalization on legal development.

1.2.6 Dialectics Between Legal Systems: Fostering Cross-Fertilization

On an international scale, globalization fosters dynamic interactions between legal systems through the interface of various jurisdictions. Legal systems – whether national, sub-national

29 Gontier, *Legal Diplomacy*.

(such as U.S. federal states), or supranational – are increasingly influencing each other and co-operating in a globally interconnected legal landscape.

One important consequence of this interconnectedness is that courts now have greater access to foreign judicial decisions, which can influence their own reasoning and rulings. As discussed in Section 3, this judicial cross-reference contributes to the gradual harmonization of legal principles. A notable example is the 2002 U.S. Supreme Court case *Atkins v. Virginia*, in which the Court ruled that executing individuals with intellectual disabilities violates the Eighth Amendment's ban on cruel and unusual punishment. In delivering the opinion, Justice Stevens pointed out that the Court's view aligned with the opinions of the international community, highlighting how global consensus can inform domestic constitutional interpretation.

These cross-border judicial interactions also help address the complexities that arise when legal communities overlap. In his work on global legal pluralism, Paul Schiff Berman, Walter S. Cox Professor of Law at George Washington University, discusses the case of *Loewen Group, Inc. v. United States*.[30] In this NAFTA dispute, a tribunal criticized the conduct of Mississippi state courts in handling contract and antitrust claims. While the tribunal lacked authority to directly change the practices of Mississippi courts – since only the federal government is party to NAFTA – it led to federal pressure being placed on state institutions. This case illustrates how legal dialogue can take place across different levels of governance, especially in the area of international business and dispute resolution.

Further examples of this global legal dialogue involve interactions with international courts. In one case, the Oklahoma Court of Criminal Appeals issued a stay of execution that was influenced, in part, by a prior decision of the International Court of Justice.[31] Even though the ICJ lacks direct enforcement power over state-level courts in the United States, its rulings can still shape domestic legal outcomes, especially in cases involving International Law or human rights.

Altogether, these examples reflect a growing trend of procedural harmonization across legal systems, driven by legal transplants, borrowing, and cross-fertilization. As judges and courts engage more frequently with international norms and decisions from foreign jurisdictions, globalization continues to shape how law is developed, interpreted, and applied around the world.

2 The Debate Over Legal Transplants

This section explores the ongoing debate surrounding the concept of legal transplants, which came to prominence in 1974 through the opposing views of Alan Watson and Otto Kahn-Freund. It examines their contrasting positions on whether legal transplants are a feasible and effective way to develop legal systems and considers the broader implications of their arguments. The section also looks at how legal borrowing and cross-fertilization contribute to legal evolution, offering a critical perspective on the strengths and limitations of these processes.

2.1 1974: A Clash of Opinions

The debate over legal transplants gained prominence in 1974 with the publication of two opposing theories on their achievability and value. This part examines the clash between two influential scholars: Alan Watson, who supported the viability and significance of legal transplants, and

30 Berman, Paul Schiff, 2012, *Global Legal Pluralism: A Jurisprudence of Law Beyond Borders*, 3rd ed., Cambridge University Press.

31 Berman, *Global Legal Pluralism.*

Otto Kahn-Freund, who expressed strong doubts about their effectiveness and warned of their possible drawbacks. Their differing views helped shape an important academic discussion that continues today, focusing on the complexities, risks, and conditions that influence the success or failure of transferring legal norms between different legal systems.

2.1.1 Alan Watson's Theory of Legal Transplants

In 1974, Alan Watson published a book titled *Legal Transplants*,[32] in which he introduced and coined the very expression "legal transplant." The book has since been translated into several languages and remains a foundational work in comparative law. Watson's central argument is that legal rules can be separated from the social, political, and institutional context in which they were originally created. For clarity, we can refer to this idea as the principle of "separability."

According to Watson, even though a legal rule may change after being adopted in a new legal system, this does not prevent its transfer. In fact, he acknowledges that once a rule is transplanted, it becomes different in its new environment. To better understand this idea, we can add – especially for pedagogical purposes – that "there is no transportation without transformation."

Watson continued to defend this position in many of his later writings. He consistently argued that legal transplants are not only possible but are a major source of legal development, and that the evolution of legal systems often depends more on external borrowing than on internal social change:

> I have long held that a transplanted rule is not the same thing as it was in its previous home. Nor need I stress my long-held view that it is rules – not just statutory rules – institutions, legal concepts, and structures that are borrowed, not the spirit of a legal system.[33]

Watson argues that laws often develop through transplants because lawmakers are aware of the potential benefits that can be gained from adopting foreign statutes or case law. In his view, a legal rule that is relevant and effective in one country retains its value even when introduced into a different legal system. For Watson, transplanting a law is not only possible but practical – it is something that can be done and has been done throughout legal history.

Alan Watson is an expert in Scottish law and comparative legal history. He serves as a research professor at the University of Georgia School of Law, where he holds the Ernest P. Rogers Chair. In recognition of his contributions to the field of comparative law, the University of Belgrade established the Alan Watson Foundation (AWF) in 2005. The foundation is a nonprofit academic organization dedicated to promoting interdisciplinary legal scholarship, with a particular focus on the relationship between law and society.[34]

Watson highlights that much of a nation's legal framework – its rules, institutions, concepts, and structures – often results from borrowing, particularly through processes of cross-fertilization. He stresses that legal ideas and notions of legal propriety do not necessarily align with national borders. For instance, he remarks that "a small farmer in the Belgian Ardennes will be closer in his legal conceptions to a small farmer in neighboring Germany than to a businessman from Brussels."

32 Watson, Alan, 1974, *Legal Transplants: An Approach to Comparative Law*, Scottish Academic Press, Edinburgh.

33 Watson, Alan, 2000, "Legal Transplants and European Private Law," in *Ius Commune Lectures on European Private Law*, Unigraphic, Maastricht.

34 See Alan Watson Official Website, online. Available at: https://www.alanwatson.org.

Watson further observes that in many areas of law, individuals are largely free to arrange their affairs in ways that diverge from statutory law. He gives the examples of contracts, marriage agreements, and testate succession, suggesting that legal rules in such areas are flexible enough to accommodate personal arrangements. Based on this, Watson argues that legal provisions can be unified in a common code while still allowing for local variation – something already demonstrated by the legal systems of Germany and Switzerland.

According to Professor Thierry Rambaud, Watson maintains that economic, cultural, political, or social differences do not prevent legal transplants from succeeding. Watson views transplants as a natural and essential part of legal development, and he draws on historical examples to support this view. He refers to the role of Roman law in shaping Scottish law and the development of American law through the adoption of English Common Law.

In line with the long-term historical perspective of Fernand Braudel, Watson believes that legal change is largely driven by imitation, mimicry, and the replication of existing models. From this perspective, the political, social, or cultural context should not be overstated when analyzing legal transfers.[35]

Rambaud illustrates this with the example of Japan in the 19th century. During its period of modernization, Japan adopted many legal rules from both French and German legal traditions. The success of these transplants, he explains, was due to Japan's strong will to reform and modernize its legal system – a process that was not significantly hindered by cultural or social differences.[36]

2.1.2 Otto Kahn-Freund's Contrasting Perspective

In 1974, Otto Kahn-Freund (1900–1979) – a scholar in labor law and comparative law, who held professorships at both the London School of Economics and the University of Oxford – developed a view that directly opposed Alan Watson's theory of legal transplants.[37] While Watson argued that laws could be separated from their social, political, and cultural context and successfully transplanted, Kahn-Freund strongly disagreed. For him, laws are deeply embedded in the society that produces them, and separating a legal rule from its original environment risks distorting its purpose and function. He believed that legal norms are closely linked to the institutions, power structures, and values of the state and society in which they were developed.

According to Kahn-Freund, a successful legal transplant is rare and largely a matter of chance. He warned that laws created in one context often fail to work properly in another because they do not align with the local institutional, cultural, and social realities. As Montesquieu famously argued in *The Spirit of Laws* (1748), political and Civil Laws must be tailored to the specific characteristics of a nation – its government, climate, geography, religion, history, and traditions. Kahn-Freund cited this idea to emphasize the difficulty, if not the impossibility, of transferring legal rules across societies without significant adaptation.

To illustrate this idea, Professor Thierry Rambaud offers a striking example from the Indian legal system. In India, he explains, there is a longstanding tradition of arranging marriages for children at a very young age. This practice is rooted in the belief that marriage is a sacred rite

35 Alan Watson Official Website.
36 Alan Watson Official Website.
37 Kahn-Freund, Otto, 1974, "On Use and Misuse of Comparative Law," *Modern Law Review*, vol. 37.

necessary for salvation, leading many parents to ensure their children are married before their own death to secure their spiritual future.

During colonial rule, British law sought to ban such practices by establishing a legal minimum marriage age – 18 for boys and 15 for girls. However, in reality, the average age of marriage for girls in many Indian states remained around 12, and the legal prohibitions had little practical effect. As Rambaud notes, the law was widely ignored, and effective enforcement proved nearly impossible. This example highlights the challenges of transplanting foreign legal norms into societies with deeply rooted cultural and religious traditions.

Beyond technical difficulties, Kahn-Freund also raised ethical and political objections to legal transplants. First, he pointed out that transplants imposed through colonization are undemocratic and often represent a form of legal imperialism. Second, such transplants may interfere with the authority and legal autonomy of the recipient state. Third, they often occur without internal reform or local participation, which leads to rejection or failure.

A modern example of the failure of legal transplants through external imposition is the 2003 U.S. invasion of Iraq. The Bush administration introduced an entirely new legal framework in a country with deeply complex political and social structures. The attempt was widely criticized for being superficial and for ignoring local realities.

Kahn-Freund's arguments highlight the close connection between legal and political transplants. Since laws reflect the values and structures of a society, the question of whether a law can be exported is also a question about the exportability of political systems – especially democracy.[38] Transplanting legal rules, in his view, cannot be separated from the broader cultural and institutional environment.

His position anticipated the rise of what is now called *cultural relativism* in legal theory, which holds that the success of a legal transplant depends heavily on local context. Supporting this view, the German scholar Gunther Teubner introduced the concept of *legal irritants* to describe how foreign legal norms, once introduced into a new system, rarely function as they did in their place of origin. Instead of being fully adopted or smoothly integrated, they disrupt the local legal culture and generate new, often unpredictable developments.[39]

Teubner explains that "when a foreign rule is imposed on a domestic culture, it is not transplanted into another organism; rather, it works as a fundamental irritation which triggers a whole series of new and unexpected events." Such rules are not simply adapted but transformed, and they may cause broader changes in both the rule itself and the legal environment receiving it.

Professor Thierry Rambaud illustrates this with the example of mergers and acquisitions law in Central and Eastern Europe. Many of these countries have adopted Anglo-American legal models, which do not always align well with their legal traditions. This use of "ready-made" legal solutions, according to Rambaud, carries risks and may even weaken the coherence of national legal systems.

Some legal systems have explicitly pushed back against such transplants. For example, Article 3 of the Civil Code of the canton of Vaud in Switzerland (1819) prohibited judges from referring to foreign laws or sources in their decisions. Similarly, the Indian Supreme Court ruled in *State of Madras v. Menon* (1954) that any law incompatible with the status of an independent India could not be considered applicable.

38 Interview with Fareed Zakaria on the exportability of democracy, online. Available at: https://www.youtube.com.

39 Teubner, Gunther, 1998, "Legal Irritants: Good Faith in British Law or How Unifying Law Ends up in New Divergences," *Modern Law Review*, vol. 61.

The debate continued into the late 20th century with Pierre Legrand, a French jurist and Professor of Comparative Legal Culture at Tilburg University.[40] In his article *The Impossibility of Legal Transplants*,[41] Legrand offered a strong critique of Watson's theory. While Watson relied on comparative legal history to support his claims, Legrand emphasized legal philosophy and culture. He argued that law is deeply tied to the language, values, and structures of a society, and that meaning is inevitably lost or changed when legal texts move between systems.

Interestingly, both Watson and Legrand agree on a fundamental point: that a rule, even if it appears identical in wording, is not the same law when applied in a different country. They agree that "context is everything" and that "a rule once transplanted is different in its new home." Still, while Watson sees this transformation as a manageable and even normal part of legal evolution, Legrand sees it as evidence of the limits – and even the impossibility – of true legal transplantation.

Two Swiss scholars,[42] Drolshammer and Weber, have contributed to the discussion from a more practical perspective. Drawing on their experience in international legal practice and academia, they approach the movement of law across borders not from a theoretical angle but from the ground up. They argue that the success of Watson's *Legal Transplants* lies less in its originality than in its provocative and accessible style, which attracted wide attention – particularly in the United States. Though much has been written on the topic since 1974, recent years have seen a decline in interest, possibly because scholars feel the subject has already been thoroughly explored.[43]

Nevertheless, the legacy of the Watson–Kahn-Freund debate continues to influence how we understand the possibilities and limitations of transferring legal norms between different societies. It reminds us that while legal borrowing is common and often necessary, it is not a neutral or purely technical process – it involves questions of power, identity, and cultural compatibility.

2.2 The Effectiveness of Legal Transplants: A Critical Analysis

Do legal transplants ever work? The debate surrounding the effectiveness of legal transplants – where a legal rule or institution from one country is adopted and applied in another – has attracted considerable attention among legal scholars and practitioners. The core question remains: can a legal system, or parts of it, be successfully transferred from one jurisdiction to another, and under what conditions do such transplants succeed?

This discussion examines the views of leading scholars and considers the broader implications of legal borrowing and cross-fertilization. It also highlights the role of adaptation, context, and legal creativity in shaping the outcomes of these transfers.

40 Pierre Legrand is a French international jurist who became a lawyer at the Ontario Bar in Canada in 1992. He has held positions as a law professor at Tilburg University in the Netherlands and Lille 2 University in 1999, and later, in 2006, became a professor at Paris 1 University, where he directed specialized training in comparative legal studies. In 2017, he was appointed professor at the Sorbonne Law School (Université Paris 1 Panthéon-Sorbonne) and a researcher at the Sorbonne Institute of Legal and Philosophical Sciences (ISJPS, UMR 8103). He also teaches at universities across Europe, North America, Australia, and China.

41 Legrand, Pierre, 1997, "The Impossibility of Legal Transplants," *Maastricht Journal of European and Comparative Law*, vol. 4, no. 2.

42 Drolshammer, Jakob and Weber, Rolf H., 2019, *Wie das Recht auf Reisen geht: Eine Übersichtsdarstellung internationaler Rechtstransfers am Beispiel des schweizerischen Rechts- und Kulturraums*, Stämpfli, Bern.

43 Reimann, Mathias W., 2020, "A Bottom-Up View of Legal Transplants," *American Journal of Comparative Law*, vol. 68, no. 3, online. https://doi.org/10.1093/ajcl/avaa021.

2.2.1 The Dynamics of Legal Transplants: Success and Failure Factors

As explained by Daniel Berkowitz, Katharina Pistor, and Jean-François Richard in a major 2003 article on the "transplant effect," the effectiveness of legal transplants depends on more than simply adopting a foreign legal model.[44] Rather than focusing on how laws are imposed, their research sought to identify the conditions under which legal transplants succeed or fail. Through an empirical analysis based on several assumptions, the authors aimed to understand what determines the success of transplanted legal systems.

Daniel Berkowitz is a professor of comparative institutions, development, and applied microeconomics at the University of Pittsburgh; Katharina Pistor is a professor of comparative law at Columbia University; and Jean-François Richard is a professor of economics, also at the University of Pittsburgh. In their study, they classified 49 countries, distinguishing between those with original (or endogenous) legal systems and those with transplanted ones. According to their classification, countries like England, France, Austria, Germany, and Switzerland were considered to have original legal systems – a categorization that can, of course, be debated. The aim was not to define origins rigidly, but to explore the structural factors that shape the outcome of legal transfers.

Importantly, the authors challenged the idea that the success of a legal transplant is tied to whether a country follows a Common Law or Civil Law tradition. Instead, they assessed 39 countries using five key indicators: judicial effectiveness, Rule of Law, absence of corruption, low risk of contract repudiation, and low risk of government expropriation. These criteria, applied to data from 1980 to 1995, helped them differentiate between "legality states" – where a culture of Rule of Law is stronger – and "illegality states," where it is weaker.

Their findings suggest that legal transplants are more likely to succeed in legality states, where public officials, legal institutions, and the broader population are more familiar with and supportive of the legal system. In such contexts, legal intermediaries such as judges, lawyers, and civil servants are willing and able to implement and adapt transplanted laws. A crucial element of success, then, is the *receptivity* of the recipient state – not just whether the law is formally adopted, but whether it is understood, accepted, and adapted to local realities.

For example, if a legal rule developed in an industrialized country is transplanted into an agricultural society, adjustments may be needed to align it with existing tax, land, and subsidy systems. In this sense, successful transplants often depend on thoughtful adaptation rather than direct imitation.

While some of these conclusions might appear intuitive – such as the idea that a transplant is more likely to succeed where institutions are already functioning effectively – the authors stress that these preconditions are often overlooked in practice. Katharina Pistor, in particular, draws on her experience with legal reform projects in post-Soviet and Eastern European states. She notes that both successful and unsuccessful cases reveal the importance of tailoring legal transplants to the specific needs and capacities of the recipient country.

However, this raises a broader question: how should we define the success of a legal transplant? Is it enough for the transplanted law to function legally and avoid problems like corruption or expropriation? The authors note that even a transplant that meets formal criteria could support an undesirable legal or political regime. For instance, if a totalitarian state successfully imposes its laws on another, the transplant may function in terms of compliance but still result in repression and illegality in a broader normative sense.

44 Berkowitz, Daniel, Pistor, Katharina and Richard, Jean-Francois, 2003, "Economic Development, Legality, and the Transplant Effect," in *European Economic Review*, Elsevier, vol. 47(1), pp. 165–195.

Therefore, the authors argue that success should be linked not only to institutional performance but also to the promotion of the Rule of Law and respect for rights. Legal transplants should aim to improve the quality of governance and support legal legitimacy, not simply achieve technical implementation.

The research also acknowledges the difficulty of defining what counts as a legal origin or when a system ceases to be "original." These assumptions complicate empirical comparisons but are necessary for analyzing long-term legal change.

In conclusion, Berkowitz, Pistor, and Richard highlight that legal transplants are complex, uncertain, and context-dependent. Their success cannot be guaranteed, and many factors –both legal and non-legal – play a role. For policymakers, reformers, and legal experts involved in exporting legal models, particularly in countries undergoing transition, these findings offer a crucial reminder: the transplantation of law requires careful consideration of local institutional realities, legal culture, and political context.

2.2.2 Legal Borrowing, Cross-Fertilization, and the Evolution of Legal Systems

The debate on the effectiveness of legal transplants has gained renewed attention with the increasing Europeanization and internationalization of law. In this context, John Bell – Emeritus Professor of Law at Pembroke College and expert in comparative law in Western Europe – draws a useful distinction between two key concepts: *borrowing* and *cross-fertilization*. Borrowing, according to Bell, refers to the direct transfer of a legal doctrine from one legal system to another, often with minimal adaptation. In contrast, cross-fertilization involves a more indirect and dynamic process, where the imported legal idea is modified and reshaped to suit the institutional and cultural framework of the receiving system.

Rodolfo Sacco and Pier Giuseppe Monateri, both professors of law at the University of Turin, offer a complementary perspective. They argue that borrowing and imitation are not only common but natural aspects of legal development. Genuine innovation, in their view, is relatively rare. Instead, legal systems evolve through a continuous process of *contamination*, a term they use to describe the blending of legal traditions and the layering of influences that occurs through legal interaction.[45]

Thierry Rambaud builds on these ideas by emphasizing that legal borrowing is often a creative act. Because law is closely tied to a society's cultural, political, and economic environment, any act of importing legal concepts involves reinterpreting and adapting them to new conditions. He proposes that legal borrowing should be seen as a process of *mixing* and *reappropriation*, rather than simple transfer.[46]

One example Rambaud highlights is the integration of public-private partnership (PPP) contracts into French law via the Ordinance of June 17, 2004. These contracts were inspired by the British Private Finance Initiative (PFI), itself originally influenced by a French legal institution: the *concession de service public* (service concession arrangement).[47] This circular exchange il-

45 See Monateri, Pier Giuseppe, 2002, "The Weak Law: Contaminations and Legal Cultures," *Global Jurist Advances*, vol. 1, no. 3, online. https://doi.org/10.2202/1535-1661.1043. See also Sacco, Rodolfo, 1991, "Legal Formants: A Dynamic Approach to Comparative Law (Installment I of II)," *American Journal of Comparative Law*, vol. 39, no. 1.

46 Rambaud, *Introduction au droit comparé*.

47 A service concession arrangement is an agreement between a government or public sector body (the grantor) and a private company (the operator), in which the operator manages and operates infrastructure owned by the grantor – such as airports, toll roads, bridges, tunnels, prisons, or hospitals – for a set period. During this time, the operator may be paid by the grantor for providing the service, or may collect payments directly from users of the service.

lustrates the reciprocal nature of legal transplants and the creative reinterpretation that can occur through such processes. Rather than a one-way adoption, the development of PPPs in France represents an example of legal cross-fertilization, where ideas circulate between systems, are transformed, and then reintroduced in new forms.

Rambaud argues that this type of exchange is particularly visible in administrative law and supports using the term *cross-fertilizations* in the plural to reflect the diversity and complexity of legal influences. He raises several important questions about these processes: How do foreign legal elements influence domestic legal traditions? How are they reshaped to meet local needs? What role do existing legal concepts and interpretations play in this integration? Are some legal systems more open or adaptable than others? And finally, can we observe shifts in the boundaries of legal categories – for instance, the privatization of Public Law or the publicization of private law – as a result of these interactions?

These questions point to the fluid and evolving nature of law in a global context. Legal systems are no longer isolated entities, but part of a larger network of exchanges, reinterpretations, and mutual influences. Legal borrowing and cross-fertilization are not only technical processes but also cultural and political ones, reflecting the broader context in which legal systems develop and transform.

3 Key Issues in Legal Transplants: Success Factors and the Role of Foreign Precedents in Judicial Decisions

This section examines the key factors that influence the success of legal transplants and considers the use of foreign precedents in judicial decision-making. It begins by outlining the main conditions for a successful legal transplant, such as the openness of the receiving society, political alignment, and institutional compatibility. The discussion then turns to the ongoing debate over whether national courts – particularly in the United States – should refer to foreign judicial decisions. It presents the main arguments both for and against the use of foreign precedents.

In conclusion, the two central practical questions that arise from the study of legal borrowings and transplants are: under what conditions can a legal transplant succeed, and to what extent should judges rely on foreign precedents? These questions are at the heart of this complex and evolving area of law.

3.1 Essential Criteria for Successful Legal Transplants

This subsection highlights the main factors required for a legal transplant to succeed. It considers the importance of how open and receptive the receiving society is to new legal ideas, the political similarities between the donor and recipient countries, and the degree to which existing institutions can support and implement the transplanted law. These elements are essential in deciding whether a transplanted legal norm can be effectively adopted and maintained within a different legal system.

3.1.1 The Receptivity of the Receiving Society

According to Watson, the most important factor for a successful legal transplant is the presence of internal demand.[48] The population must genuinely want the foreign legal rule. If the society

48 Watson, *Legal Transplants*.

is not receptive, the transplanted law is unlikely to take root. This internal demand encourages voluntary compliance, which is essential for the law to function effectively.

For example, imagine a country called "Novaria" that is undergoing major reforms to modernize its economy. As part of this effort, Novaria considers adopting environmental protection laws similar to those in a nearby country, "Ecodia," known for its strong green regulations. In Novaria, there is growing public concern about pollution and climate change, and civil society groups are actively campaigning for stricter environmental standards.

Because the population of Novaria is already aware of and supportive of such reforms, the government decides to transplant Ecodia's environmental laws. The new rules are widely accepted, actively enforced, and even improved upon to suit local conditions. This success is largely due to the internal demand for environmental protection – without it, the same law might have failed or been ignored.

Watson uses this idea to argue that legal transplants thrive when they respond to social expectations, political priorities, or pressing practical needs within the receiving country. A foreign rule cannot function merely by being imposed; it must resonate with local values or address a widely recognized problem. Internal demand thus acts as a bridge connecting the transplanted law to the society that adopts it, thereby increasing legitimacy, encouraging enforcement, and facilitating long-term integration into the legal system.

3.1.2 Cultural Proximity of Two Legal Systems

Quoting a foreign legal system in judicial reasoning or legislative drafting is not simply a matter of legal relevance – it also depends heavily on shared cultural, linguistic, and institutional foundations. When two legal systems share a common language, similar legal traditions, and comparable social and economic contexts, legal borrowing becomes more accessible and more meaningful.

For example, a judge or lawyer in Boston (Massachusetts, USA), working within a Common Law system, would find it far more practical and intuitive to cite a case from Virginia – a fellow U.S. state with a shared legal heritage, common language, and similar socio-economic conditions – than from Nicaragua, which operates within a Civil Law tradition, speaks Spanish, and is shaped by very different historical and institutional contexts.

The legal principles, terminology, procedural mechanisms, and interpretative methods in Virginia are likely to be closely aligned with those in Massachusetts, making the case law not only easier to understand but also more persuasive in argument. In contrast, a decision from Nicaragua may use unfamiliar legal reasoning, derive from a different conception of judicial authority, and reflect societal values or legal purposes that do not align with those of a U.S. court.

Therefore, the more two systems resemble each other in legal culture, language, and institutional setting, the easier and more effective legal transplants or references become. This explains why most comparative citations and borrowings occur between countries or jurisdictions that are already connected by strong cultural and historical ties.

3.1.3 Political Affinities Between Donor and Recipient Countries

Political similarities between countries play a key role in determining whether legal transplants can succeed. Legal systems are deeply rooted in political structures and values, so laws from one country are more likely to work in another if both share similar forms of governance and underlying principles.

For example, a democracy is unlikely to adopt laws from an authoritarian regime, because the assumptions behind the laws – such as individual rights, accountability, and the Separation of Powers – are fundamentally different. This is why the United States would not refer to Cuban legal precedents: the two systems reflect opposing political ideologies.

Otto Kahn-Freund strongly argued that political compatibility is essential for successful legal transplants.[49] He believed that laws are shaped by the political context in which they developed; therefore, they cannot be easily transferred to a system with different political values. Without this alignment, transplanted laws may not function as intended and could even be rejected or ignored.

A clear example of this principle can be seen in the early 1990s, when many Eastern European countries transitioned from communist regimes to democratic governance. These countries were able to adopt legal models from Western democracies with relative success, largely because they were also adopting the political values that support those legal frameworks. On the other hand, if democratic legal norms were introduced into a tightly controlled authoritarian system – such as North Korea – they would likely fail, as the political environment does not support the legal culture required for those laws to operate effectively.

In short, political similarity between donor and recipient countries increases the likelihood that transplanted laws will be accepted, applied, and sustained.

3.1.4 Institutional Compatibility and Support

Institutional factors play a major role in whether legal transplants succeed. These include the structure and function of legal institutions, such as courts, judges, legal education, and the sources of law used in a country – like legislation, case law, or even religious rules. The more similar these elements are between the donor and recipient countries, the more likely it is that a foreign legal rule will be understood, accepted, and properly applied.

David Nelken, Professor of Legal Institutions and Social Change at the University of Macerata, emphasizes that for a transplant to succeed, one must understand "the place of law in society."[50] In other words, a rule cannot be taken out of its original context and inserted into another system without considering how law functions socially and culturally in the new setting.

Jan Smits, Professor of European Private Law at Maastricht University, argues that the effectiveness of a legal transplant should be measured by its outcome – specifically, whether it helps bring about uniformity between legal systems. He points to commercial contract law in Europe as an area where legal transplants have generally worked, helping build common standards across borders. In contrast, he notes that property law remains fragmented, suggesting that transplants in that area have been less successful.[51]

Smits shares this critical and context-sensitive view with other contemporary scholars of comparative law in a changing world, like Nelken, Esin Örücü, Nigel Foster, and Peter de Cruz. These scholars tend to challenge the more optimistic positions of figures like Alan Watson, who believes in the wide applicability of legal transplants, or Pierre Legrand and Gunther Teubner, who stress cultural and systemic differences.

49 Kahn-Freund, *On Use and Misuse of Comparative Law*.

50 Nelken, David, 2003, "Legal Transplants and Beyond: Of Disciplines and Metaphors," in *Comparative Law for the 21st Century*, eds. Andrew Harding and Esin Örücü, Kluwer, The Hague.

51 Smits, Jan, 2002, "On Successful Legal Transplants in a Future Ius Commune Europaeum," in *W.G. Hart Legal Workshop Series: Comparative Law in the 21st Century*, eds. Andrew Harding and Esin Örücü, Kluwer Academic Publishers.

Overall, the debate on legal transplants continues to divide scholars. While some see legal borrowing as a flexible and useful tool, others warn that ignoring institutional and cultural differences can lead to transplant failure.

3.2 The Role of Foreign Precedents in National Courts

Should national courts refer to foreign decisions and opinions? This question has sparked debate among legal scholars and judges, especially in systems like that of the United States. This subsection looks at the arguments for and against using foreign precedents in national courts and explores how global legal dialogue is shaping judicial practices.

3.2.1 Transplants vs. Influence: Debating the Use of Foreign Law in U.S. Courts

This section examines an important distinction between legal transplants and foreign influence. The issue here is not about comparative law, conflict of laws, or simple transplantation. It is more subtle: should judges allow themselves to be influenced by foreign judicial decisions? In Europe, some scholars argue that it is inappropriate to seek guidance from the constitutional law of another country. In other regions, however, it is common for lawmakers to examine foreign legal systems before drafting new legislation.

In the United States, this issue has become a particularly intense topic of debate, especially among judges. Why is this the case? Legal scholars across American universities often ask: is it legitimate for one country's constitutional law to be influenced by another's? From this debate, three major views have emerged: (a) the "tempest in a teapot" view, suggesting this issue is overblown and not truly significant; (b) a moderate concern that acknowledges the issue as important and worth examining seriously; and (c) the "road to perdition" view, which sees foreign legal influence as dangerous, leading to the erosion of national legal identity and values.

Some U.S. Supreme Court Justices have referenced foreign law in their decisions. Justice Sandra Day O'Connor, for example, accepted that foreign sources could be useful if applied cautiously. Others, like Justice Antonin Scalia, strongly rejected any reference to foreign law in constitutional interpretation, viewing it as illegitimate.

One of the most cited examples is the Supreme Court's ruling in *Roper v. Simmons* (2005),[52] where the Court had to decide whether sentencing a person to death for a crime committed under the age of 18 violated the Eighth Amendment, which prohibits cruel and unusual punishments.

In 1989, in *Stanford v. Kentucky*, the Court upheld such sentences.[53] However, by 2005, in *Roper*, it reversed course. Justice Anthony Kennedy wrote the majority opinion, stating that there was a growing national consensus against executing minors, and noted that the U.S. was one of the only countries still doing so. He referred to international norms – not as the basis for the ruling, but to reinforce the point that America was increasingly isolated in its practice. His use of foreign law wasn't outcome-determinative but rather a means of confirming that the U.S.

52 *Roper v. Simmons* 543 U.S. 551 (2005).

53 *Stanford v. Kentucky*, 492 U.S. 361 (1989), followed by *Roper v. Simmons*, 543 U.S. 551 (2005), which overruled *Stanford* and held that all juvenile offenders older than 15 but younger than 18 are exempt from the death penalty. In 2003, the Governor of Kentucky, Paul E. Patton, commuted Kevin Stanford's death sentence, an action later supported by the Supreme Court's decision in *Roper*.

was out of step with global practices. The methodological answer is one that is discussed in the article *International and Foreign Law Sources: Siren Song for U.S. Judges*.[54]

If foreign law does influence outcomes, even subtly, then how should judges decide which legal systems to cite? This is where methodological concerns arise. Judges may "cherry-pick" countries that support their position, ignoring those that don't. There is no obligation, as in conflict of laws, to refer to any specific foreign law, so references can be selective and biased. Often, judges do not conduct this research themselves – clerks or legal briefs bring the material to their attention.

To address this, scholars suggest that courts should: (a) Clearly explain why they cited certain countries; (b) Ensure a fair and representative sample of foreign law; and (c) Be transparent about their sources to avoid accusations of manipulation.

Another issue: Should courts consult every country's law on every issue? Likely not. For example, in free speech cases, referencing a country without strong speech protections could lead to outcomes inconsistent with democratic values.

In less politicized fields, such as copyright law, U.S. courts frequently and uncontroversially reference foreign systems. For example, definitions of "fair use" may draw on international practice, since standards of fairness are broadly similar across liberal democracies.

Some scholars argue that the same logic could be extended to constitutional law if the foreign system shares similar philosophical foundations. But when dealing with issues like privacy, dignity, or abortion, the debate becomes more heated.

National legal culture and historical context play a major role. For example, Germany's abortion laws mandate the criminal prosecution of those involved in abortion procedures, a stance rooted in its unique history and values. Similarly, the South African Constitutional Court, interpreting rights in a post-apartheid context, considered applying constitutional rights horizontally (between private parties). While courts in the U.S., Canada, and Germany saw rights as applying only vertically (against the State), one South African judge argued that the country's particular history justified a different approach.

Such examples suggest that not all legal systems are equally relevant. Courts should ideally restrict their analysis to countries with comparable values or shared historical experiences.

This debate has had real political consequences. At one point, a bill in the U.S. Congress proposed to make it a crime for judges to cite foreign law. Though never passed, it reflects the deep suspicion some American lawmakers have toward international legal influence.

Justice Scalia was a vocal opponent of citing foreign law, arguing that a country's constitution should be interpreted only according to domestic values, without external influence.

Foreign legal influence on constitutional interpretation remains a complex and controversial topic, especially in the U.S. While globalization has encouraged greater dialogue between legal systems, the selective use of foreign precedents, methodological inconsistencies, and value-based concerns make this a delicate issue.

Courts should approach foreign law with caution, transparency, and respect for national values.

The broader challenge is to balance domestic legal identity with global legal insights in a way that supports, rather than undermines, the legitimacy of national legal systems.

54 Keitner, Chimène, 2009, "International and Foreign Law Sources: Siren Song for U.S. Judges?," *Advance: The Journal of the ACS Issue Groups*, vol. 3, no. 1, online. Available at: https://ssrn.com.

3.2.2 Arguments For and Against Using Foreign Precedents

This section looks at the main arguments for and against using foreign legal decisions in national court rulings. It starts by explaining why some judges and scholars support this practice, especially when legal systems share common values or face similar issues due to globalization. Then it presents the main concerns of those who oppose it, such as the risk of weakening national legal traditions, differences in legal culture, and the possibility of using foreign rulings in a selective or biased way. Overall, the debate raises important questions about how much influence foreign law should have on a country's legal system.

3.2.2.1 SUPPORTING THE USE OF FOREIGN PRECEDENTS

One key argument in favor of using foreign precedents is that courts in many democratic countries face similar constitutional questions, such as freedom of speech, privacy, or the Separation of Powers. These are shared legal challenges. For example, both the U.S. Supreme Court and the Constitutional Court of South Africa have addressed free speech issues, especially how to balance expression with public safety concerns like incitement to violence. In such cases, foreign rulings can offer useful insights.

A second argument for using foreign precedents is practical: If a complex legal issue has already been addressed by a foreign court, national judges can learn from that reasoning instead of starting from scratch.

A good example of this is the U.S. Supreme Court case *Lawrence v. Texas* (2003). The case began when Houston police responded to a false report about a weapons disturbance at the home of John Lawrence. Upon entering his apartment, the officers found Lawrence and another man, Tyron Garner, engaging in consensual sexual activity. Both men were arrested under a Texas law that specifically criminalized sexual conduct between people of the same sex. The law did not apply to opposite-sex couples, meaning it singled out same-sex intimacy for punishment.

Lawrence and Garner challenged their convictions, arguing that the law violated their constitutional rights. The Texas Court of Appeals upheld the convictions, citing the U.S. Supreme Court's earlier decision in *Bowers v. Hardwick* (1986), which had ruled that states could criminalize same-sex sexual activity.

When the case reached the U.S. Supreme Court, the justices were asked to consider whether the Texas law violated the Equal Protection Clause or the Due Process Clause of the Fourteenth Amendment. They were also asked whether the Court should overturn its earlier ruling in Bowers.

The Supreme Court ruled in favor of Lawrence and Garner. The majority held that the Texas law was unconstitutional because it violated the Due Process Clause, which protects the right to privacy and personal liberty. The Court emphasized that consenting adults have the right to engage in private, intimate conduct without interference from the government. In doing so, the Court also overruled *Bowers v. Hardwick*, stating that it had been wrongly decided and failed to respect the dignity of same-sex couples.

This landmark decision marked a significant step forward for LGBTQ+ rights in the United States, reinforcing the principle that private, consensual relationships between adults are protected under the Constitution.

In its reasoning, the Court cited a foreign precedent: the European Court of Human Rights case *Dudgeon v. United Kingdom* (1981). In that case, Jeffrey Dudgeon, a shipping clerk and gay activist living in Northern Ireland, brought a complaint against the UK. At the time, homosexual acts between men were still criminal offenses in Northern Ireland, even though such laws had already been repealed in England and Wales. Dudgeon argued that this law violated his right to private life under Article 8 of the European Convention on Human Rights.

The European Court agreed with Dudgeon, ruling that criminalizing private consensual sexual acts between adults was a disproportionate interference with the right to privacy.

By referencing Dudgeon, the U.S. Supreme Court in *Lawrence v. Texas* showed that there was already international recognition that laws criminalizing same-sex intimacy violate basic rights. While the U.S. Court did not base its decision on the European case, it used it to reinforce the idea that privacy and dignity are essential legal principles shared across democratic societies.

A third reason is that considering different legal perspectives can lead to more thoughtful and fair decisions. When courts look at how others have handled similar cases, they are more likely to protect fundamental rights effectively. The Canadian Supreme Court, for example, often cites U.S. and European rulings, especially in cases about privacy or Indigenous rights, to make sure its decisions meet the highest standards of justice.

Overall, using foreign precedents can help judges make better decisions and strengthen the protection of rights.

3.2.2.2 OPPOSING THE USE OF FOREIGN PRECEDENTS

One common criticism of using foreign legal precedents is that comparative analysis is more useful when drafting new laws or constitutions than when interpreting existing ones. Critics argue that legal systems differ too much from country to country for foreign decisions to be helpful in interpreting specific legal rules. For example, when South Africa adopted a new constitution after the end of apartheid, it looked at legal models from countries like Germany and Canada. This was seen as helpful because the country was building a new legal system. However, opponents argue that once a legal system is in place, continued reliance on foreign examples may not fit the local legal and cultural context.

Another concern is that referring to foreign rulings might threaten the independence and authority of national courts. Critics believe that allowing foreign influence in court decisions can be seen as giving up part of a country's legal sovereignty. This concern is especially strong in the United States, where some judges and lawmakers believe that courts should only follow American law. In the case of *Roper v. Simmons* (2005), the U.S. Supreme Court referenced foreign laws when deciding that executing minors was unconstitutional. This sparked controversy, with opponents saying that foreign opinions should not shape American constitutional interpretation.

A final objection is the risk of "cherry-picking" – when judges selectively cite foreign rulings that support their personal views while ignoring others that might offer a different opinion. For example, a judge might choose a decision from a foreign country that aligns with their stance on privacy rights, without considering rulings from other countries that take a different approach. This selective use of foreign law may appear biased and undermine the credibility of the court's reasoning.

Overall, while foreign legal precedents can offer valuable insights, critics emphasize the need for caution. They argue that differences in legal culture, national identity, and political values must be taken seriously to avoid weakening the authority and independence of national courts.

3.2.3 Globalization and Judicial Networks: Enhancing Legal Dialogue

Legal borrowing and the exchange of ideas help legal professionals gain a deeper understanding of different legal systems. Today, globalization and modern communication technologies make the rapid sharing of legal information much easier. Judges, lawyers, and scholars can now connect across borders more efficiently than ever before.

Online legal databases provide quick access to national laws, court decisions, and even international legal materials such as those from UNCITRAL. This digital access allows legal professionals to explore how other systems address similar legal challenges. In addition to online tools, judges also meet in person through international networks and forums where they exchange views and experiences.

For example, U.S. Supreme Court Justices often meet with judges and legal experts from countries like France, the United Kingdom, Germany, and India. At the same time, international courts – such as the European Court of Justice, the International Court of Justice, and the European Court of Human Rights – bring together judges from a wide range of legal traditions.

Overall, globalization encourages dialogue and collaboration between courts, helping legal systems influence one another and adopt useful practices from different traditions.

This growing interaction contributes to a more interconnected legal landscape in which ideas circulate quickly and widely. Comparative insights are increasingly used to interpret statutes, design reforms, and resolve complex transnational disputes. Although each legal system remains sovereign, this global exchange fosters mutual learning and can lead to the gradual harmonization of certain principles and practices. In this sense, globalization not only accelerates the movement of legal concepts across borders but also strengthens a shared understanding of fundamental legal values.

Conclusion

In conclusion, it is clear that foreign laws have a significant impact on domestic legal systems. A central issue in this debate is the legitimacy of referencing, quoting, using, or applying elements from foreign legal systems. However, in today's interconnected world, the focus has shifted from questioning the acceptance of foreign influence to recognizing its necessity. For example, Turkey's adoption of the entire Swiss Civil Code highlights how countries may integrate foreign legal systems in their entirety. The real question now is not whether such practices are legitimate, but rather which countries can be considered as models or, to use an economic term, "suppliers" of legal norms, judicial decisions, or institutions.

This perspective is reinforced by international legal frameworks, such as Article 9 of the Statute of the International Court of Justice, which mandates that elected judges represent the major civilizations and legal systems of the world. Similarly, Article 2 of the Statute of the International Tribunal for the Law of the Sea ensures a fair geographical distribution and representation of the world's principal legal systems. These provisions highlight the importance of diverse legal influences in shaping global legal practices, further emphasizing the interconnected nature of our legal systems today.

Selected Bibliography

Breda, V., (Ed.), 2019, *Legal Transplants in East Asia and Oceania*, Cambridge University Press, 352 pages.

Drolshammer, J., & Weber, R. H., 2019, *Wie das Recht auf Reisen geht: Eine Übersichtsdarstellung internationaler Rechtstransfers am Beispiel des schweizerischen Rechts- und Kulturraums*, Stämpfli, Bern, 486 pages. (Transl. *How Law Travels: An Overview of International Legal Transfers Using the Example of the Swiss Legal and Cultural Sphere*, Bern: Stämpfli, 486 pages).

Kahn-Freund, O., 1974, On Use and Misuse of Comparative Law. *Modern Law Review*, 37, 1.

Prado, Mariana Mota, 2020, December 15, Diffusion, Reception, and Transplantation, in Cane, Peter, and others (Eds.), *The Oxford Handbook of Comparative Administrative Law*, Oxford Academic.

Ragone, S., & Smorto, G., 2023, *Comparative Law: A Very Short Introduction*, Oxford University Press, 176 pages.
Reimann, M. W., 2020, A Bottom-up View of Legal Transplants. *The American Journal of Comparative Law*, 68(3), 689–694.
Solinas, M., 2017, The Debate on the Diffusion of Law, in *Legal Evolution and Hybridisation*, (IUS Commune: European and Comparative Law Series), Intersentia.
Watson, A., 1993, *Legal Transplants: An Approach to Comparative Law*, University of Georgia Press, 144 pages. (First published in 1974).
Zweigert, Konrad, & Kötz, Hein, 2011, *An Introduction to Comparative Law* (3rd ed.), Clarendon Press Oxford, 742 pages.

Part Three

International Law in Its Many Aspects

9 What Is International Law and How Is It Made?

Treaties, you see, are like roses and young girls: they last while they last.
Charles de Gaulle, Speech at Elysée Palace, July 2, 1963

This statement by Charles de Gaulle reflects his pragmatic and somewhat cynical view of international relations. By comparing treaties to "young girls and roses," de Gaulle implied that treaties are inherently impermanent – they are temporary and don't last forever.

This chapter explores International Law – a system of rules that governs relations among states and other global actors, helping to establish order, cooperation, and peace on a global scale. Unlike national laws, which are enforced by a central authority, International Law operates without a single global government. Instead, states and other actors collaborate to create, interpret, and enforce these rules, aiming to maintain a balance between state independence and global order.

International Law is defined in various ways, highlighting its broad scope and unique structure. Each definition of International Law highlights different aspects, such as the subjects it deals with and the relationships it regulates. At its simplest, International Law can be defined as the set of rules that govern relations between states. However, in reality, it is much more complex, shaped by political, diplomatic, and socio-economic factors.

International Law refers to the set of rules that govern legal relationships between nations and states.[1] More broadly, *Public International Law* covers various aspects of state-to-state relations, ranging from issues like war and diplomacy to areas such as satellite use and the functioning of international organizations.[2] It primarily focuses on how agreements between states are formed and implemented, how states interact under legal frameworks, and occasionally includes certain domestic issues. However, it does not include rules dealing with *Private International Law*, which concerns individuals and corporations across borders.[3]

These definitions show that while International Law is fundamentally about governing relations between states, it also includes many layers of complexity in its application and scope.

A significant contribution to the theoretical understanding of International Law was made by Hans Kelsen (1881–1973), the prominent Austrian legal theorist and founder of the *Pure Theory*

1 See Klabbers, Jan, 2020, *International Law*, 2nd ed., Cambridge University Press.
2 See Shaw, Malcolm N., 2021, *International Law*, 9th ed., Cambridge University Press, p. 2.
3 Combacau, Jean and Sur, Serge, 2012, *Droit international public*, 10e éd., Montchrestien, Paris. p. 17.

DOI: 10.4324/9781003393047-13

of Law. Kelsen offers a profound analysis of the structural differences between international and national legal systems. He observes:

> The most important difference between international and national law consists in the fact that the former is a relatively decentralized, the latter a relatively centralized coercive order. This difference manifests itself in the methods by which the norms of the two orders are created and applied. . . . [The International community], constituted by general International Law, being completely decentralized, has no special organs for the creation and application of the law.[4]

In view of this decentralized structure, a broad yet flexible definition captures the essence of International Law: "International Law is a set of rules applicable to international society."[5] This definition embraces the diverse elements and the inherent "internationality" of these norms, setting them apart from national legal systems.

International Law primarily refers to *Public International Law,* governing relations between states and international entities, as opposed to *Private International Law,* which involves domestic legal systems addressing private disputes with a foreign element. Private International Law is outside this chapter's focus, as it functions within national systems to resolve conflicts between domestic and foreign legal jurisdictions. In Chapter 7, we examined *Private International Law* – also known as the *conflict of laws* – by addressing the central question: *When and why do courts apply the law of a foreign jurisdiction?*

Building on these foundational definitions and perspectives, International Law can be understood as a unique and evolving legal system – developed by the international community, for the international community. It provides a structured framework of rules and principles designed to guide the conduct of states and other international actors in their interactions.

This understanding raises several important questions that guide the study of International Law: Who are the subjects of International Law? Why are shared legal rules necessary at the global level, and who is responsible for creating them? What kinds of issues fall within the scope of International Law? Where are these rules recorded or codified?

Exploring these questions helps to clarify the nature, purpose, and scope of International Law. It also highlights the opportunities and challenges involved in applying legal norms in a world characterized by increasing interdependence and global complexity.

This chapter begins by examining the subjects of International Law – those to whom international legal rules apply – including states, international organizations, and, in certain cases, individuals (Section 1). It then explores the sources of International Law, such as treaties, customary International Law, and general principles of law recognized by nations (Section 2). Following this, the chapter outlines the main areas regulated by International Law, including issues such as territorial sovereignty, the Law of the Sea, and diplomatic relations (Section 3).

Attention then turns to contemporary challenges, such as the evolving limits of state sovereignty in an increasingly globalized world (Section 4) and the expanding scope of international human rights protection (Section 5). The chapter concludes by addressing the rules governing

4 Kelsen, Hans, 1949, *The Law of the United Nations: A Critical Analysis of Its Fundamental Problems*, Stevens, London.

5 Rousseau, Charles, *Droit international public*, t. I, n. 1, p. 13. See also Daillier, Patrick, Forteau, Mathias and Pellet, Alain, 2009, *Droit international public*, 8e éd., LGDJ, Paris, p. 43.

the use of force, and the legal consequences of breaches of International Law, including the doctrines of state responsibility and universal jurisdiction (Section 6).

1 Subjects of International Law

Who is subject to International Law? The "Who?" dimension addresses questions like whose actions are governed by International Law, who establishes international norms, and to whom International Law applies. These are referred to as "subjects of International Law" or "international legal persons," meaning entities whose actions are regulated by International Law. These actors are directly bound by international norms, granted specific rights and duties, and may have particular legal capacities, such as the ability to assert their rights through international claims or participate in norm-making. This legal status varies in degree and form, reflecting the diverse members of the international community.

1.1 States as Primary Actors in International Law

States are the foundation of International Law, originally created to govern their interactions. From regulating diplomacy to creating treaties, states have been both the main subjects and creators of legal norms. This part examines their historical role and unique position in shaping International Law.

1.1.1 The Origins of State-Focused International Law

Traditionally, international society was understood as an *inter-state* system, where only the relations between sovereign states were governed by international legal norms. Early International Law focused primarily on regulating interactions between states, whether through peaceful diplomacy or armed conflict. One of the earliest and most enduring areas of International Law is diplomatic law, which governs the establishment, conduct, and termination of diplomatic relations between states.

In this early framework, states were the sole subjects of International Law. They were considered the central actors in the international legal system, with exclusive authority over individuals and legal entities within their territory. Non-state actors – such as individuals, corporations, or other organizations – were not recognized as direct subjects of International Law and were instead governed entirely by domestic legal systems.

This structure reinforced the central role of states in shaping and enforcing international legal norms, marking them as the only entities capable of possessing rights and obligations under International Law.

This traditional, state-centred model reflected a world in which international law existed mainly to manage relations between governments. Its rules were limited in scope and focused on issues like treaties, territory, and war. Over time, however, global developments challenged this narrow view, gradually opening the door for new actors and new areas of international regulation.

1.1.2 The Full Legal Personality and Dual Role of States

States are the original and primary subjects of International Law. As such, they possess full international legal personality, meaning they are recognized as entities capable of holding rights and obligations under International Law. This status allows states to be the direct addressees of international legal norms. Both treaties and customary International Law establish rules that apply directly to states, regulating their conduct in the international sphere.

A clear example of this can be found in the Charter of the United Nations, a foundational multilateral treaty. The Charter is addressed to member states, and it imposes binding legal obligations upon them. For instance, Article 2, paragraph 4 of the UN Charter states: "All Members shall refrain in their international relations from the threat or use of force against the territorial integrity or political independence of any state," and Article 18 lays down that "Each member of the General Assembly shall have one vote."

A bilateral treaty signed by the USA and France on avoidance of double taxation opens up with the following formula:

> The Government of the United States of America and the Government of the French Republic, desiring to conclude a new convention for the avoidance of double taxation and the prevention of fiscal evasion with respect to taxes on income and capital, have agreed as follows:[6]

A detailed legal regime is outlined in the subsequent provisions to which the two contracting parties legally engage.

In addition to that, states enjoy full range of legal capacities on the international level, namely the capacity to go to court and make claims in respect of breaches of International Law (active capacity) and the capacity to be legally responsible for the violation of International Law and to be sued before an international court (passive capacity). States also possess the capacity to create International Law, for example, to conclude treaties and to give rise to international custom, and to enjoy privileges and immunities from national jurisdictions.

In short, states have a special double role in International Law: they are both the ones who follow the rules and the ones who create them. By making treaties and developing customs, states help shape what International Law is and how it works. In this way, they define the overall structure of the international legal system.

Rony Abraham, a prominent French jurist and former President of the International Court of Justice (ICJ), has emphasized the dual role of states as both creators and subjects of International Law. He noted that states are fundamental actors in the development of legal norms, particularly through treaties and customary practices.As emphasized by Rony Abraham in his address before the Sixth Committee of the United Nations General Assembly, the exercise of State sovereignty takes place within a framework of legal constraints, including the need to take into account the legal interests of other States. This perspective underscores the balance between state independence and their duties under the international legal system.[7]

An emerging and underexplored concept in the study of international relations is Legal Diplomacy. Developed through recent academic research, legal diplomacy refers to the way in which states use their legal systems, traditions, and institutions as instruments of international influence.[8] While traditional diplomacy has focused on areas such as economics, culture, and

6 Convention Between the Government of the United States of America and the Government of the French Republic for the Avoidance of Double Taxation and the Prevention of Fiscal Evasion with Respect to Taxes on Income and Capital General Effective Date under Article 33: 1 January 1996.

7 Abraham, Rony, 2017, *Speech before the Sixth Committee of the United Nations General Assembly*, International Court of Justice.

8 See Gontier, Jean-Yves, 2023, *Legal Diplomacy – Defense and Illustration of French Law and Continental Law in Global Law Through the Examples of Mediation and International Arbitration*, thesis defended on 30 January 2023, Paris-Saclay University.

security, legal diplomacy recognizes that legal norms and frameworks also function as tools of soft power.

Other ways to refer to legal diplomacy highlight different aspects of how law and diplomacy interact. For instance, Diplomacy of Law emphasizes law as the subject or domain of diplomacy. Whereas Diplomacy by Law focuses on law as the means or instrument of diplomacy.

All of these terms point to the same idea: that law is not just a set of rules to follow, but also a powerful way for states to shape global discussions, promote their values, and support their foreign policy goals. In sum, they reflect the growing role of legal systems not only in regulating global relations but also in shaping foreign policy and soft power strategies.

Imagine Country A, a nation known for its strong legal system and independent courts. Country A creates a program to help other countries recover from war or internal conflict. As part of this effort, it sends legal experts – like constitutional lawyers and justice advisors – to help Country B, which is rebuilding its government and legal institutions. These experts give advice on human rights, judicial reform, and creating fair and accountable institutions.

While this program is a genuine form of humanitarian aid – as it directly contributes to the recovery and stabilization of societies emerging from conflict – it also allows Country A to promote its own legal values, such as due process, judicial independence, and the Rule of Law. By sharing its legal system abroad, Country A strengthens its global image, builds good diplomatic relationships, and shows leadership in the international community.

Similarly, consider Country A leads a group of states at the United Nations to propose a new international treaty on digital rights and artificial intelligence ethics, based on its own national laws. Even though Country B is not a close political partner, it supports the treaty because aligning with the proposed legal standards would improve its access to Country A's digital markets and attract foreign investment.

This shows how Country A uses legal innovation as a form of diplomacy, helping to shape international rules and increase its influence, not through pressure, but by setting legal standards others want to follow.

1.2 International Organizations as Functional Subjects of International Law

International organizations arose as states recognized the need to work together on problems no single country can solve alone, shared interests, and global challenges such as peace and security, economic development, public health, climate change, and humanitarian crises.

These entities are created to carry out specific functions, with their powers and responsibilities defined by the treaties that establish them. For example, the United Nations works to maintain international peace and security, while the World Health Organization focuses on global health issues. Although important, their roles are limited to the purposes set out in their founding agreements.

1.2.1 The Role and Legal Personality of International Organizations

States, recognizing shared interests and values, created international organizations to address global needs and manage common projects. Organizations, such as the Universal Postal Union for communication, the International Maritime Organization for shipping safety, and the United Nations for global peace and cooperation, serve specialized or broad purposes. Some focus on regional goals, like ASEAN for South Asia, while others, like the World Bank and NATO, have global mandates for development and security.

International organizations are formed through treaties and have legal personalities distinct from their member states. They function as partial subjects of International Law, with powers defined by their founding agreements. For example, the WHO focuses on health, while the ICC addresses war crimes, with their roles strictly outlined in the WHO Convention and the Rome Statute.

While they are bound by international norms, their legal capacities are limited to their missions. They can contract, own property, and engage in legal proceedings, but lack general powers like states. They can address disputes, including arbitration, and be held accountable for wrongful acts, just as they can hold states responsible for breaches of International Law.

A landmark case on this issue is the 1949 case Reparation for Injuries Suffered in the Service of the United Nations. The International Court of Justice held public hearings on March 7, 1949, at the Peace Palace in The Hague to answer a question from the United Nations General Assembly about whether the UN could claim compensation for injuries suffered by its staff while working for the organization.[9]

In the Reparation for Injuries Suffered in the Service of the United Nations case, the International Court of Justice gave an advisory opinion in response to a question from the United Nations General Assembly. The question was whether the UN could bring a legal claim against a state to ask for reparation and compensation when one of its staff members is harmed while carrying out official duties. This issue arose after Count Folke Bernadotte, a UN mediator working in Palestine, was killed in 1948.

The Court said yes – the UN can bring such a claim. It explained that the United Nations is an international legal person. This means that, although it is not a state, it has some legal rights and responsibilities under International Law. One of these responsibilities and rights is to protect its staff and ask for compensation when they are harmed in the line of duty.

The Court added that this capacity is important because the UN carries out key missions such as peacekeeping. To do this work effectively, it must be able to protect its officials. The UN can request reparation both for the harm done to the organization and for the damage suffered by the staff member or their family. The Court also said that the UN and the staff member's home country can work together to decide who should bring the claim.

This case showed that international organizations like the UN have their own legal identity and can act independently to protect their interests and staff members.

1.2.2 The Rise and Role of Regional Integration Organizations

The degree of powers transferred by states to international organizations differs and can even lead to the creation of Regional Integration Organizations (RIO). This kind of international organization has been given a lot of power by its member states. The states agree to let the organization make decisions or take actions for them in certain areas.

An example of an R-I-O is the European Union, which is an intergovernmental organization established by the Treaty on European Union. As laid down in the Treaty, EU member states "resolved to mark a new stage in the process of European integration" and conferred on the European Union "competences to attain objectives they have in common."[10] It is a political and

9 International Court of Justice, 1949, *Reparation for Injuries Suffered in the Service of the United Nations*, Advisory Opinion, ICJ Reports 1949, p. 174.

10 Treaty on the European Union, Preamble, Article 1.

economic union that functions via a system of supranational independent institutions and intergovernmental decision-making processes by the member states.

Member states have given the European Union exclusive powers in certain areas, meaning only the Union can make laws and take binding decisions. These areas include the customs union, competition rules, Eurozone monetary policy, fisheries conservation, and the common commercial policy.[11] States may act only if the Union allows it or to carry out Union rules.

The European Union can make laws that apply directly to people and companies within member states without needing each country to pass a separate law to make them work. This is different from most international organizations, where rules usually need to be turned into national law before they take effect.

The many types of international organizations show that states have different goals and needs. Some organizations focus on regional issues, while others work at the global level. Their structure and powers depend on what the member states want them to do. This variety also illustrates how flexible international cooperation has become. Some organizations, like the EU, take on a supranational role and can shape domestic legal systems, while others operate more traditionally by coordinating policies between states. The choice of structure reflects how willing states are to share or pool their sovereignty. As a result, international organizations today play a wide range of functions, from simple coordination to deep integration, showing how international law adapts to the evolving needs of global and regional governance.

1.3 Individuals' Rise to International Law

The inclusion of individuals in International Law marks an important change in its development. Initially focused only on states, International Law began to address issues within states, granting protections to individuals. This section looks at how individuals' rights are recognized and at their growing responsibilities, including accountability for major crimes.

1.3.1 Recognition of Individual Rights in International Law

The number of subjects of International Law has continued to grow, not only through the creation of international organizations as supra-state actors, but also by including individuals. The idea of *internationality* has moved beyond relations between states and reached inside states to address the rights of individuals. In this way, individuals are no longer seen only as subjects under national law but also as holders of rights under International Law.

They are no longer fully dependent on their State for legal protection when it comes to their fundamental rights and freedoms. Important rights such as the right to life, the right to liberty and security, the prohibition of torture, and freedom of expression are now protected by international legal rules. This means that individuals can be directly protected by International Law, especially in areas related to human rights.

Individuals have seen their basic human rights recognized for example in the International Covenant on Civil and Political Rights (ICCPR, 1966), the International Covenant on Economic, Social and Cultural Rights (ICESCR, 1966), the European Convention for the Protection of Human Rights and Fundamental Freedoms (ECHR, 1950), the American Convention on Human Rights (1969), the African Charter on Human and Peoples' Rights (1981) and in a wide range of particular human rights treaties like the International Convention on the Elimination

11 Treaty on the Functioning of the European Union, Articles 2 and 3.

of All Forms of Racial Discrimination (1966) or the Convention on the Rights of the Child (1989). This international protection evidences a progressive maturation of international society towards common values of humanity that transcend frontiers and unite in common legal principles. Placing the core of human existence under international safeguard represents one of the milestones in International Law.

This development is still ongoing. The level of international protection individuals receive depends largely on the willingness of states to accept and apply international human rights rules. As a result, human rights protection around the world remains uneven and fragmented. Although many human rights treaties give direct rights to individuals – for example, "Every human being has the inherent right to life" (Article 6, ICCPR), or "Everyone is entitled to a fair and public hearing within a reasonable time by an independent and impartial tribunal established by law" (Article 6, paragraph 1, ECHR) – not all states have agreed to these treaties. States that have not signed or ratified a treaty are generally not bound by it, and the rights it contains do not apply to people under their jurisdiction.

For instance, 168 states are parties to the International Covenant on Civil and Political Rights (ICCPR), while 155 states have ratified the Convention against Torture and Other Cruel, Inhuman or Degrading Treatment or Punishment (1984). This shows that while many states accept these obligations, not all individuals worldwide benefit equally from the same legal protections.

Surely, this does not exclude that some human rights apply erga omnes to all states via international customs, but their number is more restricted.

Moreover, the access of individuals to international courts is not fully guaranteed, as there exists no international human rights court, and regional courts have limited geographical scope and restricted accessibility.

An example of a case related to individual rights is the 2010, ICJ, *Ahmadou Sadio Diallo* case.[12] The case of *Ahmadou Sadio Diallo* happened when Mr. Diallo, a businessman from Guinea, was unfairly arrested, arbitrarily detained, and expelled from the Democratic Republic of the Congo (DRC) by the DRC authorities. Mr. Diallo prompted Guinea to exercise diplomatic protection on his behalf. Guinea brought the case to the International Court of Justice, claiming his rights under international treaties, like the right to fair treatment and protection against arbitrary actions, were violated.

The International Court of Justice found that the DRC violated Diallo's rights under the International Covenant on Civil and Political Rights (ICCPR) and the African Charter on Human and Peoples' Rights, including his right to liberty, fair trial, and protection against arbitrary expulsion. The Court ruled that the DRC was responsible and obligated to provide reparation to Guinea for the harm caused to its national. This case affirmed the enforceability of individual rights under International Law and the role of states in protecting their nationals. Thus, the case of *Ahmadou Sadio Diallo* highlighted the recognition of individual rights under International Law.

Building on the broader recognition of individual rights in International Law, feminist legal scholars have reshaped how legal systems engage with issues of gender, power, and inequality. In the United States, scholars such as Catharine MacKinnon, Kimberlé Crenshaw, Martha Fineman, Patricia Williams, Joan Williams, Angela Harris, and Janet Halley have led critical debates on sexual harassment, intersectionality, family law, race, and the boundaries of feminist theory. In Europe, figures like Carol Smart and Nicola Lacey in the United Kingdom, Geneviève

12 International Court of Justice, *Ahmadou Sadio Diallo (Republic of Guinea v. Democratic Republic of the Congo)*, Judgment, ICJ Reports 2010, p. 639.

Fraisse, Marie Mercat-Bruns, and Irène Théry in France, and Ruth Rubio-Marín in Spain have advanced feminist legal theory across diverse legal traditions, focusing on topics such as gender bias, workplace discrimination, and gendered justice in post-conflict settings.

At the international level, scholars like Christine Chinkin[13] and Hilary Charlesworth have challenged the male-dominated structures of global governance[14] and helped integrate gender perspectives into human rights and international criminal law. Their work has strengthened concepts such as intersectionality and emphasized the need to address overlapping forms of discrimination. Collectively, these scholars have offered critical tools to understand how legal systems perpetuate inequality and how they might be transformed to promote greater inclusivity and justice.

Feminist and gender theories have also profoundly influenced the recognition of individual rights in International Law by highlighting systemic inequalities and advocating for the protection of marginalized genders. For example, by emphasizing how traditional International Law often overlooks issues like gender-based violence and reproductive rights, feminist scholars contributed to a key milestone: the 1979 Convention on the Elimination of All Forms of Discrimination Against Women (CEDAW), which set standards for achieving gender equality.

The Convention on the Elimination of All Forms of Discrimination against Women, adopted by the UN General Assembly on December 18, 1979, came into force on September 3, 1981. It serves as a global framework for eliminating gender discrimination and advancing women's rights, building on decades of efforts by the UN Commission on the Status of Women.

CEDAW defines discrimination broadly and requires states to enact laws and policies promoting gender equality in areas like education, employment, political participation, and family life. It emphasizes reproductive rights, equal responsibilities in child-rearing, and access to family planning, while challenging cultural stereotypes that sustain inequality.

Implementation is overseen by the CEDAW Committee, a group of 23 experts who review regular reports from states and provide recommendations. This ensures accountability and progress in addressing discrimination globally, making CEDAW a cornerstone of international efforts for women's rights and equality.

Gender theories have also shaped the development of frameworks like UN Security Council Resolution 1325 (2000), which stresses the importance of women's participation in peace processes and the protection of women during armed conflicts (Otto, 2006).

At the same time, new challenges to International Law are emerging from non-state actors, especially in the digital space. The influence of major tech companies has expanded debates on freedom of expression and the regulation of online content. Platforms like Meta (formerly Facebook) serve as global arenas for public debate, impacting billions of individuals.

Meta – the company behind Facebook, Instagram, and WhatsApp – ended its third-party fact-checking program for Facebook in the United States in early 2024. The transition began around early 2024, when Meta announced it would no longer work with third-party fact-checkers in the U.S., shifting instead to a community-based moderation approach similar to Twitter's (now X) "Community Notes." This shift drew attention due to concerns about misinformation and the weakening of structured fact-checking ahead of the 2024 U.S. elections.

13 Chinkin, Christine, 1999, "Women: The Forgotten Victims of Armed Conflict?," in *The Changing Face of Conflict and the Efficacy of International Humanitarian Law*, eds. Helen Durham and Tim McCormack, Martinus Nijhoff Publishers, Dordrecht.

14 Charlesworth, Hilary, Chinkin, Christine and Wright, Shelley, 1991, "Feminist Approaches to International Law," *American Journal of International Law*, vol. 85, no. 4.

Meta's decision to end fact-checking partnerships highlights the tension between corporate interests and the responsibility to protect freedom of expression and fight against misinformation. It shows how private companies now influence global standards for individual rights, underlining the need for international rules to guide their role in public communication.

1.3.2 Individuals' Responsibilities and Limited Legal Personality

In contrast, the recognition of individuals' passive legal capacity – that is, the ability to be held legally responsible under International Law – marked a major step forward with the creation of the International Criminal Court (ICC) in The Hague, based on the Rome Statute adopted in 1998. The ICC has the authority to prosecute individuals accused of committing the most serious crimes of international concern, including genocide, crimes against humanity, war crimes, and the crime of aggression. This development reflects a shift in International Law, where not only states but also individuals can be held directly accountable before an international court.

A case that illustrates the theme of individuals' responsibilities under International Law is *Prosecutor v. Thomas Lubanga Dyilo* (ICC, 2012). Thomas Lubanga Dyilo, a leader in the Democratic Republic of the Congo, was convicted by the International Criminal Court (ICC) for forcing children under 15 to become soldiers in his armed group during a conflict from 2002 to 2003. These children were trained in harsh conditions and sent to fight or act as bodyguards. The court found him guilty of war crimes and sentenced him to 14 years in prison. Lubanga was also ordered to pay for programs to help the child victims, including education and health care. This was the first case completed by the ICC, showing that using child soldiers is a serious crime. While other courts and tribunals, such as the International Criminal Tribunal for the former Yugoslavia (ICTY) and the Special Court for Sierra Leone (SCSL), had previously tried individuals for crimes involving child soldiers and other international crimes, the Lubanga case was unique because it was the ICC's first trial. It also specifically focused solely on the crime of enlisting and using child soldiers, setting an important precedent in international criminal law. So, while the ICC built upon principles already established by earlier tribunals, this case was its first milestone.

The case of *The Prosecutor v. Thomas Lubanga Dyilo* shows that individuals can be held accountable for violations of International Law, highlighting their international responsibilities. However, while individuals may be prosecuted for serious crimes such as war crimes and crimes against humanity, their overall role in International Law remains limited.

Unlike states and, to some extent, international organizations, individuals do not have the capacity to create legal norms or conclude treaties. They also generally lack standing to bring claims for violations of international treaties. Although international human rights law offers some protection to individuals, it remains limited and depends on whether states have accepted specific legal obligations. At the national level, human rights may be better protected, but the level of protection varies from one country to another.

In addition, International Law offers protection to certain categories of individuals, such as national minorities, refugees, stateless persons, and migrant workers, recognizing their particular vulnerability in the international system.

1.4 Other Actors Recognized by International Law

Alongside states, international organizations, and individuals, other entities can also gain recognition in International Law for certain roles or functions. These actors are sometimes granted limited legal status to respond to specific needs, such as delivering humanitarian aid, supporting self-determination, or engaging in diplomacy. This section focuses on two main groups: organizations with special legal status, such as non-governmental organizations (NGOs), and non-state actors, including insurgent groups and national liberation movements.

1.4.1 Organizations With Special Legal Status

To give a full picture of international society, it is important to mention that some actors other than states, international organizations, or individuals can also be actors with specific rights and duties under International Law.

These actors may receive limited legal status for special purposes – such as helping in humanitarian situations, supporting diplomacy, or promoting self-determination. In some cases, International Law gives them recognition because of their special role or skills.

Some non-governmental or religious organizations have been recognized for their unique contributions. One example is the International Committee of the Red Cross (ICRC), a private organization based in Switzerland. The ICRC was given a special role under the Geneva Conventions of 1949 to protect and assist victims of war. It can also sign agreements with international bodies, such as the World Food Programme or the International Criminal Court. The ICRC has rights and protections similar to those of the United Nations.

Another example is the Holy See, which is linked to the Vatican City State. The Holy See is the governing body of the Catholic Church and a subject of International Law, while Vatican City is the independent State that serves as its territorial base. It has diplomatic relations with many countries, signs international agreements, and is a member of several international organizations like the Organization for Security and Co-operation in Europe (OSCE), the International Atomic Energy Agency (IAEA), and the United Nations High Commissioner for Refugees (UNHCR).

In the Lateran Treaty of 1929, Italy recognized the state of the Vatican City and "the sovereignty of the Holy See in the international domain as an attribute inherent in its nature, in accordance with its tradition and with the requirements of its mission in the world."[15] The Vatican City is also party to several international treaties and a member of the Universal Postal Union (UPU) and the International Telecommunication Union (ITU).

1.4.2 Insurgents, Liberation Movements, and International Legal Recognition

Insurgents and liberation movements, although not traditional subjects of International Law like states, can receive limited recognition under certain conditions. These non-state actors are often involved in armed conflicts or struggles for self-determination, and their legal status depends on the nature of their actions and how the international community responds.

Insurgents, who take part in internal armed conflicts or rebellions, may be bound by international humanitarian law. For example, the Geneva Conventions apply to all parties in an armed conflict, including insurgent groups. This means they are required to respect rules such as the humane treatment of prisoners and the protection of civilians. In some situations, insurgents may also enter into agreements, such as ceasefire arrangements or local governance deals, allowing them to gain a limited form of legal recognition in practice.

For example, the FARC (Revolutionary Armed Forces of Colombia) negotiated peace agreements with the Colombian Government, which led to the demobilization of its forces

15 *Lateran Treaty*, 1929, Art. 2.

and partial integration into the political process. In civil wars, insurgent groups often make temporary agreements with states or international organizations to allow humanitarian aid or enforce ceasefires.

National liberation movements represent people living under colonial rule, foreign occupation, or racist regimes. These groups fight for their right to self-determination, a principle recognized by International Law. When their cause gains support from states or international organizations, they may receive limited recognition as subjects of International Law. This recognition often depends on the legitimacy of their struggle and how closely it aligns with the principles of self-determination set out in international legal instruments.

Key examples include the African National Congress (ANC) during its struggle against apartheid in South Africa, which was supported by the United Nations and recognized as the legitimate representative of the oppressed majority. After the end of apartheid, the ANC became the ruling political party in South Africa and has remained in power since 1994, transforming from a liberation movement into a central actor in national governance.

The Palestine Liberation Organization (PLO), recognized by the United Nations as the representative of the Palestinian people and granted observer status in the General Assembly, continues to participate in international diplomacy. The PLO represents Palestine in various international forums, including the United Nations, where the State of Palestine was granted non-member observer state status in 2012. However, peace negotiations with Israel remain stalled, and political divisions between Palestinian groups have complicated its role.

In 2024 and 2025, several countries, including France, Spain, Ireland, and Norway, formally recognized the State of Palestine.[16] This move aimed to support a two-state solution and increase international pressure for a peaceful resolution to the Israeli-Palestinian conflict. These recognitions add to growing global support for Palestinian statehood, although major powers remain divided, and the situation on the ground remains unstable. The recognitions also reflect broader debates about self-determination and the role of recognition in International Law.

While insurgents and liberation movements do not possess full international legal personality, their actions can have international legal consequences. They are bound by international norms like the Geneva Conventions, and their recognition by international entities or states grants them a limited legal standing. However, their legal rights and obligations are often contingent on the specific context of their activities and the degree of international support they receive.

A case that exemplifies insurgents, liberation movements, and international legal recognition is the Western Sahara Advisory Opinion (1975) of the International Court of Justice.[17] This case focused on whether the people of Western Sahara had the right to decide their own future (self-determination). The ICJ examined claims by Morocco and Mauritania over the territory and concluded that the people of Western Sahara, represented by their liberation movement, had a right to self-determination under International Law. This means they should decide if they want to form their own country or join another. The case highlighted how International Law supports the rights of people under colonial rule to have their voices heard. In recent years, the situation remains unresolved, with the Polisario Front continuing to claim independence, while Morocco controls most of the territory. Some states have begun to shift their recognition or open consulates in Moroccan-controlled areas, raising further legal and political debates.

16 In 2025, 156 countries recognized the State of Palestine. This represents more than three-quarters of the 193 member states of the United Nations.

17 *Western Sahara, Advisory Opinion*, ICJ Reports 1975, p. 12.

Another important example is the 2005 case Armed Activities on the Territory of the Congo, which deals with the role of insurgent groups and international legal responsibility.[18] The Democratic Republic of the Congo accused Uganda of helping rebel groups inside its borders and violating International Law by engaging in armed conflict in Congolese territory. The International Court of Justice found Uganda guilty of supporting the rebels and violating Congo's sovereignty. The Court also highlighted that even non-state groups, like insurgents, must follow International Laws during conflicts. In 2022, the ICJ ruled that Uganda must pay $325 million in reparations to the DRC, showing that legal responsibility can extend to both states and the non-state actors they support.

An ongoing case illustrating this theme is *The Gambia v. Myanmar*,[19] which focuses on Myanmar's alleged genocide against the Rohingya people, a minority group. The International Court of Justice is currently examining whether Myanmar violated International Laws by harming the Rohingya. Some groups within the Rohingya community have started resisting the government, which raises questions about how International Law protects and recognizes oppressed groups. In 2022, the ICJ rejected Myanmar's objections and confirmed that the case can proceed, marking a significant step toward accountability. While the case is ongoing, it highlights how International Law addresses the rights and struggles of non-state groups in situations involving mass atrocities and displacement.

2 Sources of International Law

The dynamic nature of International Law raises important questions: Where do we find its rules? How can we determine whether a state's actions comply with International Law? What human rights are protected? Is a military intervention lawful? Must a State follow an environmental treaty? Why do states sometimes sign formal treaties, while in other cases they allow legal norms to develop gradually through custom and state practice?

Understanding the sources of International Law is essential for identifying which rules apply in a given situation. These sources reflect a balance between formal legal commitments and evolving practices. They show how states shape and respond to legal obligations over time.

The Statute of the International Court of Justice provides a general – though not exhaustive – framework for identifying the sources of International Law. Article 38 of the ICJ Statute lists the legal materials the Court relies on when settling international disputes:

1. The Court, whose function is to decide in accordance with International Law such disputes as are submitted to it, shall apply:

   a. international conventions, whether general or particular, establishing rules expressly recognized by the contesting states;
   b. international custom, as evidence of a general practice accepted as law;
   c. the general principles of law recognized by civilized nations;
   d. subject to the provisions of Article 59, judicial decisions and the teachings of the most highly qualified publicists of the various nations, as subsidiary means for the determination of rules of law.

18 *Armed Activities on the Territory of the Congo (Democratic Republic of the Congo v. Uganda)*, Judgment, ICJ Reports 2005, p. 168.

19 *The Gambia v. Myanmar* (Application of the Convention on the Prevention and Punishment of the Crime of Genocide), ICJ Reports 2022 (ongoing).

2. This provision shall not prejudice the power of the Court to decide a case *ex aequo et bono*, if the parties agree thereto.

This framework provides a legal basis for identifying and applying international norms, helping scholars, courts, and policymakers navigate the complex and evolving structure of International Law.

2.1 Treaties and International Agreements

Treaties are key instruments of International Law. They create binding agreements between states and help ensure legal certainty and stability. This section examines what treaties are, how they function, and their role in maintaining international legal order.

2.1.1 Defining and Structuring Treaties

The 1969 Vienna Convention on the Law of Treaties defines a treaty in Article 2(1)(a) as "an international agreement concluded between states in written form and governed by International Law, whether embodied in a single instrument or in two or more related instruments and whatever its particular designation."

A treaty creates legal obligations only for the states that clearly agree to be bound by it. Its written form ensures legal certainty and clarity, supported by detailed rules on how treaties are made, interpreted, modified, suspended, or terminated. The core principle that gives treaties their binding force is *pacta sunt servanda*, a customary rule meaning that agreements must be kept. While the use of treaties is rooted in long-standing custom, modern treaty law has been systematized and developed in the 1969 Vienna Convention on the Law of Treaties.

Treaties can cover any matter of international concern and contain specific rules agreed upon by the parties. For example, the 1944 Convention on International Civil Aviation (the Chicago Convention) sets binding rules for international air travel, aircraft safety, and registration. A bilateral extradition treaty between two states allows for the surrender of individuals accused of crimes. The 1992 Convention on Biological Diversity establishes rules on the conservation and sustainable use of biodiversity, and the fair sharing of benefits from genetic resources.

States also conclude law-making treaties, which regulate entire branches of International Law and set out general rules of conduct, for example, the 1961 Vienna Convention on Diplomatic Relations (1961) or the 1982 United Nations Convention on the Law of the Sea. However, most treaties are of a particular nature, addressing specific legal relationships or issues.

Treaties can be further classified by the number of parties involved (bilateral or multilateral) or by the procedure used (formal treaties vs. simplified agreements). In practice, terms such as *treaty*, *agreement*, and *convention* are often used interchangeably. Other labels include *pacts*, *acts*, *charters*, *protocols*, *statutes*, *memoranda of understanding*, *modus vivendi*, and *declarations* – each chosen based on context, legal intent, and diplomatic preference.

The International Court of Justice confirmed that "international agreements may take a number of forms and be given a diversity of names."[20] The vocabulary used is not decisive, for it is always the content that defines the legal regime.

20 Maritime Delimitation and Territorial Questions between Qatar and Bahrain (*Qatar v. Bahrain*), judgment of July 1, 1994, ICJ Reports 1994, p.120.

2.1.2 Types and Scope of Treaties

States use treaties to create legal rules that help them cooperate. Some treaties set up broad frameworks, like the 1961 Vienna Convention on Diplomatic Relations, which protects diplomats around the world, or the 1982 United Nations Convention on the Law of the Sea, which sets rules about who controls which parts of the ocean. Other treaties deal with more specific topics, such as extradition, trade, or environmental protection.

One important example is the South China Sea Arbitration (*Philippines v. China*). In this case, the Philippines brought a legal complaint against China in 2013 under the rules of the Law of the Sea Treaty (UNCLOS).[21] The Philippines argued that China was making unfair claims over parts of the South China Sea, an area that has important fishing grounds and oil reserves. China claimed large parts of the sea using a "nine-dash line" drawn on its maps – a unilateral sea boundary. But in 2016, the international tribunal decided that China's claims had no legal basis, and that some of the islands China claimed were too small to have special sea zones. This case showed how treaties like UNCLOS can be used to solve international disputes fairly and peacefully.

Another example is the Extradition Treaty between the United States and the United Kingdom (1972). This treaty helps both countries send people accused of crimes back to the country where they are wanted. For instance, in the case of Julian Assange, the U.S. asked the UK to extradite him under this treaty because he was accused of criminal charges in the United States. The case went through the British courts, which had to check whether the request followed the rules of the treaty.

Julian Assange, an Australian computer hacker and founder of WikiLeaks, became internationally known for publishing large volumes of classified U.S. Government documents, including military reports from the wars in Iraq and Afghanistan, and diplomatic cables revealing sensitive political communications. His actions sparked intense legal and political debates about transparency, national security, and press freedom. After taking asylum in the Ecuadorian Embassy in London for seven years, he was arrested in 2019 and held in Belmarsh Prison. The U.S. sought his extradition on charges under the Espionage Act for conspiring to obtain and publish classified materials. In June 2024, the case concluded when Assange accepted a plea deal with the U.S. Department of Justice. He pleaded guilty in a U.S. court on the island of Saipan –avoiding formal extradition – and was sentenced to time served (about five years in a UK prison). Following the ruling, he was released and returned to Australia. While the case ended without imprisonment in the U.S., it remains a landmark in discussions about the limits of free speech, digital activism, and international legal cooperation.

The case of Julian Assange shows how extradition treaties help countries cooperate on criminal justice while following legal procedures. The South China Sea Arbitration and the Julian Assange case both show how treaties – whether broad or focused on a single issue – play a key role in organizing International Law, solving conflicts, and building trust between countries.

Treaties can be bilateral or multilateral and may follow formal or simplified procedures. Terms like *treaty*, *agreement*, or *convention* are often used interchangeably, alongside others like charters or protocols. To recall, the International Court of Justice emphasizes that a treaty's content, not its name, defines its legal status. By creating clear rules and mutual obligations, treaties are essential for maintaining stability and predictability in international relations.

21 Permanent Court of Arbitration, "The South China Sea Arbitration (The Republic of Philippines v. The People's Republic of China)," Award of 12 July 2016, PCA Case No. 2013-19.

2.2 Customs: Turning Practices Into Legal Standards

Many students view custom in International Law as outdated or abstract, but it continues to play a key role today. Although treaties have become more common since the 20th century, certain legal rules still develop through customary practice, especially in areas where no formal treaty exists or where universal agreement is difficult. For instance, the principle of sovereign immunity, that a state cannot be sued in another state's courts without its consent, is mostly based on custom, not on treaty law.

Customary International Law has the same legal value as treaties, and many treaty rules eventually become customary, applying even to states that have not signed them. For this reason, understanding both treaties and customs is essential when interpreting International Law or resolving disputes.

The International Court of Justice, in the *Continental Shelf* case, explained that customary law is found mainly in the practice of states and in their belief that such practice is legally required (*opinio juris*).[22] These are the two elements of custom: (1) consistent State practice (*usus longaevus* or *consuetudo*); and (2) belief that the behavior is a legal obligation (*opinio juris sive necessitatis*).

A helpful way to imagine this is like a path formed in a park: if many people walk the same shortcut to a tram station, over time it becomes an accepted route – even if it wasn't officially planned. In International Law, when states regularly behave in a certain way and believe it is required by law, this behavior may become a legal custom. For example, before formal treaties existed to regulate the Law of the Sea, many rules – like those on maritime boundaries or resource use – developed through custom. In this way, custom turns repeated actions and shared beliefs into legal obligations. In other words, customs tend to transform factual reality into legal reality.

> [International custom] is a phenomenon above all sociologic, which either arises from logical necessity or it responds to a social need. . . . Most often . . . customary rule corresponds to an equilibrium of international forces existing at a given moment, to a confrontation of legal subjects with an international problem. The spontaneous creation of such rules is accomplished as a result of collective legal conscience of social necessity.[23]

The International Law Commission, a subsidiary organ of the United Nations General Assembly responsible for codifying and progressively developing International Law, has included the topic "Identification of customary International Law" in its long-term programme of work since 2011. Aware of the uncertainty surrounding how customary International Law is formed, the Commission aims to examine the legal requirements for the creation of customary rules, as well as the material evidence used to identify them.[24] This work is expected to provide an updated view of customary International Law in light of modern state practice.

Given this ongoing process, it is essential to examine the basic elements that make up international customs.

22 *Continental Shelf (Libyan Arab Jamahiriya v. Malta)*, Judgment of 3 June 1985, ICJ Reports 1985, p. 29.

23 Daillier, Forteau and Pellet, *Droit International Public*, 355 (author's translation).

24 *Report of the International Law Commission*, Sixty-fourth session, General Assembly Official Records, Sixty-seventh session, Supplement No. 10 (A/67/10), p. 108.

2.2.1 The Meaning of Actual Practice in International Law

A comprehensive definition of state practice, which forms one of the key elements of international custom, was provided by the International Court of Justice (ICJ) in its judgment of February 20, 1969, in the North Sea Continental Shelf cases. The Court stated that:

> [A]n indispensable requirement would be that within the period in question, short though it might be, state practice, including that of states whose interests are specially affected, should have been both extensive and virtually uniform.[25]

This definition highlights three key features of customary practice: it must be uniform, constant, and general.

What does uniformity mean in practice? Uniformity refers to the consistency of a state's actions. A state must act in a coherent way, repeating similar conduct over time. If a state's actions are contradictory or unclear, they cannot be considered as part of a consistent practice and therefore do not support the formation of a custom.

How frequent or long must a practice be? There is no strict number of times a state must repeat a certain action, nor is there a fixed time frame. While customs used to take a long time to develop, the ICJ recognized that, due to the increased pace of international relations, a customary rule may emerge quickly, as long as there are enough opportunities to adopt and repeat the conduct.[26] As the Court noted, "the passage of only a short period of time is not necessarily, or of itself, a bar to the formation of a new rule of customary International Law."[27]

How many states must participate? To form a valid international custom, practice must be general, meaning that it should be widespread and representative, especially among states most affected by the issue. Full participation of all states is not necessary. The ICJ explained that a smaller number of specially affected states could establish a custom if their actions are clear and consistent. The silence or lack of opposition by other states can be seen as acquiescence – a form of tacit agreement.

An example is provided by space law. Only a few states actively operate in outer space, but their practices – if consistent – can help form customary space law. Other states may not actively participate but can accept (or reject) these developments through their silence or actions. In this way, custom can supplement or even change existing space treaties.

Can a state avoid being bound by a custom it disagrees with? Yes, but only under certain conditions. International Law is built on the idea of consent, and a state may avoid the effects of a new custom if it clearly objects to it from the beginning and maintains its objection over time. This is known as the persistent objector rule. In the Anglo-Norwegian Fisheries Case (1951), the ICJ ruled that Norway was not bound by a rule setting territorial sea limits at ten miles because it had consistently rejected the rule from the outset. The Court found that "the ten-mile rule would

25 North Sea Continental Shelf (*Federal Republic of Germany v. Netherlands*) (*Federal Republic of Germany v. Denmark*), judgment of 20 February 1969, ICJ Reports 1969, p. 43.

26 This invokes the question of an "instant custom," i.e., whether an isolated precedent can give rise to a customary rule. Some authors claim that, in view of the dynamics of global progress and new situations international society faces, prompt rule-formation in exceptional cases of urgent necessity and absence of contrary rules could be accepted. For example, Bernhardt notes: "I would even accept that in exceptional circumstances no practice is necessary if a certain rule according to which a certain behaviour is either necessary or prohibited has been universally approved. In so far I would accept the possibility of 'instant law.'" Bernhardt, Rudolf, 1987, "Custom and Treaty in the Law of the Sea," *RCADI*, vol. 205, p. 266.

27 ICJ, *North Sea Continental Shelf.*

appear to be inapplicable as against Norway inasmuch as she has always opposed any attempt to apply it to the Norwegian coast."[28]

The limits of this rule are that a state can only object to general customary rules. In contrast, regional or bilateral customs, which develop among specific groups of states, require common agreement and cannot be avoided unilaterally.

2.2.2 Why Opinio Juris *Matters in International Law*

If states become accustomed to behaving in a certain way, why is *opinio juris* still necessary? The psychological element – namely, the belief that a specific practice is legally required – is essential because it turns a habit into a binding legal rule. States may engage in many practices, but not all of them are legally obligatory. For example, states often choose to provide humanitarian aid or take part in mediating international disputes. However, these actions are typically voluntary and can be withdrawn or altered at any time, depending on the state's preferences.

A similar situation exists in diplomatic relations, where many long-standing traditions are followed out of courtesy or protocol rather than legal obligation. As the International Law Commission has noted, "There are many international acts, e.g., in the field of ceremonial and protocol, which are performed almost invariably, but which are motivated only by considerations of courtesy, convenience or tradition, and not by any sense of legal duty."[29]

Therefore, what sets customary International Law apart from mere diplomatic or voluntary conduct is *opinio juris* – the belief that the behavior is carried out because the law requires it. This belief transforms consistent state practice into a binding legal norm.

Without *opinio juris*, repeated actions remain only patterns of behavior, similar to habits or traditions. The psychological element shows that states are consciously acting out of a sense of legal obligation and not simply repeating a convenient or traditional practice. This distinction is crucial because it explains why some repeated behaviors crystallize into customary law while others do not. In this way, *opinio juris* functions as the normative foundation that elevates practice into law and secures the authority of customary rules within the international legal system.

2.3 General Principles of Law vs. General Principles of International Law

General principles play an important role in International Law by filling gaps where neither treaties nor customary rules offer clear answers. It is important, however, to distinguish between general principles of law, which are drawn from common elements found in national legal systems,[30] and general principles of International Law, which reflect broader values and norms already recognized in international legal practice. This section looks at how these principles arise, why they matter, and how they are used in legal reasoning.

2.3.1 General Principles of Law Derived From National Legal Systems

International Law can sometimes rely on national legal systems to extract common legal principles and apply them at the international level. In cases where neither treaties nor customary rules

28 *Fisheries (United Kingdom v. Norway)*, Judgment of 18 December 1951, ICJ Reports 1951, p. 131.

29 ICJ, *North Sea Continental Shelf.*

30 Formulation "general principles of law recognized by civilized nations" utilized in Art. 38 of the ICJ Statute reflects the international scene at that time and is now largely regarded as a vestige of the past.

provide clear answers, and to avoid a situation of *non liquet* (where no applicable law exists), general principles of law found in domestic systems may be used. These principles serve as an auxiliary source of law. For such a principle to be transferred to the international legal system, two conditions must be met: the principle must be common to several national legal systems and its nature must allow for its adaptation to the international context.

Examples of such general principles of law include legal certainty and the protection of legitimate expectations, the principle of *res judicata* (finality of judgments), and the principle of full compensation for damage. These principles are especially relevant in developing areas of International Law where legal gaps are more likely to appear, such as international criminal law, which often involves elements traditionally handled at the national level.

General principles derived from domestic legal systems show the influence of national legal traditions on International Law. However, many of these principles originate from Western legal systems, which shaped much of International Law during the colonial period. As a result, International Law has faced criticism for being rooted in Western values and for lacking representation of the legal diversity found across the globe. This criticism highlights the colonial legacy of International Law and raises ongoing concerns about its inclusiveness and fairness.

Legal scholar Antony Anghie, Professor of Law at the National University of Singapore Faculty of Law and Secretary General of the Asian Society of International Law, in *Imperialism, Sovereignty and the Making of International Law* (2005), argues that the foundations of International Law were shaped during the colonial era. He explains how principles such as sovereignty and the "standard of civilization" were used to legitimize imperial control. Anghie challenges the idea that International Law is neutral, showing instead how it supported global inequality and control over non-European territories. His work calls for a rethinking of international legal structures to promote a more equitable global system.

Likewise, B. S. Chimni, Professor of International Law at Jindal Global University, Haryana, India, in *International Law and World Order: A Critique of Contemporary Approaches* (2017),[31] criticizes the Eurocentric nature of International Law. He argues that it often serves the interests of powerful states and multinational corporations, while marginalizing the voices of the Global South. Drawing on Marxist and postcolonial theory, Chimni advocates for the "Third World Approach to International Law" (TWAIL), which aims to reform International Law by addressing the historical injustices of colonialism and promoting a more just world order.

Sundhya Pahuja, a prominent International Law scholar and Fellow of the Australian Academy of the Social Sciences, in *Decolonising International Law: Development, Economic Growth and the Politics of Universality* (2011), further criticizes how development policies often reinforce colonial-era power dynamics. Her work stresses the importance of adopting decolonial approaches to reshape International Law in a way that prioritizes fairness and inclusivity.

2.3.2 General Principles of International Law Reflect Existing International Rules

General principles of law are often mistaken for general principles of International Law, though the two differ in both origin and function. General principles of International Law do not operate as an independent source of law but instead emerge from the generalization of existing

31 Chimni, B. S., 2017, *International Law and World Order: A Critique of Contemporary Approaches*, Cambridge University Press.

treaty-based or customary norms. These principles are characterized by their high degree of abstraction and generality, reducing complex legal norms to concise formulations.[32]

They encapsulate the foundational values of the international community and embody the underlying spirit of international legal norms. Their purpose includes enhancing the coherence of International Law, filling normative gaps, and guiding legal interpretation. For instance, the International Court of Justice has recognized that the prohibition of the use of force, as articulated in Article 2(4) of the UN Charter, is not only a customary rule but also a cardinal principle of International Law.[33]

Similar recognition is given to principles such as *pacta sunt servanda*, which obliges states to respect their treaty commitments, and the principle of sovereign equality. The latter ensures that all states, regardless of their differences, are equal members of the international community. Sovereign equality includes specific legal elements:

(a) States are legally equal.
(b) Each state enjoys the rights of full sovereignty.
(c) Each state must respect the legal personality of other states.
(d) States' territorial integrity and political independence are inviolable.
(e) States have the right to choose and develop their own systems freely.
(f) States must fulfil their international obligations in good faith and promote peaceful coexistence.[34]

These principles collectively support the stability, predictability, and legitimacy of the international legal system.

2.3.3 *Equity as a Corrective Element in Law*

Equity has given rise to different interpretations and arguments in legal thought. In general terms, equity means fairness and impartiality – "the quality of being fair and impartial."[35] In legal systems, especially International Law, equity serves to make justice more concrete and adaptable within legal rules.[36]

In International Law, equity has two main roles. First, it may guide the interpretation and application of existing legal rules. Second, it may act as an independent basis for deciding disputes, as mentioned in Article 38(2) of the Statute of the International Court of Justice (ICJ).

This article allows the Court to decide cases *ex aequo et bono*, meaning according to what is fair and good, rather than strictly applying legal rules. However, many scholars debate whether equity is truly a separate source of International Law, though they agree it plays an important role in its development.

32 Dupuy, Pierre-Marie and Kerbrat, Yann, 2012, *Droit International Public*, 11e éd., Paris, Dalloz, p. 378.

33 Military and Paramilitary Activities in and against Nicaragua (*Nicaragua v. United States of America*), Judgment of 27 June 1986, ICJ Reports 1986, p. 100.

34 UN General Assembly Resolution 2625 (XXV), Annex, Declaration on Principles of International Law concerning Friendly Relations and Co-operation among states in accordance with the Charter of the United Nations.

35 *Oxford Dictionary of English*, 2013, 3rd ed., ed. Angus Stevenson, Oxford University Press.

36 For historical context, see Chapter 3 – The Common Law Tradition, particularly section 1.2 "Equity: Its Emergence and Role as a Common Law Complement," and the landmark Earl of Oxford's Case (1615), where the principle that equity prevails over Common Law was firmly established.

From the first perspective, scholars see equity in three ways: (1) as a corrective tool to ensure the fair application of law; (2) as a feature or characteristic of the legal system itself; and (3) as a set of equitable principles reflected in treaties or customary law.

The ICJ has applied equity, especially in maritime boundary cases, to support the use of fair methods such as the equidistance principle when drawing maritime borders. For example, in the Continental Shelf (*Tunisia v. Libya*) case, the Court stated that it must apply equitable principles as part of International Law. It must balance relevant factors to reach a fair result, but this does not mean the Court is free to act based on personal judgment or to engage in distributive justice.

> [I]t is bound to apply equitable principles as part of International Law, and to balance up the various considerations which it regards as relevant in order to produce an equitable result. While it is clear that no rigid rules exist as to the exact weight to be attached to each element in the case, this is very far from being an exercise of discretion or conciliation; nor is it an operation of distributive justice.[37]

Equity here remains grounded in law.

2.3.4 Equity as an Autonomous Basis for Dispute Settlement

The second perspective, under which equity is an autonomous basis for judicial settlement of disputes, is best illustrated in the ICJ Statute that gives in Article 38, paragraph 2, the power to the Court to decide a case *ex aequo et bono*, "if the parties agree thereto." In the Court's view, in this situation, "the Court is then freed from the strict application of legal rules in order to bring about an appropriate settlement."[38] In all cases, the main question is how far equity can go. Can it replace existing legal rules or even go against them – produce effects *contra legem* (against the law)? Or is equity only meant to fill gaps in the law or make unfair laws less harsh in certain cases? Equity can have a stronger effect when both parties clearly agree to use it.

In practice, most international courts apply equity only within the limits of the existing legal framework: they use equitable principles to interpret vague rules, to adjust rigid norms, or to resolve issues not expressly covered by treaties or customary law. However, when the parties explicitly authorize a court to decide *ex aequo et bono*, equity becomes a true alternative to law. In such cases, the judge may depart from the legal rules and focus on achieving a fair and reasonable outcome for both parties. This exceptional mechanism illustrates the flexible role that equity can play in international dispute settlement, while also confirming that its strongest effects depend on the express consent of the states involved.

2.4 Unilateral Acts

A unilateral act is an action taken by a state on its own without needing agreement from others, which can legally bind that state under certain conditions. These acts, such as declarations, recognitions, or promises, reflect the state's intention to commit itself to legal obligations. This section explores the legal impact of unilateral acts and how they are applied in practice.

37 *Continental Shelf (Tunisia v. Libyan Arab Jamahiriya)*, Judgment of 24 February 1982, ICJ Reports 1982, p. 60.
38 ICJ, *Continental Shelf (Tunisia v. Libya)*.

2.4.1 Legal Impact of Unilateral Acts

A unilateral act by a state can, in certain situations, create legal obligations. States may issue declarations, make recognitions or promises, and deliver official statements or notifications. If such an act clearly reflects the state's will and is made with the intention to be legally bound, it can produce binding legal effects for that state.

In the Nuclear Tests Case (1974), France promised to stop testing nuclear weapons in the Pacific Ocean. They made this promise publicly, and other countries trusted that France would keep its word. The International Court of Justice (ICJ) said France's promise was legally binding because it was clear, public, and made with serious intent. A series of official statements made publicly by France in the course of 1974 concerning the holding of atmospheric tests of nuclear weapons in the Pacific Ocean was qualified by the International Court of Justice as evidence of "its intention effectively to terminate [its atmospheric] tests."[39] In the judgment in *Nuclear tests* Case, the Court decided that "[h]aving regard to their intention and to the circumstances in which they were made," the statements "must be held to constitute an engagement of the State."[40] "It was bound to assume that other states might take note of these statements and rely on their being effective."[41] The Court concluded that France had undertaken an obligation concerning the effective termination of the tests.

The Court's statement highlights the main principle behind the binding nature of unilateral acts: a state has the freedom to intentionally create legal commitments that generate effects for other states. For such acts to have legal force, publicity or clear communication of the act is important, as well as the good faith of the state making the declaration. Importantly, the acceptance or approval of other states is not required for the act to be legally binding.

2.4.2 Role of Unilateral Acts in International Law

Unilateral acts play an important role in areas such as territorial recognition, declarations of neutrality, or promises related to environmental protection.

The binding nature of these acts depends on the clear intention of the state and the context in which they are made. Once a state makes such an act with clear intent, it becomes legally binding. However, the act must also follow the principles of good faith and be made public to ensure transparency and build trust. These principles help make unilateral acts a valuable tool in International Law, offering both flexibility and accountability.

Here are some examples of cases where countries made unilateral promises or statements that became legally binding:

In the Eastern Greenland Case (1933), Norway made a promise that Denmark could have control over a place called Eastern Greenland. The court decided that Norway's promise was legally binding because it was made clearly and in good faith. This case showed that countries' promises can be trusted and relied on.[42]

In the Temple of Preah Vihear Case (1962), Thailand accepted a map showing that a temple belonged to Cambodia. Later, Thailand tried to change its mind, but the ICJ ruled that Thailand's earlier acceptance was a legal promise. It was binding because Cambodia had trusted and relied on that promise.[43]

39 *Nuclear Tests (Australia v. France) (New Zealand v. France)*, Judgment of 20 December 1974, ICJ Reports 1974, p. 269.

40 ICJ, *Nuclear Tests*.

41 ICJ, *Nuclear Tests*.

42 *Legal Status of Eastern Greenland*, PCIJ Series A/B, No. 53, 1933.

43 *Temple of Preah Vihear (Cambodia v. Thailand)*, ICJ Reports 1962, p. 6.

In the *Burkina Faso v. Mali Frontier Dispute Case* (1986), two countries, Burkina Faso and Mali, promised to resolve a border disagreement peacefully. The ICJ said their promises were legally binding because they were made publicly and in good faith. This showed how countries' promises can help avoid conflict.[44]

In the Fisheries Jurisdiction Case (1974), Iceland said it would extend its fishing areas. The ICJ looked at the promise but didn't find it legally binding in this case. However, the Court explained how promises made by countries can become binding if they are clear, public, and meant to be relied on.[45]

These cases show that when a country makes a clear and serious promise, it can become legally binding if other countries trust and rely on it.

2.5 How Judicial Decisions and Scholars Help Shape International Law

Judicial decisions and academic writings do not, by themselves, create International Law. However, they play an important role in explaining, clarifying, and interpreting the law. Through their reasoning and analysis, courts and scholars help states and other actors understand how existing legal rules apply in specific situations. This section discusses the ways in which judicial decisions and academic writings contribute to the development and practical application of International Law.

2.5.1 Judicial Decisions: Shaping International Law

"Judicial decisions and the teachings of the most highly qualified publicists of the various nations," as referred to in Article 38 of the Statute of the International Court of Justice, are not themselves formal sources of International Law.[46] Court decisions, arbitral awards, and academic writings do not create legal rules but rather assist in identifying, interpreting, and applying existing law. As the ICJ stated in an advisory opinion, "it states the existing law and does not legislate. This is so even if, in stating and applying the law, the Court necessarily has to specify its scope and sometimes note its general trend."

Despite this limitation, judicial decisions and scholarly writings make a significant contribution to the development of International Law. For instance, although the decisions of the International Court of Justice are only binding on the parties involved and for the specific case at hand, they have a strong influence on the broader understanding and interpretation of the legal principles in question. As Shaw notes,

> while the doctrine of precedent as it is known in the Common Law, whereby the rulings of certain courts must be followed by other courts, does not exist in International Law, one still finds that states in disputes and textbook writers quote judgments of the Permanent Court and the International Court of Justice as authoritative decisions.[47]

In this sense, they function as persuasive authorities: they help clarify ambiguities, consolidate emerging interpretations, and provide reasoned guidance where treaty provisions or customary rules remain uncertain. Over time, repeated reliance on these authorities can influence state practice and even contribute indirectly to the crystallization of customary norms. Thus,

44 *Frontier Dispute (Burkina Faso v. Mali)*, ICJ Reports 1986, p. 554.

45 *Fisheries Jurisdiction (United Kingdom v. Iceland)*, ICJ Reports 1974, p. 3.

46 *Legality of the Threat or Use of Nuclear Weapons*, advisory opinion of 8 July 1996, ICJ Reports 1996, para. 18.

47 Shaw, *International Law*, p. 110.

although they are not formal sources of law, judicial decisions and scholarly writings help ensure coherence, predictability, and intellectual rigor within the international legal system.

Similarly, the works of leading scholars are frequently cited by international courts and invoked by states in diplomatic practice. This shows that both judicial decisions and academic writings, while not law-making in themselves, play an important role in shaping the perception, development, and application of international legal norms.

2.5.2 Teachings: The Role of Scholars in International Law

Academic writings by respected legal scholars play a key role in shaping International Law. Although they do not create legal rules, these writings are often used in court decisions and cited by states to explain or support their legal positions. This relationship between judicial rulings and scholarly opinion reflects how International Law evolves through ongoing interpretation, helping to clarify legal norms and make them more accessible.

Several legal scholars have made lasting contributions to the development of International Law:

Hugo Grotius, often regarded as the father of International Law, laid the foundations of the field in his work *De Jure Belli ac Pacis* (On the Law of War and Peace) published in 1625. He introduced the idea of natural law as the basis for relations among states, emphasizing justice and fairness. His teachings strongly influenced the legal principles governing war and peace, which remain central today.

Emer de Vattel's *The Law of Nations* (1758) helped to popularize the concepts of state sovereignty and the equality of states. These ideas became core principles of International Law and are reflected in key instruments such as the United Nations Charter.

Hersch Lauterpacht contributed significantly to the development of international human rights. In his influential book *The Function of Law in the International Community* (1933), he argued for the recognition of individuals as subjects of International Law. His work influenced key documents like the Universal Declaration of Human Rights (1948) and the International Covenant on Civil and Political Rights (1966).

Oppenheim's International Law (9th ed., 1992) remains one of the most authoritative and frequently cited textbooks in the field. It offers detailed guidance on major areas of International Law, including treaties, State responsibility, and the Law of the Sea. Courts such as the International Court of Justice regularly reference it.

Antonio Cassese's contributions to international criminal law, especially in his book *International Criminal Law* (2003), were instrumental in developing this area. His work supported the creation of international tribunals like the International Criminal Tribunal for the Former Yugoslavia (ICTY) and the International Criminal Court (ICC).

James Crawford's book *The International Law Commission's Articles on State Responsibility* (2002) clarified the legal rules surrounding state accountability for internationally wrongful acts. His analysis has been widely cited in international litigation and continues to shape how breaches of International Law are addressed.

2.6 Equality of Sources vs. Hierarchy of Norms in International Law

Understanding the relationship between sources and norms in International Law is essential. The concept of "sources" refers to the origin or mechanisms that create legal rules, while "norms" are the actual rules or principles that regulate behavior. These two concepts are distinct and do not overlap. Sources are acts, agreements, or practices – such as treaties, customs, or general principles of law – that generate the legal content. Norms are the legal obligations or rights that emerge from those sources.

In simpler terms, sources provide the framework of International Law, and norms are the substantive rules within that framework. For example, a treaty (source) may contain provisions on environmental protection (norms), or a customary practice (source) may give rise to a legal ban on slavery (norm). Thus, sources give rise to legal rules, while norms guide and regulate conduct in international relations.

The diversity of sources reflects the varying interests and needs of states. Each source comes with specific legal and procedural features and serves a particular function. For example, a bilateral trade agreement may be the most efficient tool for regulating economic exchange between two neighboring countries. On the other hand, a multilateral treaty on the use of force to protect citizens abroad in emergency situations may require broader consensus and could gradually develop through state practice and *opinio juris* before becoming a binding rule.

This diversity supports the principle of equality among the sources of International Law. There is no formal hierarchy – customary International Law is not subordinate to treaties, nor are general principles less authoritative. States are obligated to follow applicable legal norms regardless of their source. What matters is not how the rule was formed, but that it is valid and binding in International Law.

2.6.1 Resolving Conflicts Between Norms: Special and New Rules

When two norms come into conflict, International Law applies legal maxims to resolve the issue. The principle *lex specialis derogat generali* means that a more specific rule prevails over a general one, while *lex posterior derogat priori* gives priority to the rule that was adopted later in time. These principles help preserve coherence in the legal system when norms overlap or contradict each other.

When international norms conflict – whether they arise from the same legal source or from different sources – these maxims are typically applied. According to *lex specialis derogat generali*, the more specific rule overrides the general rule. Under *lex posterior derogat priori*, the newer rule takes precedence over the older one. For instance, a general regional agreement on cooperation in the fishing industry would be overridden by a specific treaty establishing fishing limits to protect endangered species.

These maxims provide practical guidance for courts and states by clarifying which norm should be applied in situations of overlap. They do not create new obligations but help interpret existing ones in a way that reflects the presumed intentions of the parties. In this sense, lex specialis and lex posterior function as interpretive tools that support the stability and predictability of International Law, ensuring that conflicting texts can be reconciled without undermining the overall coherence of the legal system.

2.6.2 The Unique Status of Jus Cogens *Norms*

Unlike other rules, *jus cogens* norms hold a higher and binding status in International Law. These are fundamental principles that all states must respect, even if they do not agree to them. As defined in Article 53 of the Vienna Convention on the Law of Treaties, *jus cogens* norms are rules accepted by the international community as non-derogable. This means no treaty or rule can go against them. Examples include the prohibition of genocide, slavery, torture, and the illegal use of force.

The term *jus cogens* comes from Latin and means "compelling law." These norms represent the most basic and widely accepted values in the international legal system. They protect human dignity and aim to uphold the global public order. For example, a treaty that allows slavery or genocide would have no legal effect, as it would violate *jus cogens*.

Courts have supported the special nature of *jus cogens* norms. In the 1970 *Barcelona Traction* case, the International Court of Justice introduced the idea of obligations *erga omnes* – duties owed to all states. The Court explained that some international obligations, like the ban on genocide and racial discrimination, go beyond the interests of two states and protect the shared values of the international community.

In *Belgium v. Senegal* (2012), the ICJ ruled on Senegal's failure to prosecute or extradite Hissène Habré, a former president accused of torture. Belgium claimed Senegal had violated its duty under the 1984 Convention against Torture. The Court confirmed that the duty to fight torture reflects a *jus cogens* norm and must be respected by all states.

Although some countries, such as the United States, China, and Russia, have expressed concerns about the lack of a clear authority to define *jus cogens* norms, these principles remain essential. They promote common values and help protect fundamental human rights across all nations. By limiting state actions that violate basic human dignity, *jus cogens* norms play a key role in shaping a just and lawful international order.

3 Issues Regulated by International Law

What issues does International Law regulate?

International Law plays a key role in regulating the global community. Just like national law organizes relationships within a country, International Law helps manage relations between states and other international actors. Its purpose is to promote order, justice, and cooperation while helping to resolve conflicts peacefully.

In the international society, relationships are shaped by both cooperation and conflict. States may share common goals, but they also have different interests, needs, and values. These differences can lead to tensions. At the same time, states often work together in areas such as trade, security, or the environment. This constant shift between cooperation and disagreement shows why agreed-upon "rules of the game" are necessary.

International Law helps manage this balance. It provides a framework that guides how states behave, resolve disputes, and work together. In today's globalized world, international interaction is more complex than ever. As a result, International Law covers a wide and growing range of issues, from climate change and human rights to armed conflict and internet governance. In recent years, it has also begun addressing new and complex areas such as cybersecurity, artificial intelligence, data privacy, space activities, global health emergencies like pandemics, and the regulation of emerging technologies. These developments show how International Law continues to evolve in response to scientific progress, digital transformation, and the changing needs of the global community.

One way to understand the wide scope of International Law is to look at it from two angles: the law of cooperation and the law of dispute settlement. The law of cooperation includes rules on trade, environment, health, development, and more – areas where states work together for common goals. The law of dispute settlement focuses on peaceful ways to resolve conflicts between states, including through courts, arbitration, and negotiations.

This diversity and flexibility are what make International Law dynamic and responsive to the changing realities of the world.

3.1 Law of Cooperation and Diplomacy

The law of cooperation and diplomacy is like a guidebook for countries to work together, talk, and live side-by-side peacefully. It sets rules to protect each country's independence, decide who controls what land, and make agreements between nations. These rules cover many areas, like protecting the environment, trading goods, and even exploring space. This section looks at two big ideas: the basic rules for countries to cooperate and the special laws made for solving global problems.

3.1.1 Foundational Principles of International Cooperation

International cooperation is built on key principles that protect state sovereignty, territorial integrity, and political independence. International Law defines the boundaries of state authority and the criteria for recognizing states.[48] Historically, rules for treating diplomats laid the groundwork for modern diplomatic and consular law, which ensures privileges and immunities necessary for international dialogue.

Today, International Law extends to areas like maritime rules, airspace regulation, and human rights, allowing states to coexist peacefully while addressing shared global issues. It also covers areas such as environmental protection, climate change, international trade, global health, migration and refugees, the regulation of armed conflict, terrorism, cybercrime, artificial intelligence, data protection, outer space activities, nuclear non-proliferation, and the use of natural resources.

Diplomacy plays a crucial role in international cooperation by helping states negotiate solutions and ensure compliance with international rules. According to France's Ministry for Europe and Foreign Affairs (France Diplomatie), diplomacy is the practice of dialogue and negotiation between sovereign states, operating without coercion.[49]

Alicia Cebada Romero, Professor of International Law and International Relations at Universidad Carlos II of Madrid, emphasizes the value of nonbinding diplomatic methods, like negotiation and mediation, in resolving disputes.[50]

While binding methods such as court decisions often receive the most attention in International Law, nonbinding approaches are also very important. These include soft law instruments like declarations, guidelines, and codes of conduct. Although not legally enforceable, they show how states interact, help interpret international rules, and influence the development of new legal norms. Over time, such practices can shape the evolution of International Law.

Legal diplomacy also plays a key role in international cooperation. It allows states to build consensus, promote shared goals, and influence international discussions. By sharing their legal traditions and promoting national legal norms, states can contribute to the creation of international frameworks in areas such as biodiversity protection, sustainable development, and human rights. Through this process, a state can position its legal system as a model for others, increasing its influence and encouraging cooperation among countries. This shows how law is becoming an essential tool in modern diplomacy and a strategic part of shaping global relations.

A notable example of legal diplomacy is the European Union's General Data Protection Regulation (GDPR). Although it is a domestic law, it has had a strong international impact.

48 See Shaw, *International Law*.

49 *France Diplomatie*. Available at: https://www.diplomatie.gouv.fr.

50 See UN SG Report on Enhancing Mediation and Its Support Activities, S/2009/189, p. 3.

Since its implementation in 2018, the GDPR has introduced strict rules on data protection, such as consent-based data collection, the right to be forgotten, and heavy fines for violations. Many countries and companies around the world have followed its standards, making it a global reference point for privacy and data regulation.

The influence of the General Data Protection Regulation extends far beyond Europe, inspiring a wave of similar data privacy laws worldwide.[51] For instance, Brazil's Lei Geral de Proteção de Dados (LGPD), implemented in 2020, closely mirrors the GDPR by requiring consent for data processing and imposing fines of up to 50 million BRL (approximately 11.8 million EUR) for violations. Similarly, China's Personal Information Protection Law (PIPL), which came into force in 2021, establishes extraterritorial obligations and penalties of up to 50 million CNY (around 6 million EUR) or 5% of global turnover, resembling GDPR's approach.

In India, the Personal Data Protection Bill (PDPB) proposed in 2019 includes GDPR-inspired provisions such as data subject consent, breach notifications, and fines of up to 4% of global turnover. Likewise, South Africa's Protection of Personal Information Act (POPIA), effective from 2020, aligns with GDPR standards but adds criminal penalties, including imprisonment, alongside financial fines of up to 10 million ZAR (approximately 500,000 EUR).

Other countries, such as Thailand with its Personal Data Protection Act (PDPA) (2019) and Canada with the Digital Charter Implementation Act (2020), have also incorporated GDPR-like frameworks. These laws emphasize consent, data protection measures, and penalties for non-compliance, furthering the global trend of harmonizing data privacy standards to safeguard individual rights in the digital age.

This global adoption underscores the GDPR's role as a cornerstone of modern data privacy legislation and the increasing necessity for international cooperation in the regulatory landscape.

3.1.2 Specialized Regimes in Shared Global Concerns

International cooperation has developed to respond to increasingly specialized issues that require collective action. For example, the law of the sea regulates maritime navigation, the use of marine resources, and environmental protection in ocean spaces. Similarly, international space law sets rules to ensure the peaceful use of outer space and prevent militarization, while the Antarctic Treaty System preserves Antarctica for scientific research and bans military activities. Each of these regimes emerged because no single state can effectively regulate such vast or sensitive areas alone. They illustrate how International Law evolves to manage shared spaces that lie beyond national jurisdiction and, therefore, require coordinated governance.

In the field of environmental protection, International Law plays a key role in addressing global challenges such as climate change, biodiversity loss, and pollution. These legal frameworks aim to promote sustainable development and coordinate global responses to environmental threats.

Environmental treaties demonstrate how states increasingly rely on collective commitments – such as emission reduction targets or biodiversity conservation measures – to address problems that transcend borders and cannot be solved domestically.

In the area of economic cooperation, international legal rules govern trade, foreign investment, financial assistance, and development aid. Institutional mechanisms, such as international organizations, help to manage shared policies and implement joint projects. Additionally, treaty law provides structured procedures for the negotiation, interpretation, enforcement, and revision

51 Granmar, Claes G., 2021, "Global Applicability of the GDPR in Context," *International Data Privacy Law*, vol. 11, no. 3, online. https://doi.org/10.1093/idpl/ipab012.

of international agreements. These mechanisms strengthen predictability and reduce conflicts by ensuring that economic exchanges occur within a stable and transparent legal framework. They also allow states to coordinate their economic interests while maintaining oversight through binding or semi-binding commitments.

These specialized legal regimes show how International Law adapts to the complex and changing needs of an interconnected global society. By creating specific rules for diverse areas of cooperation, International Law supports stability, coordination, and long-term problem-solving among states. They reveal a gradual shift from a purely state-centered system toward a more functional and issue-driven approach where legal norms are tailored to meet the technical, environmental, and economic realities of global interdependence.

3.2 Law of Dispute Settlement

Interaction among states often involves competing interests, which can lead to disagreements and disputes. International Law provides peaceful methods for resolving these conflicts, helping to maintain order and prevent escalation. This section examines two key aspects of dispute settlement: first, the peaceful means available to states, such as negotiation, mediation, arbitration, and adjudication; and second, the conditions under which International Law permits the use of coercive measures, such as countermeasures or sanctions, to encourage a state to comply with its legal obligations. Together, these mechanisms reflect the balance between cooperation and enforcement in the international legal system.

3.2.1 Peaceful Settlement of Disputes

International Law places great importance on the peaceful settlement of disputes. It sets out rules and procedures that help states resolve conflicts without resorting to force. These rules apply at all stages of a conflict, from the early signs of disagreement to more serious confrontations. The peaceful resolution of disputes is not just a legal principle – it is a fundamental norm of International Law that all countries must follow and cannot break.

This principle is clearly stated in Article 2(3) of the United Nations Charter, which requires all member states to settle their disputes by peaceful means. It is further developed in the United Nations General Assembly Resolution 2625 (XXV) on the Principles of International Law concerning Friendly Relations and Cooperation among States. The goal is to maintain international peace and security, uphold the Rule of Law, and promote cooperation between states.

Article 33 of the UN Charter provides a non-exhaustive list of peaceful methods for resolving disputes. These include negotiation, inquiry, mediation, conciliation, arbitration, judicial settlement, and the use of regional mechanisms. States are free to choose any peaceful means that suit the situation.

Article 33 of the UN Charter

1. The parties to any dispute, the continuation of which is likely to endanger the maintenance of international peace and security, shall, first of all, seek a solution by negotiation, inquiry, mediation, conciliation, arbitration, judicial settlement, resort to regional agencies or arrangements, or other peaceful means of their own choice.
2. The Security Council shall, when it deems necessary, call upon the parties to settle their dispute by such means.

   If the parties fail to resolve their dispute using these methods, Article 37 of the UN Charter requires them to refer the matter to the Security Council.

Article 37 of the UN Charter

1. Should the parties to a dispute of the nature referred to in Article 33 fail to settle it by the means indicated in that Article, they shall refer it to the Security Council.
2. If the Security Council determines that the dispute is likely to threaten international peace and security, it may take action under Article 36 or recommend suitable terms for a settlement.

In addition to diplomatic efforts, international judicial bodies also play a key role in dispute settlement. Courts such as the International Court of Justice in The Hague and the European Court of Human Rights in Strasbourg are responsible for delivering legally binding judgments. These courts ensure that International Law is applied fairly and consistently.

They are supported by arbitral tribunals and other diplomatic mechanisms that offer flexible and peaceful solutions. Together, these methods and institutions show how International Law provides both structure and tools for resolving conflicts without violence, helping to preserve international order and stability.

For example, in 2021, the International Court of Justice (ICJ) resolved a maritime boundary dispute between Somalia and Kenya in the Indian Ocean.[52] Somalia claimed that Kenya had violated its rights by unilaterally setting the boundary, which affected access to valuable resources such as oil and gas. Kenya argued that the boundary was already agreed upon. The ICJ ruled in favor of Somalia, drawing the boundary based on international legal principles. This decision helped resolve the conflict peacefully and demonstrated how International Law can fairly settle disputes between states.

In a 2015 address to the Sixth Committee of the United Nations General Assembly, Ronny Abraham, then-President of the ICJ, emphasized the Court's important role in shaping the legal framework of the United Nations. He referred to key cases such as *Reparations for Injuries Suffered in the Service of the United Nations* (1949) and *Legal Consequences of the Construction of a Wall in the Occupied Palestinian Territory* (2004). In these decisions, the ICJ clarified the legal identity of the UN and the complementary roles of its main organs, such as the General Assembly and the Security Council. Abraham underlined the Court's contribution to strengthening the Rule of Law and adapting legal norms to the evolving needs of the international community.

Beyond judicial settlement, other peaceful methods listed in Article 33 of the UN Charter have been effectively used in international practice. Negotiation played a central role in the *Camp David Accords* (1978),[53] where Egypt and Israel, with support from the United States, reached a peace agreement that led to Israel's withdrawal from the Sinai Peninsula.

Enquiry has also been significant. In the *Dogger Bank Incident* (1904),[54] a commission investigated an incident in which Russian naval ships mistakenly fired on British fishing vessels. The enquiry helped reduce tensions and avoid further conflict.

Mediation proved effective in the *Dayton Accords* (1995),[55] where U.S.-led negotiations helped end the Bosnian War by facilitating an agreement among Bosnia, Croatia, and Serbia.

52 International Court of Justice, *Maritime Delimitation in the Indian Ocean (Somalia v. Kenya)*, Judgment, ICJ Reports 2021.

53 Carter, Jimmy, 1982, *Keeping Faith: Memoirs of a President*, Bantam Books.

54 Scott, James Brown, 1907, *The Hague Peace Conferences of 1899 and 1907: A Series of Lectures Delivered Before the Johns Hopkins University*, Johns Hopkins Press.

55 Franchini, Daniel and Tzanakopoulos, Antonios, 2017, "The Kosovo Crisis (1999)," in *International Law and the Use of Force: A Case-Based Approach*, eds. Olivier Corten and Tom Ruys, Oxford University Press, 2018, online. Available at: https://ssrn.com/abstract=2960294.

Conciliation was used in the *Beagle Channel Dispute* (1971–1984), where Argentina and Chile accepted the Vatican's proposal to peacefully resolve a territorial disagreement and avoid armed conflict.[56]

Arbitration is well illustrated by the *Alabama Claims Arbitration* (1872), in which an international tribunal settled a dispute between the United States and the United Kingdom over damages caused by British-built Confederate ships during the American Civil War. This case set a key precedent for the use of arbitration in International Law.

These examples demonstrate the practical use of peaceful dispute settlement methods under Article 33 of the UN Charter. They show how different legal and diplomatic tools have been successfully used to resolve conflicts, promote cooperation, and maintain international peace and security in various historical and political contexts.

3.2.2 Understanding Coercive Measures in Context

International sanctions are political or economic restrictions used by states or international organizations to influence the actions of other states, groups, or individuals. These measures are generally imposed to protect national security, uphold International Law, or respond to serious violations such as threats to peace or breaches of sovereignty. Sanctions may include economic restrictions (such as trade bans), diplomatic measures (like cutting off diplomatic relations), and targeted actions (such as freezing assets or travel bans for specific individuals).[57]

Sanctions can be imposed by the United Nations Security Council, which acts with international legal authority, or unilaterally by individual states acting in their own strategic interest.[58] In other words, sanctions may be applied either by one state against another (unilateral sanctions) or collectively by a group of states through an international organization like the United Nations (collective sanctions).

These non-military coercive measures aim to put pressure on the wrongdoer to change their behavior, comply with international rules, or prevent further violations. They serve as a way to express international disapproval while keeping open the possibility for diplomatic negotiation and peaceful resolution.

The effectiveness of sanctions varies. In some cases, they have helped prevent larger conflicts, such as in the former Yugoslavia during the 1990s. However, they are also widely criticized for their unintended humanitarian consequences. For example, sanctions against Iraq in the 1990s were blamed for contributing to the suffering of civilians. To reduce such impacts, some sanctions now include humanitarian exemptions, also known as "carve-outs," to ensure access to essential goods like food and medicine.

The debate over sanctions includes concerns about their ethical use, their fairness, and whether they are truly effective. Nevertheless, sanctions remain a key instrument of international diplomacy and law enforcement.

A major scholarly contribution to the study of sanctions is Jean Combacau's 1974 thesis, *The Sanctioning Power of the UN: Theoretical Study of Non-Military Coercion*.[59]

56 Garrett, James L., 1985, "The Beagle Channel Dispute: Confrontation and Negotiation in the Southern Cone," *Journal of Interamerican Studies and World Affairs*, vol. 27, no. 3, online. https://doi.org/10.2307/165601.

57 Joyner, Christopher C., 1995, "Sanctions as Peaceful Coercion: Lessons from the United Nations Experience," *Australian Year Book of International Law*, vol. 16.

58 See Combacau, Jean, 1974, *The Sanctioning Power of the UN: Theoretical Study of Non-Military Coercion*, no. 23 of Publications of the Revue Générale de Droit International Public, A. Pedone, Paris.

59 Combacau, *The Sanctioning Power of the UN*.

Jean Combacau is a prominent French scholar and emeritus professor of International Law, widely recognized for his deep contributions to the theory and practice of international legal systems. His work explores the United Nations' legal authority to use sanctions to influence state behavior without using force. Combacau examines the balance between international pressure and respect for state sovereignty, the humanitarian risks of sanctions, and the evolution from broad embargoes to more targeted approaches. His work remains influential in understanding the legal and political role of sanctions.

Although his thesis was written in 1974, Jean Combacau's *The Sanctioning Power of the UN: Theoretical Study of Non-Military Coercion* remains a key reference on the subject. It is still widely cited for its in-depth analysis of non-military coercive power within the framework of International Law, particularly in relation to actions taken by the United Nations.

Recent examples show how sanctions are used in practice. In 2016 and 2017, the United Nations imposed sanctions on North Korea to pressure it to stop its nuclear weapons program. These sanctions targeted exports like seafood, textiles, and minerals. However, they also affected North Korean civilians by limiting trade with China, which provides essential goods to local markets.[60]

Another example is the response to Russia's annexation of Crimea in 2014. The European Union and the United States imposed sanctions on Russian individuals and organizations. These included asset freezes, travel bans, and restrictions on banking. The goal was to pressure Russia to respect Ukraine's territorial integrity. The legal basis for these actions included EU Council Decision 2014/145/CFSP and U.S. Executive Order 13661.[61]

Following Russia's full-scale invasion of Ukraine on February 24, 2022, the international community faced a major crisis. The invasion violated Article 2(4) of the United Nations Charter, which prohibits the use of force against the sovereignty of another state. The war resulted in thousands of deaths, the displacement of millions of Ukrainians, and serious violations of International Law. Due to Russia's veto power in the Security Council, the UN was unable to adopt binding resolutions to stop the conflict. Instead, the General Assembly adopted non-binding resolutions calling for the withdrawal of Russian forces.[62]

This situation demonstrates the limits of International Law enforcement, especially when powerful states block action through the veto system. Similar challenges have appeared in past conflicts, including Kosovo (1999), Iraq (2003), and Libya (2011), where questions of legality, legitimacy, and enforcement were widely debated.

To sum up, coercive measures are non-military tools used to influence the conduct of states or other international actors without the use of armed force. These measures can include economic, diplomatic, or cultural restrictions and are designed to promote compliance with International Law and resolve disputes peacefully. However, when such measures fail, the international community may consider the use of force under the framework of collective security.

According to Article 42 of the United Nations Charter, military force may only be used as a last resort and with authorization from the Security Council in order to maintain or restore international peace and security. The shift from non-military sanctions to military action is a serious

60 Voice of America (VOA), "Are Sanctions Worsening Conditions for North Koreans?," *VOA News*. Available at: https://www.voanews.com. Accessed 11 January 2025.

61 European Union, *Council Decision 2014/145/CFSP of 17 March 2014 Concerning Restrictive Measures in Respect of Actions Undermining or Threatening the Territorial Integrity, Sovereignty and Independence of Ukraine*, Official Journal of the European Union, L 78/16.

62 United Nations General Assembly, *Resolution A/ES-11/L.7 of 23 February 2023: Territorial Integrity of Ukraine: Defending the Principles of the Charter of the United Nations*, Official Records.

legal step and is strictly governed by International Law. It must meet conditions of legality, legitimacy, and necessity.

4 Sovereignty and Its Limits in International Law

Sovereignty – the authority of a state to govern itself – is a fundamental principle of International Law. However, this authority is not without limits. In theory, sovereignty defines both the internal power of a government over its territory and its independence in external relations. Yet in practice, various legal and political mechanisms place limits on this power to prevent abuse and protect individual rights. These include constitutional review, the Separation of Powers, and other forms of accountability. This section explores the meaning of sovereignty, its significance in International Law, and how it is balanced and constrained through legal and institutional checks.

4.1 The Theoretical and Legal Definitions of State Sovereignty

Sovereignty is a state's supreme authority to govern itself. As described by philosophers like Jean-Jacques Rousseau, it represents the highest form of political power. However, when sovereignty is left unchecked, it can lead to abuses of power. This section explores the meaning of sovereignty, both within a State and in its external relations, and examines how it is balanced through legal and institutional mechanisms, such as judicial review and respect for international norms.

4.1.1 Understanding Sovereignty

Sovereignty refers to the ultimate authority of a State to govern its people and manage its affairs. It operates on two levels, internally and externally.

Internally, sovereignty means the State has full control over its territory, population, and legal system.

Externally, sovereignty means the State can act independently in international relations without interference from other states.

While Rousseau described sovereignty as absolute, modern legal systems recognize that such power must be limited. Constitutional checks and balances, the Separation of Powers, and judicial review are essential to ensure that sovereignty is exercised responsibly and in a way that protects individual rights.[63]

In the international sphere, sovereignty includes a state's ability to establish diplomatic relations, enter into treaties, and maintain embassies. These rights are protected by International Law, particularly the 1961 Vienna Convention on Diplomatic Relations. Sovereignty also includes territorial integrity, a principle enshrined in Article 2(4) of the United Nations Charter, which prohibits the use of force against the territorial independence of another state. A clear example of this principle in action was the global condemnation of Iraq's invasion of Kuwait in 1990, where the violation of Kuwaiti sovereignty led to a UN-authorized military response.

Sovereignty often intersects with complex geopolitical disputes. A notable case is the ongoing conflict over Western Sahara, a territory claimed by Morocco. In recent years, several

63 For an exploration of sovereignty internally, focusing on governance within a state's territory, constitutional authority, and the role of judicial checks, refer to Chapter 5 on Constitutionalism and Judicial Review. Chapter 5 delves into how internal sovereignty operates within constitutional democracies, balancing state authority with individual rights and legal accountability.

international actors have shifted their positions. During a 2024 state visit, French President Emmanuel Macron expressed support for Morocco's autonomy plan, aligning with earlier endorsements by the United States and Spain. These moves challenge Algeria's backing of the Polisario Front, which advocates for Sahrawi self-determination. While Morocco continues to strengthen its position through regional partnerships and diplomatic recognition, the legal status of Western Sahara remains unresolved under International Law.

The European Court of Justice has issued important rulings on this issue. It emphasized that Western Sahara has a separate and distinct status from Morocco. For example, the ECJ concluded that the EU-Morocco Association Agreement does not apply to Western Sahara unless the people of the territory give their consent.[64] The Court also annulled parts of EU–Morocco trade and fisheries agreements because they were applied to Western Sahara without respecting the right of the Sahrawi people to self-determination.[65] These rulings reinforce the idea that sovereignty must operate within the framework of International Law and respect the rights of peoples under occupation or dispute.

4.1.2 Implications of Sovereignty

The absolute nature of sovereignty requires safeguards to prevent its abuse. Thinkers like Montesquieu argued for the Separation of Powers among the Executive, Legislative, and Judicial branches to ensure that no single institution holds unchecked authority. One of the most important tools to preserve this balance is judicial review, which ensures that constitutional norms are respected. Through judicial review, courts can invalidate laws or government actions that violate constitutional rights, helping to protect individual freedoms and maintain accountability.

At the international level, sovereignty reflects two key principles that guide relations among states. The first is the equality of states, which means that all countries, regardless of their size, power, or wealth, are considered legally equal under International Law. This principle ensures that every state has the same legal rights and obligations and promotes mutual respect and cooperation. For example, a small state holds the same legal status as a major power in international forums like the United Nations. International rules – such as respecting borders, complying with treaties, and observing international norms – help maintain stability and fairness in global relations. In addition, customary rules, such as the prohibitions on genocide and slavery, apply to all states, even if they have not signed specific treaties.

The second principle is non-interference in internal affairs, which protects each state's right to govern its territory and people without outside interference. This principle means that no other state or international organization can intervene in a country's domestic matters – such as its political system, laws, or cultural practices – unless International Law provides a legal basis for doing so. For example, external intervention may only be permitted with the state's consent, through a treaty, or in exceptional cases such as humanitarian intervention recognized under International Law.

Together, the principles of equality and non-interference help maintain the independence and autonomy of states while supporting an international system based on respect and cooperation. External sovereignty allows each state to operate freely, but within a shared legal framework that promotes peaceful relations and respect for self-determination.

At the same time, sovereignty also implies responsibility. States that violate international rules can face consequences, such as sanctions or legal proceedings. In this way, sovereignty

64 CJUE, *Conseil contre Front Polisario*, n° C-104/16 P.
65 CJUE, gr. ch., 27 févr. 2018, Western Sahara Campaign UK, n° C-266/16.

combines the right to self-govern with the duty to respect International Law. It offers states independence but within a system that encourages accountability, fairness, and global cooperation.

4.2 The Legal and Practical Limits to State Sovereignty

While sovereignty gives states broad authority to govern their own affairs, it is not unlimited. Various mechanisms exist to ensure accountability and prevent the misuse of power. Constitutional justice, in particular, plays a key role by allowing courts to enforce constitutional principles and safeguard individual rights. In addition, counter-powers such as civil society organizations, independent media, and economic forces can influence state behavior and promote transparency. These internal and external checks help balance the exercise of sovereignty with the need for cooperation, legal responsibility, and the protection of fundamental rights.

4.2.1 Constitutional Justice and the Evolution of Sovereignty

Chapter 5 of this textbook discusses constitutional law in detail, including a full explanation of constitutional justice. In this section, we briefly explain how constitutional justice acts as a practical limit on state sovereignty.

Professor Guillaume Tusseau, a legal scholar at Sciences Po, has explored the role of constitutions in shaping political power and protecting fundamental rights. In his book *Comparative Constitutional Litigation*,[66] he examines how courts in different countries enforce constitutional norms to ensure that governments respect the Separation of Powers and safeguard citizens' rights.[67] However, he also cautions that even authoritarian regimes can adopt constitutional systems, which means their effectiveness must be evaluated critically and not assumed.

Beyond national systems, the idea of global constitutionalism has developed as a broader framework influencing legal systems around the world. This concept seeks to integrate domestic constitutional principles with international norms to address shared global challenges, such as human rights, environmental protection, and transnational governance. Scholars have proposed different models of global constitutionalism. For example, Gunter Teubner – a German legal scholar and sociologist, best known for his work in the field of the Social Theory of Law, where he explores how legal systems interact with social structures and how law evolves within complex, pluralistic societies – supports a version led by civil society, focusing on decentralized participation and the growing influence of digital platforms and private actors. In contrast, Philip Allott – Emeritus Professor of International Public Law at the University of Cambridge Faculty of Law and a Fellow of Trinity College – argues for a more transformative vision of global order that reimagines the relationship between International Law and world society.

Global constitutionalism aims to strengthen the Rule of Law, promote human rights, and encourage a fair distribution of power across borders. It supports international cooperation and attempts to correct power imbalances between states, contributing to the development of a more just and democratic international system.

However, critics of global constitutionalism raise important concerns. Some argue that it may weaken national sovereignty, place too much emphasis on liberal democratic values, and overlook the political and cultural diversity of states. Other concerns include the risks of judicial

66 Tusseau, Guillaume, 2021, *Contentieux constitutionnel comparé. Une introduction au droit processuel constitutionnel*, LJDG.

67 Sciences Po, "Faire appliquer les constitutions: un engagement démocratique," *Cogito – Le magazine de la recherche*, online. Available at: https://www.sciencespo.fr. Accessed 2 May 2023.

overreach, the growing influence of private actors in setting global norms, and the potential for democratic erosion when international standards are imposed without local legitimacy.

In conclusion, while constitutional justice and global constitutionalism both seek to promote accountability, cooperation, and the protection of rights, their effectiveness depends on how they are implemented. A careful balance must be maintained between sovereignty, democracy, and the evolving needs of the global community.

4.2.2 Alternative Forces Challenging State Sovereignty

A counter-power is a force that challenges established authority. It can take political, economic, cultural, or social forms and seeks to limit sovereign power while proposing alternative perspectives or solutions. These counter-powers do not replace state authority but influence how it is exercised, especially in a globalized and interconnected world. This section provides three key examples of practical counter-powers to state sovereignty: (1) international civil society and the international community; (2) the Internet and global media; and (3) foreign direct investment and economic actors.

International civil society refers to non-governmental organizations (NGOs), advocacy groups, and social movements that operate across borders to influence global governance. These actors work to promote democratic values, human rights, environmental protection, and social justice. A joint seminar organized by the European Commission in Brussels in the early 2010s, titled *The Role of Civil Society in Global Governance*, concluded that global civil society has become a significant actor in international affairs.[68] Since the end of the Cold War, civil society organizations (CSOs) have contributed to agenda-setting, International Law-making, transnational diplomacy (especially in informal diplomatic channels), and the monitoring of global issues ranging from trade and development to peace, security, and digital governance.

CSOs function as advocates, service providers, knowledge brokers, and watchdogs. Their influence has grown through a combination of institutional support, socio-economic change, and technological innovation. They act as practical counter-powers by challenging state decisions, proposing alternatives, and holding authorities accountable on the international stage.

The international community, in contrast, is a broader and more formal concept. It is primarily composed of states and institutions, especially the United Nations system, donor agencies, and intergovernmental organizations. While the international community often works through consensus and diplomacy, it also exercises pressure through legal instruments, sanctions, and humanitarian intervention, thereby acting as a collective check on unilateral state actions.

The Internet has transformed how information is shared, how diplomacy is conducted, and how public opinion is shaped. It plays a dual role in international relations – facilitating dialogue and transparency while also posing risks to national security and social cohesion. Governments such as France recognize the strategic role of the Internet in diplomacy, highlighting its use in activism, advocacy, and international communication.[69]

Digital platforms like Facebook and X (formerly Twitter) have enabled what is often called "Twitter diplomacy," allowing states and non-state actors to communicate directly with global

68 Marchetti, Raffaele, 2010, "Report on the Joint Seminar Organized by the EUISS, the European Commission / DG Research, and UNU-CRIS (Brussels, 1 October 2010)," online. Available at: https://www.iss.europa.eu.

69 République française – Vie publique, "En quoi Internet influence-t-il la scène internationale?", online. Available at: https://www.vie-publique.fr. Accessed 2 May 2023.

audiences. Whistleblowers such as Edward Snowden have used the Internet to disclose sensitive information, sparking international debates on surveillance, privacy, and government accountability. Social movements such as the Arab Spring demonstrated the Internet's power to mobilize mass protests and influence regime change.

At the same time, the Internet presents serious challenges, including cyberattacks, disinformation (fake news), digital propaganda, and illegal activities such as trafficking or money laundering. These risks have led to the rise of cybersecurity strategies aimed at protecting digital sovereignty. In this way, the Internet acts as both a tool of empowerment and a threat, challenging traditional forms of state control and reshaping the global public sphere.

In addition to the role of users, major technology corporations also function as powerful global actors. Companies like Meta (formerly Facebook) and Tesla, led by influential figures such as Elon Musk, shape social, economic, and regulatory landscapes. Their decisions on content moderation, privacy, and compliance with national laws directly affect global norms and public debate. As transnational entities, they often operate beyond the reach of national jurisdictions, demonstrating how private economic power can dilute or bypass traditional sovereignty.

Foreign direct investment (FDI) is another important counter-power that influences state sovereignty, particularly in shaping economic policy and legal frameworks. In open economies, FDI plays a crucial role in funding infrastructure, promoting development, and supporting innovation. However, in order to attract investment, states must offer stable legal environments that protect investor rights. This places pressure on governments to align national laws with international standards, effectively limiting their freedom to regulate without consequences.

After the collapse of the Soviet Union, many Central and Eastern European countries restructured their legal systems to attract FDI.[70] They adopted legal models based on Western European standards to reassure investors of the Rule of Law and economic stability. Similarly, France's economic diplomacy strategy includes efforts to support exports, attract foreign capital, and harmonize national regulations with European and International Law, particularly in support of emerging sectors like technology and green energy.

The globalization of the economy and the rise of economic diplomacy have fostered the emergence of global legal frameworks and transnational litigation, creating competition among legal systems and traditions.[71] This underscores how economic forces, particularly FDI, challenge traditional notions of sovereignty and reshape international relations.

In conclusion, while sovereignty remains a core principle of International Law, it is increasingly shaped and constrained by counter-powers. Civil society, global media, digital technologies, multinational corporations, and foreign investors all exert influence that affects how states govern, both internally and externally. These forces promote accountability, transparency, and participation, but also raise complex challenges for maintaining democratic legitimacy, national sovereignty, and global cooperation in a rapidly changing world.

5 Individual Rights and Responsibilities

Since the mid-20th century, the protection of individual rights has made significant progress in two important areas: international human rights law and international criminal law.

70 Berkowitz, Daniel, Pistor, Katharina and Richard, Jean-François, 2003, "The Transplant Effect," *American Journal of Comparative Law*, vol. 51.

71 Gontier, *Legal Diplomacy*.

International human rights law focuses on ensuring that states – and in some cases non-state actors – respect the rights guaranteed by treaties, customary International Law, and other legal instruments. According to the United Nations' International, Impartial and Independent Mechanism (IIIM),[72] these rights are universally applicable, including in times of peace. Some rights, such as the right to life, may be interpreted differently in situations of armed conflict, where international humanitarian law also applies.

International Criminal Law, as defined by the European Center for Constitutional and Human Rights, addresses the most serious crimes under International Law, such as genocide, war crimes, and crimes against humanity. It seeks to hold individuals criminally responsible for these acts, whether through national courts or international institutions such as the International Criminal Court (ICC).[73]

Although these two areas of law are distinct, they are closely linked. The United Nations' International Law Commission has emphasized that human rights law aims to protect individuals, while criminal law ensures that violations of those rights do not go unpunished.[74] This connection is reflected in the work of international courts. For instance, Article 21(3) of the Rome Statute of the ICC requires that the Court interpret and apply the law in accordance with internationally recognized human rights. This integration strengthens the relationship between individual protection and legal accountability, creating a more comprehensive and consistent approach to justice at the international level.[75]

5.1 International Human Rights Law

International human rights law provides the global framework for protecting the fundamental rights and freedoms of individuals and groups. It sets out the legal standards that states must follow to ensure dignity, equality, and justice for all people. This section explores the main legal instruments that form the foundation of human rights protection, such as international treaties and declarations. It also examines the mechanisms established to prevent violations, monitor compliance, and respond effectively when rights are threatened or abused.

5.1.1 The Instruments of the International Human Rights Framework

The United Nations established most of the instruments that form the international human rights framework in the aftermath of World War II. This framework is based on three key principles: (1) All people, everywhere, have the same rights by virtue of our shared humanity; (2) Everyone is equally entitled to these rights without discrimination; and (3) All human rights are interrelated, interdependent, and indivisible.

In 1946, the United Nations General Assembly created the United Nations International Children's Emergency Fund (UNICEF) to provide emergency food and healthcare to children and mothers in countries devastated by the war.

72 The IIIM has been established by the United Nations to assist in the Investigation and prosecution of Persons Responsible for the most serious crimes under International Law committed in the Syrian Arab Republic since March 2011.

73 European Center for Constitutional and Human Rights (ECCHR), "Glossary – International Criminal Law," online. Available at: https://www.ecchr.eu. Accessed 2 May 2023.

74 International Law Commission (ILC), "Mandate and Establishment by the UN General Assembly (1947)," online. Available at: https://legal.un.org.

75 See Kersten, Mark, 2021, "Arenas of Interaction: The Relationship between International Criminal Law and International Human Rights Law," online. Available at: https://justiceinconflict.org. Accessed 2 May 2023.

Two years later, in 1948, the United Nations adopted the Universal Declaration of Human Rights (UDHR), which set out a common standard for human rights protection. Although the UDHR is not a binding legal instrument, it carries significant moral authority. As UNICEF explains, its global acceptance gives strong moral weight to the idea that all people – regardless of nationality, place of residence, sex, ethnicity, color, religion, language, or any other status – should be treated equally and with respect.[76]

Since the adoption of the UDHR, the United Nations has developed a number of legally binding treaties and agreements that make up the core of the international human rights framework. These include nine core international human rights treaties:

The 1965 International Convention on the Elimination of All Forms of Racial Discrimination
The 1966 International Covenant on Civil and Political Rights
The 1966 International Covenant on Economic, Social and Cultural Rights
The 1979 Convention on the Elimination of All Forms of Discrimination against Women
The 1984 Convention against Torture and Other Cruel, Inhuman or Degrading Treatment or Punishment
The 1989 Convention on the Rights of the Child
The 1990 International Convention on the Protection of the Rights of All Migrant Workers and Members of Their Families
The 2007 Convention on the Rights of Persons with Disabilities
The 2010 International Convention for the Protection of All Persons from Enforced Disappearance

Every country in the world has ratified at least one of these core treaties, and many states have ratified several, if not most, of them. These instruments are key legal tools that hold governments accountable for respecting, protecting, and fulfilling the rights of individuals within their jurisdiction.

According to the United Nations, understanding this framework is essential for the promotion, protection, and realization of human rights. For states that ratify these treaties, the principles and rights they contain become legal obligations. The framework also establishes legal and institutional mechanisms that can be used to hold governments accountable if they violate these rights.

5.1.2 Mechanisms to Prevent, Report, and Sanction Violations of Human Rights

To ensure that governments are held accountable for human rights violations, the international human rights framework has developed a range of mechanisms aimed at preventing, monitoring, and addressing abuses. These mechanisms function within the broader United Nations system, particularly through the leadership of the Office of the High Commissioner for Human Rights (OHCHR). This framework relies on three key components: the development and promotion of international norms, the monitoring and reporting of human rights situations, and technical cooperation with states to improve legal and institutional practices.

An example of a preventive mechanism is the Optional Protocol to the Convention against Torture (OPCAT), which allows for confidential reporting and access to places of detention. Such tools are designed to reduce the risk of torture and ill-treatment through early intervention and transparency.

76 United Nations International Children's Emergency Fund (UNICEF), online. Available at: https://www.unicef.org. Accessed 7 May 2023.

Accountability is a key principle for deterring future violations. National-level measures such as judicial independence, human rights education, and codes of conduct for public officials help build a culture of respect for rights. Within the UN system, tools such as the Due Diligence Policy aim to ensure that UN-supported operations do not contribute to human rights violations.

However, experts in international sanctions for human rights violations, such as Muriel Sognigbé Sangbana – an academic affiliated with the University of Poitiers and the University of Lomé – have argued that the United Nations should adopt stronger and more effective sanctioning mechanisms.[77]

In her view, existing procedures often lack enforceability, especially when states fail to cooperate or refuse to implement recommendations.

At the regional level, institutions like the European Court of Human Rights (ECHR) provide more robust protections through binding legal judgments. These regional mechanisms demonstrate the importance of effective national implementation. Without it, even the strongest international or regional decisions may have limited impact. Therefore, the success of human rights protections ultimately depends on how well they are integrated into national legal systems.

In the digital age, new challenges have emerged, particularly regarding the role of private actors in shaping public discourse. The concentration of power in the hands of tech leaders such as Elon Musk, Jeff Bezos, and Mark Zuckerberg raises serious concerns for democratic societies. Their platforms have a wide reach and significant influence over global public opinion.

For example, Meta's decision to end its partnerships with independent fact-checking organizations raises questions about how effectively misinformation is being addressed. This issue has implications for the protection of human rights online, especially in relation to access to reliable information and freedom of expression. The lack of binding international rules that apply to digital platforms makes it difficult to hold them accountable for the spread of harmful or false content.

This situation highlights the growing dependence on private companies to uphold basic rights in the online space, even though they are not bound by the same legal obligations as states. As a result, stronger cooperation between governments, international organizations, and technology companies is essential. Such collaboration is necessary to create more effective mechanisms for protecting human rights in the digital environment and ensuring that online spaces remain safe, fair, and transparent.

5.2 International Criminal Law

International criminal law deals with the most serious offenses under International Law, including genocide, war crimes, and crimes against humanity. It focuses on individual responsibility for acts that threaten peace, security, and human dignity on a global scale. This section examines the foundational principles of international criminal law and the role of the International Criminal Court in ensuring justice and accountability for these grave crimes.

5.2.1 What Is International Criminal Law?

International criminal law is the branch of law that defines and regulates the prosecution of the most serious crimes affecting the international community. These crimes include genocide,

77 Sangbana Muriel, Sognigbé, 2018, *La sanction internationale de la violation des droits de l'homme*, Fondation René Cassin Collection, Publications de l'Institut International des Droits de l'Homme, vol. 38, Pedone, Paris.

crimes against humanity, war crimes, and the crime of aggression. Its primary purpose is to hold individuals – not just states – accountable for actions that violate fundamental human values and cause widespread harm.

The origins of international criminal law can be traced back to the aftermath of World War II, particularly the Nuremberg and Tokyo Trials. These were the first instances where individuals were prosecuted at the international level for war crimes and crimes against peace. These trials established the principle that individuals, including political and military leaders, can be held personally responsible for serious violations of International Law, regardless of their official status.

In the 1990s, special international tribunals were established to address crimes committed during specific conflicts. The International Criminal Tribunal for the former Yugoslavia (ICTY) and the International Criminal Tribunal for Rwanda (ICTR) played key roles in developing the legal standards and procedures that continue to influence the field today. These tribunals demonstrated the need for a permanent institution to ensure accountability on a global scale.

This led to the creation of the International Criminal Court (ICC) in 1998 through the adoption of the Rome Statute. The ICC, based in The Hague, is the first permanent international court with the mandate to investigate and prosecute individuals for the most serious international crimes. It operates independently from the United Nations, although it maintains a cooperative relationship with the UN system.

In recent years, international criminal law has continued to grow and adapt. Many countries, such as France, have adopted domestic legislation allowing for the prosecution of international crimes committed abroad, based on the principle of universal jurisdiction. This development reflects a broader commitment to ensuring accountability beyond national borders.

However, the international criminal justice system faces challenges. These include limited cooperation from states, political resistance, and debates about the fairness and efficiency of international prosecutions. Some states have refused to join the ICC or have withdrawn from it, citing concerns about national sovereignty or perceived bias.

At the same time, new legal and academic discussions are emerging around how international criminal law can address contemporary issues such as cybercrime, environmental destruction (also referred to as ecocide), and the criminal liability of non-state actors, including multinational corporations and armed groups.

Scholars provide valuable contributions to this evolving field. Some focus on the core legal principles and structures of international criminal law, offering general introductions and analyses of key legal texts and case law.[78] Others highlight the political dimensions of international criminal justice, examining how international legal mechanisms function in practice, the role of power in shaping enforcement, and the challenges of achieving impartial justice.[79]

Together, these perspectives demonstrate the growing importance of international criminal law as a tool for promoting justice, preventing impunity, and addressing emerging global threats.

5.2.2 The International Criminal Court

The International Criminal Court (ICC), established by Article 1 of the Rome Statute, is a permanent international institution responsible for prosecuting individuals for the most serious

78 See, for example, Stahn, Carsten, 2018, *A Critical Introduction to International Criminal Law*, Cambridge University Press, p. 464; Cryer, Robert, 2019, *An Introduction to International Criminal Law and Procedure*, Cambridge University Press, p. 640.

79 See, for example, Fernandez, Julian, 2020, *Droit international pénal*, L.G.D.J., Paris, p. 246.

crimes under International Law: genocide, war crimes, crimes against humanity, and the crime of aggression, as defined in Article 5. The ICC operates on the principle of complementarity, meaning it intervenes only when national jurisdictions are unwilling or unable to carry out genuine investigations or prosecutions, as set out in Article 17. Headquartered in The Hague, Netherlands, the Court holds international legal personality under Article 4 and functions with the mandate to ensure justice and accountability on a global scale. This structure reflects a deliberate balance between respecting state sovereignty and providing an international safety net to ensure that the gravest crimes do not go unpunished. The ICC is therefore designed not to replace domestic courts, but to act when they fail to deliver credible and impartial justice.

The Court's operations are governed by detailed procedural rules. Article 15 allows the Prosecutor to initiate investigations on their own initiative (*proprio motu*) based on reliable information. Article 20 guarantees the principle of ne bis in idem, ensuring that no individual is tried twice for the same conduct. Sanctions under Article 77 include imprisonment, fines, and the forfeiture of assets, depending on the gravity and circumstances of the offense. These provisions collectively establish a coherent procedural framework that safeguards both the effectiveness of prosecution and the rights of the accused. They also illustrate the ICC's hybrid character, blending civil law and common law influences to create a unique and internationally acceptable model of criminal procedure.

Several landmark cases demonstrate the practical application of these legal provisions. In the Al Mahdi case,[80] the ICC convicted Ahmad Al Faqi Al Mahdi under Article 8 for intentionally directing attacks against cultural and religious monuments in Timbuktu, Mali. He was sentenced to nine years in prison and ordered to pay €2.7 million in reparations to the affected community under Article 75. This decision was notable for being the first ICC case focused exclusively on cultural heritage destruction, affirming that such acts constitute serious war crimes under international humanitarian law.

In contrast, the Court's handling of the Gbagbo and Blé Goudé case resulted in an acquittal. Both individuals were charged with crimes against humanity, but the Trial Chamber – and later the Appeals Chamber – determined that the prosecution had not met the evidentiary standards required under the Statute.[81] The case illustrates the high burden of proof required by the Court and its commitment to ensuring that convictions rest on solid, persuasive evidence. It also highlights the ICC's willingness to acquit when prosecutorial shortcomings undermine the credibility of the case, thereby reinforcing the institution's legitimacy and procedural rigor.

The ICC's legal structure, encompassing jurisdiction, legal principles, and procedural safeguards, reflects its mission to address crimes that deeply harm the international community, while strictly adhering to the Rule of Law and principles of due process. By combining substantive international criminal norms with robust procedural protections, the Court aims to deliver justice that is not only punitive but also principled, fair, and consistent with global legal standards.

6 The Use of Force and the Consequences of Violating International Law

The use of force and the consequences of violating International Law are closely linked. International Law imposes a near-absolute prohibition on the use of force, as stated in Article 2(4) of the United Nations Charter, in order to preserve international peace and security. However,

80 International Criminal Court, *Case No. ICC-01/12-01/15.*

81 International Criminal Court, *Case No. ICC-02/11-01/15 (Gbagbo)* and *Case No. ICC-02/11-02/15 (Blé Goudé).*

when this fundamental rule is breached – through acts of aggression or unlawful military interventions – International Law provides a range of mechanisms to address such violations. These include narrowly defined exceptions permitting the lawful use of force as well as consequences for wrongful acts, such as the attribution of international responsibility, the imposition of sanctions, and the activation of dispute resolution processes.

This section examines the legal framework governing the use of force, the specific conditions under which it may be lawfully exercised, and the legal and political consequences that arise when states breach these rules.

6.1 The Legal Framework Governing the Use of Force

International Law establishes a general prohibition on the use of force, as set out in the United Nations Charter, to safeguard state sovereignty and promote peaceful coexistence among nations. However, there are limited and regulated exceptions to this rule. These include the inherent right of self-defense under Article 51 of the Charter and the use of force authorized by the UN Security Council under Chapter VII in response to threats to international peace. In recent years, contemporary debates have introduced additional justifications – such as humanitarian intervention or the responsibility to protect – which reflect the evolving complexities of maintaining global security and addressing large-scale human rights violations.

6.1.1 Prohibition of the Use of Force

The cornerstone of the international legal framework is Article 2(4) of the UN Charter, which prohibits the threat or use of force against the territorial integrity or political independence of any state. Article 2(4) of the UN Charter explicitly states: "All Members shall refrain in their international relations from the threat or use of force against the territorial integrity or political independence of any state, or in any other manner inconsistent with the Purposes of the United Nations." This prohibition ensures respect for sovereignty and promotes peaceful coexistence among nations. It establishes a clear legal boundary for state behavior, signaling that force is no longer an acceptable tool for advancing national interests except under strictly defined circumstances.

Adopted in 1945, in the wake of two world wars, Article 2(4) of the United Nations Charter embodies the international community's resolve to prevent the recurrence of large-scale armed conflict. It represents a collective commitment to uphold the principles of sovereignty, non-intervention, and peaceful dispute resolution, in line with the broader objectives of the United Nations – particularly the maintenance of international peace and security. In this sense, Article 2(4) is not merely a legal provision but a foundational norm that reshaped international relations by privileging diplomacy, negotiation, and collective security mechanisms over unilateral military action.

The prohibition outlined in Article 2(4) is broad in scope. It not only bans direct military aggression but also includes indirect forms of coercion, such as supporting armed groups within another state or employing economic pressure to destabilize a government. The specific reference to "territorial integrity" and "political independence" underscores the protection of state borders and the right of nations to manage their internal affairs without external interference. This broad interpretation reflects the recognition that modern conflicts often unfold through hybrid or indirect strategies, which can threaten state stability just as seriously as conventional warfare. Additionally, the phrase "in any other manner inconsistent with the Purposes of the United Nations" ensures that the prohibition applies to any conduct – regardless of form – that undermines the UN's fundamental goals, including the promotion of peace, justice, and international cooperation. This open-ended formulation gives Article 2(4) a flexible and evolving character, allowing it to adapt to new forms of coercion or conflict that were not foreseen in 1945, while preserving its central purpose: safeguarding peace through law.

6.1.2 Exceptions to the Prohibition

Despite the broad prohibition on the use of force, International Law recognizes two main exceptions that allow for lawful military action in specific circumstances: self-defense under Article 51 of the United Nations Charter and authorization by the UN Security Council under Chapter VII. A state may resort to force in self-defense if it has been subjected to an armed attack, provided that the response is both necessary and proportionate. This right is grounded in customary International Law and is reaffirmed in the Charter.

The scope of self-defense, however, remains a subject of considerable debate. Pre-emptive self-defense – responding to an imminent threat before an actual attack – has gained some support in legal discourse and state practice, although it remains controversial. In contrast, preventive self-defense – using force against a non-imminent or hypothetical threat – is generally considered incompatible with the Charter and lacks broad legal acceptance.

Under Chapter VII, the Security Council is empowered to determine the existence of a threat to peace, a breach of peace, or an act of aggression. Once such a situation is identified, it can authorize coercive measures, including the use of force, to restore or maintain international peace and security. This reflects the UN's collective security system, intended to prevent unilateral military action and ensure that the use of force serves the shared interests of the international community.

These exceptions seek to strike a balance between maintaining global peace and allowing states to defend themselves when necessary. Their legitimacy depends on strict adherence to legal criteria, ongoing interpretation of International Law, and adaptation to emerging challenges, such as terrorism and cyber threats.

In this evolving landscape, states must justify any use of force with clear legal reasoning, while international institutions continually refine the boundaries of permissible action. This dynamic interaction between state practice and legal oversight helps maintain the integrity of Article 2(4), ensuring that exceptions remain truly exceptional and do not undermine the overall prohibition on the use of force.

6.1.3 Arguments Supporting the Use of Force Beyond the UN Charter

Some scholars and states have proposed additional justifications for the use of force beyond those expressly recognized in the UN Charter. These include concepts such as pre-emptive self-defense against imminent threats and humanitarian intervention to prevent mass atrocities. While these arguments remain highly contested, they reflect ongoing debates within International Law, particularly in response to evolving global security and humanitarian challenges.

The prohibition on the use of force under Article 2(4) of the UN Charter is a foundational norm in International Law. Nevertheless, its interpretation has been challenged by new threats and situations. One key area of debate concerns pre-emptive self-defense. For example, the 2003 U.S.-led invasion of Iraq was justified on the basis of pre-emptive self-defense against alleged weapons of mass destruction.

Although widely criticized and lacking explicit support under Article 51, the notion of pre-emptive self-defense has been explored in legal scholarship, such as in *War Law: Understanding*

International Law and Armed Conflict by Michael Byers, a renowned professor of political science at the University of British Columbia. His work examines how such justifications for the use of force attempt to fit within or challenge the broader legal framework established by International Law.[82]

Humanitarian intervention is another contentious justification. NATO's 1999 intervention in Kosovo, undertaken without Security Council authorization, aimed to halt ethnic cleansing. While it raised concerns over the violation of state sovereignty, it also prompted international debate on the moral and legal duty to protect civilians. This discourse contributed to the emergence of the Responsibility to Protect (R2P) doctrine, later invoked in the 2011 Libya intervention under UN Security Council Resolution 1973.[83]

Preventive strikes have also been used as a justification for force. In 1981, Israel bombed Iraq's Osirak nuclear reactor, claiming it was necessary to prevent a future threat. The action was widely condemned by the international community and highlighted the controversy surrounding anticipatory uses of force.[84]

In addition, the fight against non-state actors, especially in the context of terrorism, has further complicated the legal landscape. U.S. drone strikes targeting groups like Al-Qaeda in countries such as Pakistan have been framed as acts of self-defense. These operations raise significant questions about the scope of self-defense, the role of state consent, and the erosion of traditional sovereignty norms.[85]

Taken together, these debates illustrate how modern threats – ranging from weapons proliferation to mass atrocities and transnational terrorism – are challenging the established legal framework governing the use of force and prompting a re-examination of its core principles.

6.1.4 Collective Security System

The prohibition on the use of force lies at the heart of the system of collective security that forms the basis of today's protection of international peace and security. It is a system whereby a community of states, seeking to prevent the use of force against any one of them, undertakes to settle disputes peacefully, ensuring that each member benefits from a collective guarantee through coordinated action. In other words, the international security system established by the United Nations is based on the premise that an individual state's interest is best served by ensuring that the interest of the community of states is preserved. It is a system "where a collective measure is taken against a member of a community that has violated certain community defined values"[86] – here, the protection of international peace and security.

Article 1 of the UN Charter rules that "to keep international peace and security" – which is the main goal of the United Nations – "the UN can take action to prevent or stop threats to peace,

82 Byers, Michael, 2005, *War Law: Understanding International Law and Armed Conflict*, Grove Press.

83 The *Responsibility to Protect* doctrine (R2P) is discussed in *Gareth Evans's* book, *The Responsibility to Protect: Ending Mass Atrocity Crimes Once and For All*. The 2011 Libya intervention under UN Resolution 1973 serves as a key case study. See Evans, Gareth, 2008, *Responsibility to Protect: Ending Mass Atrocity Crimes Once and for All*, Brookings Institution Press.

84 Dinstein, Yoram, 2017, *War, Aggression and Self-Defense*, 6th ed., Cambridge University Press.

85 Deeks, Ashley, 2012, "'Unwilling or Unable': Toward a Normative Framework for Extra-Territorial Self-Defense," *Virginia Journal of International Law*, vol. 52, no. 3, online. Available at: https://ssrn.com.

86 Sarooshi, Danesh, 1999, *The United Nations and the Development of Collective Security*, Oxford, Oxford University Press, p. 5.

deal with acts of aggression, and solve disputes or problems peacefully, following the rules of justice and International Law."

The collective security system is a complex mechanism that relies on a range of political, economic, and military tools, supported by methods for the peaceful settlement of disputes and additional measures aimed at safeguarding international peace. The central responsibility for maintaining peace and security at the global level has been assigned to the United Nations Security Council, as established in Article 24 of the UN Charter. The Council stands at the top of the collective security framework.

To make this system effective, states have voluntarily transferred significant powers to the Security Council, especially under Chapter VII of the Charter. These powers include the authority to impose economic or political sanctions – such as embargoes or the freezing of assets – against those who threaten or breach international peace. Most importantly, the Security Council alone has the legal authority to authorize the use of force in such situations. By doing so, states have agreed to limit their own right to use force, placing that responsibility in the hands of the Security Council to ensure that any military action serves the collective interest of international stability and security.

The key provision in the UN Charter activating the collective security measures, including the use of force, is Article 39, which accords the Security Council "the discretion to qualify a situation anywhere in the world as constituting a threat to the peace, breach of the peace, or act of aggression." This act of qualification opens the gate to the wide array of coercive tools. While originally, such dangerous situations triggering the reaction of the international community, including military action, were limited to inter-state disputes, gradually the perception has transformed to broaden the scope and capture "disturbances, conflicts and clashes within states [which are today] recognized as the major factors of the disruption of the peace at the international level."[87] The UN Security Council expressed this shift already in 1992:

> The absence of war and military conflicts amongst states does not in itself ensure international peace and security. The non-military sources of instability in the economic, social, humanitarian and ecological fields have become threats to peace and security.[88]

While the United Nations Security Council initially required a clear connection between a situation and its impact on regional or international stability to qualify as a threat to peace, this threshold has evolved. Contemporary practice shows that the presence of cross-border elements is no longer a necessary condition. The Security Council now regularly recognizes that internal conflicts – particularly those marked by serious violations of human rights or international humanitarian law, unconstitutional changes of government (*coups d'État*), terrorism, or piracy – can constitute a "threat to the peace, breach of the peace, or act of aggression" under Chapter VII of the UN Charter. These determinations have increasingly justified the Council's authorization of military interventions or other coercive measures, even when the crisis remains largely domestic in scope.

In short, the collective security system empowers the UN Security Council to respond to both international and internal threats to peace, reflecting an evolving understanding of what endangers global stability. This shift underscores the community-based approach to safeguarding

87 Gowlland-Debbas, Vera, 2005, "Article 1, paragraphe 1," in *La Charte des Nations Unies: Commentaire article par article*, 3e éd., eds. Jean-Pierre Cot and Alain Pellet, Economica, Paris, p. 328.

88 Security Council Statement, S/23500, 11 February 1992.

peace. As global conditions continue to change, the United Nations and its member states face the challenge of addressing new and complex threats to international peace and security.

6.1.5 New Threats to International Peace and Security

New threats to international security are reshaping the global landscape, challenging traditional frameworks and responses. These threats extend beyond conventional military conflicts, encompassing cyberattacks, terrorism, organized crime, climate change, and pandemics. For example, cyberattacks can disrupt essential infrastructure like electricity grids or communication networks, while terrorism spreads fear and destabilizes regions. Climate change intensifies resource scarcity, drives displacement, and fuels conflict. These modern challenges require co-operative international responses, flexible strategies, and innovative tools to uphold peace in an increasingly interconnected world.[89]

Given the flexible and evolving interpretation of Article 39 of the UN Charter, it is reasonable to ask why cyber threats could not be recognized as threats to international peace and security. The destructive potential of a cyberattack can equal or surpass that of conventional military actions. For instance, if a cyber operation disables or manipulates the control systems of a dam, causing flooding and casualties, its effects would be nearly identical to a traditional military bombing. Similarly, a cyberattack on an air traffic control system could result in mass casualties, comparable to a missile strike on commercial aircraft. In both cases, the consequences are severe – yet only the latter is traditionally viewed through the lens of international peace and security. As Marco Roscini – Professor of International Law at the University of Westminster and Senior Fellow at NATO Cooperative Cyber Defence Centre of Excellence (CCDCOE) – notes, "cyber operations . . . could certainly potentially amount to a 'threat to the peace'."[90] The UN General Assembly has repeatedly acknowledged that cyber technologies "can potentially be used for purposes that are inconsistent with the objectives of maintaining international stability and security."[91]

This raises further questions about the Security Council's powers under Article 42. If it authorizes the use of "all necessary measures," does this include cyber defense by states or regional organizations? Could a conventional military response be justified against a cyberattack – and vice versa? These issues challenge the current understanding of collective security and require thoughtful legal interpretation.

Similar concerns may emerge from the growing use of outer space. The increasing number of satellites and space-based technologies introduces new risks, including cyber-warfare and the weaponization of space. Though space has traditionally been a peaceful domain, it is not immune to the Rule of Law. The principles of the UN Charter and the collective security system may need to be applied in this rapidly evolving domain.

These developments also impact the interpretation of the right of self-defence under Article 51 of the UN Charter. A State is no longer threatened only by traditional armed forces; cyber operations now represent a credible form of aggression. The International Court of Justice (ICJ) has refrained from providing a strict definition of "armed attack," instead referring to general

89 See Société Française pour le Droit International (S.F.D.I.), 2004, *Les nouvelles menaces contre la paix et la sécurité internationales – New Threats to International Peace and Security. Journée franco-allemande – Contributions en français et en anglais*, Collection Société Française pour le Droit International, Pedone, Paris.

90 Roscini, Marco, 2014, *Cyber Operations and the Use of Force in International Law*, Oxford University Press, Oxford, p. 111.

91 United Nations General Assembly, Resolution 66/24 of 2 December 2011.

agreement about its nature. This includes not only cross-border actions by regular forces but also indirect acts like the use of armed bands or mercenaries. If such indirect methods can qualify as armed attacks, cyber operations with similarly grave consequences could also meet that threshold.

The recognition of the 2001 terrorist attacks in the United States as "armed attacks" demonstrated the adaptability of Article 51. Despite being non-traditional in nature, their scale and impact led to broad international acceptance of self-defence in response. Likewise, the destructive potential of cyber operations suggests that the concept of "armed attack" may continue to expand.

In sum, as International Law evolves to meet new challenges, the understanding of concepts like "threat to the peace" and "armed attack" must also adapt. This evolution reinforces the idea that the UN Charter is a living instrument – capable of preserving its fundamental goals of peace and security in the face of rapidly changing global threats.

6.2 International Responsibility

States are obligated to honor the international treaties they sign. When a state violates these commitments, it breaches International Law and must take responsibility for its actions. In this context, *responsibility* means the obligation to uphold legal duties, while *accountability* involves explaining those actions and facing any resulting consequences. These principles work together to support international responsibility and help uphold the Rule of Law in global relations.

Two key areas of international responsibility are central to this framework: (1) the principle that states must be held accountable for their internationally wrongful acts; and (2) the growing use of *universal jurisdiction* to address the most serious crimes, such as genocide, torture, and war crimes, even when they occur outside a state's borders.

6.2.1 The Foundational Principle of State Accountability

Renowned French scholar Alain Pellet, former President of the United Nations International Law Commission, emphasized the importance of state responsibility in International Law.[92] Citing Charles de Visscher (1884–1973),[93] Pellet underlined that responsibility is "the necessary corollary of the equality of states" and, more broadly, of International Law itself.

Without responsibility, there can be no international legal order – as de Visscher famously stated: "No responsibility, no International Law."[94]

The principle of state accountability in International Law affirms that sovereignty does not exempt states from legal responsibility. Rather, it reinforces their obligation to act in accordance with international legal norms. A foundational case illustrating this is the Corfu Channel Case (*United Kingdom v. Albania*, 1949).[95] In this case, British warships struck naval mines in Albanian waters, leading to casualties and damages. The United Kingdom argued that Albania was

92 Pellet, Alain, 2010, "The Definition of Responsibility in International Law," in *The Law of International Responsibility*, eds. James Crawford, Alain Pellet, Simon Olleson and Kate Parlett, Oxford Commentaries on International Law, online ed., Oxford Academic. Accessed 11 January 2025.

93 Charles De Visscher was a prominent Belgian jurist who, influenced by World War I, shifted from Civil and Labor Law to International Law. He taught at the universities of Ghent and Louvain and as a visiting professor in Chicago and The Hague. He held high-ranking positions, including judge at both the Permanent Court of International Justice (1937–1945) and the International Court of Justice (1946–1952), where he remains the only Belgian to have served.

94 Pellet, *The Definition of Responsibility in International Law*; De Visscher, Charles, 1924, *La responsabilité des États*, Bibliotheca Visseriana, Leiden, p. 90.

95 International Court of Justice, *Corfu Channel (United Kingdom v. Albania)*, Judgment, ICJ Reports 1949.

responsible for failing to warn them of the danger. The International Court of Justice agreed, holding Albania liable and emphasizing the duty of states to prevent harm within their territory. This ruling became a key precedent in defining state responsibility.

Another landmark case is *Nicaragua v. United States* (1986), in which Nicaragua accused the United States of violating International Law by supporting Contra rebels and mining its harbors. The ICJ ruled in favor of Nicaragua, reinforcing the principles of non-intervention and the prohibition of the use of force, and again emphasized that states cannot invoke sovereignty to escape accountability for internationally wrongful acts.[96]

A more recent example is the Application of the Genocide Convention (the *Gambia v. Myanmar*, 2019).[97] The Gambia brought a case before the ICJ accusing Myanmar of committing genocide against the Rohingya population. The Court ordered provisional measures requiring Myanmar to prevent genocidal acts, highlighting that states must comply with international obligations under human rights and humanitarian law, even in sensitive matters of sovereignty.

These cases collectively reinforce the idea that sovereignty carries with it legal duties, particularly in preventing harm and respecting human rights. This principle has been strongly upheld by figures like Ronny Abraham, a former ICJ President, who consistently argued for balancing state sovereignty with the duty to prevent atrocities and uphold international norms.[98]

Moreover, feminist and gender perspectives have expanded the scope of international responsibility by highlighting gender-based crimes in conflict. The Rome Statute of the International Criminal Court (1998) includes crimes such as rape, sexual slavery, and forced sterilization as war crimes and crimes against humanity. These inclusions reflect feminist efforts to ensure accountability for sexual and gender-based violence. In support, UN Security Council Resolution 1820 (2008) recognizes sexual violence in conflict as a threat to peace and security, affirming the global commitment to justice and accountability in such contexts.

Together, these legal developments and perspectives demonstrate the evolution of state accountability as a central pillar of International Law, encompassing not only state conduct in conflict but also broader obligations to uphold human dignity and rights.

6.2.2 Ensuring Universal Jurisdiction

Universal jurisdiction is a legal principle that allows states to prosecute individuals for serious crimes such as genocide, war crimes, and crimes against humanity, regardless of where the crimes took place or the nationalities involved. Its main purpose is to prevent impunity and provide justice for victims, making it an important tool in International Law.

The Geneva Conventions and Additional Protocol I of 1977 require states to adopt national laws that enable universal jurisdiction over certain war crimes, especially grave breaches[99] committed during international armed conflicts. This reflects the global commitment to hold perpetrators of serious crimes accountable.

96 International Court of Justice, *Case Concerning Military and Paramilitary Activities in and Against Nicaragua (Nicaragua v. United States of America)*, Merits, Judgment of 27 June 1986, I.C.J. Reports 1986.

97 International Court of Justice, *Application of the Convention on the Prevention and Punishment of the Crime of Genocide (The Gambia v. Myanmar)*, Provisional Measures, Order of 23 January 2020, I.C.J. Reports 2020.

98 Abraham, Rony, 2016, "The Role of the International Court of Justice in Resolving Disputes Between States," Speech at the ICJ.

99 Protocol Additional to the Geneva Conventions of August 12, 1949, and Relating to the Protection of Victims of International Armed Conflicts (Protocol I), 8 June 1977.

The principle of universal jurisdiction has been under discussion in the United Nations General Assembly's Sixth Committee since 2009, following a proposal introduced by Tanzania on behalf of the African Group. Many states recognize its value as a complement to national and international legal systems. However, there are concerns about its potential misuse. Countries have emphasized the importance of respecting state sovereignty, territorial integrity, and non-interference, as stated in the UN Charter.

Debates continue over which crimes should fall under universal jurisdiction. Some states support limiting it to the most serious crimes, while others are cautious about expanding its scope too broadly. To avoid political misuse, states have stressed the need for safeguards, including fair trials, independent judicial processes, and respect for legal procedures.

In response to these concerns, the Sixth Committee established a working group to explore the issue further. In 2016, the UN General Assembly invited member states and observers to share legal practices and treaty obligations related to universal jurisdiction.

Two notable cases before the International Court of Justice show the complexity of this principle. In the Arrest Warrant case (*Democratic Republic of the Congo v. Belgium*, 2000), Belgium issued an arrest warrant for the Congolese Foreign Minister, accusing him of war crimes and crimes against humanity.[100] The ICJ ruled that high-ranking officials have immunity from prosecution in foreign courts while in office, though this does not mean they are free from responsibility for serious crimes.

In another case, Certain Criminal Proceedings in France (*Republic of the Congo v. France*), the Republic of the Congo objected to France's use of universal jurisdiction to investigate crimes allegedly committed by Congolese officials.[101] The case was later withdrawn in 2010, leaving important legal questions unresolved.

These examples show the legal tension between universal jurisdiction, state sovereignty, and official immunity. As the principle continues to develop, the international community must work to balance the goals of justice with respect for international legal norms.

Conclusion

This chapter explored the key aspects of International Law, which help maintain order, cooperation, and accountability among states and other global actors. It showed how International Law is built on various sources, like treaties, customs, and general principles, and how these rules address issues such as diplomacy, human rights, the use of force, and dispute resolution.

International Law balances the independence of states with the need for global rules. It holds states and individuals accountable for serious violations through principles like international responsibility and universal jurisdiction. While challenges like ensuring compliance and respecting sovereignty remain, the system is essential for promoting justice and cooperation in today's interconnected and global world.

Although there is no central global authority to enforce International Law, its success depends on the commitment of states and other actors to follow its rules. As the world faces new issues like climate change, cyber threats, and the growing influence of artificial intelligence, International Law must continue to adapt to meet these challenges and support a fairer, more peaceful global community.

100 Arrest Warrant of 11 April 2000 (*Democratic Republic of the Congo v. Belgium*), Judgment, I.C.J. Reports 2002.

101 Certain Criminal Proceedings in France (*Republic of the Congo v. France*), Order of 16 November 2010, Discontinuance, I.C.J. Reports 2010.

Selected Bibliography

Anghie, Antony, 2005, *Imperialism, Sovereignty and the Making of International Law*, Cambridge University Press, 384 pages.

Arvidsson, Matilda, and Jones, Emily, (Eds.), 2024, *International Law and Posthuman Theory* (1st ed.), Routledge, 334 pages.

Asteriti, Alessandra, 2024, *Gender Identity in International Law: A Certain Inconvenience* (1st ed.), Cambridge Scholars Publishing, 289 pages.

Crawford, Emily, and Alison Pert, 2024, *International Humanitarian Law* (3rd ed.), Cambridge University Press, 450 pages.

Crawford, J., 2019, *Brownlie's Principles of Public International Law* (9th ed.), Oxford University Press, 872 pages.

Daillier, P., Pellet, A., Forteau, M., & Miron, A., 2022, *Droit International Public*, LGDJ, 2048 pages.

de la Rasilla, Ignacio & Cai, Congyan, (Eds.), 2024, *The Cambridge Handbook of China and International Law*, Cambridge University Press, 610 pages.

Dixon, M., McCorquodale, R., Williams, S., 2016, *Cases & Materials on International Law* (6th ed.), Oxford University Press, 732 pages.

Evans, M. D., (Ed.), 2021, *International Law* (6th ed.), Oxford University Press, 1024 pages.

Gardiner, Richard, 2023, *Treaties*, Oxford University Press, 256 pages.

Gibney, Mark, 2020, *International Law: Our Common Future* (1st ed.), Routledge, 456 pages.

González Hauck, Sué, Kunz, Raffaela, & Milas, Max, (Eds.), 2024, *Public International Law: A Multi-Perspective Approach*, Routledge, 694 pages.

Hall, Stephen, 2022, *Principles of International Law* (7th ed.), LexisNexis Butterworths, 947 pages.

Heathcote, Sarah, 2019, *Public International Law, LexisNexis WorkBook*, LexisNexis Butterworths, 132 pages.

Henriksen, Anders, 2023, *International Law*, Oxford University Press, 392 pages.

Hollis, Duncan B., (Ed.), 2020, *The Oxford Guide to Treaties* (2nd ed.), Oxford University Press, 896 pages.

Hough, Peter, Pilbeam, Bruce, and Stokes, Wendy, 2021, *International Security Studies: Theory and Practice* (2nd ed.), Routledge, 540 pages.

Kaczorowska-Ireland, Alina, 2024, *Public International Law* (6th ed.), Routledge, 910 pages.

Klabbers, Jan, 2023, *International Law*, Cambridge University Press, 421 pages.

Lowe, Vaughan, 2015, *International Law: A Very Short Introduction*, Oxford University Press, 144 pages.

Pellet, A., Olleson, S., Crawford, J., (Eds.), 2010, *The Law of International Responsibility*, Oxford University Press, 1296 pages.

Rose, Cecily, 2022, *An Introduction to Public International Law*, Cambridge University Press, 396 pages.

Shaw, M.N., 2021, *International Law* (9th ed.), Cambridge University Press, 1308 pages.

Sjoberg, Laura, (Ed.), 2010, *Gender and International Security: Feminist Perspectives* (1st ed.), Routledge, 304 pages.

Thirlway, Hugh, 2014, *The Sources of International Law*, Oxford University Press, 264 pages.

Wolfrum, R., (Ed.), 2011, *The Max Planck Encyclopedia of Public International Law* (12 vols), Oxford University Press, 11724 pages.

10 The Interface of National and International Law

International Law is part of the Law of the land.
Old Anglo-Saxon precept

We cannot expect over 200 countries to have the same practices or laws. Given the diversity of legal systems across the world, complete uniformity is neither realistic nor feasible – and perhaps not even desirable. Legal diversity allows states to tailor their laws to unique political, social, and cultural contexts. Moreover, it would be impossible for every scholar, lawyer, or judge to be familiar with the laws of every single jurisdiction. Therefore, when analyzing the law, one looks for trends and patterns – not absolute consistency.

The preceding chapter explored the foundations of International Law, including its origins in treaties, the consistent practices of states, and general legal principles derived from national legal systems worldwide. This chapter offers a structured analysis of the relationship between domestic and International Law, combining theoretical perspectives with practical applications. It shifts the focus from abstract concepts to more concrete issues, particularly emphasizing the critical question of enforcement within the international legal framework.

A central challenge in the international legal order is the absence of a centralized enforcement mechanism. In the absence of such a system, the implementation of International Law relies heavily on national legal frameworks. States must ensure that their domestic legal systems are capable of giving effect to international legal obligations; otherwise, enforcement becomes impossible in cases of violation. When domestic courts and institutions fail to uphold International Law, breaches may go unremedied, and states or individuals may face no consequences for their violations.

This chapter explores the intricate relationship between domestic and international legal orders. Section 1 begins by examining how and why these systems interact, laying the foundation for understanding both their autonomy and their interdependence in practice.

Building on this foundation, Section 2 offers an in-depth analysis of *monism* and *dualism* – two pivotal theories that frame the relationship between national and international legal orders. This discussion not only enriches our theoretical understanding but also deepens our grasp of the legal complexities involved in navigating multiple legal orders.

Finally, Section 3 considers the effects of globalization on this dynamic relationship, using global forced displacement as a case study. This example illustrates the practical challenges and legal intricacies of integrating international norms into domestic frameworks.

DOI: 10.4324/9781003393047-14

1 How and Why Domestic and International Legal Orders Interact

Around the world, many different legal systems exist. These systems coexist, and at times, overlap or conflict.

This phenomenon is called *legal pluralism*, where laws from different levels – like national, regional, and international – can all apply at the same time.

Interconnectivity – and the broader notion of legal connectivity – plays a central role in this dynamic: legal systems are not only linked, but often rely on one another for legitimacy, enforcement, and adaptation.

Treaties require domestic implementation, national courts increasingly reference international norms, and regional organizations influence domestic legislation, all of which illustrate the deep interdependence among legal frameworks.

In this section, we examine the interaction between domestic and international legal frameworks, analyzing both how and why they intersect. This inquiry lays the foundation for understanding their respective autonomy and mutual interdependence in today's complex and multiple legal landscape.

1.1 How Domestic and International Legal Orders Interact

Domestic and international legal systems are closely interconnected, continuously influencing one another.

International Law influences national legal systems, notably through treaties, customary rules, and international court decisions. In turn, national legal systems shape International Law notably by guiding state practice and interpreting treaty obligations. Legal diplomacy also matters, as states rely on their domestic laws to negotiate, influence, and shape international rules.[1]

This section explores the main mechanisms of this interaction – such as treaty implementation, customary International Law, judicial decisions, self-executing norms, and the harmonization of laws – underscoring the reciprocal nature of legal influence across jurisdictions.

1.1.1 Treaty Implementation

When countries enter into international treaties, they agree to abide by the rules set forth in those treaties. To give these rules effect at home, they must pass domestic laws that incorporate the treaty obligations into their national legal systems.

This process, known as ratification and incorporation, is essential for the effectiveness of international treaties. Ratification occurs when a state, after approval through its own internal processes, informs the other parties of its agreement to be bound by the treaty's terms. This official act makes the treaty legally binding on that state. Ratification ensures that the provisions of international treaties are not just intentions but are enforceable within the jurisdictions of the signatory states.[2]

1 See Gontier, Jean-Yves, 2023, *Legal Diplomacy – Defense and Illustration of French Law and Continental Law in Global Law Through the Examples of Mediation and International Arbitration*, thesis defended on 30 January 2023, Paris-Saclay University.

2 For an overview of ratification principles, refer to Chapter 9, "What is International Law and How is it Made?", and see Hollis, Duncan B. (ed.), 2020, *The Oxford Guide to Treaties*, 2nd ed., Oxford University Press, as well as Kaczorowska-Ireland, Alina, 2023, *Public International Law*, Routledge.

To incorporate treaty obligations into national law, countries may adopt a variety of approaches depending on their legal systems and constitutional requirements.

Some nations follow a monistic system, where international treaties automatically become part of domestic law once ratified, without the need for additional legislation.

Imagine Country X, which has a monist legal system. It ratifies an international treaty banning the use of certain toxic pesticides. As soon as the treaty is ratified, its provisions automatically become part of Country X's domestic law. Farmers in Country X are immediately prohibited from using those pesticides, even without any new national legislation.

However, most countries operate under a dualistic system, which requires explicit legislative action to incorporate treaty provisions into their national legal codes. This often involves the adoption of new laws or amendments to existing laws that explicitly incorporate the treaty obligations into the domestic legal order.

Consider Country Y, which follows a dualist system. It ratifies the same treaty banning toxic pesticides. However, in Country Y, the treaty does not automatically apply. The parliament must pass a new law or amend existing environmental legislation to ban the pesticides domestically. Until that legislative step is taken, the treaty's rules cannot be enforced in Country Y's courts.

The process of treaty ratification and incorporation varies from country to country, but generally it involves several key steps from the initial signing of the treaty to the treaty becoming a part of national law. This process can be observed in many areas of International Law, such as human rights, environmental protection, sustainable development, the Law of the Sea, outer space, arms control, refugee and migration issues, global communications, and international trade. A clear example is the Paris Agreement, a legally binding international treaty on climate change. Its main goal is to limit the increase in global average temperature to 1.5°C.[3]

The Agreement is significant because it brought together almost all countries in a joint effort to address climate change and its impacts. The first step in the process was the signing of the Agreement. It was adopted by consensus on December 12, 2015, and opened for signature on April 22, 2016, at a ceremony in New York. By signing, countries showed their intention to review the treaty at the national level and consider ratification.

Before ratifying, each country must follow its domestic legal procedures, which often involve the national legislature, though this is not always required. For example, in the United States, Senate approval was not required for the U.S. to join the Paris Agreement. This is because Article 4 of the Agreement does not introduce new legal obligations. It simply repeats what was already agreed under Article 4 of the 1992 United Nations Framework Convention on Climate Change (UNFCCC). Since the U.S. had already joined the UNFCCC with Senate approval in 1992, no further approval was needed for the Paris Agreement.

The United States' involvement in the Paris Agreement has undergone significant changes, especially under the administrations of Presidents Donald Trump and Joe Biden, reflecting shifts in U.S. climate policy.

In June 2017, President Trump announced the United States' intention to withdraw from the Paris Agreement, arguing that the treaty would harm the U.S. economy and disadvantage key industries, particularly the energy sector. The formal withdrawal process began in November 2019, and the U.S. officially exited the Agreement on November 4, 2020, becoming the first and only country to leave the Paris Agreement.

3 According to the UN's Intergovernmental Panel on Climate Change, to stay within the 1.5°C limit, emissions must peak by 2025 and fall 43% by 2030. For information on the United Nations Framework Convention on Climate Change, see UNFCCC, online. Available at: https://unfccc.int/. Accessed 18 November 2025.

This position was reversed with the election of President Joe Biden, who made rejoining the Paris Agreement one of his first acts in office on January 20, 2021. The Biden administration presented this decision as a renewed commitment to climate action and multilateral cooperation.

The different approaches taken by the Trump and Biden administrations show that the United States is divided on climate policy. They also reveal how U.S. involvement in international climate agreements can change depending on who is in power.[4]

Following the COP29 summit in Baku, Azerbaijan, in November 2024, global concerns grew about the future of international climate cooperation. This concern intensified following the outcome of the U.S. presidential election, in which Donald Trump was re-elected.

As expected, on his first day back in office on January 20, 2025, President Trump signed executive orders to withdraw the United States from the Paris Agreement. This second U.S. withdrawal created uncertainty around the strength of international climate commitments and drew increased attention to COP30, which took place in November 2025 in Belém, Brazil. At this summit, countries met under the United Nations Framework Convention on Climate Change to review progress and plan the next steps in global climate action.

Each country joining the Paris Agreement followed its own domestic approval procedures. For example, the European Union needed approval from both the European Parliament and the Council of the European Union. After domestic approval, countries ratified the Agreement by depositing official documents, called instruments of ratification, with the United Nations Secretary-General. The Agreement required at least 55 countries, representing 55% of global emissions, to ratify it before it could enter into force. These conditions were met, and the Agreement became effective on November 4, 2016.

Once ratified, countries were responsible for implementing the Agreement in their national legal systems. This often required passing new laws or adjusting existing ones. One of the main duties under the Agreement is for countries to submit Nationally Determined Contributions, which outline national plans to reduce emissions and adapt to climate change.

The Paris Agreement shows how complex international treaties can be. The process involves international negotiation, domestic approval, and national implementation, all of which can be strongly influenced by political leadership and changes in government priorities.

1.1.2 Customary International Law

As explained in Chapter 9 – *What is International Law and How is it Made?*, the combination of consistent actions by states (known as *precedents*) and the belief that these actions are legally required (*opinio juris*) helps form customary International Law. This process can be compared to how a footpath forms across a park: imagine a city park where people begin cutting across the grass to reach a tram station. At first, it's just a shortcut, but as more people use it daily, the path becomes clear and accepted. Eventually, the city may even pave it, turning it into an official walkway.

In the same way, when states repeatedly act in a certain manner and believe they are legally obligated to do so, a customary rule may develop at the international level. This shows how international and domestic legal systems interact. The actions and policies of individual states help shape international norms, while the application of international customs by those states reinforces their legal obligations.

4 United States Rejoins the Paris Agreement on Climate Change: Options for Congress, Congressional Research Service, 25 February 2021, online. Available at: https://crsreports.congress.gov/. Accessed 18 November 2025.

Once established, customary International Law becomes binding. Many states incorporate it into their own legal systems – either directly, by treating it as part of domestic law, or indirectly, by passing laws that align with international customs. When national courts apply these rules, they help demonstrate how International Law influences domestic legal systems and enforcement mechanisms.

To understand the process of how international customs are formed, imagine the following scenarios: Imagine that more and more countries begin to remove old satellites and space debris after completing their missions. At first, this is done for safety and environmental reasons. However, as the practice continues, states start making public statements that all nations are responsible for keeping space clean. Over time, this shared practice and belief can evolve into a customary legal rule: countries have a legal obligation to manage their space waste.

Similarly, consider a situation where several coastal nations begin banning the fishing of an endangered fish species, even outside their national waters. Other countries follow this example. Eventually, states begin to criticize those who continue such fishing, claiming it violates international responsibility. As this expectation grows and is repeated widely, it may lead to a customary rule requiring the protection of certain marine species, even without a treaty.

Customary International Law can change over time as states act differently and global norms develop. This flexibility ensures that both international and domestic legal orders can respond effectively to new challenges and developments, maintaining a coherent and relevant legal framework.

Customary International Law further plays a crucial role in the resolution of disputes between states, providing a set of norms and principles that are recognized beyond formal treaties. This facilitates a shared understanding and framework for resolving international disputes, which can have direct implications for domestic legal systems.

Imagine that an offshore oil platform operated by State A accidentally causes a large oil spill, and the pollution reaches the coast of State B, damaging its marine environment and affecting local communities. There is no specific treaty between the two states covering environmental damage of this kind.

However, over the years, many states have responded to similar incidents by accepting responsibility, offering compensation, and cooperating in clean-up efforts – based on the customary principle that states must prevent environmental harm to other states (a principle recognized in cases like Trail Smelter Arbitration and widely accepted in practice).

Because this principle is now part of customary International Law, State B invokes it in international negotiations and demands compensation. State A accepts the claim, citing its own domestic law that incorporates international environmental norms. The courts in State A also recognize the customary rule as binding and enforce compensation through national legal channels.

To sum up, customary International Law exemplifies the interaction between international and domestic legal orders by showing how state practices contribute to the development of global legal norms, how these norms influence domestic law, and how the legal systems at both levels adapt to and reinforce each other.

An example of customary International Law that exemplifies the interaction between international and domestic legal orders is the principle of diplomatic immunity. This principle, which has been a part of international relations for centuries, is recognized in both International Law and the domestic law of most countries around the world. It establishes that diplomats from foreign countries are not subject to the jurisdiction of the host country's courts and laws, ensuring their safe passage and unimpeded function while on diplomatic duties.[5]

5 United States Department of State, Office of Foreign Missions, *Diplomatic and Consular Immunity: Guidance for Law Enforcement and Judicial Authorities*, online. Available at: https://www.state.gov/wp-content/uploads/2019/07/2018-DipConImm_v5_Web.pdf. Accessed 18 November 2025.

In practice, this means that when a diplomat violates the law in a host country, that country cannot arrest, detain, or prosecute the diplomat as it would a normal foreigner or citizen. Instead, it must resort to diplomatic channels to resolve the issue, such as declaring the diplomat persona non grata (unwelcome) and requesting their removal by the sending state. The sending state may then choose to waive immunity and allow prosecution or take disciplinary action internally.

For example, imagine that a diplomat from Country A, stationed in Country B, is involved in a car accident while speeding in the capital city of Country B. The accident causes minor injuries to a local pedestrian. Under Country B's domestic laws, the act would normally lead to criminal charges and possibly a court trial. However, because the driver is a diplomat from Country A, local authorities in Country B are legally prohibited from initiating prosecution. Instead, Country B's Ministry of Foreign Affairs sends a formal complaint to Country A's embassy and requests the diplomat's recall. Country A responds by apologizing and withdrawing the diplomat, while also initiating internal disciplinary procedures.

Comparably, imagine that a diplomat from Country A, posted at its embassy in Country B, is suspected of shoplifting from a luxury store in the capital. Security footage appears to show the diplomat placing items in their bag without paying. The store files a police report, and local authorities launch a criminal investigation.

However, because the individual is accredited as a diplomat, Country B's police are not allowed to search their home, arrest them, or conduct interrogations, even with strong evidence. The Ministry of Foreign Affairs of Country B contacts the embassy of Country A to raise the issue. Country A, while not waiving immunity, recalls the diplomat and launches its own investigation back home.

This scenario demonstrates how criminal immunity protects diplomats from the host country's criminal justice system, and how issues must be handled through diplomatic – not judicial – channels, as prescribed by customary International Law and reflected in domestic procedures.

These fictional cases highlight how a customary international rule, like diplomatic immunity, is embedded in the legal systems of individual states and applied in real-world scenarios. It shows how international legal norms influence domestic legal outcomes, reinforcing cooperation and legal consistency between states.

Primarily based on custom and international practice until quite recently, the principle of diplomatic immunity is codified in international treaties such as the Vienna Convention on Diplomatic Relations of 1961, which many countries have ratified, incorporating its provisions into their domestic legal systems.

This example demonstrates how customary International Law interacts with domestic legal orders by requiring states to adjust their legal systems to respect the principles of diplomatic immunity, balancing between upholding international norms and exercising national sovereignty.

1.1.3 Judicial Decisions

Court decisions around the world show how domestic and International Law interact. Many national courts use International Law, including rulings from international courts, to support their decisions, especially in areas like human rights and environmental law, where global standards are strong. At the same time, national courts help put these international rules into practice, making the hierarchy of norms effective within their own legal systems.[6]

Imagine, for example, a constitutional court in State X invoking the Refugee Convention to strike down a domestic law that restricts asylum rights.

6 For an overview of the hierarchy of norms principles, refer to Chapter 1 – *What is Law? What Forms Does Law Take?*

Similarly, in the 2015 *Urgenda* case, the Dutch Supreme Court relied on the European Convention on Human Rights to require the government to reduce greenhouse gas emissions, linking international human rights obligations with domestic climate policy. These examples show how international norms can override conflicting national measures.

National courts help enforce international norms, shaping how they operate in domestic legal systems. But the link between international and national law differs across countries and raises both theoretical and practical challenges. Theories like monism and dualism try to explain such a relationship, but in practice, states adopt more mixed approaches.

For example, the interaction between International Law and India's domestic legislation[7] is complex and not always clear-cut. The Indian Constitution lays out a foundational structure for incorporating international treaty obligations within its legal framework. Still, India's approach to implementing International Law varies according to circumstances.[8]

Some scholars argue that there is a need for a new legal framework for better implementation of International Law in India.[9] Acknowledging that India tried to incorporate and utilize International Law in several judgments and decisions when they are consistent with the domestic laws, they argue that judges can use the principle of systemic integration and carry out an integrationist interpretation of International Law. They suggest that Indian courts should cite treaties more often and argue that it will strengthen the Indian domestic laws, that signing more treaties will make India resilient in implementing International Law, and that developing a new legal document to define a new legal framework specifically for the implementation of International Law in India. Therefore, judges in India could potentially elevate themselves into architects of the consistency of the international legal system.[10]

Unlike the UK or Italy, which have maintained a dualist stance requiring a specific law to incorporate treaties into the domestic realm, France's constitutional arrangements facilitate the direct incorporation of International Law.[11]

Nevertheless, some treaties or treaty provisions, designed to create obligations solely between states, do not automatically translate into domestic law. The Judiciary plays a critical role in determining whether a treaty clause has direct domestic applicability, taking into account the treaty's overall objectives, content, and the parties' intentions, as outlined by the Council of State in its April 11, 2012, Gisti decision.[12]

While the Constitution places treaties above domestic laws, it leaves the specifics of enforcing this hierarchy largely to judicial interpretation. Over time, case law has progressively reinforced the primacy of treaties over domestic legislation, thereby maintaining the constitutional supremacy within France's legal order.

Chapter 8 – *The Transplant Debate* – delves into the complexities and nuances of how national courts, specifically within the United States, engage with foreign decisions and opinions.

7 The Common Law system was established in India through British influence.

8 Chandra, Aparna, 2017, "India and International Law: Formal Dualism, Functional Monism," *Indian Journal of International Law*, vol. 57, online. Available at: https://link.springer.com/article/10.1007/s40901-017-0069-0. Accessed 18 November 2025.

9 Sehrawat, Vivek, 2021, "Implementation of International Law in Indian Legal System," *Florida Journal of International Law*, vol. 31, no. 1, Article 4, online. Available at: https://scholarship.law.ufl.edu/fjil/vol31/iss1/4. Accessed 18 November 2025.

10 Sehrawat, *Implementation of International Law in Indian Legal System*.

11 Stirn, Bernard, 2016, "The French Judge and International Law," presentation delivered on 21 March 2016 at the Academy of Moral and Political Sciences, online. Available at: https://academiesciencesmoralesetpolitiques.fr/2016/03/21/le-juge-francais-et-le-droit-international/. Accessed 18 November 2025.

12 Stirn, *The French Judge and International Law*.

This engagement is framed within two distinct scenarios: *the transplant scenario* and *the influence scenario*. The distinction is critical in understanding how legal ideas and precedents cross national borders, illuminating the interaction between international and national legal orders.[13]

In the transplant scenario, there is a direct adoption or transplantation of foreign legal principles into the national legal system which is relatively rare and involves explicit legislative or judicial action to incorporate foreign laws. On the other hand, the influence scenario is more subtle and involves national courts looking to foreign jurisprudence for guidance, inspiration, or confirmation of their decisions without formally incorporating these foreign laws into the national legal framework. This scenario is more common and reflects a form of legal globalization where ideas and principles flow between jurisdictions, contributing to a shared global understanding of legal concepts while respecting the sovereignty of national legal systems.

As described in Chapter 8, the debate over the use of foreign precedents in the U.S. is emblematic of broader questions about national sovereignty, judicial independence, and the global convergence of legal norms.

The case *Roper v. Simmons* illustrates this dynamic. The U.S. Supreme Court struck down the death penalty for minors and referred to international consensus as support for its reasoning. This did not dictate the Court's decision but provided a comparative perspective that reinforced its reasoning.

This use of foreign law reflects an influence scenario where international legal norms contribute to the evolving understanding of constitutional principles in the U.S., such as the interpretation of cruel and unusual punishments under the Eighth Amendment.

In summary, this discussion shows how national and international legal systems interact in complex ways, especially through the influence of foreign case law on domestic court decisions.

1.1.4 Self-Executing Norms

In some countries, the legal system permits the direct application of International Law within domestic courts. This means that international treaties and conventions may be invoked and enforced without requiring specific implementing legislation. This approach is known as *monism*. However, it is important to distinguish monism from the concept of *self-executing norms* (or *direct applicability/direct effect*), as the two represent separate legal doctrines concerning the interaction between international and national law.[14]

Monism is a legal theory that explains the relationship between International Law and domestic law. In a monist system, both are viewed as part of a single, unified legal order. As a result, once an international treaty is ratified, it becomes directly applicable within the domestic legal system without the need for additional legislation.

In monist countries, like the Netherlands, international treaties automatically become part of domestic law once ratified, and can be directly applied by courts.

For instance, imagine that in 2025, a Dutch activist is fined €5,000 for criticizing a police operation during a peaceful protest, under a domestic law prohibiting "public insults against state institutions." She challenges the fine in court, arguing that it violates her right to freedom of expression under Article 10 of the European Convention on Human Rights, which the Netherlands has ratified.

13 Refer to Chapter 8 for an overview of the Transplant Debate.

14 Nollkaemper, André, 201, "Direct Effect, National Courts and the International Rule of Law," *Oxford Academic*, online. https://doi.org/10.1093/acprof:oso/9780199236671.003.0006. Accessed 27 February 2024.

Because the Netherlands follows a monist legal approach, the court applies the ECHR directly. It finds that the activist's criticism constitutes protected speech and rules that the fine is disproportionate. As a result, the fine is overturned.

This example illustrates how, in monist legal systems, individuals can invoke international human rights law directly before domestic courts.

Self-executing norms are provisions within international treaties that have immediate legal effect within a state's domestic legal system, without the need for additional legislation. A provision is considered self-executing if it is clear, precise, and unconditional enough for individuals to rely on it directly before national courts. Whether a provision is self-executing depends on the wording of the treaty and the intention of the parties. Importantly, not all treaty provisions are self-executing; some require implementing legislation to take effect domestically.

For example, imagine a fictional international treaty on the protection of cultural heritage, which includes the following clause:

> Each state party shall ensure that all individuals within its jurisdiction have free access to public national museums on the first Sunday of every month.

This provision is clear (specifies the right of access), precise (defines the time and scope), and unconditional (requires no further action or conditions for implementation). Therefore, in a monist country, an individual could directly invoke this right before a domestic court if denied access on the designated day. The court could enforce this treaty provision without needing additional national legislation.

Direct applicability (or direct effect), by contrast, is a principle primarily associated with European Union law. A norm has a direct effect when it can be invoked by individuals or companies before national courts without any need for national implementation. This ensures that EU treaties and regulations create enforceable rights and obligations at the national level, even in the absence of domestic legislation.[15]

Monism, by contrast, is not about the nature of specific treaty provisions, but rather about a state's overall legal approach to International Law. In a monist legal system, international treaties become part of domestic law upon ratification and can be applied by courts without the need for separate implementing legislation. However, even in monist systems, only self-executing treaty provisions can be directly enforced by individuals. In other words, monism allows for the possibility of direct application, but self-execution determines whether a specific treaty norm can actually be relied upon in court.

1.1.5 Harmonization of Laws

To facilitate international trade, fight transnational crime, and protect human rights, nations often work together to harmonize their domestic laws with international standards, adopting similar legal frameworks and regulations.

Legal harmonization, which merges laws from different countries, highlights the interaction between international and national legal orders and frameworks. This effort, largely driven by economic interests, involves merging national laws into broader, agreed-upon legal frameworks. A notable example is the global agreement on trade, known as the United Nations Convention on Contracts for the International Sale of Goods, which standardizes legal practices in trade across countries (UNCITRAL).

15 Nollkaemper, *Direct Effect, National Courts and the International Rule of Law*.

Organizations like the Organization for the Harmonization of Business Law in Africa (OHADA) and the European Union (EU) play significant roles in unifying legal systems to ease trade and economic integration. OHADA, which is 30 years old, aligns business laws in mainly 17 West and Central African countries, whereas the EU's initiatives aim to make its member states' laws more consistent, particularly through regulations and directives that member states must adopt.

OHADA was founded during a period of acute economic crisis and a significant decrease in investments in Africa, where legal and judicial insecurity were pinpointed as the main causes of investor skepticism. The outdatedness, inconsistency, and inaccessibility of the rules that regulate economic operations caused legal uncertainty, characterized by doubts about the applicable law, while the lack of resources in the courts, a shortage of judicial staff, their inadequate training in economic law, judicial delays, and ethical issues were the roots of judicial insecurity, leading to unpredictable judicial decisions. To address these problems, OHADA was tasked with streamlining the business legal environment to ensure legal and judicial security for economic activities, with the goal of encouraging investment and creating a new development center in Africa.[16]

From OHADA's uniform acts to the EU's legislative efforts to harmonize contract laws and discuss a unified Civil Code, these initiatives underscore the dynamic relationship between international legal orders and national legal orders. This illustrates how international and regional organizations mix legal practices from various countries. It highlights the complex ways in which laws from different places come together.

In practice, a blend of national legal solutions takes place within regional or international organizations, such as the European Union, either through a desire for compromise during negotiations or through the actions of individuals and chance, for example, when selecting specific solutions to emerging problems. This process often leads to complex combinations of norms and legal practices through a mechanism of hybridization of national laws, particularly within global and regional institutions, which serve as prime venues for legal influence and the melding of national laws.

Furthermore, the exchange of legal information across borders, facilitated by globalization of information and technological advancements, also illustrates the interaction of international and national legal frameworks. This has led to a more interconnected legal landscape where judges and legal scholars have unprecedented access to foreign legal materials, enabling a more informed and nuanced dialogue between national and international legal orders.

We have outlined these examples – treaty implementation, customary International Law, judicial decisions, self-executing norms, and harmonization of laws – as illustrations of the interaction between international and national legal orders.

International Law interacts with national legal systems in many ways beyond treaties. These include, notably, international arbitration awards, financial standards, mutual recognition agreements, and legal diplomacy. International arbitration awards are binding decisions from international tribunals in cross-border disputes. Many countries enforce them under treaties like the New York Convention. International Financial Standards are guidelines for banking, money laundering, and financial transparency. Though not binding, countries often adopt them to align with global practices. Mutual Recognition Agreements are deals between countries to accept each other's rules – for example, in product safety or professional qualifications – making trade and cooperation easier.

16 Beauchard, Renaud and Mahutodji Jimmy Vital Kodo, 2011, "Can OHADA Increase Legal Certainty in Africa?", *Justice and Development Working Paper Series*, The International Bank for Reconstruction and Development / The World Bank, online. Available at: https://documents1.worldbank.org/. Accessed 27 February 2024.

Legal diplomacy refers to the strategic use of legal systems, norms, and institutions as tools of international influence and statecraft.[17] Unlike traditional diplomacy, which focuses on political, economic, and cultural relations, legal diplomacy involves promoting a country's legal model, values, and standards abroad – particularly in areas like arbitration, legal harmonization, contract law, and dispute resolution. It recognizes that a state's ability to export its legal framework – such as Civil Law or Common Law traditions – is directly linked to its economic influence and soft power. For example, the widespread adoption of Anglo-American arbitration practices or mediation clauses in international contracts may challenge the presence of Civil Law systems like those based on French legal traditions.

Legal diplomacy aims to promote a nation's legal system internationally, resist the dominance of foreign legal models, preserve legal diversity, and integrate legal influence into foreign and economic policy.

While the interaction between international and domestic legal systems is often viewed as a one-way flow – from international to national law – it is essential to recognize that influence can also move in the opposite direction. National courts, legislatures, and legal practices can play an active role in shaping International Law. Through consistent state practice, judicial decisions, and legislative developments, domestic legal systems contribute to the formation and evolution of global legal norms. In this sense, states are not merely passive recipients of International Law but also active participants in its development.

For example, the 2023 Brazilian Supreme Court ruling on Indigenous and ancestral land rights had a significant impact on international discussions regarding Indigenous rights and environmental protection. The court's decision to uphold Indigenous claims by rejecting time restrictions on ancestral land rights was widely seen as a positive step toward strengthening Indigenous protections.

Another example is the 2015 legalization of same-sex marriage in the U.S. (*Obergefell v. Hodges*), which contributed to global momentum for LGBTQ rights, influencing legal reforms in other countries like Australia, Taiwan, and Thailand.

France was not directly influenced by the 2015 U.S. Supreme Court decision in *Obergefell v. Hodges*, as France had already legalized same-sex marriage before that ruling. France legalized same-sex marriage on May 18, 2013, through the adoption of the *Mariage pour tous* law under President François Hollande. This made France the 14th country in the world to recognize marriage equality.

While *Obergefell v. Hodges* helped strengthen the global momentum for LGBTQ rights, France was already ahead in this regard, influencing other European countries instead. France was influenced by several countries that had already legalized same-sex marriage before 2013. The main influences came from The Netherlands (2001), the first country in the world to legalize same-sex marriage, setting a precedent in Europe and beyond, and Belgium (2003), a neighboring country to France. Belgium's legalization demonstrated how marriage equality could be successfully implemented within a Civil Law system similar to France's.

1.2 Why Domestic and International Legal Orders Interact

Previous discussions focused on the technical ways in which international and domestic legal systems interact. This section takes a step further by exploring why these legal systems interact in the first place.

17 See Gontier, *Legal Diplomacy*.

In a globalized world, multiple legal systems exist side by side. As international exchanges grow, legal orders become more connected – and sometimes compete with one another. This interaction is not random; it is shaped by several key factors.

States often need to adjust their domestic legal and administrative systems to meet international obligations. In many cases, international rules are specifically designed to operate within national legal systems, especially when they concern individual rights, trade regulations, or environmental standards.

1.2.1 Navigating a World of Interconnected and Competing Legal Orders

The world is shaped by multiple, interconnected, and sometimes competing legal orders. These systems – domestic, regional, international, and increasingly digital – are interdependent, a condition often described as *connectivity*. This concept is essential for understanding how legal orders interact, overlap, and influence one another.

The rise of the digital legal order marks a significant shift in this landscape. Legal norms now emerge not only from states and international organizations, but also from private tech actors, global platforms, algorithmic governance systems, and cross-border data regulation frameworks. This evolution challenges traditional distinctions between public and private law, national and international jurisdiction, and even between formal and informal legal sources.

This complex interplay illustrates the idea of *legal pluralism*, which acknowledges that law arises from multiple sources, not solely from the State. Today's international legal environment is multi-centered, shaped by both sovereign states and non-state actors –including digital platforms, transnational corporations, and regulatory networks. As legal systems evolve within this environment, new regulatory mechanisms are needed to manage overlapping competencies and to respond to rapid technological change.

To better understand these developments, several prominent scholars have explored how globalization, legal complexity, and technological transformation affect the legal order.

Thierry Rambaud, Professor of Public Law at Université Paris Cité, argues that globalization reframes and even absorbs many traditional functions of the State, a process now intensified by digital governance.[18] Jean-Bernard Auby, Emeritus Professor at Sciences Po Paris, notes that globalization reshapes not only the issues of Comparative Law but also its methods – especially in response to the influence of digital norms and cross-border regulation.[19]

From a historical standpoint, Jean-Baptiste Duroselle (1917–1994) distinguished between two aspects of international relations: *international policy*, driven by states (diplomacy, war), and *international life*, shaped by private actors (tourism, sports, trade). This framework is especially relevant today, as private digital actors – platforms, payment systems, AI developers – play an increasingly public role in shaping law-like norms across borders.[20]

Finally, Professor Mireille Delmas-Marty (1941–2022), a leading figure in comparative and International Law, proposed the concept of *ordered pluralism* – a vision of legal evolution that balances diversity and unity. She warned against both anarchic globalization and overly rigid legal harmonization, advocating instead for a dynamic and flexible approach to global legal integration.[21]

18 Rambaud, Thierry, 2014, *Introduction au droit comparé. Les grandes traditions juridiques dans le monde*, PUF.
19 Auby, Jean-Bernard, 2010, *La globalisation, le droit et l'État*, L.G.D.J.
20 Lefebvre, Maxime, 2013, *Le jeu du droit et de la puissance*, 4e éd., PUF.
21 Delmas-Marty, Mireille, 2011, *Les forces imaginantes du droit: Vers une communauté de valeurs*, Seuil.

Imagine a 12-year-old boy named Leo, living in France. One afternoon, he records a video of his homemade drone flying over a neighbor's backyard and uploads it to a popular global social media platform. Within hours, the platform removes the video, stating that it violates its privacy policy related to the unauthorized filming of private property.

Leo's parents are confused. Under French law, Leo hasn't broken any rules – his drone flight complies with local aviation regulations, and there is no clear violation of national privacy law. However, the platform operates under its own community standards, shaped by its headquarters in the United States, and enforced by automated moderation systems.

Soon after, Leo's parents receive a notification that their data is being processed under the platform's terms of service, which refer to EU data protection rules (GDPR), U.S. commercial practices, and internal company policies. They realize that their son's simple video has activated a complex web of legal orders – national, regional, international, and digital.

This example shows how Domestic law (French drone and privacy laws), Regional law (EU data protection), Private digital governance (platform rules and algorithms), and transnational influences (U.S.-based platform operations) all interact simultaneously. Leo's case illustrates the reality of legal connectivity and legal pluralism in the digital age, where multiple legal actors – states, platforms, regulators – converge on everyday actions.

It also echoes Professor Delmas-Marty's vision of ordered pluralism: a legal landscape that is no longer defined solely by national borders, but by overlapping systems that must be balanced to preserve fairness, accountability, and legal coherence in a globalized world.

Imagine a teenager named Amina, living in Morocco. She tries to buy a pair of sneakers from an international e-commerce website headquartered in the United States. When she visits the site, the price shown is significantly higher than what her cousin in Belgium sees for the same item. Curious, Amina uses a VPN to simulate a Belgian IP address – and the price drops.

Unknowingly, Amina has encountered algorithmic price discrimination, where the platform uses personal data and geolocation to set different prices based on region. She contacts customer service, but the platform refers her to its terms and conditions, which state that pricing is governed by U.S. law, while data handling is subject to GDPR for EU users, and local rules elsewhere.

Amina and her family reach out to the Moroccan consumer protection authority, only to find that no specific regulation currently addresses this kind of cross-border algorithmic pricing. The platform, however, is facing regulatory scrutiny in the EU for similar practices and must comply with upcoming EU digital market rules, which are not yet enforceable in Morocco.

This everyday act of online shopping involves National law (Moroccan consumer protection), Foreign regional law (EU digital regulation), International business standards (platform codes of conduct), and automated digital governance (algorithms and terms of service).

Amina's experience highlights the blurring of public/private and national/international legal boundaries. It shows how private digital actors exercise regulatory power, often beyond the reach of national governments, while regional blocs like the EU attempt to extend legal protections beyond their borders.

This case echoes the concerns raised by scholars like Rambaud, Auby, and Delmas-Marty – that in a globalized and digitized world, states must either adapt their regulatory models or risk being sidelined by private or foreign legal systems. It highlights the urgent need for coherent yet adaptable legal frameworks capable of managing legal pluralism without compromising fairness or legal certainty.

This shift in the legal landscape not only reflects deep transformations in global governance but also helps explain how, why, and under what conditions domestic, regional, and international legal orders interact. Grasping this evolving dynamic is essential for understanding and navigating the legal complexity of the 21st century.

A significant case that highlights the complexity of interconnected legal systems is *Google Spain SL and Google Inc. v. Agencia Española de Protección de Datos (AEPD) and Mario Costeja González* (2014). This case, decided by the Court of Justice of the European Union (CJEU), illustrates how domestic, regional, and international legal frameworks interact, particularly in the realm of digital governance and data protection.[22]

The dispute arose when Mario Costeja González, a Spanish citizen, requested that Google remove search results linking to outdated legal notices about his financial difficulties. He argued that these links infringed on his right to privacy under Spain's national data protection law, which was based on EU Directive 95/46/EC on data protection. Google, however, contended that as a U.S.-based company, it was not subject to EU laws and that Spain's data protection authority had no jurisdiction over it. This conflict highlighted the clash between national laws (Spain), regional regulations (EU), and corporate governance principles applied by a multinational entity (Google).

The CJEU ruled in favor of González, recognizing the *right to be forgotten* under EU law. The court determined that Google, despite being headquartered in the U.S., had to comply with EU data protection laws since it operated a subsidiary (Google Spain) within the EU. As a result, Google was required to remove links to outdated personal data when individuals requested it, provided there was no overriding public interest in keeping the information accessible. This ruling established a precedent where regional legal standards could be enforced against global companies, even if their headquarters were outside the legal jurisdiction.

This case illustrates several key aspects of legal pluralism and global legal interactions. First, it demonstrates how competing legal orders – national, regional, and international – intersect, sometimes leading to jurisdictional conflicts. Second, it underscores the connectivity of legal frameworks, as EU regulations extended beyond its borders to influence the policies of a global tech company. Third, it highlights the balancing of interests between privacy rights (protected under EU law) and free expression or access to information (defended by Google). Finally, the ruling had a ripple effect beyond the EU, as countries such as Canada and Japan began considering similar *right to be forgotten policies*, illustrating how one legal order can shape others.

Overall, this case is a prime example of how legal orders interact in a globalized and digitalized world. It showcases the challenges of navigating multiple, interconnected, and sometimes competing legal frameworks where domestic regulations, regional governance, and international corporate policies must find a way to coexist.

1.2.2 State Obligations and the Role of National Administration in Enforcing International Law

States have international obligations, and to fulfill their international obligations, they must often involve their own administration and public services. One key aspect of state obligations is the duty to respect human rights by refraining from actions that interfere with fundamental freedoms.

As described in Chapter 9 – *What Is International Law and How Is It Made?* – International Human Rights Law lays down obligations that states are bound to respect. The UN Human Rights Office emphasizes that when countries sign international treaties, they agree to respect, protect, and fulfill human rights. This means they must not interfere with people's rights, prevent abuses, and take action to ensure basic rights are upheld. Governments must also update

22 Court of Justice of the European Union, *Google Spain SL and Google Inc. v. Agencia Española de Protección de Datos (AEPD) and Mario Costeja González*, Case C-131/12, Judgment of 13 May 2014.

their laws to match these commitments. If national systems fail to address violations, people can seek help through international and regional channels to enforce human rights.[23]

A clear example is *Marper v. the United Kingdom* (2008), where the European Court of Human Rights ruled against the UK Government for retaining DNA profiles of individuals who had been acquitted of criminal charges. The court found this practice to be a violation of the right to privacy under Article 8 of the European Convention on Human Rights. The ruling emphasized that states must ensure that their policies and legal frameworks do not infringe on individual rights, demonstrating the importance of aligning domestic law with international human rights standards.

The obligation to protect human rights requires states to take proactive measures to safeguard individuals from abuses, including by investigating and preventing violations. This principle was affirmed in *Velásquez Rodríguez v. Honduras* (1988), a landmark case before the Inter-American Court of Human Rights. The court found Honduras responsible for the disappearance of a citizen during the 1980s and held that the State failed in its duty to protect the right to life, liberty, and security. This case set a precedent that states are not only responsible for direct human rights violations but also for failing to prevent and investigate abuses committed by non-state actors.

The role of national administrations in enforcing International Law is also evident in cases involving the implementation of treaty obligations. In *Medellín v. Texas* (2008), the U.S. Supreme Court examined whether the U.S. was required to enforce a ruling by the International Court of Justice (ICJ), which had determined that the rights of a Mexican national under the Vienna Convention on Consular Relations had been violated. The Supreme Court ruled that international treaties do not automatically override domestic law unless explicitly implemented by Congress. This case highlighted the challenges of translating international obligations into national legal frameworks and demonstrated the need for clear domestic legislation to enforce treaty commitments.

Other examples of how states involve their administration to fulfill international obligations include, for instance, climate change agreements, trade agreements, or anti-money laundering standards. When a country signs climate agreements like the Paris Agreement, it must enforce rules to cut emissions, such as limits on pollution and support for renewable energy. International commitments often require states to adapt their domestic laws and policies. The United States–Mexico–Canada Agreement (USMCA), which replaced NAFTA in 2020, shows how trade agreements extend beyond tariffs to include rules on intellectual property, labor, and the environment. Similarly, the Comprehensive and Progressive Agreement for Trans-Pacific Partnership (CPTPP) brings together 11 Asia-Pacific countries to regulate not only tariffs but also investment, digital trade, and labor standards. In the financial field, membership in the Financial Action Task Force (FATF) requires states to introduce anti-money laundering rules for banks. In all these cases, states must adjust their legal systems to honor international obligations.

1.2.3 Localizing Global Norms: Adapting International Rules to National Contexts

As outlined in the preceding discussions, international legal norms may operate within domestic legal systems, particularly when they relate to individual rights and protections. Traditionally, Public International Law governed state-to-state relations, with individuals acting only through their nationality and State representation. However, the evolution of human rights law

23 Office of the High Commissioner for Human Rights, United Nations.

has increasingly recognized individuals as direct subjects of International Law, particularly in the aftermath of World War II. This shift led to the adoption of key legal instruments such as the Universal Declaration of Human Rights (1948) and the European Convention on Human Rights (1950), which established enforceable rights at the international level.

A significant case illustrating the direct application of International Law to individuals is *LaGrand* (*Germany v. United States*, 2001), decided by the International Court of Justice.[24] In this case, Germany sued the United States, alleging that U.S. authorities had violated Article 36 of the Vienna Convention on Consular Relations (1963) when they failed to inform two German nationals, Karl and Walter LaGrand, of their right to consular assistance following their arrest and death sentence in Arizona. Germany argued that this failure prevented it from providing diplomatic protection and violated the brothers' individual rights under International Law.

The *LaGrand* case concerned two German brothers, Karl and Walter LaGrand, who had moved to the United States as children. In 1982, they were arrested in Arizona for an attempted armed bank robbery during which a man was killed. Both were convicted of murder and sentenced to death. At no point during their arrest or trial were they informed of their right to consular assistance under Article 36 of the Vienna Convention on Consular Relations (1963), which would have allowed them to contact the German consulate for legal and diplomatic support.

Years later, when the executions were imminent, Germany became aware of the violation and sought to intervene. It argued before the International Court of Justice (ICJ) that the United States had breached its obligations under the Vienna Convention and deprived the LaGrand brothers of their individual rights under International Law. Germany also requested provisional measures to halt the executions. Nevertheless, despite an ICJ order to stay the execution, Arizona proceeded, and Walter LaGrand was executed in 1999 (Karl having already been executed earlier).

In its judgment, the ICJ ruled in favor of Germany. It affirmed that Article 36 of the Vienna Convention confers enforceable individual rights, including the right to be informed promptly of the entitlement to contact consular officials when detained. The Court rejected the U.S. position that consular notification obligations existed only between states, confirming instead that individuals could directly invoke these rights. It also declared that ICJ provisional measures are legally binding, strengthening the Court's authority in principle.

At the same time, the case exposed the limits of International Law in practice. The execution of Walter LaGrand, despite the ICJ's order, showed that international rulings ultimately depend on the willingness of states to comply. Without strong enforcement mechanisms, international courts face significant challenges when confronted with state or subnational defiance.

Thus, the *LaGrand* case illustrates both the promise of International Law – by granting individuals rights and shaping domestic practice – and its limits, as the absence of coercive enforcement leaves compliance vulnerable to political will.

2 The Debate Between Monism and Dualism

Examining the interface and interplay between the two can be approached from different perspectives. From the standpoint of International Law, International Law prevails over national law. From the perspective of domestic law, however, the hierarchy of norms depends on each state's constitutional framework and on how national courts receive International Law. This second perspective raises the well-known contrast between monism and dualism. This second point of view confronts two opposite doctrines, monism and dualism.

24 International Court of Justice, *LaGrand Case (Germany v. United States)*, Judgment of 27 June 2001.

2.1 The International Law Perspective: The Supremacy of International Law Over National Law

We may repeat ourselves slightly at this stage, but this is necessary in order to introduce the major international cases that have shaped the principle of the supremacy of International Law over national law.

As previously discussed, certain international norms are directly applicable, meaning that individuals can invoke them before national courts without the need for additional implementing legislation. These are known as self-executing norms, as they create enforceable rights within domestic legal systems. Whether a norm is self-executing depends on the constitutional framework of each state and on how its courts interpret the integration of International Law.

For a norm to qualify as self-executing, it must be clear, precise, and specific in defining rights and obligations. By contrast, norms that are broad or programmatic require national legislation before they can be enforced, making them non-self-executing. This distinction is particularly relevant in monist systems, where International Law automatically forms part of domestic law, whereas in dualist systems, international norms generally require legislative incorporation before they take effect.

From the standpoint of International Law, international obligations take precedence over domestic law, since states voluntarily commit to them through treaties and conventions. Yet in practice, the effectiveness of this principle depends on how states adapt their national laws and institutions to align with their international commitments. Without such adaptation, the supremacy of International Law would remain a formal principle with little practical effect.

2.1.1 The Alabama Claims *of 1872: A Landmark for International Law Supremacy*

There was a famous case, known as the *Alabama Claims*, in the 1870s, which was related to a diplomatic dispute between the United States and Great Britain that arose out of the U.S. Civil War.

The U.S. federal Government claimed damages from the UK Government for secretly aiding the Confederate States of America during the Civil War, in violation of the British Neutrality Act.

England was blamed for helping to extend the Civil War by supplying the Confederacy with warships, among them the ship *Alabama*, despite laws requiring neutrality. The *Alabama*, known for capturing 58 Union ships, was eventually sunk by a U.S. warship in 1864, highlighting its role in the conflict and the broader issue of British involvement.

The United States, which had requested from the United Kingdom either two billion U.S. dollars or the cession of Canada, received 15.5 million U.S. dollars, which was paid by the United Kingdom in 1872.

Those substantial damages were awarded to the United States by an international arbitration court which was established by the Treaty of Washington in 1871 and which met in the town hall of Geneva to assess the merit of U.S. financial claims on Britain. The arbitration tribunal, which issued its decision in September 1872, rejected American claims for indirect damages but ordered Britain to pay the United States $15.5 million as compensation for the *Alabama Claims*.

In the sentence on the *Alabama Claims* of 1872, the arbitration court considered that a state could not invoke the insufficiencies of its domestic law to avoid its international responsibility.[25]

25 Alabama Claims of the United States of America Against Great Britain, Award rendered on 14 September 1872 by the tribunal of arbitration established by Article I of the Treaty of Washington of 8 May 1871. *Reports of International Arbitral Awards*, Volume XXIX, pp. 125–134, United Nations.

The decision of the arbitration court is the first example of the use of a supra-national court, the beginning of the modern history of international arbitration, and is a precursor of the International Court of Justice, the judicial body of the United Nations.

The Permanent Court of International Justice has adopted the same reasoning: it ruled that the supremacy of International Law over domestic law is a *generally recognized principle of International Law*.

2.1.2 The Treatment of Polish Nationals in the Danzig Territory Case of 1932: International Protection of Minority Rights

Danzig was a Polish city, in northern Poland, situated at the mouth of the Vistula River on the Baltic Sea. Danzig is the German name of the city; in Polish it is Gdansk. From 1919 to 1939, the city of Danzig had the status of a free city under the Treaty of Versailles, with Poland having administrative governance over it.

The request for an opinion on to the treatment of Polish nationals in the Danzig territory (which involved questions concerning education, labor, acquisition of land, police registration, etc.) was made by the League Council on the proposal of the High Commissioner for Danzig who had been asked by the diplomatic representative of Poland in Danzig for a decision in regard to the unfavorable treatment of Polish nationals in the free city.

The Court needed to decide if the treatment of Polish people in Danzig was a matter for the Treaty of Versailles and the Paris Convention of 1920, or if the laws of Danzig itself could also be considered. The decision was that only issues breaking Danzig's international agreements could be taken up with the High Commissioner, not those just about Danzig's own laws. However, Danzig had agreed to treat Polish people living there fairly, just as Poland had promised to treat minorities well under a 1919 treaty.

In an advisory opinion of February 4, 1932, the Permanent Court of International Justice affirmed the supremacy of International Law over domestic law. The Court held:

> It should however be observed that, while on the one hand, according to generally accepted principles, a State cannot rely, as against another State, on the provisions of the latter's Constitution, but only on International Law and international obligations duly accepted, on the other hand and conversely, a State cannot adduce as against another State its own Constitution with a view to evading obligations incumbent upon it under International Law or treaties in force. Applying these principles to the present case, it results that the question of the treatment of Polish nationals or other persons of Polish origin or speech must be settled exclusively on the bases of the rules of International Law and the treaty provisions in force between Poland and Danzig.[26]

In other words, the Permanent Court of International Justice explained that, under generally accepted principles, a State cannot rely on the provisions of another State's constitution, but only on International Law and obligations validly undertaken. Likewise, a State cannot invoke its own constitution to evade responsibilities arising from International Law or treaties in force.

The Court thus affirmed the supremacy of International Law over national law as a generally recognized principle of International Law. A country cannot use either its own domestic laws or those of another State to justify actions in international matters or to escape international

26 Permanent Court of International Justice, *Treatment of Polish Nationals and Other Persons of Polish Origin or Speech in the Danzig Territory*, Advisory Opinion of February 4, 1932, Series A/B, No. 44, XXIIIrd Session.

obligations. Instead, decisions in international disputes must be based solely on International Law and applicable treaties. Accordingly, in the Danzig case, the treatment of Polish nationals had to be determined by International Law and the treaties binding Poland and Danzig, not by their respective domestic laws.

2.1.3 *The* Greco-Bulgarian Communities *Case of 1930: Resolving Cross-Border Legal Disputes*

The Permanent Court of International Justice reaffirmed the principle of supremacy of International Law over domestic law, in a second Advisory Opinion of July 31, 1930, in the case *Greco-Bulgarian Communities*.

The 1919 Convention between Greece and Bulgaria established guidelines for emigration rights and property rights of individuals and *communities*, a term encompassing churches, monasteries, schools, and similar entities. The Permanent Court of International Justice's Advisory Opinion on July 31, 1930, clarified these guidelines, focusing on how properties belonging to these communities should be handled if abandoned or liquidated. This Opinion resolved ambiguities in the Convention, ensuring fair treatment of community properties in both countries and highlighting the Court's role in interpreting and applying International Law.

The Court held:

> In the first place, it is a generally accepted principle of International Law that in the relations between Powers who are contracting Parties to a treaty, the provisions of municipal law cannot prevail over those of the treaty.[27]
>
> In the second place, according to Article 2, paragraph 1, and Article 15 of the Greco-Bulgarian Convention, the two Governments have undertaken not to place any restriction on the right of emigration, notwithstanding any municipal laws or regulations to the contrary, and to modify their legislation in so far as may be necessary to secure the execution of the Convention.
>
> In these circumstances, if a proper application of the Convention were in conflict with some local law, the latter would not prevail over the Convention.

This judgment affirmed the supremacy of treaty obligations over conflicting domestic law. Once a state undertakes international commitments, it must adapt its legislation accordingly, and it cannot rely on national law to avoid compliance. The International Court of Justice has regularly reaffirmed this principle as a *fundamental principle of International Law*.

2.1.4 *The* Jurisdiction of the Courts of Danzig *Case of 1928: Sovereignty vs. International Oversight*

In the case *Jurisdiction of the Courts of Danzig* of 1928, the Permanent Court of International Justice ruled that International Law does not apply directly to individuals. The State acts like a sort of screen between International Law and private individuals.

In an Advisory Opinion of March 3, 1928, the PCIJ was required to examine the question of whether a past international agreement between Poland and the Free City of Danzig created

27 Permanent Court of International Justice, *The Greco-Bulgarian Communities*, Advisory Opinion, July 31, 1930, Series B, No. 77.

for the benefit of the railway officials, rights that these could directly invoke before the courts of Danzig.[28]

The Court ruled that the most relevant criterion to determine whether rights granted by an international agreement can be directly invoked by private individuals before national courts or not depends on the intention of the contracting state parties.

In its Advisory Opinion, the PCIJ held:

> Since the Beamtenabkommen, according to its contents, deals precisely with the regime which Poland is bound under International Law to grant to its railway officials taken over from Danzig, and since the Beamtenabkommen is an agreement to execute, amongst others, the Decision of September 5th, 1921, which established the jurisdiction of the Danzig tribunals, the applicability of the Beamtenabkommen by those tribunals must be considered as being in conformity with International Law, unless the contrary is proved.
>
> Such proof could have been given in the international proceedings by showing that the Beamtenabkommen, as an agreement between Danzig and Poland, was, in the intention of the Parties, not intended to constitute a part of the "contract of service" or otherwise to be applied directly by the Danzig tribunals. The Court, for the reasons given above, has rejected such a construction of the Beamtenabkommen.
>
> No other arguments have been adduced by Poland which, in the opinion of the Court, could preclude the Danzig tribunals from applying the Beamtenabkommen as substantive law to the pecuniary claims of the Railways officials. If, as seems to appear from some of the documents before the Court and especially from a legal opinion submitted on behalf of the Polish Government, Poland would contend that the Danzig Courts could not apply the provisions of the Beamtenabkommen because they were not duly inserted in the Polish national law, the Court would have to observe that, at any rate, Poland could not avail herself of an objection which, according to the construction placed upon the Beamtenabkommen by the Court, would amount to relying upon the non-fulfilment of an obligation imposed upon her by an international engagement.
>
> From the foregoing considerations, it follows that the Decision of the High Commissioner of April 8th, 1927, is not well founded in law in so far as it does not give satisfaction to the requests which Danzig has made. The conclusion reached upon an examination of the nature and extent of the jurisdiction established by the Decision of September 5th, 1921, fully confirms that which is based exclusively upon an examination of the nature and legal effect of the Beamtenabkommen in connection with the first part of the High Commissioner's Decision of April 8th, 1927.

Poland argued against the applicability of the *Beamtenabkommen* by the Danzig tribunals, but failed to prove that the agreement was not intended to be part of the contract of service or to be directly applied by these tribunals. Hence, the Court rejected this interpretation. Poland also argued that Danzig courts could not apply the *Beamtenabkommen* because its provisions were not properly integrated into Polish national law. However, the Court indicated that Poland could not

28 Permanent Court of International Justice, *Jurisdiction of the Courts of Danzig (Pecuniary Claims of Danzig Railway Officials Who Have Passed into the Polish Service, Against the Polish Railways Administration)*, Advisory Opinion, 3 March 1928, Series B, No. 75.

use this argument since it would essentially be admitting to not fulfilling its obligations under an international agreement.

In summary, the Court argued that the *Beamtenabkommen* should be considered valid and applicable by Danzig tribunals in accordance with International Law. Poland's objections, based on the agreement's integration into its national law or its intentions regarding the *Beamtenabkommen*'s application, were not sufficient to prevent its application by Danzig tribunals.

Consistently, international courts and arbitral tribunals have held that states cannot invoke national law as a justification for failing to honor their international commitments. This principle has become a cornerstone of International Law and is codified in the 1969 Vienna Convention on the Law of Treaties.

Vienna Convention on the Law of Treaties (1969)
Part III – Observance, Application and Interpretation of Treaties
Section 1 – Observance of Treaties
Article 27 – Internal law of states, rules of international organizations and observance of treaties
A state party to a treaty may not invoke the provisions of its internal law as justification for its failure to perform the treaty.

This provision makes clear that International Law binds the state, even when its domestic law conflicts with treaty obligations. However, this does not mean that an international court or tribunal will annul a national law inconsistent with International Law. Rather, such a law will be treated as ineffective to the extent that it produces effects on the international level – a situation that arises only rarely in practice.

Imagine a country signs a treaty banning child labor. However, its domestic law still allows children under 14 to work in factories. If that country is brought before an international court, the court will not strike down or cancel the national law. Instead, the court will rule that the country cannot use its domestic law as an excuse for violating the treaty. In other words, if children under 14 are found working, the state will be held internationally responsible, even though its own national law permits it.

2.2 *The Domestic Law Perspective: Constitutional Frameworks and Judicial Interpretation*

From the perspective of domestic law, the relationship with International Law depends on each state's constitutional framework and on how judges interpret the role of international norms within the national legal order. The approach of national courts to the applicability of international rules is shaped above all by whether the State follows a monist or a dualist model.

Although this debate is less prominent today, it remains significant for understanding the ways in which national and International Law interact.

2.2.1 *Monism vs. Dualism: Tracing the Origins of a Foundational Legal Debate*

Most states recognize the supremacy of International Law over domestic law, a principle often summarized in the Anglo-Saxon maxim: "International Law is part of the Law of the land." According to Blackstone's 1765 doctrine,[29] this supremacy constitutes a customary rule, par-

29 Sir William Blackstone (1723–1780) was an English judge and legal scholar. He is most famous for his book *Commentaries on the Laws of England* (1765–1769), which explained English Common Law in a clear and organized way. His work shaped legal thinking in Britain and the United States for centuries.

ticularly in countries without a written constitution. In practice, however, difficulties arise when domestic courts are unfamiliar with International Law. Judges may hesitate to apply it directly or may defer to government interpretations, especially in cases involving treaty compliance.

Imagine, for instance, a country that signs a treaty banning toxic chemicals. If its domestic law still allows certain chemicals to be produced, a national court may hesitate to strike down the local rule unless it clearly recognizes the supremacy of International Law. In a monist system, the judge could apply the treaty directly and declare the national law ineffective. In a dualist system, however, the court would likely wait until the legislature passes new domestic legislation before enforcing the treaty, even though the State is already bound internationally.

Similarly, imagine a country that has ratified the Convention Against Torture. Its domestic Criminal Code, however, contains no explicit law punishing torture by public officials. If a victim brings a case before a national court, the judge faces a dilemma: in a monist system, the treaty obligation can be applied directly, and the court could recognize the victim's right and condemn the act as unlawful under International Law. In a dualist system, by contrast, the judge cannot act unless the national legislature has passed a specific law criminalizing torture, even though the country is already bound by the treaty at the international level.

The monism–dualism debate emerged less from purely legal reasoning than from broader political and moral concerns. In the 19th century, dualism – shaped by Hegelian thought – was the dominant view. It emphasized state sovereignty and rejected the idea that International Law could limit state power. Monism, by contrast, developed as a response, prioritizing individual rights and democracy. Monist theorists argued that states should be subject to a universal legal order, ensuring that International Law acts as a check on state actions. Put simply, dualism viewed the State as the highest authority, free from international constraints, while monism saw International Law as an overarching system binding states and safeguarding universal legal principles and human rights.

States are expected to respect International Law. Yet the conditions under which treaties are incorporated and applied within national legal systems are largely determined by each state. This reflects the central role of sovereignty in shaping national approaches to International Law. From these conceptions arise the two opposing doctrines of monism and dualism, which continue to structure debates about the relationship between legal orders at the international and domestic levels.

2.2.2 The Dualist Approach: Distinct Legal Spheres of International and Domestic Law

The dualist approach views international and domestic law as distinct legal systems, each operating independently. In dualist states, international treaties and norms do not automatically become part of national law; they must first be incorporated through legislation. This section explores the core principles of dualism, highlights constitutional provisions that reflect this approach, and provides examples of how different countries apply it in practice.

2.2.2.1 INTERNATIONAL LAW AND DOMESTIC LAW CONSTITUTE TWO SEPARATE LEGAL ORDERS

Dualism views the domestic legal system and the international legal system as two entirely separate orders. Each is considered distinct and independent, as though an impermeable barrier – comparable to a coral reef or a waterproof wall – stood between them. This barrier prevents interaction, since dualism treats national and International Law as fundamentally different and unrelated.

Monism, by contrast, rejects this separation. It sees national and International Law as part of a single, unified legal order, where international rules can directly enter and operate within domestic legal systems.

Imagine, for example, that a country signs an international treaty banning plastic bags. In a monist system, the treaty becomes part of national law immediately, and a court could stop a shop from distributing plastic bags on the basis of the treaty itself. In a dualist system, however, the court could not act until the national parliament passed a specific law banning plastic bags, even though the treaty was already binding internationally.

Historically, dualism predates monism. The dualist school of thought was developed at the end of the 19th century by the German jurist and legal philosopher Heinrich Triepel (1868–1946), Professor of Law in Berlin. Triepel gained international recognition through his 1899 work *International Law and National Law (Völkerrecht und Landesrecht)*, where he set out the foundations of dualist theory.

According to Triepel, International Law and national law are two separate legal systems. Each operates independently, with sovereignty ensuring that states remain the ultimate authority within their domestic legal orders. This view stood in contrast to the emerging theory of monism, later defended by Hans Kelsen in 1923, which saw international and national law as part of a unified legal order.

Historically, dualism predates monism. The dualist school of thought was founded at the end of the 19th century, based on the writings of a German jurist and legal philosopher, Heinrich Triepel, who was a Professor of law in Berlin. Triepel first gained lasting international recognition in the field of International Law through his 1899 work *International Law and National Law* (*Völkerrecht und Landesrecht*).[30]

Triepel introduced the dualist theory, which views International Law and national law as separate legal systems, in opposition to monism, a view supported by Hans Kelsen in 1923. This theory suggests that countries have their own sovereignty that keeps their legal systems independent of International Laws.

Dionisio Anzilotti (1867–1950), an influential Italian jurist and President of the Permanent Court of International Justice in the early 20th century, further expanded on Triepel's ideas. Anzilotti played a significant role as a judge and president during important cases in the court, such as the *Jurisdiction of the Courts of Danzig* in 1928, and strongly advocated for the dualist approach. He also elaborated on Triepel's theory in his widely translated International Law textbook, *Corso Di Diritto Internazionale*, first published in 1912.[31]

From the dualist point of view, the international legal order and national legal orders are separate and self-contained systems. Within each system, only the norms created inside it are valid. The two differ because they have different sources, objects, and subjects: International Law governs relations between states, while national law governs relations between individuals.

Dualism also seeks to preserve state sovereignty. It conceives Public International Law as the "external Public Law" of sovereign states. As a result, International Law cannot automatically bind domestic legal systems. It must first pass through national procedures – such as incorporation or legislative translation – before becoming applicable at the domestic level.

30 Triepel, Heinrich, 1899, *Völkerrecht und Landesrecht*, C.L. Hirschfeld, Leipzig.

31 Anzilotti, Dionisio, 1912, *Corso di diritto internazionale*, vol. I: *Introduzione e teorie generali*, 3rd ed., Rome, Athenaeum, 1928.

In practice, this means that in a dualist system, treaties and international regulations are not directly enforceable in national courts. They must first be transposed into domestic law by the national legislature before individuals or judges can rely on them.

It is important to recognize that Heinrich Triepel, Dionisio Anzilotti, along with scholars such as Paul Heilborn[32] and Georg Jellinek,[33] developed the dualist perspective toward the end of the 19th century. This was a period defined by the dominance of nation-states and a strong emphasis on state sovereignty. In a dualist system, International Law – including treaties – does not automatically become part of domestic law. Instead, it must be formally incorporated or implemented by the parliament or legislative body.

From this perspective, International Law is treated as a separate legal system, distinct from domestic law. It only becomes part of the national legal order through explicit approval, usually by legislative action. This often involves a process of transposition and incorporation, ensuring that international rules are given effect within the domestic legal framework. Though somewhat traditional, this approach provides a clear framework for understanding the relationship between the two systems.

In dualism, the mere negotiation, signing, or ratification of a treaty is not enough; the treaty must be officially transformed into domestic law through legislation before individuals or courts can rely on it. Theoretically, this avoids conflicts between international and national law, since they operate independently within their own legal spheres. If differences arise, they remain separate unless the State deliberately integrates the international rule into domestic law, at which point the national system is adjusted to avoid contradiction.

Imagine a country signs an international treaty that requires the protection of wetlands. Wetlands are land areas often saturated with water, supporting distinct ecosystems with marshes, swamps, and bogs. They filter pollutants, offer habitats for diverse flora and fauna, protect against floods by absorbing excess water, and store carbon, contributing to climate change mitigation. Examples of wetlands include the Everglades, situated in Florida, in the U.S.A., which is a vast network of tropical wetlands, famous for their unique ecosystem and diverse wildlife, including alligators and a wide variety of bird species. The Camargue, situated in France, which is Europe's largest river delta, is famous for its saline wetlands, flamingos, wild horses, and bulls. The Sundarbans, which is the largest mangrove forest in the world, is located at the delta of the Ganges, Brahmaputra, and Meghna rivers on the Bay of Bengal, spanning India and Bangladesh. It is known for its unique biodiversity, including the Bengal tiger.

In a dualist system, a treaty about protecting wetlands doesn't automatically change a country's own laws. So, if a country's laws currently allow building in wetlands, there is no issue between its laws and the international treaty because they're seen as separate. But, if the country wants to follow the treaty, its government can make new laws that stop building in wetlands,

32 Paul Heilborn (1861–1932) was a German jurist and legal scholar specializing in international and commercial law. He taught in Berlin and wrote extensively on the relationship between international and domestic legal systems, contributing to the development of the dualist school of thought in the late 19th and early 20th centuries. Heilborn's works emphasized the independence of national legal orders and the importance of state sovereignty in shaping the application of International Law.

33 Georg Jellinek (1851–1911) was a German jurist and Public Law scholar, often regarded as one of the most influential figures in constitutional and International Law at the turn of the 20th century. He spent much of his career in Austria and has been described as the leading exponent of Public Law in Austria. Jellinek's writings on state theory, sovereignty, and the relationship between international and domestic law strongly shaped the development of the dualist school of thought.

which means the treaty's rules become part of the country's laws. After these new laws are made, the country's rules will match the treaty's demands, so there is no clash between them. Until these new laws are made, the treaty and the country's building laws exist side by side without affecting each other, even though they have different views on protecting the environment.

This setup implies that International Law must be formally integrated into the domestic legal framework to have any effect. This process is sometimes referred to as *domesticating* International Law.

2.2.2.2 EXAMPLES OF DUALIST CONSTITUTIONAL PROVISIONS

In the United Kingdom, international treaties do not automatically become part of domestic law. Since the UK follows a dualist system, treaties signed by the government must be incorporated through an Act of Parliament before they have legal effect. For example, the Human Rights Act of 1998 was passed to integrate the European Convention on Human Rights (ECHR) into UK law. Before this, even though the UK had signed the ECHR, its provisions were not directly enforceable in British courts. This highlights how, in a dualist system, treaties create obligations between states but do not immediately grant rights or impose duties on individuals within national law. Furthermore, UK courts cannot strike down domestic laws that contradict international treaties, ensuring that national legislation remains supreme unless parliament explicitly incorporates the treaty provisions.

In Germany, Article 59(2) of the Basic Law (Grundgesetz) requires that treaties affecting political relations or federal legislation must be approved through a federal law. This provision ensures that international agreements are not automatically binding but must go through a legislative process before becoming enforceable. However, Germany follows a unique approach, where ratification often implies incorporation, meaning that once parliament approves a treaty, it generally becomes part of domestic law. This allows Germany to maintain sovereignty over the process while ensuring compliance with international obligations.

In India, Article 253 of the Constitution gives parliament the power to pass laws necessary to implement treaties and international agreements. However, treaties do not automatically become part of Indian law upon ratification. Instead, they require specific legislation to take effect domestically. This ensures that international commitments align with India's constitutional framework and legislative approval process before being enforced.

In Canada, international treaties must be implemented through either federal or provincial legislation, depending on the subject matter. This practice stems from the Constitution Act of 1867, which divides powers between the federal and provincial governments. Unlike monist systems, where treaties are automatically binding, Canada follows a strict dualist approach, requiring explicit legislative action for treaties to have domestic legal effect.

In Australia, Section 51of the Constitution grants the Commonwealth Parliament the power to legislate on external affairs, including treaty implementation. However, similar to other dualist countries, treaties do not automatically become part of domestic law upon signing or ratification. Instead, the government must pass legislation to incorporate treaty obligations into national law.

In Italy, treaties are incorporated through ratification laws, ensuring they comply with the Constitution. Italian courts have full independence in interpreting treaty provisions, meaning they are not bound by government interpretations. Additionally, international customary law is automatically integrated into Italy's legal system, giving it the same legal standing as constitutional law.

In France, while often considered a monist system, the Constitution requires that treaties have higher authority than domestic laws only if the other party also complies. Article 55 of the French

Constitution states that duly ratified treaties take precedence over national laws, but they do not automatically override the Constitution. This means that in some cases, constitutional amendments are required to ensure compatibility with international commitments. The *Conseil d'État*, France's highest administrative court, has also ruled that treaties must be sufficiently clear and precise to be directly applicable, adding an element of dualist reasoning to the legal system.

These examples illustrate how dualist countries maintain a separation between international and domestic law, ensuring that treaties undergo a legislative process before they become enforceable at the national level.

2.2.3 The Monist Approach: Unifying Legal Systems Under One Order

The monist approach views international and domestic law as part of a single legal system, where international treaties and norms automatically become part of national law without requiring additional legislation. However, monism can take different forms – some systems prioritize domestic law over International Law, while others grant International Law supremacy over national legislation. This section explores these variations and provides examples of states that follow the monist approach.

2.2.3.1 INTERNATIONAL LAW AND DOMESTIC LAW CONSTITUTE ONE SAME LEGAL ORDER

In the monist conception, International Law and domestic law form a single legal order. This means that the rules of International Law and the rules of domestic law can interact directly with one another. But what happens when there is a conflict? What if International Law and national law stand in opposition – for example, when a piece of domestic legislation contradicts an international treaty?

Imagine a country that ratifies an international treaty protecting freedom of the press. A few years later, its parliament adopts a domestic law banning criticism of government policies on social media. This domestic law directly contradicts the state's international obligation to safeguard free expression.

The maxim placed at the head of the chapter – *International Law is part of the Law of the land* – expresses precisely this monist intuition. This old Anglo-Saxon precept captures the idea that international norms automatically form part of the domestic legal order without requiring further transformation. In other words, it reflects the monist belief that International Law and national law coexist within a single unified system.

This raises a central question: which takes precedence, national law or International Law? Within monism, two different interpretations have emerged in response to this question, leading to two distinct strands of the doctrine.

The first strand considers International Law superior to domestic law. Under this view, a conflicting national statute must be set aside or interpreted in a way that complies with the state's international obligations. The second strand takes the opposite approach, arguing that domestic law remains supreme within the national legal system, even if this leads to a breach of International Law. These two positions reflect deeper debates about sovereignty, constitutional hierarchy, and the role of international commitments in shaping domestic legislation.

2.2.3.2 MONISM WITH PRIMACY OF DOMESTIC LAW OVER INTERNATIONAL LAW

In this version of monism, domestic law overrides International Law. In case of discrepancy, discordance, or incompatibility between a national legal norm and an international legal norm like a treaty, for instance, the national law will outweigh the treaty. And so the judge will put aside the treaty and apply the domestic legal norm to settle the dispute he has to settle.

This school of thought has been developed in Germany by the School of Bonn and authors like Albert Zorn, Erich Kaufmann, Max Wenzel in the 1920s; and in France by authors such as Georges-Michel-André Decencière-Ferrandière (1901–1936)[34] who have largely inspired the Soviet conception of International Law.[35]

This theory considers that International Law follows national law, that International Law is subordinate to national law, and that domestic law is above International Law. An internal norm can override an international norm. Hence, through these lenses, International Law exists only as a reflection and projection of each internal order and amounts to an outer leg of the domestic law of each State. In other words, International Law is regarded as a sort of external Public Law of the State.

If we take the example mentioned before of a country that ratifies an international treaty protecting freedom of the press, and later adopts a domestic law banning criticism of government policies on social media, the conflict becomes clear. Although the domestic law directly contradicts the state's international obligation to safeguard free expression, under this version of monism, the judge applies the domestic law and disregards the treaty. International Law remains part of the legal order, but it is subordinated to national legislation whenever the two clash.

The arguments developed by the proponents of this theory are principally that in the absence of a super state authority, the state freely determines its international obligations and is the sole judge of how it executes those commitments.

The other argument put forward by the School of Bonn is that the State holds its competence to conclude treaties on a constitutional basis, that is, on the basis of an internal legal norm.

This theory is largely criticized. Firstly, because no international commitment can really be assured. The *Pacta sunt servanda* principle, the concept of international commitment of the state itself, loses all significance in the name of absolute sovereignty.

Secondly, because this doctrine also has an internal contradiction. It is based on an assumption: the unity of the legal system. So it concludes that there are as many International Laws as there are states; therefore, there is no International Law at all.

2.2.3.3 MONISM WITH PRIMACY OF INTERNATIONAL LAW OVER NATIONAL LAW

In this version of monism, International Law overrides domestic law. In case of discordance or incompatibility between a national legal norm and an international norm like a treaty, the treaty will override the national norm. And so the judge will put aside the domestic legal norm and apply the treaty to settle the dispute he has to settle.

If we take the example mentioned before of a country that ratifies an international treaty protecting freedom of the press and later adopts a domestic law banning criticism of government policies on social media, under this version of monism, the judge sets aside the domestic law and applies the treaty. International Law remains part of the legal order, but it is accorded precedence whenever it conflicts with national legislation.

34 Décencière-Ferrandière was a French legal scholar and professor of law at the Faculty of Poitiers who specialized in International Law and published several notable works.

35 Décencière-Ferrandière, A., 1933, "Considérations sur le droit international dans ses rapports avec le droit de l'État," *Revue Générale de Droit International Public* (RGDIP), vol. 40.

This version of monism claims that the unity of the legal system should benefit international rules. International commitments should take precedence over the internal rules. And so a treaty must prevail over an internal law, and customary International Law must prevail over the constitution, for example.

Consider another simple scenario: a country has a law that allows hunting certain wildlife species, but it has also signed an international treaty that protects these same species from being hunted.

Under the version of monism that favors International Law, if a country's domestic hunting law conflicts with an international treaty protecting certain species, the treaty takes priority. This means that, despite what the national law permits, individuals in that country are prohibited from hunting the protected species, since the international obligation prevails over the domestic rule.

In this view, even if the country's constitution normally protects the right to hunt, the treaty that prohibits hunting the protected species would override it. So, in practice, the treaty's rules would be enforced over the national constitution or any other domestic laws regarding hunting.

This school of thought is based on the writings of two authors in particular, the Austrian jurist and legal philosopher Hans Kelsen (1881–1973) and the French theorist of International Law and former member of the International Law Commission of the United Nations George Scelle (1878–1961).

Hans Kelsen and the *normativist Austrian school* developed a normativist vision of law. According to Kelsen, domestic law is derived from International Law, which sets out the powers of the states, and so domestic law cannot be contrary to International Law. This settles a hierarchical relationship between International Law and national law, with precedence of International Law over national law. The overall derives from a hypothetical fundamental norm, which can only be assumed but which is not directly included in positive law.

The French legal scholar George Scelle formulated a more objectivist theory – that is, a theory grounded in the notion that certain entities, particularly moral truths, exist objectively and independently of human knowledge or perception of them.

According to George Scelle, the hierarchy between International Law and national law must be expressed through a universal federalism, which is still under construction. Conceptually, states implement International Law and ensure its supremacy over national law on behalf of the international order.[36] What George Scelle argues is that states and governments are invested with a dual role. They act as national governments when operating in the domestic legal order, and they act as international actors when acting in the international legal order. This is what he calls the fundamental principle of *functional duplication.*

To illustrate, let's revisit the earlier example regarding a country's laws on hunting wildlife and its participation in an international treaty protecting certain species. In Scelle's view, states have the obligation to observe international conservation standards not just because they've agreed to them but because these standards represent objective moral truths about preserving biodiversity. The State, therefore, has a responsibility to enforce these international norms domestically. If a national law permits hunting a protected species, the law would need to be amended to align with international treaties, which are seen as expressions of these higher moral truths.

This version of monism, according to which International Law overrides domestic law, has known an important development for ideological, moral, and practical reasons, since the end of World War II.

36 Scelle, Georges, 1932–1934, *Précis de droit des gens (Principes et systématique)*, 2 volumes, Sirey, Paris.

The interface between International Law and national law operates a little bit like federal law and state law in a federal state.

This theory only applies to international norms that are directly applicable, self-executing norms. As explained previously, such norms are the international norms that grant individual persons rights that they may invoke directly before the national courts in their domestic legal order. Other treaties must be transposed to be applicable (and so we have to switch back to dualism). This theory is difficult to put into practice, and this is why dualism has emerged.

Santi Romano, the renowned Italian legal scholar on legal orders, is primarily associated with legal pluralism rather than strictly with monism or dualism.[37] He argued that law is not limited to a single legal system, such as state law, but instead operates through multiple, overlapping frameworks, including international, national, and social or institutional legal orders.

However, in the monism-dualism debate, his views are closer to dualism as he emphasized the independence of different legal systems. He rejected the notion of a single, hierarchical legal order where International Law automatically prevails over domestic law. Instead, he viewed legal systems as coexisting and interacting without necessarily being unified under one framework.

Thus, while not a strict dualist, his concept of legal pluralism aligns more with dualism than monism, particularly in the context of the relationship between international and domestic law.

2.2.3.4 EXAMPLES OF MONIST STATES

Some constitutions are explicitly monist in nature, incorporating International Law directly into the domestic legal system and often giving it precedence over national legislation.

In the Netherlands, Articles 93 and 94 of the Dutch Constitution establish that treaties and resolutions of international institutions become binding upon publication and that national laws conflicting with these treaties cannot be applied. This ensures that International Law is automatically enforceable within the Dutch legal order without the need for additional legislative action.

Similarly, Portugal's Constitution, under Article 8, states that ratified international conventions become part of national law upon official publication and remain binding as long as they apply internationally. It also allows norms issued by international organizations, including the European Union, to be directly effective within Portugal's legal framework.

In Costa Rica, Article 7 of the Constitution explicitly grants public treaties, international agreements, and concordats higher authority than domestic laws once enacted. Additionally, agreements related to territorial integrity or political organization require a supermajority approval from the legislative assembly and additional ratification by a Constituent Assembly.

Spain follows a similar approach, as Article 96 of the Spanish Constitution states that validly ratified international treaties automatically become part of domestic law upon official publication. These treaties can only be amended or suspended following the procedures outlined in the treaties themselves or under general International Law, reinforcing the direct effect of international commitments within Spain's legal system.

37 Santi Romano (1875–1947) was an Italian jurist, legal philosopher, and professor of law best known for his theory of the *plurality of legal orders*. In his influential 1918 work *L'ordinamento giuridico* (*The Legal Order*), he argued that law is not limited to the state but can arise from multiple sources – such as social groups, institutions, and international organizations – each creating its own legal order. This idea of legal pluralism strongly influenced 20th-century legal thought and remains a key reference in debates on the relationship between domestic and International Law. See Chapter 1 – *What Is Law? What Forms Does Law Take?*

These constitutional provisions illustrate how monist states readily integrate International Law, eliminating the need for additional legislation to enforce treaty obligations. This aligns with the monist view that international and national laws form a unified legal framework.

The United States takes a mixed approach, incorporating both monist and dualist elements. The Supremacy Clause in Article VI, Clause 2 of the U.S. Constitution states that the Constitution, federal laws, and treaties are the "supreme law of the land," binding on all states. This suggests a monist perspective, as treaties become part of federal law once ratified.

However, in practice, treaties often require implementing legislation before they can be enforced domestically. U.S. law distinguishes between self-executing treaties, which become immediately enforceable upon ratification, and non-self-executing treaties, which require additional congressional action. This dualist element ensures that not all international commitments directly alter domestic law.

The *Medellín v. Texas* (2008) case illustrates this principle. José Medellín, a Mexican national, was sentenced to death in Texas without being informed of his Vienna Convention rights to consular access. The International Court of Justice ruled in the Avena case that the U.S. had violated the treaty and should review Medellín's case. However, the U.S. Supreme Court ruled that the treaty was not self-executing and required congressional implementation before it could be enforced in domestic courts. Consequently, Medellín was executed despite the ICJ ruling, highlighting the limits of monism in the U.S. legal system.

The integration of International Law into domestic systems varies widely. Unlike the European Union, which has the European Court of Justice to ensure compliance, no global body enforces uniform international legal application. Each country determines how it engages with International Law, leading to diverse approaches.

The *Kadi* case (2008) before the European Court of Justice[38] demonstrated this complexity. Mr. Kadi challenged an EU regulation implementing a UN Security Council resolution, which froze his assets due to alleged links to terrorism. He argued that the EU's actions violated his right to a fair hearing under EU law. The court ruled in favor of Kadi, asserting that EU fundamental rights take precedence over UN resolutions. This decision highlighted how some courts prioritize regional or national legal principles over international commitments, a stance often seen in dualist legal systems.

The way International Law is incorporated into national legal systems varies significantly. The Netherlands, for example, automatically integrates treaties, while the UK requires parliament to enact them into law. Countries like France and the U.S. follow a hybrid approach, blending monist and dualist principles.

Although monism and dualism were extensively debated in the early 20th century, these concepts do not fully capture how International Law operates within states today. The main reason is that modern legal systems are far more complex and cannot be neatly placed into one model or the other.

First, states often adopt a mixed approach. A country may follow a monist approach for certain treaties, like human rights conventions, allowing them to be directly applied by courts, while requiring legislative incorporation for others, such as trade or investment treaties.

Second, the rise of supranational legal orders – most notably the European Union – has blurred the distinction. EU law, for example, has direct effect and supremacy, but its relationship with national constitutions is unique and cannot be explained simply as monist or dualist.

38 Court of Justice of the European Union (CJEU), Joined Cases C-402/05 P and C-415/05 P, *Kadi and Al Barakaat International Foundation v. Council and Commission*, Judgment of 3 September 2008.

Third, globalization and digitalization have multiplied legal actors beyond states. International standards now come not only from treaties but also from transnational networks, arbitral tribunals, and even private regulators. These sources interact with domestic law in ways that go beyond the classical state-centered frameworks of monism and dualism.

Finally, judicial practice shows that courts frequently engage in balancing acts rather than applying a rigid theory. Cases such as *Kadi* and *Medellín v. Texas* illustrate how judges navigate between sovereignty and international obligations, often crafting pragmatic solutions that do not fit neatly into either monist or dualist categories.

For these reasons, monism and dualism are best seen today as analytical tools – helpful for framing the discussion, but insufficient to explain the full diversity of state practice in the 21st century.

3 Refugee Law as a Case Study: The Interplay Between Domestic and International Legal Orders

In 2021, PluriCourts and the Faculty of Law at the University of Oslo launched a research initiative on the interface between international and national law, with a focus on Norwegian law.[39] The initiative examined how International Law is implemented in domestic legislation, administration, and case law, incorporating both normative and political perspectives.

A key issue explored was the impact of globalization on the interaction between domestic and international legal orders. Global trends such as forced displacement, climate change, cybersecurity, trade, human rights, and security challenges influence this relationship. Migration, border control, and forced displacement particularly highlight how international treaties, like the Refugee Convention, shape national immigration laws.

In 2023, over 117 million people (1.5% of humanity) were forcibly displaced, yet fewer than 32 million were recognized as refugees under UNHCR's mandate.[40]

International Law plays a crucial role in defining categories of forced migrants and shaping legal protections. This section illustrates the chapter's central theme by using global forced displacement as a case study to examine the interaction between international and domestic legal orders. It explores how national legal systems incorporate and interpret international refugee law, the influence of national case law on international norms, and the broader legal and ethical challenges in managing forced displacement within this dynamic legal framework.

3.1 The Evolution of International Refugee Law and Its Impact on Domestic Legal Systems

The evolution of international refugee law exemplifies the interconnectedness of domestic and international legal systems. This part explores how refugee law developed in response to historical challenges, particularly the shortcomings of human rights protections during World War II, and how its principles continue to shape domestic legal frameworks today.

39 PluriCourts was a center of excellence for the study of the legitimate roles of the Judiciary in the global order at the University of Oslo. The center was funded by the Research Council of Norway for the period 2013–2023. The primary research objective of PluriCourts was to analyze and assess the legitimate present and future roles of the plurality of international courts. University of Oslo, The Faculty of Law, PluriCourts – Centre for the Study of the Legitimate Roles of the Judiciary in the Global Order, [online], consulted on May 9, 2023. Available at: https://www.jus.uio.no/ior/english/pluricourts.

40 UNHCR, *Global Trends: Forced Displacement in 2023*, pp. 2–6.

3.1.1 The Origins and Foundations of MODERN International Refugee Law

The Second World War laid bare the critical limitations of international human rights law, which failed to protect those persecuted by their State and stripped of their citizenship.

As political theorist Hannah Arendt (1906–1975) argues, when refugees and stateless people lost their citizen rights, they simultaneously lost their human rights, as *the former inevitably entailed the latter*.[41] Formerly stateless herself, Arendt conceptualizes citizenship as *the right to have rights*.[42]

In a similar vein, Italian philosopher Giorgio Agamben observes that

> in the system of the nation-state, the so-called sacred and inalienable rights of man show themselves to lack every protection and reality at the moment in which they can no longer take the form of rights belonging to citizens of a State.[43]

Agamben continues: "rights are attributed to man (or originate in him) solely to the extent that man is the immediately vanishing ground . . . of the citizen."[44]

By decoupling the figure of the "human" from that of the "citizen," refugees painfully expose human rights' shortcomings. Acknowledging the need to be recognized and protected by a State in order to exercise one's fundamental human rights, the modern refugee regime emerged. Its cornerstone, the 1951 Convention Relating to the Status of Refugees, defines a refugee as a person who:

> As a result of events occurring before 1 January 1951 and owing to well-founded fear of being persecuted for reasons of race, religion, nationality, membership of a particular social group or political opinion, is outside the country of his nationality and is unable or, owing to such fear, is unwilling to avail himself of the protection of that country.[45]

Several core elements constitute this definition. A refugee must have crossed an international border, thereby excluding internally displaced persons.

Moreover, a refugee must flee a *well-founded fear of persecution*, with persecution often interpreted as both serious harm and failure of state protection. The *well-founded fear* standard of proof has been interpreted differently across jurisdictions, ranging from a "serious possibility" in the *Sivakumaran* case[46] to a "reasonable degree of likelihood" in *INS v. Cardoza-Fonseca*.[47]

Canadian-American Refugee law scholar, James Hathaway, notes that the "well-founded fear" standard aims to

> identify situations of risk that fall significantly below a probability of harm, but which give rise to more than a speculative chance that persecution may ensue. The test is ordinarily met by some combination of credible testimony and country data.[48]

41 Arendt, Hannah, 1994, *The Origins of Totalitarianism*, Harcourt Books, New York.

42 Arendt, *The Origins of Totalitarianism*.

43 Agamben, Giorgio, 1998, *Homo Sacer: Sovereign Power and Bare Life*, Stanford University Press, Stanford.

44 Agamben, *Homo Sacer*.

45 Article 1.A.2.

46 *R v. Secretary of State for the Home Department, ex parte Sivakumaran*, House of Lords, 16 December 1987.

47 *Immigration and Naturalization Service v. Cardoza-Fonseca*, 480 U.S. 421, March 9, 1987.

48 Hathaway, James, 2012, "Refugees and Asylum," in *Foundations of International Migration Law*, eds. Brian Opeskin, Richard Perruchoud and Jilyanne Redpath-Cross, Cambridge University Press.

Indeed, a typical asylum application is comprised of both a personal declaration describing the particular events having caused the applicant's flight, as well as a country conditions report which substantiates that the applicant's fear is reasonable and that the harm feared has previously occurred in comparable situations.

In addition, the feared persecution must be inflicted on the basis of at least one of five grounds: "race, religion, nationality, membership of a particular social group or political opinion." This, therefore, excludes those fleeing generalized and indiscriminate violence.

Finally, the formulation used to present the definition, "the term refugee shall apply to," renders refugee status declaratory and not constitutive. In other words, a person is a refugee as soon as these conditions are fulfilled and, as such, "does not become a refugee because of recognition, but is recognized because he is a refugee."[49]

Imagine a journalist from Country X who belongs to a small ethnic minority. After writing articles criticizing the government, she is arrested several times and threatened with death. Fearing for her life, she flees across the border into Country Y. In her asylum application, she explains her arrests and threats (personal testimony) and submits reports from international NGOs confirming that Country X systematically persecutes journalists from her minority group (country conditions report). Her claim is based on "political opinion" and "membership of a particular social group," two of the five grounds listed in the 1951 Refugee Convention. Although she has not yet been officially recognized as a refugee, under International Law, she already qualifies, since refugee status is declaratory: she is recognized because she is a refugee, not the other way around.

This example also illustrates the interaction between national and international legal orders. The journalist's right to refugee protection derives from the 1951 Refugee Convention, an instrument of International Law that sets out binding obligations for states. However, the decision on her asylum application will be made by the national authorities of Country Y, applying their domestic asylum procedures. In doing so, they must interpret and enforce the Convention's definition of a refugee, often by combining international sources (treaty law, UNHCR guidelines, NGO reports) with domestic legal mechanisms (administrative procedures, judicial review).

Thus, while her refugee status exists under International Law, it becomes effective only once it is recognized and implemented within the national legal system of Country Y. This shows how international norms and domestic law are interdependent: International Law provides the normative basis, while national law provides the institutional framework for its implementation.

When first adopted, the 1951 Refugee Convention contained a temporal limitation: it applied only to persons who became refugees "as a result of events occurring before 1 January 1951." This restriction reflected the historical context in which the treaty was drafted, as it was primarily designed to address the mass displacement caused by the Second World War and its immediate aftermath. States could also choose to limit the Convention's application geographically to "events in Europe."

This temporal restriction was later removed by the 1967 New-York Protocol Relating to the Status of Refugees, which universalized the refugee definition by eliminating both the temporal and geographical limitations. Since then, the Convention has applied to refugees worldwide, regardless of when or where the events causing their flight occurred. We will return to this point later.

3.1.2 *The Impact of International Refugee Law on Domestic Legal Systems*

While the 1951 Refugee Convention remains the cornerstone of refugee law, it was created in response to specific historical circumstances. Today, domestic legal systems incorporate and interpret its principles in diverse ways, adapting to modern challenges such as mass displacement

49 UNHCR, *Handbook on Procedures and Criteria for Determining Refugee Status under the 1951 Convention and the 1967 Protocol relating to the Status of Refugees*, para. 28. First published in 1979; reissued in 1992 and 2019.

and generalized violence. National authorities, therefore, play a decisive role in translating international obligations into concrete administrative procedures, evidentiary standards, and judicial safeguards. As a result, refugee protection varies considerably from one country to another, despite the common international framework.

Refugee protection mechanisms in national legal systems often involve asylum procedures, where applicants must provide both personal testimony and supporting country reports to substantiate their claims. They also involve Judicial interpretations, where courts assess the "well-founded fear" standard, influencing how national laws align with international obligations. Through case law, courts clarify key concepts such as persecution, membership of a particular social group, or the relevance of gender-based and non-state violence, thereby shaping the practical reach of the Convention. Finally, refugee protection mechanisms in national legal systems involve legislative adaptations, with some countries expanding the definition of refugees to include those fleeing broader forms of violence or environmental disasters.

By bridging the gap between human rights and state sovereignty, international refugee law shapes national policies and legal decisions. However, ongoing debates persist regarding its scope, application, and adequacy in addressing contemporary displacement crises.

To conclude, the development of international refugee law, particularly through the 1951 Convention, addresses the human rights gaps exposed during World War II. By defining refugee status and establishing protection criteria, this legal framework influences domestic legal systems, reinforcing the fundamental link between citizenship, human rights, and state responsibility. Its continuing importance comes from the fact that it helps states protect people who do not benefit from the usual safeguards of citizenship. At the same time, the system is not static: it evolves through national legislation, court decisions, and ongoing interpretation by international bodies. In this way, refugee law remains flexible enough to respond to new forms of displacement and the changing realities faced by those in need of protection.

3.2 Defining Refugees: The Challenge of Applying International Standards in National Contexts

The definition of a refugee has changed over time, shaping both international and national laws. While the 1951 Refugee Convention remains the main legal framework, debates continue about whether it adequately addresses modern displacement, including people fleeing war, environmental disasters, and state failure. This section explores how different legal systems interpret the refugee definition and the challenges of applying it today.

3.2.1 How the Refugee Definition Has Evolved

The following discussion delves into how the definition of refugees has changed over time and its impact on both domestic and International Laws.

Ratified by 146 States, the 1951 Convention remains the basis of refugee law today.[50] However, the Convention intended to cover those displaced by the events of the Second World War, and when ratifying the Convention, states could also choose to restrict it geographically to Europe, setting both temporal and geographical limitations to the definition.[51] As displacement persisted, states agreed to expand the definition through the 1967 Protocol Relating to the Status of Refugees. This Protocol maintained the 1951 definition but removed the temporal and geographic restrictions.

50 United Nations Treaty Collection, *Convention relating to the Status of Refugees*. Available at: https://treaties.un.org.
51 Article 1.A.2. and Article 1.B.1.

Yet, as Hathaway notes, "While the Protocol is sometimes said to have universalized the Refugee Convention, it did not in fact vary the criteria of the Convention . . . or broaden its rights guarantees."[52] As such, targeted persecution remains the requisite for protection today, although we witness growing factors of forced displacement, including state fragility and climate change.

Was it sufficient to remove the temporal and geographic restrictions? Is the definition itself a product of its time? This constitutes a fervent debate in refugee law studies.

Persecution-centered approaches argue there is something unique about the severance of the bond between state and citizen, considering refugees as "the most deserving of the deserving."

Deprivation-centered approaches present other arguments. In *Survival Migration*, Alexander Betts[53] argues: "New drivers of cross-border displacement emerged, especially outside Europe. Factors such as generalized violence, environmental change and food insecurity – and their interaction – underpin a significant and growing proportion of cross-border displacement in many parts of the world."[54]

These drivers, triggered by state actions or omissions, can lead to extreme deprivation and lack of subsistence. If, according to Arendt, citizenship represents "the right to have rights," subsistence can similarly be said to represent the ability to enjoy rights. Accordingly, Henry Shue frames subsistence as a "basic right," a right without which one cannot enjoy the substance of any other right.[55]

It follows that subsistence rights are "everyone's minimum reasonable demands upon the rest of humanity."[56]

Yet, deprivation of subsistence is often due to the state's failure to protect its citizens' rights as opposed to its active and voluntary violation of those rights. Consequently, people fleeing subsistence deprivation fall through the cracks of international protection.

Alexander Betts argues that the refugee regime must broaden its scope to incorporate state omissions. He sustains that

> in addition to protecting people fleeing the acts of states against their own populations, the refugee regime must also protect people fleeing the omissions of states, whether due to the unwillingness or the inability to provide for their citizens' most fundamental human rights.[57]

This debate is reflected in law. Compare, for example, the restrictive European Union instruments with other regional instruments attempting to expand the definition: e.g., the Organization of African Unity's 1969 Refugee Convention,

> The term "refugee" shall also apply to every person who, owing to external aggression, occupation, foreign domination or events seriously disturbing public order is compelled to leave his place of habitual residence in order to seek refuge in another place outside his country of origin or nationality.[58]

52 Hathaway, *Refugees and Asylum*, p. 179.

53 Alexander Betts is Professor of Forced Migration and International Affairs at the University of Oxford and a leading scholar on refugee and migration studies.

54 Betts, Alexander, 2013, *Survival Migration: Failed Governance and the Crisis of Displacement*, Cornell University Press, Ithaca, NY, p. 2.

55 Shue, Henry, 1996, *Basic Rights: Subsistence, Affluence, and U.S. Foreign Policy*, Princeton University Press, Princeton, p. 31.

56 Shue, *Basic Rights*, p. 1.

57 Betts, *Survival Migration*, p. 19.

58 Organization of African Unity, *Convention Governing the Specific Aspects of Refugee Problems in Africa*, Article 1(2).

The Cartagena Declaration on Refugees further extends protection to "persons who have fled their country because their lives, safety or freedom have been threatened by generalized violence, foreign aggression, internal conflicts, massive violations of human rights or other circumstances which have seriously disturbed public order."[59]

These examples show that different regions adapt refugee law to their specific challenges, interpreting international standards in different ways.

3.2.2 New Challenges: Environmental Displacement and Legal Gaps

Every year, millions of people are displaced by climate change, environmental degradation, and natural hazards, posing a growing legal challenge.[60] Yet, climate refugees are particularly difficult to fit under the current framework as environmental displacement is often internal, targeted persecution is near-impossible to prove, and the boundaries between the persecuting state and the state of refuge are blurred, as in the Ioane Teitiota case.[61]

Ioane Teitiota, a native of the Kiribati Islands, an archipelagic state in the Pacific Ocean, took the New Zealand Government to the UN Human Rights Committee in February 2016 after being denied asylum as a climate refugee. He was deported back to Kiribati in September 2015. Teitiota argued that land conflicts and a lack of clean water due to climate change forced him to seek refuge in New Zealand with his family when his visa expired in 2010.

The Human Rights Committee – which is the body of independent experts that monitors implementation of the 1966 International Covenant on Civil and Political Rights by its states parties – acknowledged that while the man's deportation wasn't illegal due to the absence of an immediate threat to his life in Kiribati, it recognized climate change as a serious threat to the right to life.

Decision-makers were encouraged to consider the impact of climate change on the rights of individuals when assessing deportation appeals. This suggests that such appeals may have a higher chance of success in the future if evidence proves the risks involved, thereby outlining a possible "pathway for future environmental migrants."[62]

The definition of a refugee affects how national governments apply their asylum laws, leading to ongoing debates about who deserves protection. As forced displacement evolves beyond persecution-based claims, International Law must adapt to new realities, including state failure, generalized violence, and climate change. The key question remains: can refugee law expand to protect more displaced people while maintaining its core principles?

3.3 Refugee Status Determination: National and International Interaction

While the 1951 Refugee Convention outlines the definition and rights of refugees, it does not specify the process for determining who qualifies. This has led to major challenges, as each country applies its own process for refugee status determination (RSD).

This section looks at three key problems in this process: lack of clear procedures, political influence, and inconsistent decisions. These issues show the difficulties in applying international refugee law within different national legal systems.

59 *Cartagena Declaration on Refugees*, Article III(3).

60 International Organization for Migration (IOM), 2024, *Legal Aspects of Protecting Migrants' Rights in the Context of Disasters, Climate Change and Environmental Degradation*, IOM, Geneva, p. 3.

61 *Ioane Teitiota v. New Zealand*, views of 24 October 2019, United Nations Human Rights Committee.

62 International Organization for Migration (IOM), *Legal Aspects of Protecting Migrants' Rights in the Context of Disasters, Climate Change and Environmental Degradation*, p. 7.

3.3.1 Challenges in Refugee Status Determination

While stipulating the definition of a refugee and the rights associated with status recognition, the 1951 Convention omits the critical question: through which process does one come to be recognized as a refugee? The process of refugee status determination remains to be laid out in international refugee law.

The following discussion deals with the gaps and challenges within the international refugee law framework, particularly in terms of the process for determining refugee status. It highlights three main challenges: the lack of due process in refugee status determination, the politicization of asylum at the state level, and the variability in decision-making at the individual level.

From the Convention's very inception, the preferential treatment of individuals subjected to persecution by state-sponsored violations of civil and political rights, as opposed to those subjected to severe socio-economic deprivations, bears the legacy of Cold War geopolitics and the Western diplomatic interests in admitting refugees from the Eastern Bloc. During the Cold War, refugees from Eastern States were largely admitted in the West as "escapees who crossed over to the West 'voted with their feet' and represented a significant political and ideological asset for the West."[63]

These historical dynamics continue to influence refugee law today. They help explain why individuals fleeing classic political persecution still fit more easily within the Convention definition than those escaping generalized violence, climate-related displacement, or extreme poverty. As a result, states retain significant discretion in interpreting who qualifies as a refugee, which contributes to inconsistent outcomes and unequal access to protection. This structural imbalance highlights the need for clearer procedural safeguards and a more inclusive understanding of contemporary forms of forced displacement.

3.3.2 Individual Subjectivity and Variability in Decision-Making

Beyond historical trends, there is also great variability in the way individual adjudicators process asylum claims. In *Refugee Roulette*, Ramji-Nogales et al.[64] study the disparities in the rates at which asylum applicants are granted status in the United States. They write:

> the very essence of the Rule of Law, embodied in the Due Process Clause of the Fifth Amendment, is that individual cases should be disposed of by reference to standardized norms. . . . But how about a situation in which one judge is 1820% more likely to grant an application for important relief than another judge in the same courthouse? Or where one U.S. Court of Appeals is 1148% more likely to rule in favor of a petitioner than another U.S. Court of Appeals considering similar cases? Welcome to the world of asylum law.[65]

Beyond the random assignment of immigration judges, outcomes also depend "in very large measure by the quality of an applicant's legal representation, by the gender of the immigration judge, and by the immigration judge's work experience prior to appointment."[66]

63 Betts, Alexander, Loescher, Gil and Milner, James, 2012, *UNHCR: The Politics and Practice of Refugee Protection*, 2nd ed., Routledge, London.

64 Jaya Ramji-Nogales is Professor of Law and Associate Dean for Research at Temple University's Beasley School of Law in Philadelphia, where she teaches Refugee Law and Policy.

65 Ramji-Nogales, Jaya, Schoenholtz, Andrew I. and Schrag, Philip G., 2007, "Refugee Roulette: Disparities in Asylum Adjudication," *Stanford Law Review*, vol. 60, no. 2.

66 Ramji-Nogales, Schoenholtz and Schrag, "Refugee Roulette," p. 296.

These challenges show how complex and uncertain asylum processes can be, affecting the rights and results for asylum seekers. They also emphasize that countries should adjust their laws to match international standards to treat refugees fairly. They also highlight the need for clearer procedures and better safeguards to reduce these disparities. Making decision-making more consistent and improving access to legal assistance would help ensure that asylum outcomes depend less on chance and more on the merits of each case.

3.4 Enforcing Asylum Rights: National Sovereignty vs. International Legal Commitments

The 1951 Refugee Convention emphasizes the need for international cooperation in protecting refugees. However, responsibility-sharing among countries is typically voluntary, leaving most responsibilities to neighboring states and developing regions. This section examines the gap between international legal commitments and national sovereignty, focusing on the challenges of global cooperation and legal enforcement.

3.4.1 The Challenge of Global Cooperation in Refugee Protection

The Preamble of the 1951 Convention Relating to the Status of Refugees recognizes that "the international scope and nature [of asylum] cannot be achieved without international cooperation."

Yet, international cooperation today, often referred to as "burden-sharing" and "responsibility-sharing," is typically predicated on voluntary participation. Beyond non-refoulement, which most directly applies to neighboring states, states have few obligations towards claimants for international protection.

B. S. Chimni argues that the "non-entrée regime which came to be consolidated after the end of the Cold War" creates structural inequalities within the international refugee regime, confining and containing asylum seekers in the Global South.[67] Today, 75% of refugees are hosted in low- and middle-income countries,[68] creating what Betts terms a "North-South Impasse" whereby the majority of refugees originate and remain within the "South," while states in the Global North have "few obligations or incentives" to engage in cooperative behavior.[69]

UNHCR tried to encourage cooperation through *solidarity conferences* like the International Conferences on Assistance to Refugees in Africa (ICARA I and II) in 1981 and 1984, the International Conference on Central American Refugees (CIREFCA) in 1989, the Indo-Chinese Comprehensive Plan of Action (CPA). These meetings only worked well when countries had their own reasons to solve the crises together. Gil Loescher[70] (1945–2020), who was an American political scientist, argues: "The global refugee problem is not a humanitarian problem requiring charity but is a political problem requiring political solutions."[71] While UNHCR was

67 Chimni, B. S., 1998, "The Geopolitics of Refugee Studies: A View from the South," *Journal of Refugee Studies*, vol. 11, no. 4.

68 UNHCR, *Global Trends: Forced Displacement in 2023*, p. 2.

69 Betts, Alexander, 2011, "International Cooperation in the Refugee Regime," in *Refugees in International Relations*, eds. Alexander Betts and Gil Loescher, Oxford University Press, Oxford.

70 Gil Loescher was an American political scientist with a doctorate from the London School of Economics. After teaching at Notre Dame, he worked with the European Council on Refugees and Exiles, the International Institute for Strategic Studies, and *openDemocracy*. Since 2003, he was a visiting fellow at Oxford's Refugee Studies Centre.

71 Loescher, Gil, 1994, "The International Refugee Regime: Stretched to the Limit?," *Journal of International Affairs*, vol. 47, no. 2.

created as a non-political organization, its capacity to promote and uphold refugee protection norms relies on its strategic navigation of political spaces.

Other scholars, such as Tendayi Achiume, challenge the dominant approach to refugee responsibility-sharing as a form of distributive justice, grounding it instead in reparative justice claims. Achiume argues that certain states have special obligations "to those they displace through [imperial] domination and intervention."[72] This reframes the debate from states "failing to *share* responsibility for conditions outside of their control" to states "failing to *take* responsibility for conditions of their making."[73]

3.4.2 Legal Enforcement: The Absence of a Binding International Refugee Court

The evolution of International Refugee Law is marked by the fact that it lacks an international refugee court to provide authoritative statements on the interpretation of the 1951 Convention on the Status of Refugees.[74]

Instead, it relies on soft law guidelines produced by the United Nations High Commissioner for Refugees (UNHCR), case law emitted at the national level by refugee tribunals, administrative agencies, and other courts; as well as decisions from international courts from other regimes, such as human rights or international criminal law. There are initiatives to promote transnational judicial dialogues, such as the International Association of Refugee Law Judges, but this has been criticized as having "no real impact" at the European level.[75]

This discussion shows how international and national laws intersect in dealing with refugee issues. While there is recognition of the need for global cooperation in refugee protection, there is no solid legal framework for it. Efforts by organizations like UNHCR to encourage cooperation have had mixed success, often depending on countries' own interests. Additionally, there is a lack of a dedicated international refugee court, so decisions rely on soft law, national case law, and judgments from other international courts.

In conclusion, this section delves into the nuanced relationship between International Law and national law, especially in the context of globalization's impact on legal frameworks.

The challenges and debates around refugee law vividly illustrate the ongoing tension between the universalist aspirations of International Law and the particularistic tendencies of national legal systems.

Our discussion serves as a key example of how international norms and standards are tested, resisted, or adopted within national contexts, further illuminating the practical implications of globalization on legal practices and the protection of human rights.

Connecting the theoretical foundations of this chapter to real-world situations where these theories are applied and examined strengthens the overall clarity and significance of our exploration.

72 Achiume, E. Tendayi, 2022, "Empire, Borders, and Refugee Responsibility Sharing," *California Law Review*, vol. 110, p. 1017.

73 Achiume, *Empire, Borders, and Refugee Responsibility Sharing*, p. 1029.

74 Bailliet, Cecilia M., 2014, *National Case Law as a Generator of International Refugee Law: Rectifying an Imbalance within the UNHCR Guidelines on International Protection*, September 4, European Society of International Law, 10th Anniversary Conference, Vienna, 4–6 September 2014, Conference Paper No. 7/2014. Available at SSRN: https://ssrn.com/abstract=2545473.

75 Goodwin-Gill, Guy S. and Lambert, Hélène, 2010, "The Limits of Transnational Law – Refugee Law, Policy Harmonization and Judicial Dialogue in the European Union," in *The Limits of Transnational Law – Refugee Law, Policy Harmonization and Judicial Dialogue in the European Union*, eds. Guy S. Goodwin-Gill and Hélène Lambert, Cambridge University Press.

Conclusion

The interaction between domestic and international legal orders is both a legal necessity and a political challenge, shaped by the tension between national sovereignty and international commitments. This chapter has shown that while International Law aspires to create universal norms, its actual impact depends on how states interpret, implement, and sometimes resist these norms within their domestic legal frameworks.

One of the core insights from this discussion is that the relationship between domestic and International Law is not uniform across states. Some legal systems, particularly monist ones, integrate International Law automatically, granting it direct effect within their national courts. Others, particularly dualist states, require explicit domestic legislation to implement international norms, leading to potential gaps, delays, or even selective application of international legal obligations. This divergence underscores the political dimensions of legal harmonization – states adopt International Law not only based on legal principles but also according to political will, national interests, and historical legal traditions.

The absence of a binding enforcement mechanism in many areas of International Law leads to inconsistencies and selective compliance. Unlike fields such as trade law, where enforcement is institutionalized, international legal commitments in areas like human rights, environmental law, and refugee protection often rely on voluntary cooperation. This results in fragmented applications, where states may choose to embrace, reinterpret, or ignore international obligations based on domestic priorities.

Despite these challenges, domestic legal systems play a crucial role in shaping International Law's impact. Courts, administrative agencies, and legal practitioners influence how global norms are integrated into national law, sometimes reinforcing international commitments even when governments hesitate. This dynamic process underscores the tension between national sovereignty and global legal frameworks, demonstrating that legal integration is not absolute but constantly negotiated.

Ultimately, the relationship between domestic and international legal orders reflects the broader realities of globalization, political will, and legal adaptation. As legal systems continue to evolve, the challenge remains: how can International Law maintain its authority while respecting national autonomy, ensuring both legal consistency and meaningful enforcement?

Selected Bibliography

Bjorge, Eirik, & Miles, Cameron, 2017, *Landmark Cases in Public International Law*, Hart Publishing, 640 pages.

Björgvinsson, Davíd T., 2015, *The Intersection of International Law and Domestic Law: A Theoretical and Practical Analysis*, Edward Elgar Publishing, Incorporated, 200 pages.

Boas, Gideon, 2023, *Public International Law: Contemporary Principles*, Edward Elgar Publishing, 395 pages.

Charlesworth, Hilary, Chiam, Madelaine, Hovell, Devika, and Williams, George, (Eds.), 2005, *The Fluid State: International Law and National Legal Systems*, Sydney, Australia: Federation Press, 304 pages.

Denza, Eileen, 2006, The Relationship between International and National Law, in Evans, Malcolm (Ed.), *International Law* (4th ed.), Oxford: Oxford University Press, pp. 412–440.

Ferrari-Bravo, Luigi, 1983, International and Municipal Law: The Complementarity of Legal Systems, in Macdonald, R. S. J. and Johnston, Douglas M. (Eds.), *The Structure and Process of International Law*, Dordrecht, The Netherlands: Martinus Nijhoff, pp. 715–744.

Kaczorowska-Ireland, Alina, 2024, *Public International Law* (6th ed.), Routledge, 910 pages.

Nijmann, Janne, & Nollkaemper, Andre, eds, 2007, *New Perspectives on the Divide between National and International Law*, Oxford: Oxford University Press, 406 pages.

Shaw, Malcolm N., 2021, *International Law*, Cambridge University Press, 1308 pages.
Shelton, Dinah, (Ed.), *International Law and Domestic Legal Systems: Incorporation, Transformation, and Persuasion*, Oxford University Press, 2011, 676 pages.
Thirlway, Hugh, 2014, *The Sources of International Law*, Oxford University Press, 264 pages.
Tritto, Nunzio Mario, 2023, *Public International Law and European Union Law*, Milchester Publishing, 430 pages.

11 Supranationalism

The European Union

A day will come when all nations on our continent will form a European brotherhood. . . . A day will come when we shall see . . . the United States of America and the United States of Europe face to face, reaching out for each other across the seas.

Victor Hugo, speech delivered at the International Peace Congress in Paris in 1849

This chapter discusses supranationalism using the European Union as an example.

European Union Law is a vast and complex subject when delving into the details of institutional procedures and the technicalities of the European Union. Our goal is to provide students and learners from around the world with short, clear, and accessible explanations on supranationalism and the main areas of European Union Law. Many academic textbooks provide a more in-depth study of the subject.

A structured approach to understanding the European Union covers its foundations, policy areas, governance structure, and global engagement, while also addressing contemporary challenges and issues.

Supranationalism refers to a form of governance where multiple countries willingly transfer or share some degree of sovereignty and competencies to a higher authority or organization, for mutual benefit and cooperation.

Supranationalism emerged as a response to the devastation of World War II and the desire for peace, stability, and economic cooperation in Europe. However, various forms of supranational cooperation and integration exist across different regions of the world with different purposes.

The African Union (AU), for example, is a continental union consisting of 55 member states across Africa. It aims at promoting political and economic integration, peace, and security throughout the African continent.

The North Atlantic Treaty Organization (NATO) is a military alliance comprising 30 member countries from North America and Europe. It operates on the principle of collective defense, where member states commit to mutual defense in response to an attack against any member.

The Association of Southeast Asian Nations (ASEAN) is a regional intergovernmental organization comprising ten Southeast Asian countries. It promotes economic, political, and security cooperation among its member states.

The Mercosur is a regional trade bloc in South America, consisting of Argentina, Brazil, Paraguay, and Uruguay, with Venezuela as a suspended member. It aims to promote economic integration and political cooperation among member states.

DOI: 10.4324/9781003393047-15

While not traditionally viewed as a supranational organization, the United Nations (UN) serves as a platform for international cooperation and collective decision-making on issues such as peacekeeping, humanitarian aid, and global development.

Thus, besides the European Union, there exist many examples of supranational entities.

The present chapter focuses on the European Union as the primary and most comprehensive model of supranational governance.

The EU is a unique model of supranational governance. The motto of the EU – *United in diversity* – illustrates the principle of unity among its member states despite their diverse cultural, linguistic, and historical backgrounds. Jacques Delors (1925–2023), former president of the European Commission, referred to the uniqueness of the EU and the risk for it to become a sort of Unidentified Political Object:

> For we must face the fact that in 30 or 40 years Europe will constitute a UPO – a sort of unidentified political object – unless we weld it into an entity enabling each of our countries to benefit from the European dimension and to prosper internally as well as hold its own externally.[1]

This analogy captures the complexity and distinctiveness of the European project. It stresses the need for unity and cohesion among the member states to prosper both domestically and internationally.

This chapter is structured into four sections, each offering insights into different aspects of the European Union's functioning and significance.

We begin by presenting the foundations of the European Union, including EU Law and legal framework (Section 1). Subsequently, we delve into a discussion related to policy areas and economic integration (Section 2). Following that, we explore governance, democracy, and citizenship within the European Union (Section 3). Lastly, we address the global role and challenges encountered by the European Union (Section 4).

1 Foundations of the European Union

This section on the foundations of the European Union is like building the groundwork for a strong house. It helps understand the basic ideas that formed the EU and how it grew over time.

The different theories about how Europe should work together, like federalism and functionalism, are presented and explained. As well as the principles of supranationalism, which is the big idea that guides the EU's actions. Plus, a detailed examination of the EU's core components, such as its institutions and legal framework, is provided to help understand its functioning.

By studying these basics, readers will gain a deeper insight into how the EU came to be and why it works the way it does.

1.1 History of European Integration

Understanding the origins and evolution of the European Union from its beginnings to the present day is crucial to grasping how this unique model of supranational governance operates and how it shapes regional and global dynamics. The vision of its founding fathers and the timeline of the European Union's evolution provide invaluable insights into the organization's development and its guiding principles.

1 Jacques Delors, Speech (Luxembourg, 9 September 1985), Bulletin of the European Communities, September 1985, No. 9 (Luxembourg: Office for Official Publications of the European Communities). Available at: http://www.cvce.eu/obj/speech_by_jacques_delors_luxembourg_9_september_1985-en-423d6913-b4e2-4395-9157-fe70b3ca8521.html. Accessed 20 October 2023.

1.1.1 Founding Fathers and Visionaries: Shaping the European Union

While there were many individuals involved in the creation and development of the European Union, some key figures played crucial roles in this process.[2] The pioneers or founding fathers of the European Union are historical figures whose actions, ideas, and contributions were decisive in the creation and development of the European Union as we know it today.

Often referred to as the "Father of Europe," Jean Monnet was a French diplomat and economist who played a fundamental role in the establishment of the European Coal and Steel Community (ECSC) in 1951, which was one of the precursors to the European Union. His vision of pooling coal and steel resources among European nations aimed to prevent future conflicts by fostering economic interdependence.

Monnet believed that the pooling of these key industries would make it more difficult for any one country to wage war independently, as control over coal and steel production is vital for military purposes. However, the goal of pooling coal and steel resources was primarily economic and aimed at building a foundation for peace and cooperation, rather than directly establishing a military arm industry. The underlying idea was to integrate these industries in such a way that they would serve the common interest of all participating countries, thereby promoting stability and preventing the resurgence of nationalist tensions that had led to past conflicts.

The European continent's history is marked by centuries of wars and conflicts, which have shaped its political landscape. Key conflicts include the Hundred Years' War (1337–1453) between England and France over French throne control, the Thirty Years' War (1618–1648), evolving from religious disputes into broader European conflict, and the Napoleonic Wars (1803–1815) driven by Napoleon's expansionism. World War I (1914–1918) and World War II (1939–1945) brought devastating consequences, leading to the collapse of empires and reshaping the global order. The Cold War (1947–1991), though not a conventional war, divided Europe into rival spheres, fueling tensions and conflicts between Western and Eastern blocs.

Another key figure in the early stages of European integration, Robert Schuman was the French Foreign Minister. He is best known for proposing the Schuman Declaration in 1950, which laid out the initial blueprint for the creation of the European Coal and Steel Community. This declaration is celebrated as Europe Day on May 9th each year.

As the first Chancellor of West Germany after World War II, Konrad Adenauer played a vital role in promoting European integration. He supported initiatives such as the European Coal and Steel Community and the European Economic Community (EEC), which eventually led to the formation of the European Union.

An Italian statesman and politician, Alcide De Gasperi is also one of the founding fathers of the European Union. He served as the Prime Minister of Italy and was highly active in the establishment of the European Coal and Steel Community. De Gasperi's commitment to European unity and reconciliation between nations greatly contributed to the formation of the EU.

While primarily known for his role as the British Prime Minister during World War II, Winston Churchill also advocated for European unity in his famous Zurich speech in 1946. He envisioned a united Europe as a means to prevent future conflicts and promote peace and prosperity on the continent.

Eighteenth-century philosophers and writers like Immanuel Kant and Victor Hugo also laid the groundwork for European unity through their visionary ideas and writings. Immanuel Kant's philosophy, particularly his concept of perpetual peace, influenced the principles of the

2 Arnull, Anthony, 2017, *European Union Law: A Very Short Introduction*, Oxford University Press.

European Union. Kant argued for republican government, International Law, and a federation of states as means to achieve lasting peace. Similarly, Victor Hugo envisioned a "United States of Europe" to prevent future conflicts and promote unity. Though their visions weren't directly realized, they inspired the pursuit of peace and cooperation in Europe.

1.1.2 Timeline of the European Union's Evolution

The evolution of the European Union is marked by key moments and transformative changes.[3]

After World War II, cooperation began to take root with the creation of the European Coal and Steel Community (ECSC) in 1951, setting the stage for deeper integration.

The Treaties of Rome solidified this commitment, accompanied by the birth of the European Parliament, symbolizing democratic representation. The Treaties of Rome were signed in 1957 by six countries: Belgium, France, Italy, Luxembourg, the Netherlands, and West Germany. These treaties created the European Economic Community (EEC) and the European Atomic Energy Community (EURATOM). The EEC aimed to make it easier for these countries to trade with each other by creating a common market. This marked an important step toward working together more closely in Europe.

During the 1960s, as the economy grew, the EU worked harder to bring countries together, promoting economic collaboration and expanding its global influence.

The 1970s saw the addition of new members such as Denmark, Ireland, and the United Kingdom, alongside the development of institutional frameworks to address regional disparities.

The 1980s witnessed transformative changes with the expansion of EU membership and the launch of initiatives like the Erasmus program, fostering cultural exchange. The single market further propelled integration, fostering economic prosperity and mobility.

As the 1990s unfolded, the EU embraced globalization with the introduction of a single currency and advancements in the single market. Expansion continued, welcoming new members and fostering closer ties among European nations. The Maastricht Treaty, signed in 1992, laid the groundwork for the formation of the European Union. It established the EU as a political and economic union, introducing the single currency, the euro, and promoting closer cooperation in areas such as justice, foreign policy, and defense among member states.

In the early 2000s, the EU saw further enlargement with 12 new countries joining its ranks. Institutional reforms, exemplified by the Lisbon Treaty, aimed to simplify decision-making processes and strengthen cohesion. The Lisbon Treaty, ratified in 2009, made it easier for the European Union to make decisions and become more efficient and democratic. It also increased the power of the European Parliament and created the role of President of the European Council.

During the next ten years, the European Union faced difficulties. It had to deal with economic problems and the complex issues surrounding Brexit. The term Brexit refers to the United Kingdom's decision to leave the European Union. In a referendum held in June 2016, a majority of UK voters chose to exit the EU. This decision led to a series of negotiations between the UK and the EU to determine the terms of their future relationship. Brexit became official on January 31, 2020, when the UK formally left the EU.

Despite these challenges, the EU showed strength and resilience. It took action to tackle crises such as the COVID-19 pandemic and continued to emphasize its dedication to working together and staying united.

3 Arnull, *European Union Law*.

As time moves forward, the EU persists in managing intricate global challenges, addressing conflict, and promoting efforts to tackle climate change. In early 2022, Ukraine, Moldova, and Georgia applied to join the EU, and they've been granted candidate status. However, the integration process is lengthy and complex. The process sped up after Russia's invasion of Ukraine in February 2022, the EU having promptly expressed its support for Kyiv.

Despite the obstacles encountered, the European Union serves as a symbol of the lasting commitment to cooperation and unity among its member states.

1.2 European Integration Theories

European integration refers to the process of bringing together European countries in various dimensions, such as economic, political, legal, social, and cultural aspects. The theories of European integration provide frameworks for understanding and explaining the complex process of European integration.

These theories help guide policymakers in creating rules, organizations, and plans that promote cooperation and unity among European nations. They help scholars and policymakers understand the drivers, mechanisms, and outcomes of European integration. Theories of European integration also provide a basis for making predictions about future developments in the integration process.

This part describes and explains the main theories of European integration.[4]

1.2.1 Functionalism

A Working Peace System is one of the most renowned international relations and political science textbooks.[5] Its author, David Mitrany, suggests that integration should occur through functional cooperation in specific policy areas, rather than through overarching political agreements. In this sense, the functional method distinguishes itself from a constitutional approach.[6] According to this theory, cooperation in functional areas (such as trade, transportation, or energy) would lead to interdependence and gradually foster a sense of community among nations.

The European Coal and Steel Community (ECSC) is often cited as an early example of functionalist integration.

Federal functionalism is a type of functionalism associated with Jean Monnet. It mixes functionalism and federalism, focusing on functional cooperation to slowly bring about political integration. Instead of immediately creating a federal state, Monnet suggested making supranational institutions to handle specific tasks, like the European Coal and Steel Community (ECSC) and the European Economic Community (EEC), which later became the European Union.

In short, functionalism sees integration as a gradual and practical process: cooperation in one sector encourages further cooperation and slowly brings states closer together.

1.2.2 Federalism

The Federalist theory, advocated by figures like Altiero Spinelli, proposes the creation of a federal European state with significant central authority. It envisions the transfer of certain powers

4 For more details, see Wiener, Antje, Börzel, Tanja A. and Risse, Thomas, 2018, *European Integration Theory*, 3rd ed., Oxford University Press.

5 Mitrany, David, 1966, *A Working Peace System*, Quadrangle Books.

6 Devin, Guillaume, 2008, "Que reste-t-il du fonctionnalisme international? Relire David Mitrany (1888–1975)," *Critique internationale*, vol. 38, no. 1, pp. 137–152.

from member states to supranational European institutions, allowing for common policies in areas such as defense, foreign affairs, and economic regulation. The idea is to create a unified political entity akin to a federation of states, with a single government representing all citizens.

Spinelli (1907–1986), the Italian politician and advocate for European federalism, known for co-authoring the *Ventotene Manifesto* and contributing to the drafting of the Treaty of Rome, laid the groundwork for the European Union. The Ventotene Manifesto was a document written by Spinelli and Ernesto Rossi[7] in 1941 while they were imprisoned by the fascist regime on the island of Ventotene. It called for the establishment of a federal Europe as a means to prevent future wars and promote peace and prosperity on the continent.[8]

The Federalist theory believes that when European countries work together closely, it helps bring peace, stability, and wealth to the continent. Supporters say creating a federal European government would not only make Europe stronger in the world but also spread important values like democracy and human rights. But making this happen is not without challenges and complexities. It means dealing with complicated politics, cultures, and power-sharing. Plus, each country has its own ideas and interests. Despite these challenges, the Federalist theory keeps sparking discussions in the European Union about how to make Europe more unified and strong in a changing world.

Thus, federalism sees integration as a political project: building a united Europe through shared institutions and common authority. Supporters of the Federalist theory include politicians, activists, academics, and citizens who advocate for deeper European integration and the establishment of a federal European state.

1.2.3 Neofunctionalism

Neofunctionalism, developed by Ernst Haas[9] and furthered by scholars like Leon Lindberg,[10] builds upon functionalism by emphasizing the spillover effect. It suggests that successful cooperation in one policy area creates momentum for integration in other areas. Neofunctionalism highlights the role of supranational institutions, such as the European Commission and the European Court of Justice, in driving integration by promoting common policies and resolving disputes.[11]

The single market, Schengen area, and Eurozone exemplify the spillover effect in neofunctionalism. By removing trade barriers, the single market led to common standards, promoting integration in services, capital, and labor markets. By eliminating border controls, the Schengen area fostered law enforcement cooperation and joint security measures. By sharing a currency, the Eurozone led to fiscal policy coordination and banking regulation to ensure financial stability. Neofunctionalism, therefore, explains integration as a dynamic process, where initial cooperation generates pressures for further integration. It captures the logic by which technical agreements gradually produce deeper political transformation.

7 Ernesto Rossi (1897–1967) was an Italian anti-fascist politician and journalist. He contributed to the re-establishment of the *Partito d'Azione* and later to the creation of the *Partito Radicale*.

8 Vayssière, Bertrand, 2005, "Le manifeste de Ventotene (1941): acte de naissance du fédéralisme européen," *Guerres mondiales et conflits contemporains*, no. 217, pp. 69–76.

9 Ernst Haas (1924–2003) was Robson Research Professor of Government at the University of California, Berkeley.

10 Leon Lindberg is an American political scientist and Emeritus Professor at the University of Wisconsin–Madison, renowned for his studies of regional and political integration, as well as neofunctionalism.

11 Haas, Ernst B., 2004, *The Uniting of Europe: Political, Social, and Economic Forces, 1950–1957*, University of Notre Dame Press.

1.2.4 Intergovernmentalism

Intergovernmentalism, in contrast to supranational approaches, emphasizes the central role of national governments in the integration process. According to this theory, member states retain control over key policy decisions, with intergovernmental negotiations driving integration forward.[12]

States cooperate mainly by making treaties and agreements, with the European Council acting as the main authority for decision-making in the EU. For example, the Common Foreign and Security Policy (CFSP) is an intergovernmental area where member states coordinate their foreign and security policies. Decision-making in this area requires unanimity among member states, highlighting the central role of national governments. For instance, when imposing sanctions on a non-EU country, such as Iran or Russia, member states must agree through intergovernmental negotiations.

Justice and Home Affairs (JHA) cooperation involves areas such as law enforcement, immigration, and asylum policies. Member states collaborate through treaties and agreements to address common challenges, such as fighting cross-border crime or managing migration flows. The European Arrest Warrant is an example of intergovernmental cooperation in this field, allowing for the extradition of criminal suspects between EU countries. Intergovernmentalism thus interprets the EU as a system where states remain the dominant actors. Integration progresses only when governments agree, highlighting sovereignty and national preference as key drivers.

1.2.5 Liberal Intergovernmentalism

This theory, developed by Andrew Moravcsik, Professor of Politics and International Affairs at Princeton University, integrates elements of both neofunctionalism and intergovernmentalism.[13] Liberal intergovernmentalism emphasizes the dominance of national interests in EU decision-making, with states cooperating based on a rational calculation of costs and benefits. Liberal intergovernmentalism views European integration as primarily driven by the preferences and bargaining power of member states, with supranational institutions playing a secondary role.

The theories of European integration offer diverse perspectives on the dynamics, mechanisms, and outcomes of European integration, reflecting the complex interplay of economic, political, and social factors shaping the European project. This approach stresses rational choice: states integrate when it maximizes national benefits. It remains one of the most influential theories for explaining major EU treaties and negotiations.

Together, these theories provide complementary insights into the forces shaping European integration. Functionalist and neofunctionalist approaches emphasize gradual, institution-driven change; federalism presents a normative blueprint for political union; while intergovernmental theories highlight the strategic choices of sovereign states. Understanding their interplay is essential for grasping the complexity and evolution of the European project.

12 Verdun, Amy, 2020, "Intergovernmentalism: Old, Liberal, and New," in *Oxford Research Encyclopedia of Politics*, Oxford University Press. Available at: https://oxfordre.com/politics/view/10.1093/acrefore/9780190228637.001.0001/acrefore-9780190228637-e-1489. Accessed 6 April 2024.

13 Moravcsik, Andrew, 2020, "Liberal Intergovernmentalism," in *Oxford Research Encyclopedia of Politics*, Oxford University Press.

1.3 Principles of Supranationalism

By presenting the principles of supranationalism, we provide a conceptual framework for understanding the fundamental principles that underpin the creation and functioning of the European Union.

Supranationalism is a concept where nations agree to work together by sharing some of their power and decision-making authority with a central organization or authority beyond their own borders. This cooperation allows them to address common challenges and create unified policies that benefit all members involved.

Essentially, countries voluntarily come together to form a higher authority that can make decisions on behalf of the collective group, rather than each country acting independently.

Supranationalism is a concept commonly associated with institutions like the European Union, but it can also be observed in organizations such as the African Union, the Andean Community, the Economic Community of West African States (ECOWAS), and the Mercosur (Southern Common Market), each of which incorporates supranational elements to varying degrees.

Some principles commonly associated with supranationalism include pooling sovereignty, shared institutions, Rule of Law, integration, subsidiarity, democratic governance, peace and stability, and flexibility and adaptability.

1.3.1 Pooling Sovereignty

Supranational organizations involve member states pooling some of their sovereign powers to the central authority. This pooling of sovereignty allows decisions to be made collectively, rather than unilaterally by individual member states.[14]

In other words, pooling of sovereignty means that countries in international cooperation agree to share decision-making power. In the European Union, for example, member states give some decision-making authority to institutions like the Council. They make decisions on many issues by a majority vote rather than everyone having to agree. This allows decisions to be made even if some countries disagree. Countries do this to avoid disagreements and to make progress on common goals, like creating a single market. However, on sensitive issues, countries may still keep the power to veto decisions.

Imagine a group of five small island nations that pool sovereignty over fisheries management. Instead of each country setting national quotas independently, they establish a supranational authority empowered to determine fishing quotas for the entire region. This collective framework not only prevents overfishing but also enhances their bargaining power with global seafood corporations and ensures the long-term sustainability of shared marine resources.

Consider a coalition of European and Asian mid-sized countries vulnerable to cyberattacks. To strengthen their defenses, they pool sovereignty by creating a supranational *Cybersecurity Alliance*. Instead of each government developing fragmented national regulations, decision-making authority over digital infrastructure security is transferred to a central agency. This supranational body is empowered to impose common technical standards, operate joint monitoring systems, and coordinate responses to large-scale cyber incidents. By pooling sovereignty, member states can deter cyber threats far more effectively than if they acted in isolation.

14 "Pooled Sovereignty," *Oxford Reference*, online. Available at: https://www.oxfordreference.com/view/10.1093/oi/authority.20110803100336931. Accessed 10 April 2024.

Some examples of pooling sovereignty within the European Union include the European Single Market, Eurozone, Schengen area, Common Agricultural Policy (CAP), and Environmental Policy.

1.3.2 Shared Institutions

Supranationalism typically involves the creation of shared institutions with authority over member states. Shared institutions are organizations or bodies created by multiple countries to help them work together on specific issues. These institutions often include a legislative body, such as the European Parliament in the case of the EU, as well as executive and judicial branches.

Some examples of shared institutions in the EU include:

- the European Commission, which helps EU countries coordinate policies and implement decisions;
- the European Parliament, which represents the people of EU countries and helps make laws for the EU;
- the Council of the European Union, made up of government representatives from EU countries, which makes decisions on EU laws and policies.

Shared institutions in supranational organizations other than the EU, like NATO and the United Nations, that help member countries work together effectively, include, for example:

- the North Atlantic Council (NAC), which makes political decisions for NATO;
- the Military Committee that advises on military matters;
- NATO Headquarters that coordinates NATO's activities;
- NATO Defense Planning Process (NDPP), which coordinates defense planning among members.

Shared institutions in the United Nations include:

- the General Assembly that makes decisions on global issues;
- the Security Council that maintains peace and security, and can authorize peacekeeping missions and sanctions;
- the Secretariat, which handles administrative tasks;
- the International Court of Justice (ICJ) that resolves legal disputes between countries.

These institutions are essential for countries to work together effectively on common challenges and goals.

1.3.3 Rule of Law

Supranational organizations operate under the Rule of Law, with legal frameworks and procedures that govern the behavior of member states and individuals within the organization.

These legal structures help to ensure consistency and fairness in decision-making. They encompass elements such as the balance of powers, hierarchy of legal norms, independence of judges, and principles like equal treatment under the law. These concepts are thoroughly presented and explained in Chapter 5, which focuses on Constitutionalism and Judicial Review.

In a supranational context, the Rule of Law further manifests through several key elements like legal certainty, respect for Human rights, compliance, and enforcement.

Supranational entities establish clear and predictable legal frameworks, enabling people to understand their rights and obligations.

The Rule of Law within supranationalism encompasses the protection of human rights as enshrined in international treaties and conventions. This includes safeguarding individuals' rights to due process, freedom from arbitrary detention, and access to justice.

Supranational entities must have mechanisms in place to ensure compliance with their legal frameworks and to enforce judgments or decisions. This may involve sanctions for non-compliance and measures to uphold the authority of the law.

For instance, imagine a journalist in Country X held without trial after criticizing the government. A supranational court orders her release and compensation. When the State refuses, it faces escalating fines and suspension of voting rights in the supranational assembly until compliance restores the authority of the law.

In a different context, consider a migrant worker in Country Y denied access to local courts for an unfair dismissal claim. A supranational tribunal requires the State to amend its laws. When authorities delay, trade sanctions are imposed, reinforcing the binding character of supranational rulings.

Similarly, take the case of a state allowing factories to pollute a cross-border river. A supranational authority orders clean-up measures and stricter controls. Non-compliance triggers suspension of development funds, ensuring respect for collective environmental standards.

Overall, the Rule of Law as a principle of supranationalism underscores the importance of legality, accountability, and fairness in the governance of transnational issues and relations.

The Rule of Law in supranationalism builds trust in how these global organizations operate. It encourages different groups to work together smoothly and agree on common goals.

1.3.4 Integration

Supranationalism aims to promote integration among member states by fostering cooperation in various areas, such as trade, security, and social policy. Integration serves as a foundational principle of supranationalism. It can lead to increased economic efficiency, political stability, and cultural exchange among member states.

Integration fosters the removal of trade barriers, harmonization of regulations, and the creation of a single market, resulting in enhanced economic efficiency.[15]

For example, the establishment of the European Single Market allows goods, services, capital, and people to move freely across borders within the EU. This has led to increased competition, economies of scale, and specialization, thereby boosting productivity and economic growth.

To illustrate the free movement of goods, consider a company in Portugal producing solar panels that can sell them easily in Germany without customs barriers or complex regulations. This access to a larger market enables the firm to scale up production, lower costs, and compete more effectively at the international level.

Similarly, to illustrate the free movement of people, consider a young engineer from Poland who moves to France for work. He finds better opportunities, while France benefits from his skills.

15 See McCormick, John, 2018, *The European Union: Politics and Policies*, Westview Press.

In the same way, to illustrate the free movement of services, consider an architect from Italy who provides design services for a project in the Netherlands without facing additional licensing requirements. This flexibility allows expertise to flow where it is most needed.

Finally, to illustrate the free movement of capital, consider an investor in Spain who easily transfers funds to establish a start-up in Belgium. This encourages cross-border investment and fosters innovation across the Union.

These examples show how economic integration operates in practice, supported by broader mechanisms such as the EU's Customs Union, which eliminates tariffs and customs duties to facilitate smoother trade and reduce transaction costs for companies. Beyond the economic dimension, integration also promotes closer cooperation among member states on political issues, thereby contributing to regional stability.[16]

Initiatives like the Common Security and Defense Policy (CSDP) promote cooperation in areas such as crisis management, peacekeeping operations, and counterterrorism efforts, enhancing the collective security of EU member states. For instance, under the EU's Common Security and Defense Policy, Operation Atalanta was launched in 2008 to fight against piracy in the Gulf of Aden and the Indian Ocean, where pirates operated from the Somali coast. This naval mission, involving ships and personnel from several member states, has protected commercial vessels, escorted humanitarian shipments, and significantly reduced piracy, demonstrating how the CSDP strengthens collective security through coordinated action.

Institutions like the European Council and the European External Action Service (EEAS) provide platforms for diplomatic dialogue and conflict resolution, helping to prevent and mitigate disputes among member states.

Integration facilitates cultural exchange and mutual understanding among member states, enriching the diversity of European society. For example, the Erasmus program promotes student and staff mobility across European universities, facilitating cultural exchange, language learning, and academic collaboration.

The European Capitals of Culture initiative highlights the cultural diversity and heritage of different EU cities, promoting cross-cultural dialogue, artistic exchange, and community engagement.

In summary, integration in the EU brings benefits like better economics, peace, and cultural sharing among countries. This happens because countries work closely together, trade barriers disappear, people can move freely, and cultures mix. These make the EU stronger and more united.

1.3.5 Subsidiarity

The principle of subsidiarity, enshrined in the Treaty on European Union, guides when action should be taken by the EU rather than member states in areas where the EU lacks exclusive competence. It ensures decisions are made at the most appropriate level of governance, whether local, regional, or central. The principle of subsidiarity serves to regulate the exercise of the European Union's non-exclusive powers.[17]

16 McCormick, *The European Union.*

17 Klamert, Marcus, 2019, "Article 5 TEU," in *The EU Treaties and the Charter of Fundamental Rights: A Commentary*, eds. Manuel Kellerbauer, Marcus Klamert and Jonathan Tomkin, Oxford Academic, New York. Accessed 28 April 2024.

The legal basis of the principle of subsidiarity in the EU is Article 5(3) of the Treaty on European Union (TEU) and Protocol (No 2) on the application of the principles of subsidiarity and proportionality. It rules that:

> in areas in which the European Union does not have exclusive competence, the principle of subsidiarity, laid down in the Treaty on European Union, defines the circumstances in which it is preferable for action to be taken by the Union, rather than the member states.

Under Article 5(3) of the TEU, this principle involves three conditions: (1) action is not within exclusive EU competence; (2) objectives cannot be adequately achieved by member states alone; and (3) EU action adds value due to scale or effects.

The Treaty of Lisbon reinforced this principle, emphasizing the role of national parliaments in its enforcement. National parliaments can issue reasoned opinions on proposed legislation, triggering review mechanisms. Additionally, the European Parliament plays a key role in promoting and monitoring subsidiarity within the EU legislative process, supported by interinstitutional agreements and resolutions.

The idea behind subsidiarity is to let local or lower-level authorities have some independence from higher ones, like central governments. It means sharing power among different levels of government, which is how federal states work.[18]

Some practical examples of subsidiarity in action include education curriculum, healthcare, environmental protection, and transportation.

In the European context, subsidiarity might mean that decisions about school curriculum and teaching methods are primarily made by local or regional authorities rather than by the EU. This allows for tailoring education to the specific needs and preferences of communities.

For example, in Germany, each federal state (*Land*) designs its own education programs, ensuring that teaching methods and curricula reflect local needs and cultural preferences, in line with the principle of subsidiarity.

Subsidiarity could also mean that each member state manages its own healthcare system according to its cultural, social, and economic factors. While the EU might provide guidelines or support for cross-border healthcare cooperation, decisions about the structure and operation of healthcare systems remain at the national level.

In healthcare, subsidiarity means that while the EU can coordinate responses to cross-border health threats, the organization and delivery of healthcare services remain the responsibility of member states.

Imagine a flu outbreak in Country X: the EU coordinates information-sharing and joint vaccine procurement, but Country X decides how many hospitals to mobilize and what vaccination strategy to apply, reflecting subsidiarity in practice.

For instance, during the COVID-19 pandemic, the EU supported vaccine procurement and distribution, but national governments decided on lockdown measures, hospital management, and vaccination strategies tailored to their populations.

When it comes to environmental policies, subsidiarity could involve the EU setting overarching goals and standards, while individual member states determine specific measures to achieve these goals based on their unique environmental challenges and resources.

For example, consider waste management in Country A: the EU sets common recycling targets, while regional authorities decide whether to build recycling plants, run public campaigns, or introduce local collection systems, ensuring solutions fit local conditions.

18 Kaczorowska-Ireland, Alina, 2016, *European Union Law*, 4th ed., Routledge, Chapter 6: "Competences of the EU."

Subsidiarity in transportation means that while the EU sets safety and emission standards for roads, each country gets to plan its own road networks and public transportation systems to fit its unique geography and population. For example, consider transport in Country Y: the EU sets general rules on vehicle emissions and safety, while City Z decides to expand bike lanes and limit traffic in the city center, showing subsidiarity in practice.

1.3.6 Democratic Governance

Supranational organizations often strive for democratic governance, with mechanisms in place to ensure representation and accountability. This may involve direct elections for certain positions, such as members of the European Parliament, as well as mechanisms for oversight and checks and balances.

Supranationalism is a vertical form of Separation of Powers in which powers are shared, in accordance with the principle of subsidiarity, between the local level and the supranational level. Indeed, that is one of the reasons why democracy is one of the principles of supranationalism.

Thus, democratic governance is a principle of supranationalism because it ensures that decisions are made with the participation and consent of the people they affect, promoting fairness and accountability.

Examples of supranational organizations that prioritize democratic governance include the European Union and the United Nations. In the EU, decisions are made through democratic processes involving elected representatives from member states, such as the European Parliament. On May 8, 2025, the European Parliament voted to downgrade the protection status of wolves from "strictly protected" to "protected" across all 27 EU member states, aligning EU legislation with the Bern Convention and thereby allowing some of these animals to be hunted. The vote passed with 371 in favor, 162 against, and 37 abstentions.

Similarly, within the UN, member states participate in decision-making through bodies like the General Assembly, where each member has equal representation and voting rights. These democratic structures aim to ensure that decisions reflect the collective will and interests of the participating nations or citizens. For example, on September 12, 2025, the UNGA voted 142 in favor, ten against, and 12 abstentions to endorse a declaration backing a two-state solution between Israel and Palestine, condemning Hamas's attacks, and calling for a Palestinian Authority Government.

1.3.7 Peace and Stability

One of the underlying goals of supranationalism is to promote peace and stability among member states by fostering closer ties and reducing the likelihood of conflict. By creating shared interests and institutions, supranational organizations aim to mitigate tensions and promote cooperation.[19]

Examples of supranational organizations promoting peace and stability among member states include the European Union, the African Union, and the Association of Southeast Asian Nations.

The European Union was formed after World War II with the aim of fostering economic cooperation and preventing future conflicts in Europe. Through initiatives like the European Coal

19 Lindseth, Peter L., 2016, "Supranational Organizations," in *The Oxford Handbook of International Organizations*, eds. Jacob Katz Cogan, Ian Hurd and Ian Johnstone, Oxford Handbooks. Online edition: Oxford Academic, 6 November 2017. Accessed 7 July 2024.

and Steel Community (ECSC) and the European Economic Community (EEC), which later evolved into the EU, member states have developed strong economic and political ties, reducing the likelihood of armed conflict among them.

The African Union (AU) was established in 2002 – as a successor to the Organization of African Unity (OAU, 1963–1999) – to promote unity, peace, and security across the African continent. The AU intervenes in conflicts, mediates disputes between member states, and supports peacekeeping operations through bodies like the African Peace and Security Architecture (APSA) and the African Standby Force (ASF).

The African Union has repeatedly intervened to uphold peace and security on the continent. In Somalia, it deployed the Transition Mission (ATMIS) from 2022 to 2024, followed by the Support and Stabilization Mission (AUSSOM) in 2025, to combat Al-Shabaab and help Somali forces take over security responsibilities. In Sudan, the AU has engaged in mediation efforts since 2023, calling for ceasefires and inclusive dialogue to end the conflict. Earlier, in 2003, the AU launched the Mission in Burundi (AMIB) to stabilize the country after its civil war, demonstrating its capacity to act through both peacekeeping and political initiatives.

As regards the Association of Southeast Asian Nations (ASEAN), it was established in 1967 in Bangkok, Thailand, to promote political and economic cooperation among Southeast Asian nations. ASEAN facilitates dialogue, conflict resolution, and cooperation on security issues through mechanisms like the ASEAN Regional Forum (ARF) and the Treaty of Amity and Cooperation (TAC), contributing to peace and stability in the region.

For example, it mediated tensions in the South China Sea through the ASEAN-China Code of Conduct negotiations, fostering dialogue among claimant states. During the COVID-19 pandemic, ASEAN coordinated a regional response, including the establishment of the COVID-19 Response Fund to support member states. More recently, since 2021, ASEAN has sought to address the crisis in Myanmar by adopting a Five-Point Consensus and appointing a special envoy to encourage dialogue and reduce violence.

These examples illustrate how supranational organizations work to prevent conflicts, build trust, and foster cooperation among member states, ultimately promoting peace and stability in their respective regions.

1.3.8 Flexibility and Adaptability

Supranationalism requires a degree of flexibility and adaptability to respond to changing circumstances and member state preferences. This may involve amending treaties, adjusting policies, or expanding the scope of cooperation in response to new challenges or opportunities.

Examples of flexibility and adaptability in supranationalism include treaty amendments in the European Union, expansion of cooperation in the World Trade Organization, and flexible response mechanisms in the United Nations.

The EU has amended its founding treaties multiple times to accommodate new member states, address emerging issues, and deepen integration. For example, the Treaty of Lisbon, which came into force in 2009, amended previous treaties to streamline decision-making processes, enhance the role of the European Parliament, and establish new policy areas like the Common Foreign and Security Policy (CFSP).

The World Trade Organization regularly updates its rules and agreements to adapt to changes in the global economy and trade landscape. Member states negotiate new agreements and expand the scope of cooperation to address emerging issues such as digital trade, environmental protection, and intellectual property rights.

With regard to the United Nations, it employs flexible response mechanisms to address evolving security challenges and humanitarian crises. For example, the Security Council can adapt its peacekeeping mandates to respond to changing circumstances on the ground, and UN agencies can mobilize resources and expertise to address new humanitarian emergencies, such as natural disasters or refugee crises.

These examples demonstrate how supranational organizations remain responsive to member state preferences and changing circumstances by adjusting treaties, policies, and cooperation mechanisms to meet the needs of their constituents better.

All these principles guide the functioning and development of supranational organizations, shaping their objectives, decision-making processes, and relationships with member states and other international actors.

1.4 Institutions of the European Union

The European Union is a unique supranational organization comprising multiple institutions that collectively govern the affairs of its member states. These institutions are designed to ensure democratic representation, legislative oversight, policy formulation, and implementation across the EU.

Key among these institutions are the European Commission, the European Parliament, the Council of the European Union, the European Council, the Court of Justice of the European Union, and the European Central Bank. Each institution plays a distinct role in the EU's decision-making process, contributing to its functioning as a complex, multi-layered governance system.

1.4.1 The European Commission

At the heart of the EU's Executive branch lies the European Commission. Comprised of one commissioner from each member state, the Commission acts as the EU's principal initiator and executor of legislation. It holds the exclusive right to propose new laws, oversee their implementation, and manage the EU's day-to-day operations. The Commission is led by a President, elected by the European Parliament, who coordinates its activities and represents the EU on the global stage.

As the executive body of the European Union, the European Commission is responsible for developing and implementing EU policies. Its work is overseen by a college of commissioners led by the President of the Commission. Commissioners focus on specific policy priorities defined by the President.

The Commission is led by a group of 27 commissioners known as the *college*. Together, they decide on the political and strategic direction of the Commission. A new college of commissioners is appointed every five years.

The commissioners of the European Commission are appointed by the governments of each EU member country. They are chosen based on their expertise. Once selected, they're approved by the European Parliament. Each commissioner represents the EU as a whole, not just their own country.

The Commission's organization consists of specialized services called Directorates-General (DGs), each responsible for a specific area of action. These services develop, implement, and manage EU policies, legislation, and funding programs. There are also executive agencies responsible for managing Commission programs.

The Commission has offices in all EU countries, as well as delegations outside the EU, managed by the European External Action Service. These offices and delegations represent and promote EU interests and policies, providing information on its activities.

Commission staff is part of the European civil service, with approximately 32,000 people holding permanent or temporary positions. They fulfill various roles, such as policy managers, researchers, lawyers, and translators, and must adhere to a strict code of conduct.

The European Commission participates in the EU's overall strategy by proposing new legislation and policies, monitoring their implementation, and managing the Union's budget. It also contributes to international development and provides humanitarian aid.

In terms of areas of action, the EU intervenes in specific domains defined by the European treaties, based on three principles: attribution, proportionality, and subsidiarity. These principles determine in which areas the EU can legislate alone, in collaboration with member states, or in support of member states' actions.[20]

The European Commission is accountable to the European Parliament, which approves its appointment and can dismiss it through a vote of no confidence. If two-thirds of MEPs support such a motion, the entire Commission must resign. This has never formally happened, but in 1999, the Santer Commission resigned collectively after strong criticism and the threat of censure from Parliament over allegations of fraud and mismanagement.

1.4.2 The European Parliament

The European Parliament is the EU's directly elected legislative body, representing the interests of its citizens. Members of the European Parliament (MEPs) are elected by the citizens of each member state, with seats allocated proportionally based on population size. The Parliament shares legislative power with the Council of the European Union, scrutinizing and amending proposals put forward by the Commission. Its responsibilities encompass approving the EU budget, monitoring the Commission's activities, and shaping EU policies across various domains.

The European Parliament, having evolved over the years through successive treaty amendments, has gained extensive legislative and budgetary powers. It collaborates with representatives of member state governments in the Council to set the direction for the European project. The European Parliament acts as a co-legislator, sharing the power to adopt and amend legislative proposals and approve the European Union's budget with the Council. It also oversees the work of the European Commission and other EU bodies, and cooperates with national parliaments of member states.

The Parliament strives to enhance democratic decision-making in Europe and globally. It is committed to defending democracy, freedom of expression, and free and fair elections worldwide. Over time, the Parliament has continually gained new powers through treaty revisions, enhancing the influence of the only directly elected EU institution. Thus, it has emerged as a major player in the EU decision-making process.

MEPs, or Members of the European Parliament, are elected through a process that occurs every five years since the first direct elections in 1979. Currently, there are 720 MEPs (which increased from 705 after the 2024 elections).[21] The allocation of seats per country is established by EU treaties.

Each member state of the European Union returns a specific number of MEPs. The number varies depending on the population size of the country. For example, smaller member states like

20 Horspool, Margot and Humphreys, Matthew, 2021, *European Union Law*, Oxford University Press, Chapter 3: "The Institutions of the Union."

21 See 6–9 June 2024 European Elections Official Website. Available at: https://elections.europa.eu/en. Accessed 4 May 2024.

Malta, Luxembourg, and Cyprus return six MEPs, while larger states like Germany return up to 96 MEPs. To ensure fair representation, the principle of *degressive proportionality* is applied. This means that while countries with larger populations return more MEPs, there's also a consideration to allocate a relatively higher number of seats per capita to less populous member states.

The electoral process for European Parliament elections is largely governed by national electoral laws and traditions of each member state. However, there are some common EU rules established in the Electoral Act of 1976, ensuring consistency and fairness across member states.

Overall, the election of MEPs involves a combination of national electoral practices and EU regulations, aiming to uphold democratic principles and ensure proportional representation at the European level.

In summary, the European Parliament, as the sole directly elected EU body, plays a crucial role in shaping legislation and budgets, overseeing EU institutions, and promoting democracy and human rights. Through its evolution, it has become a cornerstone of European integration, representing the interests of Europeans while upholding fundamental rights and democratic principles.[22]

1.4.3 The Council of the European Union

The Council of the European Union, often referred to as the Council of Ministers, represents the member states' governments and serves as the EU's main decision-making body. It consists of ministers from each member state, with the composition varying depending on the policy area under discussion.

The Council, together with the European Parliament, adopts EU laws, coordinates economic policies, and develops the EU's common foreign and security policies. Its presidency rotates among member states every six months, ensuring a balanced and inclusive approach to decision-making.

The Council of the European Union holds a central role in EU decision-making, influencing legislative direction and fostering cooperation among member states. Its key functions include legislative authority, policy coordination, foreign and security policy development, policy coordination, foreign and security policy development, international agreements, and budget adoption.

The Council negotiates and adopts EU laws, often in collaboration with the European Parliament, using the ordinary legislative procedure, also known as *codecision*. This process applies to policy areas where the EU has exclusive or shared competence with member states, with the Council working on proposals from the European Commission.

The COVID-19 pandemic seems to have contributed to quicker decision-making at lower levels of the Council, to a certain extent, at the expense of transparency.[23]

The Council coordinates member states' policies across various sectors, including economic and fiscal policies, education, culture, youth, sport, and employment policy. Guided by directives from the European Council, the Council shapes and implements the EU's common foreign and security policies. This involves areas such as development aid, defense, and trade, with a focus on maintaining unity and efficacy in external actions, in collaboration with the High Representative of the Union for Foreign Affairs and Security Policy.

22 Horspool and Humphreys, *European Union Law*.
23 Doležel, Ondřej, 2024, "Decision-Making in the Council of the European Union during the COVID-19 Pandemic," *European Politics and Society*, pp. 1–17.

The Council empowers the European Commission to negotiate agreements between the EU and non-EU entities, deciding on their signing and conclusion based on Commission proposals. Once Parliament consent (required in co-decision areas) and ratification from all member states are obtained, the Council finalizes agreements, covering diverse sectors like trade, cooperation, or specialized domains such as textiles or transport.[24]

Alongside the Parliament, the Council approves the EU budget, typically for a calendar year. Adoption usually occurs in December, with implementation beginning on January 1 of the following year.

1.4.4 The European Council

The European Council is one of the seven institutions of the EU. It consists of the heads of state or government of the 27 EU member states, the President of the European Council, and the President of the European Commission. Together, they determine the short and long-term political orientations and priorities of the EU, thus establishing the action program.

This is typically done by adopting conclusions at each European Council meeting. These conclusions address issues of particular importance to the EU and indicate specific measures to be taken or objectives to be achieved. European Council conclusions may also set deadlines for reaching agreement on specific points or for presenting legislative proposals.

The European Council does not participate in legislative negotiations or their adoption. However, while not a legislative institution, the European Council plays a crucial role in shaping the EU's agenda, particularly during times of crisis or significant change. It convenes regular summits to discuss pressing matters and facilitate consensus among member states. For instance, the European Council has recently discussed pressing matters such as Russia's war against Ukraine, the EU's response to the energy crisis, migration management, and strategies for tackling climate change. It also set the overall direction for enlargement talks with countries like Ukraine and Moldova, and coordinated the Union's position on relations with China and the Middle East.

The European Council was established in 1974 as an informal forum for discussion among the heads of state or government of the EU member states. The 1992 Maastricht Treaty conferred official status upon the European Council and assigned it the function of providing impetus and defining the general political orientations of the EU. Following changes introduced by the Lisbon Treaty, the European Council became one of the seven institutions of the EU in 2009.

1.4.5 The Court of Justice of the European Union

As the EU's judicial authority, the Court of Justice of the European Union (CJEU) ensures the uniform interpretation and application of EU law. Comprising the Court of Justice, the General Court, and specialized courts, the CJEU resolves legal disputes between member states, EU institutions, businesses, and individuals.

Because the Treaties of the European Union have vested the CJEU with exclusive authority over the interpretation of EU law, it reinforces the principle of supremacy, where EU law prevails over national laws, and protects the fundamental rights of EU citizens within the Union's legal structure.[25]

24 Horspool and Humphreys, *European Union Law*.

25 Tridimas, Takis, 2018, "The Court of Justice of the European Union," in *Oxford Principles of European Union Law: The European Union Legal Order*, eds. Robert Schütze and Takis Tridimas, vol. 1, Oxford Academic, UK. Accessed 5 May 2024.

The Court of Justice of the EU is pivotal in ensuring consistent interpretation and application of EU law across member states, while also resolving legal disputes involving national governments and EU institutions.

The CJEU handles various types of cases:

(1) Interpreting the law (Preliminary rulings): National courts in EU countries may seek clarification on EU law interpretation or validity. This process ensures the uniform application of EU law and assesses its compatibility with national laws or practices.
(2) Enforcing the law (Infringement proceedings): Cases can be initiated against national governments for failing to comply with EU law. This may lead to fines if non-compliance persists, with proceedings initiated by the European Commission or another EU country.
(3) Annulment of EU legal acts (Actions for annulment): The CJEU can be petitioned to annul EU acts violating treaties or fundamental rights. This action can be initiated by an EU Government, the Council of the EU, the European Commission, or in certain cases, the European Parliament. Private individuals may also challenge EU acts directly affecting them.
(4) Ensuring EU action (Actions for failure to act): The CJEU may compel the Parliament, Council, and Commission to fulfill their obligations. Complaints can be lodged by EU Governments, other EU institutions, or, under certain conditions, individuals or companies if these institutions fail to act.
(5) Sanctioning EU institutions (Actions for damages): Individuals or companies affected by EU action or inaction may seek redress through the CJEU.

The CJEU consists of two courts:

The Court of Justice deals with preliminary rulings, certain actions for annulment, and appeals.

The General Court adjudicates on actions for annulment primarily concerning individuals, companies, and in some cases, EU Governments, with a focus on specific areas like competition law, state aid, trade, agriculture, and trademarks.

Each judge and advocate general[26] serves a renewable six-year term, appointed jointly by national governments. Presidents of each court are selected by the judges for renewable three-year terms.

Cases undergo two stages. A written stage where parties submit written statements, summarized by the judge, and discussed at the Court's general meeting, which decides on the case's handling and the need for an oral hearing. An oral stage (public hearing), where Lawyers present arguments, and judges may question them. If necessary, the advocate general provides an opinion after the hearing. The judges then deliberate and deliver their verdict.

Private individuals or companies affected by EU institutions' actions or inactions can seek recourse indirectly through national courts or directly before the General Court if an EU institution's decision directly affects them. Complaints about EU law infringements by national authorities must follow official procedures.

1.4.6 The European Central Bank

Responsible for monetary policy within the Eurozone, the European Central Bank (ECB) maintains price stability and supports the economic objectives of the EU. Operating independently

26 Advocates General hold a distinct role within the Court of Justice of the European Union. They are not judges or prosecutors, but they assist in each case by presenting independent opinions on the legal questions at issue.

of national governments, the ECB sets interest rates, conducts monetary operations, and supervises financial institutions to ensure the stability of the euro currency. It plays a critical role in safeguarding the EU's economic and financial stability, particularly during periods of economic uncertainty or financial crisis.

The ECB is a key EU institution within the Eurosystem and Single Supervisory Mechanism. With over 5,000 employees and trainees from across Europe based in Frankfurt, Germany, the ECB collaborates closely with national central banks in the Eurosystem and with national supervisors in the Single Supervisory Mechanism to carry out various tasks.

Beyond its core monetary mandate, the ECB also plays a key role in maintaining financial stability in the Eurozone. During major crises – such as the 2008 financial crisis, the Eurozone debt crisis, and the recent economic disruptions linked to the COVID-19 pandemic – the ECB acted to stabilize markets by using unconventional tools like large asset-purchase programmes and special lending measures. These actions helped keep credit available, avoid deflation, and support economic recovery across member states.

The ECB's supervisory role has also grown. Through the Single Supervisory Mechanism, it monitors the largest European banks to ensure they remain financially sound and to reduce the risk of future banking crises. By applying common rules and working closely with national authorities, the ECB strengthens the overall stability and integration of the European financial system.

A crucial aspect of the ECB is its independence from political influence. Although it works with EU institutions and national governments, the ECB must base its decisions solely on its mandate to maintain price stability. This independence ensures that monetary policy is guided by long-term economic considerations rather than short-term political pressures.

To sum up, the Institutions of the European Union form a complex, yet interconnected system of governance, reflecting the EU's commitment to democracy, Rule of Law, and cooperation among its member states. Through their respective roles and responsibilities, these institutions uphold the principles of transparency, accountability, and solidarity, driving the EU's evolution as a dynamic and influential global actor. Despite occasional challenges and divergent interests, the EU's institutional framework remains essential for promoting peace, prosperity, and progress across Europe and beyond.

2 EU Law and Legal Framework

This section provides a comprehensive presentation of the sources of EU law as well as the main procedures governing their adoption and application.

Based on the Rule of Law, the European Union implies that every action taken by the EU is founded on treaties that have been approved democratically by its members. EU laws help to achieve the objectives of the EU treaties and put EU policies into practice.

There are two main types of EU law – primary and secondary. Treaties are the starting point for EU law and are known as primary law. The body of law originating from the treaties is known as secondary law and includes regulations, directives, decisions, recommendations, and opinions.

2.1 Sources of European Union Law

European Union law is based on a structured legal framework that guides its institutions and member states. This section outlines the main sources of EU law, including primary law (treaties), secondary law (regulations and directives), case law from the Court of Justice of the

European Union (CJEU), and general legal principles. These sources shape the legal system of the EU and define how its laws are enacted, interpreted, and applied.

2.1.1 Primary Law

Primary law is the supreme source of law in the European Union. It comes mainly from the founding treaties, notably the 1957 Treaty of Rome (which evolved into the Treaty of the Functioning of the European Union) and the 1992 Treaty of Maastricht (also called the Treaty on European Union).

Primary law delineates the allocation of powers between the EU and its member states, establishing the legal framework within which EU institutions devise and execute policies.

Primary law encompasses founding treaties, amending treaties, accession treaties, protocols appended to these treaties, supplementary agreements amending specific sections of the founding treaties, and The Charter of Fundamental Rights (since the Treaty of Lisbon).

Founding treaties include:

- The 1951Treaty of Paris establishing the European Coal and Steel Community
- The 1957 Treaty of Rome establishing the European Economic Community
- The 1957 Euratom Treaty
- The 1992 Treaty of Maastricht

Amending treaties encompass:

- The 1986 Single European Act[27]
- The 1997 Amsterdam Treaty[28]
- The 2001 Treaty of Nice[29]
- The 2007 Treaty of Lisbon[30]

Accession treaties involve member states such as Denmark, Ireland, the United Kingdom (1972), Greece (1979), Spain, Portugal (1985), Austria, Finland, Sweden (1994), Czech Republic, Cyprus, Estonia, Hungary, Latvia, Lithuania, Malta, Poland, Slovakia, Slovenia (2003), Romania, Bulgaria (2005), and Croatia (2012).

Supplementary agreements consist of:

- The 1965 Treaty of Brussels (Merger Treaty)
- Treaties amending budgetary and financial provisions
- The 1976 Act on the election of members of the European Parliament by direct universal suffrage

27 The Single European Act established the goal of creating a single market by 1992 and introduced procedures for deeper integration.

28 The Amsterdam Treaty expanded EU activities to include new policy areas, strengthened democratic institutions, and incorporated the Schengen Agreement.

29 The Treaty of Nice reformed EU institutions to prepare for enlargement, adjusted voting rules, and expanded qualified majority voting.

30 The Treaty of Lisbon modernized EU institutions, strengthened democracy, introduced the Charter of Fundamental Rights, and created new positions for enhanced external representation.

In short, primary law forms the constitutional backbone of the EU, setting the fundamental rules from which all other EU legislation derives.

2.1.2 Secondary Law

The objectives outlined in the EU treaties are realized through various types of legal instruments. While some possess binding force, others do not. Some legal acts apply to all EU countries, while others only affect a few.

Therefore, in addition to primary law, EU law comprises secondary sources such as regulations, directives, decisions, opinions, and recommendations.

These are the five types of legal acts that European Union institutions can adopt, as defined in Article 288 of the Treaty on the Functioning of the European Union (TFEU).[31] While regulations, directives, and decisions carry legal obligations, opinions and recommendations are non-binding.

Article 288 TFEU (ex Article 249 TEC).

> To exercise the Union's competences, the institutions shall adopt regulations, directives, decisions, recommendations and opinions.
>
> A regulation shall have general application. It shall be binding in its entirety and directly applicable in all member states.
>
> A directive shall be binding, as to the result to be achieved, upon each member state to which it is addressed, but shall leave to the national authorities the choice of form and methods.
>
> A decision shall be binding in its entirety. A decision which specifies those to whom it is addressed shall be binding only on them.
>
> *Recommendations and opinions shall have no binding force.*

In short, secondary law applies the treaties in practice, allowing the EU to make rules and manage policies across the Union.

2.1.2.1 REGULATIONS

A regulation within the European Union is a type of legal act that holds the highest level of authority and is binding on all member states. Unlike directives, which set out objectives for member states to achieve, regulations are directly applicable without the need for national legislation to implement them. This means that once a regulation is adopted, it automatically becomes law in all EU countries, and it must be followed in its entirety. For example, if the EU introduces a regulation to standardize product safety requirements across member states, all countries in the EU must comply with these safety standards without making any changes or adaptations at the national level.

As a matter of fact, the EU introduced Regulation (EU) 2023/988, known as the General Product Safety Regulation (GPSR), on May 23, 2023, replacing the General Product Safety Directive (GPSD). It aims to update and harmonize product safety rules across member states,

31 The TFEU originates from the Treaty of Rome (the EC Treaty, 1957). The Maastricht Treaty (1992) created the EU and introduced a three-pillar structure: (1) European Communities (economy, euro, trade); (2) Common Foreign and Security Policy; and (3) Justice and Home Affairs. Maastricht also gave its name to the Treaty on European Union (TEU). The Lisbon Treaty (2007/2009) renamed the EC Treaty as the TFEU and merged the pillars into a single EU unified framework. Today, together with the TEU, the TFEU forms the legal foundation of the EU.

applying from December 13, 2024.[32] The GPSR broadens product safety regulations, standardizes recall procedures, and defines roles for economic operators. It emphasizes risk assessments, labeling, and instructions for use to ensure product safety. Overall, the GPSR aims to enhance consumer protection and market efficiency within the EU.

Similarly, if there is a regulation governing environmental protection or data privacy, it applies uniformly across the entire EU, ensuring a consistent approach and level playing field within the single market.

In essence, regulations serve as powerful tools for harmonizing laws and regulations across the EU, promoting legal certainty, and facilitating the functioning of the internal market by removing barriers to trade and ensuring a level playing field for businesses and citizens across member states.

2.1.2.2 DIRECTIVES

A directive is a rule from the EU that tells countries what they need to accomplish. It is a legislative act that sets out a goal that EU countries must achieve. But each country can decide how to reach those goals by making its own laws. It is up to the individual countries to devise their own laws on how to reach these goals.

For instance, the EU single-use plastics directive wants to cut down on certain plastics that harm the environment.[33] Each country can choose how to reduce or even stop using things like plastic plates, straws, and cups for drinks.

Similarly, imagine a directive on renewable energy requiring 40% of electricity from renewables by 2030: one country might expand wind farms, while another invests in solar power to meet the target.

Directives must be transposed into national law within a set deadline, meaning each member state passes its own legislation to implement the EU goal. Directives offer flexibility and allow for national differences, while regulations ensure immediate and consistent harmonization across the EU. Regulations are directly applicable, leading to uniform interpretation and implementation. However, their strict nature may limit consideration for national specifics.

2.1.2.3 DECISIONS

A decision is a type of legal act in the EU that has binding force on the specific entities it is directed to, such as an EU country or an individual company. This means that the entities addressed by the decision are required to comply with its terms. Unlike directives, decisions do not need to be transposed into national law by member states because they are directly applicable. Due to its direct applicability, it goes into effect right away without needing to be turned into law by each country. This allows for immediate implementation of the decision's provisions without the need for further action at the national level.

For example, a decision made by the European Commission on January 31, 2024, called Commission Implementing Decision (EU) 2024/411, is about creating a list of shipping companies and deciding which EU country is responsible for overseeing each one.[34] This list helps

32 Regulation (EU) 2023/988 of the European Parliament and of the Council of 10 May 2023 on general product safety, amending Regulation (EU) No 1025/2012 of the European Parliament and of the Council and Directive (EU) 2020/1828 of the European Parliament and the Council, and repealing Directive 2001/95/EC of the European Parliament and of the Council and Council Directive 87/357/EEC.

33 Directive (EU) 2019/904 on reducing the impact of certain plastic products on the environment.

34 Commission implementing decision (EU) 2024/411 of 30 January 2024 on the list of shipping companies specifying the administering authority in respect of a shipping company in accordance with directive 2003/87/ec of the European Parliament and of the Council.

reduce administrative work for shipping companies and EU member states. It also includes identification numbers for each shipping company.

This shows how decisions directly impose obligations on specific countries or companies without requiring further legislative steps. Importantly, decisions are not binding on all EU member states but only on those to whom they are addressed, which may include individuals, companies, or specific states.

2.1.2.4 OPINIONS

An opinion is a statement made by EU institutions, like the Commission or Parliament, in a non-binding way. This means that it doesn't force anyone to do or not do something. It is just sharing thoughts or advice.

An opinion is among the five legal acts that European Union institutions can adopt, as outlined in Article 288 of the Treaty on the Functioning of the European Union. Opinions, like recommendations, are non-binding. Examples of opinions issued by EU institutions, as defined in Article 288 TFEU, include opinions provided by the European Commission when a country seeks to join the EU, as requested by the Council of the European Union.

Other examples include opinions provided by the Council on member states' economic partnership programs under Regulation (EU) No 473/2013, which monitors budgetary plans and corrects excessive deficits in euro area countries.

Although opinions do not create obligations, they help guide decision-making and influence the direction of EU policies.

2.1.2.5 RECOMMENDATIONS

A recommendation is a non-binding instrument used by the EU institutions to express their views and suggest actions without imposing any legal obligations on the recipients.

For instance, when the Commission recommended that media service providers in EU countries enhance their ownership transparency and protect their editorial independence, it did not carry any legal consequences.

Another example of a recommendation is when the European Commission issues guidance on best practices for renewable energy implementation to EU member states, aiming to promote sustainable energy policies without legally obligating the countries to follow the recommendations.

When the European Commission suggests that EU countries enhance cybersecurity measures, this is also a recommendation. This doesn't force the countries to act, but it offers guidance on best practices. Overall, recommendations help coordinate national policies and encourage convergence within the EU, even though they do not create enforceable duties.

Supplementary sources of EU law comprise case law from the Court of Justice of the EU and general legal principles.

2.1.3 Case Law of the Court of Justice of the European Union

The CJEU plays a key role in the European legal landscape. Its decisions wield significant importance and authority. *Binding Effect, Supremacy of EU Law, Ensuring Uniform Application, Guardian of the Treaties* are the four principles that underscore the CJEU's pivotal role in shaping and upholding the European legal order.

CJEU decisions are binding on all EU member states. This means that national courts must interpret and apply EU law in accordance with CJEU rulings.

CJEU decisions uphold the supremacy of EU law over national laws. This principle, established in the landmark case of *Costa v. ENEL* (1964), asserts that EU law takes precedence over conflicting national laws.

CJEU decisions contribute to the uniform application and interpretation of EU law across member states, fostering legal certainty and consistency.

The CJEU acts as the guardian of the EU treaties, ensuring that member states and EU institutions comply with their obligations under EU law. The treaties also gave the Court of Justice of the European Union the exclusive authority to interpret EU treaties and legislation. This happens mainly through the preliminary ruling procedure, where national courts send questions to the CJEU about how to interpret EU law. Because it holds this monopoly on interpretation, the Court has been able to impose its case law consistently across all member states, creating an integrated legal order that takes precedence over national law.

These principles encapsulate the fundamental pillars upon which the CJEU operates, ensuring coherence, consistency, and the supremacy of EU law across member states. Through its rulings, the CJEU not only resolves legal disputes but also drives European integration and safeguards fundamental rights. As such, its decisions resonate far beyond individual cases, shaping the trajectory of European law and governance.

European case law is essentially made through preliminary rulings, direct actions, and appeals.

National courts can refer questions on the interpretation or validity of EU law to the CJEU for a *preliminary ruling*. This mechanism, outlined in Article 267 TFEU, allows the CJEU to provide authoritative interpretations of EU law.

Individuals, businesses, and member states can bring *direct actions* before the CJEU, challenging the legality of EU legislation or the actions of EU institutions.

The CJEU hears *appeals* against decisions of the General Court, the lower court in the EU judicial system, in certain cases.

Examples of landmark cases and their impact include the following.

Van Gend en Loos (1963): In this highly important case, the CJEU established the principle of direct effect, which allows individuals to invoke certain provisions of EU law before national courts, even in the absence of implementing measures. In this case, a Dutch transport company challenged a customs duty imposed by the Netherlands, and the Court ruled that EU law could be invoked directly by individuals before national courts, establishing the principle of direct effect. The CJEU held that "The Community constitutes a new legal order of International Law for the benefit of which the states have limited their sovereign rights, and the subjects of which comprise not only member states but also their nationals."[35]

Costa v. ENEL (1964): This major case affirmed the supremacy of EU law over conflicting national laws, establishing a fundamental principle of the EU legal system. Here, an Italian citizen contested the nationalization of the electricity company ENEL, arguing it conflicted with Community law, and the Court affirmed the supremacy of EU law over national legislation. The CJEU established that

> By creating a Community of unlimited duration, having its own institutions, its own personality, its own legal capacity . . . the member states have limited their sovereign rights . . . and have thus created a body of law which binds both their nationals and themselves.[36]

35 Case C-26/62, *Van Gend en Loos v. Nederlandse Administratie der Belastingen* [1963] ECR 1, in which the Court established the principle of direct effect.

36 Case 6/64, *Costa v. ENEL* [1964] ECR 585, where the Court affirmed the supremacy of EU law over national laws.

Factortame (1990): The CJEU ruled that national courts must set aside national legislation conflicting with EU law, even if it conflicts with constitutional principles of the member state. This case arose when Spanish fishermen objected to UK rules restricting their fishing rights, and the Court held that national courts must set aside domestic laws conflicting with EU law, even constitutional ones. The CJEU affirmed that

> A national court which, in a case before it, is called upon to apply provisions of Community law is under a duty to give full effect to those provisions, if necessary refusing of its own motion to apply any conflicting provision of national legislation.[37]

Marleasing (1990): The CJEU introduced the principle of Marleasing obligation, requiring national courts to interpret domestic law in conformity with EU law, whenever possible. In this case, a Spanish company was sued for nullity under national law that conflicted with an EU directive, and the Court required judges to interpret national law in conformity with EU directives whenever possible. The CJEU affirmed that "In applying national law . . . the national court is required to interpret it in the light of the wording and the purpose of the directive in order to achieve the result pursued by the directive."[38]

Cassis de Dijon (1979): This case established the principle of mutual recognition, facilitating the free movement of goods within the EU by requiring member states to accept products legally marketed in another member state, unless justified on certain grounds. This case arose when German authorities refused to allow the import of a French liqueur due to alcohol content rules, and the Court introduced the principle of mutual recognition, ensuring goods lawfully marketed in one member state can circulate freely in others. The CJEU concluded that "There is therefore no valid reason why, provided that they have been lawfully produced and marketed in one of the member states, alcoholic beverages should not be introduced into any other member state."[39]

These landmark cases have had far-reaching implications, shaping the development of EU law and deepening the integration of the European legal order. They illustrate the CJEU's role as a key architect of European case law.

2.1.4 General Principles of European Union Law

The General Principles of European Law play a pivotal role within EU law. They act as supplementary legal foundations alongside treaties and legislation. These principles serve as tools for both states and individuals to contest Community actions and seek compensation for damages. The European Court of Justice integrates these principles into its judgments to ensure adherence to legal standards.

These General Principles encompass various key areas such as fundamental human rights, equality and non-discrimination, and procedural rights.

Examples of fundamental principles of EU law include: fundamental rights, legal certainty, proportionality, misuse of powers, subsidiarity, and equality before the law.

37 Case C-213/89, *Factortame Ltd. v. Secretary of State for Transport* [1990] ECR I-2433, where the Court ruled on the supremacy of EU law over national legislation.

38 Case C-106/89, *Marleasing SA v. La Comercial Internacional de Alimentación SA* [1990] ECR I-4135, where the Court introduced the principle of Marleasing obligation.

39 Case 120/78, *Rewe-Zentral AG v. Bundesmonopolverwaltung für Branntwein (Cassis de Dijon)* [1979] ECR 649, which established the principle of mutual recognition.

Fundamental rights are a core component of these general principles. Initially recognized in the case *Stauder v. City of Ulm* (1969), the ECJ affirmed that EU measures must not violate fundamental human rights, a stance further solidified in *International Handelsgesellschaft* (1970) and *J Nold v. Commission* (1974).[40]

The Charter of Fundamental Rights of the European Union, formalized in the 2007 Lisbon Treaty, now codifies these rights, integrating them into EU law and giving them the same legal standing as the treaties.

Consider a worker in Country A who is dismissed because of her pregnancy. She invokes the EU Charter's protection against discrimination, and the national court, applying EU law, rules in her favor. This shows how the Charter gives individuals enforceable rights equal in status to the treaties.

Legal certainty ensures that laws are clear, precise, and foreseeable, particularly concerning financial obligations. This principle prohibits retroactive laws and requires sufficient public information to enable compliance.

Suppose Country B introduces a new tax law and tries to apply it retroactively to transactions completed the year before. The national court strikes it down, citing the principle of legal certainty: people must be able to foresee their financial obligations and rely on existing law.

The doctrine of legitimate expectation protects those who act in good faith based on existing laws, ensuring that EU institutions cannot break promises that led parties to take specific actions, as seen in *Mulder v. Minister van Landbouw en Visserij* (1988).[41] This case arose when Mr. Mulder, a Dutch farmer, stopped milk production under an EU scheme that offered incentives to farmers who temporarily ceased production. Later, when milk quotas were introduced, he was refused a quota because he had taken part in that earlier scheme. He challenged this refusal, arguing it was unfair. The Court ruled that the EU institutions had violated the principle of legitimate expectations: farmers who had lawfully stopped production under an EU measure could not be penalized later by being excluded from the new quota system.

The principle of proportionality mandates that EU actions must be appropriate and necessary to achieve their objectives. First articulated in Federation Charbonniere de Belgique (1954), this principle ensures that measures do not excessively impact individuals.[42]

The dispute originated when Belgian coal traders challenged EU rules on coal pricing. They argued the measures went beyond what was necessary to regulate the market. The Court recognized for the first time that EU institutions must respect the principle of proportionality, ensuring their actions are not excessive compared to their aims.

The ECJ employs a three-part test to evaluate proportionality: suitability, necessity, and balance between the measure's impact and its objectives, as illustrated in cases like Fedesa (1990) and *Germany v. Council* (1993).[43]

The Fedesa case concerned a Council directive banning certain hormonal substances used in livestock farming. Farmers and industry groups argued the ban was disproportionate because it damaged their business. The Court upheld the directive, applying a three-part proportionality

40 Case 29/69 *Stauder v. City of Ulm* [1969] ECR 419, Case 11/70 Internationale *Handelsgesellschaft mbH v. Einfuhr- und Vorratsstelle für Getreide und Futtermittel* [1970] ECR 1125, Case 4/73 *J Nold KG v. Commission of the European Communities* [1974] ECR 491.

41 Case 120/86 *Mulder v. Minister van Landbouw en Visserij* [1988] ECR 2321.

42 Case 8/55 *Federation Charbonniere de Belgique v. High Authority of the European Coal and Steel Community* [1954] ECR 245.

43 Case C-331/88 *R v. Minister of Agriculture, Fisheries and Food, ex parte Fedesa* [1990] ECR I-4023; Case C-426/93 *Germany v. Council of the European Communities* [1995] ECR I-3723.

test: the measure was suitable for protecting public health, necessary given scientific uncertainty, and its burdens did not outweigh its objectives.

In the *Germany v. Council* case, Germany contested an EU regulation on agricultural subsidies, claiming it was too restrictive and violated proportionality. The Court found the regulation valid, stressing that while EU institutions have wide discretion in economic and agricultural policy, their measures must still be appropriate and necessary to achieve legitimate goals, without imposing excessive burdens.

This principle prevents the exercise of lawful power for purposes other than those intended. A decision by an EU institution constitutes a misuse of power if it primarily aims to achieve ends not stated in its mandate. An example is *Giuffrida v. Commission* (1976), where the ECJ found misuse of powers.[44]

The dispute concerned Mr. Giuffrida, an official at the European Commission, who challenged a staffing decision regarding his career progression. He argued that the Commission had acted for reasons other than those provided by the rules. The Court found that the Commission had indeed engaged in a misuse of powers, meaning it exercised its authority for purposes different from those for which it had been conferred. This case reinforced the principle that EU institutions must act strictly within the scope and purpose of their legal powers.

Subsidiarity ensures that decisions are made as closely as possible to the citizens, allocating action to the EU level only when more effective than national or local levels. Equality before the law mandates non-discrimination and equal treatment for all individuals under EU law.

The general principles of EU law, including fundamental rights, legal certainty, legitimate expectation, proportionality, and misuse of powers, ensure fairness and consistency in applying EU laws. These principles help maintain justice and respect for human rights across the Union.

2.2 *Procedures of European Union Law*

The European Union operates through well-defined legal procedures that ensure the creation, enforcement, and revision of its laws. This section explores key processes, including how EU legislation is adopted, how compliance with EU law is reviewed, the legal remedies available to individuals, and how treaties are revised. These procedures help maintain the effectiveness and consistency of EU law across member states.

2.2.1 *European Legislative Procedure*

In this part, we analyze the ordinary legislative procedure and the respective roles of the European Parliament, the Council of the EU, and the European Commission.

The ordinary legislative procedure, previously known as the codecision procedure, was introduced in 1992 and expanded in 1999. It was renamed following the adoption of the Lisbon Treaty, becoming the main method for adopting EU legislation. This procedure involves three key institutions: the European Commission, which holds the right of legislative initiative, and the Council of the EU and the European Parliament, which act as co-legislators. It applies to around 85 policy areas, ensuring a collaborative approach to law-making within the EU.

These policy areas cover a wide range of fields, including the internal market, consumer protection, environment, transport, energy, asylum and immigration, and the free movement of workers. In all these domains, the European Parliament and the Council act as co-legislators under the ordinary legislative procedure.

44 *Giuffrida v. Commission of the European Communities Case* 105/75 [1976] ECR 1395.

The legal base of the ordinary legislative procedure is Articles 289 and 294 of the Treaty on the Functioning of the European Union.

The process begins with the European Commission submitting a proposal to both the Council and the Parliament. During the first reading, the Parliament reviews and can amend the proposal, which the Council then either accepts or modifies, sending it back for a second reading. If disagreements persist after the second reading, a conciliation committee is formed to reach a consensus. If both institutions approve the joint text from this committee, the legislative act is adopted. If a proposal is rejected at any stage, the procedure ends and must be restarted with a new proposal from the Commission.

This structured approach balances input from various EU bodies to create comprehensive and agreed-upon legislation.

Special methods of European legislation: consultation procedure and cooperation procedure.

Under Article 289 of the Treaty on the Functioning of the European Union (TFEU), the consultation procedure is a special legislative process that serves as an exception to the ordinary legislative procedure outlined in Article 294.

Article 289

1. The ordinary legislative procedure shall consist in the joint adoption by the European Parliament and the Council of a regulation, directive or decision on a proposal from the Commission. This procedure is defined in Article 294.
2. In the specific cases provided for by the Treaties, the adoption of a regulation, directive or decision by the European Parliament with the participation of the Council, or by the latter with the participation of the European Parliament, shall constitute a special legislative procedure.
3. Legal acts adopted by legislative procedure shall constitute legislative acts.
4. In the specific cases provided for by the Treaties, legislative acts may be adopted on the initiative of a group of member states or of the European Parliament, on a recommendation from the European Central Bank or at the request of the Court of Justice or the European Investment Bank.

This procedure requires the Council to consider the opinion of the European Parliament and, where specified in the Treaties, the opinions of the European Economic and Social Committee, the Committee of the Regions, and the European Central Bank.

While the Council must consult the Parliament, it is not obliged to follow the Parliament's recommendations. If the Council fails to consult the Parliament, the resulting act can be deemed illegal and subject to annulment by the Court of Justice. Additionally, if the Council intends to make significant changes to the proposal, it must consult the Parliament again.

This procedure is used in a limited range of policy areas, such as exemptions from internal market rules, competition law, financial matters, intellectual property, and administrative issues. It also applies to the adoption of instruments like recommendations and opinions issued by the Council and the Commission.

The 2007 Treaty of Lisbon has abrogated the cooperation procedure, primarily employed in economic and monetary domains. Even though the European Parliament had substantial influence, it couldn't stop legislative proposals completely in this system. Basically, the process involved several steps: the European Commission made proposals, then the European Parliament gave its opinion, and finally, the Council of Ministers made a decision. The European Parliament could agree or disagree with the Council, and then the Council would vote on the proposal, either approving or rejecting it unanimously.

2.2.2 Procedure for Reviewing Compliance With EU Law

First, we examine the preliminary ruling procedure and the CJEU's role in ensuring the uniform interpretation of EU law.

The preliminary ruling procedure is used when a national court faces a question about the interpretation or validity of EU law that is essential for resolving a case. The national court can refer the question to the CJEU, which will provide a ruling that helps the national court make its final judgment.

For instance, a court in Spain is unsure whether an EU consumer protection directive applies to online contracts. The Spanish court hears a dispute between a consumer and an online retailer about whether the 14-day withdrawal period in an EU consumer protection directive applies to digital downloads. Unsure how to interpret the directive, the court refers the question to the CJEU, which clarifies the rule before the Spanish court issues its ruling.

Similarly, consider a Polish court dealing with a case where a food company challenges national rules requiring larger warning labels than those set by an EU regulation. The court doubts whether the national rules are compatible with EU law and refers the matter to the CJEU, which decides on the regulation's validity and guides the Polish court's judgment.

In a real case, the 1987 Foto-Frost case (Case 314/85), a German court questioned the validity of an EU customs decision imposing import duties. The CJEU held that although national courts may doubt the validity of EU acts, only the CJEU itself can declare them invalid, to safeguard the consistency and uniformity of EU law.

This process ensures the consistent application of EU law across member states. The national court must clearly outline the legal and factual context of the case and suspend national proceedings until the CJEU gives its ruling.

The recommendations to national courts regarding preliminary ruling proceedings aim to guide EU member states' courts on how to refer questions to the Court of Justice of the European Union (CJEU) under Article 267 of the Treaty on the Functioning of the European Union and Article 19(3) of the Treaty on European Union.

These recommendations explain the purpose of the procedure, the proper format for referrals, and the scope of the preliminary ruling process. They ensure that national courts know how to effectively seek a preliminary ruling, which is crucial for the uniform application of EU law. The recommendations emphasize the importance of clear, concise referrals and the need for national courts to keep the CJEU informed of any developments in the case.

An example of preliminary ruling procedure in action is the following scenario. Imagine a German court hears a case from a chemical company in Hamburg. The company challenges a national rule requiring factories to cut CO_2 emissions 30% more than EU law demands. It argues this is unfair because firms in other countries follow the lower EU standard. Unsure how to interpret the EU directive, the German court refers the case to the CJEU.

The steps in such a preliminary ruling procedure would be the following.

- The German company files a lawsuit in a German court, claiming that the national regulation violates EU law (Initiation of the Case).
- The German court, unsure about the interpretation of the relevant EU directive, decides that a ruling from the Court of Justice of the European Union is necessary to resolve the case. The court drafts a referral, outlining the legal and factual context and specifying the questions about the interpretation of the EU directive (National Court Referral).
- The referral is sent to the CJEU, requesting a preliminary ruling on whether the German regulation is compatible with the EU directive (Submission to the CJEU).

- The CJEU reviews the referral. It considers written observations submitted by the German Government, the European Commission, and other interested parties. The CJEU then interprets the relevant EU law (CJEU Deliberation).
- The CJEU issues a preliminary ruling, clarifying the interpretation of the EU directive. It determines that the directive sets minimum standards, allowing member states to impose stricter environmental regulations if they choose (CJEU Ruling).
- The German court receives the CJEU's ruling. It applies the interpretation provided by the CJEU to the case at hand. The court concludes that the German regulation is compatible with the EU directive, as member states are permitted to enforce stricter environmental standards (Application of the Ruling).
- The German court makes its final decision based on the CJEU's ruling, dismissing the company's claim (Final Judgment).
- We now turn to infringement proceedings, the mechanism ensuring member states' compliance with EU law.

Infringement proceedings are mechanisms used by the European Commission to ensure that EU member states comply with EU law. For example, a country that fails to implement an EU directive on air quality standards may first receive a formal notice, and if it still does not act, the case can be brought before the CJEU. Similarly, if a state introduces unlawful customs checks on goods from other EU countries, the Commission can launch proceedings to restore the free movement of goods.

A real case is *Commission v. France* (Spanish Strawberries, Case C-265/95), where the CJEU held that France had infringed EU law by failing to stop farmers from blocking imports of Spanish strawberries and Belgian tomatoes, thereby breaching the principle of free movement of goods.

According to articles 258, 259, and 260 of the TFEU, the Commission can initiate an infringement procedure against an EU country that does not implement EU law. The Commission can take the matter to the Court of Justice, which has the authority to impose financial penalties.

The process begins with an investigation into potential breaches, which can be triggered by complaints, own-initiative inquiries, or information from various sources.

Initially, the Commission often engages in an informal dialogue with the member state to clarify the issue and seek a resolution. If this informal approach does not yield results, the Commission sends a formal notice, known as a letter of formal notice, outlining the alleged breach and requesting a response from the member state.

If the member state's response is unsatisfactory, the Commission issues a reasoned opinion detailing the infringement and setting a deadline for compliance. Should the member state still fail to comply, the Commission can refer the case to the Court of Justice of the European Union (CJEU). The CJEU then examines the case and issues a judgment. If the Court finds an infringement, the member state must take necessary measures to comply. If compliance is not achieved, the Commission can request the CJEU to impose financial penalties. This structured process ensures the uniform application and enforcement of EU laws across all member states, maintaining the integrity of the EU legal framework.

2.2.3 Individual Remedies Procedure

The Individual Remedies Procedure allows individuals and companies to assert their rights under EU law before national and European courts. This procedure provides access to justice and avenues of recourse in cases where they believe their rights have been violated by a member state or an EU institution.

Individuals and companies can bring their cases to national courts, which may refer questions of EU law to the Court of Justice of the European Union (CJEU) for a preliminary ruling. They can also directly approach the CJEU if they are directly and individually affected by an EU act. This ensures that their rights under EU law are protected and enforced effectively.

Imagine a small business in Italy that imports products from another EU country. If the Italian Government imposes unfair taxes on these imports, violating EU rules on free movement of goods, the business can take action.

First, the company can go to an Italian court to challenge the taxes. If the court needs clarification on EU law, it can ask the Court of Justice of the European Union (CJEU) for a ruling. Alternatively, if the company is directly affected by an EU regulation, it can bring its case directly to the CJEU. This way, the company can seek justice and ensure that its rights under EU law are respected.

Consider an employee in Spain who works more than the maximum weekly hours set by the EU Working Time Directive. If Spanish law or practice fails to respect these limits, the worker can bring a claim before a Spanish court. The court may then refer the question to the CJEU for clarification. If the worker is directly and individually affected by an EU measure – for example, if an EU regulation excluded certain workers from protections – he could also challenge it directly before the CJEU, ensuring his rights under EU law are upheld.

The Individual Remedies Procedure under the Treaty on the Functioning of the European Union is supported by several key articles. Article 258 allows the European Commission to take action against member states that fail to comply with EU law, potentially leading to infringement proceedings. Article 259 enables member states to bring cases against each other for non-compliance. Article 260 outlines the consequences for member states that do not comply with CJEU judgments, including financial penalties. Article 263 allows individuals and companies to challenge EU acts directly before the CJEU if they are directly and individually affected. Finally, Article 267 enables national courts to refer questions of EU law to the CJEU for a preliminary ruling, ensuring consistent interpretation and application of EU law across member states.

These provisions ensure that individuals and companies can assert their rights and seek remedies under EU law.

2.2.4 Treaty Revision Procedure

The Treaty Revision Procedure outlines the mechanisms and conditions for making changes to the founding treaties of the European Union. This involves a structured process where member states negotiate and agree upon amendments to the treaties.

The legal implications of treaty revisions are significant, as they can alter the legal framework within which the EU operates. This can include changes to the distribution of powers between EU institutions and member states, as well as adjustments to the rights and obligations of both.

Politically, treaty revisions can be complex and sensitive, requiring consensus among member states and often involving extensive negotiations. The outcome of these revisions can shape the direction and functioning of the EU, impacting its policies, decision-making processes, and relationships with its member states and external partners.

The Treaty on the Functioning of the European Union does not directly outline a Treaty Revision Procedure, but the process is primarily detailed in Articles 48 to 51 of the Treaty on European Union. These articles establish a structured process for amending EU treaties, involving initiation by various EU institutions or member states, proposal through a Convention, unanimous agreement among member states, and ratification according to national constitutional requirements. This ensures a transparent and democratic approach to making changes to the EU treaties, balancing the interests of the EU institutions and member states.

We now turn to policy areas and economic integration, which define the scope of EU action.

3 Policy Areas and Economic Integration

The European Union manages a range of policies and economic initiatives to integrate and support its member states. This section covers key areas like trade, agriculture, the single market, enlargement, and Common Foreign and Security Policy. Together, these efforts aim to promote economic stability, social cohesion, and international peace.

3.1 EU Policies

The European Union oversees a comprehensive range of policies, including trade, agriculture, competition, environment, migration, and social policy. These policies shape the economic, social, and environmental landscape of the EU member states. Through regulatory frameworks and cooperation mechanisms, the EU aims to foster economic growth, ensure fair competition, promote sustainable agriculture practices, protect the environment, manage migration flows, and enhance social cohesion across its diverse member states.

3.1.1 Agriculture and Rural Development

The EU's Agriculture and Rural Development sector, overseen by the Directorate-General for Agriculture and Rural Development, supports farmers, ensures food security, protects the environment, and boosts rural economies.[45] The Common Agricultural Policy (CAP) partners with farmers to promote sustainability, income, and market stability. Each EU country implements the CAP through strategic plans, with initiatives to encourage young farmers and enhance rural development. The CAP also focuses on sustainable agriculture by combining social, environmental, and economic strategies. The EU facilitates global agricultural trade and food security, providing comprehensive data on markets, production, prices, and trade. Various initiatives and consultations aim to shape a fairer, healthier, and greener future for agriculture.

In short, the EU's agricultural policy guides how Europe produces food, protects the environment, and supports rural communities, ensuring that farming remains sustainable and resilient in the years ahead.

3.1.2 Competition and Trade Policies

Competition policy in the EU ensures companies compete fairly, benefitting consumers with better products and prices.[46] The European Commission oversees this by preventing anti-competitive practices such as abuse of dominant market positions, cartels, and unfair mergers. It also regulates state aid to avoid market distortion. Various EU institutions, including the European Parliament, the European Council, and the European Court of Justice, play roles in shaping

45 See, for example, Gelhaus, Laura, 2024, *The EU's External Governance of Agriculture and Rural Development: Shaping Rural Spaces*, 1st ed., Routledge.

46 See, for example, Gelhaus, Laura, 2024, *The EU's External Governance of Agriculture and Rural Development: Shaping Rural Spaces*, 1st ed., Routledge.

and enforcing these rules. The Commission collaborates with national competition authorities to maintain consistent application across the EU. Public consultations are used to gather input on competition-related issues, ensuring policies reflect stakeholder concerns.

Trade policy in the EU aims to help EU companies compete fairly in the global market and promote sustainable development. It involves making trade agreements with non-EU countries, setting tariffs, and protecting against unfair trade practices. The EU focuses on free and fair trade, economic growth, job creation, and also ensures environmental protection and human rights.

Together, these policies help the EU create a fair, open, and predictable economic system that benefits both businesses and consumers.

3.1.3 Environmental, Migration, and Social Policies

EU Environmental Policy, outlined in various action programs since the 1970s, currently centers around the 8th Environment Action Program (EAP) guiding policy until 2030. Aligned with the European Green Deal, the 8th EAP aims for a climate-neutral, resource-efficient economy that enhances biodiversity and reduces pollution. It emphasizes stakeholder engagement and monitoring frameworks for effective implementation across EU member states.[47] The EU is committed to reaching climate-neutrality by 2050 as part of its global climate action under the Paris Agreement.

The EU and its member states are working to create a unified, humanitarian, and safe migration policy.[48] The European Council sets priorities and mandates negotiations with non-EU countries, while also adopting laws and programs. In response to crises, the Council activated political crisis response tools in 2015. Recently, the EU adopted a pact to improve asylum procedures and solidarity among member states. The EU manages legal migration, asylum requests, and returns of illegal migrants. Migration mainly occurs through three routes: Eastern Mediterranean, Western Mediterranean and Western African, and the Western Balkans, with an additional route from Ukraine due to conflict. Data and infographics show migration trends from 2015 to 2024, highlighting EU efforts in managing migration and asylum challenges.

Alongside environmental and migration policies, the EU also pursues social objectives, as set out in Article 151 TFEU and Articles 6 and 9 TEU.

Article 151 of the Treaty on the Functioning of the European Union outlines the EU's social policy goals: promoting employment, improving working conditions, ensuring equal treatment, providing social protection, fostering social dialogue, and developing human resources for sustainable employment.[49] Article 6 of the Treaty on European Union binds the EU Charter of Fundamental Rights' social rights. Article 9 of the Treaty on the Functioning of the EU adds a social clause requiring EU policies to meet key social needs. While member states manage most social policies, the EU can set minimum standards through directives. These directives cover worker safety, conditions, social security, equality, and integrating marginalized groups into the job market, often with input from social partners.

47 See, for example, Jordan, Andrew and Gravey, Viviane, 2021, *Environmental Policy in the EU: Actors, Institutions and Processes*, 4th ed., Routledge.

48 Ceccorulli, Michela and Fassi, Elena (eds.), 2022, *The EU's External Governance of Migration: Perspectives of Justice*, 1st ed., Routledge.

49 Kyriazi, Anna, Miró, Júlia, Natili, Marcello and Ronchi, Stefano, 2024, *Social Policy and EU Polity-Building through Crises and Beyond*, 1st ed., Routledge.

3.2 Single Market and Economic Integration

At the core of the EU's economic integration efforts lies the single market, which facilitates the free movement of goods, services, capital, and labor among member states. The principles of the single market are underpinned by efforts to eliminate trade barriers, harmonize regulations, and promote competition. Furthermore, the EU has established an economic and monetary union (EMU), including the adoption of the euro currency in the Eurozone. These mechanisms play a vital role in promoting economic stability, fostering cross-border investments, and facilitating trade within the EU.[50]

3.2.1 Legal Framework and Principles

The Single Market of the EU operates under a robust legal framework primarily defined by the EU Treaties, particularly the Treaty on the Functioning of the European Union. Articles 26 to 62 of the TFEU establish principles such as non-discrimination, free movement of goods, services, establishment, and competition policy.

To implement and enforce these principles, the EU also adopts secondary legislation, including regulations, directives, and decisions. To recall, regulations are directly applicable across all member states, while directives require member states to transpose them into their national laws.

Together, the Treaties and secondary legislation provide a coherent legal structure that removes barriers, harmonizes standards, and ensures that the Single Market functions consistently throughout the EU. This framework creates a predictable legal environment for businesses and consumers, promotes economic integration, and ensures that rights granted under EU law can be exercised uniformly across member states.

3.2.2 The Court of Justice of the European Union and the Enforcement of Single Market Rules

The Court of Justice of the European Union plays a crucial role in interpreting and enforcing Single Market rules through case law. Key principles established through CJEU rulings include direct effect (allowing individuals to invoke EU law in national courts), supremacy of EU law over conflicting national laws, proportionality in member states' actions, and rules on state aid. Among the CJEU's landmark decisions that have shaped the single market rule, several cases stand out.

In *Van Gend en Loos* (1963, Case 26/62), a Dutch company contested customs duties higher than EU rules allowed, leading the Court to establish the principle of direct effect, enabling individuals to invoke EU law in national courts. In *Cassis de Dijon* (1979, Case 120/78), German authorities blocked the import of a French liqueur for not meeting local alcohol content standards; the Court responded with the principle of mutual recognition to ensure the free movement of goods. The *Bosman ruling* (1995, Case C-415/93) arose when a Belgian footballer was prevented from transferring clubs freely, prompting the Court to affirm the free movement of workers in professional sports. In *Schrems v. Data Protection Commissioner* (2015, Case C-362/14), an Austrian citizen challenged Facebook's transfer of personal data to the U.S., resulting in the

50 Egan, Michelle P., 2015, "Conclusion," in *Single Markets: Economic Integration in Europe and the United States*, online ed., Oxford Academic, Oxford, 19 March. https://doi.org/10.1093/acprof:oso/9780199280506.003.0008. Accessed 6 July 2024.

invalidation of the Safe Harbor framework and stronger data protection standards. Finally, in *European Commission v. Council* (2015, Case C-425/13), the Commission challenged a Council decision on state aid, and the Court clarified the division of powers in EU competition law.

These cases illustrate how the CJEU's decisions contribute to ensuring the coherence and effectiveness of the Single Market, promoting economic integration while upholding fundamental EU principles.

3.2.3 Economic and Monetary Union

The EU has established an Economic and Monetary Union (EMU), which includes the adoption of the euro currency in the Eurozone. The EMU aims to promote economic stability, foster cross-border investments, and facilitate trade within the EU. The euro is the second most traded currency in the world, enhancing economic cohesion among member states.

For instance, by adopting the euro, a company in France can sell goods in Spain or Italy without facing exchange rate risks or currency conversion costs. This makes cross-border trade simpler and more predictable, fostering investment and integration within the single market. Likewise, a student from Portugal studying in Germany can easily use the same currency for everyday expenses, avoiding exchange rate costs and making life abroad simpler.

The European Central Bank (ECB) manages the euro and monetary policy, working to maintain price stability and support economic growth. The Stability and Growth Pact sets fiscal rules to ensure member states maintain sound public finances.[51]

For example, if a member state's budget deficit exceeds 3% of GDP, the Stability and Growth Pact allows the European Commission to issue warnings and, if necessary, recommend sanctions to bring its finances back in line. During the Eurozone debt crisis in 2009–2010, Greece repeatedly exceeded the 3% deficit limit and breached the debt threshold set by the Stability and Growth Pact. The European Commission launched excessive deficit procedures and imposed strict monitoring, eventually linking compliance with access to EU financial assistance. In 2016, Spain and Portugal also failed to reduce their excessive deficits, leading the Commission to recommend financial sanctions for the first time, though the Council ultimately decided not to impose them.

3.3 Enlargement, Neighborhood Policy, and Regional Development

The European Union expands its influence through enlargement, partnerships with neighboring countries, and regional development initiatives. This section examines the enlargement policy, which governs how new countries join the EU, the neighborhood policy, which strengthens ties with non-member states, and regional development efforts aimed at reducing economic disparities within the EU.

3.3.1 Enlargement Policy

The EU enlargement policy aims to integrate eligible countries into the European Union, promoting stability, democracy, and economic prosperity. Candidate countries' progress in implementing EU-aligned reforms is assessed, with the EU providing financial assistance and

51 Howarth, David and Verdun, Amy (eds.), 2023, *Economic and Monetary Union at Twenty: A Stocktaking of a Tumultuous Second Decade*, 1st ed., Routledge.

supporting socio-economic development to prepare them for accession.[52] The goal is to extend EU membership benefits, foster regional cooperation, and strengthen ties with neighboring countries, enhancing peace, security, and economic growth across Europe.

The EU's enlargement policy can be seen in practice through several examples. Croatia joined the Union in 2013 after years of reforms in governance, the Rule of Law, and border management. Today, candidate countries from the Western Balkans, such as Serbia, Montenegro, North Macedonia, and Albania, continue to work on EU-aligned reforms with financial and technical support. It should also be recalled that, more recently, in 2022, Ukraine and Moldova were granted candidate status, showing how enlargement also serves as a strategic tool to promote stability and security in Europe.

These examples illustrate how enlargement strengthens both the EU and its neighbors by promoting democracy, cooperation, and shared prosperity.

3.3.2 Neighborhood Policy

The Directorate-General for Neighborhood and Enlargement Negotiations (DG NEAR) leads the EU's efforts in this regard, working closely with the European External Action Service and thematic directorates. DG NEAR implements assistance actions in Europe's eastern and southern neighborhoods, focusing on reform, democratic consolidation, prosperity, stability, and security. It also supports EU values and policies in these regions, fostering a special relationship with neighboring countries.

For example, under the European Neighborhood Policy, the EU provides financial and technical support to countries like Ukraine, Georgia, and Moldova in the east, and to Morocco, Tunisia, and Jordan in the south. These programs promote democratic reforms, economic development, and regional stability, while strengthening cooperation with the EU. Through these initiatives, the EU seeks to create a stable and cooperative neighborhood, reducing political risks at its borders and encouraging long-term partnerships that benefit both the Union and its neighboring regions.

3.3.3 Regional Development

In the enlargement process, DG NEAR assists candidate countries in meeting EU criteria and monitors their progress during accession negotiations mandated by the Council. The DG manages bilateral relations with these countries, emphasizing reforms in Rule of Law, economic governance, and public administration. Specifically for the Western Balkans, DG NEAR implements the EU's stabilization and association policy as defined by the European Council.

DG NEAR coordinates the majority of the EU's financial and technical assistance to neighborhood and enlargement countries. Headquartered in Brussels with approximately 1,650 staff members, DG NEAR operates under the oversight of Commissioner Olivér Várhelyi and Director-General Gert Jan Koopman. The 2023 Enlargement Package assesses reform progress in the Western Balkans, Turkey, Georgia, Moldova, and Ukraine, setting priorities for future reforms. A new Growth Plan for the Western Balkans aims to accelerate economic convergence with the EU, supported by a €6 billion Reform and Growth Facility for 2024–2027. Amid

52 Gateva, Eli, 2019, "Enlargement Policy and European Union Politics," *Oxford Research Encyclopedia of Politics*, online. https://doi.org/10.1093/acrefore/9780190228637.013.1104. Accessed 6 July 2024.

ongoing Russian aggression, the EU remains committed to supporting Ukraine politically, financially, and humanitarianly, with extensive sanctions in response.

3.4 European Foreign and Security Policy

The European Union plays a key role in global diplomacy and security through its foreign and security policy. This section explores the policy framework and legal basis, the EU's diplomatic efforts and missions, and the current challenges and strategic priorities shaping its global engagement.

3.4.1 Policy Framework and Legal Basis

EU foreign and security policy is designed to uphold peace, enhance international security, foster cooperation, and promote democracy, the Rule of Law, and human rights globally. This policy framework operates through diplomacy, adherence to international rules, and engages in trade, humanitarian aid, and development cooperation. The EU engages with key global players and regional groups based on mutual interests and benefits.

The legal framework for the EU's Common Foreign and Security Policy (CFSP) is set out in the Treaty on European Union, mainly in Title V (Articles 21–46 TEU). Decisions are taken jointly by the European Council, made up of EU heads of State and government, and by the Council of the EU. Most decisions in this area require unanimous agreement among all member states, reflecting the sensitivity of foreign and security matters. While the European Commission and the European Parliament have more limited roles, the High Representative of the Union for Foreign Affairs and Security Policy ensures coordination and represents the EU externally.[53]

For example, under the CFSP framework, the EU unanimously decided in 2022 to impose sanctions on Russia following its invasion of Ukraine. These measures targeted individuals, companies, and sectors of the Russian economy, showing how the EU uses foreign and security policy tools to uphold International Law, protect peace, and defend its values.

3.4.2 Diplomatic Efforts and Missions

The Common Foreign and Security Policy provides the overarching framework for the EU's external action, setting out its objectives and decision-making process. Diplomatic efforts and missions are the instruments through which this policy is put into practice. Central to this is the European External Action Service (EEAS), the EU's diplomatic arm with over 140 delegations and offices worldwide, which works to promote and safeguard EU values and interests.

In addition, under the Common Security and Defence Policy, the EU can deploy civilian and military missions, using forces contributed by member states. While the EU does not have a standing army, these missions have included peacekeeping operations, support for the Rule of Law, maintaining order in conflict zones, and providing humanitarian aid.

For example, Operation Atalanta, mentioned before and launched in 2008, has successfully protected shipping routes off the coast of Somalia and escorted humanitarian aid deliveries,

53 McNamara, Kathleen R., 2015, "European Foreign Policy," in *The Politics of Everyday Europe: Constructing Authority in the European Union*, online ed., Oxford Academic, 18 June. https://doi.org/10.1093/acprof:oso/9780198716235.003.0007. Accessed 6 July 2024.

while EULEX Kosovo has supported the Rule of Law since 2008 by assisting local authorities in strengthening police, justice, and customs institutions.

More recently, the EU established the EU Military Assistance Mission (EUMAM Ukraine) in 2022 to train Ukrainian armed forces, showing how the EU adapts its missions to current global challenges.

3.4.3 Current Challenges and Strategic Focus

Examples of EU actions in foreign policy include participating in peacekeeping missions, supporting conflict resolution efforts, providing humanitarian aid in crisis zones, and engaging in diplomatic initiatives to uphold International Law and human rights standards. The EU's foreign policy also includes strategic partnerships with emerging powers and regional groups to address global challenges effectively.

At present, Europe confronts several crises, including the ongoing Russian conflict with Ukraine, Israel's conflict with Hamas, and the Iran-backed Houthi attacks in the Red Sea, impacting global trade significantly.

At present, Europe confronts several crises close to its borders, though not within the EU itself. These include Russia's ongoing war against Ukraine, Israel's conflict with Hamas, and Iran-backed Houthi attacks in the Red Sea, which have significantly disrupted global trade. While these conflicts take place outside Europe, their proximity directly affects European security and economic stability.

The EU lacks global influence. If it were a major player, it would have a credible foreign, security, and defense policy. It could play a role in the Middle East, where it has supported the Palestinian Authority and built ties with Israel. Europe's divided response to the Israel-Hamas conflict highlights the lack of a unified foreign policy, which weakens its ability to act decisively in the Middle East. Yet, as a major regional and global actor with strong economic, diplomatic, and humanitarian tools, the EU has the potential to play a more influential role if member states align their positions.

With weak security and defense policies, Europe should focus on strengthening ties with NATO. This would enhance its security and responsibility, especially as U.S. commitments are uncertain. Better cooperation with NATO could also help Ukraine.

However, U.S. President Donald Trump's position on NATO has increased pressure on European members to increase defense spending and question the certainty of U.S. guarantees. This situation highlights the ongoing challenge for Europe to strengthen its strategic autonomy and build a more reliable security framework.

4 Governance, Democracy, and Citizenship

Having previously explored the structure and functions of EU Institutions and Decision-Making, we now turn to the broader aspects of Governance, Democracy, and Citizenship within the European Union. This section delves into the mechanisms of democratic governance, the rights and responsibilities of EU citizens, and the social and cultural dimensions that underpin the EU's commitment to creating a cohesive and inclusive European community.

4.1 Democratic Governance and Participation

Democracy is a fundamental principle of the European Union, ensuring transparency, accountability, and citizen involvement in decision-making. This section explores the EU's democratic framework, the role of European Parliament elections, the influence of political parties and groups, and the instruments used to support and strengthen democracy across the Union.

4.1.1 Democratic Framework and Legitimacy

The EU is committed to promoting democratic governance both within its member states and in its partner countries. This commitment is reflected through various initiatives and support mechanisms designed to enhance political participation, transparency, accountability, and the protection of fundamental rights.

The EU's democratic legitimacy has been debated since the late 1970s when the European Parliament was established. Initially, voter turnout for these elections was low but has varied over the years. The term *democratic deficit* arose to describe concerns about citizen participation, representation, and accountability within EU institutions. Critics point to the European Commission, which initiates legislation without direct election. Efforts to address these concerns include giving EU citizens more rights and giving greater powers to the Parliament, but low voter turnout persists. There's an ongoing debate about whether the EU needs reforms to enhance its democratic credibility.

The European Union's foundational treaties, such as the Treaty on European Union and the Treaty on the Functioning of the European Union, mandate that the election and appointment processes for EU institutions are transparent and democratic. These treaties emphasize representative democracy as the core principle of EU governance.

The guiding principles are, firstly, that citizens are directly represented at the EU level in the European Parliament; secondly, that EU countries are represented by their heads of State or government in the European Council and by their governments in the Council of the EU.

4.1.2 European Parliament Elections

The European elections are a vital part of the European Union's democratic process, allowing EU citizens to vote directly for Members of the European Parliament (MEPs). These elections are held every five years, and the most recent took place on June 6–9, 2024. The European Parliament is composed of 720 MEPs, who are elected according to national electoral laws and traditions in each EU country.

The European elections of 2024 had major political consequences in France. After the National Rally's victory, President Macron invoked Article 12 of the French Constitution to dissolve the National Assembly, claiming the country needed clarity and a renewed democratic mandate. This decision triggered early French parliamentary elections, resulting in a deeply fragmented parliament with no single party holding a majority – marking the beginning of a political crisis.

As a result, France entered a period where minority governments could be voted out by opponents, with those opponents unable to agree on forming a new government themselves. Thus, Prime Minister Michel Barnier, former French Minister of Agriculture, European Commissioner, and chief Brexit negotiator for the European Union, saw his government brought down by a no-confidence vote in December 2024. Then, Prime Minister François Bayrou, leader of the centrist MoDem party, failed to win a vote of confidence in September 2025, forcing him to resign. The former Minister of the Armed Forces, Sébastien Lecornu, was subsequently appointed Prime Minister.

This series of events shows how, in France's semi-presidential political system, dissolving parliament without a clear plan for what comes next can lead to political gridlock, economic uncertainty, and ongoing public unrest – all triggered by an election focused on European, not national, issues.

The European Parliament started as the Common Assembly of the European Coal and Steel Community (ECSC) in 1952. At first, it had no real power, but it grew in importance. By 1979, it became more influential, and the 1976 EU election act allowed members to be directly elected by voters.

The first direct elections to the European Parliament were held from June 7–10, 1979. This was historic because it was the first time citizens of the European Economic Community could directly elect their representatives.

MEPs join political groups within the Parliament based on their political affinities, although some remain "non-attached." The Parliament acts as a co-legislator, working on an equal footing with the Council of the EU on most issues. It decides on new legislation proposed by the European Commission, votes on trade agreements, and scrutinizes the EU institutions and the EU budget.

The Parliament also has significant powers of appointment, including voting for its own President and electing the President of the European Commission. The Parliament must approve the new Commission President proposed by the European Council and vet Commissioners proposed by the Council in agreement with the President-elect of the Commission. It also approves the entire European Commission through a single vote of consent and holds supervisory powers over other EU institutions, including the ability to adopt a vote of no-confidence to dismiss the Commission.

This democratic process ensures that EU citizens have a direct say in the governance of the European Union, influencing key decisions and leadership appointments through their elected representatives in the European Parliament.

4.1.3 European Political Parties and Political Groups

The Authority for European Political Parties and European Political Foundations registers and oversees political parties and foundations in the EU. It ensures they follow EU laws, promoting transparency and accountability. This Authority manages a detailed register and provides information upon request for legal or administrative purposes.

Main European political parties include:

- The European People's Party (EPP): The EPP represents the center-right in Europe, focusing on justice, solidarity, and responsibility. The EPP supports a strong EU based on democracy, a social market economy, and environmental sustainability.
- Party of European Socialists (PES): PES unites socialist and social democratic parties. PES promotes social fairness, equality, and well-being, aiming for a progressive and sustainable Europe.
- Alliance of Liberals and Democrats for Europe Party (ALDE): ALDE champions a liberal vision of freedom, democracy, entrepreneurship, and sustainability. The party strives to protect European values and build a more liberal and prosperous Europe.
- European Democratic Party (EDP): EDP brings together parties that want a closer connection between the EU and its citizens. The EDP advocates for peace, freedom, solidarity, and education.
- European Green Party (EGP): EGP focuses on environmental responsibility, social justice, and inclusion. The party works to combat climate change and social inequalities, aiming for a greener and safer Europe.
- European Free Alliance (EFA): EFA supports regions and minorities seeking greater autonomy or independence. The EFA promotes European unity, diversity, and social justice.

- European Conservatives and Reformists Party (ECR): ECR values individual liberty, national sovereignty, and limited government. The ECR seeks to reform the EU based on free trade, family values, and decentralization.
- Party of the European Left (PEL): PEL unites left-wing parties for a socially just society. PEL focuses on peace, diversity, and social justice.
- European Christian Political Movement (ECPM):s ECPM promotes Christian values in politics, focusing on human dignity, healthy families, and an economy benefiting people and the planet.

Members of the European Parliament (MEPs) are organized by political affiliation, not nationality. Currently, there are seven political groups in the European Parliament.

To form a political group, at least 23 MEPs from at least one-quarter of the EU member states are required. MEPs can only belong to one political group. Those who do not belong to any group are known as non-attached Members. Each political group manages its own internal organization, appointing a chair, a bureau, and a secretariat. Seating in the Chamber is arranged by political affiliation, from left to right, in agreement with the group chairs.

Before plenary votes, political groups review reports from parliamentary committees and propose amendments. Each group's position is determined through internal discussions. MEPs cannot be forced to vote in a particular way, ensuring individual freedom in decision-making.

Current political groups include:

- The Group of the European People's Party (Christian Democrats)
- The Group of the Progressive Alliance of Socialists and Democrats in the European Parliament
- The Renew Europe Group
- The Group of the Greens/European Free Alliance
- The European Conservatives and Reformists Group
- The Identity and Democracy Group
- The Left group in the European Parliament – GUE/NGL

Together, these parties and groups structure political debate in the European Parliament and shape the EU's legislative agenda through negotiation, coalition-building, and democratic discussion.

4.1.4 Democracy Support Instruments

The European Instrument for Democracy and Human Rights (EIDHR) is a thematic funding instrument for supporting human rights, fundamental freedoms, and democracy projects outside the EU. In short, the EIDHR is a legal and financial instrument of the EU's external action policy. It operates independently, working directly with human rights defenders and civil society organizations, addressing sensitive issues, and responding flexibly to new challenges. The EIDHR focuses on protecting human rights defenders at risk, supporting EU human rights priorities, promoting democracy, conducting EU Election Observation Missions, and supporting key actors in human rights mechanisms.[54]

54 Kurki, Milja, 2011, "Governmentality and EU Democracy Promotion: The European Instrument for Democracy and Human Rights and the Construction of Democratic Civil Societies," *International Political Sociology*, vol. 5, no. 4, December, online. https://doi.org/10.1111/j.1749-5687.2011.00139.x. Accessed 18 November 2025.

The EU provides technical and material support for electoral processes, ensuring they are inclusive, credible, and transparent. Election observation, both by domestic and international (EU) observers, plays a crucial role in this effort.

For example, in Nigeria's 2019 general elections, the EU deployed an Election Observation Mission that monitored the process and issued recommendations to improve transparency and inclusiveness. Similarly, during Ukraine's 2019 presidential and parliamentary elections, the EU sent both long-term and short-term observers to assess compliance with international standards, thereby supporting Ukraine's democratic transition.

These observation missions illustrate the EU's commitment to strengthening democratic processes abroad. Beyond elections themselves, however, democratic participation also depends on the existence of reliable civil registration systems that provide individuals with a legal identity.

Civil registration is crucial for improving democratic governance, especially for marginalized and disadvantaged people. Legal identity is essential for accessing basic rights and services. Approximately 1 billion people lack legal identity, with the majority being women and children in Sub-Saharan Africa and South Asia. The EU supports efforts to ensure that all individuals, particularly those in Sub-Saharan Africa and South Asia, have a legal identity.

4.2 EU Citizenship and Rights

EU citizenship grants individuals a set of rights and freedoms that extend beyond national borders, fostering a shared European identity. This section explores the rights of EU citizens, recent initiatives to enhance citizenship, and the social and cultural aspects that shape the European civic experience.

4.2.1 Rights and Freedoms of EU Citizens

EU citizenship grants individuals a range of rights, including the freedom to move and reside within the EU, access to consular protection, and the right to petition the European Parliament. Furthermore, the EU is dedicated to upholding human rights standards, addressing issues related to immigration, asylum, and the protection of fundamental rights for all individuals within its jurisdiction.

An individual acquires EU citizenship rights automatically upon possessing the nationality of an EU member state. In other words, if you hold the nationality of an EU country, you automatically have EU citizenship rights. These rights encompass both national laws specific to each country and EU laws that apply uniformly across all EU nations. They affect various aspects of daily life, including shopping, driving, healthcare, and family matters.

Key rights include the freedom to live and move within the EU without nationality-based discrimination, enhanced consumer protections, and access to healthcare across EU borders under certain conditions.

For example, imagine a Spanish student who moves to Germany to study and later takes a job there without needing a visa or facing restrictions based on nationality. Or imagine an Italian tourist who buys goods online from a French retailer and benefits from the EU rule that gives consumers a 14-day right to return their purchase. Likewise, a Portuguese patient who cannot access a specific surgery at home can travel to Belgium for treatment and have the costs reimbursed under EU cross-border healthcare rules.

These rights are detailed in Article 18 of the Treaty on the Functioning of the European Union and Chapter V of the Charter of Fundamental Rights.

4.2.2 Enhancing EU Citizenship

The EU Citizenship package aims to strengthen rights for EU citizens. It celebrated its 30th anniversary in 2023. The EU Citizenship package includes the Citizenship Report 2023, summarizing developments since 2020. This package proposes changes to enhance consular protection, provides guidance on free movement, electoral practices for citizens with disabilities, a Compendium of e-voting, and a Guide to EU citizenship. These initiatives support democratic engagement and reinforce EU citizens' rights to non-discrimination, free movement within the EU, consular help abroad, voting, petitioning EU institutions, and more. They ensure that EU citizens can fully exercise their rights and promote active participation in the EU's political processes.

In doing so, the package helps make EU citizenship more accessible, more visible, and more meaningful in people's daily lives. For example, imagine an Italian student studying in Belgium. Thanks to clearer information tools and improved guidance on free movement, she easily registers her residence, accesses healthcare, and votes in local elections. When she travels to a non-EU country and loses her passport, the strengthened rules on consular protection allow her to receive immediate help from the nearest EU embassy, even if Italy is not represented there. In this way, EU citizenship becomes a practical reality that directly supports her daily life and mobility.

4.2.3 Social and Cultural Dimensions of EU Citizenship

The EU promotes social cohesion and cultural diversity as fundamental pillars of European identity. Through social policies, the EU aims to ensure equal opportunities, fight against discrimination, and address social challenges such as poverty and inequality. Additionally, the EU fosters cultural exchange, preservation, and promotion, recognizing the richness of Europe's cultural heritage and the importance of cultural cooperation in building a cohesive European community.

The EU's Strategic Framework for cultural policy outlines key priorities aligned with broader EU goals. These include climate neutrality, digital empowerment, social fairness, global leadership, equality promotion, and democratic strengthening.

The New European Agenda for Culture, introduced in 2018, focuses on enhancing cultural contributions to society, the economy, and global relations. Member states collaborate through work plans to address cultural priorities, with the current 2023–2026 plan emphasizing the empowerment of cultural professionals, greater citizen participation, and sustainable cultural practices. Alongside these objectives, the EU also prioritizes cultural heritage preservation and international cultural relations to foster dialogue and development globally. Concrete initiatives include the Creative Europe programme, which funds cross-border projects connecting young artists and cultural professionals; the European Capitals of Culture, such as Elefsina (Greece), Timișoara (Romania), and Veszprém (Hungary) in 2023, which showcase Europe's diversity while boosting local development; and the European Heritage Label, which highlights sites of historical significance to strengthen a shared European identity.

Conclusion

While supranationalism can be observed in different contexts, the European Union represents its most advanced and distinctive expression, marked by an unprecedented pooling of sovereignty and a binding legal order.

The European Union plays a key role in international diplomacy and security through its Common Foreign and Security Policy and defense cooperation, aiming to stabilize its neighborhood and beyond. However, it faces significant challenges such as Brexit, migration crises, populism, climate change, and economic disparities. These issues require innovative and cooperative solutions to uphold European values.

Globally, the EU actively governs, trades, and develops policies, addressing climate change, pandemics, and promoting human rights and prosperity through multilateralism and partnerships. Economic disparities threaten social cohesion, but the EU pursues sustainable development, economic growth, and social protection policies to mitigate these challenges.

EU law, which takes precedence over national laws, ensures consistency and uniformity across member states. The Court of Justice of the European Union plays a crucial role in interpreting and enforcing EU law.

The EU's ability to address its challenges and leverage its legal framework will determine its success in promoting stability, prosperity, and unity within Europe and worldwide.

Selected Bibliography

Arnull, Anthony, 2017, *European Union Law: A Very Short Introduction*, Oxford University Press, 176 pages.

Bermann, George, Goebel, Roger, Davey, William, & Fox, Eleanor, 2010, *Cases and Materials on European Union Law (American Casebook Series)* (3rd ed.), West Academic Publishing, 1580 pages.

Chalmers, Damian, Davies, Gareth, Monti, Giorgio, & Heyvaert, Veerle, 2024, *European Union Law: Text and Materials*, Cambridge University Press, 1232 pages.

Conway, Gerard, 2016, *EU Law* (1st ed.), Routledge, 756 Pages.

Davies, Karen, van Munster, Maarten, & Düsterhöft, Isabel, 2023, *Understanding European Union Law* (8th ed.), Routledge, 272 pages.

Favret, Jean-Marc, 2023, *L'essentiel de l'Union européenne: Ses institutions et son droit*, Gualino, 112 pages.

Gruber, Annie, Jean-Louis, Clergerie, Patrick, Rambaud, & Thierry, Rambaud, 2022, *Droit institutionnel et matériel de l'Union européenne* (14th ed.), Dalloz, 1212 pages.

Horspool, Margot, Humphreys, Matthew, & Wells-Greco, Michael, 2021, *European Union Law*, Oxford University Press, 792 pages.

Jacqué, Jean-Paul, 2023, *Droit institutionnel de l'Union européenne* (10th ed.) Dalloz, 920 pages.

Kaczorowska-Ireland, Alina, 2016, *European Union Law* (4th ed.), Routledge, 1276 Pages.

Leclerc, Stéphane, 2023, *Droit de l'Union européenne: Pour connaître le Droit de l'Union européenne applicable en 2023* (8th ed.), Mementos Gualino, 244 pages.

Peers, Steve, & Barnard, Catherine, 2023, *European Union Law*, Broché: Oxford University Press, 1064 pages.

Reinfeld, Yuval, 2024, *The European Union as a Normative Power: The Role of the CJEU* (1st ed.), Routledge, 206 Pages.

Schütze, Robert, 2021, *European Union Law*, Oxford University Press, 1104 pages.

Storey, Tony, & Pimor, Alexandra, 2018, *Unlocking EU Law* (5th ed.), Routledge, 628 Pages.

Volpato, Annalisa, 2024, *Delegation of Powers in the EU Legal System* (1st ed.), Routledge, 308 Pages.

12 International Arbitration

Privatized Justice

Arbitration is not perfect, but it remains the least imperfect system for resolving international commercial disputes.
Emmanuel Gaillard (1952–2021)

Arbitration is, first and foremost, a legal discipline that has experienced rapid and remarkable expansion. Initially, it occupied only about three hours in an International Commercial Law course. Over time, it gradually expanded to cover half of the course, then evolved into a standalone subject, eventually warranting an entire university diploma, a LLM, or a Master's degree, with numerous specialized courses dedicated to both procedural and substantive aspects of the field.

As Emmanuel Gaillard (1952–2021), a French leading lawyer and scholar in international arbitration, explained during his lesson at the Academy of Moral and Political Sciences in Paris on October 17, 2016, international arbitration has expanded significantly, both in academic study and practical application.[1] Once a small part of International Commercial Law, arbitration has now become the preferred method for resolving cross-border disputes, shaping global business and legal practice.

International arbitration offers an alternative to state-controlled courts, allowing parties to settle disputes through neutral, private adjudication. Its appeal lies in its flexibility, efficiency, and enforceability, particularly through the 1958 New York Convention, which ensures that arbitral awards are recognized and enforced worldwide. This makes arbitration a powerful tool in cross-border commerce and investment, reducing legal uncertainty and fostering international cooperation.

However, arbitration does not operate entirely outside state authority. While it provides an independent forum for dispute resolution, it still depends on national courts for enforcement and is influenced by public legal frameworks. This balance between private justice and state control has shaped its evolution and continues to fuel debates on its fairness, legitimacy, and accessibility.

This chapter explores the fundamental principles, key mechanisms, and challenges of international arbitration. It begins with an examination of alternative dispute resolution (ADR), focusing on its different forms, including mediation, and their role in balancing state authority and

1 Emmanuel Gaillard, Professor at the Sciences Po Law School. Academy of Moral and Political Sciences, Session of Monday, October 17, 2016.

DOI: 10.4324/9781003393047-16

private justice (Section 1). The discussion then shifts to the fundamental notions of arbitration, distinguishing between domestic and international arbitration, analyzing arbitration agreements, and outlining the procedural steps involved in arbitration, from initiation to enforcement (Section 2). The chapter further delves into international arbitration as a transnational legal order, the concept of arbitral validity, and the interaction of arbitration with multiple legal systems, including the role of international treaties, the influence of national laws, and the link between arbitration and diplomacy in global dispute resolution. (Section 3)

By exploring arbitration's dual nature as both a privatized system of justice and a process embedded within a broader legal framework, this chapter provides a comprehensive analysis of its role in cross-border dispute resolution. It illustrates how arbitration balances party autonomy with state intervention, shaping its function as an effective mechanism for resolving international disputes.

1 Alternative Dispute Resolution: Between State Authority and Private Justice

This section examines how alternative dispute resolution (ADR), particularly mediation and arbitration, operates between state authority and private justice. It explores ADR mechanisms and practices, highlighting the dilemma of dispute resolution and the various forms of ADR.

A focused discussion on mediation follows, analyzing its role in access to justice, its distinction from arbitration, and its broader social impact. The section concludes with an examination of negotiation strategies, particularly the Best Alternative to Negotiated Agreement (BATNA) method, and its relevance in dispute resolution.

Through this analysis, we will see how ADR balances party autonomy with judicial oversight, offering efficient and flexible alternatives within modern legal systems.

1.1 Alternative Dispute Resolution: Mechanisms and Practices

This subsection explores the structure and function of Alternative Dispute Resolution (ADR) as a means of resolving conflicts outside traditional court litigation. It begins by examining the dilemma of dispute resolution, addressing the balance between efficiency, flexibility, and legal enforceability. It then outlines the different types of ADR, including mediation, arbitration, and other hybrid mechanisms, highlighting their distinct roles and applications in modern legal systems.

1.1.1 The Dilemma of Dispute Resolution

Parties to a conflict may wish to solve their dispute just by talking it through. Informal dispute resolution, often characterized by direct negotiation and discussions between parties, stands out for its accessibility and simplicity. It avoids the formalities, costs, and delays typical of judicial proceedings, presenting an attractive alternative for those scared by the complexity of legal battles. However, there are two main problems that may arise with that.

First, the conflicting parties may not be able to reach a solution that is acceptable for both. For example, X wishes to recover $100,000 for damages caused by Y, but Y, although recognizing that X should get some money for said damages, agrees to pay only $50,000.

Second, even if the conflicting parties do reach a satisfying solution to their dispute, the enforcement of the solution may be put at risk by one of the parties. For instance, the parties decide that Y should reimburse $100,000 to X, but Y does not reimburse X when the payment is due.

In both situations, informality does not offer a means to reach a binding and final solution to the dispute.

Disputes may reach an impasse if the parties cannot agree on a resolution. For instance, when one party's compensation demand is not fully met by the other, it creates a deadlock that informal negotiation alone cannot resolve. Many disputes worsen or remain unresolved due to deep emotional issues that are often ignored. Emotions play a key role in conflict, yet they are rarely addressed. A better understanding of the parties' psychology could help resolve many cases without years of litigation.

Even when parties reach an agreement, ensuring compliance poses a significant challenge. Without formal enforcement mechanisms, one party may fail to uphold their agreement, rendering the resolution inefficient.

These limitations underscore the need for a more structured approach that retains the benefits of informality while ensuring outcomes are both binding and enforceable.

It is important to recall, as outlined in the first chapter, *What Is Law? What Forms Does It Take?*, that the core of legal principles and the legal system itself is deeply rooted in the concept of *enforceability*.

Given the criticisms of court litigation – its inefficiency, costs, and bureaucratic hurdles – alongside the inadequacies of informal settlement, there has been a concerted move towards developing more effective means of resolving disputes. This effort has given rise to Alternative Dispute Resolution (ADR), a collective term for mechanisms designed to resolve legal disputes outside the traditional court system.

1.1.2 The Different Types of Alternative Dispute Resolution

Alternative Dispute Resolution (ADR) encompasses various mechanisms designed to resolve conflicts outside traditional court litigation, balancing efficiency, flexibility, and legal enforceability. Two primary forms of ADR – mediation and arbitration – offer distinct approaches to dispute resolution, reflecting different degrees of formality and binding authority.

Mediation represents a non-adversarial approach where a neutral third party, the mediator, facilitates dialogue between disputing parties to help them reach a mutually acceptable solution. Unlike judges or arbitrators, mediators do not impose decisions but guide discussions toward consensus, leading to a settlement agreement that outlines the terms of resolution. This process emphasizes cooperation and communication, offering a flexible and personalized means of resolving disputes.

Arbitration, by contrast, follows a more formal and adversarial process. An arbitrator assumes a role similar to that of a judge, with each party presenting its case before the arbitrator renders a binding decision. Unlike mediation, arbitration results in a definitive ruling that the parties have agreed to abide by, granting it a level of enforceability akin to court judgments.

While mediation and arbitration are the most well-known ADR methods, other forms of ADR also exist. Negotiation is a direct discussion between parties to reach a voluntary agreement without third-party intervention. Conciliation is similar to mediation, but the conciliator actively suggests solutions to help resolve the dispute.

Expert determination is a procedure where parties, by mutual agreement, submit a dispute or issue to one or more experts for resolution. The expert examines a technical matter and issues a decision that may be either binding or advisory, depending on the parties' agreement. By default, the decision is binding unless the parties have stipulated otherwise.

Med-Arb (Mediation-Arbitration) is a combination of mediation and arbitration, where parties first attempt to mediate, and if unsuccessful, proceed to arbitration for a binding decision.

Arb-Med (Arbitration-Mediation) follows the reverse order of Med-Arb. It begins with arbitration, usually limited to a predefined framework, where the arbitrator renders a decision that is then sealed in an envelope. The process then moves to mediation, allowing the parties to negotiate a mutual resolution. However, if mediation fails, the arbitrator's sealed decision automatically becomes binding. This approach creates strong pressure for parties to reach an agreement, as they are aware that a final decision already exists and will take effect if mediation does not succeed.

The effectiveness of ADR mechanisms hinges on their legal enforceability, which is grounded in multiple legal domains. Mediation and arbitration often rely on contractual agreements where parties consent to resolve disputes through these methods (contract law). Arbitration, in particular, follows established legal procedures to ensure fairness and due process in decision-making (procedural law). In cross-border disputes, international treaties provide a framework for recognizing and enforcing arbitration agreements and awards (International Treaty Law).

Mediation relies primarily on contract law, while arbitration is supported by contract law, procedural law, and treaty law, reinforcing its international applicability. Ultimately, ADR mechanisms derive their binding and enforceable nature from the coercive power of the state. Without state-backed enforcement, these resolutions would lack legal authority. The delegation of dispute resolution power, whether through domestic law or international agreements, highlights the state's pivotal role in legitimizing and supporting ADR.

ADR reflects the modern legal system's adaptability, offering solutions that combine the informality and accessibility of negotiation with the binding authority of formal adjudication. As societies evolve, ADR continues to play an essential role in ensuring efficient and equitable dispute resolution, marking a significant step forward in the pursuit of justice.

1.2 A Focus on Mediation

This subsection explores mediation as a key form of alternative dispute resolution, emphasizing its role in enhancing access to justice and fostering collaborative conflict resolution. It distinguishes mediation from arbitration and examines its theoretical foundations, classifications, and conceptual autonomy. Finally, it highlights mediation's broader impact beyond legal disputes, particularly in strengthening social and community bonds.

1.2.1 Enhancing Access to Justice: The Role and Impact of Mediation in Resolving Disputes

Mediation has been consistently adopted as an alternative to court litigation in Europe, Canada, and the United States for more than 40 years. Since the 1970s, legislative reforms have been conducted towards fostering mediation as a way to improve access to justice.[2] Article 3 of the European Directive on mediation of May 21, 2008 defines mediation as follows:[3]

Mediation refers to a structured process, however named or referred to, whereby two or more parties to a dispute attempt by themselves, on a voluntary basis, to reach an agreement on the settlement of their dispute with the assistance of a mediator. This process may be initiated by the parties or suggested or ordered by a court or prescribed by the law of a member state.

In essence, mediation consists of entrusting an impartial third party (the mediator) with the mission of assisting the conflicting parties to find a mutually acceptable solution to their dispute.

2 Georgakopoulos, Alexia (ed.), 2017, *The Mediation Handbook: Research, Theory, and Practice*, 1st ed., Routledge.

3 Directive 2008/52/EC of The European Parliament and of the Council of 21 May 2008 on certain aspects of mediation in civil and commercial matters.

In practice, the mediator does that by engaging in attentive listening of parties' views, by confronting their perspectives, and by reestablishing a channel of communication among the parties.[4]

The parties will play an important role in mediation. Although mediation may be commenced both through the parties' initiative and through a judge's referral, usually court-ordered mediation can only proceed if the parties provide their consent to the mediation process. This, for instance, is the rule in France, as can be seen in Article 131-1 of the French Code of Civil Procedure:

> A judge seized of litigation may, after having obtained the consent of the parties, appoint a third person who will hear them and confront their points of view to help them resolve the dispute dividing them.

Some argue that mediation is better suited to foster social peace than court litigation. Mediation is, indeed, conducive to abandoning the search for right and wrong. Within this framework, parties are invited to portray themselves as partners, not as adversaries. Furthermore, parties are invited to construe the conflict as a shared problem that needs to be resolved together.

Imagine two neighbors who disagree about a tree growing between their properties. The tree's branches block sunlight from one garden, so one neighbor wants to trim them. The other worry is that cutting the tree would ruin its appearance or reduce its value. Tension builds, and their communication becomes strained and emotional.

In a short mediation session, the mediator listens calmly to both sides. Instead of offering a solution, the mediator helps each person understand the other's concerns. Through this guided conversation, they come to an agreement: the overhanging branches will be trimmed to a certain height, and the cost will be shared.

Consider a dispute between two business partners over the division of profits from a recent project. One partner insists on an equal split, while the other argues for a larger share based on their greater contribution. Tensions rise, and the continuity of the partnership is threatened.

During mediation, a neutral third party facilitates structured dialogue. By expressing their perspectives and clarifying misunderstandings, the partners reach a mutually acceptable agreement on profit distribution and establish clearer guidelines for future collaboration.

Mediation, therefore, could be a more effective instrument in the restoration and preservation of the social bonds underlying a conflict.

The effectiveness of mediation comes precisely from the fact that the mediator has no power to impose a decision. Unlike a judge or arbitrator, the mediator does not control the outcome. Their role is to create space for the parties to speak, listen, and find common ground.

By stepping back, the mediator allows the parties to own both the problem and the solution. In this sense, the mediator's true power lies in their ability to withdraw, to remain neutral, and to trust the parties' capacity to resolve their own conflict. The mediator's power lies precisely in their lack of power.

1.2.2 Mediation Is Not a Kind of Arbitration

International arbitration and mediation have become leading approaches to settling international disputes. However, a common misconception is to regard mediation as a subset of arbitration. In the practice of International Law, it is not rare that legal actors refer expressly to mediation as "a kind of arbitration." This misunderstanding is not inconsequential.

4 Hopt, Klaus J. and Steffek, Felix, 2013, *Mediation: Principles and Regulation in Comparative Perspective*, Oxford University Press.

This conflation[5] is problematic because mediation and arbitration are two distinct methods of dispute resolution, and they are governed by different sets of rules and principles.

Mediation involves a neutral third party to help the disputing parties reach a voluntary settlement, while arbitration is a judicial-like procedure resulting in a binding decision.

The rules governing mediation emphasize confidentiality, voluntary participation, and the non-binding nature of the process, allowing parties to reach a settlement on their own. The rules governing arbitration detail the procedure for selecting arbitrators, the arbitration process, and how the decision is made and enforced.

Because their approaches, goals, and outcomes differ significantly, mediation and arbitration are governed by separate rules and practices tailored to their respective processes. Conflating mediation and arbitration in the context of international dispute resolution implies incorrectly that they are alike or function similarly, which can lead to practical, legal, and educational missteps in the field.

This mix-up contributes to what Michèle Guillaume-Hofnung, a French legal scholar, emeritus professor of Public Law, expert in mediation and ethics, describes as *Terminological Degeneration Related to Anomie*, a linguistic and terminological decay, connected to an absence of order or norms, which could, for instance, be contributing to the fading distinctions between these two methods in international dispute resolution.[6]

The concept of "anomie" (or anomy) originates from the field of sociology and was popularized by the French sociologist Émile Durkheim. It refers to a state of society or a condition where there is a breakdown of social norms and guidance. Anomie occurs when society's rules and norms are unclear or when they are in conflict with each other, causing confusion and a lack of direction for individuals. This can result in a sense of disconnection and alienation, and can lead to increased instability and disorder within a society.

In the context of law and dispute resolution, anomie can describe a similar breakdown in the clarity and application of legal norms and principles. When legal concepts are not distinctly defined and used correctly, such as the conflation of arbitration and mediation, it leads to a state of confusion – similar to anomie – where practitioners and scholars may lack clear guidelines on how to proceed in their work. This can undermine the legal process and the effectiveness of legal systems in resolving disputes.

1.2.3 Functional and Ontological Perspectives on Mediation

In the context of mediation's application and theory, a French leading figure emerges: Professor Michèle Guillaume-Hofnung, who offers an ontological perspective on mediation. This section draws on her framework, given its wide acceptance and foundational contributions to the field.

Michèle Guillaume-Hofnung is an emeritus professor of Public Law and a prominent French legal scholar, known for her expertise in mediation and legal ethics. She has significantly shaped the understanding and practice of mediation within the European Union and the Council of Europe. Author of the reference book *La Médiation*, published in the renowned French academic

5 The term *conflation* refers to the merging or blending of two or more different concepts, ideas, or entities into one, often leading to confusion or misunderstanding. In the context of legal terminology, conflation might occur when distinct legal concepts are treated as if they are interchangeable or similar, when, in fact, they have different meanings and implications.

6 Guillaume-Hofnung, Michèle, 2023, *La médiation*, 9e éd., Presses Universitaires de France.

series *Que sais-je?* (9th edition, 2023), she established the definition of social mediation for the European Union in 2000, and for the Council of Europe for intercultural dialogue in 2011.

Her definition of mediation, encapsulated within the pages of her book *La Médiation*, challenges the conventional, vague notions often associated with the concept, advocating for a precise, technical understanding of mediation as a specific process.[7]

1.2.4 Key Definitions and Classifications

Mediation is sometimes classified into various types, depending on its aims or contexts – such as prevention, conflict resolution, or relationship repair. While these distinctions may offer useful analytical tools, they risk fragmenting the concept. In contrast, Professor Guillaume-Hofnung highlights the fundamental unity of mediation, offering a comprehensive definition that treats it as a coherent and holistic process rather than a collection of separate forms.[8]

Guillaume-Hofnung's ontological definition distinguishes two primary forms of mediation – those that exist outside of conflict and those that aim to resolve disputes. She defines mediation as an ethical communication process that relies on the autonomy and responsibility of the involved parties, facilitated by a neutral, impartial third party without inherent authority.

Michèle Guillaume-Hofnung, in her textbook *La Médiation*, challenges the common yet vague understanding of mediation, arguing for its recognition as a specific, technical, and precise concept. She asserts that mediation is not a fuzzy concept but suffers from thoughtless application, emphasizing the importance of defining mediation through specific characteristics or criteria to understand and justify actions.[9]

She differentiates between social functions and acts in mediation, highlighting every mediation as a voluntary act involving parties and the mediator, thus forming a contract. She questions the idea of dividing mediation into separate types, arguing that this can hide its fundamental unity as a single, coherent process.[10]

She also underlines mediation's ternary nature in both structure and outcome, distinguishing it from negotiation and conciliation by the essential involvement of a third party, and highlighting its unique outcome that emerges from dialogue and exchange, unlike the binary outcomes of judicial decisions.

Professor Guillaume-Hofnung concludes that the definition of mediation includes the following two criteria: the involvement of a third party; the neutrality and impartiality of the third party, or the absence of any institutional or implied power of this third party.[11]

1.2.5 Conceptual Autonomy of Mediation

Highlighting the distinct nature of mediation and clarifying its separation from terms often incorrectly seen as interchangeable is essential.

Mediation is neither negotiation, arbitration, authority intervention, conciliation, transaction, nor assistance to conflicting parties, but a process that transcends and constructs beyond mere conflict resolution.

7 Guillaume-Hofnung, *La médiation*.
8 Guillaume-Hofnung, *La médiation*.
9 Guillaume-Hofnung, *La médiation*.
10 Guillaume-Hofnung, *La médiation*.
11 Guillaume-Hofnung, *La médiation*.

Mediation, requiring only a third party and its unique process, stands as a significant philosophical concept, distinct from conciliation, arbitration, or negotiation, which are merely notions. It does not inherently involve conflict or legal jurisdiction.

Guillaume-Hofnung criticizes the misuse of terminology that equates mediation with arbitration, conciliation, or negotiation, stressing that such a comparison is as erroneous as calling a pear a type of apple.[12]

Mediation distinguishes itself from conciliation, transaction, arbitration, negotiation, and conflict through its conceptual autonomy. Unlike conciliation, which is directly linked to the existence of a conflict, mediation can operate independently of any dispute, offering a creative freedom to the mediator that is absent in conciliation. Transactions focus on financial issues and have definitive legal authority, clearly differentiating them from mediation. Arbitration, a judicial process, differs in its ability to produce an enforceable decision, unlike mediation, which aims for voluntary resolution without decision-making power. Mediation also stands apart from negotiation, which directly involves the parties in the art of compromise, while mediation seeks a new and common solution. Finally, modern mediation moves away from focusing on conflict to concentrate on building and strengthening social bonds, highlighting its essential role in social cohesion.

The differences between mediation and other dispute resolution mechanisms underscore mediation's unique capacity to create or restore social bonds, beyond merely resolving conflicts. This differentiation is crucial for understanding mediation's broader implications for social cohesion and peace.

1.2.6 Mediation Beyond Conflict: Building and Strengthening the Community Bond

Modern mediation plays a vital role in fostering social peace by its ability to address the underlying causes and development of conflicts, rather than focusing solely on their consequences. By encouraging parties to view conflicts as shared problems requiring cooperative solutions, mediation promotes a shift from adversarial to partnership-based interactions.

This approach, supported by Professor Guillaume-Hofnung and reflected in her work, positions mediation as a key instrument in the maintenance and restoration of social connections, essential for the collective well-being and the foundational values of society.

This section has explored the theoretical underpinnings of mediation through the lens of functional and ontological perspectives. By examining the conceptual autonomy of mediation and its critical role in building and strengthening community bonds, we gain a deeper understanding of its importance in legal studies and practice, emphasizing the transformative potential of mediation in resolving disputes and fostering social harmony.

Transitioning from this presentation and analysis of mediation, we now turn our attention to arbitration, another critical mechanism in dispute resolution, to compare its principles, applications, and impact on legal and social frameworks. Before turning to arbitration, however, we will first examine the Best Alternative to a Negotiated Agreement (BATNA) method – an essential practical tool for evaluating options in dispute resolution.

1.3 The Best Alternative to a Negotiated Agreement (BATNA) Method

BATNA stands for Best Alternative to a Negotiated Agreement. It is a concept from negotiation theory that represents the most advantageous alternative course of action a party can take

12 Guillaume-Hofnung, *La médiation.*

if negotiations fail and an agreement cannot be reached. The concept was introduced during the 1980s by Roger Fisher and William Ury in their book *Getting to Yes: Negotiating Agreement Without Giving In,* first published in 1983.[13]

Understanding one's BATNA is crucial in negotiation because it provides a standard against which to evaluate any proposed agreement. It essentially sets the minimum acceptable value for any negotiated agreement.

This subsection is divided into two parts: first, understanding and applying BATNA in negotiation, with real-world scenarios such as job offers and contract disputes; and second, exploring its use in complex legal disputes, showing how it helps parties assess litigation risks and make strategic decisions.

1.3.1 Understanding and Applying BATNA in Negotiation

Knowing your BATNA helps you make more informed decisions during negotiations, ensuring that you do not agree to a deal that is less favorable than your best alternative.

Let's consider a job negotiation scenario:

Imagine you're currently employed, but you've received a job offer from another company. The new job offers a salary increase, but you're not entirely satisfied with the proposed terms. Before entering into negotiations with the new company, you evaluate your current job situation and find you have several alternatives:

(1) Stay at your current job, which you find satisfying and secure, but with a lower salary.
(2) Receive a counteroffer from your current employer if you mention the new job offer, potentially leading to a salary increase or improved working conditions.
(3) A third company has also shown interest in hiring you, though you haven't pursued this option seriously yet.

In this scenario, your BATNA might be the potential counteroffer from your current employer, assuming it promises the best mix of salary, job satisfaction, and security compared to the new job offer and the unexplored opportunity with the third company. Understanding that this is your best alternative to a negotiated agreement with the new company, you can negotiate more confidently, knowing you have a desirable option if the negotiation doesn't result in a satisfactory offer.

Consider another scenario involving a contract between a freelance graphic designer and a client for the design of a website. The agreement stipulates that the project must be completed within three months, with the client paying $5,000 upon completion. Two months into the project, the client decides to cancel the contract, leaving the work unfinished and the designer unpaid.

In this case, the graphic designer's BATNA involves evaluating alternatives to resolve the breach of agreement without resorting to legal action, which can be costly and time-consuming. The alternatives might include:

(1) Negotiating with the client for a partial payment reflecting the work completed to date.
(2) Offering to complete a smaller portion of the project for a reduced fee, thus saving some of the contract's value.

13 Fisher, Roger, Ury, William L. and Patton, Bruce, 1983, *Getting to Yes: Negotiating Agreement Without Giving In*, Penguin Books.

(3) Seeking another client in need of graphic design services, potentially leading to a new project that compensates for the lost income.
(4) Taking legal action against the client to claim compensation for the breach of contract (including costs incurred and lost profit) if negotiation fails and the other alternatives are less favorable.

In this scenario, the designer's BATNA would depend on which alternative offers the best outcome in terms of financial compensation, time investment, and future business relationships. If, for example, finding a new client who can offer an equal or better project is highly feasible and can be done quickly, this could represent the best alternative to continuing a dispute with the original client. This assessment helps the designer approach negotiations with a clear understanding of their most favorable course of action outside the original agreement, ensuring they do not settle for less than what their BATNA would provide.

Those examples illustrate how understanding the BATNA in a practical legal situation guides a party in choosing the most advantageous path forward, ensuring they are not forced into a less favorable position simply to resolve a dispute.[14]

1.3.2 Using BATNA in Complex Legal Disputes

In complex legal disputes, BATNA is essential for assessing litigation risks and potential settlement strategies. Consider a share transfer dispute between two companies. The seller argues that the company's financial reserves and cash flow were not included in the sale and should remain his as dividends. The buyer claims that the purchase included all company assets, including financial reserves and cash flow. Since the share transfer agreement lacks clarity, the dispute leads to civil, commercial, and even criminal litigation.

Each party assigns probabilities to their chances of success in court, which can also be applied to the amount claimed or estimated in litigation. For example, if the seller believes they have a 60% chance of proving that the transfer was invalid, they might estimate their claim at $1 million, meaning their expected value in litigation is $600,000. Meanwhile, the buyer, who estimates the seller's chances at only 30%, would value the same claim at $300,000.

This difference in perception influences their negotiation strategies, as each party assesses not only their own chances to succeed in their claim but also how the other side views the dispute. By quantifying these estimates, both parties can see the gap between their perceived success rates and the financial implications of their claims.

This exercise allows each party to objectively measure the divergence in expectations and identify a possible settlement range. A deal could be found within this gap through mutual concessions, avoiding prolonged and costly litigation while securing a resolution that aligns with both parties' risk assessments.

The BATNA method helps parties make informed decisions in disputes by assessing risks, negotiation strategies, and alternative options. It allows parties to compare litigation and settlement, helping them choose the best course of action based on their chances of success. By understanding opposing success perceptions, parties can adjust their bargaining position, preventing unrealistic expectations or missed opportunities. BATNA provides a clear structure

14 Subramanian, Guhan, 2023, "What Is BATNA? How to Find Your Best Alternative to a Negotiated Agreement," online. Available at: https://www.pon.harvard.edu/daily/batna. Accessed 12 February 2024.

for determining whether to litigate or settle, ensuring decisions are based on facts rather than emotions.

The BATNA method is an essential negotiation tool, allowing parties to assess their best alternative objectively. In both simple and complex disputes, BATNA ensures that negotiators and litigants do not settle for an outcome worse than their strongest alternative, leading to better-informed and more strategic decisions.

2 Fundamental Notions of Arbitration

This section explores the key notions of arbitration, distinguishing between domestic and international arbitration based on the parties involved, the applicable law, and the place of enforcement. It examines the different forms of international arbitration, including state-to-state, commercial, and investor-state arbitration, and the role of consent in arbitral proceedings.

The discussion then focuses on the arbitration agreement, emphasizing party autonomy, consent, and enforceability as fundamental pillars of arbitration. Finally, it outlines the unfolding of arbitration from initiation to enforcement, detailing key procedural steps such as the formation of the tribunal, conduct of proceedings, and issuance of arbitral awards.

2.1 The Distinction Between Domestic and International Arbitration

Arbitration can be either domestic or international. Respectively, domestic arbitration is connected to one single country, while in international arbitration, one or all of its elements transcend the borders of countries.[15] This distinction is important as it affects how arbitration proceedings are conducted, how arbitration agreements are interpreted, and how arbitral awards are enforced.

With the growth of international trade and cross-border interactions, international disputes have become more common. These disputes are typically resolved through litigation in national or international courts or by international arbitration, which allows parties to settle conflicts based on mutually agreed-upon rules and principles.[16] International arbitration is grounded in international treaties and domestic laws, providing a structured framework for resolving disputes while respecting party autonomy. Emmanuel Gaillard, in his book *Legal Theory of International Arbitration*, describes international arbitration as *a parallel system of justice*, allowing private parties to resolve disputes outside national courts based on agreed legal principles.[17]

2.1.1 Domestic Arbitration

Domestic arbitration is characterized by its singular connection to one country: all critical elements – involved parties, the nature of the dispute, applicable law, and enforcement location – are linked to the same jurisdiction.

Consider a dispute over a car sale, for example: if both parties are nationals of Country X, the dispute is governed by Country X's law, and the car is located within Country X, the arbitration is deemed domestic.

15 Bermann, George A., 2020, *International Commercial Arbitration in a Nutshell*, West Academic Publishing.

16 Bermann, George A., Dodge, William S. and Childress, Donald Earl III, 2021, *Transnational Litigation in a Nutshell*, West Academic Publishing.

17 Gaillard, Emmanuel, 2010, *Legal Theory of International Arbitration*, Brill Nijhoff.

In the context of French law, for example, the legal framework that governs arbitration is sophisticated and tailored to distinguish clearly between domestic and international arbitration. The foundational basis for this differentiation lies within French procedural law, particularly the principles outlined in the Code of Civil Procedure (*Code de Procédure Civile*).

Domestic arbitration in France is essentially defined by exclusion. This means that any arbitration that does not involve elements that would classify it as international falls into the category of domestic arbitration. The criteria for this classification are not explicitly stated. Thus, domestic arbitration is understood to be any arbitration that lacks the cross-border elements or the involvement of the interests of international commerce that would elevate it to the status of international arbitration.

Domestic arbitrations are governed by a set of procedural rules that are tailored to disputes that are purely internal to France. These rules cover aspects such as the appointment of arbitrators, the conduct of the arbitration proceedings, and the enforcement of arbitral awards. The emphasis is on providing a framework that is consistent with French legal traditions and practices, without the need to accommodate the complexities that arise in cross-border disputes.

2.1.2 International Arbitration

The realm of international arbitration encompasses disputes with cross-border elements, which may pertain to any or all aspects of the arbitration – parties, disputes, applicable law, and enforcement venues. To put it simply, the arbitration may be international due to the parties involved, to the dispute, to the law applicable, or to the place of enforcement.

International arbitration is regulated differently across jurisdictions, but France's approach is particularly broad and commercially oriented. In contrast with domestic arbitration, international arbitration is defined positively in French law. Under Article 1504 of the French Code of Civil Procedure, arbitration is considered international if it "involves the interests of international commerce." This flexible definition captures a wide range of cross-border disputes, regardless of the parties' nationality, the applicable law, or the arbitration venue.

Many other countries define international arbitration based on factors like the parties' nationality, the place of arbitration, or the governing law. For example, the UNCITRAL Model Law (adopted in Singapore, Canada, and other jurisdictions) defines international arbitration using criteria such as cross-border trade relationships. Switzerland considers arbitration international if the parties are from different jurisdictions. The U.S. and UK focus more on contractual autonomy and enforcement rather than defining international arbitration in broad terms.

France's commercial focus and pro-arbitration stance make it an important model, especially for jurisdictions modernizing their arbitration laws. As a leading arbitration hub, France's approach aligns with global arbitration trends and provides a valuable reference for international disputes.

2.1.2.1 INTERNATIONAL PARTIES

The parties involved in a dispute may be companies or individuals coming from different countries. For instance, the claimant could be an Indian company, while the respondent could be an American citizen.

In addition, the parties involved in a given arbitration may be two sovereign states. Indeed, Qatar and Saudi Arabia may initiate arbitration against each other in order to solve a dispute between them.

Finally, a given sovereign state may be involved in arbitration with a private person who is a non-national of that State. As an illustration, we may have Brazil and a Lebanese company involved in arbitration over a certain investment contract.

These examples show that arbitration is flexible enough to handle disputes between any combination of parties – states, companies, or individuals – regardless of nationality. This flexibility is one of the main reasons arbitration is widely used in international commerce and investment today.

2.1.2.2 APPLICABLE LAW

Arbitral tribunals may be called to apply international legal instruments to a given dispute. Notably, parties may choose international law as the governing law of the case. Also, the arbitrators may decide that international law is the most adequate law to govern the dispute.

It should be noted that there are certain international legal instruments that are often used in international arbitration, such as the United Nations Convention on the Law of the Sea,[18] the United Nations Convention on Contracts for the International Sales of Goods,[19] and Investment Treaties.[20]

Besides these formal international legal instruments, there are informal legal instruments that are quite relevant in international disputes, of which the UNIDROIT Principles on International Commercial Contracts is the best example[21].

However, in international arbitration, the applicable law does not need to be international law. Parties frequently choose a *national* law – such as English law, Swiss law, French law, or New York law – to govern their contract. This reflects the principle of party autonomy, a cornerstone of arbitration, which allows parties to select the legal system they consider most predictable and reliable. Arbitrators must respect this choice, and in cases where the parties remain silent, the tribunal itself will select the law it considers most appropriate, often by examining the connection of the dispute to a particular jurisdiction.

These tools give arbitrators a wide and reliable legal framework, helping them reach fair and predictable outcomes even when the dispute involves parties from different countries and legal systems.

2.1.2.3 THE PLACE OF ENFORCEMENT OF ARBITRAL AWARDS

Arbitral awards, which may be final or partial, are binding decisions resolving the presented dispute. While compliance is generally voluntary, enforcement may necessitate intervention by state courts, especially if the losing party resists compliance. The enforceability of an award in

18 The United Nations Convention on the Law of the Sea, adopted in 1982, creates a detailed system of regulations and governance for the world's oceans and seas, setting standards for all oceanic and maritime activities and resource use.

19 The United Nations Convention on Contracts for the International Sale of Goods (CISG), adopted in Vienna in 1980 and coming into effect on January 1, 1988, aims to establish a contemporary, standardized, and equitable framework for international goods sale contracts. By doing so, the CISG plays a crucial role in ensuring predictability in commercial transactions and reducing the costs associated with these exchanges.

20 Investment Treaties are international instruments for the protection of investors and promotion of investment. These treaties are usually bilateral (commonly referred to by the English acronym BIT – Bilateral Investment Treaty), but there are also multilateral treaties governing foreign investment (for instance, the North American Trade Agreement).

21 UNIDROIT is a private institution that fosters the unification of International Private Law. The "Principles" is a document drawn up by UNIDROIT intended to help harmonize international commercial contracts law.

jurisdictions outside the one in which it was issued (to seize assets of the non-compliant party, for example) highlights the internationalization of arbitration.

For instance, in a scenario where a car sale dispute is adjudicated in Country X but involves a car located in Country Y, an award directing the respondent to deliver the car to Country X becomes international if the respondent fails to comply and the claimant seeks enforcement in Country Y. This situation underscores the arbitral tribunal's potential need to navigate multiple legal systems to ensure the award's enforceability across relevant jurisdictions.

An arbitral award is a decision rendered by the arbitral tribunal with regard to the dispute between the parties. The award may be final or partial. Final awards solve the entire dispute presented to the tribunal, while partial awards settle parts of the dispute or convey provisional orders.

In both cases, however, the award will be binding on the parties. Although the parties usually comply voluntarily with the award of the arbitral tribunal, they may also take a different course of action and resist abiding by the award. In this respect, it should be highlighted that arbitral tribunals will rely on state courts to enforce their commands in case the parties do not comply with them voluntarily.

Also, it is important to bear in mind that arbitral awards may "travel," for the winning party may wish to enforce it where assets of the losing party are available. Accordingly, the place of enforcement of the arbitral award may lead to the internationalization of the arbitral award itself.

Consider again that dispute over the sale and purchase of a car. Imagine that the parties are nationals of country X, the law applicable is that of country X, the arbitral tribunal is seated in country X, but the car is located in country Y. Now imagine that the arbitral tribunal has ordered the respondent to bring the car to country X and deliver it to the claimant. Now imagine that the respondent failed to comply with this award. What could the claimant do?

The claimant is allowed to take this arbitral award from country X and bring it to country Y, and demand that the courts of that country seize the car. To enforce the arbitral award, the claimant must petition for an exequatur from the courts in country Y.

Exequatur is a legal procedure by which a court in one country recognizes and enforces an arbitral award issued in another country. Under the New York Convention on the Recognition and Enforcement of Foreign Arbitral Awards (1958), which has been adopted by over 170 countries, parties seeking to enforce an arbitral award in a foreign jurisdiction must obtain an exequatur from the courts of that jurisdiction. This process involves proving that the award complies with the requirements of the Convention and the local laws concerning the enforcement of foreign judgments and awards.

In the described scenario, the arbitral award crossed borders and became international.

2.1.3 Implications

Determining whether arbitration is domestic or international is crucial as it affects the legal framework, enforcement, and procedural flexibility. This distinction impacts how disputes are handled and resolved. Many countries have separate laws for domestic and international arbitration. International arbitration allows more flexibility, while domestic arbitration is often subject to stricter national regulations.

International arbitration awards benefit from the New York Convention (1958), making them easier to enforce across 170 countries. Domestic awards, however, follow local laws, which may require additional court approvals. In international arbitration, parties can select their governing law, rules, and venue, while domestic arbitration is generally bound by national procedural laws, limiting party autonomy.

International arbitration minimizes court intervention, respecting party autonomy. Domestic arbitration, however, often involves greater judicial supervision, with courts having more power to review or set aside awards. Domestic arbitration is more restricted by national laws, which may exclude consumer, labor, or family disputes. International arbitration, in contrast, enjoys broader applicability, focusing on cross-border commerce.

The distinction between domestic and international arbitration determines legal rules, enforcement, and court involvement. Understanding this is key for parties seeking efficient dispute resolution in both local and global contexts.

2.2 Varieties of International Arbitration

International arbitration can be categorized into several distinct types, each serving specific roles within the framework of global dispute resolution. These types are designed to address a wide range of disputes that arise across international borders, involving state entities, private corporations, and individuals. The primary types of international arbitration include three primary forms: state-to-state arbitration, investor-state arbitration, and commercial arbitration.[22]

These forms span the spectrum from Public Law to Private Law, with state-to-state and commercial arbitration representing the two poles, and investor-state arbitration occupying a unique middle ground.

Thus, state-to-state arbitration and international commercial arbitration may be described as two extremes of the Public Law-Private Law dichotomy, while investor-state arbitration may be perceived as a third category between both.

2.2.1 State-to-State Arbitration

State-to-state arbitration, also called interstate arbitration, involves disputes between sovereign states over elements of their sovereignty, including issues of territorial sovereignty, maritime boundaries, and treaty-related issues.

This form of arbitration operates predominantly within the realm of public international law, given its focus on state sovereignty and public legal principles. So here we see those territorial and treaty-related disputes.

Prominent state-to-state arbitration cases include the Indus Waters Kishenganga arbitration between Pakistan and India, the dispute between Ukraine and the Russian Federation concerning the detention of Ukrainian naval vessels and military personnel by the Russian Federation, and the dispute between Barbados and the Republic of Trinidad and Tobago concerning maritime boundary delimitation. We set out these cases here as examples.

2.2.1.1 PERMANENT COURT OF ARBITRATION (PCA), INDUS WATERS TREATY ARBITRATION (*PAKISTAN V. INDIA*), CASE NO. 2023–01

The dispute centers around the Kishanganga hydro-electric project initiated by the Republic of India, which the Islamic Republic of Pakistan claims diverts more water than allowed under the treaty, affecting its own water supply. The arbitration, which took place under the Indus Waters

22 The most common and widespread type of international arbitration is undeniably international commercial arbitration, followed by investor-state arbitration and then inter-state arbitration. For some statistics on international arbitration, see Altenkirch, Markus and Gremminger, Nicolas, "Parties' Preferences in International Arbitration: The Latest Statistics of the Leading Arbitral Institutions," online. Available at: https://www.globalarbitrationnews.com. Accessed 13 February 2024.

Treaty of 1960, was decided in 2013, with the final award allowing India to proceed with the project under certain conditions to ensure water flow to Pakistan.

In 2016, after unresolved negotiations, Pakistan initiated further arbitral proceedings against India under Paragraph 2(b) of Annexure G to the Indus Waters Treaty 1960. On July 6, 2023, the Court of Arbitration, after considering India's objections to its competence, unanimously rejected these objections, affirming its authority to adjudicate the disputes presented by Pakistan. This case shows the PCA's dedication to solving disputes by clarifying the application of the Indus Waters Treaty to modern water management challenges. It has not been definitively settled yet.[23]

2.2.1.2 PERMANENT COURT OF ARBITRATION (PCA), DISPUTE CONCERNING THE DETENTION OF UKRAINIAN NAVAL VESSELS AND SERVICEMEN (*UKRAINE V. THE RUSSIAN FEDERATION*), CASE NO. 2019–28

In this case, the dispute centers around the detention of Ukrainian naval vessels and military personnel by the Russian Federation. Ukraine initiated arbitration proceedings against Russia on April 1, 2019, under Annex VII of the United Nations Convention on the Law of the Sea (UNCLOS), seeking a resolution over this matter. The core of the dispute lies in Ukraine's allegations against Russia concerning the detention, which Ukraine contends violates the provisions of UNCLOS that govern the rights and obligations of states concerning the use of the world's seas and the conduct of naval vessels.[24]

Following Ukraine's initiation of arbitration by submitting a Notification and Statement of Claim under Annex VII of UNCLOS, Russia raised preliminary objections questioning the Tribunal's competence to hear the case. These objections led to a separate, preliminary phase of proceedings to determine the Tribunal's authority to decide on the dispute. This phase included the submission of written observations by Ukraine on Russia's objections and an oral hearing held at the Peace Palace in The Hague from October 11 to 15, 2021.

The Tribunal's decision on June 27, 2022, concerning Russia's preliminary objections marks a critical point in the arbitration process. However, the resolution of these objections is a preliminary step, and the case is still pending, awaiting further proceedings to address the substantive issues of the dispute under the UNCLOS framework.

The war between Ukraine and the Russian Federation has significantly affected the case in several ways. Generally speaking, in cases like this, the context of armed conflict or tense geopolitical relations makes legal cases more complex and harder to manage. The backdrop of war adds complexity to legal arguments and diplomatic negotiations, complicating the legal proceedings. Enforcement of tribunal decisions becomes difficult as the conflict affects parties' compliance willingness and ability. The war directly influences tribunal proceedings by complicating evidence gathering, participant safety, and potentially biasing tribunal legitimacy, which could delay proceedings and affect their perceived fairness. While these factors can influence the arbitration process, international tribunals like the one operating under the UNCLOS framework strive to maintain impartiality and focus on the legal merits of the case, independent of the

23 Permanent Court of Arbitration (PCA), *The Islamic Republic of Pakistan v. The Republic of India*, Case No. 2023-01, Inter-state arbitration regarding Electricity/Power under the Indus Waters Treaty, General List No. 284 [online]. Available at: https://pca-cpa.org/en/cases/284/. Accessed 13 February 2024.

24 Permanent Court of Arbitration (PCA), *Dispute Concerning the Detention of Ukrainian Naval Vessels and Servicemen (Ukraine v. the Russian Federation)*, General List No. 284, Case No. 2019-28, [online]. Available at: https://pca-cpa.org/en/cases/229/. Accessed 13 February 2024.

broader geopolitical context. However, the reality of international relations and the dynamics of conflict inevitably play a role in the broader narrative and impact of such cases.

2.2.1.3 PERMANENT COURT OF ARBITRATION (PCA), MARITIME BOUNDARY DELIMITATION (*BARBADOS V. THE REPUBLIC OF TRINIDAD AND TOBAGO*), CASE NO. 2004-02

The dispute between Barbados and the Republic of Trinidad and Tobago centered on the delimitation of the maritime boundary between the two states. The arbitration under the 1982 United Nations Convention on the Law of the Sea was initiated to establish a clearly defined maritime boundary that would delineate the respective territorial waters and exclusive economic zones of Barbados and Trinidad and Tobago. The case sought to resolve disagreements over the maritime boundary line claimed by each country, affecting the rights to exploit marine resources, conduct maritime navigation, and manage the conservation of sea life within their respective areas. The Tribunal's task was to draw a single maritime boundary that would be legally binding for both parties, taking into account equitable considerations and international law principles.

The Arbitral Tribunal's award establishes a maritime boundary differing from the claims of both parties by following the equidistance line, adjusted in the eastern Atlantic sector for the coast of Trinidad and Tobago. The Tribunal found it lacked jurisdiction over a fisheries regime in Trinidad and Tobago's Exclusive Economic Zone, but stated the duty of both states to negotiate access to fisheries.[25] The proceedings began in 2004, with hearings in London in 2005, and PCA served as the registry. The Arbitral Tribunal issued its final award in 2006.[26]

These three cases – the Indus Waters Kishenganga Arbitration (*Pakistan v. India*), the Detention of Ukrainian Naval Vessels Arbitration (*Ukraine v. Russia*), and the Maritime Boundary Delimitation Arbitration (*Barbados v. Trinidad and Tobago*) – illustrate the ongoing relevance and utility of state-to-state arbitration and that of similar dispute resolution mechanisms in addressing contemporary international disputes of territorial sovereignty, maritime boundaries, and violations of international law.

One should avoid mixing the International Court of Justice (ICJ) with the Permanent Court of Arbitration (PCA). It is important to differentiate between the two. These two prominent international institutions fulfill two distinct roles in resolving international disputes and operate under different legal frameworks. While both institutions are based in The Hague, the International Court of Justice is the principal judicial organ of the United Nations, whereas the Permanent Court of Arbitration is an independent arbitral framework established by the 1899 Hague Peace Conference.

The key differences between the ICJ and the PCA relate to jurisdiction and access, nature and scope, legal framework and flexibility, and composition.

The ICJ deals only with state-to-state disputes, whereas the PCA can handle disputes involving a variety of actors, including states, private entities, and international organizations.

The ICJ acts as a judicial body making binding decisions on international legal disputes, while the PCA provides a range of dispute resolution services, with a focus on arbitration.

The ICJ operates under a fixed legal framework provided by its Statute and the UN Charter, while the PCA offers more flexibility, allowing parties to choose the applicable arbitration rules and procedures.

25 The fishing grounds and resources within Trinidad and Tobago's Exclusive Economic Zone.

26 Permanent Court of Arbitration (PCA), *Maritime Boundary Delimitation (Barbados v. The Republic of Trinidad and Tobago)*, General List No. 104, Case No. 2004-02, [online]. Available at: https://pca-cpa.org/en/cases/104/. Accessed 13 February 2024.

The ICJ has permanent judges, whereas the PCA facilitates the formation of arbitral tribunals on an *ad hoc* basis.

Both institutions play crucial roles in the international legal order by providing fora for the peaceful resolution of disputes, but their distinct characteristics make them suitable for different types of cases and parties.

2.2.2 International Commercial Arbitration

At the other end of the spectrum of international arbitration, international commercial arbitration addresses disputes between private parties, which can include companies, individuals, or state entities, arising from commercial relationships or contracts. While this mode primarily engages with Private Law, it can also incorporate Public Law elements, for some Public Law aspects may intervene in the reasoning of the tribunal, especially through so-called public policy considerations.

International Commercial Arbitration cases often remain private, as the proceedings of arbitration are typically confidential. However, some cases become public when enforcement actions are filed in national courts or when parties disclose information about the arbitration.

Let's consider the *Dow Chemical Company v. Petrochemical Industries Company of Kuwait (PIC)*. In the *Dow Chemical v. PIC case*, the Dow Chemical Company was awarded over $2.6 billion in 2012 by the International Chamber of Commerce (ICC) International Court of Arbitration. This followed the collapse of a planned plastics joint venture between Dow and PIC, showcasing disputes that can arise from failed mergers and acquisitions. This award, issued by the International Chamber of Commerce's International Court, is considered one of the largest arbitration settlements ever.

The dispute between Dow Chemical Company and the Petrochemical Industries Company of Kuwait (PIC) is an example of international commercial arbitration because the dispute was between two corporate entities regarding a joint venture agreement, rather than a dispute between a private investor and a sovereign state, which would characterize it as investor-state arbitration. The case was heard by the International Chamber of Commerce (ICC) International Court of Arbitration, which is a common forum for resolving international commercial disputes.

A broad range of disputes illustrates the breadth of international commercial arbitration, covering sectors from energy to finance and issues from expropriation to contract disputes. They underscore the critical role of arbitration in providing a forum for resolving complex international disputes outside of national courts.

Hereunder are classical examples of types of international commercial arbitration cases that would typically be arbitrated under the ICC rules.

Disputes over International Sales Contracts: A seller in France and a buyer in Brazil have a disagreement over the quality of goods delivered under a sales contract. They might seek arbitration through the ICC.

Construction and Infrastructure Disputes: An Italian construction company and a Middle Eastern government entity arbitrate a dispute related to the construction of a highway or airport.[27]

27 Examples of scenarios where international commercial arbitration may be applied in construction cases are as follows.

Delay and Disruption Claims: A construction company from Spain and a developer from Saudi Arabia could enter into arbitration over delays and additional costs incurred due to disruptions in the construction of a hotel.

Defects and Warranty Issues: An engineering firm from Canada and a project owner in the United States might arbitrate a dispute over alleged defects in the design and construction of a bridge, including warranty claims and liability for repair costs.

Maritime and Transport Disputes: A shipping company based in Singapore and a charterer from Germany arbitrate a dispute over the terms of a shipping contract.

Energy Sector Disputes: An American energy company and an African state-owned enterprise arbitrate a dispute concerning a contract for the development of oil and gas resources.

Telecommunications and Technology Disputes: A dispute between a Korean technology firm and an Indian telecom company over a patent licensing agreement was resolved through ICC arbitration.

Joint Venture Disagreements: Two companies from different countries involved in a joint venture arbitrate a dispute about the breach, management, or profits of the joint venture, as in the *Dow Chemical Company v. Petrochemical Industries Company of Kuwait* case.

These examples highlight the diversity and complexity of international commercial disputes that can be arbitrated through International Commercial Arbitration forums like the ICC, which provides a neutral and internationally recognized forum for the resolution of such conflicts.

International commercial arbitration offers distinct advantages and disadvantages, influenced by factors such as the nature of the dispute, the preferences of the parties involved, and the specific contexts of their commercial activities.

International Commercial Arbitration offers multiple advantages for resolving cross-border commercial disputes.

(1) Neutrality: Firstly, its neutrality ensures a balanced forum that mitigates the risk of home court advantage, providing fairness to parties from diverse jurisdictions.
(2) Choice of Arbitrators: The ability to select arbitrators with specialized legal, technical, or industry knowledge directly related to the matter at hand is another significant benefit, paving the way for more informed and relevant decisions.
(3) Choice of Law: The parties may choose in advance the applicable law that will govern their dispute settlements in case any dispute arises. For example, U.S. law, and even more specifically Texas law, French law, Belgian law, OHADA law, Russian law, United Kingdom law, and so forth.
(4) Flexibility: International Commercial Arbitration is characterized by its flexibility, allowing customization of procedures to fit the specific needs of the parties involved, including choices regarding language, venue, and scheduling. The parties are free to choose the international arbitration center and rules (LCIA, ICC, SIAC, HKIAC, DIAC, SCCA, etc.) to resolve their dispute.
(5) Confidentiality: Arbitration also affords a level of confidentiality not found in public court proceedings, safeguarding trade secrets, business methodologies, and the reputations of the parties.
(6) Enforceability: A key advantage lies in the enforceability of arbitration awards, bolstered by the New York Convention, which facilitates easier recognition and enforcement in over 170 countries compared to traditional court judgments.

Payment Disputes: A subcontractor from Italy might pursue arbitration against a main contractor from the UK over non-payment for completed works in a commercial building project in London.

Termination of Contract: A South African construction firm and an Australian mining company could engage in arbitration due to the alleged wrongful termination of a contract related to the construction of mining infrastructure.

Change Order Disputes: A consortium of construction firms from different countries working on a dam project in Latin America might arbitrate disputes over the approval, valuation, and payment for change orders issued by the project owner.

(7) Finality: Lastly, the finality of arbitral awards, with very limited opportunities for appeal, streamlines dispute resolution, potentially saving time and reducing litigation costs, making international commercial arbitration an attractive option for resolving global commercial disputes.

Still, International Commercial Arbitration also comes with a number of drawbacks that parties should consider.

(1) Costs: Arbitration can be expensive, particularly for complex or prolonged disputes. Fees for arbitrators, arbitration institutions, legal representation, and additional costs (such as expert witnesses and venue) can accumulate significantly.
(2) Unpredictability: Arbitration does not create legal precedents, which can lead to unpredictability in the application of law and may not contribute to the development of legal standards in certain fields. Lack of precedent must be considered by the parties.
(3) Limited Judicial Review: The possibilities for appealing or challenging an arbitration award are very restricted, which can be complicated in cases of arbitrator error or oversight.
(4) Risk of Bias: While arbitrators are expected to be impartial, concerns about potential biases exist, especially in smaller industries or specialized areas where arbitrators and parties may frequently interact in different capacities.

The decision to opt for international commercial arbitration should be made after carefully considering these advantages and disadvantages in the context of the specific needs and circumstances of the parties involved. The choice of arbitration clauses, including the choice of law and forum, plays a crucial role in maximizing the benefits and mitigating the downsides of arbitration in international commercial transactions.

In 2016, the late Emmanuel Gaillard, who was a Professor at the Sciences Po Law School in France, delivered an insightful lecture on International Arbitration to the Academy of Moral and Political Sciences in Paris:

The appeal of arbitration does not lie, as was once written in introductions to the subject, in the fact that arbitration would be fast, inexpensive, and maintain excellent relations between the parties. There are procedures that last ten years, cost fortunes, and in which the parties detest each other. But one does not become the standard mode of dispute resolution in international trade without reason. It does not achieve this status without adopting certain characteristics of state litigation in some parts of the world. The advantage of arbitration is elsewhere. It lies in the neutrality, both geographic and in terms of nationality, of the arbitrators (no one wants to plead in the other's court), in the participation of the parties in the appointment of arbitrators and in the definition of procedures (Should witnesses be heard orally? Is one or two weeks of hearings needed?) and in the benefit of the New York Convention, under which 156 states have committed to recognize and enforce arbitral awards without reviewing them on the merits, something that has no equivalent in the realm of judgments.[28]

28 Translated from French by the author. Original text: "L'intérêt de l'arbitrage ne tient pas, comme on l'écrivait autrefois dans les introductions à la matière, au fait que l'arbitrage serait rapide, peu onéreux et maintiendrait d'excellentes relations entre les parties. On connaît des procédures qui durent dix ans, coûtent des fortunes et dans lesquelles les parties se détestent. Mais l'on ne devient pas impunément le mode normal de règlement des différends du commerce international. On ne le devient pas sans emprunter certains traits des contentieux étatiques dans certaines parties du monde. L'avantage de l'arbitrage est ailleurs. Il tient à la neutralité, géographique et en termes de nationalité, des arbitres (personne ne voulant plaider chez l'autre), à la participation des parties à la nomination

Regarding International Commercial Arbitration, it is essential to distinguish the distinct roles of closely related organizations involved.

The ICC International Court of Arbitration (ICA) is a specialized body of the International Chamber of Commerce (ICC) founded in 1923, following the establishment of the ICC in 1919. The ICA's primary role is to provide a structured and reputable forum for arbitration, which is an alternative dispute resolution process. The court aims to settle international commercial and business disputes outside the traditional court system, offering confidential, amicable, or binding solutions that are cost-effective and efficient. The ICA's arbitration process is supported by experienced mediators and arbitrators who are trained and certified, providing guidance throughout the mediation and arbitration procedures from initiation to closure. This service is available to companies both in France and internationally.

The International Chamber of Commerce (ICC) is a non-profit, private international organization that advocates for world businesses by promoting international trade, investment, and open markets, as well as the free flow of capital. Founded in 1919 with its international secretariat in Paris, the ICC works towards economic growth, job creation, and prosperity on a global scale. As a member-driven organization, it influences global business perspectives and maintains direct access to national governments through its national committees, which include ICC France, among others.

ICC France operates as a non-profit association and is recognized for its public utility. It was created in 1921. It is one of the most active national committees of the ICC, bringing together around 160 members that include major companies from the CAC 40 index, law firms, large professional organizations like Medef and AFEP, and consular bodies like CCI France. It plays a crucial role in mobilizing French companies on issues of international commerce and represents a significant portion of the French economy.

The Centre for Mediation and Arbitration of Paris (CMAP) was founded in 1995 by the Chamber of Commerce and Industry of Paris. The CMAP offers companies a conflict management and resolution center. The CMAP supports companies seeking alternative dispute resolution methods to litigation. It provides a structured array of alternative dispute resolution mechanisms, including confidential and amicable solutions, with the goal of resolving conflicts efficiently and outside the court system.

The Chamber of Commerce and Industry of the Paris Île-de-France Region represents approximately 840,000 companies, accounting for 29% of the national GDP, and is actively engaged in supporting the regional economy. Its mandate includes representing businesses to promote their growth, training individuals for future challenges, nurturing business projects, and promoting the Paris region to enhance its influence and reputation.

Each of these institutions plays a distinct but complementary role in fostering a favorable business environment by promoting trade, advocating for businesses, offering training, and providing mechanisms for alternative dispute resolution.

The United Nations Commission on International Trade Law (UNCITRAL) provides a non-exhaustive list[29] of arbitration centers that: (a) have an institutional framework inspired

---

des arbitres et à la définition des procédures (faut-il entendre les témoins oralement? avoir une semaine ou deux d'audiences?.) et au bénéfice de la Convention de New York par laquelle 156 États se sont engagés à reconnaître et exécuter les sentences arbitrales sans les réviser au fond, ce qui n'a pas d'équivalent en matière de jugements." *in* Gaillard, Emmanuel, 2016, *International Arbitration*, presentation delivered during the session on Monday, October 17, at the Academy of Moral and Political Sciences. Available at: https://academiesciencesmoralesetpolitiques.fr/2016/10/17/larbitrage-international/.

29 United Nations Commission on International Trade Law (UNCITRAL), Arbitration Centers, [online]. Available at: https://uncitral.un.org/fr/texts/arbitration/contractualtexts/arbitration/centres. Accessed 12 February 2024.

by the UNCITRAL Arbitration Rules; (b) administer arbitrations or offer administrative services under the Rules; and/or (c) fulfill the role of appointing authority in accordance with the Rules.

As we will see later, among the best-known are the Permanent Court of Arbitration (PCA) in The Hague, the International Centre for Settlement of Investment Disputes (ICSID) in Washington, the ICC International Court of Arbitration in Paris, the London Court of International Arbitration (LCIA), and the Arbitration Institute of the Stockholm Chamber of Commerce (SCC).

2.2.3 Investor-State Arbitration

Investor-state arbitration emerged in the 1980s, marked by a rise in Bilateral Investment Treaties (BITs) that aimed to protect foreign investments under the Rule of Law. This form of arbitration is distinguished by its ability to allow private investors to initiate claims against host states for damages caused by state actions. Initially, the emphasis was on its Private Law aspects. However, investor-state arbitration can be seen as a hybrid system, blending elements of both Public International Law and Private International Law. Currently, scholars prefer to stress that investor-state arbitration is a hybrid transnational normative regime.

In this respect, Anthea Roberts, Professor of Global Governance at the Australian National University's School of Regulation and Global Governance, specializes in innovative approaches to understanding dynamic and complex global areas. She judiciously compared investor-state arbitration to the Australian platypus species. Ten years ago, in 2013, she published an article in the American Journal of International Law, in which she wrote:

> When the skin of an Australian platypus was first taken to England in the 1700s, scientists thought it was a fake. It looked like someone had sewn a duck's bill onto a beaver's body; one scientist even took a pair of scissors to the skin looking for stitches. The animal had fur and was warm-blooded like a mammal, yet laid eggs and had webbed feet like a bird or a reptile. Scientists struggled to categorize this unusual creature. Was it a bird, a mammal, or a reptile? Or was it some strange hybrid of all three?
>
> Understanding and analyzing the investment treaty system has proven just as difficult. Investment treaties are clearly creatures of Public International Law: they are entered into by two or more states and are substantively governed by Public International Law. However, they are distinct from most Public International Law treaties because the vast majority of them permit investors to bring arbitral claims directly against host states based on procedural rules and enforcement mechanisms developed largely in the context of international commercial arbitration and investor-state contracts. Accordingly, the system grafts Private International Law dispute resolution mechanisms onto Public International Law treaties.[30]

Building on Anthea Roberts' insightful analogy, the very features that make the platypus so difficult to classify have also made it a symbol of uniqueness and scientific fascination. Due to its unique characteristics and because it shares traits with birds, reptiles, and mammals, the platypus has been the subject of scientific interest and study since its discovery by Europeans in the late 18th century. It is often cited as an example of a transitional form in the evolutionary process and is a symbol of biological uniqueness.

30 Roberts, Anthea, 2013, "Clash of Paradigms: Actors and Analogies Shaping the Investment-Treaty System," *The American Journal of International Law*, vol. 107, no. 1, pp. 45–94, 45.

Like the platypus, which confounded scientists with its mix of mammalian and avian-reptilian traits, investor-state arbitration incorporates the dispute resolution mechanisms of Private International Law into the treaties of Public International Law, creating a unique, hybrid system.

Investor-state arbitration cases are characterized by their involvement of a private investor and a state, and typically revolve around the investor's rights under international law as protected by treaties. These cases are distinct from international commercial arbitration, which involves disputes between private commercial entities and does not typically involve state parties or investment treaties.

What follows are examples of cases handled through investor-state arbitration.

One of the most significant cases in arbitration history is *Yukos Universal Limited (Isle of Man) v. The Russian Federation* (PCA Case No. 2005-04/AA227).[31] In this case, the former shareholders of Yukos Oil Company filed a claim against Russia under the 1994 Energy Charter Treaty, alleging unlawful expropriation and unfair treatment.

Starting in 2003, the Russian tax authorities charged Yukos with systemic and large-scale tax evasion. It imposed on Yukos very substantial tax assessments and fines, and ultimately seized Yukos' assets, as a result of which Yukos went into bankruptcy in August 2006. The Yukos shareholders claimed that the Russian Federation had thereby unlawfully expropriated most of Yukos' assets, and thus their protected investment.

The Yukos shareholders initiated three separate arbitral proceedings at the Permanent Court of Arbitration in The Hague against the Russian Federation under Article 26(4)(b) of the Energy Charter Treaty and the UNCITRAL Arbitration Rules.[32]

The proceedings began in 2005, and in 2014, the Arbitral Tribunal awarded the claimants approximately $50 billion for the expropriation of their investments, although the enforcement of this award has faced legal challenges in various jurisdictions.

The *Yukos Oil Company v. The Russian Federation* case is a historical investor-state arbitration. This case was heard in The Hague under the auspices of the Permanent Court of Arbitration. It involved claims by the shareholders of Yukos Oil Company – at the time Russia's largest oil company – that the Russian Federation had unlawfully expropriated their investments, violating the terms of the 1994 Energy Charter Treaty.

Another example is the *Vattenfall AB and others v. Federal Republic of Germany* (II), ICSID Case No. ARB/12/12. In the wake of the Fukushima disaster in 2011, Germany decided to accelerate the shutdown of its nuclear power plants through a legislative amendment known as the Thirteenth Amendment to the Atomic Energy Act. This move had direct consequences for Vattenfall, a Swedish energy company, which operated the Brunsbüttel and Krümmel nuclear plants in Germany. The amendment led to the premature closure of these plants without providing compensation to Vattenfall, despite previous legislative assurances under the Eleventh Amendment that had extended the operational lifetimes of nuclear plants. Vattenfall responded to this situation by challenging the German government's decision on two fronts: domestically, by filing a constitutional complaint, and internationally, by filing a request for arbitration before the World Bank's International Centre for Settlement of Investment Disputes (ICSID) under the Energy Charter Treaty (ECT).[33]

31 Permanent Court of Arbitration (PCA), *Yukos Universal Limited (Isle of Man) v. The Russian Federation*, Case No. 2005-04/AA227.

32 Bermann, George A., 2016, "The Yukos Annulment: Answered and Unanswered Questions," *American Review of International Arbitration*, vol. 27, no. 1.

33 *Vattenfall AB and others v. Federal Republic of Germany* (II), ICSID Case No. ARB/12/12, online. Available at: https://icsid.worldbank.org/cases/case-database/case-detail/ARB/12/12. Accessed 12 February 2024.

The German Federal Constitutional Court ruled in 2016 that the Thirteenth Amendment was unconstitutional insofar as it failed to offer compensation for investments made based on the legitimate expectation of continued plant operation. This ruling underscored the principle that while the state has considerable leeway in shaping its energy policies, especially concerning high-risk sectors like nuclear energy, it must also protect investors' legitimate expectations. However, the subsequent legislative attempts to rectify this, particularly through the Sixteenth Amendment, were deemed insufficient and failed to comply with the court's mandate, leading to further legal challenges.

Concurrently, Vattenfall's pursuit of international arbitration sought compensation for the financial losses incurred due to Germany's expedited nuclear phase-out.

The *Vattenfall v. Germany* case falls under the category of investor-state arbitration, similar to the Yukos case mentioned earlier. As explained, this type of arbitration arises when a foreign investor initiates proceedings against a sovereign state for alleged breaches of investment protection standards set out in international treaties or agreements.

The *Vattenfall v. Germany* case underscores the complex interplay between investment protection, as governed by international treaties and arbitration bodies like the ICSID, and the sovereign right of states to regulate industries for the public good, including environmental protection. It raises important questions about how countries can pursue environmental objectives without infringing on the legal rights of foreign investors, and how disputes of this nature can be resolved fairly and equitably.

In 2021, the Tribunal issued a procedural order acknowledging the discontinuance of the proceedings in accordance with ICSID Arbitration Rule 44, which means that the arbitration process was formally ended without a decision on the merits of the case.[34]

A third example of a case handled through investor-state arbitration is *ConocoPhillips Petrozuata B.V., ConocoPhillips Hamaca B.V. and ConocoPhillips Gulf of Paria B.V. v. Bolivarian Republic of Venezuela* (ICSID Case No. ARB/07/30). ConocoPhillips, an American exploration and production company headquartered in Houston, Texas, initiated proceedings against the Venezuelan government after the expropriation of its oil investments.

In this complex international arbitration case, ConocoPhillips subsidiaries filed a claim against the Bolivarian Republic of Venezuela under the auspices of the International Centre for Settlement of Investment Disputes (ICSID).

The Netherlands-Venezuela Bilateral Investment Treaty (BIT) of 1991[35] was applicable in this case because ConocoPhillips structured its investments in Venezuela through subsidiaries incorporated in the Netherlands. This is a common practice known as "treaty shopping," where investors from one country invest in another country via a third country that has a favorable investment treaty in place with the host country. This approach allows investors from one country to leverage the investment protections of a treaty between the host country and a third country with a favorable investment treaty.

The Netherlands-Venezuela BIT afforded ConocoPhillips a strong legal platform to pursue arbitration, securing rights to fair and equitable treatment, assurance against expropriation

34 Rule 44 of the ICSID Arbitration Rules allows for the discontinuance of a case when the parties involved agree to end the arbitration or when one party requests to discontinue and the other party does not object within a specified timeframe. Essentially, this procedural order signifies that the arbitration was halted by mutual agreement of the parties involved or by a unilateral decision that was not contested, without reaching a conclusion on the substantive issues of the dispute.

35 Netherlands–Venezuela BIT (1991) Agreement on encouragement and reciprocal protection of investments between the Kingdom of the Netherlands and the Republic of Venezuela.

without prompt and adequate compensation, and the freedom to transfer funds. By structuring its investments via Dutch entities, ConocoPhillips effectively availed itself of the BIT's protections, thereby invoking the treaty's provisions for its claims against Venezuela for expropriation and other treaty violations. Consequently, the BIT essentially gave the company access to international arbitration through ICSID, which is often a more neutral forum than domestic courts for resolving investment disputes.

The claim, registered on December 13, 2007, arose from disputes regarding investments in Venezuela. The arbitration tribunal was constituted on July 23, 2008, and included distinguished members from New Zealand, the UK, and Canada. The proceedings involved preliminary jurisdictional objections by Venezuela, comprehensive submissions on the merits by both parties, and several rounds of document production requests.

Following the death of an arbitrator and subsequent reconstitution of the tribunal, the case experienced procedural complexities, including requests for arbitrator disqualification and proposals for reconsideration of decisions. Despite these challenges, hearings on the merits and quantum (the amount of compensation due) took place, leading to a decision on jurisdiction and liability, with dissenting opinions reflecting the contentious nature of the case.

The original proceeding culminated in an award issued by the tribunal on March 8, 2019. The arbitration panel awarded ConocoPhillips over $8 billion, recognizing the breach of investment treaty obligations by Venezuela, which underscored the issues of government expropriation and the necessity of fair compensation within the sphere of international investments.

Subsequently, Venezuela sought rectification of the award, leading to a decision on rectification on August 29, 2019. Venezuela also applied for the annulment of the award, initiating a separate annulment proceeding that involved further procedural orders, hearings, and decisions on requests for reconsideration and the admissibility of new evidence. This annulment proceeding featured additional challenges, including proposals for the disqualification of committee members, and concluded with a hearing on annulment in Paris and via videoconference, reflecting the procedural and substantive complexity of international investment arbitration.[36]

2.2.4 Ad Hoc *vs. Institutional Arbitration*

Arbitration can be categorized as either *ad hoc* or institutional, each offering distinct advantages and challenges.

Ad hoc arbitration is a procedure set up and managed directly by the parties without institutional oversight. The parties are responsible for organizing and conducting the arbitration, relying on pre-agreed rules, such as the UNCITRAL Arbitration Rules, to govern the arbitration. In case of procedural difficulties, state courts at the arbitration seat may intervene if they have jurisdiction, but no institutional support is available.

UNCITRAL, the United Nations Commission on International Trade Law, is a key global body working to modernize and unify international trade laws. Its Arbitration Rules provide a structured framework that parties can adopt for their arbitration proceedings. These rules apply to both *ad hoc* arbitrations (where no institution is involved) and institutional arbitrations (where a body oversees the unfolding of the arbitration). They cover key aspects such as arbitrator appointment, case management, and award enforcement.

36 ConocoPhillips Petrozuata B.V., ConocoPhillips Hamaca B.V., and *ConocoPhillips Gulf of Paria B.V. v. Bolivarian Republic of Venezuela,* ICSID Case No. ARB/07/30, [online]. Available at: https://icsid.worldbank.org/cases/case-database/case-detail/ARB/07/30. Last accessed 12 February 2024.

Since their first adoption in 1976, the UNCITRAL Arbitration Rules have been widely used in commercial disputes, investor-state arbitrations, and state-to-state disputes. Over time, revisions have modernized the framework while preserving its original principles. The 2010 revision updated the UNCITRAL Arbitration Rules to reflect contemporary arbitration practices and enhance efficiency. The 2013 version introduced transparency rules for treaty-based investor-state arbitration. The 2021 version incorporated accelerated arbitration procedures for faster dispute resolution.

While *ad hoc* arbitration offers flexibility in setting procedural rules and lower costs (as it avoids institutional fees), it also carries risks. Disputes over arbitrator selection or funding issues can cause delays, as there is no institution to oversee these matters.

Institutional arbitration, in contrast, is administered by recognized arbitration institutions that provide a structured framework, support services, and procedural guidance for a fee: *International Arbitration Centers*. Though exact statistics are limited, institutional arbitration is generally more common worldwide due to its structured nature and institutional backing.

Contrary to common belief, often influenced by the diverse names these institutions carry or the misleading term "court," an arbitration institution is not a judicial body and does not hold any jurisdictional authority. These institutions are generally referred to as "Arbitration Centers," "Arbitration Courts," "Arbitration Institutes," "Arbitration Commissions," or even "International Dispute Resolution Centers." Other variations include "Arbitration Chambers" or "Councils."

Some of the most well-known arbitration institutions include the Permanent Court of Arbitration (PCA) in The Hague, the International Centre for Settlement of Investment Disputes (ICSID) in Washington, and the International Chamber of Commerce (ICC) International Court of Arbitration located in Paris. Other examples of arbitration centers include: the London Court of International Arbitration (LCIA), the Hong Kong International Arbitration Centre (HKIAC), the Swiss Chambers' Arbitration and Mediation Court, the International Court of Arbitration of the International Chamber of Commerce (ICC), the Arbitration Institute of the Stockholm Chamber of Commerce (SCC), the Côte d'Ivoire Arbitration Court (CACI), the China International Economic and Trade Arbitration Commission (CIETAC), the International Centre for Settlement of Investment Disputes (ICSID), the Bahrain Chamber for Dispute Resolution (BCDR-AAA), and the Korean Commercial Arbitration Board (KCAB).

Regardless of their name, these arbitration institutions primarily offer conciliation, mediation, and/or arbitration services to resolve disputes. In most cases, they handle conflicts related to international trade and investment (for international arbitration) or various domestic disputes (for domestic arbitration).

These institutions provide not only administrative support but also comprehensive arbitration rules that guide the entire process. Their rules typically specify the default number of arbitrators in a tribunal, the appointment process for arbitrators, and the timeframe for each phase of the arbitration.

For instance, the ICC Arbitration Rules are widely used worldwide, offering a neutral and fair framework for resolving international disputes under the supervision of the ICC International Court of Arbitration, one of the most respected arbitral bodies.

Although institutional arbitration provides structure and efficiency, it also comes with higher costs and less procedural flexibility compared to *ad hoc* arbitration. However, it ensures a smoother process by eliminating common administrative hurdles found in *ad hoc* arbitration, such as difficulties in appointing arbitrators or resolving procedural disputes.

Both *ad hoc* and institutional arbitration offer viable paths for resolving international disputes. The choice between them depends on factors such as cost considerations, procedural flexibility, and the need for institutional support. While *ad hoc* arbitration allows parties to tailor procedures to their needs, institutional arbitration provides a well-defined, structured approach that reduces the risk of procedural deadlocks. Ultimately, selecting the appropriate arbitration method depends on the nature of the dispute and the preferences of the parties involved.

2.3 Foundation of Arbitration: Agreements, Clauses, and Party Autonomy

Arbitration is a contract-based dispute resolution mechanism that relies on the mutual consent of the parties. This section explores the foundation of arbitration, focusing on arbitration agreements and clauses, which define the scope and process of arbitration, and party autonomy, which allows parties to shape key aspects of the arbitration proceedings within legal limits. Understanding these principles is essential for ensuring an effective and enforceable arbitration process.

2.3.1 Arbitration Agreements and Arbitration Clauses

Arbitration is a contract-based method of resolving disputes outside the courts. This means that parties must agree in writing to settle their disputes through arbitration. This agreement can take two forms: an arbitration clause included in a contract before a dispute arises or a separate arbitration agreement made after a dispute has already occurred.

An arbitration clause is part of a commercial contract, ensuring that any future disputes will go to arbitration instead of court. It is commonly found in business agreements such as sales, leases, and partnerships. On the other hand, an arbitration agreement is made after a dispute arises, allowing parties to decide on arbitration at that stage.

A key principle in arbitration is *separability*, which means the arbitration clause remains valid even if the main contract is cancelled or ruled invalid. This separability principle ensures the continuity and enforceability of the arbitration process, safeguarding it from disputes concerning the underlying contract.[37] Hence, this allows arbitration to continue independently of the contract.

However, arbitration agreements must follow specific legal rules, which vary between countries. Some disputes cannot be settled through arbitration, and some legal systems require arbitration agreements to follow a certain format.

Certain disputes cannot be settled through arbitration due to public interest, fundamental rights, or state authority. Legal systems often require such cases to be handled by public courts for proper oversight. Criminal cases like fraud, assault, and money laundering fall under criminal courts, as arbitration applies only to civil and commercial disputes. Similarly, family law matters such as divorce, child custody, and inheritance require court intervention due to their impact on personal rights and social policy. Employment disputes, including wrongful termination and wage claims, are often resolved through labor courts instead of arbitration. Consumer protection cases may also be restricted to prevent unfair arbitration clauses that limit consumer rights. Bankruptcy and insolvency cases require judicial supervision since they involve multiple creditors and the public interest. Likewise, competition law (antitrust) disputes often cannot be arbitrated due to their effect on the broader economy. Finally, constitutional and public law disputes, including government regulations and taxation, are generally non-arbitrable.

37 Bermann, George A., 2016, "International Arbitration and Private International Law," *Collected Courses of the Hague Academy of International Law*, vol. 381, General Course on Private International Law.

Consent is essential for arbitration. Whether in state-to-state, investor-state, or commercial arbitration, all forms of arbitration rely on parties agreeing to resolve disputes this way. In state-to-state arbitration, this agreement is usually found in treaties. In commercial arbitration, it is included in business contracts. In investor-state arbitration, governments often make a standing offer to arbitrate in treaties, which becomes binding when an investor files a claim.

Despite debates on the nature of consent in investor-state arbitration, it is generally accepted that these arbitrations also rest on a foundational agreement. Although some have considered that investor-state arbitration would be an example of arbitration without privity,[38] mainstream scholars consider it to be based on consent just as much as the other two modes of international arbitration.

Even still, one should note that the formation of the arbitration agreement follows a particular process. In this respect, scholars argue that provisions contained in investment treaties referring disputes to arbitration would represent a standing offer to arbitrate and that the arbitration agreement would be formed once the investor decided to initiate arbitration by accepting the offer contained in the treaty.[39] In this context, investment treaties function as a standing offer to arbitrate, with the agreement materializing once an investor opts to initiate arbitration.

It is essential to differentiate between the execution of arbitration agreements and the enforcement of arbitral awards, because one could mistakenly mix the enforcement of arbitration agreements with the execution of arbitral awards. The enforcement of arbitration agreements generally involves a separate legal process aimed at compelling parties to arbitrate (order compelling arbitration), rather than enforcing a final decision through exequatur. The enforcement of arbitral awards relies on the exequatur procedure, which is used to recognize and enforce arbitral awards across borders, ensuring that a winning party can enforce the award in a jurisdiction different from where the arbitration took place.

In conclusion, the arbitration agreement is the cornerstone of international arbitration. However, the legally binding nature of the arbitration agreement is proportional to the capacity that it has to be endowed with enforceable power by state courts.[40]

2.3.2 Party Autonomy in Arbitration

Party autonomy is a fundamental principle in international arbitration, which allows parties to shape the arbitration process according to their specific needs. This principle grants parties the freedom to agree on various aspects of arbitration, including procedural rules, the appointment of arbitrators, the seat of arbitration, and even the applicable substantive law.

Arbitration provides parties with an *à la carte* system where they can choose procedural rules, arbitrators, and applicable law. The DNA of arbitration is undeniably adversarial. The parties in an arbitration procedure are adversaries, not partners, each trying to advance their

38 See Paulsson, Jan, 1995, "Arbitration without Privity," *ICSID Review – Foreign Investment Law Journal*, vol. 10, no. 2, pp. 232–257.

39 With regards to arbitration provisions in investment treaties, see for example Article VII (3)(a) of the 1991 US-Argentina BIT, which stipulates: "Provided that the national or company concerned has not submitted the dispute for resolution under paragraph 2 (a) or (b) and that six months have elapsed from the date on which the dispute arose, the national or company concerned may choose to consent in writing to the submission of the dispute for settlement by binding arbitration."

40 Bermann, George A., 2017, "The Role of National Courts at the Threshold of Arbitration," *The American Review of International Arbitration*, vol. 28, no. 3.

interests as much as possible. The ideal outcome in arbitration, as in any litigation, is first and foremost to win the case.

However, a fundamental point of divergence between arbitration and litigation (and thus a point of convergence between arbitration and mediation) concerns the place of party autonomy in the dispute resolution process. Indeed, party autonomy, also called the "will of the parties," is just as central in arbitration as in mediation: arbitration is founded and organized on the basis of the autonomy of the parties and contract law. This is notably the famous *arbitration agreement* that is the legal foundation of the arbitrators' power. Consequently, consent to arbitration is an indispensable prerequisite to its commencement and development.

For Diego P. Fernández Arroyo, Professor at Sciences Po, expert in International Litigation, Arbitration, Comparative Law, Private International Law, and Public International Law, director of the LLM in Transnational Arbitration and Dispute Settlement,

> Arbitration – and even more clearly international arbitration – is known as the legal field in which party autonomy reaches its highest expression. Indeed, the parties to a legal relationship not only decide voluntarily upon the selection of arbitration as the mechanism to settle their disputes, but they also agree on the functioning details of such mechanism. In this sense, they may define the subject matters submitted to arbitration, the concrete type of arbitration under which those disputes will be solved (ad hoc or institutional), the procedure to appoint arbitrators (and, of course, the arbitrators themselves), the seat of arbitration, the language of the proceedings, the law applicable to the merits of the case, and other procedural details. In other words, they set the framework and build their own dispute resolution process. In this sense, when it comes to arbitration, party autonomy does not end with the mere choice of one of the diverse available dispute settlement mechanisms; instead the parties' will spreads – directly or indirectly – over every single element of the procedure. In sum, we find here a propitious area for the exercise of party autonomy.[41]

Arbitration is quite flexible when compared to a traditional jurisdictional procedure, given that the parties and arbitrators have almost discretionary power over the conduct of the trial. However, nowadays there is a considerable movement in favor of codifying arbitration practices.[42] This trend can be attributed to the fact that many feel the work of arbitrators is closer to

41 Fernández Arroyo, Diego P., 2016, "Arbitrator's Procedural Powers: The Last Frontier of Party Autonomy?," in *Limits to Party Autonomy in International Commercial Arbitration*, ed. Franco Ferrari, JurisNet.

42 See Kaufmann-Kohler, Gabrielle, 2010, "Soft Law in International Arbitration: Codification and Normativity," *Journal of International Dispute Settlement*. Professor Kaufmann-Kohler describes the phenomenon in the following terms: "The preceding analysis shows that there is indeed a soft law codification process in the field of arbitral procedure which combines compilation with innovation. This process is driven by the epistemic global arbitration community and is facilitated by globalization, which leaves ample room for action to non-state actors. In this context, one may wonder how the transnational consensus on international arbitration would be affected if the present political consensus which underpins globalization were to disintegrate. This is a question that only time will answer. This study has also shown that soft law carries a certain normative weight and that normativity is enhanced when soft law rules are codified. While soft codification serves a useful purpose in increasing certainty and predictability, it cannot be ignored that the prevalent influence of the epistemic community carries the inherent risk of lack of democratic legitimacy. The interests of the categories of users which are not adequately represented in the epistemic community may be left without protection. It is thus incumbent upon the state to provide appropriate safeguards for those users through legislation as part of its residual power in arbitration."

that of a judge than that of a mediator, with the same requirements in terms of responsibility and legitimacy as those governing judicial disputes.[43]

George Bermann, Professor of International Law and director of the Center for International Commercial and Investment Arbitration at Columbia Law School, has a balanced and critical approach to the field. He argues that being "pro-arbitration" does not mean accepting all aspects of arbitration uncritically.[44] Instead, he emphasizes the need for fairness, efficiency, and legitimacy to ensure arbitration remains a trusted dispute resolution mechanism. His work highlights the complex trade-offs involved in designing arbitration systems that serve both private and public interests.[45]

Through his work at Columbia Law School, contributions to ALI's Restatement on Arbitration, and active engagement in international arbitration forums, George Bermann has significantly shaped modern international arbitration.

As mentioned before, party autonomy means that parties in a dispute can decide important aspects of the arbitration process. However, how much control they have depends on the type of arbitration: commercial arbitration, investment arbitration, or interstate arbitration.

Commercial arbitration provides strong party autonomy, allowing parties to freely choose the arbitration rules, governing law, arbitrators, and seat of arbitration, with minimal restrictions limited to public policy and mandatory legal provisions. The most common forums for commercial arbitration include the International Chamber of Commerce (ICC), London Court of International Arbitration (LCIA), Singapore International Arbitration Centre (SIAC), Hong Kong International Arbitration Centre (HKIAC), American Arbitration Association – International Centre for Dispute Resolution (AAA-ICDR), China International Economic and Trade Arbitration Commission (CIETAC), Stockholm Chamber of Commerce (SCC), Dubai International Arbitration Centre (DIAC), and UNCITRAL Ad Hoc Arbitration (instead of using an institution, parties can choose ad hoc arbitration under UNCITRAL Arbitration Rules, providing more flexibility).

Investment arbitration offers limited party autonomy, as the arbitration process is largely governed by investment treaties, such as the ICSID Convention or bilateral investment treaties. Investors do not negotiate arbitration terms directly; instead, they accept the terms already agreed upon in treaties. The choice of arbitration rules, location, and governing law is often determined by the treaty, not by the parties. Although investors and states may have some flexibility in selecting arbitrators and procedural rules, states can impose restrictions, such as transparency

43 See Fouchard, Gaillard and Goldman: "Arbitrators are empowered by the parties to decide the parties' dispute. That judicial power is the principal characteristic of their role and enables arbitration to be distinguished from superficially similar concepts such as expert proceedings, conciliation and mediation." Fouchard, Philippe, Gaillard, Emmanuel and Goldman, Berthold, 1999, *International Commercial Arbitration*, Kluwer Law International, p. 560.

44 Bermann, George A., 2018, "What Does It Mean to Be 'Pro-Arbitration'?," *Arbitration International*, vol. 34, pp. 341–358. Available at: https://scholarship.law.columbia.edu/faculty_scholarship/2880.

45 One of Bermann's major areas of focus is the recognition and enforcement of arbitral awards, particularly under the 1958 New York Convention. He examines the role of national courts in enforcing or challenging arbitration decisions, with a specific emphasis on public policy exceptions and judicial review. He has contributed extensively to discussions on how courts should navigate their limited but important role in overseeing arbitration outcomes without undermining its core principles.

As the chief reporter for the American Law Institute (ALI) Restatement on U.S. Arbitration Law, Bermann has played a key role in shaping U.S. arbitration jurisprudence in relation to international standards. He advocates for greater coherence between U.S. law and global arbitration frameworks. Bermann has also been a prominent voice in debates on Investor-State Dispute Settlement (ISDS), highlighting concerns over transparency, legitimacy, and fairness.

requirements or limits on certain claims. Party autonomy exists, but it is much more limited than in commercial arbitration. The international arbitration forums most commonly provided for in bilateral investment treaties are: Arbitration under the Convention on the Settlement of Investment Disputes between States and Nationals of Other States (ICSID Arbitration), Arbitration under the Additional Facility Rules of the International Centre for the Settlement of Investment Disputes (ICSID Additional Facility Arbitration), Ad hoc arbitration conducted under the UNCITRAL Arbitration Rules (UNCITRAL Ad Hoc Arbitration), Arbitration under the Arbitration Institute of the Stockholm Chamber of Commerce (SCC Arbitration), and Arbitration conducted under the Rules of Arbitration of the International Chamber of Commerce (ICC Arbitration).

Interstate arbitration grants minimal party autonomy, as the process is primarily dictated by international treaties, customary law, and established dispute resolution mechanisms, leaving little room for states to independently shape procedural rules or arbitration terms. The common arbitration forum for interstate arbitration is the Permanent Court of Arbitration. The Permanent Court of Arbitration was established in 1899 to facilitate arbitration and dispute resolution between states. Over time, it has evolved into a modern arbitral institution that serves the international community's changing needs. The Peace Palace, constructed in 1907, serves as the headquarters of the Permanent Court of Arbitration and remains one of The Hague's most significant legal landmarks. Reflecting global trends in international dispute resolution, the PCA handles a growing number of cases, including inter-state arbitrations, investment treaty disputes, and contract-based arbitrations involving states and public entities.

As highlighted previously, party autonomy applies to all three types of arbitration, but to varying degrees and with different limitations.

2.4 The Unfolding of Arbitration

Arbitral proceedings generally follow a structured but flexible approach, incorporating elements from both Common Law and Civil Law traditions. A fundamental principle is the right of both parties to be heard, which ensures that they can present their claims, respond to opposing arguments, and submit relevant evidence. Procedural fairness requires that neither party be placed at a disadvantage, and tribunals must ensure that both sides are given equal opportunity to participate.

The arbitration begins with a *request for arbitration*, which serves as a formal notice of a party's intent to initiate proceedings. This request is typically submitted to an arbitral institution or directly to the appointed arbitrator, depending on whether the arbitration is institutional or *ad hoc*. Once the arbitration is initiated, jurisdictional questions may arise, particularly concerning the validity of the arbitration agreement and the arbitrability of the dispute under the relevant legal framework. Parties often challenge the tribunal's jurisdiction, arguing that the arbitration clause is invalid or that the dispute falls outside its scope. The principle of competence-competence allows arbitral tribunals to determine their own jurisdiction, subject to later review by national courts in some cases.

Once jurisdiction is established, arbitrators are appointed either by party agreement or through default mechanisms set by institutional rules. The appointment process is crucial in ensuring neutrality and expertise, particularly in complex international disputes. Following the constitution of the tribunal, the arbitrators set procedural timelines, defining key stages such as the submission of statements of claim and defense, document production, and scheduling of hearings. These procedural steps are usually governed by party agreements, institutional rules, or procedural orders issued by the tribunal.

Now we should explain what exactly happens in arbitral proceedings. As mentioned previously, arbitrations presuppose the existence of an arbitration agreement.

Let's imagine a very simple situation where two individuals have signed a contract of purchase and sale of a car, which, in one of its clauses, provides that any dispute arising from that contract shall be resolved through arbitration. Let's further imagine that the buyer failed to pay the agreed sum for the car. In this scenario, how exactly will the seller proceed?

2.4.1 Initiating Arbitration

Usually, the first step in arbitration is either to file a Request for Arbitration before an arbitral institution (in case your arbitration agreement provided for institutional arbitration) or to serve the opposing party a Notice of Arbitration. In both cases, these documents will consist of a written summary of the dispute and of the claimant's claims and may contain references to the constitution of the arbitral tribunal.

So initially, the claimant will file a statement of claim presenting at length the facts of the case, its arguments, and its claims. Then follows the respondent's statement of defense, presenting at length its arguments for resisting the claimant's claims. This initial phase sets the framework for the entire procedure, as it defines the scope of the dispute and clarifies the issues that the tribunal will later be asked to decide.

2.4.2 Responding to the Arbitration

Upon receipt of the arbitration notice, the respondent, here the buyer, is expected to provide a reply. The respondent's participation at this stage is crucial, as it ensures that both sides are heard from the outset and that the proceedings move forward on a balanced and transparent basis.

This reply will detail the respondent's perspective on the dispute, their defenses, any counterclaims they might have, and their views on the composition of the arbitral tribunal. With that in mind, it should be noted that a fundamental feature in the exchanges between the parties consists of discussing the topics related to the constitution of the tribunal. Hence, at this point, we may take a closer look at the constitution of the arbitral tribunal.

2.4.3 Forming the Arbitral Tribunal

The parties usually provide the number of arbitrators and the method for the appointment of arbitrators in their arbitration agreement, or instead they rely on the arbitral rules of the institution chosen to administer the arbitration (in the case of institutional arbitration).

The arbitration agreement typically specifies the number of arbitrators and the procedure for their appointment. Most commonly, an arbitral tribunal consists of three arbitrators, though a single arbitrator is not uncommon. The selection process often involves each party nominating one arbitrator, with the two appointed arbitrators then selecting a third who usually serves as the presiding arbitrator.[46]

Forming the tribunal is therefore a decisive moment, since the legitimacy and credibility of the entire process depend on having impartial, competent arbitrators trusted by both parties.

46 In this respect, it should be noted that there is a relation between the complexity of the dispute and the number of arbitrators. Thus, arbitral tribunals with a sole arbitrator are reserved for less complex disputes.

2.4.4 *Role and Responsibilities of the Arbitral Tribunal*

The arbitral tribunal, the body composed of one or more arbitrators, is the organ entrusted with the authority of settling the dispute.

Arbitrators are neutral third parties who bear the responsibility of conducting the proceedings fairly and impartially, ultimately deciding on the outcome of the dispute. Unlike mediators, who facilitate discussions, arbitrators have the authority to render binding decisions. They also have the responsibility to manage the proceedings, including setting deadlines and resolving procedural disagreements between the parties.

Also, arbitrators are entrusted with the charge to determine the conduct of the proceedings whenever the parties cannot agree on a certain point. For instance, let's imagine that one party wishes to file a certain document within the deadline X, while the opposing party wishes that the deadline be Y. In this situation, the arbitrator has the authority to set the deadline it finds most convenient.

Their task goes beyond applying the law: arbitrators must ensure efficiency, fairness, and due process, guiding the proceedings from start to finish until the final award is rendered.

2.4.5 *The Arbitration Proceedings*

Once the tribunal is constituted, the parties will then start their exchanges towards the resolution of their dispute.

The arbitration continues with the claimant and respondent exchanging detailed submissions: the statement of claim and the statement of defense, respectively. These documents lay out the facts, arguments, and claims or defenses in depth. The exchange may include further rounds of submissions, known as joinder and re-joinder. So there may be joinder and re-joinder, respectively, from the claimant and the respondent.

Meanwhile, the parties will have to produce and present evidence to support their arguments – this production of evidence is known as discovery.

The taking of evidence in arbitration varies depending on the procedural rules adopted by the parties. Documentary evidence is often central to arbitral proceedings, with document production requests being subject to limitations designed to prevent fishing expeditions. The Redfern Schedule is a structured tool used in arbitration to manage document production efficiently. It consists of columns where parties list requested documents, explain their relevance, respond to objections, and receive a ruling from the tribunal. This format helps ensure that document requests are justified and not overly broad.

Document disclosure is essential in arbitration, as it allows parties to present evidence they would not otherwise have. However, the Redfern Schedule should not be misused for fishing expeditions. Most arbitral institutions, including the IBA Rules on Taking Evidence in International Arbitration (2020), discourage speculative document requests and emphasize proportionality.

Under the IBA Rules, a request must provide a clear description of the documents sought, explain their relevance, and confirm that they are not already in the requesting party's possession. Arbitrators assess requests based on factors such as materiality, legal privilege, confidentiality, and procedural economy. They may grant full disclosure, limit the scope, or reject requests if they are excessive or unnecessary.

Redfern Schedules were introduced to streamline arbitration by reducing time and costs in document production. While some parties attempt to misuse them, the widespread adoption of IBA guidelines and keyword search tools helps curb excessive disclosure demands. Arbitrators increasingly focus on balancing transparency with efficiency, ensuring that disclosure remains fair and proportionate to the case.

Consider, for example, a dispute over defective software: one party would request internal emails and quality control reports to prove the other had been aware of the defects before delivery. The opposing party might object, arguing that the requests were too broad and included confidential information.

To manage this, the tribunal would use a Redfern Schedule to assess each request. It could allow access to emails but might limit disclosure to those discussing defects. Quality control reports would be granted with redactions to protect sensitive details. However, a request for customer complaints from other clients might be denied as irrelevant to the case.

This structured approach would ensure fair document production, balancing transparency with efficiency while preventing excessive or speculative requests.

Witness testimony is another key evidentiary tool, with fact witnesses providing accounts of events and expert witnesses offering opinions on technical or legal matters. The method of questioning witnesses differs between arbitration traditions. Some arbitrations follow the Common Law approach, where cross-examination is a significant part of the arbitration, while others adopt a Civil Law style, where tribunals take a more active role in questioning. The IBA Rules on the Taking of Evidence in International Arbitration serve as a widely accepted guideline for handling evidence, offering a balanced approach between these traditions.

Following discovery, hearings are held, providing an opportunity for oral arguments and the cross-examination of witnesses and experts.

2.4.6 Issuance and Enforcement of Arbitral Awards

The tribunal finally issues a written award, which determines the final resolution of the arbitration. This award outlines the tribunal's findings, legal reasoning, and any monetary or non-monetary remedies granted. Arbitration provides a structured yet flexible process, ensuring disputes are resolved efficiently outside traditional court systems.

Once issued, arbitral awards are binding and final, meaning parties are expected to comply without further litigation. However, in some cases, national laws permit limited challenges, typically on procedural grounds such as lack of jurisdiction, violation of due process, or exceeding the tribunal's mandate.

The New York Convention (1958) plays a key role in ensuring the global enforceability of arbitral awards. With over 170 signatory states, it obligates national courts to recognize and enforce awards unless specific exceptions apply, such as public policy violations or invalid arbitration agreements. This makes arbitration an effective tool for resolving international disputes.

Limits to arbitral authority include the fact that arbitral tribunals lack direct enforcement power and cannot compel parties to comply with awards. Unlike state courts, which have coercive authority to freeze assets, seize property, or enforce judgments, arbitrators rely on national courts for enforcement.

If a party refuses to comply, the successful party must apply to a state court for enforcement. Courts have the legal authority to issue orders compelling compliance, such as asset freezes or monetary payments. This reliance on national courts highlights the inherent limitations of arbitration and its dependence on state legal systems.

Arbitrators have the authority to issue interim measures, which are temporary rulings designed to protect parties' rights during arbitration. These may include asset freezes, injunctions, or orders to preserve evidence. However, the enforceability of interim measures varies by jurisdiction.

Some national courts readily enforce interim measures, while others require a final award before granting enforcement. The UNCITRAL Model Law (2006) provides a framework for recognizing arbitral interim measures, but its adoption is not universal. Ultimately, an arbitrator's power to impose interim relief depends on whether national courts recognize and enforce such orders.

At the same time, state courts have the power to annul arbitral awards under specific conditions. Grounds for annulment are limited and typically include procedural irregularities, lack of jurisdiction, violations of due process, or conflicts with public policy. Annulment does not review the merits of the case but ensures the arbitration process was fair and legally valid.

Arbitral awards provide a binding resolution to disputes, but their enforceability depends on national courts. While arbitration offers autonomy and flexibility and is an independent dispute resolution mechanism, its effectiveness depends on judicial support. As Gary Born aptly stated, "International arbitration works because states agreed to enforce arbitral awards, without reviewing their merits. This is a remarkable achievement of global cooperation."[47]

3 International Arbitration as a Transnational Legal Order

This section delves into the concept of international arbitration as a transnational legal order, highlighting its role in resolving cross-border disputes. It explores how arbitration transcends national boundaries, creating a framework of norms and practices that bridge diverse legal systems. The discussion examines the evolution of arbitration, the validity of arbitration agreements, and the interplay between national legal systems and a growing transnational arbitral order. The concept of *floating justice* is introduced to describe arbitration's unique position as a system that operates above the confines of individual states, relying on International Law and cooperation to deliver justice in a globalized world.

3.1 The Evolution of Arbitration as a Transnational Legal Order

This section examines how investor-state and state-to-state arbitration function as international legal orders, meeting key criteria such as norms, subjects, and adjudicators. It also explores the debate on whether international commercial arbitration qualifies as a transnational legal order, reflecting the impact of globalization on legal frameworks. By analyzing these systems, we assess arbitration's role in bridging national boundaries and addressing the complexities of global disputes.

3.1.1 Investor-State and State-to-State Arbitration as International Legal Orders

Investor-state arbitration and state-to-state arbitration can be perceived as international legal orders because they encompass the three fundamental criteria that define a legal order: norms, subjects with rights, and judges, regardless of their designation (*arbitrators* in the case of international arbitration).[48]

Both systems operate under established legal frameworks that provide the norms for the proceedings. In investor-state arbitration, these norms often derive from bilateral investment treaties (BITs), multilateral treaties like the Energy Charter Treaty, or provisions within Free Trade Agreements (FTAs) that include investment chapters. In state-to-state arbitration, these norms are generally set by other international treaties.

47 See Born, Gary B., 2021, *International Commercial Arbitration*, 3rd ed., Kluwer Law International.

48 Refer to Chapter 1 – *What Is Law? What Forms Does Law Take?* – which provides further discussion of this point.

The subjects – or parties with rights and obligations – within these legal orders are clearly defined. In investor-state arbitration, the subjects are typically private investors and the host state in which the investment is made. For state-to-state arbitration, the subjects are the states themselves, each with sovereignty and the capacity to enter into agreements under International Law.

An adjudicator is an individual who has the authority to make a judgment or decision regarding a dispute. In arbitration, this person is called an *arbitrator*. The role of an arbitrator is to make decisions that are binding on the parties, based on the law and the facts presented. This involves evaluating evidence and arguments presented by the parties involved in the dispute.

3.1.2 The Debate on International Commercial Arbitration as a Transnational Legal Order

Is international commercial arbitration a transnational legal order? This question raises significant debate within the realm of International Law and global governance, challenging scholars and practitioners alike to consider the complexities and realities of law beyond the confines of nation-states. The concept of a transnational legal order refers to a collection of practices, norms, and rules that are observed across national boundaries, influencing the behavior of states, corporations, individuals, and non-state actors in the international arena. This phenomenon is driven by globalization, the proliferation of international treaties, the activities of international organizations, and the increasing interconnectedness of economic, social, and political processes worldwide.

At the heart of the debate is the extent to which this order possesses legal authority and legitimacy, transcending the traditional Westphalian notion of sovereignty, where states are the primary law-makers and law-enforcers. Proponents like Anne-Marie Slaughter – a global leader and public intellectual, formerly a Harvard Law professor and President of the American Society of International Law – argue that a transnational legal order is emerging through various mechanisms and interactions, including interactions between international courts and national courts, transnational regulatory networks, and multilateral agreements that create cohesive legal frameworks on issues like human rights, environmental protection, and trade.

> Judicial globalization, by contrast, describes a much more diverse and messy process of judicial interaction across, above and below borders, exchanging ideas and cooperating in cases involving national as much as international law. This essay sets forth five different categories of judicial interaction: relations between national courts and the European Court of Justice in the European Union; interactions between the European Court of Human Rights and national courts; the emergence of judicial comity in transnational litigation; constitutional cross-fertilization; and face-to-face meetings among judges around the world.[49]

Opponents, however, questioned the effectiveness, enforceability, and democratic legitimacy of such an order. They highlight the disparities in power and resources among states and other actors that could lead to an uneven playing field, where the interests of more powerful entities predominate.[50] Furthermore, the lack of a centralized global government or universally recognized legal authority complicates the enforcement of transnational laws and norms, leading to inconsistencies and conflicts between different legal systems and cultures.

49 Slaughter, Anne-Marie, 2000, "Judicial Globalization," *Virginia Journal of International Law*, vol. 40, no. 4, pp. 1103–1124.

50 John Mearsheimer, for instance, an international relations theorist known for his work on realism, Professor of Political Science at the University of Chicago, questions the efficacy and fairness of international institutions, arguing that they often reflect the interests of the most powerful states rather than serving a genuinely global community.

The late and aforementioned Emmanuel Gaillard (1952–2021), who was a distinguished French practicing lawyer, a foremost expert in international commercial arbitration, and a professor of law, presented the idea of a transnational arbitral order, a theoretical framework in which the legitimacy of arbitration and the power of arbitrators are acknowledged and upheld through a consensus among nations.

The rise of a transnational legal order shows how legal norms and practices are increasingly crossing borders, challenging state sovereignty while creating new ways to address global issues.

3.2 Introduction to Arbitral Validity

Arbitration is rooted in contract. Even still, we may find in the legal literature some efforts to identify "the ultimate *source of validity* of the agreement giving arbitrators the power to judge."[51] These efforts are seemingly loyal to the basic tenets of legal positivism, as the key question in these studies is related to knowing which legal order governs the arbitral agreement. Such exploration is not merely academic but strikes at the heart of arbitration's practical efficacy and recognition across different legal systems.

One stream of scholars engaged in this type of inquiry has argued that the source of validity of arbitral agreements would be found in the law of the seat of the arbitration. The strongest version of this argument defends that "every arbitration is a national arbitration, that is to say, subject to a specific system of national law."[52]

3.2.1 National Law as the Source of Validity

A predominant view among scholars suggests that the validity of arbitral agreements is anchored in the law of the arbitration's seat. This perspective upholds that arbitration inherently adheres to the national legal framework, rendering every arbitration essentially national in character. This argument, in its most rigid form, suggests that arbitral proceedings are invariably subject to a specific national legal system.

A softer version of this explanation, carrying a "choice of law" flavor, argues that parties to arbitral agreements would choose the *lex arbitri* by choosing the place of arbitration.[53] Even still, once the seat is chosen, the corresponding system of state law would attribute and govern arbitrators' power to issue binding decisions on given disputes.

If two companies choose Paris as the seat of arbitration, they are indirectly choosing French law to govern the arbitration. This means French law will define and regulate the arbitrators' authority to make binding decisions in their dispute.

3.2.2 Multilocal and Transnational Perspectives

Venturing beyond conventional legal positivism, Emmanuel Gaillard offered an innovative perspective on the validity of arbitration agreements and, by extension, the foundational authority of arbitrators.

51 Translated from French by the author. Original text: "la source de validité de la convention donnant aux arbitres le pouvoir de juger." *in* Gaillard, Emmanuel, 2008, *Aspects philosophiques du droit de l'arbitrage international*, LGDJ, p. 72.

52 Mann, Frederick Alexander, 1986, "Lex Facit Arbitrum," *Arbitration International*, vol. 2, no. 3, pp. 241–261.

53 See, for instance, Goode, Roy, 2001, "The Role of the Lex Loci Arbitri in International Commercial Arbitration," *Arbitration International*, vol. 17, no. 1, pp. 19–39.

The first explanation, his approach to the so-called *multilocalisatrice* (multilocal) for the validity of arbitral agreements, argues that all national legal systems potentially affected by the arbitration would have a say on the validity of its constitutive act.[54] The adjective multilocal means having multiple points of origin, perspectives, or centers. It is often used in anthropology, cultural studies, or legal theory to describe phenomena that don't come from a single source but from several. Here, it indicates a concept or approach that involves multiple locations or jurisdictions. This view expands the scope of legal consideration beyond the singular law of the seat, suggesting a more integrated and pluralistic approach to arbitral validity.

Building on this, Gaillard advances the idea of a transnational arbitral order – a theoretical construct where the validity of arbitration and the authority of arbitrators are recognized and supported by a consensus among states. This second explanation, seemingly a refined version of the previous thesis, thus affirms that arbitral authority would be grounded on a transnational arbitral order, which would be created by states "that broadly agree on the conditions that an arbitration must fulfill to be considered as a mandatory mode of dispute resolution whose outcome, the arbitral award, deserves to receive the endorsement of states."[55]

This consensus broadly agrees on the conditions necessary for arbitration to be considered a mandatory dispute resolution mechanism. The transnational arbitral order, thus, is not confined to the dictates of any single national legal system but is a product of international consensus on the essential features that arbitration must satisfy to warrant state enforcement of arbitral awards.

3.2.3 Floating Justice

The discussions surrounding the *source of validity* for arbitral agreements challenge the traditional boundaries of legal positivism and invite a reassessment of arbitration's place within the global legal order. The perspectives ranging from strict adherence to national law to the embracing of a transnational arbitral order reflect the dynamic and evolving nature of international arbitration.

This evolution mirrors the growing complexity of cross-border disputes and the need for a dispute resolution mechanism that is both flexible and recognized across jurisdictions. As such, the concept of a transnational arbitral order not only enriches the academic debate but also has deep implications for the practice of international arbitration, advocating for a more harmonized and universally accepted framework.

The notion of *floating justice*[56] best characterizes transnational litigation and, more specifically, international arbitration. It conveys the idea that the justice rendered through Alternative Dispute Resolution mechanisms is not anchored to the judicial system of any single state but rather stands above and transcends them, accompanying the disputing parties across international borders.

In conclusion, international arbitration can be seen as an autonomous transnational legal order to a significant extent, with its own rules and norms that operate across national boundaries.

54 Gaillard, Emmanuel, 2007, "Souveraineté et autonomie: réflexions sur les représentations de l'arbitrage international," *Journal du Droit International*, pp. 1163–1173, 1172.

55 Translated from French by the author. Original text: "s'accordent largement sur les conditions qu'un arbitrage doit satisfaire pour être considéré comme un mode obligatoire de règlement des différends dont le résultat, la sentence arbitrale, mérite de recevoir la sanction des États." *in* Gaillard, "Souveraineté et autonomie: réflexions sur les représentations de l'arbitrage international," p. 102.

56 This notion has been discussed by several scholars and legal theorists, but it is most notably associated with the late Emmanuel Gaillard.

However, its autonomy operates within a framework established by international treaties and relies on national courts for the enforcement of awards, which interlinks it with the broader international legal system.

3.3 International Arbitration and the Interplay of Legal Systems

International arbitration functions within a complex legal framework that goes beyond national borders, combining different legal rules and standards.

This framework is essential for resolving disputes that cross national boundaries, involving states, corporations, and individuals from various jurisdictions. It is constituted by an intricate patchwork of international Public Law, domestic law, soft law, and non-state rules.

This section explores these components, their roles, and how they interact, with examples from global dispute resolution.

3.3.1 Navigating Multiple Legal Orders: The Dynamics of International Arbitration

International arbitration is a preferred dispute resolution mechanism in cross-border conflicts due to its binding nature, flexibility, and the enforceability of its awards. Unlike domestic disputes resolved within a single legal system, international arbitration must navigate the complexities of multiple legal orders, making its normative structure unique, transnational, and global.

One of the most striking aspects of international arbitration is indeed its operation within a complex mosaic of legal orders. International arbitration law is distinguished by its multiple sources. International and national sources coexist, as there is no single international convention establishing a uniform global framework for international arbitration. Arbitrators and parties involved must skillfully navigate through a labyrinth of domestic laws, international treaties, and soft law principles. This multiple legal landscape requires a solid understanding of comparative law, as well as a nuanced grasp of the legal customs and practices that shape what each party anticipates and agrees to in a contract.

The practice of international arbitration reflects a delicate balance between respecting the sovereignty of national legal systems and adhering to universally recognized principles that facilitate cross-border dispute resolution. Arbitration proceedings may be governed by the laws of the place of arbitration (*lex arbitri*), the rules chosen by the parties, and the substantive laws governing the contract.

International arbitration also exemplifies legal multiculturalism through its diverse composition and application of laws. For instance, a tribunal composed of Canadian, French, and Japanese arbitrators may conduct proceedings in English while applying U.S. law to resolve a dispute seated in Singapore. This illustrates how arbitration transcends national boundaries, integrating multiple legal traditions and languages within a single case.

The success of international arbitration relies on managing legal differences across jurisdictions. Arbitrators and lawyers must determine the right legal rules for the arbitration agreement, procedure, and dispute. This requires understanding conflicts of law, treaty obligations, and the interaction between international arbitration norms and national laws.

This interplay of multiple legal orders and traditions not only enriches the arbitration process but also poses unique challenges in ensuring consistency, fairness, and efficiency in the resolution of disputes.

3.3.2 International Treaties and Norms Governing Arbitration

Global legal instruments shaping international arbitration include treaties such as the 1958 New York Convention on the Existence and Validity of Arbitral Award (New York Convention henceforth), the 1965 Washington Convention on the Settlement of Investment Disputes between States and Nationals of other States (ICSID Convention), and the 1975 Inter-American Convention on International Commercial Arbitration (Panama Convention). These key treaties provide a foundation for the recognition and enforcement of arbitral awards across borders. They ensure that arbitration awards are respected and treated similarly to judgments from domestic courts.

The 1965 Washington Convention on the Settlement of Investment Disputes between States and Nationals of Other States, also known as the ICSID Convention, sets up a special system for resolving disputes between foreign investors and states. It allows investment disputes to be settled through arbitration without needing to go through national courts.

A key feature of the ICSID system is that arbitral awards are automatically recognized and enforced in all 158 member countries without requiring approval from local courts. This makes it easier for investors to ensure that states comply with arbitration rulings, strengthening legal certainty and investor protection in international business.

The 1958 New York Convention on the Recognition and Enforcement of Foreign Arbitral Awards is the key pillar of international arbitration. It ensures that arbitration agreements and awards are recognized and enforced across its 172 signatory states, providing a reliable and standardized legal framework that promotes international trade and investment.

The Convention mainly applies to international commercial arbitration, facilitating the enforcement of arbitral awards globally. While it may also apply to investment arbitration, this depends on whether the award is considered "commercial" under national law. However, state-to-state arbitration is generally governed by other treaties, such as the Vienna Convention on the Law of Treaties.

Two essential provisions shape the Convention's role: Article II, which ensures that arbitration agreements are in writing and enforceable, and Article V, which limits the grounds on which a court may refuse to recognize or enforce an award, such as lack of due process, invalid agreements, or violations of public policy.

The New York Convention strikes a balance between the independence of arbitration and the oversight of national courts. It allows arbitral tribunals to function effectively while ensuring state courts can intervene only under specific, limited circumstances. This framework makes arbitration a trusted and enforceable method for resolving international disputes.

The 1975 Inter-American Convention on International Commercial Arbitration – the Panama Convention – is a regional treaty that helps enforce arbitration agreements and awards between countries in the Americas. It works in a similar way to the New York Convention, ensuring that arbitration decisions made in one member country can be recognized and enforced in another. This convention promotes efficient dispute resolution in international trade across Latin America and the Caribbean.

3.3.3 National Legal Frameworks in International Arbitration

At the national level, most countries have developed their own arbitration laws, which govern both domestic and international arbitration proceedings within their territories. These laws reflect how states have adopted, adapted, or diverged from international norms.

For example, the United Kingdom's Arbitration Act of 1996 provides a comprehensive framework that covers the conduct of arbitration proceedings, the role of the Judiciary in supporting arbitration, and the enforcement of arbitral awards.

Another example is the United States 1929 Federal Arbitration Act, which establishes a statutory foundation for arbitration, enforcing arbitration agreements, and providing mechanisms for the confirmation and challenge of awards.[57]

Further examples include the French Code of Civil Procedure (Articles 1442 to 1527). France is indeed renowned for its arbitration-friendly legal regime, which is largely codified. French arbitration law distinguishes between domestic and international arbitration, offering a highly favorable legal framework for international arbitration. The law provides broad autonomy to the parties in choosing the arbitration rules, the seat of arbitration, and the applicable law to the dispute. Also, France is supportive of enforcing international arbitration decisions. It keeps the reasons for not enforcing them to a minimum, similar to what the New York Convention suggests. This arbitration-friendly environment makes France, particularly Paris, a preferred seat for international arbitrations.

Japan's approach to arbitration is included in the Japanese Arbitration Act of 2003, which is largely based on the UNCITRAL Model Law. This Act applies to both domestic and international arbitration proceedings conducted in Japan, providing a modern legal framework that supports the efficient resolution of disputes through arbitration. The Act covers various aspects of the arbitration process, including the arbitration agreement, the composition of the arbitral tribunal, the conduct of the arbitration proceedings, and the recognition and enforcement of arbitral awards. Japan's arbitration law reflects its commitment to making the country a more attractive venue for international arbitration, in line with global standards.

Like most other West African countries, Côte d'Ivoire's arbitration regime is governed by the OHADA Uniform Act on Arbitration (*Organization for the Harmonization of Corporate Law in Africa*), which applies to all member states. The OHADA Uniform Act provides a unified legal framework for arbitration within the OHADA region, aiming to promote arbitration as an effective means for dispute resolution and to facilitate the enforcement of arbitral awards across member states. The Act covers the arbitration agreement, the arbitral tribunal, the conduct of proceedings, and the recognition and enforcement of awards, ensuring that OHADA's arbitration laws are harmonized with international best practices.

The Sultanate of Oman's approach to arbitration is governed by the Omani Arbitration Law, which was issued by Royal Decree No. 47/1997. This law outlines the legal framework for both domestic and international arbitration in Oman, reflecting the country's efforts to modernize its dispute resolution mechanisms and to provide a supportive environment for arbitration.

The Omani Arbitration Law covers a wide range of aspects related to arbitration, including the arbitration agreement, the composition and jurisdiction of the arbitral tribunal, the arbitration proceedings, and the award. It stipulates that parties have the freedom to choose their arbitrators and the language of the arbitration proceedings, as well as the applicable law to the dispute. The law also details the procedures for the enforcement of arbitral awards, which are generally in line with the principles set out in the New York Convention, to which Oman is a signatory since 1999.

One of the notable features of the Omani Arbitration Law is its emphasis on the confidentiality of the arbitration process, recognizing the importance of privacy in commercial and

57 It was passed in 1929, codified in 1947, and amended in 1954 and 1970.

international disputes. Additionally, the law allows for the annulment of arbitral awards under certain conditions, such as a violation of Omani public policy.

Oman's adoption of this law demonstrates its commitment to providing an effective legal framework for arbitration, aiming to encourage the use of arbitration for the resolution of commercial disputes and to position itself as a favorable venue for international arbitration in the region. The Omani legal system's approach to arbitration is indicative of a broader trend in the Middle East towards embracing arbitration as a key mechanism for dispute resolution, aligning with international practices and standards.

These examples from the United Kingdom, United States, France, Japan, OHADA countries, and the Sultanate of Oman illustrate the diverse ways countries have structured their arbitration laws, influenced by both their unique legal traditions and the international norms that guide the practice of arbitration globally.

3.3.4 Convergence of Arbitration and Diplomacy in Global Conflict Resolution

Arbitration and diplomacy are complementary mechanisms in the international arena, each playing a unique role in the resolution of conflicts. While arbitration provides a formalized and legalistic approach, diplomacy is often characterized by negotiation and conciliation, leaning on the art of managing international relations to resolve disputes before they escalate. The relationship between arbitration and diplomacy is symbiotic. Arbitration and diplomacy are interdependent and complementary because they both serve crucial roles in the resolution of international disputes, but in different ways and at different stages of conflict resolution. In essence, while diplomacy negotiates and builds consensus, arbitration provides a formal resolution when consensus cannot be reached. Together, they offer a full spectrum of tools for international dispute resolution, from informal to formal, and from flexible to binding, which is why they are interdependent and complementary.

Arbitration agreements and choice of law clauses embedded in international commercial contracts may sometimes act as a Trojan horse for Anglo-Saxon law firms and large Anglo-Saxon corporations, subtly embedding their legal principles and standards into global commerce.[58] However, the interplay between arbitration and diplomacy is crucial. The importance of both disciplines in maintaining global harmony, as well as their joint contribution to international conflict resolution, should be highlighted more often.

Conclusion

Arbitration plays a fundamental role in modern dispute resolution, offering parties a flexible, efficient, and enforceable alternative to court litigation. Rooted in party consent, arbitration agreements and clauses establish a structured framework that allows disputes to be resolved outside national courts. This contractual foundation ensures that parties voluntarily choose arbitration, making it a cornerstone of international dispute resolution.

The enforceability of arbitration agreements and awards remains crucial, as their recognition by state courts determines their practical effectiveness. Instruments like the New York

58 Gontier, Jean-Yves, 2023, *La Diplomatie Juridique: Défense et Illustration du Droit Français et du Droit Continental dans le Droit Global à travers les Exemples de la Médiation et de l'Arbitrage International*, Doctoral Thesis in Law, Université Paris-Saclay. National Thesis Number: 2023UPASH003. Available at: https://tel.archives-ouvertes.fr/tel-04283865. Last accessed 16 February 2024.

Convention have significantly contributed to the globalization of arbitration by facilitating cross-border enforcement. Arbitration is particularly valuable in international commercial, investment, and interstate disputes across various sectors, including energy, finance, construction, maritime law, and technology.

Beyond its practical advantages, international arbitration raises broader legal questions. It operates beyond national legal orders, influencing multiple jurisdictions and contributing to the development of an autonomous transnational arbitral order. As globalization intensifies, arbitration continues to serve as a bridge between different legal traditions, adapting to the growing demand for neutral and efficient dispute resolution mechanisms.

Despite its challenges, arbitration remains indispensable for fostering international trade and investment, ensuring legal predictability, and promoting economic cooperation. As arbitration continues to evolve, it must strike a balance between efficiency, fairness, and enforceability, making it a key tool in the resolution of complex international disputes.

Selected Bibliography

Andenas, Mads, & Heidemann, Maren, (Eds.), 2024, *Commercial Contract Law and Arbitration: From Assignments to Unfair Terms*, Routledge, 256 pages.

Bermann, George A., 2016, International Arbitration and Private International Law (General Course on Private International Law, Volume 381), in *Collected Courses of the Hague Academy of International Law*, Brill Nijhoff.

Bermann, George A., 2017, The Role of National Courts at the Threshold of Arbitration. *The American Review of International Arbitration*, 28(3).

Bermann, George A., 2020, *International Commercial Arbitration in a Nutshell*, Nutshells series, West Academic Publishing, 356 pages.

Bermann, George A., Dodge, William S., & Childress, Donald Earl III, 2021, *Transnational Litigation in a Nutshell*, Faculty Books, No. 331, 534 pages.

Blackaby, Nigel K. C., Partasides, Constantine K. C., & Redfern, Alan, 2023, *Redfern and Hunter on International Arbitration* (7th ed.), Oxford University Press, 832 pages.

Born, Gary B., 2021a, *International Arbitration and Forum Selection Agreements: Drafting and Enforcing* (6th ed.), Kluwer Law International, 336 pages.

Born, Gary B., 2021b, *International Arbitration: Law and Practice*, Wolters Kluwer, 616 pages.

Born, Gary B., 2021c, *International Commercial Arbitration* (3rd ed.), Kluwer Law International, Wolters Kluwer, 4250 pages.

Cadiet, Loïc, & Clay, Thomas, 2019, *Les modes alternatifs de règlement des litiges* (3e éd., coll. Connaissance du droit), Dalloz, 180 pages.

Cole, Tony, & Ortolani, Pietro, 2019, *Understanding International Arbitration* (1st ed.), Routledge, 262 pages.

Dasser, Felix, 2021, *Soft Law in International Commercial Arbitration*, Martinus Nijhoff, 300 pages.

Fernández Arroyo, Diego P., 2016, Arbitrator's Procedural Powers: The Last Frontier of Party Autonomy? in Ferrari, Franco (Ed.), *Limits to Party Autonomy in International Commercial Arbitration*, JurisNet, LLC, 522 pages.

Fernández Arroyo, Diego P., 2019, Soft Law and Arbitral Procedure – A Conditioned but Inescapable Couple. *European International Arbitration Review*, 2019-2, 71–86.

Fernández Arroyo, Diego P., forthcoming, Legitimacy of International Arbitration: Commercial v. Investment, in Bjorklund, A., Ferrari, F., & Kröll, S. (Eds.), *Cambridge Compendium of International Commercial and Investment Arbitration*, Cambridge: Cambridge University Press.

Gaillard, Emmanuel, 2008, *Aspects philosophiques du droit de l'arbitrage international*, LGDJ, 240 pages.

Gaillard, Emmanuel, 2010, *Legal Theory of International Arbitration*, Brill Nijhoff, 204 pages.

Georgakopoulos, Alexia, (Ed.), 2017, *The Mediation Handbook: Research, Theory, and Practice* (1st ed.), Routledge, 450 pages.

Guillaume-Hofnung, M., 2023, *La médiation* (9e éd.), Que sais-je?, Presses Universitaires de France, 128 pages.

Hopt, Klaus J., & Steffek, Felix, 2013, *Mediation: Principles and Regulation in Comparative Perspective*, Oxford University Press, 1000 pages.

Kaufmann-Kohler, Gabrielle, 2010, Soft Law in International Arbitration: Codification and Normativity. *Journal of International Dispute Settlement*, 1–17.

Mainguy, Daniel, & El Ahdab, Jalal, 2021, *Droit de l'arbitrage: théorie et pratique*, LexisNexis, 2021, 1088 pages.

Muir Watt, Horatia, & Fernández Arroyo, Diego P., (Eds.), 2015, *Private International Law and Global Governance*, Law and Global Governance series, Oxford University Press, 400 pages.

Muir Watt, Horatia, Fernández Arroyo, Diego P., Radicati Di Brozolo, L. G., Banifatemi, Y., & Hascher, D., 2023, *The Hague Academy's Lectures on Emmanuel Gaillard's Legacy/Les Conférences de l'Académie sur l'héritage scientifique d'Emmanuel Gaillard*, Brill Nijhoff, 158 pages.

UNCITRAL Secretariat, Gaillard, Emmanuel, & Bermann, George A. (Eds.), 2017, *Guide on the Convention on the Recognition and Enforcement of Foreign Arbitral Awards*, New York, 1958, Brill Nijhoff.1

Index

For Product Safety Concerns and Information please contact our
EU representative GPSR@taylorandfrancis.com Taylor & Francis
Verlag GmbH, Kaufingerstraße 24, 80331 München, Germany